DECISION SUPPORT for MANAGEMENT

Ralph H. Sprague, Jr.
The University of Hawaii

Hugh J. Watson
The University of Georgia

Prentice Hall, Upper Saddle River, New Jersey 07458

Library of Congress Cataloging-in-Publication Data

SPRAGUE, RALPH H.
Decision support for management / RALPH H. SPRAGUE, Jr., HUGH J. WATSON
p. cm.
Includes bibliographical references and index.
ISBN 0-13-396268-7
1. Decision support systems. 2. Management information systems.
I. Watson, Hugh J. II. Title.
HD30.213.S68 1995
658.4 038—dc20 95-41302

Editor in chief: *Richard Wohl*
Executive editor: *P.J. Boardman*
Project management: *Edie Riker*
Cover design: *Kiwi Design*
Buyer: *Paul Smolensky*
Editorial assistant: *Jane Avery*

Printed in the United States of America

10 9 8 7 6 5 4

ISBN 0-13-396268-7

Prentice-Hall International (UK) Limited, *London*
Prentice-Hall of Australia Pty. Limited, *Sydney*
Prentice-Hall Canada Inc., *Toronto*
Prentice-Hall Hispanoamericana, S.A., *Mexico*
Prentice-Hall of India Private Limited, *New Delhi*
Prentice-Hall of Japan, Inc., *Tokyo*
Simon & Schuster Asia Pte. Ltd., *Singapore*
Editora Prentice-Hall do Brasil, Ltda., *Rio de Janerio*

CONTENTS IN BRIEF

CONTENTS

PREFACE

The use of information technology to support decision making and problem solving continues to advance. Decision Support Systems (DSS) have evolved significantly since their early development in the 1970s. The DSS "movement" initially defined the nature of computer-based systems to assist decision makers with ill-structured problems. Over the past two decades, DSS has taken on a narrower definition; while other systems have emerged to assist specific kinds of decision makers, faced with specific kinds of problems. Executive Information Systems (EIS), Expert Systems (ES), Group Decision Support Systems (GDSS), Management Support Systems (MSS), and Executive Support Systems (ESS) are examples. The result is the emergence of a *class* of computer based applications which support a variety of information workers as they deal with ill-structured decision-making and problem-solving tasks.

These so-called "support systems" have many concepts and principles in common, yet they vary in the kind of user to be supported, nature of the task, kinds of technology used, and methodology of development. They are among the most important and valuable type of computer based system, because they increase the efficiency and effectiveness of upper-level information workers who tend to be highly paid. Thus, the ability to build, develop, install, and use these systems generates higher productivity increases and business value than more traditional transaction processing or reporting systems.

We have prepared this book (1) to help students and practitioners understand the principles and concepts that guide the development and use of these systems, (2) to explore the variety and richness of these systems, the wide range of users, problems, and technologies employed, (3) to illustrate how the concepts and principles have been applied in specific systems and (4) to provide experiential learning opportunities with such systems through the use of videos, demos, tutorials, and student software.

The book is designed to be a primary text for understanding this continually developing field. We include the full range of systems and users, but with some extra emphasis on managers and their use of systems such as EIS, rather than an emphasis on management analysts who develop expert systems. The book is an integrated text that replaces our earlier readings book on this subject, but we still draw on some important articles from the literature, and special contributions which we have solicited from several leaders in the field.

SUPPLEMENTARY MATERIALS

To aid in the process of learning and understanding this important field, we have included a variety of supporting material. An *Instructor's Manual* contains a number of items that support the teaching of a decision support course. Particularly helpful are the videos and software that are available to adopters of the book. Both add variety, texture, and richness to the written text, and offer a wide range of learning and teaching opportunities. The videos range from examples of applications, to how applications are built. The software includes vendor demos, tutorials, and student software that can be used for hands-on projects and assignment. They have been made available by vendors such as IBM, Apple, Comshare, Pilot Software, Holos, Lotus, Ventana, BusinessObjects, and Andyne. These teaching aids cover decision support systems, executive information systems, group support systems, and expert systems. In addition, a companion text, *Visual IFPS/Plus for Business* by Paul Gray, is available from Prentice Hall for more extensive treatment of DSS application development.

STRUCTURE OF THE BOOK

The format and contents of the book are organized into eight parts. Listed below is an overview of the content and primary emphasis of each Part.

Part 1—These two chapters trace the emergence of the DSS movement, and identify the concepts and principles on which it is based.

Part 2—This set of chapters discusses the development methodology and usage patterns for DSS and presents detailed descriptions of real systems.

Part 3—This part develops the architecture or structure of DSS; it is based primarily on the data-dialog-modeling paradigm explained in Chapter 1.

Part 4—These chapters explain the organizational and technical environment required for the development and use of DSS.

Parts 5, 6, 7—These three parts deal extensively with each of three "special kinds" of DSS: Executive Information Systems in Part 5, Group Support Systems in Part 6, and Expert Systems in Part 7.

Part 8—This final part of the book explains the benefits that occur from the use of DSS, and how to measure and access them.

ACKNOWLEDGMENTS

We would like to express our appreciation to those who made a contribution to this book, especially those authors who responded to our invitation to prepare a chapter, and then were gracious enough to accommodate our suggested changes. We also thank: Rod Skiff, Brad Black, K. C. Kyriakou, Pamela Holden, Navendu Charu, and Matthias Rubner for further help in developing the material in the book.

Ralph H. Sprague, Jr.
Hugh J. Watson

Part 1

THE CONCEPTUAL FOUNDATION FOR DSS

Frameworks or "conceptual models" are often crucial to the understanding of a new or complex subject. A framework which identifies the parts of a topic and how they interrelate allows readers to extend and expand their mental model and extrapolate additional understandings. If a picture is worth a thousand words, a framework is worth a thousand pictures.

As decision support systems (DSS) began to appear in the early 1970s, the subject was a prime candidate for a conceptual framework. They were fundamentally different from traditional computer-based applications, served a fundamentally different set of needs, and required a different development approach. As a result, a framework was needed to communicate these differences and guide the evolution of the DSS field. Such a framework emerged from a set of driving forces, including emerging computer hardware and software technology; research efforts at leading universities; a growing awareness of how to use technology; a desire for better information; an increasingly turbulent economic environment; and stronger competitive pressures, especially from abroad. During the rest of the decade, there was a growing body of DSS research from the academic community, and an increasing number of organizations began to develop decision support systems. These experiences provided the conceptual foundation for DSS.

The purpose of this first part of the book is to explore the history, background, conceptual foundation, and likely future of decision support systems. Chapter 1 traces the origins of what became the DSS "movement" in the late 70s, in both academic endeavors and business practice. It then summarizes the key concepts and models that became the conceptual theory of

DSS. Finally, Chapter 1 outlines challenges for the future that will allow DSS to continue evolving.

Chapter 2 is a conceptual model for the future of information usage by one of America's greatest management thinkers. Peter Drucker describes the kind of information and information tools that executives really need in today's tough, competitive, global business environment. He suggests that the nature of this environment will require business executives to restructure their information and the tools that provide access to it. He suggests a shift in focus from profit making to wealth creation and identifies four kinds of internal information needed to pursue these objectives. External information also will grow in importance and change in structure. Chapter 2 is thus a thought provoking treatise on the underlying business objectives, the nature of decision making, the role of information tools in supporting the activities of executives, and therefore the structure of decision support systems in the future.

1

DSS: PAST, PRESENT, AND FUTURE

INTRODUCTION

Decision support systems (DSS) can be viewed as a third generation of computer-based applications. First, mainframe computers were used mostly for transactions processing. Then, there was a growing realization that computers and information technology could be used for purposes other than automating paper work, for example, for management reporting, so the field of management information systems (MIS) was taking hold. Meanwhile, assistance for decision making was the domain of management scientists and operations researchers who created structured models, for which computers served primarily as computation engines.

This environment was fertile soil for the paper by Gorry and Scott Morton (Gorry and Scott Morton 1971) which explored the concept of structure in decision making. They developed a now-famous matrix which showed the interaction between the level of management and the amount of structure in the decision making done at each level. As the level of management increases from the operating management to executive levels, the decision-making process becomes semi-structured, then unstructured. The thrust of their argument was that management science models were effective for structured decision making, but decision makers needed tools and technology to assist them in dealing with semi-structured or unstructured problems. This rationale set the stage for the work Scott Morton did in his thesis on what he called management decision systems (Scott Morton 1971).

During the 70s and 80s, the concept of DSS grew and evolved into a full field of research, development, and practice. DSS was both an evolution and a departure from previous types of computer support for decision making. Management Information Systems (MIS) provided 1) scheduled reports for well-defined information needs, 2) demand reports for ad hoc information requests, and 3) the ability to query a database for specific data. Operations Research/Management Science (OR/MS) employed mathematical models to better analyze and understand specific problems. Each was lacking some of the attributes needed to support decision making—attributes such as focus, development methodology, handling of managerial data, use of analytic aids, and dialog between user and system.

Initially, there were different conceptualizations about what decision support systems were. Not only did academicians give different definitions, but vendors, quick to adopt anything to help sell their products, also applied the DSS label very loosely. When the characteristics of DSS were described to a vendor, he said, "That's it! That's the name we need for our new product." The term Decision Support System had such an instant intuitive appeal that it quickly became a "buzz word."

In this chapter we explore the field of DSS, including its origin, its current status, and a look into its future. The next section explains how DSS evolved at the intersection of trends in data processing and management science modeling to play an important role in the overall mission of information systems in organizations. Then we trace the development of DSS into a "field" of practice, education, and academic research. The third section identifies current developments and trends and summarizes the status of the field. The final sections identify future challenges for the advancement of DSS, draw some conclusions, and explain how the material in the book will help the reader understand the growing field of DSS.

DSS AND OTHER SYSTEMS

As the DSS field evolved, there were continued questions about how it related to, or differed from, MIS and Management Science. The structured versus unstructured decision-making framework was helpful, but did not adequately explain the variety of activities that seemed to go beyond decision making. It became clear from conference discussions and academic papers that the focus of DSS should be higher than the decision event. Decision making is a process that involves a variety of activities, most of them dealing with the handling of information.

A Scenario of Problem Solving

To illustrate these concepts consider a scenario of a problem-solving task, and the technology that might be used to assist decision makers in handling it.

1. The vice president of marketing discovers a shortfall in sales in a region. He notices this by using the executive information system (EIS) to compare budget and actual sales.
2. He uses the capability of the EIS to "drill down" into the components of the summarized data. No apparent causes for a shortfall are revealed so he must look further.
3. He sends an e-mail message to the sales manager in the district requesting additional suggestions and explanation. The sales manager's response and a follow-up phone call revealed that there is no obvious single cause, so they must look further.
4. He then investigates several other possible causes
   a. Economic condition. Through the EIS he has access to the wire services, bank economic newsletters, current business and economic publications, and the company's internal economic report on the region in question. These sources reveal no serious downturn in the economic conditions of the region.
   b. Competitive analysis. Through the same sources he investigates whether competitors have introduced a new product, launched an effective ad campaign, or whether there are new competitors entering the market.
   c. Written sales reports. He then browses through the written reports of individual sales representatives to detect possible problems. A "concept-based" text retrieval system allows for quick searches for topics such as a concern for quality, inadequate product functionality, or obsolescence.
5. He then accesses the marketing DSS which includes a set of models to analyze sales patterns by product, by sales representative, and by major customer. Again, no clear problems are revealed.
6. He decides to hold a meeting of the regional sales managers and several of the key salespeople. They meet in an electronic meeting room supported by GDSS software such as GroupSystems by Ventana Corporation or TeamFocus from IBM. During this meeting they
   a. Examine the results of all the previous analyses using the information access and presentation technologies in the room.
   b. Brainstorm to identify possible solutions
   c. Develop an action plan
7. They decide that the best solution is a new sales campaign based on a multimedia presentation that runs on a laptop computer that sales representatives use when they visit customers.
8. A revised estimate of the sales volume, with the new sales promotion plan, is entered in the financial planning model and distributed to the sales force in the region.
9. A sales meeting is held in the GDSS room and by video conference to launch the campaign and train sales personnel in the use of the presentation.

This scenario illustrates the wide variety of activities involved in dealing with a decision-making and problem-solving task. Where does the decision making start and stop? Which are the crucial decisions? It does not really matter because all the activities are part of the overall process of solving the problem. It also illustrates the wide variety of technologies which can be used to assist decision makers and problem solvers. Which of the technology-based systems are DSS? In the broad sense, all of them are because they all improve the effectiveness or efficiency of the decision-making or problem-solving process.

The definition of DSS which evolved from these discussions, and the one that prevails today, was articulated in a "framework" paper on DSS (Sprague 1980). It defines DSS as:

- computer-based systems
- that help decision makers
- confront ill-structured problems
- through direct interaction
- with data and analysis models

Each part of this definition has a key concept that contributes to the unique character of DSS. DSS are *computer-based systems* which add to the many other approaches and tools that decision makers can use to assist in decision-making tasks. DSS *help* decision makers; they often do not deliver an optimum answer. In fact, there may be no optimum because these are *ill-structured* problems and situations so the decision must evolve through the *interaction* of decision makers with resources such as *data and analysis models.*

The Overall Mission of Information Systems in Organizations

Any debate or discussion of the similarities or differences among systems must be couched in terms of the overall mission of information systems (IS) in organizations. In the frenetic, fast-changing world of information systems, it is sometimes hard to stay focused on the true objective or mission of information systems in organizations. New terms (buzz words?) are created, new systems proposed, and new products are developed with confusing rapidity. It sometimes seems that the true objective is to enlarge the power base of the IS department, or enhance the reputation of certain academics, or increase the market share of IS vendors. These may be somewhat legitimate outcomes, but they are by-products of a more important objective. We suggest that the ultimate mission of IS in an organization is

> to improve the performance of information workers in organizations through the application of information technology.

This mission is admittedly not very specific—with ambiguous words such as "improve" and "performance"—but there are two important implications nevertheless. First, it establishes *people* as the target of IS. Systems should be built to serve people. The kind of people—information workers—are those whose job is primarily handling information. The United States Bureau of Labor Statistics shows that more than 50 percent of the employees in the country are information workers. In some industries, such as banks, the percentage is above 90.

Second, information systems should increase performance. Merely producing reports, or supporting activities, or even "getting the right information to the right person at the right time" falls short unless the result is performance improvement. Certainly there will be problems defining "performance" and "improvement," but at least the general objective is clear.

How can performance be improved? The generic word "support" has been used to infer the concept of using IS as a resource to leverage the activities of managers (management support systems, decision support systems). With information workers as the majority of employed people in the U.S. and most other advanced societies, it is clear that IS can be used in a multitude of ways to support a multitude of activities performed by information workers. In fact, some form of segmentation of information workers and their activities is required to better focus information system efforts to support them.

A Dichotomy of Information Work

An important concept in support systems is based on an intuitive dichotomy of information handling activities. The primary distinction is whether they are based on predefined procedures, or on objectives or goals (which are independent of a predefined process). Figure 1–1 summarizes the attributes of procedure-based and goal-based activities which are labeled Type I and Type II, respectively. Other key characteristics of this dichotomy include:

1. Transactions: Type I work consists of a large volume of transactions with a relatively low value (or cost) connected with each. Type II work consists of fewer transactions, but each is more costly or valuable.

2. Process: Type I work is based on well defined procedures, while Type II work is process-independent, or at least based on ill-structured or flexible procedures.

3. Output: The output from Type I work is more easily measured because it is defined by the number of iterations. The focus is on performing the necessary process or procedure quickly, efficiently, and usually many times. Type II output is not easily measured because it consists of problem solving and goal attainment. You can assign a Type I task to an information worker by explaining the sequence of steps required to accomplish it. With a Type II task, you must specify the desired outcome. Figuring out the necessary steps in the sequence is part of the job, and may be significantly different for different people.

Procedure-Based (Type I)	Goal-Based (Type II)
• High volume of transactions	• Low volume of transactions
• Low cost (value) per transaction	• High value (cost) per transaction
• Well-structured procedures	• Ill-structured procedures
• Output measures defined	• Output measures less defined
• Focus on process	• Focus on problems and goals
• Focus on efficiency	• Focus on effectiveness
• Handling of "data"	• Handling of concepts
• Predominately clerical workers	• Managers and professionals
• Examples from banking	• Examples from banking
"Back office"	Loan department
Mortgage servicing	Asset/liability management
Payroll processing	Planning department
Check processing	Corporate banking

FIGURE 1–1 A Dichotomy of Information Work

4. Data: Type I work uses data in relatively well-structured form, whereas Type II work deals primarily with concepts which are presented in less well-structured form, usually with a great deal of ambiguity.

At first glance this dichotomy looks similar to the "clerical" versus "managerial-professional" breakdown that has been used for many years. Upon closer examination, however, it is clear that some clerical personnel such as secretaries, frequently have process-independent tasks defined only by their outcome. Likewise, most managers and professionals have a certain proportion of their work which is process defined.

It can be argued that the nature of the task, (goal-based or procedure-based), is the most important characteristic in determining what kind of support is required from information systems. It should be clear that most uses of information systems in the past have been for supporting Type I tasks. It is easiest and most natural to use a process engine (computer) to support process-driven tasks.

It is also clear that the challenge of the future is to use information systems to support Type II tasks. The nature of the tasks is different, the mentality required to do them is different, and so the information support must be different from the traditional Type I approaches.

There have been several attempts to support Type II work with information systems. In most cases, however, it has been done by providing Type II workers with better access to tools that have been used for Type I tasks. For example, consider a typical breakdown of Type II functions:

1. Tracking, monitoring, alerting.
2. Problem solving, analysis, design.
3. Communication.

Systems to support each one of these clusters of activities have evolved under the names of management information systems, management science (including operations research, statistics, and mathematics), and office automation, respectively. But they tend to be separate and diverse, poorly linked, and built on completely different structures. Note also that the Type II task we have called decision making usually requires an intermixture of all three functions.

What is needed, then, is a systems effort focused on supporting Type II activities. To be specific, we should broaden our concept of DSS to include tracking-monitoring-alerting and communicating as well as the more traditional intelligence-design-choice view of decision making. This can be accomplished by merging the systems development in several areas into an amalgam of systems capabilities under the control of information workers performing Type II activities.

DSS AT THE INTERSECTION OF TRENDS

The DSS movement has become one of the most substantive on-going efforts to deal with support for Type II activities. Until recently, however, even this effort was based on using tools designed originally for Type I purposes. Traditional data base and modeling tools were integrated in a system with a facile interface for the user. The user contributed the mental capability to deal with the Type II task, while the system tools leveraged those mental skills.

A significant contribution of the DSS movement, however, was the merging and integration of previously separate tool sets into a unified whole more valuable than the sum of the parts. In fact, current DSS can be viewed as computer-based systems that lie at the intersection of two major evolutionary trends—*data processing* which has yielded a significant body of knowledge about managing data, and *management science* which has generated a significant body of knowledge about modeling. The confluence of these two trends forms the two major resources with which decision makers interact in the process of dealing with ill-structured tasks. Let us consider how evolutionary developments in data processing and management science have led to the data base and model base capability of DSS.

The Data Processing Evolution

A helpful way to define the stages in the evolution of data processing is the following:

1. Basic data processing—characterized by stand-alone EDP jobs, mostly for transaction processing, with each program having its own files. Data handling was limited to such classic data processing functions as sorting, classifying, and summarizing.
2. File management—integrated EDP jobs for related functions, sometimes sharing files across several programs. This stage included attempts to develop common software for handling files (utilities) and prescribed ways to ensure data security, integrity, backup, etc.
3. Data base management—a major capability of the MIS era, with particular emphasis on the software system for dealing with data separate from the programs that use it. The major impact of DBMS at this stage was the reduction of program maintenance, since data files could be modified without recompiling all the programs that used it. At this stage, DBMS software began to use data "models" to represent the way data were logically related.
4. Query, report generation—the addition of flexible report generators and "English-like" query languages to facilitate ad hoc requests and special reports. Emphasis here was on the direct access to data bases by non-technical people such as end users.

Note that each stage contributed a major capability that is still valuable in today's systems. In other words, we have not evolved beyond the need for the contribution of each stage but have added capabilities to increase the value.

Throughout the EDP evolution, emphasis has been on manipulating data, initially in predefined ways to accomplish structured tasks, and later in flexible ways to accommodate ad hoc requests and preferences by individual users. Sophisticated ways of manipulating data (models) were embedded in the data processing system for some well-structured problems, for example inventory management, but modeling was generally considered a separate type of application. Users dealt with less well-structured problems by querying the data base, getting special reports, and then using their judgment.

In general, the data base approach evolving from the EDP tradition seemed to be characterized by the following objectives:

1. to effectively manage a large amount of data,
2. to establish independence between the data and the programs that used it,
3. to separate the physical and logical structures of data and deal with them separately,
4. to provide flexible, easy access to data by non-programmers.

The problems and limitations of this approach were related to its dominantly accounting-oriented historical data, and its focus on information flows and summaries. Unfortunately, for an important set of problems and decisions, getting "the right information to the right person" was necessary but not sufficient. That data often needed to be analyzed, interpreted, and extended with the use of some decision models being developed from management science/operations research efforts.

The Modeling Evolution

While data processing professionals were strengthening their ability to store and handle data, management scientists and operations researchers were increasing their ability to create "models" of a problem or situation and manipulate them to shed light on how to handle that problem. A similar sequence of evolutionary steps in the development of modeling might include the following:

1. Symbolic models—The early stages of modeling were characterized by heavy use of linear and nonlinear equations, sometimes in large sets of simultaneous equations.
2. Computers as a computational engine—Computers first became important to modeling as number crunchers to reduce large amounts of data to create estimates for the equations, or as computational engines for solving sets of equations.
3. Computer models—Eventually, the computer took on a subtly different role. Rather than a device to compute a mathematical model, the computer program *became* the model. Computer variables became the symbols which were manipulated by the computer program instead of by mathematical operations. This approach led to a popular class of models that were not "solved" but rather "run" over time to observe the behavior of the model and thus shed light on the modeled situation.
4. Modeling systems—The computer became so important to modeling efforts that software systems were developed to handle classes of models. The software generally provided common data input formats, similar report for-

mats, and integrated documentation. Modeling systems for statistical analysis and mathematical programming are good examples.

5. Interactive modeling—As computers became more available in "time sharing" mode, interactive modeling became more feasible. Mini-computers and mainframes dedicated to on-line usage generally had libraries of models which could be called to do a variety of analyses. Unfortunately, it was common for the models to be stand-alone programs with different data requirements and formats and little if any linkage between the models.

Again, as in the data processing evolution, each stage yielded knowledge or a capability that contributed a valuable part of the tools available for dealing with problem solving and decision making. Also, as before, the evolution led to the modeling capabilities utilized in DSS to help decision makers deal with Type II problems.

The modeling evolution led to an increasingly close relationship between the models and computers but continued to be separate from the data which they used. This seemed to reflect model builders' preoccupation with the model as the focus of attention and their hesitance to get intimately involved with data sources and structures. In general, the modeling efforts needed major contributions from the data base efforts of systems professionals.

Evolutions Converge

Each of the two developmental tracks—in data base and in modeling—were useful in their own right. They were each significantly lacking, however, in helping information workers deal with Type II tasks. Developments in decision support systems allowed each set of capabilities to realize their potential in this area. DSS extended and combined both the data base technology and the modeling technology, and gave non-technical users access to them. The data and models were intimately linked, and both were linked with the user.

Conversely, DSS makes demands on the data base and the modeling capability that were not necessary before. Specifically, DSS makes the model management capabilities necessary. Without the integration requirements of DSS, modeling systems or libraries of interactive models would probably suffice. So as the need for model management capabilities became apparent, it was the DSS builders and researchers who began working on its development.

DEVELOPMENT OF THE DSS FIELD

Based on the trends and developments discussed above, DSS evolved as a "field" of study and practice during the 1980s. This section of the chapter discusses the principles of a theory of DSS, developments in IS departments in organizations, and academic research activities and conferences—all of which led to the formation and development of this field.

Principles of DSS

During early development of the field several principals evolved. Eventually, these principles became a widely accepted "structural theory" or framework. (Sprague and Carlson 1982). The four most important of these principles are summarized below.

The DDM Paradigm. The technology for DSS must consist of three sets of capabilities in the areas of dialog, data, and modeling, what Sprague and Carlson call the DDM paradigm. They make the point that a good DSS should have *balance* among the three capabilities. It should be *easy to use* to allow non-technical decision makers to interact fully with the system, it should have access to a *wide variety of data*, and it should provide *analysis and modeling* in a variety of ways. Many early systems adopted the name DSS when they were strong in only one area and weak in the others. Figure 1–2 shows the relationship between these components in more detail. Note that the models in the model base are linked with the data in the data base. Models can draw parameters, coefficients, and variables from the data base and enter results of the model's computation in the data base. These results can then be used by other models later in the decision-making process.

Figure 1–2 also shows the three components of the dialog function. The data base management system (DBMS) and the model base management system (MBMS) contain the necessary functions to manage the data base and model base, respectively. The dialog generation and management system (DGMS) manages the interface between the user and the rest of the system.

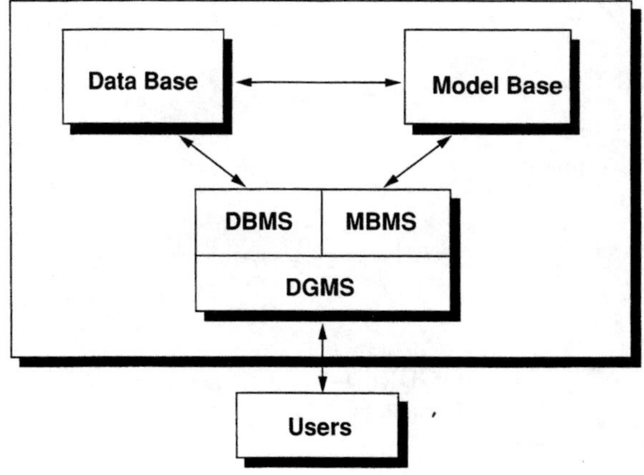

FIGURE 1–2 The Components of DSS

The DDM paradigm eventually evolved into the dominant architecture for DSS. In Part 3 of the book, we explore each of the components—the data resources and management, the dialog or interface, and the modeling—in more detail.

Levels of Technology. Three levels of technology are useful in developing DSS. This concept illustrates the usefulness of configuring *DSS tools* into a *DSS generator* which can be used to develop a variety of *specific DSS* quickly and easily to aid decision makers. (see Figure 1–3). The system which actually accomplishes the work is called the *specific DSS,* shown as the circles at the top of the diagram. It is the hardware/software that allow a specific decision maker to deal with a set of related problems. The second level of technology is called the *DSS generator.* This is a package of related hardware and software which provides a set of capabilities to quickly and easily build a specific DSS. The third level of technology is *DSS tools* which facilitate the development of either a specific DSS or a DSS generator.

DSS tools can be used to develop a specific DSS application directly, as shown on the left half of the diagram. This is the same approach used to develop most traditional applications with tools such as general purpose languages, data access software, and subroutine packages. The difficulty of this approach for developing DSS is the constant change and flexibility which characterize them. The development and use of DSS generators create a "platform" or staging area from which specific DSS can be constantly developed and modified with the cooperation of the user, and without heavy consumption of time and effort.

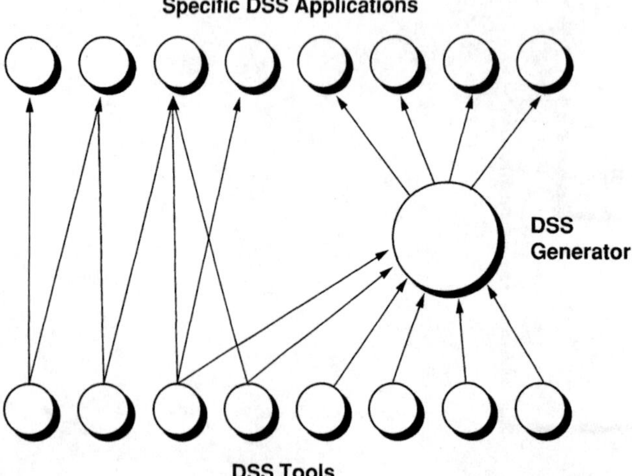

FIGURE 1–3 Three Levels of DSS Technology

Iterative Design. The nature of DSS requires a different design and development technique from traditional batch or on-line systems. Instead of a traditional development process, DSS require a form of *iterative development* which allows them to evolve and change as the problem or decision situation changes. They need to be built with short, rapid, feedback from users to ensure that development is proceeding correctly. They must be developed to permit change quickly and easily.

Organizational Environment. Effective development of DSS requires an organizational strategy to build an *environment* within which such systems can originate and evolve. The environment includes a *group of people* with interacting roles, a set of *hardware and software technology,* a set of *data sources,* and a set of *analysis models.*

Building the Organizational Environment

The concept of the organizational environment deserves further explanation. Because the technology to develop and support DSS was different from that required for MIS, different hardware and software were often required. Generally, this meant larger and better screens for workstations, better user-interface software, and perhaps specialized software to serve as a DSS generator. Enriched data sources required more external data, and internal data defined and organized to serve decision making instead of accounting needs. This meant development of an "extracted data base" separate from the traditional corporate data base. Analysis models became one of the components of a DSS, to be used by non-technical decision makers. This meant models had to be interactive, integrated with each other, and linked to the data base. Because the development methodologies for DSS were much different from the traditional system development methodologies, a new breed of analysts evolved to work with decision makers. They became partners in a team to develop and evolve DSS. This meant the evolution of a DSS support group with people dedicated to this purpose. This new DSS group was often located in the IS department, but sometimes not.

As is often the case, the technical developments were less troublesome than the organizational changes. Watson and Carr did some research which identified eight alternative locations for the DSS support group (Watson and Carr 1987). It revealed that some of the groups evolved in the IS or MIS department while others were in one of the alternative organizational locations. The alternative organizational locations were

- An Applications Group of Systems Analysts
- A Tools Group in the IS Department
- An Operations Research or Management Science Group

- Planning Departments
- Staff Analysis Groups
- Formally Charted DSS Groups
- Information Centers
- A DSS Group in End-User Services

The organizational aspects of DSS development and use are treated more fully in Parts 2 and 4. Part 2 explores the role of management in the development and use of DSS, finishing with a "classic" example of a DSS. Part 4 includes a chapter on the organizational placement of the DSS group, and a chapter on the methodology for selecting DSS software.

Vendors

Meanwhile, vendors began to realize the emerging need for software at all three levels—DSS tools, DSS generators, and specific DSS. Most of the development effort was aimed at the generator level. Products such as IFPS from Execucom and System W from COMSHARE (now combined in one product line by COMSHARE) allowed the quick development of specific DSS to help managers with certain kinds of decision-making situations. Then some vendors who had products strong in one of the three areas of functionality (data, dialog, modeling) began to add features in the other areas. SAS for instance, a strong package of statistical modeling tools, added an interactive "front-end" and graphic display to aid in dialog, and then mechanisms to define and link with data sources. By the mid 80s an entire software industry had grown up to serve the DSS movement.

Academic Developments

Meanwhile, DSS was developing as an academic field of study, research, and teaching. DSS courses began appearing in universities, textbooks were published, and conferences began.

DSS-XX. The International Conference on Decision Support Systems was first held in 1981 (DSS-81). It was an unusual conference because it identified four stakeholders or types of constituents and developed a program to bring all four together and serve them in a balanced way. The four stakeholders were

1. Academics and researchers
2. DSS developers and builders
3. Managers and users
4. Vendors

The conference was held annually from 1981 through 1992. In the latter years, reflecting a broadening perception of the topic, it was entitled "Information Technology for Executives and Managers." A newly published book contains the best papers from the conference transactions that were not previously published (Gray 1994).

HICSS. The Hawaii International Conference on System Sciences began in 1968, and in 1978, a DSS track was added. Formal refereed papers are presented and published in the *Proceedings*, but the real value for most participants are the discussion and interaction at the conference. The *Proceedings* are published yearly by the IEEE Computing Society Press (e.g., Shriver and Sprague 1995), and a recently published book contains the best papers from recent years (Blanning and King 1993).

IFIP-WG8.3. The International Federation of Information Processing (IFIP) is organized into a series of technical committees. TC8 is devoted to information systems in organizations. In 1983, TC8 formed working group 8.3 to focus on DSS. Because of its world-wide activities and European base, this group draws a very international clientele. It holds working conferences every other year, and the *Proceedings* are published in book form by North Holland. (For example McLean and Sol 1986; Sol and Vecsenyi 1991.)

DSS as a Field

By the late 80s DSS had attained the status of a pervasive "field." Universities had courses, faculty were doing research, and conferences were held at which research was presented and discussed. Organizations had hardware and software infrastructure, and DSS development or support personnel. The software market had developed with several vendors basing an entire product line on DSS. But trends in technology and organizations suggested even more developments.

CURRENT DEVELOPMENTS AND TRENDS

Throughout the 80s, there were strong advances in several areas of technology that combined to affect the field of DSS. Each of these trends had a significant effect on the growth and development of DSS; taken together their effect has proved to be dramatic. They include the following:

1. The personal computer revolution; the hardware, the software, and the emphasis on ease-of-use through common interfaces such as Windows, and common representations such as spreadsheets

2. The increasing capability and decreasing cost of telecommunications, both for wide area networks (WAN) and local area networks (LAN)
3. The increasing availability of public data bases and other sources of external data
4. The growth of artificial intelligence techniques such as expert systems and natural language processing
5. The rapid increase in end-user computing and the increasing knowledge and computer literacy of end users
6. The increasing availability of large color screens and color graphic software
7. The increasing availability of mobile computing and communication

Important Developments in DSS

The intersection of the continued progress in DSS and the trends cited above resulted in some important development in DSS. We have seen the following DSS trends:

1. Personal computer-based DSS have continued to grow. Spreadsheets took on more and more functions, eventually encompassing some of the functions previously performed by DSS generators. Newer packages for "creativity support" became more popular as extensions of analysis and decision making. These developments further strengthened the use of the PC for these applications, especially for personal support for independent thinking and decision making rather than for institutional DSS such as budgeting and financial planning.
2. For the popular institutional DSS that support sequential, interdependent decision making, the trend toward "distributed DSS"—close linkages between mainframe DSS languages and generators and the PC-based facilities. Vendors of both mainframe and PC products are now offering versions that run on, and link with, the other.
3. For interdependent decision support, "group DSS" (GDSS) has become much more prevalent in the past few years. The growing availability of local area networks and group communication services, such as electronic mail, will make this type of DSS increasingly available.
4. Decision support system products have begun to incorporate, and will eventually encompass, tools and techniques from artificial intelligence. The self-contained, stand-alone products in artificial intelligence have proven to be like the stand-alone statistical and management science models of a decade ago—they increasingly are embedded in DSS, which serve as a "delivery system" that facilitates their use. DSS will provide the mechanism for the assimilation of expert systems, knowledge representation, natural language query, voice and pattern recognition, and so on. The emerging

result is "intelligent DSS" that can "suggest," "learn," and "understand" in dealing with managerial tasks and problems.

5. Continued efforts to leverage the usefulness of DSS to gain benefit and value have resulted in focused versions targeted at specific sets of users or applications. The first strong thrust in this direction was executive information systems (EIS) aimed at top managers, primarily for flexible reporting and status monitoring. EIS use enhanced graphics and other user-friendly capabilities, less modeling and analysis capability, and more support from systems professionals to customize the system to a specific executive. Another popular "specialization" of DSS is the group DSS mentioned above.
6. DSS groups have become less like special project "commando teams" and more a part of the support team for a variety of other end-user support, perhaps as a part of an information center.
7. Cutting across all the trends given above is the continued development of user-friendly capabilities. This, more than any other feature, is what enabled early DSS. The development of dialog support hardware, such as light pens, mouse devices, touch screens, and high-resolution graphics will be further advanced by speech recognition, handwriting recognition, and voice synthesis. Dialog support software such as menus, windows, and help functions is continuing to advance. The "virtual desktop" dialog pioneered by Xerox, and currently used by Apple Macintosh computers and Microsoft Windows, embodies many user-friendly features and has nearly become a *de facto* standard.

Vendors

The software market for DSS has continued to develop and mature. Every year finds new, enhanced products in the marketplace. Students in a DSS cause are likely to work with one or more of these products.

Academic Progress

DSS continue to be a fertile ground for research and development. A 1987 survey of MIS researchers reported that DSS was one of the five most popular research themes from 1977 to 1985 (Farhoomand 1987). A more recent study reported that nearly one third of the researchers in MIS were doing DSS research (Teng and Galetta 1990).

A major study just completed developed a view of the intellectual structure of the DSS field (Eom and others 1993). A citation analysis was performed on several hundred articles which characterize the DSS field. Then a factor analysis derived the primary clusters in the literature. The authors found two contributing disciplines (management science/operations research and multi-criteria decision making) plus the following areas of DSS research:

1. Fundamental theory, frameworks, and concepts of DSS
2. Group DSS
3. Routing DSS
4. Data base and model base management systems
5. Multi-criteria DSS
6. Marketing DSS

There are several other DSS areas of research and application under development, but they have not yet been published long enough to affect this citation analysis. The authors plan to update this analysis from time to time to show these new areas as they appear.

Status

Despite all the developments of the late 80s and early 90s, DSS as a field is now at a crossroads. Because of an increased focus on special kinds of DSS, such as executive information systems, group DSS, expert systems, and other knowledge-based DSS, the field seems to be fragmenting. The connotation of the term DSS in some quarters is quite narrow: specific model-intensive systems used by technical analysts. Some functions that were once considered part of DSS are now migrating to other areas. Spreadsheet-based financial modeling and electronic meeting rooms are examples.

We use several parts of the book to examine these "special kinds" of DSS more closely. Part 5 looks at executive information systems—those systems designed for upper-level managers, primarily for status reporting, monitoring, and alerting. Part 6 explores the technology that supports decision making and problem solving by groups—group support systems. Finally, Part 7 contains four chapters on expert systems.

Although the connotation of the DSS label might be narrowing, the purpose and value of systems that fit the original definition of DSS continue to grow in importance. One reason for this apparent inconsistency is that it is increasingly difficult to identify the decision-making stages in the context of all the other activities executives and managers must perform in dealing with ill-structured problems. Likewise, decision support technology has broadened to include monitoring, tracking, and communication tools to support the overall process of ill-structured problem solving. In the next section we suggest a renewed vision for the field of DSS, based on a broad view of their purpose.

FUTURE OF DSS

Recalling our earlier discussion of the ultimate mission of information systems, the vision for DSS should be the application of a variety of technologies to improve the performance of information workers in organizations especially as they deal with ill-structured problems. Goal-based information handling activities (Type II) exist in a wide variety of forms, and systems to "support" them are equally varied.

Challenges

Several challenges will have to be met if this vision of DSS is to be realized. We pursue the connectivity necessary to link all the people who must work together in decision making and problem solving, and we must develop richer data sources and more "intelligence" in the model bases.

Integrated Architecture. The workstation on the desktop of the information worker is becoming the "window" into the world of information. A common dialog interface will allow access to all the information resources, and previously separate systems can be called and run from this common interface. The graphic user interface represented by Windows, Mac, Motiff, etc. is becoming common enough to be a "de facto" standard for this purpose, but the applications and data must be compatible enough to be accessible from this window.

Connectivity. The workstations of information workers will be connected whenever people must cooperate or communicate. Communication is recognized as an increasingly important function to be supported by technology, so it will be an integrated part of the information systems delivered through the workstation. Connectivity means first, the actual ability to connect workstations through local area networks (LANs) and across LANs through wide area networks (WANs) and gateways. It also requires a band width or data transfer rate to accommodate the interchange of large files, graphics and figures, digital images, photographs, and video. Rich communication in the process of decision making and problem solving will require rich media, and therefore high capacity communication channels.

Document Data. The well-structured data in data bases has long been valuable for decision support. Even more important may be the concepts and ideas contained in less well-structured documents. Technologies are emerging that will allow access to, and management of, documents in addition to data records. This vastly increased set of information resources will have a major impact on the strength and effectiveness of DSS. These expanded information resources are made even more valuable with new search and structuring technologies such as concept retrieval, hypertext, and multimedia. Chapter 12 discusses the growing importance of document resources in DSS.

More Intelligence. As expert systems began to develop and be used, some thought that they would replace DSS. DSS builders realized, however, that expert systems are enhanced forms of models, but if used only on a stand-alone basis, they suffer from the same limitations as stand-alone management science models. Thus, they were added to the model base and the DSS was used as a delivery system for the expert systems.

More recently, components of expert systems and other AI approaches have been integrated into DSS. The knowledge base becomes a form of combined data/model base, the inference engine can be viewed as a knowledge base management system (similar to the data base management system and dialog management system), and the language system is a part of the dialog. The future will bring much more integration and extension of the intelligence capability in DSS. Chapter 13 presents a more detailed vision of the growing role of intelligent DSS.

SUMMARY AND CONCLUSION

We have seen how DSS evolved into a field of research, development, and practice during the 1970s and 80s. That field has now grown to the point it is made up of many threads with different, but related names, such as Executive Information systems, group DSS, expert systems, expert support systems, and intelligent support systems. A broader perspective suggests that all these threads are part of the overall mission to improve the performance of people in organizations when they confront ill-structured problems and tasks. This vision can be realized if we can meet the challenges to provide an integrated architecture for the systems which includes widespread connectivity, incorporate documents in the information resources, and continue to increase the intelligence of the systems.

REFERENCES

BLANNING, ROBERT and DAVID KING. *Current Research in Decision Support Technology.* CSP Information Systems Book Series, ed. Ralph Sprague. Los Alamitos, California: IEEE Computer Society Press. 1993.

EOM, SEAN B., SANG M. LEE, and JWA K. KIM. "The Intellectual Structure of Decision Support Systems (1971–1989)." *Decision Support Systems* 10 (June 1993): 19–35.

FARHOOMAND, A. F. "Scientific Progress of Management Information Systems." *Data Base* 18 (Summer 1987): 48–56.

GORRY, M. A. and MICHAEL SCOTT MORTON. "A Framework for Management Information Systems." *Sloan Management Review* 13 (Fall 1971): 55–70.

GRAY, PAUL (ed). *Decision Support and Executive Information Systems.* Prentice Hall Series in Information Management, ed. William King. Englewood Cliffs, N.J.: Prentice Hall, 1994.

MCLEAN, EPHRAIM R. and HENK SOL, ed. *Decision Support Systems: A Decade in Perspective.* Amsterdam, Holland: Elsevier Science Publishers, B. V., 1986.

SCOTT MORTON, MICHAEL. *Management Decision Systems: Computer Support for Decision Making.* Cambridge, Mass.: Harvard University Press, 1971.

SHRIVER, BRUCE, and RALPH H. SPRAGUE, JR. (eds), "Proceedings, Hawaii International Conference on Systems Sciences." Computer Society Press. Los Alamitos, Ca., c. 1995.

SOL, HENK and J. VECSENYI, ed. *Environments for Supporting Decision Support Systems.* Amsterdam, Holland: Elsevier Science Publishers, B. V., 1991.

SPRAGUE, RALPH H. "A Framework For the Development of Decision Support Systems." *Management Information Systems Quarterly* 4 (Winter 1980): 1–26.

SPRAGUE, RALPH H. and ERIC CARLSON. *Building Effective Decision Support Systems.* Englewood Cliffs, N.J.: Prentice Hall, 1982.

SPRAGUE, RALPH H. and HUGH WATSON. *Decision Support Systems: Putting Theory into Practice.* Third ed., Englewood Cliffs, N.J.: Prentice Hall, 1993.

TENG, J. T. C. and D. F. GALETTA. "MIS Research Directions: A Survey of Researcher's Views." *Data Base* 21 (Fall 1990): 1–10.

TIMS, The Institute of Management Sciences. "Proceedings, International Conferences on DSS." Providence, Rhode Island.

WATSON, HUGH and HOUSTON CARR. "Organizing for Decision Support System Support: The End-User Services Alternative." *Journal of Management Information Systems* 4 (January 1987): 83–95.

QUESTIONS

1. What is the mission of information systems in organizations and how does DSS support it?
2. What is the difference between Type I and Type II information work?
3. Why is the distinction important to the design and use of DSS?
4. Trace the stages of the data processing and MIS evolution. What is likely to be the next stage?
5. Trace the stages of the management science evolution. What is likely to be the next stage?
6. Explain how parts of each of these evolutions have converged in DSS. What is likely to be the next stage in DSS?

7. Discuss the three levels of DSS technology. Give examples of each level.
8. Compare and contrast iterative design with the more traditional approaches (e.g., systems development life cycle).
9. Give examples of each of the components of the DDM paradigm. What is the significance of the direct link of the data and modeling components?
10. Which of the challenges for the future will be the most difficult to achieve, in your opinion.

2

THE INFORMATION EXECUTIVES TRULY NEED

Ever since the new data processing tools first emerged 30 or 40 years ago, business people have both overrated and underrated the importance of information in the organization. We—and I include myself—overrated the possibilities to the point where we talked of computer-generated "business models" that could make decisions and might even be able to run much of the business. But we also grossly underrated the new tools; we saw in them the means to do better what executives were already doing to manage their organizations.

Nobody talks of business models making economic decisions anymore. The greatest contribution of our data processing capacity so far has not even been to management. It has been to operations—for example, computer-assisted design or the marvelous software that architects now use to solve structural problems in the buildings they design.

Yet even as we both overestimated and underestimated the new tools, we failed to realize that they would drastically change the tasks to be tackled. Concepts and tools, history teaches again and again, are mutually interdependent and interactive. One changes the other. That is now happening to the concept we call a business and to the tools we call information. The new tools enable us—indeed, may force us—to see our businesses differently:

- as generators of resources, that is, as organizations that can convert business costs into yields;

This chapter is a reprint of Peter Drucker, "The Information Executives Truly Need," *Harvard Business Review*, Jan.-Feb. 1995, pp. 54–62, and is used by permission.

- as links in an economic chain, which managers need to understand as a whole in order to manage their costs;
- as society's organs for the creation of wealth; and
- as both creatures and creators of a material environment, the area outside the organization in which opportunities and results lie but in which the threats to the success and the survival of every business also originate.

This article deals with the tools executives require to generate the information they need. And it deals with the concepts underlying those tools. Some of the tools have been around for a long time, but rarely, if ever, have they been focused on the task of managing a business. Some have to be refashioned; in their present form they no longer work. For some tools that promise to be important in the future, we have so far only the briefest specifications. The tools themselves still have to be designed.

Even though we are just beginning to understand how to use information as a tool, we can outline with high probability the major parts of the information system executives need to manage their businesses. So, in turn, can we begin to understand the concepts likely to underlie the business—call it the redesigned corporation—that executives will have to manage tomorrow.

FROM COST ACCOUNTING TO YIELD CONTROL

We may have gone furthest in redesigning both business and information in the most traditional of our information systems: accounting. In fact, many businesses have already shifted from traditional cost accounting to *activity-based costing*. Activity-based costing represents both a different concept of the business process, especially for manufacturers, and different ways of measuring.

Traditional cost accounting, first developed by General Motors 70 years ago, postulates that total manufacturing cost is the sum of the costs of individual operations. Yet the cost that matters for competitiveness and profitability is the cost of the total process, and that is what the new activity-based costing records and makes manageable. Its basic premise is that manufacturing is an integrated process that starts when supplies, materials, and parts arrive at the plant's loading dock and continues even after the finished product reaches the end user. Service is still a cost of the product, and so is installation, even if the customer pays.

Traditional cost accounting measures what it costs to *do* a task, for example, to cut a screw thread. Activity-based costing also records the cost of *not doing,* such as the cost of machine downtime, the cost of waiting for a needed part or tool, the cost of inventory waiting to be shipped, and the cost of reworking or scrapping a defective part. The costs of not doing, which traditional cost accounting cannot and does not record, often equal and sometimes even exceed the costs of doing. Activity-based costing therefore gives not only much better cost control, but increasingly, it also gives *result control.*

Traditional cost accounting assumes that a certain operation—for example, heat treating—has to be done and that it has to be done where it is being done now. Activity-based costing asks, Does it have to be done? If so, where is it best done? Activity-based costing integrates what were once several activities—value analysis, process analysis, quality management, and costing—into one analysis.

Using that approach, activity-based costing can substantially lower manufacturing costs—in some instances by a full third or more. Its greatest impact, however, is likely to be in services. In most manufacturing companies, cost accounting is inadequate. But service industries—banks, retail stores, hospitals, schools, newspapers, and radio and television stations—have practically no cost information at all.

Activity-based costing shows us why traditional cost accounting has not worked for service companies. It is not because the techniques are wrong. It is because traditional cost accounting makes the wrong assumptions. Service companies cannot start with the cost of individual operations, as manufacturing companies have done with traditional cost accounting. They must start with the assumption that there is only *one* cost: that of the total system. And it is a fixed cost over any given time period. The famous distinction between fixed and variable costs, on which traditional cost accounting is based, does not make much sense in services. Neither does the basic assumption of traditional cost accounting: that capital can be substituted for labor. In fact, in knowledge-based work especially, additional capital investment will likely require more, rather than less, labor. For example, a hospital that buys a new diagnostic tool may have to add four or five people to run it. Other knowledge-based organizations have had to learn the same lesson. But that all costs are fixed over a given time period and that resources cannot be substituted for one another, so that the *total* operation has to be costed—those are precisely the assumptions with which activity-based costing starts. By applying them to services, we are beginning for the first time to get cost information and yield control.

Banks, for instance, have been trying for several decades to apply conventional cost-accounting techniques to their business—that is, to figure the costs of individual operations and services—with almost negligible results. Now they are beginning to ask, Which one *activity* is at the center of costs and of results? The answer: serving the customer. The cost per customer in any major area of banking is a fixed cost. Thus it is the *yield* per customer—both the volume of services a customer uses and the mix of those services—that determines costs and profitability. Retail discounters, especially those in Western Europe, have known that for some time. They assume that once a unit of shelf space is installed, the cost is fixed and management consists of maximizing the yield thereon over a given time span. Their focus on yield control has enabled them to increase profitability despite their low prices and low margins.

Service businesses are only beginning to apply the new costing concepts. In some areas, such as research labs, where productivity is nearly impossible to measure, we may always have to rely on assessment and judgment rather than on measurement. But for most knowledge-based and service work, we should, within 10 to 15 years, have developed reliable tools to measure and manage costs and to relate those costs to results.

Thinking more clearly about costing in services should yield new insights into the costs of getting and keeping customers in all kinds of businesses. If GM, Ford, and Chrysler had used activity-based costing, for example, they would have realized early on the utter futility of their competitive blitzes of the past few years, which offered new-car buyers spectacular discounts and hefty cash rewards. Those promotions actually cost the Big Three automakers enormous amounts of money and, worse, enormous numbers of potential customers. In fact, every one resulted in a nasty drop in market standing. But neither the costs of the special deals nor their negative yields appeared in the companies' conventional cost-accounting figures, so management never saw the damage. Conventional cost accounting shows only the costs of individual manufacturing operations in isolation, and those were not affected by the discounts and rebates in the marketplace. Also, conventional cost accounting does not show the impact of pricing decisions on such things as market share.

Activity-based costing shows—or at least attempts to show—the impact of changes in the costs and yields of every activity on the results of the whole. Had the automakers used it, it soon would have shown the damage done by the discount blitzes. In fact, because the Japanese already use a form of activity-based costing—though still a fairly primitive one—Toyota, Nissan, and Honda knew better than to compete with U.S. automakers through discounts and thus maintained both their market share and their profits.

FROM LEGAL FICTION TO ECONOMIC REALITY

Knowing the cost of your operations, however, is not enough. To succeed in the increasingly competitive global market, a company has to know the costs of its entire economic chain and has to work with other members of the chain to manage costs and maximize yield. Companies are therefore beginning to shift from costing only what goes on inside their own organizations to costing the entire economic process, in which even the biggest company is just one link.

The legal entity, the company, is a reality for shareholders, for creditors, for employees, and for tax collectors. But *economically,* it is fiction. Thirty years ago, the Coca-Cola Company was a franchisor. Independent bottlers manufactured the product. Now the company owns most of its bottling operations in the United States. But Coke drinkers—even those few who know that fact—could not care less. What matters in the marketplace is the economic reality, the costs of the entire process, regardless of who owns what.

Again and again in business history, an unknown company has come from nowhere and in a few short years overtaken the established leaders without apparently even breathing hard. The explanation always given is superior strategy, superior technology, superior marketing, or lean manufacturing. But in every single case, the newcomer also enjoys a tremendous cost advantage, usually about 30%. The reason is always the same: the new company knows and manages the costs of the entire economic chain rather than its costs alone.

Toyota is perhaps the best-publicized example of a company that knows and manages the costs of its suppliers and distributors; they are all, of course, members of its *keiretsu*. Through that network, Toyota manages the total cost of making, distributing, and servicing its cars as one cost stream, putting work where it costs the least and yields the most.

Managing the economic cost stream is not a Japanese invention, however, but a U.S. one. It began with the man who designed and built General Motors, William Durant. About 1908, Durant began to buy small, successful automobile companies—Buick, Oldsmobile, Cadillac, Chevrolet—and merged them into his new General Motors Corporation. In 1916, he set up a separate subsidiary called United Motors to buy small, successful parts companies. His first acquisitions included Delco, which held Charles Kettering's patents to the automotive self-starter.

Durant ultimately bought about 20 supplier companies; his last acquisition—in 1919, the year before he was ousted as GM's CEO—was Fisher Body. Durant deliberately brought the parts and accessories makers into the design process of a new automobile model right from the start. Doing so allowed him to manage the total costs of the finished car as one cost stream. In fact, Durant invented the keiretsu.

However, between 1950 and 1960, Durant's keiretsu became an albatross around the company's neck, as unionization imposed higher labor costs on GM's parts divisions than on their independent competitors. As the outside customers, the independent automobile companies such as Packard and Studebaker, which had bought 50% of the output of GM's parts divisions, disappeared one by one, GM's control over both the costs and quality of its main suppliers disappeared with them. But for 40 years or more, GM's systems costing gave it an unbeatable advantage over even the most efficient of its competitors, which for most of that time was Studebaker.

Sears, Roebuck and Company was the first to copy Durant's system. In the 1920s, it established long-term contracts with its suppliers and bought minority interests in them. Sears was then able to consult with suppliers as they designed the product and to understand and manage the entire cost stream. That gave the company an unbeatable cost advantage for decades.

In the early 1930s, London-based department store Marks & Spencer copied Sears with the same result. Twenty years later, the Japanese, led by Toyota, studied and copied both Sears and Marks & Spencer. Then in the 1980s, Wal-Mart

Stores adapted the approach by allowing suppliers to stock products directly on store shelves, thereby eliminating warehouse inventories and with them nearly one-third of the cost of traditional retailing.

But those companies are still rare exceptions. Although economists have known the importance of costing the entire economic chain since Alfred Marshall wrote about it in the late 1890s, most businesspeople still consider it theoretical abstraction. Increasingly, however, managing the economic cost chain will become a necessity. In their article, "From Lean Production to the Lean Enterprise" (*HBR*, March-April 1994), James P. Womack and Daniel T. Jones argue persuasively that executives need to organize and manage not only the cost chain but also everything else—especially corporate strategy and product planning—as one economic whole, regardless of the legal boundaries of individual companies.

A powerful force driving companies toward economic-chain costing will be the shift from cost-led pricing to price-led costing. Traditionally, Western companies have started with costs, put a desired profit margin on top, and arrived at a price. They practiced cost-led pricing. Sears and Marks & Spencer long ago switched to price-led costing, in which the price the customer is willing to pay determines allowable costs, beginning with the design stage. Until recently, those companies were the exceptions. Now price-led costing is becoming the rule. The Japanese first adopted it for their exports. Now Wal-Mart and all the discounters in the United States, Japan, and Europe are practicing price-led costing. It underlies Chrysler's success with its recent models and the success of GM's Saturn. Companies can practice price-led costing, however, only if they know and manage the *entire* cost of the economic chain.

The same ideas apply to outsourcing, alliances, and joint ventures—indeed, to any business structure that is built on partnership rather than control. And such entities, rather than the traditional model of a parent company with wholly owned subsidiaries, are increasingly becoming the models for growth, especially in the global economy.

Still, it will be painful for most businesses to switch to economic-chain costing. Doing so requires uniform or at least compatible accounting systems at companies along the entire chain. Yet each one does its accounting in its own way, and each is convinced that its system is the only possible one. Moreover, economic-chain costing requires information sharing across companies, and even within the same company, people tend to resist information sharing. Despite those challenges, companies can find ways to practice economic-chain costing now, as Procter & Gamble is demonstrating. Using the way Wal-Mart develops close relationships with suppliers as a model, P&G is initiating information sharing and economic-chain management with the 300 large retailers that distribute the bulk of its products worldwide.

Whatever the obstacles, economic-chain costing is going to be done. Otherwise, even the most efficient company will suffer from an increasing cost disadvantage.

INFORMATION FOR WEALTH CREATION

Enterprises are paid to create wealth, not control costs. But that obvious fact is not reflected in traditional measurements. First-year accounting students are taught that the balance sheet portrays the liquidation value of the enterprise and provides creditors with worst-case information. But enterprises are not normally run to be liquidated. They have to be managed as going concerns, that is, for *wealth creation.* To do that requires information that enables executives to make informed judgments. It requires four sets of diagnostic tools: foundation information, productivity information, competence information, and information about the allocation of scarce resources. Together, they constitute the executive's tool kit for managing the current business.

Foundation Information. The oldest and most widely used set of diagnostic management tools are cash-flow and liquidity projections and such standard measurements as the ratio between dealers' inventories and sales of new cars; the earnings coverage for the interest payments on a bond issue; and the ratios between receivables outstanding more than six months, total receivables, and sales. Those may be likened to the measurements a doctor takes at a routine physical: weight, pulse, temperature, blood pressure, and urine analysis. If those readings are normal, they do not tell us much. If they are abnormal, they indicate a problem that needs to be identified and treated. Those measurements might be called foundation information.

Productivity Information. The second set of tools for business diagnosis deals with the productivity of key resources. The oldest of them—of World War II vintage—measures the productivity of manual labor. Now we are slowly developing measurements, though still quite primitive ones, for the productivity of knowledge-based and service work. However, measuring only the productivity of workers, whether blue or white collar, no longer gives us adequate information about productivity. We need data on total-factor productivity.

That explains the growing popularity of economic value-added analysis. EVA is based on something we have known for a long time: what we generally call profits, the money left to service equity, is usually not profit at all.[1] Until a business returns a profit that is greater than its cost of capital, it operates at a loss. Never mind that it pays taxes as if it had a genuine profit. The enterprise still returns less to the economy than it devours in resources. It does not cover its full costs unless the reported profit exceeds the cost of capital. Until then, it does not

[1]I discussed EVA at considerable length in my 1964 book, *Managing for Results,* but the last generation of classical economists, Alfred Marshall in England and Eugen Böhm-Bswerk in Austria, were already discussing it in the late 1890s.

create wealth; it destroys it. By that measurement, incidentally, few U.S. businesses have been profitable since World War II.

By measuring the value added over *all* costs, including the cost of capital, EVA measures, in effect, the productivity of *all* factors of production. It does not, by itself, tell us why a certain product or a certain service does not add value or what to do about it. But it shows us what we need to find out and whether we need to take remedial action. EVA should also be used to find out what works. It does show which product, service, operation, or activity has unusually high productivity and adds unusually high value. Then we should ask ourselves, What can we learn from those successes?

The most recent of the tools used to obtain productivity information is benchmarking—comparing one's performance with the best performance in the industry or, better yet, with the best anywhere in business. Benchmarking assumes correctly that what one organization does, any other organization can do as well. And it assumes, also correctly, that being at least as good as the leader is a prerequisite to being competitive. Together, EVA and benchmarking provide the diagnostic tools to measure total-factor productivity and to manage it.

Competence Information. A third set of tools deals with competencies. Ever since C.K. Prahalad and Gary Hamel's pathbreaking article, "The Core Competence of the Corporation" (*HBR*, May-June 1990), we have known that leadership rests on being able to do something others cannot do at all or find difficult to do even poorly. It rests on core competencies that meld market or customer value with a special ability of the producer or supplier.

Some examples: the ability of the Japanese to miniaturize electronic components, which is based on their 300-year-old artistic tradition of putting landscape paintings on a tiny lacquer box, called an *inro,* and of carving a whole zoo of animals on the even tinier button that holds the box on the wearer's belt, called a *netsuke;* or the almost unique ability GM has had for 80 years to make successful acquisitions; or Marks & Spencer's also unique ability to design packaged and ready-to-eat luxury meals for middle-class budgets. But how does one identify both the core competencies one has already and those the business needs in order to take and maintain a leadership position? How does one find out whether one's core competence is improving or weakening? Or whether it is still the right core competence and what changes it might need?

So far the discussion of core competencies has been largely anecdotal. But a number of highly specialized midsize companies—a Swedish pharmaceutical producer and a U.S. producer of specialty tools, to name two—are developing the methodology to measure and manage core competencies. The first step is to keep careful track of one's own and one's competitors' performances, looking especially for unexpected successes and unexpected poor performance in areas where one should have done well. The successes demonstrate what the market values and will pay for. They indicate where the business enjoys a leadership advantage.

The nonsuccesses should be viewed as the first indication either that the marker is changing or that the company's competencies are weakening.

That analysis allows for the early recognition of opportunities. For example, by carefully tracking an unexpected success, a U.S. toolmaker found that small Japanese machine shops were buying its high-tech, high-priced tools, even though it had not designed the tools with them in mind or made sales calls to them. That allowed the company to recognize a new core competence: the Japanese were attracted to its products because they were easy to maintain and repair despite their technical complexity. When that insight was applied to designing products, the company gained leadership in the small-plant and machine-shop markets in the United States and Western Europe, huge markets where it had done practically no business before.

Core competencies are different for every organization; they are, so to speak, part of an organization's personality. But every organization—not just businesses—needs one core competence: *innovation.* And every organization needs a way to record and appraise its *innovative performance.* In organizations already doing that—among them several topflight pharmaceutical manufacturers—the starting point is not the company's own performance. It is a careful record of the innovations in the entire field during a given period. Which of them were truly successful? How many of them were ours? Is our performance commensurate with our objectives? With the direction of the market? With our market standing? With our research spending? Are our successful innovations in the areas of greatest growth and opportunity? How many of the truly important innovation opportunities did we miss? Why? Because we did not see them? Or because we saw them but dismissed them? Or because we botched them? And how well do we convert an innovation into a commercial product? A good deal of that, admittedly, is assessment rather than measurement. It raises rather than answers questions, but it raises the right questions.

Resource-Allocation Information. The last area in which diagnostic information is needed to manage the current business for wealth creation is the allocation of scarce resources: capital and performing people. Those two convert into action whatever information management has about its business. They determine whether the enterprise will do well or do poorly.

GM developed the first systematic capital-appropriations process about 70 years ago. Today practically every business has a capital-appropriations process, but few use it correctly. Companies typically measure their proposed capital appropriations by only one or two of the following yardsticks: return on investment, payback period, cash flow, or discounted present value. But we have known for a long time—since the early 1930s—that none of those is *the* right method. To understand a proposed investment, a company needs to look at *all* four. Sixty years ago, that would have required endless number crunching. Now a laptop computer can provide the information within a few minutes. We also have known for 60 years that managers should never look at just one proposed capital appropriation in isolation but should instead choose the projects that show the best ratio between opportunity and risks. That requires a capital-appropriations *budget* to display the choices—again, something far too many businesses do not do. Most serious, however, is that most capital-appropriations processes do not even ask for two vital pieces of information:

- What will happen if the proposed investment fails to produce the promised results, as do three out of every five? Would it seriously hurt the company, or would it be just a flea bite?
- If the investment is successful—and especially if it is more successful than we expect—what will it commit us to? No one at GM seems to have asked what Saturn's success would commit the company to. As a result, the company may end up killing its own success because of its inability to finance it.

In addition, a capital-appropriations request requires specific deadlines: When should we expect what results? Then the results—successes, near successes, near failures, and failures—need to be reported and analyzed. There is no better way to improve an organization's performance than to measure the results of capital appropriations against the promises and expectations that led to their authorization. How much better off the United States would be today had such feedback on government programs been standard practice for the past 50 years.

Capital, however, is only one key resource of the organization, and it is by no means the scarcest one. The scarcest resources in any organization are performing people. Since World War II, the U.S. military—and so far no one else—has learned to test its placement decisions. It now thinks through what it expects of senior officers before it puts them into key commands. It then appraises their performance against those expectations. And it constantly appraises its own process for selecting senior commanders against the successes and failures of its appointments. In business, by contrast, placement with specific expectations as to what the appointee should achieve and systematic appraisal of the outcome are virtually unknown. In the effort to create wealth, managers need to allocate human resources as purposefully and as thoughtfully as they do capital. And the outcomes of those decisions ought to be recorded and studied as carefully.

WHERE THE RESULTS ARE

Those four kinds of information tell us only about the current business. They inform and direct *tactics*. For *strategy*, we need organized information about the environment. Strategy has to be based on information about markets, customers, and noncustomers; about technology in one's own industry and others; about worldwide finance; and about the changing world economy. For that is where the results are. Inside an organization, there are only cost centers. The only profit center is a customer whose check has not bounced.

Major changes also start outside an organization. A retailer may know a great deal about the people who shop at its stores. But no matter how successful it is, no retailer ever has more than a small fraction of the market as its customers; the great majority are noncustomers. It is always with noncustomers that basic changes begin and become significant.

At least half the important new technologies that have transformed an industry in the past 50 years came from outside the industry itself. Commercial paper, which has revolutionized finance in the United States, did not originate with the banks. Molecular biology and genetic engineering were not developed by the pharmaceutical industry. Though the great majority of businesses will continue to operate only locally or regionally, they all face, at least potentially, global competition from places they have never even heard of before.

Not all of the needed information about the outside is available, to be sure. There is no information—not even unreliable information—on economic conditions in most of China, for instance, or on legal conditions in most of the successor states to the Soviet empire. But even where information is readily available, many businesses are oblivious to it. Many U.S. companies went into Europe in the 1960s without even asking about labor legislation. European companies have been just as blind and ill informed in their ventures into the United States. A major cause of the Japanese real estate investment debacle in California during the 1990s was the failure to find out elementary facts about zoning and taxes.

A serious cause of business failure is the common assumption that conditions—taxes, social legislation, market preferences, distribution channels, intellectual property rights, and many others —*must* be what we think they are or at least what we think they *should* be. An adequate information system has to include information that makes executives question that assumption. It must lead them to ask the right questions, not just feed them the information they expect. That presupposes first that executives know what information they need. It demands further that they obtain that information on a regular basis. It finally requires that they systematically integrate the information into their decision making.

A few multinationals—Unilever, Coca-Cola, Nestlé, the big Japanese trading companies, and a few big construction companies—have been working hard on building systems to gather and organize outside information. But in general, the majority of enterprises have yet to start the job.

Even big companies, in large part, will have to hire outsiders to help them. To think through what the business needs requires somebody who knows and understands the highly specialized information field. There is far too much information for any but specialists to find their way around. The sources are totally diverse. Companies can generate some of the information themselves, such as information about customers and noncustomers or about the technology in one's own field. But most of what enterprises need to know about the environment is obtainable only from outside sources—from all kinds of data banks and data services, from journals in many languages, from trade associations, from government publications, from World Bank reports and scientific papers, and from specialized studies.

Another reason there is need for outside help is that the information has to be organized so it questions and challenges a company's strategy. To supply data is not enough. The data have to be integrated with strategy, they have to test a company's assumptions, and they must challenge a company's current outlook. One way to do that may be a new kind of software, information tailored to a specific group—say, to hospitals or to casualty insurance companies. The Lexis data base supplies such information to lawyers, but it only gives answers; it does not ask questions. What we need are services that make specific suggestions about how to use the information, ask specific questions regarding the users' business and practices, and perhaps provide interactive consultation. Or we might "outsource" the outside-information system. Maybe the most popular provider of the outside-information system, especially for smaller enterprises, will be that "inside outsider," the independent consultant.

Whichever way we satisfy it, the need for information on the environment where the major threats and opportunities are likely to arise will become increasingly urgent.

It may be argued that few of those information needs are new, and that is largely true. Conceptually, many of the new measurements have been discussed for many years and in many places. What is new is the technical data processing ability. It enables us to do quickly and cheaply what, only a few short years ago, would have been laborious and very expensive. Seventy years ago, the time-and-motion study made traditional cost accounting possible. Computers have now made activity-based cost accounting possible; without them, it would be practically impossible.

But that argument misses the point. What is important is not the tools. It is the concepts behind them. They convert what were always seen as discrete techniques to be used in isolation and for separate purposes into one integrated information system. That system then makes possible business diagnosis, business strategy, and business decisions. That is a new and radically different view of the meaning and purpose of information: as a measurement on which to base future action rather than as a postmortem and a record of what has already happened.

The command-and-control organization that first emerged in the 1870s might be compared to an organism held together by its shell. The corporation that is now emerging is being designed around a skeleton: *information,* both the corporation's new integrating system and its articulation.

Our traditional mind-set—even if we use sophisticated mathematical techniques and impenetrable sociological jargon—has always somehow perceived business as buying cheap and selling dear. The new approach defines a business as the organization that adds value and creates wealth.

QUESTIONS

1. What are the major changes in the ways executives will need to look at their organizations and their objectives?
2. Summarize the four kinds of information that will be needed for executives to manage the modern business. Give some examples of each.
3. What kinds of "outside information" will be needed? How should it be organized? Give some examples.
4. What guidelines or suggestions for the design of DSS and EIS can you derive from the kind of information, both inside and outside, that will be needed by the modern manager?

Part 2

DEVELOPING AND USING DECISION SUPPORT APPLICATIONS

A number of activities are required before a decision support application is ready for use. First, approval has to be given for the project. This step requires that the potential benefits and costs be assessed. While the costs can normally be estimated without too much difficulty, determining the benefits is more problematic, because they tend to be "soft" in nature. It is difficult to put a dollar value on benefits such as "more timely information" or " more concise information." Unlike transaction processing applications where the benefits involve increased transaction processing efficiency, such as reduced clerical expenses, decision support applications generate benefits that are not so easily quantified.

The next step is to determine the information requirements for the application. It might seem that this is as easy as asking the user what information is needed. Unfortunately, it is seldom as simple as this. Even if a user has a good understanding of the requirements, he or she may have a difficult time articulating them completely, or indicating the best format for their presentation. Even more likely, the user may not fully understand what information is needed. This more complete understanding may come only after using the system for awhile. Compounding the problem is that users and developers alike may have a difficult time communicating with and understanding one another. In a worse case scenario, the user may not understand the "techno speak" of the developer and the developer may not be able to adequately understand what the user wants.

Decision support applications require a different development methodology than transaction processing systems. Rather than using the system's development life cycle, with its distinct information requirements, logical systems design, physical systems design, programming, testing, and implementation phases, decision support applications use methodologies which go by names such as "adaptive," "evolutionary," "prototyping," and "iterative" design, where all the development steps are compressed in time and iterated as the requirements for the system become better understood. Recent hardware and software advances have made this development approach feasible.

Decision support applications require more user involvement than other kinds of applications. Because this system must meet the user's needs and these needs only become understood over time, the user should be involved during the entire development process. The user is best viewed as being a member of the development team.

The four chapters in this part of the book are designed to provide an initial understanding of how decision support applications are developed and used. Management becomes involved with decision support applications in a variety of ways: as an approver or administrator, developer, operator, and user of output. Chapter 3 provides a realistic analysis of management practices in each of these areas.

A critical early step in developing any kind of application is determining the information requirements. Most of what follows is shaped by this step. As has been suggested, for many decision support applications, specifying the information requirements is difficult. Chapter 4 explores determining the information requirements for an executive information system. It discusses why it is a difficult process, the traditional approaches employed, and the findings from a study that identified methods that can be used. While the methods are specifically for EIS, they suggest how the information requirements for other kinds of decision support applications can be determined.

The conventional wisdom is that decision support applications require a unique development approach. Chapter 5 discusses this approach and illustrates it for a real estate DSS. It also shows how a DSS can be used.

A computer-aided train dispatching application is discussed in Chapter 6. It illustrates that some DSS are developed using a more structured methodology than adaptive design. It also shows how a DSS can be developed and used by operational personnel.

3

MANAGEMENT INVOLVEMENT IN DECISION SUPPORT SYSTEMS

The purpose of a decision support system (DSS) is to support managerial decision making. This support may come about indirectly through staff operation of the DSS or as a result of hands-on use by management. Because a DSS is designed and developed for a specific decision-making task and decision maker(s), the need for management involvement is substantial. In fact, management is involved with a DSS from the initial inception of the idea to its ongoing use.

One way to think about the role of management in DSS is through a logical segmentation of management's tasks, which include

- Approval and administration;
- Development;
- Operation; and
- Utilization of output.

As an approver, the manager is functioning in a way that is consistent with other planning activities. It is generally the responsibility of management to judge the relative merits of alternative organizational investments and to approve those investments that are of the greatest potential value to the organization. In addition, DSS development may require a new organizational unit with a position within the organization's structure, requiring relationships with other organizational units and submitting them to the administrative control of management.

This chapter was written by Jack T. Hogue.

Once a DSS project has been approved, the system must be brought into being; that is, it must be developed. Given that the purpose of a DSS is to support the manager's decision-making responsibilities, and given that decision making is often a difficult task to specify or structure, it is logical that considerable management involvement is required during the development of a DSS. Because there is a high level of managerial ownership of DSS (discussed later), management involvement during development goes well beyond the usual specification of information requirements.

The actual operation of a DSS may require skills not possessed by many managers. In these cases, an intermediary may operate the system for the user. However, there are also instances where the manager will want to operate the DSS personally.

When making decisions, managers typically make use of a variety of sources of information. Depending on the manager's own personal style, the emphasis placed on different information will, of course, vary. The purpose of the DSS is to support the manager in the decision-making process by supplying needed information. In the final analysis, it is the output of the DSS that the manager is most interested in.

Insights about managements' involvement in DSS related activities are provided by several studies that were largely conducted during the 1980s. This chapter summarizes and puts into perspective much of what was learned.

APPROVER AND ADMINISTRATOR OF THE DSS

Who Defines DSS Policy?

The conventional wisdom says that information system applications should be centrally monitored and controlled; however, in practice, planning for the development of a DSS tends to be more of a decentralized, ad hoc process. Sprague and Carlson [1982] indicate that DSS planning should be incorporated into corporate planning processes. Alavi [1985] has focused on the need for coordination and control of end-user computing (EUC). Table 3–1 provides a description of the main issues that are involved.

While many of the EUC issues apply to DSS as well (since most DSS are examples of EUC), decision support systems are distinct from the EUC category in terms of initiating and championing the application. Virtually all DSS have strong management support and involvement, whereas many EUC applications are built by and for staff personnel. The strong commitment to and involvement in "their" DSS leads to a sense of ownership of DSS by managers. It may be this decentralized ownership which has perpetuated the "hands-off" philosophy regarding DSS administration. Thus, formal planning for DSS is the exception.

TABLE 3-1 Organizational Risks Associated with Different Stages of End-User Application Life Cycle

	End-user life cycle stages	Risks
Analysis	Analysis of end-user tools	Ineffective use of monetary resources Incompatible use of monetary tools Threats to data security and integrity
	Analysis of end-user applications	Over analysis and inefficient search in the problem space Solving the wrong problem
Design	Conceptual design of end-user applications	Applying the wrong model Mismatch between the tools and applications
	Development of end-user applications	Little or no documentation Lack of extensive testing Lack of validation and quality assurance checks Inefficient expenditure of non-data processing personnel Redundant development effort
Implementation	Operation of end-user applications	Threats to data integrity Threats to security Taxing the mainframe computer resources
	Maintenance of end-user applications	Failure to document and test medications Failure to upgrade the applications

(Adapted from Maryam Alavi and Ira Weis, "Managing the Risks Associated with End-User Computing," *Journal of Management Information Systems,* Winter 1985–86, pp. 6–20.)

While DSS are occasionally administered by a corporate steering committee, local managers generally control their DSS directly and through their immediate staff. Corporate master plans for DSS development rarely exist; rather, policies are usually informally set by middle and/or upper managers within the DSS user group. Even though administrative policies are generally set at the departmental level, they often reflect corporate policy. When the departmental manager tries to define an administrative policy for DSS applications, corporate procedures are often copied.

Three basic planning approaches for the development of DSSs are described by Sprague and Carlson [1982]. The *quick-hit* approach consists of the development of a single DSS application with little or no thought given to subsequent applications. With a *staged development* approach, the effort expended in creating the first system is reused in developing the second. This can affect the selection of a DSS generator, so that it is appropriate for use with multiple applications. The final approach is a *complete DSS* approach, where prior to the development of any specific DSS, a complete set of DSS tools and generators is acquired, and organizational issues related to DSS are decided. Among the alternatives, the evidence is clear that the first two approaches are most commonly used by companies.

How Are Resources Allocated and Controlled?

The financial evaluations of DSS are difficult due to the basic nature of the applications for which DSS are developed. The value created by a DSS is in the improvement in decision making that results from using the DSS. In order to fully evaluate DSS benefits, it is necessary to know the value to the organization of a decision both with and without the proposed DSS. This is, of course, not possible. The only practical approach to benefit analysis is to estimate the expected value of an improved decision, assuming that the proposed DSS improves the decision. Cost evaluation can proceed in a traditional fashion, by comparing the current cost of decision support with the cost of developing the DSS. The resources required for development of a DSS include traditional components, such as hardware, software, and management and staff development time. Because management and staff personnel devote a significant amount of time to developing a DSS, this cost should not be overlooked.

A common approach to evaluating the desirability of developing a DSS involves an intuitive assessment of the costs and benefits [Hogue, 1987]. Benefits are often difficult to quantify. Even though costs are more easily estimated, it may be that a perceived low level of costs relative to potential benefits may eliminate a more formal analysis. This intuition-based approach to cost-benefit analysis is very close to the method described by Keen, which is referred to as "value analysis" [Keen, 1983]. In part, value analysis prescribes the establishment of a "cost threshold" which the intuitively estimated benefits must exceed in order for the DSS to be approved.

The specific resources utilized by DSS can be categorized as technical and application. Technical resources include hardware, development software, and communications capabilities. Both the source and control of these resources tend to vary depending on whether the application is PC or mainframe-based. For PC-based DSS, technical resources are supplied and controlled in a collaborative fashion between the user area and the information system (IS) function. Mainframe-based DSS have their technical resources supplied and controlled by IS. Application resources include data input, application logic, and application maintenance. Application resources tend to be both supplied and controlled by the user area (with support from IS).

DEVELOPER OF THE DSS

How Much and When Is Management Involved?

The development process for a DSS includes the same basic steps that are required for most applications—idea generation and approval, information requirements determination, design, development, and maintenance. However, DSS applications tend to rely heavily upon an iterative development process which involves multiple executions of a combined analysis-design-implementation effort [Keen, 1980; Naumann and Jenkins, 1982]. In order to examine the specific points of management involvement in DSS development, it is useful to categorize the development process somewhat differently, and to examine it in terms of the different levels of management; see Table 3–2. The design and development steps are combined into the single step labeled "building."

Most DSS are developed for and by middle and upper management. While upper management is very often involved in the development process of a DSS, it tends to be less directly involved in the physical, hands-on process of building the DSS. Top management often has the idea for developing the DSS, participates in determining information requirements, and later accepts the application.

Middle management involvement is often different from upper-management involvement in DSS development. Middle management often takes the leadership role during the development process. This role is especially noteworthy during the physical building process. It is not limited to situations where the DSS is being developed for a middle management decision-making process, but rather extends into applications for upper management as well. It may be logically expected that more direct management involvement in system building results from employing more user-friendly development tools (i.e., DSS generator rather than DSS tools). Research has shown a general tendency for DSS applications which have been developed using a DSS generator to have been developed by the end users of the system, and those developed from DSS tools to be more likely to have been developed by IS [Hogue and Watson, 1983].

The time required for the development of a DSS can range from one week to three months for narrowly defined, quick hit DSS, and often take six months to two years for larger-scale, organization-wide DSS. While the total time for DSS development varies considerably, the percentage of managements' time devoted to the development effort is relatively unaffected by the total duration. For the

TABLE 3–2 Management Involvement in the Development of DSS

	Management level			
Stage	Lower	Middle	Top	All
Idea	0%	61%	61%	100%
Information Requirements	0	78	61	100
Building	11	72	6	78
Testing	11	72	6	83
Demonstration	11	78	28	89
Acceptance	0	72	67	100

Adapted from Jack T. Hogue and Hugh J. Watson, "Current Practices in the Development of Decision Support Systems," *Proceedings of the Fifth International Conference on Information Systems*, Tucson, Arizona, November 28–30, 1983, pp. 117–127.

manager(s) who tends to have primary responsibility for the project, typical time requirements are in the 25 to 75 percent range.

How Is Management Style Incorporated into the DSS?

Considerable attention has been given to the issue of personal decision-making process and style, and the accommodation of that process and style by IS applications (e.g., the intuitive-rational dichotomy [McKenney & Keen, 1974]). Because DSS are typically built for a relatively few individuals' use, the opportunity exists to tailor a DSS to the specific individual(s) who will be using it. There is an appeal to this idea but it suffers from one major problem. If the DSS was developed around the specific process and style of one decision maker, considerable revision could be required when a new individual assumes the job. The problem would be greater for a DSS modeled directly upon a decision process. Here the revision in code would require a major application revision. Consequently, DSS are rarely developed as a model of the decision maker.

The incorporation of decision style into a system usually focuses on the user interface, the level of expertise in use of the application assumed of the user, and the presentation format of DSS outputs. All of these can easily be tailored to the style of a user; however, the problem of multiple users or new users again presents itself. Most DSS accommodate user style through multiple options for different kinds of users. For example, the user may choose from novice or experienced user interfaces, and from various levels of detail/summary and graphical/tabular reporting options.

OPERATION OF THE DSS

How Much Does Management Operate the DSS?

A decision-making process is often a semistructured, ad hoc process by which a manager identifies possible scenarios, considers the impact of the scenarios, and chooses a final course of action. A DSS is an aid to assist with this process, and may be operated directly by the manager or delegated by the manager to a staff intermediary. It may not make any real difference to the success of the decision-making process whether it is the manager or an intermediary who operates the DSS, and in fact, most DSS are operated by both managers and their intermediaries.

How Is the Manager's Decision Approach Maintained by the DSS?

A DSS should function, to some degree, as an extension of the manager(s) for which it is built. When a manager operates the DSS directly, maintenance of the decision approach is not an issue, assuming the DSS has been designed to accommodate the variations in the form of the user interface, the level of expertise in use of the application assumed of the user, and the presentation format of DSS outputs. The user is able to personally choose the sequencing of activities and methods of information presentation. This manager-DSS utilization process could be impacted if a manager were to make extensive use of intermediaries, since the utilization process would in this case seem to be more driven by the intermediary than the manager. In a study of 18 DSS, managers indicated that decision-maker style/approach is maintained acceptably if there is

- easy access of the intermediary to the manager;
- easy access of the intermediary to the DSS; and
- fast turnaround time on DSS output [Hogue and Watson, 1985].

These three items taken together indicate that the key to maintaining a decision maker's style when intermediaries are used is flexibility of operation rather than a design that replicates a single manager's decision-making process. The speed of response between the point in time when a manager requests support from the DSS and the point in time when the response is provided to the manager is critical when an intermediary is used.

UTILIZATION OF DSS OUTPUT

Is Use of the DSS Required?

Once a DSS is operational, its use may either be mandated, or more typically, be at the discretion of management. Further, there may be a question about whether the outputs must be "obeyed." There may be a managerial mandate to operate the DSS, but it is rare to have a situation where the system's recommendation must be followed. This latter situation is in keeping with the spirit of decision support rather than decision automation.

The requirement to use a DSS may arise from two situations. First, operation of the DSS may be mandated to provide information to management. Second, management may perceive the value of a DSS to be so high as to require its operation by lower-level managers. A case in point is Southern Railway, where operational personnel make routing decisions for trains. The operation of the train dispatching DSS is mandated by middle management; however, dispatchers are not obligated to follow the recommendations of the DSS. This application is discussed in depth in Chapter 6.

What Levels of Management Utilize the DSS?

All levels of management are actively engaged in decision making on a routine basis. The differences in the nature of decision making (and the nature of the information required) have been commonly noted to include such dimensions as:

- Decision structure (structured/unstructured);
- Source of information (internal/external);
- Accuracy of information (deterministic/probablistic, present/future); and
- Scope of decision (narrow/broad).

It is generally agreed that the more routine and structured the decision-making process is, the more successful transaction processing systems (TPS) and management information systems (MIS) are in satisfying the information requirements of the decision maker. Also, there will be less need for the ad hoc, investigative capabilities of a DSS. Therefore, while all levels of management can benefit from the use of DSS capabilities, the highest level of support is usually for middle and upper management.

How Does a Traditional DSS Support Individual and Group Processes?

Decision making can be categorized as:

- Independent;
- Sequential interdependent; or
- Pooled interdependent [Keen and Scott Morton, 1978]

Independent decision making involves one decision maker using a DSS to reach a decision without the need for input from other managers. While this form of DSS use is found occasionally, it is the exception, because of the common need for collaboration with other managers. Sequential interdependent decisions involve decision making at a decision point, followed by a subsequent decision at another point. In this case the decision at one point becomes the input to the decision at another point. A common example would be corporate planning and budgeting where a department formulates a plan which then becomes an input to the development of the budget. DSS are frequently used in support of sequential dependent decision making, but not as frequently as pooled interdependent decision making.

Pooled interdependent decision making is a joint, collaborative decision-making process in which all managers work together on the task. A group of marketing managers getting together to develop a marketing plan is an example of this type of decision. Specialized hardware, software, and processes have been developed to support pooled interdependent decision making. It is a type of group support system that is discussed in detail in Part 6 of the book.

How Does the DSS Support the Phases of Decision Making?

The decision-making process is generally considered to consist of a set of steps or phases which are carried out in the course of making a decision. The process can be conceptualized as consisting of intelligence, design, and choice phases [Simon, 1960]. Intelligence involves the identification of a problem (or opportunity) that requires a decision, and the collection of information relevant to the decision. Design involves the creation and evaluation of alternative courses of action. Choice is the selection of a course of action.

A DSS is typically developed to address a specific problem or opportunity which has been identified. Therefore, it is often unnecessary for a DSS to support the intelligence phase, especially for ad hoc DSS, where the DSS is created in response to the specific problem. For institutional DSS, which provide on-going decision support, a DSS may trigger an exception report which signals the need to address a problem.

The ability to support the design phase of decision making is the true test of a DSS. The real core of any DSS is the model base which has been built to analyze a problem or decision. The primary value to a decision maker of a DSS is the ability of the decision maker and the DSS to explore the models interactively as a means to identify and evaluate alternative courses of action. This is of tremendous value to the decision maker and represents the DSS's capability to support the design phase. Specifically, the most prevalent support for the choice phase by DSS is through "what-if" analysis and goal seeking.

The choice phase of decision making is the most variable in terms of support from DSS. In general, choice has been supported only occasionally by a DSS, traditionally because DSS were not designed to make a decision, but rather to show the impact of a defined scenario. Some DSS include models which identify a best choice (e.g., linear programming), but they are not the rule.

FACTORS AFFECTING MANAGEMENT INVOLVEMENT

While management involvement in DSS is often substantial, the level of involvement is a function of three factors which have a significant impact: the level of DSS technology employed for development of the DSS, the characteristics of the decision-making task, and whether the decision task involves independent or interdependent decision making.

In general, the availability of a DSS generator increases the amount of managerial involvement in the development of DSS. Because a DSS generator often supports application development in departmental/functional areas, managers and their staff become more involved in all stages of the developmental process. This is less likely to occur when DSS tools are used.

More structured decision tasks tend to require less managerial involvement. This is especially true with regard to the specification (and respecification) of information requirements. Consequently, DSS for strategic planning and management control applications usually demand more user involvement than those for operational control.

Finally, because group decision making normally requires more discussion than does individual decision making, this leads to greater management involvement for DSS which support group rather than individual decisions. It follows then that DSS for pooled interdependent and sequential interdependent decision making have greater management involvement than those which support independent decision making.

EVALUATION OF DSS SUCCESS

The evaluation of a DSS suffers from the same difficulties as does the initial assessment of the desirability of developing the DSS; specifically, it is difficult to determine the benefits from improved decision making due to the DSS. There are two basic approaches that management can employ in evaluating the success of a DSS—the formative evaluation and the post implementation audit.

The formative evaluation process consists of four phases—domain evaluation, design evaluation, implementation evaluation, and outcome evaluation [Athappilly, 1985]. Domain evaluation calls for a nonquantitative, expert examination of the project prior to development. Design evaluation is descriptive in nature and defines the essential components to be developed in the DSS. Implementation evaluation examines the DSS design and provides feedback for modifications. Outcome evaluation compares the goals of the DSS with the resulting product.

The more common form of evaluation of DSS success is the post-implementation audit. This is similar to the outcome evaluation phase of the formative evaluation process. Traditionally, the post-implementation audit of information systems takes the form of a structured cost-benefit analysis (or other similar procedure). However, the often qualitative nature of decision improvement resulting from the DSS typically results in an intuitive assessment of system success. One approach which has been recommended specifically for the evaluation of DSS success considers elements which are measurable and common sense [Welsch, 1980]. These measures include perceived satisfaction of management with the "final" product, acceptability of the DSS to management, and frequency of use (if use is voluntary). A formal EIS evaluation methodology is provided in Chapter 29.

THE IMPACT OF DSS ON MANAGEMENT

The most obvious impact of DSS on management is an improvement in decision making. DSS provide better access to information, and in particular, better access to models which permit an examination of the options which exist but were less amenable to analysis without computer support. Specifically, a DSS can increase the number of alternatives evaluated, improve confidence in decisions, and speed up the decision-making process. In today's business environment, computer support is needed by all levels of management.

There is another aspect of DSS utilization which affects management—the basic nature of what managers do. Upper-level managers are now interacting directly with computer output, and in many cases, with the computer itself. This hands-on utilization of computers by senior management has a very positive effect on the perceived value of IS in general. Middle management may be the most significantly affected category of management, because they often fill multiple roles with regard to DSS. First, they develop and use their own DSS and thus are affected in the same ways as upper management. But secondly, middle managers often serve as intermediaries to upper managers. In this situation, they often become project leaders for critical, corporate level projects. This provides valuable cross-departmental experience, both functionally and in the development of computer-based applications.

CONCLUSION

The involvement of managers in DSS is greater than their involvement with other kinds of IS applications. Management is actively involved with the approval, development, operation, use, and administration of DSS. This direct involvement becomes possible due to the ease of use of development tools, the frequently narrow scope of the applications being developed, and other factors. The importance of the DSS to the manager's decision-making tasks, and the involvement of the manager and staff generally result in a sense of ownership of the DSS which results in overall administrative control of the application.

QUESTIONS

1. When today's generation of students achieves managerial positions, what impact do you think that this will have on direct (i.e., hands-on) use of DSS? Are computer skills the only thing that affects management's direct use of computers? Discuss.
2. It has been suggested that differences in decision-making styles and preferences should be accommodated through flexibility in the software rather than being "hard wired" into the application. What does this mean? Give examples of how it might be done.
3. Is it more difficult to be a benefit/cost analysis for a DSS than a transaction processing application? Why?

REFERENCES

ALAVI, MARYAM and IRA R. WEISS. "Managing the Risks Associated with End-User Computing," *Journal of Management Information Systems.* Vol. 2, No. 3 (Winter 1985–86), pp. 5–20.

ATHAPPILLY, K. "Successful Decision Making Starts with DSS Evaluation," *Data Management.* (February 1985).

HOGUE, JACK T. "A Framework for Management Involvement in Decision Support Systems," *Journal of Management Information Systems.* Vol. 4, No. 1 (Summer 1987), pp. 96–110.

HOGUE, JACK T. and HUGH J. WATSON. "Current Practices in the Development of Decision Support Systems," *Proceedings of the Fifth International Conference on Information Systems,* Tucson, Arizona. (November 28–30, 1983), pp. 117–127.

HOGUE, JACK T. and HUGH J. WATSON. "An Examination of Decision Maker's Utilization of Decision System Output," *Information & Management.* Vol. 8, No. 4 (April 1985), pp. 205–212.

KEEN, PETER G. W. "Decision Support Systems: Translating Analytic Techniques into Useful Tools," *Sloan Management Review.* Vol. 22, No. 3 (Spring 1980), pp. 33–44.

KEEN, PETER G. W. "Value Analysis: Justifying Decision Support Systems." *MIS Quarterly.* Vol. 7, No. 2 (June 1983), pp. 1–16.

KEEN, PETER G. W. and M. S. SCOTT MORTON. *Decision Support Systems: An Organizational Perspective.* Reading, MA: Addison-Wesley, 1978.

MCKENNEY, JAMES L. and PETER G. W. KEEN. "How Managers' Minds Work," *Harvard Business Review.* Vol. 52, No. 3 (May–June 1974), pp. 79–90.

NAUMANN, J. D. and MILT A. JENKINS. "Prototyping: The New Paradigm for Systems Development," *MIS Quarterly.* Vol. 6, No. 3 (September 1982), pp. 29–44.

SIMON, H. A. *The New Science of Management Decision.* New York: Harper & Row, 1960.

SPRAGUE, R. H. and E. D. CARLSON. *Building Effective Decision Support Systems.* Englewood Cliffs, NJ: Prentice Hall, 1982.

TURBAN, EFRAIM. *Decision Support and Expert Systems: Management Support Systems.* New York: Macmillan Publishing Company, 1993.

WELSCH, GEMMA M. *Successful Implementation of Decision Support System: PreInstallation Factors, Service Factors, and the Role of the Information Transfer Specialist,* unpublished Ph.D. Dissertation. Evanston, IL: Northwestern University, 1980.

4

DETERMINING INFORMATION REQUIREMENTS FOR AN EIS

An increasing number of organizations are implementing executive information systems (EISs), or executive support systems (ESSs) as they are sometimes called. These systems are used to access news, stock prices, and information about competitors, customers, key performance indicators, and internal operations (Watson, et al., 1991).

There are many EIS success stories, but an EIS must still be viewed as a high-risk system (Houdeshel and Watson, 1987; Rockart and DeLong, 1988). One study of 50 EISs found that 21 of them had experienced an EIS failure prior to the development of a successful system (Watson et al., 1991). When developing an EIS, there are a myriad of potential organizational, developmental, and technical problems to overcome. For example, an EIS often serves users who have little previous computer training and experience, have been successful without using computers in the past, and may feel that they have little need to use computers now. System developers often have a limited understanding of the nature of executive work and information needs, have little experience in developing applications of this kind, and must work with new technology.

A major developmental problem is determining what information to include in the system. At the EIS Institute '88 and '89, practitioners ranked "getting executives to specify what they want" as their number one concern in implementing an EIS. Also on their list of worries was "keeping abreast of executives' changing information needs and desires" (Stecklow, 1989).

This chapter is adopted from Hugh J. Watson and Mark N. Frolick, "Determining Information Requirements for an EIS," *MIS Quarterly*, Vol. 17, No. 3, September 1993, pp. 255–269.

This concern is not unique to EIS; executives often have a difficult time articulating their information needs. As Ronald Compton, president of Aetna Life and Casualty, says, "The major problem in the implementation of technology is not the technicians, nor the programmers, nor the systems analysts. The major problem is the business-person who does not know what he or she wants and is unable to accurately communicate what little they can figure out" (McClatchy, 1990).

Systems analysts and researchers have a long-standing interest in how to identify information requirements. Even though it has been heavily researched, new types of applications can require modifications to traditional methods, the development of additional methods, and research on the effectiveness of various methods. In their discussion of methods for determining information requirements, Byrd, et al., (1992) call for "investigations into how certain elicitation methods seem to be better suited to certain problem domains, examinations of the synergistic effects of elicitation techniques, and developments of new elicitation techniques for emerging needs" (p. 118).

To better understand how to determine the information requirements for an EIS, we conducted a multi-stage study. The study revealed a large number of methods (i.e., approaches or techniques) that can be used, judgments about the methods' usefulness, and insights about what makes them useful or not useful. These findings can improve EIS developers' ability to determine information requirements. While the study focused on EISs, the findings provide insights about determining the information requirements for any kind of decision support application.

SATISFYING EXECUTIVES' INFORMATION NEEDS

Over the years, a growing, but still incomplete, understanding of the nature of executive work has evolved. We know that executives have a demanding workload and an unrelenting work pace, and they think about their work constantly. Executive work activities are usually diverse, brief, and fragmented. Verbal communications are preferred, in part, because of the opportunity for the exchange of soft information—gossip, ideas, opinions, predictions, and explanations. Additionally, executive work is more unstructured, non-routine, and long-range in nature than other managerial work (Mintzberg, 1975). Much of executive work centers around developing agendas—goals, priorities, strategies, and plans that may not be documented, and network building—and developing cooperative relationships with people inside and outside the organization who may play a role in developing and implementing the emerging agenda (Kotter, 1982).

In order to perform their job responsibilities, executives need external and internal information (Aguilar, 1967; Daft and Lengel, 1986). Trade journals, friends in the industry, and customers are important sources of external information. Scheduled meetings, unscheduled meetings, and tours are highly valued sources of internal information. Organization information systems are not usually perceived to be the most important sources of external or internal information (Jones and McLeod, 1986).

The nature of both executive work and information needs provides insights into why EIS developers worry about determining information requirements. Executives are unlikely to have much time to spend with analysts, and when they do, they may find it difficult to specify their requirements. The requirements, when identified, are often for information that is external, soft, not machine-resident, and not from readily identified sources. Thus, analysts must deal with a very different type of user, with unique information needs, and with information sources different from other types of applications.

Analysts consider two levels of information requirements: (1) organizational-level information requirements and (2) application-level information requirements (Davis, 1982). The first level defines an overall information systems structure for an organization and specifies a portfolio of applications and data bases. The second level defines and documents the information needs for specific applications, such as EISs.

There are four generic strategies for identifying organizational or application-level information requirements: (1) asking, (2) deriving from an existing information system, (3) synthesizing from characteristics of the utilizing system, and (4) discovering from experimentation with an evolving information system (Davis, 1982). The first strategy is to obtain information requirements by asking people about their information needs (Telem, 1988a; 1988b). The second strategy is to derive information requirements from an existing information system (Byrd, et al., 1992). The third is to develop information requirements based on the characteristics of the system being served (i.e., the object system). The requirements for information stem from the activities of the object system. A variety of methods are based on this strategy: normative analysis (Davis, 1982), strategy set formulation (Davis, 1982; King, 1978), critical success factor analysis (Rockart, 1979; Zahedi, 1987), process analysis (Davis, 1982; Valusek and Fryback, 1987), decision analysis (Ackoff, 1967; Jenkins, et al., 1984), socio-technical analysis (Bostrom, 1989; Bostrom and Heinen, 1977), and input-process-output analysis (Davis, 1982). The final strategy is to establish an initial system, then refine it as information requirements become better understood. Prototyping (Nauman and Jenkins, 1982), iterative design (Sprague, 1980), and heuristic development (Berresford and Wetherbe, 1979) are based on this approach.

Each approach poses some difficulties. The asking strategy requires that system users (in this case the firm's executives) be available and capable of articulating their information needs. As discussed previously, this may be problematic.

In many firms, the EIS differs considerably from existing systems. It is the inability of these existing systems to deliver the information executives need that typically motivates the development of an EIS (Houdeshel and Watson, 1987). Consequently, deriving information requirements from existing systems may be of limited value.

For EIS, the critical success factor (CSF) method is the most frequently mentioned approach of the methods that determine information requirements based on the characteristics of the object system. However, not all users of the CSF methodology report success (Burkan, 1988). It requires considerable executive involvement for several days and a skilled leader. Also, EISs contain more than CSF related information.

Basing information requirements on experimentation with an evolving system requires that an existing system already be in place. Consequently, this approach is useful for the ongoing but not the initial version of an EIS.

Because of the variety of problems associated with identifying executives' information requirements, organizations have used a variety of methods. These include participation in strategic planning sessions, formal CSF sessions, discussions with executives, tracking executive activities (e.g., executive logs), discussions with executive support personnel, examinations of computer-generated information, examinations of non-computer-generated information, attendance at meetings by the EIS support staff, software tracking of EIS usage, and the strategic business objectives method (Volonino and Watson; 1990–91; Watson and Frolick, 1992). No single method appears adequate, but the use of multiple methods triangulates on information needs.

The development of an EIS can be thought of as an ongoing journey rather than as a destination. The system continues to evolve over time in response to market, industry, and organizational changes that affect executives' information needs. It is useful, however, to focus on two phases in the lifetime of an EIS (Houdeshel, 1990; Watson et al., 1991). In the initial phase, a set of screens or applications are rolled out to an initial set of users. In the ongoing or sustaining phase, the initial screens or applications are maintained while new screens or applications are added to the system. Additional users and system capabilities (e.g., access to external news services) are also likely. The ongoing phase continues throughout the lifetime of the EIS as the system continues to evolve.

Some of the methods for determining information requirements are better or uniquely suited to either the initial or ongoing phases. For example, examining the reports currently received by executives is usually more helpful in the initial phase, because once this review is completed, little value is received from reviewing them again. Software tracking of system usage, on the other hand, is only feasible for the ongoing phase because it can only be used after an initial system is established.

To summarize, the preceding discussion has briefly explored the nature of executive work. This work results in information requirements that an EIS may partially satisfy. It is necessary that these information requirements be correctly identified by EIS developers. This task is complicated, however, by the very nature of executive work. Traditional elicitation methods may not be appropriate or may need to be modified and new methods may need to be employed. What works with the initial version of an EIS may not work well with the ongoing version and vice versa. The need to learn about this area motivated the study described next.

THE STUDY

Through a multi-stage study, issues associated with identifying the information requirements for an EIS were investigated. Specifically, the following questions were addressed:

- What methods are used for determining information requirements for both initial and ongoing EIS?
- How frequently are the various information requirements methods used?
- How useful are the various methods?
- In what situations are the methods useful or not useful?

In the first stage of the study, EIS developers were interviewed by phone. The three-part interviews consisted of (1) a description of the study and a definition of terms; (2) a request for demographic data about the respondents, their firms, and their EISs; and (3) the collection of data relevant to the study questions. Telephone interviews were conducted with a single person in each of 54 organizations.

The interviews were open-ended. Respondents were asked what methods were used rather than to respond to a predefined list. This approach was chosen because a comprehensive list of methods was not known in advance of the study and because it eliminated any possible pressure to indicate that a method was used when it actually was not. The limitation of this approach was that methods were likely to be under-reported because a method may have been used but the respondent failed to recall or mention it during the interview.

The interviews uncovered 16 methods that organizations use to identify information requirements for either the initial version of an EIS or when it enters the ongoing support phase. The interviews also provided insights about what makes the methods useful or not useful.

The second part of the study was designed to obtain a more accurate assessment of the use of various methods, to increase the sample size, and to possibly surface additional methods. The survey questionnaire consisted of five parts: (1) a description of the study and a definition of terms; (2) a request for organizational data, including background data about the firm's EIS; (3) the collection of data about the determination of information requirements for the initial version of the EIS; (4) the collection of data about the ongoing determination of information requirements; and (5) a request for personal information about the respondent. Three hundred questionnaires were sent to firms. A first and follow-up mailing generated 133 (44 percent) responses, including 98 (33 percent) completed responses from organizations with an EIS and 35 responses from organizations without one. Twenty-six firms participated in both the telephone interview and survey questionnaire phases of the study. A comparison of the interview and questionnaire data confirmed the belief that the respondents were unlikely to recall in the telephone interviews all the methods used. Consequently, the telephone interviews were most useful for generating descriptive and anecdotal information, and the survey questionnaire was most useful for providing quantitative data.

FINDINGS AND DISCUSSION

Demographics

Both the telephone interviews and the survey questionnaires generated data about the organizations, their EISs, and the respondents' backgrounds. The companies studied are geographically dispersed, although nearly all are from North America. Virtually all industries were represented, with the highest percentage being manufacturing. Responding firms tended to be large, with mean assets and gross revenues in excess of two billion dollars; however, a few firms had less than one million dollars in assets and revenues. The age of the EISs ranged from one month to five years, with a mean age of two and a half years; as anticipated, an EIS is a relatively new type of application in most organizations. Most of the respondents were either EIS managers or part of the EIS support staff; however, a few executives, functional area analysts (who help identify information requirements), and information systems (IS) professionals (who provide technical support) also participated in the study. Respondents tended to have considerable work and IS experience. The length of their EIS experience closely mirrored the amount of time the EIS has existed in their organization.

Telephone Survey

The telephone interviews were structured but included open-ended questions so that the methods could be fully understood. The respondents identified and discussed 16 methods that were used to determine the information requirements for either the initial or the ongoing version of their EIS. The 16 methods provide a rich portfolio for determining information requirements.

Survey Questionnaire

The survey questionnaire asked the respondents to identify what methods were used for the initial and ongoing versions of their EIS. Respondents were given the summary descriptions presented in Table 4–1. If a method was employed, they were asked to judge its usefulness. A useful method was described as one that is easy to use, reveals information requirements quickly, and provides a clear understanding of these requirements. These suggestions for usefulness were based on the work of Davis (1989) and Davis (1974). These characteristics were also provided in the telephone interviews on those few occasions when a respondent asked for a characterization of a useful method. A five-point anchored scale was employed, where a response of "1" indicated that a method had a low level of usefulness and a "5" a high level. Separate ratings were requested when the method was employed for both the initial and ongoing versions of the system. Table 4.1 presents the frequency with which the methods were used and their mean usefulness scores. The numbers for the top three methods in each category are shown in boldface (there is a three-way tie for second for the mean usefulness of the ongoing version).

Respondents were also asked to identify methods that were not listed on the questionnaire. They provided three additional methods: EIS executive steering committees, developing online prototypes with the executive, and executive sponsorship of functional area information. Where necessary, follow-up telephone calls were made in order to understand these methods. Executive steering committees provide high-level guidance on the overall information contents of the system. The development of an online prototype allows executives to quickly assess whether the information provided and its presentation format are appropriate. Where there is executive sponsorship of functional area information, executives in each functional area develop a proposal of what information from their functional area should be included in the system. The proposals are then reviewed at meetings with executives from throughout the organization to ensure that the information provides an appropriate organizationwide perspective.

Discussion of the Methods

This section discusses the methods for determining information requirements for an EIS. These methods are based on the telephone interviews and the questionnaire findings, the researchers' informal discussions with EIS developers over the years, the EIS literature, and our own EIS development experiences. The numerical information comes from the questionnaires. The discussion and anecdotal information draw upon all sources, thus providing the greatest insights into how to determine EIS information requirements.

Discussions with Executives. Discussions with executives are vital to determining EIS information requirements. That only 62.2 percent of the respondents indicated that this happened with the initial version is both surprising and troublesome. An organization is well advised not to develop an EIS if its executives are unwilling to spend time with the developers. Other studies have identified lack of executive support as a major reason for EIS failure (Watson and Glover, 1989).

Once an EIS enters the ongoing support phase, the percentage of firms that use this method jumps to 95 percent, but its mean usefulness score falls from 4.2 to 3.8. This decrease is probably due to executives' difficulties in expressing their information needs and problems in gaining sufficient executive time.

TABLE 4–1 Summary Descriptions, Frequency of Use, and Perceived Usefulness of the Methods for Determining Information Requirements for the Initial and Ongoing Versions of an EIS

Method	Initial Version		Ongoing Version	
	Percentage Using the Method	Mean Perceived Usefulness	Percentage Using the Method	Mean Perceived Usefulness
Discussions with executives. The analyst probes for information needs by asking about job responsibilities, problems currently being experienced, and commonly used information. These discussions vary from formally scheduled, heavily scripted interviews to informal, ad hoc conversations.	62.2	4.2	**94.6**	3.8
EIS planning meetings. EIS planning meetings are used to plot the course of an organization's EIS. The individuals involved in these meetings include the EIS support staff; IS personnel; and functional area personnel, including, on occasion, executives. These meetings are used to evaluate the EIS and to decide and prioritize changes to the system.	58.1	3.8	**74.6**	4.6
Examinations of computer-generated information. Analysts study what computer-generated information executives currently receive that should be included in the EIS. Missing information is also identified and the presentation of the information is discussed.	56.1	3.8	34.6	3.1
Discussions with support personnel. The EIS support staff meets with secretaries, administrative assistants, and other executive support staff who have a good understanding of what information is important to the executives. Support personnel can often help identify what information was recently requested and who the executive talks to in order to gain information.	51.0	3.9	**76.0**	**4.7**
Volunteered Information. Executives make recommendations concerning information they would like to see included in the EIS.	47.9	3.8	69.3	4.5
Examinations of other organizations' EIS. The EIS support staff looks at other organizations' EISs to get ideas about what information to include in their EIS. They also gain a better understanding of how useful different kinds of information might be.	44.9	3.9	6.6	3.0
Examinations of non-computer-generated information. Analysts study the non-computer-related materials that executives refer to or need on a regular basis. Possible sources of information include newspapers, books, articles, government publications, newsletters,	40.8	3.6	52.0	4.6

Critical success factors sessions. Sessions are held in which organizational goals are identified, the CSFs that underlie the goals are discussed, measures of the CSFs are explored, and methods for providing information relevant to the CSFs are discussed.	38.7	3.9	28.0	4.0
Participation in strategic planning sessions. Strategic planning sessions are used to develop long-range plans for the organization. When analysts sit in on these sessions, they are better able to supply information that supports the accomplishment of the strategic plans.	26.5	4.1	29.3	**4.7**
Strategic business objectives method. The EIS is designed to focus attention on and to provide support for the organization's strategic business objectives. After the strategic business objectives are established, the business processes related to their accomplishment are identified. Information related to monitoring the strategic business objectives and to supporting the execution of the business processes is provided. This method provides an organizationwide approach to EIS design.	26.5	4.1	42.6	**4.7**
Attendance at meetings. EIS support staff attend meetings they think might enhance their understanding of what information executives need. Project status reviews, public relations briefings to the media, and customer review sessions are examples of meetings that might be attended.	24.4	4.6	48.0	**4.8**
Information systems teams working in isolation. The EIS support staff develop the EIS without executive input. The system's information contents is based on what the analysts believe would be useful to the organization's executives.	22.0	2.7	17.0	1.6
Examination of the strategic plan. The EIS support staff examine the strategic plan in order to identify information needed to carry out and monitor the execution of the plan.	15.3	4.5	10.6	4.4
Tracking executive activity. The activities of executives are tracked in order to gain a better understanding of how they work and the information they use. This can be accomplished by either accompanying executives throughout the day or having the executive or executive support staff maintain logs of the executives' activities.	9.1	3.6	2.6	2.2
Software tracking at EIS usage. The EIS maintains a log of executives' use of the system. This information helps identify how the system might be changed in order to make it more useful.	0	N/A	29.3	3.2
Formal change requests. Executives indicate any changes they want made to the EIS in either a paper or an electronic-based form. The EIS support staff review, prioritize, and schedule the changes to the system.	0	N/A	2.66	3.0

Developers differed widely in their descriptions of executives' willingness to spend time discussing information requirements. Some reported that little or no time is given, while others indicated that they have good access to the executives they support. One EIS manager provided an interesting insight, noting that the amount of time an analyst gets is often related to how well the analyst knows the business. Analysts who know the business well, and consequently are perceived to be capable of understanding the executives' information needs, are likely to get time with the executive, while less knowledgeable analysts are quickly dismissed and not given further access.

Developers should try to have as much contact with executives as possible. Another EIS manager said that he learned the CEO spent his lunch hour walking on the treadmill in the company gym. He now makes a point of joining the workout in order to have a better opportunity to discuss how the EIS might support the CEO. Yet another EIS manager said that her office is on the same floor as many of the firm's executives and that chance conversations in the hallway are very helpful in identifying information requirements.

Executive interviews must be conducted carefully. Simply asking the executive what information is wanted is unlikely to result in a comprehensive description of information needs (Burkan, 1992). Answers will be influenced by what information the executive has seen recently, the contents of existing reports, current problems, and the executive's limited understanding of what can be done with information technology. A more fruitful approach is to first gain a better understanding of the executive's job—how the executive spends his or her day; what information is currently being used by the executive; what important issues or problems are facing the executive; what factors make the executive successful; and what information about the external environment, the marketplace, and competitors would be helpful. Questions that address these issues can be posed in interesting ways. For example, "When you return from a two-week trip, what information do you want to see first when you get back?" "If you were dropped into a competitor's office, what information would you most like to see?" "Three years from now, if a *Harvard Business Review* article described how you led the company to success, what would it say?"

One EIS manager described an approach that he uses to meet with executives who are seldom available. He schedules a very short meeting, and after a brief opening, presents a small number of sample screens that he believes are pertinent. The executive is asked three questions: Which of the screens are of greatest value? How would you like to have them changed? What additional information would be helpful? The sample screens add structure to the interview and, if time runs out for the meeting, the executive can mark up the screens at a later time and return them to the EIS support staff.

EIS Planning Meetings. These meetings are useful for bringing a team approach to EIS development, and they serve a variety of purposes—planning and controlling the system's evolution, identifying information requirements, and discussing problems with the system. All parties with a stake in the EIS—the EIS support staff, IS personnel, functional area personnel, and executives—should participate in the meetings, although executive participation may not always be necessary, such as when technical topics are discussed. EIS planning meetings with group executive participation are especially helpful in identifying information requirements about cross-functional systems because they bring a joint application design approach to the sessions (Wetherbe, 1991). The survey data indicate that while EIS planning meetings are common and useful for the initial version of the EIS (58 percent of the firms and a mean usefulness of 3.8), they become more common (75 percent) and useful (4.6) for the ongoing support of the system.

Examinations of Computer Generated Information. Most executives already receive considerable computer-generated information. The problem is that it may not be timely, accurate, relevant, concise, easy to find, or in the right format. Nonetheless, looking at existing computer-based information flows is a logical starting point for developing an EIS. This approach was used by many organizations for the initial version of the system (56.1 percent) with reasonably good results (mean usefulness of 3.8). It is less frequently employed and is perceived to be less useful for the ongoing phase (34.6 percent and 3.1). These decreases are not surprising because most of the value of looking at existing information flows is realized during the first reviews.

Existing reports can be analyzed by placing them into three categories: those that are used regularly; those that are used sometimes; and those that are seldom or never used (Houdeshel, 1990). Attention should be focused first on those reports that are used regularly. The executive is asked to identify what information on the reports is most important and should be included in the EIS. There should also be discussions about what format to use (e.g., graphs, tables) when presenting the information. Less frequently used reports are examined later as need and time permit.

Discussions with Support Personnel. Executive time is scarce, so analysts are unlikely to get the time necessary to fully identify the executive's information requirements. The executive's support staff, especially the executive's secretary, can be very helpful in this case. The support staff typically knows the executive's work habits, such as what the executive does the first thing in the morning (e.g., read the *Wall Street Journal,* look at overnight flash reports, or schedule appointments). The support staff also knows what information is requested regularly, to whom the executive talks, whose opinions are valued, as well as the current issues of concern.

Discussions with the executive's support staff are common and useful for the initial version of the system (51 percent and 3.9), and become more common and useful over time (76 percent and 4.7). A major reason for these increases is that a good working relationship evolves between the EIS support group and the executive's support staff. In some organizations, the executive's support staff is formally assigned the responsibility of working with the EIS staff.

Volunteered Information. It is common for executives to suggest that specific information be included in the EIS. This practice tends to increase as the system moves from the initial to the ongoing support phase (48 to 69 percent), as does its mean usefulness rating (3.8 to 4.5). As executives become more familiar with the system and its EIS support staff, they initiate recommendations about the system's contents. While this method has value, executives will occasionally make recommendations based more on what will make them or their organizational unit look good rather than on legitimate information needs. The EIS support staff must then handle such recommendations judiciously.

Examinations of Other Organizations' EIS. About 45 percent of the firms looked at other organizations' EISs while building their first version. The mean usefulness of doing this was 3.9. Visits to other organizations can help generate ideas about information to include, assess the value of different kinds of information, and provide insights about other issues (e.g., the best way to provide navigation through the system). Executives' participation in these visits can increase their understanding of EISs, spark discussions about information requirements, and increase support for the project. Far fewer firms visit other organizations (6.6 percent) and find it less useful (3.0) after the initial version is implemented.

Examinations of Non Computer Generated Information. To monitor what is happening in the firm's internal and external environments, executives need to have a variety of information, much of it not available within the organization's current information systems. Internal information sources include memos, documents, and e-mail. Books, articles, government and industry publications, correspondence, and marketing research information are all possible external sources. Discussions with the executive and the executive's support staff can help identify useful information. Many executives are unfamiliar with the technology options that currently exist for capturing, delivering, and presenting information, so the analyst may need to suggest what can be done. Examples include providing current stock prices that are publicly transmitted by FM signals, delivering news stories from external databases, optically scanning photographs of employees to include on the firm's organization charts, and adding voice annotations to screens to provide meaning and interpretation to the information displayed.

Almost 41 percent of the organizations reported examining non-computer-generated information when developing the initial version of the EIS. The mean usefulness was 3.6. These numbers increase to 52 percent and 4.6, respectively, for the ongoing support phase. Because many firms focus on including "harder" information (e.g., information from existing reports, financial information) initially, softer information is often left for later, although executives typically find this softer information to be valuable (Watson et al., 1992).

Critical Success Factor Sessions. The EIS literature frequently states that an EIS should provide information relevant to the organization's critical success factors or key performance indicators (Burkan, 1988; Rockart and Treacy, 1982; Zmud, 1986). These are those few things "that must be done right" if the organization is to be successful (Rockart, 1979). Almost 39 percent of the organizations indicated that they used critical success factor sessions when developing the initial version of their system, with a mean usefulness score of 3.9. When formally applied, the CSF methodology requires a broad level of participation by company executives over several days. A facilitator (from within or outside the organization) leads a discussion about company goals, the critical success factors relevant to achieving the goals, and how the CSFs might be best measured. Displays for the CSF-related information are then developed, discussed, and ultimately approved. Some CSFs can be measured using hard measures (e.g., return on assets), while others may require surrogate measures (e.g., employee turnover or sick leave for employee morale).

CSF sessions can also be used to identify critical failure factors (CFFs). These are developments that can significantly impair performance. For example, a strike or environmental damage are potential CFFs for many firms. A CFF may not come readily to mind when thinking of success, but its occurrence can have disastrous consequences.

A somewhat smaller percentage of firms (28 percent) use CSF sessions during the ongoing phase of their EIS. Its mean usefulness increases slightly, however, to 4.0. Those firms that used it only for the initial version often mentioned either the difficulty of getting executives to participate in the sessions on a continuing basis or that it was not that useful.

Participation in Strategic Planning Sessions. If an EIS is to support the accomplishment of an organization's strategic objectives, it is important for the EIS support staff to clearly understand the objectives. One way to accomplish this is to allow the support staff to attend strategic planning sessions. About 26 percent of the organizations did this when developing the initial version of their system and 29.3 percent did it with the ongoing version. This method is perceived to be useful as evidenced by the 4.1 and 4.7 mean usefulness scores. The biggest barrier to using this method is that the strategic planning group may not give the EIS support team access to the meetings because of confidentiality concerns. This is one of several situations (e.g., monitoring executive usage of the system, getting information providers to release information that indicates problems in their areas) where it is important that the EIS support staff be trusted to perform their jobs in a professional manner.

Strategic Business Objectives Methods. The strategic business objectives method focuses attention on the firm's strategic business objectives and the critical business processes required to accomplish these objectives. Typically, these business processes cross several functional areas. For example, if a strategic business objective is to respond more rapidly to changing customer needs, the business processes necessary to accomplish this objective include sales, distribution, inventory, production, and product design. Appropriate information is made available to all organizational personnel who are responsible for doing the work in the business processes as well as to the firm's executives. Because information is no longer the executives' sole province, some organizations now refer to their EIS as "everybody's information system" or the "enterprise information system."

The strategic business objectives method can be contrasted with the critical success factors method. The latter identifies *what* the CSFs are and the information needed to monitor them, but it does not systematically explore *how* they are to be accomplished. The strategic business objectives (SBO) method does. An analogy illustrates this difference: Some EISs are like the dashboard of a car that indicates how far the car has gone and its current speed, but it fails to provide information about the car's pedal that is responsible for what appears on the dashboard (Bittlestone, 1991).

Approximately 27 percent of the firms used the SBO method for the initial version of their EISs and judged its mean usefulness to be 4.1. These numbers increased to 43 percent and 4.7 when the system entered the ongoing support phase. A challenge in using this method is that it potentially requires a new way of viewing the organization (i.e., looking at business processes that cut across functional areas rather than looking at functional areas themselves). But once internalized, the results appear to be good. It helps satisfy a key to EIS success: a clear link to business objectives (Rockart and DeLong, 1988).

Attendance at Meetings. This is the most highly rated method for both the initial (mean of 4.6) and the ongoing (mean of 4.8) version of the EIS. It was used by 24.4 percent of the firms for the initial version and grows to 48.0 percent with the ongoing version. By participating in meetings, the EIS support staff is well positioned to identify information gaps and new information needs. A side benefit of this method is that the support staff can serve as a valuable source of information during meetings because of their detailed knowledge of information about the firm.

The usefulness of this method may be related to the organization structure for the EIS support group. Some organizations have a centralized structure, where all of the staff members are in a geographically centralized location. In order to attend a meeting, the staff member must be aware of it, gain permission to attend, and physically go to the meeting's location. Other organizations are decentralized, with a small central staff and with other personnel scattered throughout the organization, usually performing EIS support services as only a small part of their overall job responsibilities. Because these people are located where the meetings are held, attendance is easier to arrange and is often part of their job responsibilities.

Information Systems Teams Working in Isolation. In 22 percent of the organizations, the EIS support staff was expected to develop the initial version of the system with no executive participation in determining information requirements. This lack of involvement was also found in 17 percent of the organizations for the ongoing support phase. In most cases, the support team was told to work with the executives' subordinates. The unsatisfactory nature of this arrangement is seen in the 2.7 and 1.6 mean usefulness scores. These numbers may even overstate the usefulness of this method because of the likelihood that organizations that took this approach had an EIS failure and were not included in the survey responses.

Examination of the Strategic Plan. Another way for the EIS support staff to be familiar with the organization's strategic plans is to give the staff access to the written strategic plan or to have regular meetings with a representative of the strategic planning group. These approaches may be considered preferable to having a staff member attend strategic planning sessions because it avoids the chance that someone from outside the executive group will hear their differences of opinion. Slightly over 15 percent of the organizations used this method with the initial version of their EIS and 10.6 percent employ it with the ongoing version. Respondents indicated that this method is quite useful, giving it mean usefulness scores of 4.5 and 4.4, respectively. In some organizations, the strategic plan is included as part of the contents of the EIS.

Tracking Executive Activity. A small number of organizations (9.1 percent for the initial and 2.6 percent for the ongoing version) tracked how executives spend their days. This can be done by unobtrusively accompanying the executives, asking questions where appropriate, or by having the executives or someone such as the executives' secretaries maintain logs of how the executives spend their time and the information the executives need throughout the day. While this method was judged to be reasonably useful for the initial version of the system (a mean of 3.6), the small number of organizations that employ it for the ongoing version gave it poor marks (a mean of 2.2). Respondents indicated that most of the value from its use was gained the first time around. It was relatively time consuming to employ, and executives were not supportive of its use.

Software Tracking of EIS Usage. Some EISs collect data on how the firm's executives use the systems. By logging executive activity on the system, it is possible to identify which executives are and are not using the system; where problems in using the system are occurring; which displays are important to particular executives and the user group as a whole; and what displays are not being used and thus, are candidates for modification or deletion. Because this method requires that an EIS be in place, it can only be employed with the ongoing version. Twenty-nine percent of the firms reported using this method and gave it a 3.2 mean usefulness score.

The ability to track EIS activity is a potentially powerful capability. Two firms in the study—one with a software tracking capability and the other without—illustrate this point. In the first firm, system-generated reports on screen use ultimately result in 30 to 50 percent of the screens being either modified or deleted each year, and the total number of screens in the system is kept between 500 and 700. Furthermore, the logs of individual executive use of the system allow trouble spots to be identified and corrected. In contrast, the other firm had developed a system with over 1500 screens in only a year and a half, and the EIS manager lamented about not knowing which screens were actually important to executives. EISs with unnecessary screens are not only difficult and costly to maintain but make navigation through the system difficult.

Few EIS vendors provide software tracking of system usage capabilities. When asked about this, they often indicate that it will be "in the next release of the software." Because this never seems to happen, firms that want this capability typically must develop it themselves. Often companies do not appreciate the importance of this capability until their EIS has been in operation for awhile. Consequently, vendors may not see it as a help in making the initial sale.

Formal Change Requests. A common information systems practice is to have users submit written requests for changes. About 27 percent of the organizations reported doing this with the ongoing version of their EIS and gave it a 3.0 mean usefulness score. The rationale is that an executive may think of a change to improve the system while using it and is more likely to remember and communicate the idea if a mechanism is available to do it easily. Some change request systems are paper based, while computerized versions allow a preformatted screen to be called up, the requested change to be entered, and the request to be electronically communicated to the EIS support staff where it is considered and, if accepted, scheduled for implementation.

It is worth noting that some organizations have an informal rather than a formal change system. As one EIS manager described it "An executive calls me up and tells me the changes that he wants made; that's as formal as it gets."

Why the Methods Are or Are Not Useful

The previous discussion of the methods for determining EIS information requirements included many of the reasons why the various methods are useful or not useful. However, there are additional ones. Rather than discussing the reasons individually, we deemed it more useful to identify common themes (i.e., global constructs) that apply across different methods. To illustrate, time constraints is a common problem with many methods. For example, discussing information needs with executives is limited by the availability of executive time. Also, examining the noncomputer-generated information used by executives is a problem because of the time required of executives, the executives' support staff, and the EIS support group.

The global reasons for why the methods are useful reaffirm what is already known: they work well. They include the following. First, nearly all of the methods provide access to people who can identify information requirements (such as discussions with executives). Second, many of them support the development of good working relationships between the sources of information requirements and the EIS support staff (such as discussions with support personnel). Third, some methods provide helpful insights into how executives work (such as discussions with the executives' support staff). Finally, all of the methods help determine the information contents of the system and how it is presented.

The global reasons for why the methods are not useful are particularly insightful. First, as suggested previously, a common reason is time constraints, especially time with executives. Second, some sources of information requirements, such as networks of people outside of the organization, may be inaccessible. Third, people often have problems articulating their information needs. Simply asking "what information do you want" usually is inappropriate with executives because of the unstructured nature of their jobs. Consequently, carefully planned and prepared executive interviews are important, as are specific methodologies such as CSF sessions and the strategic business objectives method. Fourth, it is not always easy to identify all the sources of information for an EIS. Executives rely on people inside and outside the organization to provide information, and these sources can be difficult to identify. Fifth, executives, analysts, and information sources sometimes misunderstand each other and/or have misunderstandings about the EIS. For example, executives may not understand how completely they must state their information requirements in order for needed information to be included in the system. Sixth, executives' information needs change rapidly. As an illustration, some respondents felt that the CSF method was too labor intensive to justify its use because by the time the CSF sessions were completed, some of the CSFs had already changed. Finally, an EIS often encounters political resistance, which may hamper usage of some of the methods. For example, the executives' support staff may fear that the EIS will decrease their importance to the executives; consequently, they may not be fully cooperative in helping identify the executives' information needs.

CONCLUSION

Determining the information requirements for an EIS is a challenging task that can seldom be successfully completed using a single method. Rather, a mixture of methods should be used in response to organizational and executive contingencies. For example, some methods such as attendance at strategic planning meetings, formal CSF sessions, and informal discussions with executives are highly useful for determining external information needs. However, analysts must have access to strategic planning meetings for this method to succeed. As another example, discussions with executives are very useful for understanding what an executive does and what information needs exist, but if the executive is unwilling to spend much time with the analyst, discussions with support personnel will need to be an important method.

The study explored the determination of information requirements through the eyes of the EIS professional. Other stakeholders who can improve our understanding of the requirements determination process include the executive users of these systems and the internal and external advisors that serve them. They may provide a much different perspective on this process. For instance, an executive user might, because of time constraints, view participation in requirements interviews with less enthusiasm than systems professionals. Some research has already begun to explore these alternative perspectives (Bergeron, et al., 1992).

QUESTIONS

1. Is it important to distinguish between methods for determining the information requirements for the initial version of an EIS and one that has been in operation for awhile? Discuss.
2. It is not unusual for the initial version of an EIS to contain many reports that were previously available in paper form. Why might this be the case? Is this a good practice? Discuss.
3. Executives sometimes have a difficult time describing the information they need. Why might this be the case? Do you think that they are better able to express their needs after seeing a prototype? Discuss.
4. How might you respond to an executive who says, "I'm too busy to meet with you. Talk to my assistant, Bill. He knows what information I need."

REFERENCES

ACKOFF, R.L. "Management Misinformation Systems," *Management Science* (14:4), December 1967, pp. B147–B156.

AGUILAR, F. *Scanning the Business Environment,* Macmillan, New York, NY, 1967.

BERGERON, F., RAYMOND, L., and RIVARD, S. "Understanding EIS Use: An Empirical Test of a Behavioral Model," in *Proceedings of the Twenty-Fifth Annual Hawaii International Conference on Systems Sciences,* Vol. 3, J.F. Nunamaker (ed.), IEEE Computer Society, Kauai, HI, January 1992, pp. 157–165.

BERRESFORD, T.R. and WETHERBE, J.C. "Heuristic Development: A Redesign of Systems Design," *MIS Quarterly* (3:1), March 1979. pp. 11–19.

BITTLESTONE, R. "Information Technology: Are You Unhappy With Your Company's IT PAYBACK," *Chief Executive*, Issue 51, May/June 1991, pp. 38–41.

BOSTROM, R.P. "Successful Application of Communication Techniques to Improve the Systems Development Process," *Information & Management* (16:5), May 1989, pp. 279–295.

BOSTROM, R.P. and HEINEN, J.S. "MIS Problems and Failures: A Socio-Technical Perspective: Part I," *MIS Quarterly* (1:3), September 1977, pp. 17–33.

BURKAN, W.C. "Making EIS Work," in *DSS-88 Transactions*, The Institute of Management Sciences, E. Sue Weber (ed.), Providence, RI, 1988, pp. 121–136.

BURKAN, W.C. "The New Role of `Executive' Information Systems," *I/S Analyzer* (30:1), January 1992, pp. 2–14.

BYRD, T.A., COSSICK, K.L., and ZMUD, R.W. "A Synthesis of Research on Requirements Analysis and Knowledge Acquisition Techniques." *MIS Quarterly* (16:1), March 1992, pp. 117–138.

DAFT, R. and LENGEL, R. "Organizational Information Requirements, Media Richness and Structural Design," *Management Science* (32:4), May 1986, pp. 554–571.

DAVIS, F.D. "Perceived Usefulness, Perceived Ease of Use, and User Acceptance of Information Technology," *MIS Quarterly* (13:3), September 1989, pp. 319–340.

DAVIS, G.B. *Management Information Systems*, McGraw-Hill, New York, NY, 1974.

DAVIS, G.B. "Strategies for Information Requirements Determination," *IBM Systems Journal* (21:1), 1982, pp. 4–32.

HOUDESHEL, G. "Selecting Information for an EIS: Experiences at Lockheed-Georgia," in *Proceedings of the Twenty-Third Annual International Conference on System Sciences*, Vol. 3, J.F. Nunamaker (ed.), IEEE Computer Society, Kailua-Kona, HI, January 1990, pp. 178–185.

HOUDESHEL, G. and WATSON, H.J. "The Management Information and Decision Support (MIDS) System at Lockheed-Georgia," *MIS Quarterly* (11:1), March 1987, pp. 127–140.

JENKINS, A.M., NAUMANN, J.D., and WETHERBE, J.C. "Empirical Investigation: Systems Development Practices and Results," *Information & Management* (7:2), April 1984, pp. 73–82.

JONES, J.W. and McLEOD, R. "The Structure of Executive Information Systems: An Exploratory Study," *Decision Sciences* (17:2), Spring 1986, pp. 220–249.

KING, W.R. "Strategic Planning for Management Information Systems," *MIS Quarterly* (2:2), March 1978, pp. 27–37.

KOTTER, J.P. "What Effective General Managers Really Do," *Harvard Business Review* (60:6), November–December 1982, p. 160.

McCLATCHY, W. "Meadows the CEO," *Information Week*, November 5, 1990, p. 34.

MINTZBERG, H. "The Manager's Job: Folklore and Fact," *Harvard Business Review* (53:4), July–August 1975, pp. 49–61.

NAUMANN, J.D. and JENKINS, A.M. "Prototyping: The New Paradigm for Systems Development," *MIS Quarterly* (6:3), September 1982, pp. 29–44.

ROCKART, J.F. "Chief Executives Define Their Own Data Needs," *Harvard Business Review* (57:2) March–April 1979, pp. 81–93.

ROCKART, J.F. and DELONG, D.W. *Executive Support Systems: The Emergence of Top Management Computer Use,* Dow Jones-Irwin, Homewood, IL, 1988.

ROCKART, J.F. and TREACY, M.E. "The CEO Goes On-Line," *Harvard Business Review* (60:1), January–February 1982, pp. 82–88.

SPRAGUE, R.H. "A Framework for the Development of Decision Support Systems," *MIS Quarterly* (4:4), December 1980, pp. 1–26.

STECKLOW, S. "The New Executive Information Systems," *Lotus,* April 1989, pp. 51–53.

TELEM, M. "Information Requirements Specifications I: Brainstorming Collective Decision-Making Approach," *Information Processing and Management* (24:5), 1988a, pp. 549–557.

TELEM, M. "Information Requirements Specifications II: Brainstorming Collective Decision-Making Approach," *Information Processing and Management* (24:5), 1988b, pp. 559–566.

VALUSEK, J.R. and FRYBACK, D.G. "Information Requirement Determination: Obstacles Within, Among, and Between Participants," in *Information Analysis: Selected Readings,* R. Galliers (ed.), Addison-Wesley, Reading, MA, 1987, pp. 139–151.

VOLONINO, L. and WATSON, H.J. "The Strategic Business Objectives Method for Guiding Executive Information Systems Development," *Journal of Management Information Systems* (4:4), Winter 1990–91, pp. 27–39.

WATSON, H.J. and FROLICK, M.N. "Determining Information Requirements for an Executive Information System," *Journal of Information Systems Management* (9:2), Spring 1992, pp. 37–43.

WATSON, H.J. and GLOVER, H. "Common and Avoidable Causes of EIS Failure," *Computerworld,* December 4, 1989, pp. 90–91.

WATSON, H.J., RAINER, K., and KOH, C. "Executive Information Systems: A Framework for Development and a Survey of Current Practices," *MIS Quarterly* (15:1), March 1991, pp. 13–30.

WATSON, H.J., HARP, C.G., KELLY, G.G., and O'HARA, M.T. "Adding Value to Your EIS Through Soft Information," *EIS and Information Delivery Systems Report* (5:6), June 1992, pp. 3–7.

WETHERBE, J.C. "Executive Information Requirements: Getting It Right," *MIS Quarterly* (15:1), March 1991, pp. 51–65.

ZAHEDI, F. "Reliability of Information Systems Based on Critical Success Factors-Formulation," *MIS Quarterly* (11:2), June 1987, pp. 187–204.

ZMUD, R.W. "Supporting Senior Executives Through Decision Support Technologies: A Review and Directions for Future Research," in *Decision Support Systems: A Decade in Perspective,* E.R. McLean and H.G. Sol (eds.), Elsevier, North-Holland, Amsterdam, 1986, pp. 87–101.

5

APPLYING ADAPTIVE DESIGN TO A REAL ESTATE DSS

INTRODUCTION

Decision support systems (DSS) are computer-based systems designed to enhance the effectiveness of decision makers in performing semistructured tasks. With such tasks, the decision maker is uncertain about the nature of the problem/opportunity, the alternative solutions and/or the criteria or value for making a choice. Hence, the primary role of a DSS is to aid the judgment processes as the decision maker contends with poorly defined problems.

The way of designing a DSS is different from that of a transaction processing system. A fundamental assumption in the traditional "life cycle" approach is that the requirements can be determined prior to the start of the design and development process. However, Sprague [14] stated that DSS designers literally "cannot get to first base" because the decision maker or user cannot define the functional requirements of the DSS in advance. Also, as an inherent part of the DSS design and implementation process, the user and designer will "learn" about the decision task and environment, thereby identifying new and unanticipated functional requirements.

Generally, DSS designers have recognized that this circumstance calls for a departure from tradition: adaptive design. This chapter focuses on the adaptive design approach. First, conceptual issues of adaptive design are explored and

This chapter is a reprint of Maryam Alavi and H. Albert Napier, "An Experiment in Applying the Adaptive Design Approach to DSS Development," *Information & Management*, Volume 7, Number 1, February 1984, pp. 21–28.

discussed. Then a case study is presented. The empirical findings of this provide some insight into the application and the effectiveness of the approach.

THE ADAPTIVE DESIGN PROCESS

In an adaptive design approach, the four traditional system development activities (requirements analysis, design, development, and implementation) are combined into a single phase, which is iteratively repeated in a relatively short time [14]. The process is described in the context of the framework of Keen [9]. According to this framework, the major components of adaptive design include the builder, the user, and the technical system (DSS). During the design process, these elements interact with ("influence") each other. Hence, three adaptive links are established in this framework: the user-system, the user-builder, and the builder-system.

In this framework, the user is either the manager or individual faced with a problem or opportunity. The user is responsible for taking action and its consequences. In some cases, the user may not directly interact with the technical system. Then, an intermediary provides the interface between the user and the system. The intermediary may play a clerical role (interact with the terminal to obtain user specified outputs) or play the role of a "staff assistant" (interact with the user and make suggestions) [14].

The DSS builder is the individual who develops the specific DSS with which the user or intermediary interacts. The builder should be knowledgeable about information systems technology and capabilities, and become familiar with the task for which the DSS is being designed. In some cases the builder may also play the role of user intermediary.

In the adaptive design framework, the technical system is the hardware/software provided to the user. A technical system is "configured" from DSS generator and/or DSS tools. A generator is a "package" which provides a set of capabilities to build a specific DSS quickly and easily [14]. An example of a DSS generator is the Executive Information System (EIS) marketed by Boeing Computer Services [4]. EIS capabilities include report generation, graphics, inquiry, and modeling languages which are available through a common command language. DSS tools are hardware and software elements applied to the development of a specific DSS or a DSS generator. Examples of DSS tools include general purpose programming languages, database management systems, and financial planning languages. Many early DSS were developed by direct application of DSS tools.

User-System Interactions

The user-system link deals with the effect of a user's characteristics on the system utilization. Research by Dickson, Chervany and Senn [6] established that some individual characteristics, such as problem solving style, experience, background and skills, influence the quality and quantity of system utilization. Alavi and Henderson [1] showed that individuals with an "analytical problem solving" style are more willing and inclined to use DSS than "intuitive" individuals.

This link reflects user learning as a result of using the system. It is argued that through interaction with the DSS, the user's understanding and perception of the decision task and potential solutions are enhanced. Case studies [9] have shown this.

The builder-system link occurs as the builder adds new capabilities and functions to the system. System evaluation and change is feasible only if system architecture is flexible; i.e., new capabilities can be added with little expenditure of time and resources. The system-builder link concerns the demand placed on the builder for system evolution resulting from user and builder learning and changes in the decision environment.

User-Builder Interactions

User-builder interactions involve communication and collaboration between the user and builder during the DSS development process. Through these interactions, the user learns about the capabilities and possibilities for decision support and the designer learns about user requirements and builds credibility. Effective communication and collaboration between user and builder are key aspects of adaptive design.

CASE STUDY

Background

The system discussed here has been implemented in a southwestern U.S. real estate development and management firm which had revenues of about 50 million dollars in 1982. Prior to development and implementation of the system, the firm had some experience related to computers, but none with DSS. The firm had an in-house IBM System 34 computer that was used primarily for transaction processing applications. The company purchased this computer in 1979.

Elements of Adaptive Design. The elements of adaptive design: The user, builder, and DSS in the case are depicted in Figure 5–1.

The Users. The primary users of the decision support system, a corporate cash flow analysis, and projection system are the chief executive officer (CEO), the controller, the administrative vice president, and the manager of operations. The CEO uses the system through an intermediary (the controller). Summary cash flow projection reports and sensitivity analysis results are used by the CEO

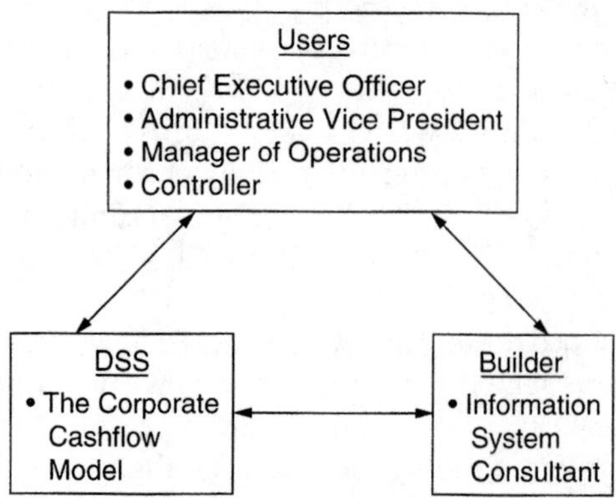

FIGURE 5–1 The Elements of Adaptive Design in the Case

for support of financial decisions, such as: identifying times when cash is needed and when surpluses are available, making "hold" or "sell" decisions for existing properties, and in making investment decisions for new real estate development projects. The controller is a "hands-on" user; the system outputs and its "what-if" capabilities are used to assist in activities such as the determination of the timing of construction draws and major cash payment and tax planning. The administrative vice president and the manager of operations use the system in budgeting activities for individual projects. Clerical staff personnel perform the role of intermediary for the vice president and the manager. Some demographic characteristics of these users are summarized in Table 5–1. Prior to the implementation of the DSS, the users had no familiarity with decision support systems.

The Builder. The DSS builder was an information systems consultant. The builder configured a cash flow model (the specific DSS) from a DSS generator, the Interactive Financial Planning System (IFPS) marketed by Execucom Systems

TABLE 5–1 Parameters of the DSS Users

Organizational Title	Number of Years in the Current Position	Educational Background	Age	DSS Utilization Mode
1. Chief Executive Officer	19	Engineering	45	Through an intermediary (the controller)
2. Administrative Vice President	4	Engineering	48	Through an intermediary (a clerk)
3. Manager of Operations	7	Mathematics	37	Through an intermediary (a clerk)
4. Controller	7	Accounting	32	"Hands-on"

Corporation (now Comshare) [8]. In the early stages of the project, the builder also acted as an intermediary to the CEO and the controller.

The DSS: The Corporate Cash Flow System. The corporate cash flow system consists of seven models and a set of datafiles, as illustrated in Figure 5–2. The DSS was developed using the IFPS modeling language and is processed on the Control Data Corporation (CDC) Cybernet timesharing system.

Model PPBS (Project Planning and Budgeting System) is used to project the cash flow operations for each real estate project. The datafiles for the model are prepared by the vice president of administration and the manager of operations. An intermediary, in this case a secretary, inputs the various datafiles and processes the Model PPBS using these files. Model Partner is processed for each property and a partnership report is printed. The datafiles for Model Partner are prepared by the controller. This requires the controller to obtain information from various operations personnel. After the datafiles are prepared, an intermediary, the controller's secretary, enters the data and processes Model Partner using the datafiles. The Model for Detailed Reports (MDR) generates detailed management reports and schedules for sources and uses of cash. The data for Model MDR is generated automatically by Model Partner. This model also generates the datafile CFPART, which is an input to the corporate cash flow model. Model Notes Receivable (MNOTREC) generates a note receivable report and a datafile (CFNTREC) of the totals by month for notes receivable. The input file to Model MNOTREC is the datafile NOTEREC. This input file is prepared by the accounting department and contains payment amounts for the notes receivable accounts. The controller's secretary enters this data and processes Model MNOTREC. The Model MNOTPAY generates a notes payable report. The accounting department prepares datafile (NOTEPAY), containing relevant payments to other organizations and individuals. The totals by month for notes payable are stored in file CFNTEPY which is used as input for the Corporate Cash flow model. The controller's secretary enters this data and processes Model NOTEPAY. Model Investment (MINV) produces a detailed report for other company financial activities. Totals by month for projected sales and projected costs and expenses are stored on datafile CFINV. The input file to Model MINV is datafile INVC which contains the projected revenues and expenses for the relevant business interests. The datafile is prepared by the accounting department. Again, the secretary of the controller acts as an intermediary by entering the datafile and processing Model MINV.

The Model Cash Flow (CASHFLO) provides a projection of cash flow and a report on sources and applications of cash. The cash flow model is developed with input files generated by the other 6 models contained in the system. In addition to these input files, the datafile MISC provides other necessary input to the cash flow model. The controller prepares and inputs the datafile MISC, and processes Model CASHFLO.

It should be noted that as the various models and datafiles were initially being developed, the DSS builder and user (the controller) did most of the data

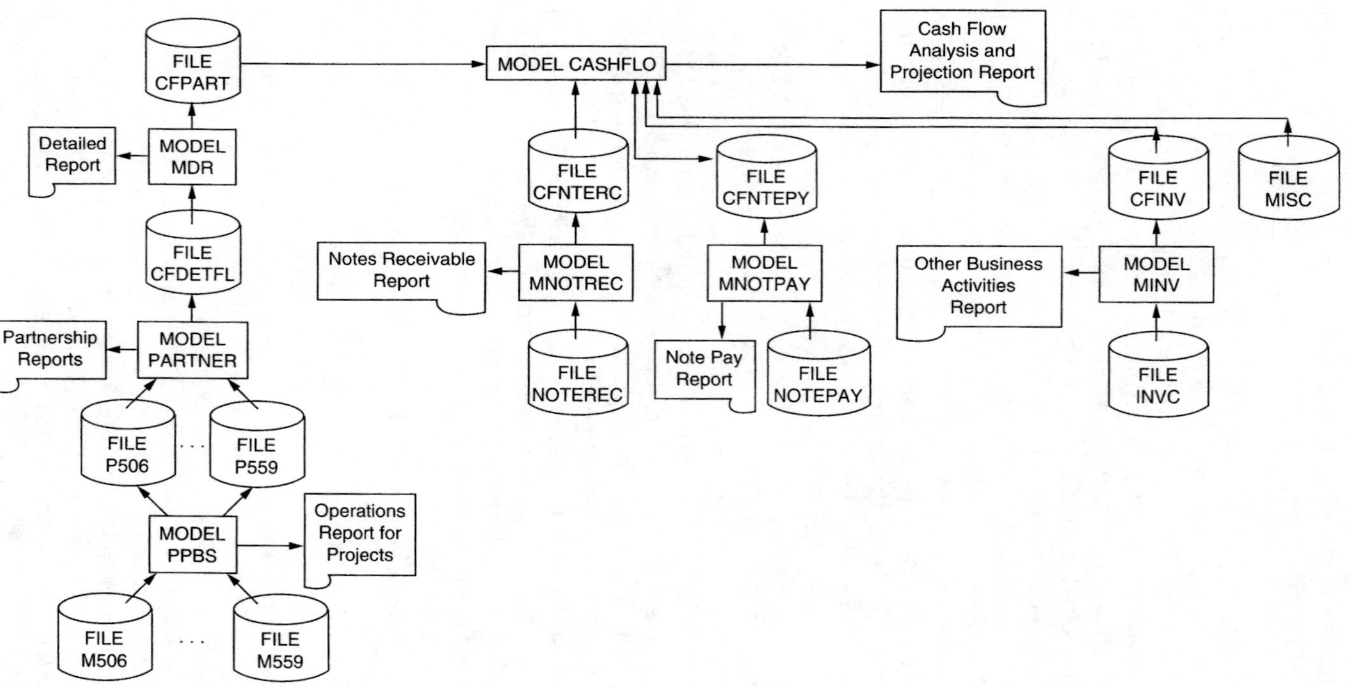

FIGURE 5–2 The DSS: Corporate Cash Flow System

entry and all the model processing. After the system was well defined and procedures developed, more intermediaries were used by the controller. Furthermore, after each of the various key processing steps occurred (completion of Model PPBS for all projects, processing of Model Partner for all projects, etc.) the controller and personnel responsible for various operations reviewed the reports and data to make sure it was correct before going to the next step in processing the system.

The cash flow system is processed monthly. Additional cash flow reports are run, as necessary, to facilitate decision making using various parameters. These additional reports are processed using the "what-if" capability of IFPS. This decision support system evolved in an iterative fashion over a period of 2½ months.

Application of Adaptive Design Approach

Prior to development and implementation of the DSS, cash flow analysis and projections were performed manually. The process was time consuming, error prone, and did not provide opportunities for sensitivity analysis. The DSS development process was initiated by the CEO, who approached the builder and expressed the need for improving the effectiveness and timeliness of the cash flow projections. During an informal session with the builder that lasted about one hour, the CEO briefly described the dynamics of real estate financing, the characteristics of his business, and his perceived need for timely, accurate information and the ability to perform sensitivity analysis.

Based on the chief executive officer's basic requirements, the builder developed a simple cash flow projection model. This model served two primary purposes:

- It demonstrated the potential for decision support and the essential features of a DSS.
- It enhanced the builder's understanding of the user's business and the environment.

Through the use of the simple cash flow model, with the builder acting as the intermediary, the chief executive officer quickly learned about the possible capabilities and features of the system. For example, the IFPS "What-If" and "Goal Seeking" commands were demonstrated by making various changes in model assumptions and parameters. After trying the initial system and entering some "What-If" commands, the chief executive officer perceived that a DSS could be built to assist in the projection and analysis of cash flow for his organization. The builder was then asked to develop and implement a cash flow system for the firm.

First Iteration. After the decision to build the cash flow system was made, but prior to initiating the development process, a 3-hour seminar providing an overview of financial planning and IFPS capabilities was conducted by the builder.

At the outset of the development process, the controller was somewhat hesitant about the attainment of the potential benefits and capabilities of the system. She also thought that the use of such a system might require more work than the manual system. To overcome this hesitancy, during the initial stage of the development process, the builder also assumed the role of educator. Specific examples of the potential capabilities and features of the system were provided to illustrate time savings and sensitivity analysis. The controller assumed a proactive role during the design process by providing information and input about the financial operations of the firm and the desired features of the system. Through this collaborative effort, with the builder providing the modeling expertise and the user (controller) providing the business expertise, the first version of the corporate cash flow system was created. The first version consisted of the following components:

1. The model CASHFLO, which generated the summary cash flow reports and projections for the CEO.
2. Models MNOTREC, MNOTPAY, MINV, and PARTNER and the associated datafiles.

The CEO was closely involved in the development of the first version of the cash flow system by monitoring the progress of the development effort and evaluating the system outputs. The first iteration of the cash flow model required 49 hours of the DSS builder's time, 25 hours of the controller's time, and 10 hours of the chief executive officer's time. The first iteration of the system was completed in one month of elapsed time.

Second Iteration. All the users (the chief executive officer, the controller, the vice president of administration, and manager of operations) actively participated in the second iteration of the system. This phase involved the development of Model PPBS and creation of the input files which contained detailed operational and financial data on individual properties. The level of effort spent in this phase was 31.5 hours of the DSS builder's time, 15 hours each of the vice president and the manager's time, and 10 hours of the controller's time. The CEO spent 5 hours during the second iteration.

The CEO's role at this time involved monitoring the project activities and progress. The controller, vice president of administration, and manager of operations assisted in defining the output reports and the processing logic. They also developed the necessary input datafiles.

Third Iteration. At the completion of the second iteration, the functional requirements were all satisfied. However, operational use of the system indicated that the approach taken in the creation of the detailed reports (using model

MDR) needed modification and refinement. A single model with a large matrix size was used to create the detail reports. If some of the detail reports had to be regenerated due to an error, the large model had to be reprocessed and all the detail reports regenerated. This was highly inefficient in terms of user time and computing resources. Hence, in the third iteration, the single large model was replaced by a set of 12 models that collectively generated the detailed report datafiles. These smaller models were more efficient. Furthermore, if one report had to be regenerated, only one small model had to be processed. "Command" files which automated the processing of the various processing segments were also developed to enhance the operation of the DSS.

The third iteration phase of the system was concluded by documenting the system and the operational procedures. The level of the effort spent at this iteration consisted of 60 hours of the builder's time and 20 hours of the controller's time.

CASE SUMMARY

The case involved the actual design and implementation of a decision support system for cash flow projections and analysis. The user group consisted of four decision makers: the CEO, the controller, the vice president of administration, and the manager of operations.

The design process can be best characterized as an iterative cycling between the DSS generator (IFPS) and the specific corporate cash flow system. With each cycle, the cash flow system was enhanced and new components were added. In each iteration, the typical systems development steps (analysis, design, construction, and implementation) were united.

The user group was closely involved in the process of development and implementation. The total level of user effort was 90 person-hours. The cash flow system has been in operation for the past 1½ years. The system is operated solely by the users and is under their control.

The users are satisfied with the system and perceive it as a valuable and beneficial tool for use in cash flow decisions. Their perceived benefits of the system include: obtaining better control over the operations; ability to respond to environmental changes (e.g., in the interest rates) in a timely manner; and increased capability for decision analysis.

OBSERVATIONS ON THE CASE STUDY

During the development of the corporate cash flow decision support system, the following observations were made on the effectiveness and requirements of the adaptive design approach.

1. The adaptive design approach requires a high level of user participation and involvement. In this project, the users spent 90 person-hours in the development process compared to 140.5 person-hours spent by the builder. User involvement and cooperation seem to be a necessary condition for effective application of the approach. Hence, it may not be applicable to those design situations in which the user is unable or unwilling to participate actively in the design process.
2. During the early stages of the development process, there was rapid progress toward defining the user requirements and developing DSS capabilities to meet them. There were cycles of discussion, development, review of the output, and further development. Such rapid progress resulted in positive user attitudes. Furthermore, providing quick and tangible output in early stages established credibility for the DSS builder and helped in obtaining user cooperation.
3. Availability of a program generator and interactive computing resource were critical factors in the application of the approach. Capabilities provided by IFPS (self-documentation, ease of coding and making changes, data storage and retrieval, report generation, etc.) allowed rapid response to requirements and the iterative and modular development process used to develop the cash flow system.
4. Except for a 3-hour introductory seminar on financial planning languages and IFPS conducted at the outset, no other formal user training programs were needed. The interactions among the user, builder, and system, and the proactive role of the users in the design process decreased the requirements for formal user training.
5. The perceived need and usefulness of the system seemed to be the incentive for its adoption. No attempts at an explicit and formal cost/benefit analysis were made. Perceived value was established at the outset by using and evaluating a prototype cash flow system.

SUMMARY

The adaptive design approach seems to be useful and effective for DSS development. However, further experimentation and evaluation are required before suggesting it is universally applicable. The following are some areas in which research or investigation must be conducted to increase understanding of the approach and its applicability:

1. What are the advantages and disadvantages of the adaptive design approach relative to others?

2. What contextual variables (e.g., organizational and task) seem to impact the process of adaptive design? What variables enhance or constrain its application?
3. What is the impact of the adaptive design approach on the user? Is there user-related psychological satisfaction or dissatisfaction derived from this approach?
4. What is the impact of the adaptive design approach on the DSS builder?
5. What training and skills are required of the builder for successful application of the approach?
6. What technological tools and resources are required?

Adaptive design may only be effective given certain contingencies: it may work well in one environment but not in another. However, preliminary findings from this case study suggest that the approach has high potential for developing effective decision support systems.

QUESTIONS

1. What is it about DSS applications that requires an adaptive rather than a traditional development approach?
2. Describe the activities of the organizational personnel who were involved in the development of the corporate cash flow system. Discuss how the organizational roles of manager, intermediary, DSS builder, technical supporter, and toolsmith were filled.
3. Discuss the three iterations in the development of the corporate cash flow system.

REFERENCES

1. ALAVI, M., and J. C. HENDERSON "An Evolutionary Strategy for Implementing a Decision Support System," *Management Science*, 27, no. 11 (November 1981).
2. BALLY, L., J. BRITTAN, and K. H. WAYNER "A Prototype Approach to Information System Design and Development," *Information & Management*, 1 (1977), 21–26.
3. BERRISFORD, T., and J. C. WETHERBE "Heuristic Development: A Redesign of Systems Design," *MIS Quarterly*, March 1979, 11–19.
4. BOEING COMPUTER SERVICES c/o Mr. Park Thoreson, P.O. Box 24346, Seattle, WA 98124.
5. BOLAND R. J., JR. "The Process and Product of System Design," *Management Science*, 24, no. 9 (1978), 887–98.

6. DICKSON, G. W., N. L. CHERVANY, and J. A. SENN "Research in Management Information Systems: The Minnesota Experiments," *Management Science,* 23, no. 9 (May 1977).
7. HAWGOOD, J., ed., *Evolutionary Information Systems.* Proceedings of the IFIP TC 8 Working Conference on Evolutionary Information Systems, Budapest, Hungary, September 1–3, 1981 (Amsterdam: North Holland Publishing, 1982; ISBN: 0-444-86359-1).
8. IFPS USERS MANUAL EXECUCOM SYSTEMS CORPORATION P.O. Box 9758, Austin, TX 78766.
9. KEEN, P. G. W. "Adaptive Design for DSS," *Database,* 12, nos. 1 and 2 (Fall (1980), 15–25.
10. KEEN, P. G. W. "Value Analysis: Justifying Decision Support Systems," *MIS Quarterly,* March 1981, 1–15.
11. LIVARI, J. "Taxonomy of the Experimental and Evolutionary Approaches to the Systemeering," in J. Hawgood, *Evolutionary Information Systems.* Proceedings of the IFIP TC 8 Working Conference on Evolutionary Information Systems, Budapest, Hungary, September 1–3, 1981 (Amsterdam: North Holland Publishing, 1982: ISBN 0-444-83539-1).
12. LUCAS, H. C. "The Evolution of an Information System: From Key-Man to Every Person," *Sloan Management Review,* Winter 1978.
13. NAUMAN, J. G., and M. A. JENKINS "Prototyping: The New Paradigm for Systems Development," *MIS Quarterly,* 6, no. 3 (September 1982), 29–4.
14. SPRAGUE, R. H., JR. "A Framework for the Development of Decision Support Systems," *MIS Quarterly,* December 1980, 1–26.
15. ZMUD, R. W. "Individual Differences and MIS Success: A Review of the Empirical Literature," *Management Science,* 25, no. 10 (1979).

6

DECISION SUPPORT FOR TRAIN DISPATCHING

INTRODUCTION

In Chapter 5, adaptive design (also called evolutionary or iterative design) was discussed and illustrated. While adaptive design is appropriate for most DSS work, it is not always the best choice. There are factors that can lead to the use of a more structured methodology, and in extreme cases, even to the use of the systems development life cycle. The following factors may lead to the use of a more structured development methodology:

1. company-wide use of the system
2. company-wide data requirements
3. the use of DSS tools rather than generators
4. well-defined information requirements
5. system development by IS professionals
6. the required technology is not currently available in the company
7. high cost systems

This chapter is adapted from Richard L. Sander and William M. Westerman, "Computer Aided Train Dispatching: Decision Support Through Optimization," *Interfaces*, Volume 13, Number 6, December 1983, pp. 24–37.

This chapter describes the development of the computer aided train dispatching system at Southern Railway. The DSS is an interesting application in its own right, but how it was developed provides an interesting contrast to the DSS described in Chapter 5 and helps illustrate the range of DSS development methodologies.

TRAIN DISPATCHING AT SOUTHERN RAILWAY

A mini-computer based information system with on-line optimal route planning capability was developed to assist dispatchers on the complex northern portion of Southern Railway's Alabama Division. The routing plan is revised automatically as conditions change. Since implementation in September 1980, train delay has been more than 15 percent lower, reflecting annual savings of $316,000.

The dispatching support system is now being expanded to all other Southern Railway operating divisions with $3,000,000 annual savings expected from reduced train delay.

Southern Railway Company operating throughout the southeastern United States is one of the nation's largest railroads. For years it has been a leader in profitability in the industry. In 1981 Southern's after tax profits totaled $212 million from revenues of $1.87 billion.

In June 1982, Southern Railway and the Norfolk and Western Railway merged to form the Norfolk Southern Corporation. The combined system provides efficient single system service throughout the South, East, and Midwest. The Norfolk Southern Corporation is now the nation's fifth largest and most profitable railway system. Had it existed in 1981, it would have produced revenue of $3.59 billion and realized profits of $500 million. Even in the 1982 recession year, after tax profits, on a pro forma basis, amounted to $411 million.

Southern Railway and the Norfolk and Western operate as autonomous organizations whose activities are coordinated at the holding company level. Each railroad is divided into two operating regions, and each region, headed by a general manager, contains five operating divisions.

Daily operations are controlled at the division headquarters level. Although movement of trains between divisions is coordinated through a centralized operations control center, the responsibility for the safe and efficient movement of trains over the division lies principally in the division dispatching office. Directly accountable to the division superintendent, the dispatching office is headed by an assistant superintendent, the "Super Chief"; reporting to him is a chief dispatcher and a staff of train dispatchers.

Dispatching trains is complex and demanding. In a typical eight-hour shift, a train dispatcher will control the movement of 20 to 30 trains over territories spanning three to six hundred miles. In most cases, these trains operate over single tracks and opposing trains must meet at strategically placed passing sidings. The dispatcher arranges these "meets" with safety the paramount consideration.

He also must safely coordinate movements of roadway maintenance gangs, signal maintenance crews, industrial switch engines, and motor car inspection crews.

The dispatcher is also in constant contact with yard personnel at freight terminals who report essential information regarding trains that will move over the division. Once trains reach their destinations, they report operating and delay statistics for the dispatcher to record. Federal law requires that the dispatcher maintain this "train sheet." Finally, the train dispatcher interacts and coordinates with other dispatchers, as well as the chief dispatcher, giving and taking information about the operation of his territory.

Southern Railway's Alabama Division (Figure 6–1) is a complex operating division. Headquartered at Birmingham, Alabama, its most heavily traveled routes extend from Atlanta through Birmingham to Sheffield, Alabama, near Memphis. It interfaces with other operating divisions at each of these locations. Other major routes extend from Birmingham south to Mobile and from Birmingham southeast to Columbus, Georgia. Altogether, mainline trackage exceeds 800 miles and 80 to 90 trains operate daily. The division employs more than 1,200 persons, mostly in train and engine service.

Two train dispatchers are on duty around the clock at the Birmingham headquarters. One controls the high density Birmingham-Sheffield corridor (the North Alabama District) and the line south to Mobile. The other controls the Birmingham-Atlanta route (the East End District) and the line into southwest Georgia.

Both the North Alabama and the East End Districts operate under Centralized Traffic Control (CTC). This provides a failsafe system of signals and switches in the field controlled centrally by the dispatcher who monitors all field activity on an electronic display board. The other lines on the division have no signal control. In these "dark" territories, train movement is controlled solely by the dispatcher issuing stringent orders to train crews.

Until the mid-1970s, the operation of the Alabama Division was not overly complex; in fact, there was no centralized traffic control whatsoever. Then in 1974 with the opening of a large freight yard facility at Sheffield, merchandise traffic levels began to grow steadily, making the North Alabama District a major gateway to and from the Midwest. A coal loading facility near Sheffield was opened in 1977, further congesting the line. Unit trains (trains with up to seven locomotives and 96 loaded coal cars) began operating to key power plants in Georgia and Alabama. These trains operate on 40 hour "cycles," that is, moving loaded to their destination, unloading, and returning empty over the reverse route for reloading. Up to four such trains operate concurrently.

Management foresaw the need for centralized traffic control to assist dispatchers and began installation in 1976.

The research and development project to provide computer assistance for the dispatcher was in progress independently during this same period. As the CTC installation neared completion and as the R&D project began to show

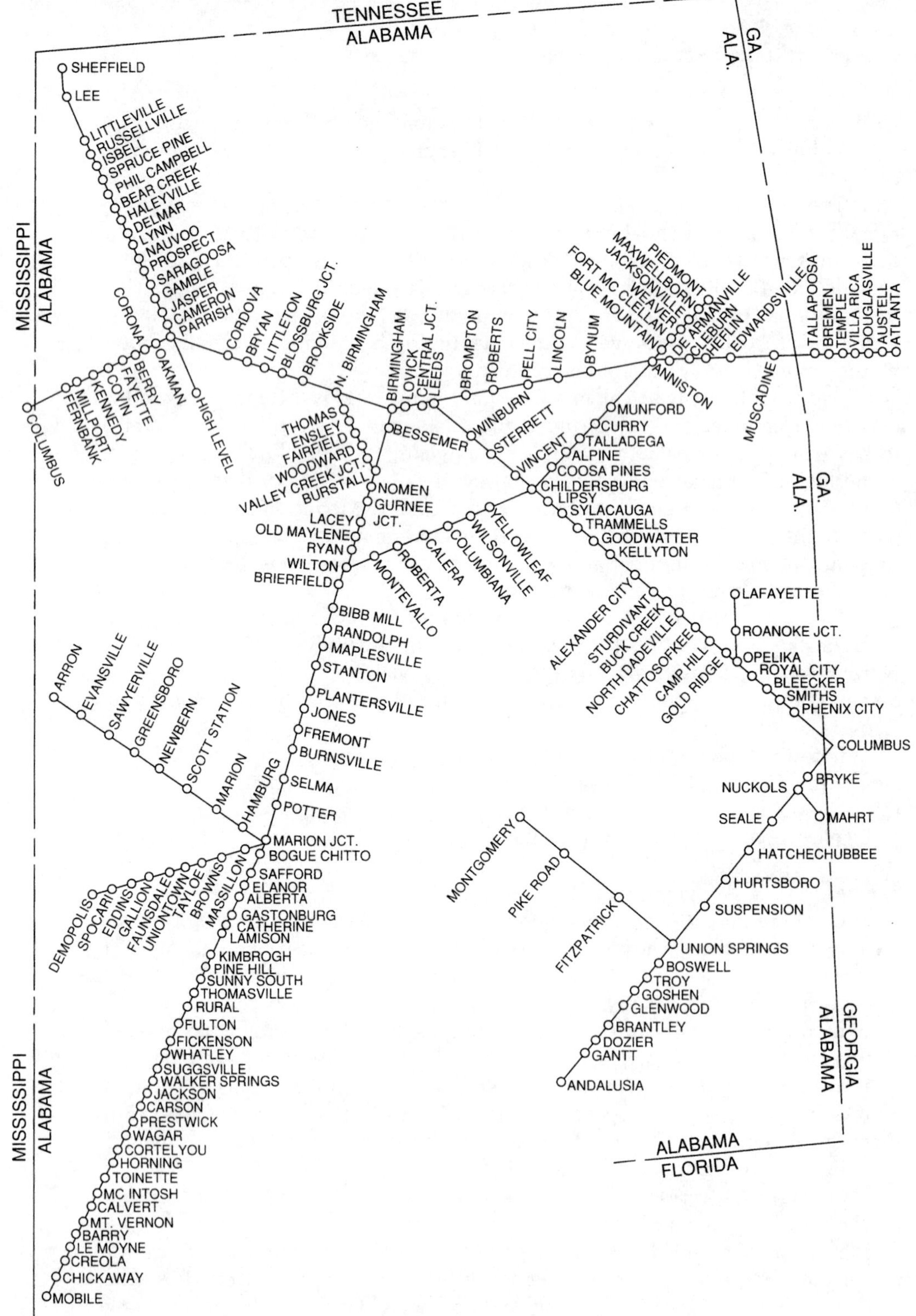

Figure 6–1 Southern Railway's Alabama Division

promise, it became clear that the Alabama Division was a logical location for determining how computer aided dispatching could further improve performance.

DEVELOPMENT OF THE SUPPORT SYSTEM

Southern Railway's operations research staff (which is now the Norfolk Southern Corporation's OR staff) has existed since the mid-1960s. Originally oriented toward computer model development, the operations research group by the early 1970s had become a corporate consulting staff providing *applications* support using tested analytical techniques, on one hand, and supporting *research and development* on the other.

The development staff began to investigate computer aid for the train dispatcher in 1975. Information systems for yard and terminal operations were already in place at many locations on the railroad. Extensions to this system requiring chief dispatchers to report realtime status of key trains were already envisioned. No other division-level systems were then being contemplated.

Concurrently, several signal manufacturers started selling turn-key systems to support CTC operations, providing features such as automatic "OS-ing (On Station reporting of the time a train passed a key location). Some systems permitted automated record keeping. One system even incorporated a rudimentary planning capability, tracing the routes of two opposing trains to determine when they would meet.

Operations research personnel reviewed a number of these systems and rejected them as being too inflexible. They saw the potential for automating the vast amount of division level information being manually recorded and for integrating this with other information systems. With extensive experience using simulation models to analyze line changes, they also foresaw the real possibility of on-line predictive planning aids for the dispatcher. They proposed that a computerized physical simulator be developed to explore these possibilities. Southern's top management computer usage committee approved the R&D project in late 1976.

The mini-computer based simulator, built and thoroughly tested over a three-year period, emulated a centralized-traffic-control-office environment and permitted designers and dispatchers alike to play and replay real-life scenarios, refining features that could eventually be installed in a division office. The simulator contained a bank of four color CRT's. Two displayed the track layout of the territory being studied. A simulation model was written to emulate movement of trains over the territory and it displayed movement of trains on the two track-layout CRT's based on route decisions interactively keyed by the "dispatcher."

A third CRT served as a work sheet for updating automated train-data files. A specially designed function keyboard permitted screen formats to be displayed which allowed dispatchers to update train sheets, reports of delay, locomotive failures, weather conditions, and many other records, all of which were then kept manually at division offices. The computerized system did not change what was being recorded; it merely changed the manner in which data was being recorded. A fourth CRT was reserved for displaying how trains should be routed—a capability which was being developed at the same time.

The potential for an on-line planning algorithm lay in considering all feasible future train meets throughout the territory and advising the dispatcher of that combination which would minimize total train delay. This "meet/pass plan," as it was labeled, had to account for all realistic operating conditions: travel times between sidings based on power and tonnage, speed limits, speed restrictions, train length compared with siding length, the ability of a train to start once stopped in a siding, train adherence to schedule, special cargo requiring special handling, work locations, and so forth. It also had to respond to dynamically changing conditions and display its latest recommended plan of action to the dispatcher in a manner he could readily comprehend.

The time-distance graph shown in Figure 6–2 is a standard method for displaying train meeting points and associated delay. Even in this simplified example involving five sidings and four eastbound and five westbound trains, there are thousands of meet combinations that could occur. The meet-pass plan was designed to reevaluate the combination at any time conditions changed and to display this new plan starting at the current time (8:30 am in the Figure 6–2 example) and projecting six to eight hours into the future.

Also incorporated was the ability for the dispatcher to override the plan by stating specific meet locations, by taking track out of service and by forcing trains in one direction to be stopped in sidings prior to the arrival of an opposing train. This permitted dispatcher experience and judgment to be reflected in the plan. It also formed the basis for a "what if" planning capability!

The first attempt to model the process evaluated feasible train routes with a decomposition approach incorporating a shortest path algorithm and a linear programming formulation. Although optimal solutions were obtainable, more often than not, convergence time was excessive and suboptimal solutions resulted. This method was subsequently replaced with a branch-and-bound technique enumerating all feasible meet locations and this approach did insure optimal results in a highly responsive fashion.

The meet/pass plan was integrated into the simulator, and its use for on-line tactical planning was evaluated in detail. Possibly its most significant use was predicting the impact of the system operating in a real environment. During a periodic review of the project's status, the computer usage committee directed the operations research group to evaluate the potential of the system on the North Alabama District.

Operation was simulated both with and without computer-aided planning, and the impact on resulting train delay was measured. Train sheets for the North Alabama line were reviewed, and a typically heavy, yet normal, day of operation was selected. Train-meet delay for the first eight-hour shift on that day had

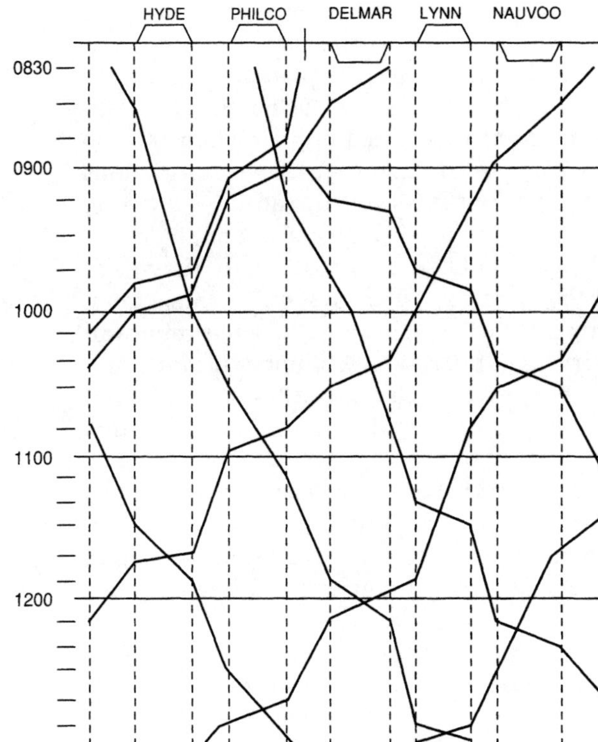

Figure 6–2 A time-distance graph displaying train movement through a five siding network in a four and one-half hour time frame. Four eastbound trains move diagonally from left to right meeting five westbound trains where the lines intersect.

amounted to 457 minutes. An Alabama Division dispatcher operated that same shift of operation in the simulator. The session began with train locations shown and information available concerning oncoming trains. The dispatcher worked the entire shift with no planning assistance, and the delay recorded at the conclusion of the session amounted to 455 minutes—a two-minute difference.

The dispatcher then replayed the shift, this time following meets recommended by the plan. The resulting delay, 300 minutes, reflected a reduction of 34 percent. Reductions in other scenarios subsequently simulated ranged from 22 to 38 percent. When the OR group presented these findings, the committee, perceiving that if even half of these benefits could be realized they would create a significant performance impact, immediately approved the project. The North Alabama pilot project was underway.

IMPLEMENTATION AND ITS IMPACT

Interfacing the mini-computers and the CTC system was the only significant task involved in converting from a simulated to an on-line environment. CRT's were added to the North Alabama dispatcher's work station to complement the CTC display board: two "work" CRT's were installed to provide flexibility and backup, and a third CRT was installed solely for meet/pass plan display.

Installation and parallel testing of the North Alabama system began in January 1980. On September 15, 1980, the system was placed in production and the dispatcher's manual train sheets were removed. Six weeks later, instructions were issued to dispatchers to utilize the computer-generated plan.

Earlier in 1980, groundwork had been laid for installing a second, independent system to support the East End Alabama Division dispatcher. In the meantime, Data General Corporation, the minicomputer system manufacturer, announced an advanced operating system that would permit a *single* minicomputer, with additional internal memory, to support a large number of users and work stations simultaneously. The desirability of such a single system that could support two or more dispatchers and any others needing access to the system was evident.

Conversion of the system started in mid-1981, with East End operations added to the dispatching system in March 1982. A final system supporting all territories on the Alabama Division became a reality in September. What had begun as a system to support a single train dispatcher had now evolved into one supporting all division operations.

Auditing operating performance as the system gained acceptance and comparing it with prior performance experience was a vital step in measuring the impact of computer-aided dispatching. The improvement predicted in the simulator experiment now had to be verified. For two full years since implementation, performance statistics have been compiled daily reflecting the total numbers of trains operating, train meets, and the total delay caused by these meets. Reviewing manual train sheets for a full year of operation starting in September 1979 provided similar data for pre-implementation comparison.

Forty weeks of operations in each of these periods were then selected for a comparison study (a choice made necessary to compensate for a ten-week coal strike in 1981). Corresponding weeks were used for the year before implementation (the base period) and the year after. In the second year of operation, the first 40 contiguous weeks, beginning September 15, 1981, were used, thereby eliminating from consideration a period when business took a sharp downturn during the latter half of 1982.

Stringent guidelines were developed for analyzing delay reports to insure consistent measurement across periods:

1. Only delay within the limits controlled by the dispatcher was included.
2. Only delay that the dispatcher's planning would influence was considered.
3. Days reflecting highly abnormal operation, such as during a derailment, were excluded and replaced with an average for the same day in the four previous weeks. The operating statistics for the three measured periods are summarized in Table 6–1.

TABLE 6–1 North Alabama District Operating Statistics for the Three-Year Period Starting September 15, 1979

	Period A	Period B	Period C
	Year Prior to Implementation	First Year since Implementation	Second Year since Implementation
Average Weekly Meet Delay (Minutes)	8893	8290 (–6.8%)	6645 (–25.3%)
Trains Operated (Weekly)	147.4	156.9 (+8.5%)	147.7 (+0.2%)
Train Meets (Weekly)	245.9	262.1 (+6.6%)	226.3 (+8.0%)
Meets Per Train Operated	1.67	1.67	1.53
Delay Per Train (Minutes)	60.3	52.8 (–12.4%)	45.0 (–25.4%)
Delay Per Meet (Minutes)	36.2	31.6 (–12.7%)	29.4 (–18.8%)

By comparing the first year of implementation with the previous year, traffic increased nearly nine percent, yet delay per train operated and delay per meet were down more than twelve percent. Traffic in the second year of operation returned to pre-implementation levels. The average number of trains operating weekly is nearly identical in the two periods, yet delay is more than 25 percent less in the 1981–1982 period.

Of the two measures, delay/train and delay/meet, the latter is more meaningful because division personnel have some control in scheduling trains to avoid meets but have little control over the numbers of trains operating. This ability to plan and control meets is evident in the figures for the second year of operation when delay per meet was reduced 18.8 percent. Overall, combining the 80 weeks of measured operation since computer-aided dispatching was placed on line, delay per meet has improved 15.5 percent. In addition, as Figure 6–3 shows, the operation is more consistent. In the year prior to implementation delay per meet ranged from 31.0 to 44.4 minutes. In the first year after implementation, it ranged from 26.6 to 40.2 and in the second, from 26.2 to 33.7 minutes.

Optimal planning together with information availability has improved performance significantly, and the resulting operation is a more consistent one. Several of the reasons are:

1. *A cleaner, neater, more professional operation.* Information is mechanically and electronically recorded, replacing hand-scrawled and often altered massive documents.

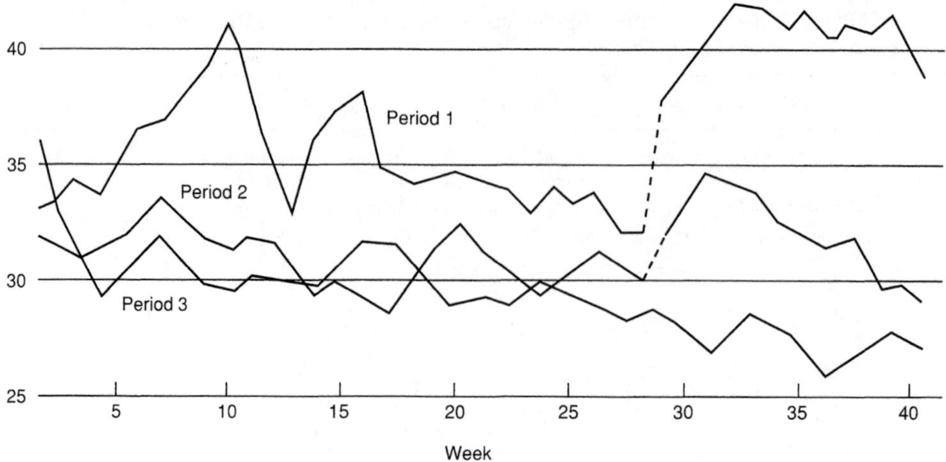

Figure 6–3 Minutes of Delay per Meet, a Three-Week Moving Average

2. *A readily accessible information base.* Information recorded by the dispatcher is readily available and functional in inquiry form to all division personnel. Train information can also be transferred from one dispatcher's territory to another, reducing manual recording.
3. *An optimal plan clearly reflecting management policy.* The meet/pass plan considers management directives regarding key priorities for dispatching trains. The continually updated nature of the plan ensures compliance with this policy under dynamic conditions.
4. *An equitable attitude toward dispatcher responsibility and action.* As should be expected, dispatchers are severely criticized for delays caused by poor planning or inattention, for example if a high-priority train is delayed because a low-priority opposing train blocks its movement. A common dispatching solution had been to clear the low-priority train into a siding far in advance to minimize possibility of delaying the hot train. Computer aided dispatching has virtually eliminated this waste. Dispatchers are encouraged to use the plan and are not hauled on the carpet if they follow it, even should a delay occur.

In addition to freeing the dispatcher from complex, diversionary, time-consuming calculations and risks, this computerized system has ancillary benefits. For instance, train crews now make their runs in consistently less time, giving them more time at home and substantially improving morale. By the same token, locomotive fuel and equipment requirements are cut, thereby effecting a measurable reduction in mechanical costs.

Reduction in train delay translates directly to cost savings. One hour of train operation equates to more than $240 using a formula which considers fuel consumption, crew costs, locomotive availability and utilization, freight car ownership costs, revenue producing potential, and a variety of other factors. The more than 15 percent reduction in delay experienced in the 80 measured weeks of performance directly reflects savings of $316,000 in each of the first two years of operation.

What are the anticipated divisionwide savings now that the system does in fact support all operating districts on the division? It is reasonable to expect similar percentage savings on the East End CTC line between Atlanta and Birmingham. On the non-CTC portion of the division, some lesser improvement will occur from better planning and train scheduling. On this basis, future savings for the Alabama Division, when traffic returns to pre-1982 levels, are estimated at $675,000 annually. In addition, a proposed new passing siding on the North Alabama line, at a cost of $1,500,000, has been postponed indefinitely as a direct result of the greater dispatching efficiency.

Another monetary saving which cannot be easily quantified is additional track time for various types of maintenance crews. The dispatcher can now more quickly and efficiently allocate working time, because he can adjust the locations of train delays to accommodate these crews. Using the meet/pass plan's "what-if" capability, he can determine the best times to allocate, maximizing on-track working time yet minimizing train delay.

BEYOND THE BASIC SYSTEM

On the same basis that expected divisionwide savings were estimated for the Alabama Division, implementation of the computer-aided dispatching system on all Southern Railway divisions will produce cost savings of $3,000,000 annually in train delay reduction alone.

On September 27, 1982, a memo sent to the Executive Vice President for Administration, Norfolk Southern, from the President of the Southern Railway read in part:

> I am very much interested in extending this system to other divisions. I feel the results on the Alabama Division have been even better than we anticipated, and I believe we should move now to the north end of the Georgia Division between Chattanooga and Atlanta. . .

Computer hardware to support the Georgia Division operation was delivered in the last week of December. Starting in early January, operations research analysts, working with Georgia Division personnel, "defined" the division, using interactive file definition programs. On January 27, the Georgia Division support system was put on-line to begin dispatcher training and no computer program changes were required to transfer the existing Alabama Division support system to the Georgia Division.

Training continued through February, and on March 18 manual train sheets for the north end of the Georgia Division, Atlanta to Chattanooga, were removed. The total conversion effort required less than six operations-research man weeks, and less than three Georgia Division man weeks, including system support and training.

Systems for three additional Southern Railway divisions are budgeted for the remainder of 1983. In January of 1983, the President of Southern Railway convened a task force representing transportation, engineering, operations research, and data processing to produce an implementation plan that considers real installation costs matched against previously derived benefits. At the present time, it is expected that total installation cost at each division, except for one that requires new building facilities, will be less than $300,000.

The system described to this point is in operation and results have been demonstrated. The need for some new features became evident in working with the implemented system and they will be implemented soon.

First is formal planning assistance for the chief dispatcher. Improved efficiency in his duties has already been achieved through the information processing capabilities of the system. The meet/pass plans now used by the train dispatchers are tactical plans that consider trains now on the territory and trains whose arrival is imminent. In a new approach, appropriately dubbed "SUPERPLAN," the individual meet/pass plans for each dispatching territory will provide input to a divisionwide planning process and allow the chief dispatcher to adjust train schedules and work assignments to avoid unnecessary train meets and traffic congestion.

A second innovation provides information transfer among division offices. This step ties together each of the divisions through Southern Railway's central computer complex in Atlanta. This feature, first of all, eases the chief dispatcher's clerical effort in reporting key train movements. More important, it provides the basis for "SUPERPLAN-II"—optimal planning among divisions. The ultimate capability, now a potential reality, is vastly improved planning among divisions, at the general manager level and at the system control and coordination level. What was once a blue-sky dream of optimizing systemwide operation is now within reach because the basic building block, the division-level computer-aided dispatching system, works!

SUMMARY

Today the working computer-aided dispatching system continues to demonstrate significant dollar impact. Direction to expand the application to other territories testifies to the faith management has in the future benefits of the system. From a management scientist's viewpoint, the dispatching system is a marriage of information processing and management science. It is a distributed system and a decision support system. Proven management science optimization techniques form the basis of the system which around the clock provides dispatchers and managers alike the real time key to improving productivity and expanding profitability.

QUESTIONS

1. Describe the responsibilities of a train dispatcher.
2. Describe the development approach for the train-dispatching DSS at Southern Railway.
3. What factors influenced the development approach used?
4. Does Southern Railway's train-dispatching DSS support or automate decision making? Discuss.
5. Discuss the benefits that have resulted from the implementation of Southern Railway's train-dispatching DSS.

Part 3

THE ARCHITECTURE FOR DECISION SUPPORT APPLICATIONS

Part 1 of the book established the conceptual foundations which became the theory of DSS. One of the central conceptual models of DSS is the Data-Dialog-Modeling (DDM) paradigm presented in Figure 1–2. Its importance lies in its ability to describe the main components of DSS and explain how they interrelate. The three components are the database, the modelbase, and the dialog. Data and models are the two primary resources provided by a DSS, and the dialog component is what allows the decision maker to access and utilize them.

The dialog component is a software interface through which the user directs the actions and receives the output from the DSS. It gets its name because it supports the *dialog* between the user and the system. The database component serves such functions as providing information in response to queries from the user; supplying data for the building, updating, and running of models; and storing intermediate and final results from analyses that are made. Finally there is the model base component. This component includes permanent models as well as modeling capabilities for building and updating models.

The DDM conceptual model is described in Chapter 1 in a few paragraphs. Part 3 of the book devotes seven chapters to the architecture for DSS, defined primarily by the DDM model. The topic deserves this much attention because it is the structure of DSS which becomes the infrastructure which must be built to support an on-going DSS effort. It also provides the terminology and framework for communication among the primary stakeholders in the DSS movement. Users and managers define the functionality they need in dialog, data, and models while the builders and vendors use the same framework to develop the technology to deliver those services.

The seven chapters in Part 3 describe more fully the attributes of the three components of the DSS architecture and provide additional insights through examples. Chapter 7 deals with the data-dialog-modeling components of the DSS architecture in more detail. Each of the three components provides capabilities and functions beyond those which are first apparent. The dialog component can be broken down into what the user *can do* (the action language), *must know* (the knowledge base), and *can see* (the presentation language). Specific combinations of attributes for each of these functions form a "dialog style" that specifies how the system and the user interact. The data component must deal not just with traditional data, but also with a full range of information resources. And the modeling component goes beyond traditional models to incorporate advanced techniques from the field of artificial intelligence. Chapter 7 also explains the important characteristics of the direct linkage between the database and the modelbase. Model parameters are stored in, or derived from, the database. And intermediate results of a submodel are stored in the database for subsequent use by other models.

Chapter 8 discusses requirements in the database component for ad hoc and institutional DSS. Ad hoc DSS are used infrequently, usually on a project basis, while institutional DSS are used regularly for repetitive decision making. This chapter describes the database component of two institutional and ad hoc DSS and suggests database differences that seem to exist between these two types of decision support systems. An understanding of these differences can facilitate the design of a DSS database.

Chapter 9 continues the discussion of the data component by presenting multi-dimensional databases, with emphasis on how they differ from traditional databases for transaction processing and routine reporting. The multi-dimensional database structure is intuitively comfortable for executives. Consequently it has grown rapidly in DSS and EIS.

Chapter 10 is an example of a DSS for vehicle routing that clearly illustrates the three components of the DSS architecture, and the capabilities of each. It also explains why a balance among the three is necessary, and that a strong modeling component, even for a traditional linear programming application, does not replace the need for the other two components.

Chapter 11 returns to the interface or dialog component with guidelines for the design of the interface capabilities for EIS used by executives. The chapter shows that these guidelines are proving to be appropriate for other types of DSS also.

An important new aspect of the database component is the growing use of documents. It is easy to see how the data and information contained in documents, reports, memos, and even phone messages can be an extremely important resource for DSS. New technologies are now evolving that will make it possible to manage this data resource better, as explained in Chapter 12.

The final chapter in this part provides a look at the important developments in the field of artificial intelligence and the impact they are likely to have in the future of DSS. Especially important are the new developments in software agents, which are featured in this chapter. These impacts will be significant both in the modeling and the dialog components of the DSS architecture.

7

ARCHITECTURE FOR DSS

INTRODUCTION

A useful way of thinking about the component parts of a decision support system (DSS) and the relationships among the parts is to use the dialog, data, and models (DDM) paradigm described in Chapter 1 (see Figure 1–2). In this conceptualization, there is the *dialog* (D) between the user and the system, the *data* (D) that support the system, and the *models* (M) that provide the analysis capabilities. While the components differ somewhat from application to application, they always exist in some form. Figure 7–1, an expansion of Figure 1–2, provides a pictorial representation of the component parts of a DSS.

For users and DSS builders, it is important to understand how each component can be designed. For users, it creates an awareness of what can be requested in a DSS. For DSS builders, it suggests what can be delivered.

New technology continues to affect the dialog, data, and models components. For example, icon-based, touchscreen systems provide new options for directing the system. Relational database technology, and more recently object-oriented databases, and data warehousing are influencing how data are stored, updated, and retrieved. Drawing from artificial intelligence advances, there is the potential for representing and using models in new ways.

Our purpose in this chapter is to explore the component parts of a DSS. We will attempt to describe the richness of what is currently possible and suggest emerging technologies that will continue to expand this domain.

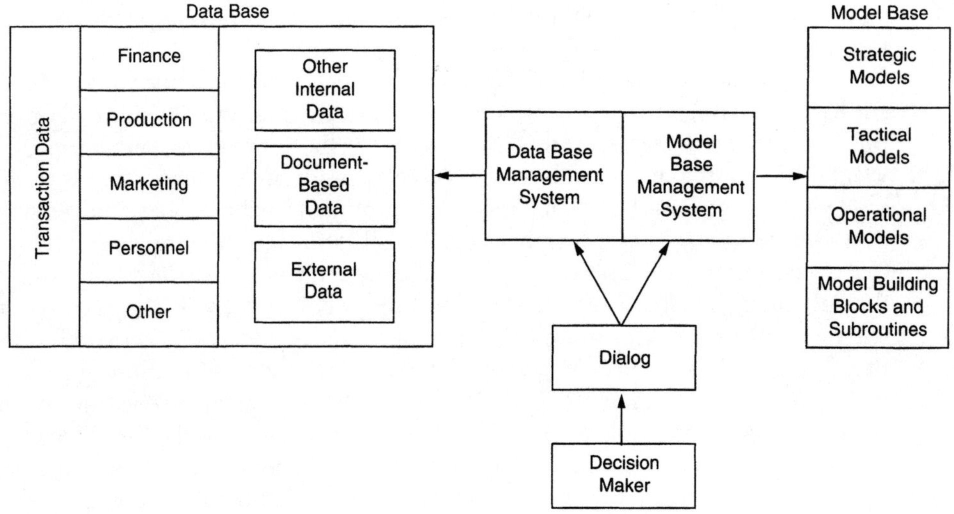

Figure 7–1 The Components of a DSS

THE DIALOG COMPONENT

An appreciation of the importance of the dialog component is gained by recognizing that from the user's perspective, the dialog *is* the system. What the user has to *know in order to use the system*, the options for *directing the system's actions*, and the alternative *presentations of the system's responses* are what is important. Bennett [1] refers to these dialog components as the *knowledge base*, the *action language*, and the *presentation language*, respectively. Unless they affect the dialog, the user typically has little interest in such considerations as the hardware and software used, how data are stored in memory, and the algorithms employed by the models. Such factors are often transparent to the user; that is, they are neither seen nor recognized.

General Considerations

When designing the DSS dialog, it is important to recognize who the potential users are. In some instances, there is a single user; more typically, the DSS has multiple users [4]. While much of the writing on DSS emphasizes its usefulness for supporting the poorly structured decision-making tasks of top management [7], the reality is that middle management and especially professional staff (e.g., financial planners, marketing researchers) are the hands-on users of DSS [4]. This does not mean that DSS is not used by top management. Rather, what often happens is that senior executives request information from a staff assistant who uses a DSS to obtain the information. Operating this way, the assistant is an extension of the DSS. As will be seen, this arrangement has important implications for dialog design.

It should be recognized that a dialog involves *simplicity* versus *flexibility* trade-offs. Dialogs that are simple to use typically offer less flexibility. For example, the old *question-answer* approach requires the user to respond to questions. While this approach is simple and is often appropriate for novice users performing well-structured tasks, it does not provide flexibility beyond what was planned by the system's designers. In this situation, the system is largely in control. *Menu*-oriented systems impose the same kind of structure on the user even though they provide a different dialog approach. By way of contrast, *command languages* place the user more in control but require additional knowledge to use the system. Command languages normally employ a verb-noun syntax (e.g., RUN SIMULATION, PRINT REPORT). Most DSS generators use variations of the command language approach. While DSS generators simplify the development and operation of a DSS, they require training and a frequency of use sufficient to remember their syntax. It is for these reasons that most top managers are not hands-on DSS users. They are unwilling or unable to take the time to be trained properly and have job responsibilities that do not allow frequent use.

When a DSS supports several uses, multiple dialog options can be designed for the system. This is sometimes referred to as a *tiered* dialog approach because there are several levels of dialog options. Novice users can employ the system in one way and more experienced ones can use it in another way. The availability of multiple dialog options also supports differences in cognitive style among users. A person's *cognitive style* refers to the systematic and pervasive way that data are perceived and analyzed. For example, a *systematic* person processes data in a structured, step-by-step process, whereas an *intuitive* person may jump from one analysis process to another. A systematic person may feel comfortable with a menu-oriented dialog, but an intuitive person may want the flexibility offered by a command language.

Another dialog consideration is whether the DSS will be operated by the decision maker or an intermediary (sometimes called the *chauffeur*). With chauffeur-driven systems, the emphasis can be on the power and flexibility of the dialog. Ease-of-use features that might be critical to nonspecialists can be omitted, resulting in systems with less software "overhead."

The Knowledge Base

The knowledge base includes what the user knows about the decision and about how to use the DSS. Note that this is not the definition of *knowledge base* that is prevalent in the field of artificial intelligence. It is, rather, Bennett's term to represent what knowledge the user must bring to the system in order to interact with it in dealing with the problem area or making the necessary decisions.

The user's knowledge of the problem is largely learned external to the DSS. The DSS allows the user to understand better the decision, but much about the problem must already be known. A notable exception is when a DSS is used to train new decision makers. In this case, the DSS is an educational vehicle.

Users can be trained in the use of a DSS in multiple ways [8]. The *one-on-one tutorial* is commonly employed with senior executives. *Classes* and *lectures* are efficient when many users require training. *Programmed* and *computer-aided instruction* are economical approaches when the DSS is expected to have a long life span and serve many users. A *resident expert* can respond to specific requests for help.

The DSS can include features that make it easier to use. Instruction manuals can be made available on-line. Any time during a session, a user can receive help by pressing a single key. The help can be made *context sensitive;* that is, depending on where the decision maker is in the use of the DSS, the system provides help that is customized for the situation.

Command or *sequence files* are useful to novice or infrequent users. These files contain preprogrammed instructions that are activated by a few simple keystrokes. Consequently, a user does not have to know any of the underlying commands; only how to execute the command file. As an example of a command file, at the end of each month, a senior manager may want to compare projected versus actual cash flow. Such an analysis is common with many financial DSS but often requires the user to enter a series of commands. In order to make it easy for the manager to obtain the analysis, the required commands might be put into a command file.

Comprehensive DSS generators usually support the creation and use of command files. Some have a "capture" feature, which functions by recording and saving all commands entered. The user issues a command to evoke the capture feature, enters the commands to be saved, and provides an appropriate filename.

The Action Language

The actions that the user can take to control the DSS can be described in a variety of ways, depending on the system's design. Question-answer, menu-oriented, and command language approaches have already been discussed. Other options exist, and additional attractive alternatives continue to appear.

Some DSS use an input-output form approach. The user is provided an input form and enters the required data. After all the data are input, the DSS performs the analysis and presents the results.

The visual-oriented interfaces developed originally by Xerox, and later adapted by Apple for the Macintosh, are growing in popularity. These interfaces use "icons," or pictorial symbols to represent familiar objects, such as a document, file folder, outbasket, or trash bin. The action language is usually implemented by using a mouse to move icons or to perform actions on them by selecting choices from a menu.

Voice input is the ultimate in ease of use. While important advances in voice input are being made, currently it is not a popular option for DSS. Existing technology supports only a limited vocabulary, must be typically calibrated to the user's voice, and offers discrete rather than continuous speech recognition. These limitations tend to make voice input only appropriate for individual DSS that are used in a highly structured manner. As the technology improves, however, more voice-oriented systems can be expected.

The physical actions required to direct a DSS have also undergone change. Keyboard input is no longer the only choice. Touchscreen and especially mouse-driven systems are common. These are attractive alternatives for executives who do not want to type.

The Presentation Language

The PC or workstation used on a stand-alone basis, as a device on a local area network, or as an intelligent terminal connected to a mainframe has significantly expanded and enhanced how output from a DSS is presented. Printed reports are now the less-preferred output option. In fact, in many instances there is no hard copy output. Instead, the output is presented on the screen, internalized by the decision maker, and discarded. The DSS can be rerun if the user needs to see the output again.

One of the greatest contributions of the PC is its superior *graphics* capabilities. Used with graphics software, a variety of graphs, in three dimensions and in color, are easily created. The current research on chip technology promises to improve graphics quality even more, providing nearly perfect resolution. Even though research has not clearly established the superiority of graphics over tabular output [5], its popularity speaks for its perceived usefulness.

Animation is beginning to be used for DSS output, especially for applications that involve the simulation of physical systems. A research group at Delft University of Technology, for example, has developed several DSS projects using automation. One shows the flow of trucks, goods, and the required paperwork for a shipping and loading application at the Port of Rotterdam. Watching the trucks and ships move on the screen while the documents are processed in the offices gives the decision maker a sense of the dynamics of the problem that would not be possible without the animation. See for example, reference [6].

Voice output is also a possibility, even though it is not currently being used for DSS. As an example of its potential, consider a financial DSS where not only exception reports are provided, but a voice overlay also describes or explains the exceptions.

Dialog Styles

Combinations or sets of options for implementing the knowledge base, the action language, and the presentation language, taken together, can be called a "dialog style." For example, one dialog style results from a system that requires users to keep a reference card (knowledge base) and to remember which commands to

remember that a certain document is about one-third of the way down in the pile on the left side of the desk. The interface includes "content retrieval" algorithms which permit clustering of documents into piles based on their contents.

More advanced elements of the action and presentation language are still under development. Voice input and output are improving but are not as yet common. Still experimental are eye movement control of cursors, and large flat panel displays that could replace desktop surfaces and permit handwritten input. It is clear from the developments of the past few years, however, that the dialog or interface component of DSS will continue to improve in the future.

THE DATA COMPONENT

Data play an important role in a DSS. Data are either accessed directly by the user or are an input to the models for processing. Care must be taken to ensure their availability.

Data Sources

As the importance of DSS has grown, it is becoming increasingly critical for the DSS to use all the important data sources within the organization, and from external sources also. Indeed, the concept of data sources must be expanded to *information sources*—moving beyond traditional access to database records, to include documents containing concepts, ideas, and opinions that are so important to decision making.

To characterize the full scope of information sources relevant to DSS, and to explore some of its ramifications, it is helpful to consider four types of information. First, there are two types of information generated and managed internally in the organization: (1) information based on data records such as is found in data files, and (2) document-based information such as reports, opinions, memos, and estimates.

The first type of internal information pertains primarily to entities, such as individual employees, customers, parts, or accounting codes. Well-structured data records are used to hold a set of attributes that describes each entity. The second category of information pertains primarily to *concepts*—ideas, thoughts, and opinions. Less-structured documents or messages, with a wide variety of information forms, are used to describe these.

The same two types of information are also generated externally to the organization. There is external record-based information, such as government data on economic and financial conditions, stock price quotations, and airline schedules. There is also external document-based information, such as opinions about economic forecasts or rumors. Figure 7–2 shows these four types of information in a simple matrix along with the information management activity that has characterized each in the past. Internal record-based information has been the

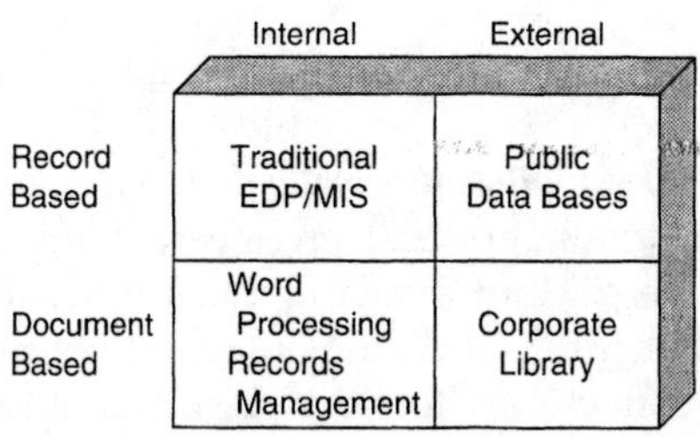

Figure 7–2 Four Types of Information

focus of attention of information systems because that is the type of information computer-based application systems generate and manage easily. External record-based information has become more popular recently in the form of public databases; end users themselves have generally handled the procurement of these data, often using outside time-sharing services. Until recently, practically no attention has been given by DSS builders or vendors to document-based information, either internal or external, as an information resource for DSS. Those areas have been the responsibility of either the administrative vice president or the corporate library. Chapter 12 discusses the increasing availability of document resources for DSS.

Few DSS need data at the transaction level. Summarized data are more typically required and can be obtained in several ways. One way is to have the database management system (DBMS) for the transaction processing system extract the transaction data, summarize them, and make the data available to the DSS. Another option is to extract the data but have the processing done external to the DBMS. While this is ideally a computerized process, some DSS rely on manual processing. This may be appropriate when the processing requires little effort or when the DSS is needed quickly and a more "elegant" solution cannot be implemented in a timely manner.

Some organizations give only end users access to *extract files*. These are files maintained externally to the DBMS and are created specifically to meet the data needs of end users. Extract files are used for security, ease of access, and data integrity reasons. In organizations with extract files, the DSS obtains data from these files.

The previous comments suggest that the database for a DSS may be separate from the transaction processing database, and, for several reasons, this indeed is the case in most organizations. The same line of thinking that leads to extract files also supports the idea of a separate DSS database. Many people believe that it is best to not intermix the rather different worlds of end-user and information systems computing. Also, most DBMS for handling transaction data (e.g., IBM's IMS, and later DB/2) were created for information systems specialists rather than end users and require considerable training. Also end users expect fast response times, and this may be a problem when they are competing with transaction processing applications for machine cycles. Because of the need for fast response times, organizations often dedicate a specific machine for end-user applications.

In addition to transaction data, *other internal data* may be needed. For example, subjective estimates from managers and engineering-related data may be needed. These kinds of data are seldom available from normal data processing activities. In order to have other internal data available, they must be collected, entered, and maintained. The collection effort may be difficult and time consuming because it requires a special initiative. If the data must be available on an ongoing basis, specific methods and procedures must be developed for keeping the data up to date. A good DBMS is required to support the entering, maintenance, and extraction of data.

External data may also be needed, especially for decision support at the upper managerial levels. Examples of external data include national and regional economic data, industry data, and competitive data. Like internal data, making external data available requires special efforts. Unlike internal data, external data may be purchased. For example, marketing data can be purchased from firms such as A. C. Nielson, Market Research Corporation of America, and Brand Rating Index Corporation. The data are extracted from the commercial database, communicated to the user's organization, and entered into the organization's database.

Researchers and organizations are exploring how to include yet another type of data in a DSS: *document-based data.* Organizations have a wealth of data contained in documents such as memos, letters, contracts, and organization charts. If the contents of these documents can be electronically stored and then retrieved by key characteristics (e.g., topic, date, location), a powerful new source of information for decision support can be supplied to decision makers.

Data Warehouses, OLAP, and Software Agents

Separate databases for decision support applications are being developed through the creation of data warehouses. These are special databases that are designed to allow decision makers to do their own analyses. They are also sometimes referred to as information databases. With the typical data warehouse, needed data are first extracted from mainframe and other databases; see Figure 7–3. Prior to being placed in the data warehouse, the data are processed (i.e., "cleaned") to make them more usable for decision support. Several vendors provide software specifically for this purpose (e.g., Prism from Prism Solutions). The data are then maintained on a file server, and special-purpose software is often used to support DSS activities better. Very popular are multi-dimensional databases (e.g., Lightship Server from Pilot Software) that provide fast response times for complex queries (e.g., multiple joins) against large files. End users then employ yet more specialized software (e.g., Visualizer from IBM) to do their own decision analyses. It commonly allows users to "slice and dice" the data by pointing and checking rather than writing SQL queries.

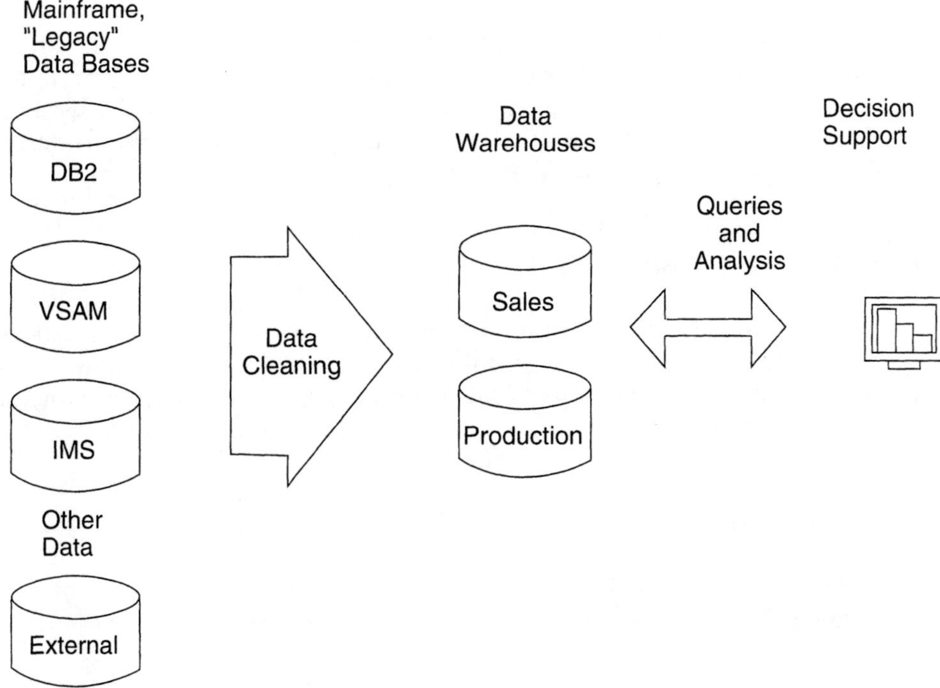

Figure 7–3 Creating and Using a Data Warehouse

Managers and professionals doing decision support analyses without help from intermediaries or information systems professionals is commonly referred to as on-line analytical processing (OLAP). It is in contrast to on-line transaction processing (OLTP). OLAP is driven by the need for information; the emergence of software that supports the building, maintenance, and use of data warehouses; and more computer proficient end users who are able and willing to do their own decision support. Figure 7–3 illustrates this process.

It is interesting to note that while (often complex) mathematical models are commonly associated with DSS, the kinds of analyses needed by managers and professionals are often much simpler. They often want answers to questions such as "which of our new sales reps on the West coast exceeded their quotas by 50 percent" or "how did pretzels on promotion sell in Atlanta this week?" Answers to questions such as these are found by sorting through large data files.

Even though decision makers are better equipped than ever before to analyze the vast quantities of data stored by organizations, this is increasingly being recognized as not being good enough, because important information is often available only when actively sought. Important developments may go undetected because no one is looking for them. In response to this problem, vendors now offer software agents (also known as intelligent agents) which continually send queries to databases in order to find exceptional conditions. When one is found, it is automatically sent to the appropriate person, often through e-mail. Software agents provide a "detect and alert" capability and are discussed in more detail in Chapter 13. They reflect an exciting integration of an artificial intelligence capabilities into decision support.

THE MODEL COMPONENT

Models provide the analysis capabilities for a DSS. Using a mathematical representation of the problem, algorithmic processes are employed to generate information to support decision making. For example, a linear programming model of a production blending problem might reveal the cheapest way to blend a product while meeting product specifications.

Types of Models

There are many different types of models and various ways that they can be categorized. Important distinctions can be made on the basis of their *purpose, treatment of randomness,* and *generality of application.*

The purpose of a model can be either optimization or description. An *optimization model* is one that seeks to identify points of maximization or minimization. For example, management often wants to know what actions will lead to a profit or a revenue maximization or a cost minimization. Optimization models provide this information. A *descriptive model* describes the behavior of a system. In a sense, any model is a descriptive model if it is a valid representation of reality. But a descriptive model describes *only* the system's behavior; it does not suggest optimizing conditions.

Regarding randomness, nearly all systems are probabilistic. That is, the behavior of the system cannot be predicted with certainty because a degree of randomness is present. A *probabilistic model* attempts to capture the probabilistic nature of the system by requiring probabilistic data inputs and by generating probabilistic outputs. Even though most systems are probabilistic, most mathematical models are *deterministic. Deterministic models* employ single-valued estimates for the variables in the model and generate single-valued outputs. Deterministic models are more popular than probabilistic ones because they are less expensive, less difficult, and less time consuming to build and use, and they often provide satisfactory information to support decision making.

In terms of generality of application, a model can be developed for use with only one system (a *custom-built* model) or a model may be applicable to many systems (*ready-built* models). In general, custom-built models describe a particular system and, consequently, provide a better description than a ready-built model. However, they are generally more expensive for the organization, because they have to be built "from the ground up."

Model Base

The models in a DSS can be thought of as a *model base*. As Figure 7–1 shows, a variety of models can be included: strategic, tactical, and operational models and model-building blocks and subroutines. Each type of model has unique characteristics.

The *strategic models* are used by top management to help determine the objectives of the organization, the resources needed to accomplish those objectives, and the policies to govern the acquisition, use, and disposition of these resources. They might be used for company objectives planning, plant location selection, environmental impact planning, or similar types of applications. Strategic models tend to be broad in scope with many variables expressed in compressed, aggregated form. Much of the data required to fuel the models are external and subjective. The time horizons for the models are often measured in years, as are top management's strategic planning responsibilities. The models are usually deterministic, descriptive, and custom-built for the particular organization.

The *tactical models* are commonly employed by middle management to assist in allocating and controlling the use of the organization's resources. Applications include financial planning, worker requirements planning, sales promotion planning, and plant layout determination. The models are usually only applicable to a subset of the organization, like production, and there is some aggregation of variables. Their time horizon varies from one month to less than two years. Some subjective and external data are needed, but the greatest requirements are for internal data. The models tend to be deterministic, and in comparison to strategic models are more likely to provide optimality information and to be ready-built.

The *operational models* are usually employed to support the short-term decisions (e.g., daily, weekly) commonly found at lower organizational levels. Potential applications include credit scoring, media selection, production scheduling, and inventory control. Operational models normally use internal data in their operation. They are typically deterministic, often ready-built, and provide optimization information.

In addition to strategic, tactical, and operational models, the model base contains *model-building blocks and subroutines*. They might include linear programming, time-series analysis, regression analysis, and Monte Carlo sampling procedures. In form and size, these tools might range from a subroutine for calculating an internal rate of return to a packaged set of programs for exploring a generic class of problems (e.g., SAS for statistical analysis problems). The model-building blocks and subroutines can be used separately for ad hoc decision support, or together to construct and maintain more comprehensive models.

Problems with Traditional Modeling

From a historical perspective, organizations' experiences with models are mixed. While there are many successes, there are often many failures. With hindsight, it is possible to identify the problems that lead to failure:

- Difficulties in obtaining input data for the models.
- Difficulties in understanding how to apply the output from models.
- Difficulties in keeping the models up to date.
- Lack of confidence in the models by users; therefore, the models are not trusted.
- Little integration among models.
- Poor interaction between the models and users.
- Difficulty for users to create their own models.
- The models' little explanation for their output.

The DSS Approach to Modeling

The DSS approach to modeling attempts to minimize the traditional modeling problems by emphasizing that a *system* (e.g., dialog, data, and models working together) to support decision making is required.

The database is important to solving many of the problems. It provides the data required to build, use, and maintain the models. The output from the models is placed in the database, thus making the output accessible to other models and providing integration among the models.

A well-designed dialog enhances the likelihood that users will be able to develop their own models, operate the system successfully, keep it up to date, and apply the output to decision-making tasks. These considerations, along with high levels of involvement during the system development process, lead to greater confidence in the models.

The models in a DSS are likely to be useful because they are adequately supported by the data and dialog components. An interesting new development in modeling is the inclusion of artificial intelligence capabilities through which the models explain the factors that led to the output. For example, it might be explained that a decrease in profits is due to the drop in market share in the western region.

The DSS approach to modeling requires a model base management system (MBMS) with capabilities analogous to a DBMS. The most important capabilities include:

- A flexible mechanism for building models.
- Ease of use of the models to obtain needed decision support.
- Methods for saving models that will be used again.
- Procedures for updating models.
- Methods for making output from a model available to other models as input.

Unlike a DBMS, a MBMS is not commercially available as a stand-alone product. Rather, it exists as a component capability of DSS generators. Consider, IFPS as an example. It has an English-like syntax with built-in functions that facilitate the building and updating of models (e.g., VALUE = INFLOWS – OUTFLOWS). Specifications for directing model execution are easily understood (e.g., SOLVE, MONTE CARLO). Models can be saved for future use (e.g., SAVE).

Considerable research is being conducted in MBMS. One stream of research focuses on applying and extending the relational model for DBMS to MBMS [2]. Another approach is to apply artificial intelligence concepts to model management [3]. Chapter 13 by Dave King provides a good survey of the emerging technologies from the field of artificial intelligence, and their contribution to model management and other capabilities of DSS.

CONCLUSION

The dialog, data, and models paradigm provides a powerful conceptual model for understanding the components and relationships in a DSS. Each is critical if a DSS is to live up to its decision support potential. The DDM paradigm is useful in understanding and assessing the capabilities of DSS generators, and to some extent has influenced the evolution of these products. Current DSS research can also be understood in the context of the DDM model.

QUESTIONS

1. What is meant by "From the user's perspective, the dialog *is* the system"? Do you agree with this statement? Discuss.
2. What constitutes a dialog style? What are the new technologies that are creating new dialog styles?
3. What information sources may be required by a DSS? To what extent are the data machine-readable? Discuss.
4. Compare and contrast the traditional and DSS approaches to modeling.

REFERENCES

1. BENNETT, J. "User-Oriented Graphics, Systems for Support in Unstructured Tasks," in *User Oriented Design of Interactive Graphics Systems,* S. Treu (ed.). New York: Association for Computing Machinery, 1977.
2. BLANNING, ROBERT W. "A Relational Theory of Model Management," in *Decision Support Systems: Theory and Application.* Clyde W. Holsapple and Andrew Winston (eds.). Berlin: Springer-Verlag, 1987.
3. ELAM, JOYCE J., and BENN KONSYNSKI. "Using Artificial Intelligence Techniques to Enhance the Capabilities of Model Management Systems," *Decision Sciences* (Summer 1987), 487–502.
4. HOGUE, JACK T. "A Framework for the Examination of Management Involvement in Decision Support Systems," *Journal of Management Information Systems,* no. 1 (1987), 96–110. (Reprinted as Reading 3 in this book.)
5. JARVENPAA, SIRKA L., GARY W. DICKSON, and GERARDINE DE SANCTIS. "Methodological Issues in Experimental IS Research: Experiences and Recommendations," *MIS Quarterly* (June 1985), 141–56.
6. SCHRIJVER, P. R., and H. G. SOL. "A Fleet Management System for Road Transportation," *Proceedings of the Second International Conference on Applications of Advanced Technologies in Transportation Engineering,* Minneapolis, 1991.
7. SPRAGUE, RALPH H. "A Framework for the Development of Decision Support Systems," *MIS Quarterly* (December 1980), 1–26.
8. SPRAGUE, RALPH H., and ERIC D. CARLSON. *Building Effective Decision Support Systems* (Englewood Cliffs, N.J.: Prentice Hall, 1982.

8

DATA BASE REQUIREMENTS FOR INSTITUTIONAL AND AD HOC DSS

INTRODUCTION

A growing number of organizations have developed decision support systems (DSS). The applications include financial planning [19], portfolio management [6], marketing-mix decision making [13, 14], plant capacity planning [17], and joint venture analysis [12]. As one studies various DSS applications, it becomes clear that decision support systems can differ considerably. They can be used for operational control, management control, or strategic planning. They can vary in the structuredness of the decision-making task which they support. They can be used for one time or recurring decision making. Because of the variations which exist, one might expect to find differences in their component parts, including the database component.

The authors recently investigated four decision support systems developed for budgeting and resource allocation, train dispatching, pricing, and acquisition applications. Two of the DSS studied are used on a recurring basis while the other two were used for a one-time decision. Donovan and Madnick [4] refer to these as institutional and ad hoc DSS, respectively. The primary area of investigation was whether there are differences in the database component of the DSS based on the institutional and ad hoc distinction. This study suggests that there are differences with practical implications for DSS designers.

This chapter is adapted from Carleen Garnto and Hugh J. Watson, "An Investigation of Data Base Requirements for Institutional and Ad Hoc DSS," *DATABASE*, Summer 1985.

THE CONCEPTUAL FRAMEWORK

Gorry and Scott Morton [7] combined Anthony's [2] categories of managerial activity (that is, operational control, management control, and strategic planning) with Simon's [15] concepts of structured and unstructured decision making to provide a framework for viewing information systems. This framework has proven useful in understanding information requirements and the type of information system needed to support decision making. For example, information requirements vary with managerial activity. Keen and Scott Morton [11] identify accuracy, age of information, level of detail, time horizon, frequency of use, source, scope of information, and type of information as aspects of information requirements which vary with managerial activity. In another example, the type of information system needed, that is, electronic data processing (EDP), management information system (MIS), or (DSS), is related to the structuredness of the decision-making task. While EDP and to a great extent MIS are recognized as useful for supporting structured decisions, DSS are appropriate for supporting semistrucured and unstructured decision making. And as a final example, the type of information system needed is related to managerial activity. Most frequently, EDP best serves operational control, MIS is oriented to management control, and DSS supports strategic planning.

While Gorry and Scott Morton's framework suggests useful generalizations, there are many exceptions. Of particular interest to this study is that DSS can be used for operational control, management control, or strategic planning. This being the case, it follows that different types of DSS may be appropriate for various managerial activities. The work of Donovan and Madnick supports this contention. They suggest that DSS can be divided meaningfully into two categories: institutional DSS which deal with decisions of a recurring nature, and ad hoc DSS which deal with specific decisions which are not usually anticipated or recurring. The characteristics of each type of DSS are summarized in Table 8–1. Donovan and Madnick suggest that these characteristics of institutional and ad hoc DSS lead to the conclusion that institutional DSS are most appropriate for operational control applications, ad hoc DSS are most useful for strategic planning applications, and there is an area of overlap in regard to management control applications.

Keen and Scott Morton indicate that just as information requirements vary with managerial activity, so do data requirements. Because institutional and ad hoc DSS tend to be associated with different managerial activities, it might be expected that the database component would differ. While DSS database requirements have been considered in a variety of contexts, no research has been conducted on the specific database requirements for institutional and ad hoc DSS. Given that the institutional and ad hoc DSS dichotomy seems to be a useful way of looking at DSS, such research might potentially provide helpful guidelines for DSS database design. Sprague and Carlson [16] have developed a list of general requirements common to DSS databases which is presented in Table 8–2. It is used in this study as a basis for exploring the database requirements for institutional and ad hoc DSS.

TABLE 8-1 Comparison of Institutional and Ad Hoc Decision Support Systems

	Institutional DSS	Ad hoc DSS
Number of decision occurrences for a decision type	many	few
Number of decision types	few	many
Number of people making decisions of same type	many	few
Range of decisions supported	narrow	wide
Range of users supported	narrow	wide
Range of issues addressed	narrow	wide
Specific data needed known in advance	usually	rarely
Problems are recurring	usually	rarely
Importance of operational efficiency	high	low
Duration of specific type of problem being addressed	long	short
Need for rapid development	low	high

SOURCE: J. Donovan and S. Madnick, "Institutional and Ad Hoc DSS and Their Effective Use," *DATABASE,* 8, no. 3 (Winter 1977), 82.

TABLE 8-2 General Requirements for DSS Data Bases

- Support for Memories
- Data Reduction
- Varying Levels of Detail
- Varying Amounts of Data
- Multiple Sources
- Catalog of Sources
- Wide Time Frame
- Public and Private Data Bases
- Varying Degrees of Accuracy
- Set Operations
- Random Access
- Support for Relationships and Views
- Performance
- Interface to Other DSS Components
- End-User Interface

SOURCE: Ralph H. Sprague, Jr., and Eric D. Carlson, *Building Effective Decision Support Systems* (Englewood Cliffs, N.J.: Prentice Hall, 1982).

THE STUDY METHOD

Purpose

The purpose of this study was to gather and analyze data about the database component of institutional and ad hoc DSS based on the general requirements proposed by Sprague and Carlson. This information is used to suggest generalizations about database requirements for institutional and ad hoc DSS. The findings should prove helpful to interested researchers and to those considering the development of decision support systems.

Research Methodology

The research method selected for this study was the field study. A structured interview was conducted with a knowledgeable individual in the company about a specific application of an institutional or ad hoc DSS in order to gain information related to each of the database requirements identified by Sprague and Carlson.

Sample Selection

Four companies in Atlanta, Georgia, who are developing and using DSS participated in the study. The criteria for including a specific DSS in the study were the same as those used by Hogue and Watson [9] in their study of management's role in the approval and administration of DSS. Each of the four companies had developed a DSS which met the following essential criteria:

- Supports but does not replace decision making.
- Directed toward semistructured and/or unstructured decision-making tasks.
- Data and models organized around the decision.
- Easy to use software interface.

In addition, each of the four DSS satisfied most of the following additional criteria:

- Interactive processing.
- DSS use and control determined by the user.
- Flexible and adaptable to changes in the environment and decision-maker's style.
- Quick ad hoc DSS building capabilities.

The DSS was judged to be either institutional or ad hoc based on the characteristics provided by Donovan and Madnick. For the purpose of the study, two institutional and two ad hoc systems were identified. Each was considered successful by users and developers.

The Interview

Interviews were conducted at each organization with a member or members of the DSS development team. The interviews were tape recorded so that the information could be carefully analyzed and categorized.

The interviews consisted of two parts. The first part was designed to gather background information on the company and on the development and use of the DSS. It included questions related to the corporate business sector, conditions

that led to the creation of the DSS, developmental history, and
The second part of the interview focused on the database compo
Specific questions were designed to obtain information related to
eral requirements proposed by Sprague and Carlson. This inforr
to prepare case studies, descriptions, and summary tables regardi
and ad hoc database requirements.

FOUR CASE STUDIES

Brief descriptions follow for the four DSS, two institutional and two ad hoc, selected for this study of database requirements. All DSS met the requirements for DSS as defined by Hogue and Watson, each could be classified as institutional or ad hoc based on the characteristics set forth by Donovan and Madnick, and each was considered successful.

Collectively, the systems support all of Anthony's levels of managerial activity. The train dispatching system aids in the area of operational control, while a majority of AIMS capabilities focus on managerial control. Both ad hoc systems, the pricing model and the acquisition model, support strategic planning.

Train Dispatching System

The train dispatching system used by the Norfolk Southern Corporation is an example of an institutional DSS. It is an on-line, real-time, operational DSS that is used daily by train dispatchers of the Norfolk and Southern Railroad. It was developed to assist dispatchers on the northern portion of the Alabama Division and is now being expanded to include the nine other divisions of the Norfolk and Southern Railway. (See detailed description in Chapter 6).

Each dispatcher is typically responsible for the movement of twenty to thirty trains over three- to six-hundred miles of track. Most of this is single track and requires that the routes of opposing trains be safely coordinated so that the trains meet at strategically placed passing sidings. In addition, the dispatcher must safely coordinate the movement of work and inspection crews along these same tracks. The dispatcher is also in constant contact with freight terminals for information regarding trains that will move over the division and for information on trains that have arrived at their destination. The system developed by the operations research staff was designed to assist the dispatchers with these activities.

The train dispatching system now in use provides for more accurate and timely entry of federal reporting information directly into the system by the dispatchers and allows the dispatchers ready access to the information needed for train and work crew dispatching.

Specialized algorithms and models were developed by the operations research staff specifically for train dispatching and related decisions. The models take into account thousands of possible meet/pass combinations that could occur for the trains and suggest the optimal solution. As information is entered regarding changes in track or train conditions, a new optimal solution is displayed along with projections of future conditions over a six- to eight-hour period. All train information is current and changes as conditions change. While the system offers an optimal solution for each dispatching decision, the dispatcher has the ability to override each plan to reflect his experience and judgment. His decision can be entered into the system which results in new projections.

The mini-computer based system involved approximately three years of prototype work. The system at a division office includes four color CRTs. Two display track layout and the movement of trains along the tracks. A third CRT displays screen formats which serve as work sheets for updating the train data by the dispatchers. The fourth CRT displays how trains should be routed based on calculations of the models.

Automated Information Management System (AIMS)

In January 1984, BellSouth began operation as the parent company for Southern Bell and South Central Bell. This brought the two divisions which supply local telephone service to the southern United States under a single managing body separate from American Telephone and Telegraph. This proved to be a great opportunity and challenge for BellSouth. Top management saw the need for an extensive management support system to aid largely in management control decision making. As a result, a systems analysis group was formed at BellSouth to develop such a system. The first prototype of the Automated Information Management System (AIMS) was installed approximately six weeks later. AIMS is a corporate planning model used for budgeting, resource allocation, and strategic planning. It utilizes forecasting, graphics, and spreadsheet packages along with a sophisticated database management package to provide needed information and analysis capabilities at different managerial levels. It has approximately 4000 users at the district, state, and headquarters level and combines features of office automation and information resource management as well as decision support.

At the district level, managers use the system to evaluate daily operations. They can analyze present performance in terms of past performance and can view projected performance generated from preprogrammed models. This information is used to keep service to customers in line with company standards and to see that budget restrictions are maintained. The district data is used by managers at the state level to prepare preliminary budgets and to forecast resource needs using additional models.

At the corporate level managers consolidate the state budgets and develop a corporate budget and corporate resource forecasts. They serve as intermediaries for the CEO by preparing reports, identifying problem areas, and exploring "what if" performance and budgeting scenarios. These budgets and reports are stored in a private database accessible only by the CEO and used at his discretion for strategic planning decisions.

Pricing Model

Coca-Cola® USA is the producer and marketer of all Coca-Cola domestic beverages. Rather than marketing a finished product, however, Coca-Cola USA supplies the beverage syrup and sweetening agent to individual bottling franchises and fountain operations where it is then mixed for bottling and final sale.

In early 1983 Coca-Cola USA geared for the introduction of Diet Coke, a new diet product, into the market. All market research and testing had been completed for the product, but the Vice President of Strategic Planning faced a problem. What price would bottlers be charged for the Diet Coke syrup and Aspartame sweetener? Would the syrup be priced at the Tab rate, the rate for Coca-Cola USA's other diet product, or would it be priced, as the bottlers hoped, at the rate for original Coke? There were also questions about the pricing of the sweetener Aspartame. The Vice President for Strategic Planning also had to consider how the pricing of the Diet Coke syrup and sweetener would affect Tab's market share.

To assist him in making the pricing decision, the Vice President requested the creation of a model that would allow him to manipulate the model's parameters in order to evaluate possible pricing combinations. As a result of working with the model, a pricing proposal would then be prepared and presented to the bottlers. A three-person, in-house team was selected to develop the model. The group was composed of a financial analyst, a builder/intermediary, and the Vice President for Strategic Planning. The Vice President was important in determining the parameters necessary for the decision and was the ultimate user of the information provided by the model. The financial analyst determined the financial relationships necessary for the model, and the builder/intermediary actually created and coded the model using available tools. The builder intermediary also operated the model to obtain results for the Vice President.

The model was created using EXPRESS, a DSS generator equipped with a high-level, non-procedural programming language, financial and statistical analysis capabilities, graphics, and database management capabilities. The initial creation of the model took approximately one week. The model was refined as new parameters were identified and as additional considerations were raised by the bottlers.

Acquisition Model

Since its founding in 1933, Gold Kist, Inc., has become the leader in the Southeast's agribusiness industry. At the present time, Gold Kist is considering adding to its holdings through the acquisition of a company in a related area of business. The Executive Committee instructed the Director of Corporate Planning and Economic Research to recommend the best company for such an acquisition. The Executive Committee provided the Director with basic parameters the selected company should meet, including the price range Gold Kist would pay to acquire the company, the volume of business the company should maintain, and the company's contribution to the Gold Kist profit picture. Even with these guidelines the Director faced a big job. Many companies met the requirements specified by the Executive Committee. Selecting the one best company from as many as twenty-five possibilities would require careful analysis of each company's performance based on information from knowledgeable individuals at all levels within the company, as well as financial information.

The Director wanted financial information that reflected the company's future performance should an acquisition by Gold Kist take place. This information could be easily identified and analyzed once basic fundamental reports such as balance sheets and income statements had been prepared. Therefore, the Director wanted a model that would formulate these reports for each company under study. Using PROFIT II, a DSS generator that combines a high-level programming language with financial and statistical analysis capabilities, graphics, and data management capabilities, the Director set out to develop such a model. After one week, the Director had a working model that produced an income statement, cash flow statement, working capital statement, and source and use of funds statement, as well as financial ratios and forecasting ratios for each company being considered.

FINDINGS AND DISCUSSION

As was expected, differences were found in the database component of the four DSS studied. In general, the differences can be explained by the institutional and ad hoc DSS distinction. Of course, the differences are also related to the managerial activity supported by the DSS. Consider now the database differences using the general DSS database requirements suggested by Sprague and Carlson.

Multiple Sources

Data for the train dispatching system is largely transaction data gathered as a result of daily dispatching operations. The remainder of the data is also internal. The data for AIMS comes from a variety of sources. It includes transaction data obtained from operations, internal data from corporate personnel databases and from corporate planning, and external population data purchased outside of the organization. All the data for Coca-Cola USA's pricing model was internally generated and gathered by different departments within the company. This data reflected external factors such as consumer preferences, market demand, and economic conditions. The data was prepared to reflect total corporate performance before its inclusion in the database. Likewise, all data included in Gold Kist's acquisition model was based on information gained from external sources. This

TABLE 8–3 Sources of Data for Each System

	Transaction	Internal	External
Institutional			
Train Dispatching System	X	X	
AIMS	X	X	X
Ad hoc			
Pricing Model		X	X
Acquisition Model		X	X

external information was modified during planning and evaluation. The internally generated results were then included in the database.

The use of transaction, other internal, and external data by the institutional and ad hoc DSS is presented in Table 8–3. The general impression is that institutional DSS rely primarily on transaction and other internal data while ad hoc DSS employ non-transaction internal data and external data. The data requirements for the four DSS also correspond with what one would expect based on Anthony's levels of managerial activity.

Wide Time Frame

While all data in Gold Kist's acquisition model was based on historical data, the actual data included in the database were projections of performance. A similar situation existed for Coca-Cola USA's pricing model; however, one time period of historical data was included for projection purposes. The train dispatching system relies exclusively on current data, while AIMS uses data from all three time frames: historical, current, and projected.

The time frame for the data used in the four DSS does not appear to be strongly related to the type of DSS. However, as can be seen in Table 8–4, both ad hoc DSS employ projected data. There seems to be a stronger relationship between the data's time frame and the level of managerial activity.

TABLE 8–4 Time Frame for Data for Each System

	Historical	Current	Projected
Institutional			
Train Dispatching System	X		
AIMS	X	X	X
Ad hoc			
Pricing Model	X		X
Acquisition			X

Data Reduction

Based on Sprague and Carlson's definition, very little data reduction took place in the ad hoc systems studied. In the pricing model and the acquisition model all data reduction manipulations were performed on the data before their inclusion in data files. The data management capabilities of the DSS generators serve to limit the extent to which these features can be included in the ad hoc systems.

On the other hand, the institutional systems studied rely heavily on data reduction. AIMS aggregates data at each level of use, while the train dispatching system relies on subsetting and combination to represent the movement of all trains over a division. These capabilities necessitate the use of packaged or in-house created database management systems.

Various Levels of Detail

It follows from the data reduction requirements that institutional and ad hoc systems would vary in the level of detail of data necessary to support the systems. For the ad hoc systems no attempt was made to maintain detailed data in the database. A request for this type of information was beyond the scope of each of the ad hoc systems.

The institutional DSS studied do maintain data at different levels of detail. With AIMS, if a question arises regarding a figure in the corporate budget, the data used to arrive at that figure can be traced to the district level through data maintained in the database. Likewise, a question about a division's performance can be investigated by viewing data on each train dispatched in the division during a specific shift. In both cases, the decisions supported by the systems call for this type of capability. The institutional systems have a commitment of resources and technology that make these levels of data easier to maintain.

Varying Amounts of Data

Varying amounts of data are also maintained and used in institutional and ad hoc DSS. This follows from the previous requirements regarding data reduction and varying levels of detail. The ad hoc systems studied maintained only those data which were actually used for the decision-making process. In contrast, the institutional systems maintained a large amount of data. Both AIMS and the train dispatching system maintain a large volume of potentially relevant data in varying levels of detail. As mentioned earlier, this facilitates the explanation of aggregate data should a question arise. It also results in much data being maintained which is seldom used.

Varying Degrees of Accuracy

Absolute accuracy was not required of the data included in the ad hoc systems. It is difficult to verify the accuracy of the data for these systems since both relied on aggregate, projected data.

Related to accuracy is the idea of currency of the data. For both ad hoc systems, all data included were based on historical data. With Gold Kist's acquisition model, data were based on the latest financial reports available for a company. In many cases these were as much as a year old. This data was, therefore, subject to a certain amount of inaccuracy due to the lack of currency of the historical data. The increasing age of the information on which the projections were based would tend to decrease the accuracy.

By the same argument, the institutional systems tended to have a much higher degree of accuracy. The long-range projections included in AIMS and short-range, shift projections included in the train dispatching system are based on current information. The operational natures of the dispatching decision for Norfolk and Southern and district service for BellSouth require a high degree of accuracy.

Support for Memories

Sprague and Carlson suggest four kinds of memory aids that the DSS database should support. Table 8–5 illustrates the types of memory aids that are found in the database component of each of the systems studied.

Both the institutional and ad hoc systems were organized around the "scratch pad" concept. All four systems provided workspaces where calculations could be performed and displayed. Each system also provided libraries for saving intermediate results for later use.

The institutional database components provide additional memory support in the form of links and triggers. With the train dispatching system, a particular train can be identified from a list of those dispatched during a shift. All information relevant to that train can be stored in link memory for use with another workspace. A blinking asterisk also appears in the corner of the display screen if

TABLE 8–5 Memory Aids Provided by Each System

	Workspaces	Libraries	Links	Triggers
Institutional				
Train Dispatching System	X	X	X	X
AIMS	X	X	X	X
Ad hoc				
Pricing Model	X	X		
Acquisition Model	X	X		

changing track conditions result in a new meet/pass plan. This triggers a new decision situation for the dispatcher. Similarly, with AIMS, blinking, reverse screen figures indicate when a budgetary or service figure is out of range.

Support for Relationships and Views

While both types of systems provided support in this area, the ad hoc systems tended to provide the best support for relationships and views. The "what if" capabilities of the DSS generators used by each of the ad hoc systems allowed the managers to test alternate scenarios quickly and with relative ease. This flexibility was essential due to the ill-defined nature of the ad hoc decisions.

The institutional systems studied, on the other hand, do not exhibit this degree of flexibility. Due to the better defined nature of the decision, alternate relationships and ways of viewing the data were designed at the time of system development. While "what if" scenarios may be carried out on AIMS by certain skilled managers at the headquarters level, "what if" options beyond those originally developed for the train dispatching system must be handled by the OR development team.

Random Access

Database components of both the ad hoc and institutional DSS were found to support random access. This access proved to be more sophisticated for the institutional DSS. Their database management capabilities allowed access to data that the decision maker did not expect to need and to data that was not related to the data currently being used.

Security and Private Databases

No specific measures were taken to protect the data included in the database component of either of the ad hoc systems studied. Both systems were designed for personal support for a single user. Therefore, data security was not a primary concern.

The institutional systems studied, on the other hand, are accessible by many people. As a result, measures were taken to secure certain data. While any dispatcher can access and view any train information during his shift, only certain dispatchers can alter specific train data. Likewise, AIMS provides a private database, accessible only by the CEO, where sensitive budgets and reports are stored.

End-User Interface

Differences were observed in the end-user interface for the institutional and ad hoc DSS. The interfaces for the institutional systems were designed to be "transparent" to the user. Users need to know nothing of the internal structure of the

DSS. Both DSS employ menus and function keys which facilitate the use of each system by many users.

In contrast, no special end-user interfaces were designed for the ad hoc systems studied other than the standard prompt interfaces provided by each DSS generator.

CONCLUSION

Based on the characteristics of the database components of the systems studied, generalizations can be proposed for the specific database requirements for institutional and ad hoc systems. Table 8–6 summarizes these requirements as they apply to the general database requirements for DSS.

From these requirements we see that the nature of the decision, whether or not it is recurring, does indeed affect the type of DSS support chosen and the database requirements for the DSS. Recurring, well-defined decisions call for institutional systems. These are developed by highly technical and experienced development teams using a sophisticated collection of DSS tools. Institutional DSS provides organizational support to a large number of users. Consequently, considerable time and money are spent making the system as complete and easy to use as possible. This is illustrated by the data requirements for memory aids, varying amounts of data, public and private databases, and easy to use end-user interface. As a result, flexibility to change and to create new views of the data is limited.

The one-shot decisions are difficult to anticipate and define and call for ad hoc support. This support must be provided quickly and cost effectively. As a

TABLE 8-6 Database Requirements for Institutional and Ad Hoc DSS

	Institutional	Ad Hoc
Multiple sources	internal	external
Wide time frame	no relationship found	
Data reduction	extensive	minor
Varying levels of detail	many	few
Varying amounts of data	large	small
Varying degree of accuracy	high	low
Security & private databases	common	rare
Support for memories	broad	narrow
Support for relationships and views	limited	extensive
Random access	complex	simple
End-user interface	fixed	variable

result, the ad hoc system is normally developed by a small development team using a DSS generator. The system's data management capabilities are limited to the data management capabilities of the DSS generator. Therefore, much preparatory work is usually done on the data before it is included in the database.

Ad hoc systems tend to provide personal support to single users. Consequently, only data handling features essential for the decision are included in the system. The user's familiarity with the system or an intermediary to operate the system for the decision maker reduces the data management features necessary, as well as the development time. The DSS generator does provide a great deal of flexibility for making changes and viewing data in many ways. The ill-defined nature of ad hoc problems makes this essential.

The database components for these two types of DSS are different. These differences reflect the nature of the decision involved as well as characteristics of the system itself. These requirements facilitate the storage and transformation of data for decisions unique to each type of system.

QUESTIONS

1. What are the differences between institutional and ad hoc DSS?
2. Describe the general requirements for a DSS database.
3. Describe the database component of the train dispatching DSS at Southern Railway, the automated information management system (AIMS) at BellSouth, the pricing model at Coca-Cola USA, and the acquisition model at Gold Kist.
4. Discuss the differences in database requirements for institutional and ad hoc DSS.

REFERENCES

1. ALTER, STEVEN L. *Decision Support Systems: Current Practices and Continuing Challenges.* Reading, Mass.: Addison-Wesley, 1980.
2. ANTHONY, R. N. *Planning and Control Systems: A Framework for Analysis,* Harvard University Graduate School of Business Administration, Boston, 1965.
3. BENNETT, JOHN L., ed. *Building Decision Support Systems.* Reading, Mass.: Addison-Wesley, 1983.
4. DONOVAN, J., and S. MADNICK. "Institutional and Ad Hoc DSS and Their Effective Use," *Data Base,* 8, no. 3 (Winter 1977), 79–88.
5. FICK, GLORIA, and RALPH H. SPRAGUE, JR., eds. *Decision Support Systems: Issues and Challenges.* London: Pergamon Press, 1980.

6. GERRITY, THOMAS P. "Design of Man-Machine Decision Systems: An Application to Portfolio Management," *Sloan Management Review,* 12, no. 2 (Winter 1971), 59–75.
7. GORRY, G. A., and M. S. SCOTT MORTON. "A Framework for Management Information Systems," *Sloan Management Review,* 12, no. 1 (Fall 1971), 55–70.
8. HACKATHORN, RICHARD D., and PETER G. W. KEEN. "Organizational Strategies for Personal Computing in Decision Support Systems," *MIS Quarterly,* 5, no. 3 (September 1981), 21–26.
9. HOGUE, JACK T., and HUGH J. WATSON. "Management's Role in the Approval and Administration of Decision Support Systems," *MIS Quarterly,* 7, no. 2 (June 1983), 15–25.
10. KEEN, PETER G. W. "Interactive Computer Systems for Managers: A Modest Proposal," *Sloan Management Review,* 18, no. 1 (Fall 1976), 1–17.
11. KEEN, PETER G. W., and MICHAEL S. SCOTT MORTON. *Decision Support Systems: An Organizational Perspective.* Reading, Mass.: Addison-Wesley, 1978.
12. KEEN, PETER G. W., and GERALD R. WAGNER. "DSS: An Executive Mind-Support System," *Datamation,* 25, no. 12 (November 1979), 117–22.
13. LITTLE, JOHN D. C. "BRANDAID: A Marketing-Mix Model, Part I: Structure," *Operations Research,* 23, no. 4 (July–August 1975), 628–55.
14. LITTLE, JOHN D. C. "BRANDAID: A Marketing-Mix Model, Part 2: Implementation, Calibration, and Case Study," *Operations Research,* 23, no. 4 (July–August 1975), 656–73.
15. SIMON, HERBERT A. *The New Science of Management Decision.* New York: Harper & Row, 1960.
16. SPRAGUE, RALPH H., JR., and ERIC D. CARLSON. *Building Effective Decision Support Systems.* Englewood Cliffs, N.J.: Prentice Hall, 1982.
17. SPRAGUE RALPH H., JR., and HUGH J. WATSON. "Bit by Bit: Toward Decision Support Systems," *California Management Review,* 22, no. 1 (Fall 1979), 60–68.
18. SPRAGUE, RALPH H., JR., and HUGH J. WATSON. "MIS Concepts: Part II," *Journal of Systems Management,* 26, no. 2 (February 1975), 35–40.
19. SPRAGUE, RALPH H., JR., and RON L. OLSEN. "The Financial Planning System at the Louisiana National Bank," *MIS Quarterly,* 3, no. 3 (September 1979), 1–11.

9

MULTIDIMENSIONAL DATA BASES FOR DSS

Sixty executives want answers, and they want them now. Not tomorrow, not next week, certainly not in those familiar old monthly reports. They work in sales, in marketing, in finance. They don't even know what they want to know, except that they want to know it right away, before their counterparts in competing companies get the jump on them. Millions of dollars, hundreds of jobs, entire careers may depend on whether they make a quick but informed decision. Those 60 executives don't want to know that it will take legions of your programmers many hours banging away at report writers and spreadsheets to keep them fed with information. They want to know the answers.

And at the Chicago-based *Quaker Oats Co.,* they get the answers. Themselves. Because IS managers like David Breig gave decision makers tools that let them ask their own questions—even the gnarly ones—with less fear of tying up database servers in endless joins, without having to master Structured Query Language and without a lot of assistance from IS.

Food giant Pet Inc. has been using one of these new multi-dimensional analysis tools to better understand point-of-sale and competitive data from outside agencies and from Pet's mainframe applications, says vice president of MIS Bob Drury.

"It's really given us an insight we never had," says Drury. "We can outmaneuver our competitors and win fights for retail shelf space like never before. Five of our brand managers get together on a regular basis and try to find out

This chapter is a reprint of Ricciuti, Mike, "Winning the Competitive Game," *Datamation*, Feb. 15, 1994, pp 21–28 and is used here by permission.

what price points are being lowered by our competitors and why. Or to examine consumer acceptance or use of coupons. We couldn't look at these things before."

Drury says that St. Louis-based Pet, which sells foodstuffs under the Progresso and Old El Paso labels, among others, uses *Express from IRI* Software (the same package Quaker uses) to analyze about 50 gigabytes worth of data now, and "it may easily be 500 gigabytes at some point, no question."

Breig and Drury are among a growing group of IS managers who recognize that it's no longer enough to provide business managers with a single static report that cuts sales data by territory, or revenue by quarter—questions that may be easily posed to a relational database through Structured Query Language. A more competitive world working on thinner profit margins requires better, more flexible on-the-fly data analyses and the tools to deliver them.

"Trying to force this type of ad hoc data analysis on a relational model doesn't work," says Peter Kastner, an analyst with the Aberdeen Group Inc. in Boston. "Human beings ask questions that are very straightforward, like 'What is our 12-month sales total?' That's a question any executive will ask. And the IS guy turns around and says, 'Well, that's going to take three months to program.' Give me a break!"

This new style of multidimensional data analysis makes perfect sense to users, but not to most production database management systems. Older hierarchical DBMSs, of course, don't lend themselves to ad hoc querying at all, and certainly combining data from multiple hierarchical DBMSs in a query is not for the faint of heart. Even RDBMSs, touted for their flexibility, are not malleable enough to meet many end users' demands for complex ad hoc queries, either because they involve nested queries or require multiple joins. Nor do executive information systems solve the problem: standard mainframe EISs are best at generating a series of canned reports.

A flood of SQL-based query-by-example front-end tools have come on the market in recent years, many of which can be used directly by end users. There's no question that they can simplify many queries, but they quickly run out of steam for three-, four- and more-way selects. And even if end users develop the skills and patience to do nested QBEs, they still need to know where the data they're after reside. And should they clear that hurdle, they might inadvertently bring the server and network to its knees with the wrong kind of queries.

Just as it took transaction monitors and other tools to transform DBMSs into on-line transaction-processing systems, it takes special tools to enable on-line analytical processing (OLAP), as this style of computing is called by Dr. E.F. Codd of the San Jose-based consulting firm Codd and Date Inc., the noted RDBMS expert who defined the requirements for relational technology back in 1985.

OLAP tools fall into three product groups: multidimensional spreadsheets, multidimensional query tools for standard RDBMSs, and fully multidimensional DBMSs. Probably the most critical element in choosing an approach is database size—the larger the database, the more a fully multidimensional approach makes sense.

At the most basic level are multidimensional spreadsheets. For example, Computer Associates International Inc.'s CA-SuperCalc For Windows combines the Islandia, N.Y.-based software giant's CA-SuperCalc spreadsheet with its Compete! multidimensional analysis tool. Another example is Improv from Lotus Development Corp. of Cambridge, Mass. Standard spreadsheets like Redmond, Wash.-based Microsoft Corp.'s new Excel 5.0 increasingly include multidimensional tools and intelligent-querying capabilities to make data analysis easier.

Still, spreadsheets are strictly for desktop multidimensional data analysis. To get data into them, you need to establish the same SQL links you need for traditional spreadsheets or SQL tools, or you'll have to populate them by hand.

Then there are tools designed to model multidimensional relationships in separate databases. These tools—like Pablo from Andyne Computing Ltd. of Kingston, Ontario and Prism from Comshare Inc. of Ann Arbor, Mich.—use a multidimensional view of data residing in RDBMSs, flat file systems and in financial or human resource applications. Comshare's tool works only with the company's EIS, whereas Pablo is designed to work with almost any RDBMS by creating and storing multidimensional views of relational data on users' PCs.

Another data access and analysis product, BusinessObjects from Business Objects Inc. of Cupertino, Calif., uses an ordinary RDBMS on the server but includes a multidimensional client data analysis tool and report writer.

Tom Youlnik, a systems analyst at Eli Lilly and Co., the pharmaceutical company in Indianapolis, says he installed BusinessObjects just for its ability to get him out of the report-writing business. But when he and his users discovered BusinessObjects' multidimensional tool, "it made our socks roll up and down.

THE VIEWS FROM THIS DATABASE ARE SPECTACULAR!

- Imagine a company that sells four products—bananas, oranges, apples, and pears—in three regions—East, West, and Central. Product managers want to know actual sales by product in each region, but they also need to compare them to projected sales. Easy—create two spreadsheets, print them out, and compare them, right? But with multidimensional analysis tools, a single entity can contain all the data and do all the analysis without the complex queries that a purely relational tool would require.
- Conceptually, stack the "actual" matrix (the original example) on to a new "projected" matrix to form a cube with six faces (there are actually only four unique views). Now you've built a multidimensional model that provides ready answers to common questions without repeated querying. Instead of doubling the number of rows, so you have one for actual and one for projected, or adding another column, as you would with an RDBMS, you make the two-dimensional matrix a three-dimensional matrix.

We had data extracted from Oracle and DB2 on the mainframe, and we had millions of years' and thousands of lives' worth of Excel macros just to get the data into spreadsheets. But this is just a few clicks for users after IS sets it up."

Tools like BusinessObjects don't eliminate the problems of executing complex queries and multiple joins of RDBMSs. They simply hide the difficulty of formulating them from users. If the resulting performance is not up to snuff, you need to consider changing the back-end database as well.

Several high-end packages combine a specialized server multidimensional database with client front-end tools. Such products include eSSbase from Santa Clara-based Arbor Software Corp.; Express from IRI Software of Waltham, Mass.; Acumate Enterprise Solution (ES) from Kenan Technologies of Cambridge, Mass.; and LightShip Server from Boston-based Pilot Software Inc. Comshare also resells eSSbase and embeds it into its latest executive information system.

It's that last group that fulfills the potential of OLAP, says Richard Finkelstein, president of Performance Computing Inc. of Chicago. "It's not simply getting an interface that works and makes it easier to work with the data. It's fundamentally changing the way the data is stored, so that it is easily and quickly accessible."

Tools like Acumate ES, eSSbase, Express, and LightShip Server incorporate a server database that stores data in a multidimensional matrix so that users can access, aggregate, analyze and view large amounts of data quickly, in an ad hoc manner.

"Multidimensional tools let you get the data in a form you want without having to do a data dump through a spreadsheet. You're operating on the whole database, instead of dumping data out of a relational format into tables," says Quaker's Breig. He's been using Express for over five years to do financial reporting, budgeting and forecasting for Quaker's U.S.-based operations (see box on page 136), "Oatmeal, Sliced and Diced".

Users say to get the same level of flexibility from relational databases, you would literally have to join all of your database tables together so that you could scan all of your data simultaneously. A two-gigabyte relational database could quickly become a terabyte or more of data, if joined this way.

That's because relational data are organized to minimize sparse data—empty holes in tables—and to represent data only once. You wouldn't store separate totals for individual regions' sales and also store total sales in an RDBMS, since, ideally, RDBMS data are normalized—represented only once in the most flexible way possible so that they can be combined later on.

"What the relational vendors try to do is throw a lot of big hardware at the problem, with new parallel database servers. But you're talking about millions of dollars' worth of hardware to solve a problem best handled through software," says Finkelstein.

Products like eSSbase, Express, and LightShip Server can be had for a fraction of the cost, at around $40,000 or less. They keep database size to a minimum on the server through data compression. And while that big relational table and

Oatmeal, Sliced and Diced

Want to see a real-world example of what multidimensional data analysis can do? There it is, right there on the supermarket shelf in the blue and red boxes with the wise old gentleman's picture on it—Quaker Oats.

How those boxes of oatmeal got there, how many are stacked on that shelf, who buys them and why—and how much profit was made on each—are all parameters tracked by Chicago-based Quaker Oats Co. Quaker uses Express from IRI Software, a multidimensional database and toolset, to analyze sales, marketing, and financial data, says David Breig, manager of finance and planning systems in Quaker's financial-planning group.

And not just for oatmeal: Gatorade, Life cereal, Cap'n Crunch, Rice-A-Roni—Quaker can now analyze data on all of its food products worldwide. That's something it just couldn't do before.

"We now have an overall worldwide competitive picture that we never had before. We now know where we stand relative to our competitors, and we understand our total profitability picture. We used to know how much we sold in total in Germany or France, but we really couldn't break that down for each product in those countries or anywhere else. We just didn't have the tools to do that," says Breig.

Using that analysis, Quaker can now decide almost instantly which products it should market and in what part of the world—and at what price—to beat its competitors. Quaker began using Express five years ago, and it is gradually replacing an aging mainframe-based EIS system that relied on hard-coded analyses and only serviced a few of the top brass.

Now Quaker has rolled out Express to about 60 users in marketing, sales, and financial divisions. Whereas the previous system showed general trends in Quaker's overall business, Express lets users drill down to produce details by brand and even by product bar code.

End-of-period financial closings and consolidations are still done on a general ledger system and on Excell spreadsheets, but "that's really one of the bottlenecks in the entire process, right now," said Breig. "We'll soon handle all of this with Express. When you're doing analytics on data, everything fits nicely in a two-dimensional world. But if you want to sort by region, by channel, by customer etc., and keep shifting the data, relational systems do not fit that model."

Breig says that eventually all of Quaker's financial data will be contained in a single multidimensional database. End users can then tap into the database using multidimensional analytical tools.

Despite the success Breig's group and other similar groups at Quaker have had, Breig says his own department still isn't sold on multidimensional technology. "Our IS department has been immersed in transactional systems. So there is still a bit of a bias" toward relational systems.

"One of the things a typical IS organization overlooks is that data by itself doesn't always mean a lot to end users," he says. "Dumping data onto somebody's PC is okay, but you need a system that can do some baseline analysis for you."

expensive hardware will take a team of specialists months to set up, users report that OLAP tools can be on line in a matter of weeks.

Users say eSSbase is one of the easiest of the OLAP tools to configure. "To really get value out of the product, you need a computer guy to set it up. But a really sharp accountant or someone with a flair for spreadsheets could set it up. It's pretty easy," says Eric Klusman, first vice president of applied systems at brokerage Cantor Fitzgerald LP in New York City. The company installed eSSbase last year to provide revenue and expense reports.

ESSbase's multidimensional DBMS is installed on a server running OS/2 or Windows NT. Defining data relationships in the database can be done in two ways. The first involves using an outliner, similar to an outliner in a word-processing program, to define data dimensions, like time, accounts, products, or markets. Formulas can also be defined in the outline. Or, data can be fed into the eSSbase server from any ASCII file, spreadsheet file or SQL database. All that is required is telling the server the rules for looking at the data, such as the first column equals sales.

On the front end, eSSbase works through spreadsheets like Excel or 1-2-3 and appears as a menu choice. Or, Arbor supplies an application-programming interface to the server database so that IS can create custom front ends with tools like Visual Basic.

LightShip Server is set up in a similar way, while Acumate ES and Express require a bit more programming to set up initially, say users. All allow a variety of clients to tap into multidimensional servers with a minimum of training or IS Intervention.

"The beautiful thing about any of these [OLAP] products is that they allow me to distribute data directly to end users who don't have to go to class, who don't have to learn a query language and who don't have to work with spreadsheet retrieval techniques," says Cantor Fitzgerald's Klusman. "Some of that stuff is just a little too cumbersome for most spreadsheet users. [We] have accountants who are ready to burst into tears at how beautiful this tool is."

Used correctly, OLAP tools can also give your company a competitive advantage and can pump up that bottom line.

"Lots of people are using these tools for competitive advantages," says Kastner. "Your competitors may not be bragging about it, but rest assured they are using them. And if you're not, you may wind up behind the eight ball."

QUESTIONS

1. What are the three product groupings for on-line analytic processing? What are distinctions among them?
2. What are the specific advantages of an OLAP tool compared to a normal relational DBMS? What are the disadvantages?
3. What business benefits does Quaker Oats derive from the use of EXPRESS? How specifically does the system generate those benefits?

10

A DSS FOR VEHICLE ROUTING

INTRODUCTION

In this chapter we describe a PC-based DSS, called FleetManager, which addresses the milk tanker routing scenario in the New Zealand dairy industry. It incorporates vehicle routing and judgmental models. The purpose of the system is to help the vehicle schedulers of the dairy companies build the schedules using their experience and preferences, and it can also be used as a strategic planning tool. The DSS uses multiple, resizable, overlapping windows to assist schedulers in their tasks. Users can also interact with the system through a graphical interface which displays a road map of the area and the location of the milk processing plants and milk suppliers. FleetManager also contains the option of automatically creating vehicle routes, which can be modified by the users. The system can be used to analyze a wide variety of "What-if?" scenarios with potential cost impacts. The system evolved as a result of several years of collaboration between vehicle schedulers and researchers at the Department of Management Systems, The University of Waikato, New Zealand.

In the first part of the chapter, we present a description of the New Zealand dairy industry focusing on the issue of efficient milk tanker routing. We then discuss possible methodologies to address this issue. The second part of the chapter describes the formulation and development of a DSS for this environment.

This chapter is adapted from Basnet, Chuda, Les Foulds, and Magid Igbaria, "FleetManager: A Microcomputer-Based Decision Support System for Vehicle Routing, Decision Support Systems," forthcoming.

Finally, we illustrate how the DSS was used in practice to improve tanker routing efficiency.

OVERVIEW OF MILK TANKER SCHEDULING

Throughout New Zealand, dairy companies are faced with the question of how to collect milk from their supplier farms efficiently, using road milk tankers, and have it delivered to their factories for processing. The dairy companies operate one or more factories, each of which has a daily demand for milk that must be satisfied. They also operate fleets of milk tankers over two shifts per day. The bases, where the tanker fleets are maintained, may be at sites other than factories. Each company has contracts with hundreds of farmers (suppliers) to supply milk usually (but not always) daily to the company. The amount of milk produced by each supplier varies daily and must be estimated. The company's vehicle schedulers operate the tanker fleet within location, budget and other constraints attempting, among other objectives, to minimize the cost per kilogram of milk delivered to the factories.

In order to achieve this objective, suppliers are grouped together into what is called a run: a sequence of suppliers which are visited by a tanker in a specific order (the complete set of runs for a shift is called a schedule). The runs must be developed and then allocated to the factories so as to satisfy the demands of each factory. This also involves assigning a tanker to each run. The initial run for each tanker begins at its base, visits the suppliers of the run in the order specified, and then ends at the factory for that run (which may be at a different location from the initial base). Subsequent runs of the tanker will begin at that factory and may well end at another factory. It is usually efficient to attempt to orchestrate the final run of the shift for each tanker to end at its base (when the base is a factory with positive demand) in order to minimize empty running. Because some suppliers have a relatively low output at certain times of the season, it is not considered worthwhile to visit them daily. Thus part of the allocation problem is the identification of which suppliers are to be visited in the current shift. There is also the question of the accurate prediction of supplier output. Further, a judgment has to be made as to when frequency of visiting a particular supplier is to be either increased or decreased, due to a change in output.

Tanker schedulers often approach these issues by first establishing which suppliers are to be visited during a given shift and then allocating them to the different factories in order to satisfy factory demand. If there has been no significant change from a previous similar shift, the runs of that shift are usually modified in order to generate the runs for the present shift. In examining previous runs, schedulers often ask themselves two key questions:

1. What are the requirements of a new schedule which differ from the previous schedule?

2. How should the previous schedule be modified in order to create a satisfactory new schedule?

The first question usually involves constraints governing the feasibility of any new schedule. The second question involves not only these constraints but also the measurement of how satisfactory the new schedule is, in terms of various objectives. The New Zealand dairy company vehicle schedulers have traditionally used a large-scale map together with colored pins displaying the suppliers. A manual file system was used for handling the information concerning the suppliers and the tankers, and for creating the schedule.

The dairy industry in New Zealand has been restructured and as a result many companies have been consolidated. The vehicle routing problem therefore became even more complex because of the significant increase in the number of suppliers, tankers, and factories. This has often led to a drastic decrease in the quality and timeliness of the schedules generated by the manual system. The dairy companies invited us to study their operations and vehicle routing methods and recommend areas for improvement. We now describe the approaches that we considered.

THE MATHEMATICAL PROGRAMMING APPROACH

Traditionally vehicle routing scenarios have been modeled as mixed integer programs to be solved by advanced mathematical programming techniques. The classical vehicle routing problem (VRP) is concerned with the efficient routing of a fleet of vehicles which must visit, from a central depot, a collection of clients to collect or deliver some commodity or perform some service. An excellent survey of the VRP has been given by Bodin [2] who discussed important concepts, approaches for solving practical problems, and other issues. Milk tanker routing is an example, where milk tankers need to be assigned to dairy farms for the collection and transportation of milk to factories for processing. For a description of a model of this scenario see [1]. We discuss below some problems with this approach.

Dairy company vehicle schedulers are often faced with problems which cannot be represented by a single well-defined optimality criterion, together with families of well-defined constraints, expressed in mathematical form. Their decisions are based not only on objective data points and formulas which can be optimized, but also on their subjective judgment. The total cost of servicing all the customers is only one of many considerations in the comparison of possible routing options. Often it is only a secondary consideration of the busy planner who is under pressure to produce a satisfactory schedule. Combinations of other factors often need to be considered: the level of customer satisfaction, equity of route generation including driving and visiting times, rostering arrangements for drivers, efficient vehicle and driver utilization, the total schedule time, company financial strategies, access problems including certain vehicle-customer combinations, road inclinations in winter conditions, queuing of tankers returning to factories, accidents and breakdowns, geographical obstacles which complicate distance and time estimation, vehicle cleaning and servicing, union rules, labor and traffic codes, company and customer policies, and human error. Thus the dairy company scheduler is typically faced with a multitude of ill-defined objectives and constraints, the relative priorities of which, may change markedly in a short space of time. There are goal programming and other approaches available for this scenario, but these approaches are computationally complex, and are usually not suitable for practical problems of a relatively large size.

Some commercial packages, based on mathematical programming, such as some of those discussed by Golden et al. [4], are available to address vehicle scheduling problems; however they usually suffer from major deficiencies when applied to practical milk tanker routing scenarios. The major difficulty with these packages for the milk tanker scenario is their inflexibility, in view of the factors mentioned above. Most of these packages ignore the talents of the experienced schedulers and do not lend themselves very well to manual "tweaking" of the routes suggested by the package.

To summarize, the problem remained, and the vehicle schedulers still required a system that would support their decision making concerning milk tanker routing. They required schedules which incorporated both quantitative and qualitative considerations. A system which follows their daily human decision-making processes and takes into account some of the non-quantitative considerations would be useful for them. Recognizing the importance of both models and judgmental considerations, the dairy companies together with the authors studied the companies' operations and vehicle routing methods and decided to develop a DSS to address the issue of milk tanker routing. We now present a DSS designed to aid the vehicle schedulers of the dairy companies.

THE DSS ENVIRONMENT

The traditional large-scale map, together with colored pins displaying the farms, is a very useful visual aid and, in order to gain acceptance, it is productive for a DSS to contain a computerized map which is used in place of the large-scale map. Geographical features and all relevant locations can be represented on the screen as a result of digitizing their coordinates. Relevant factory, milk tanker, and supplier information can be represented by using a color graphics display system with windows and pull-down menus. This allows a complementary combination of skills. The schedulers have the skill, superior to that of the computer, to recognize patterns in the location of suppliers and routes. Based on these patterns, the scheduler can create or modify the schedules. The use of a computerized map permits the computer to present immediately to the scheduler the consequences of these options. The scheduler then chooses an option, and the computer updates the schedule. Such a scheduler-computer combination marries the pattern recognition skills and the specialized knowledge that the experienced scheduler usually has, along with the numerical and recall ability of the PC.

To develop the DSS, we held a series of discussions with vehicle schedulers and other concerned individuals over a period of time. This helped us to understand their needs and requirements. In order to meet the schedulers' needs and requirements and follow their decision-making processes, possible main-menu functions of a DSS were developed. These functions are needed by the schedulers to identify the requirements of the new schedule and to create a satisfactory new schedule.

1. File open/close: In order to begin the process of new schedule generation, based on a previous schedule, the scheduler must first be able to access the previous schedule. Schedulers should be able to open and manipulate all the data files: suppliers, tankers, road network, and so on.

2. Schedule checking: There should be some means whereby the scheduler can ascertain how well a schedule will meet the requirements of the scheduler. A schedule may be checked for tanker capacity, amount of milk collected from individual suppliers, amount of milk remaining in the vats of suppliers, and distance traveled.

3. Schedule modification: Having pinpointed where a schedule is deficient, the scheduler must then devise modifications to it which produce a satisfactory new schedule. The system must allow for modification of existing schedules by such means as

- adding a new supplier to a run;
- deleting a supplier from a run;
- transferring a supplier from one run to another;
- interchanging suppliers between different runs; and
- creating a new run.

These functions should be guided by the provision of relevant statistics associated with them, such as tanker capacity utilization and run duration. Naturally, there must be a mechanism whereby the new schedule can be recorded.

It is also desirable that the DSS can be used to respond to enquiries and to address questions concerning changes to the size of the tanker fleet base, the acquisition of new suppliers or the location of a new factory. In these cases, and other similar inquiries and questions, it is not a modification of an existing schedule, rather a construction of a complete schedule from scratch. This is appropriate in a start-up situation, or when there are significant changes in the conditions or data which trigger a rationalization of resources. This task can be accomplished by carrying out systematically the clustering of suppliers into subregions. We now introduce the system structure of our DSS which has been devised for the New Zealand dairy industry.

THE SYSTEM STRUCTURE

The DSS (called FleetManager) was developed at the University of Waikato for use by New Zealand milk tanker schedulers. It can be categorized as a Specific DSS (SDSS) according to Figure 1–3 in Chapter 1. The TOOLS used to develop the Specific DSS were Turbo Pascal version 6.0 for an IBM-compatible PC with a high-resolution color monitor. It also conforms to the DDM paradigm shown in Figure 1–2 of Chapter 1. The three components are the user interface, the model base, and the database. The integration of the three components, that is, the structure of our SDSS, is presented in Figure 10–1. We made several revisions to make the system more robust and user-friendly. Currently it is used as a PC-based decision support system with the capability of communicating with the company mainframe computer, mainly to import the information necessary to support it, including the updating of supplier outputs. We also incorporated some strategic planning tools to create runs and examine the effects of changes in the milk yield, factory demands, shifts, and tanker capacities. The system includes a digitized map of the area of operations of the dairy company which shows all relevant locations and roads. The system is composed of pull-down menus, windows which display factory, suppliers, and milk tanker information, and is user-friendly and mouse-driven. It can be used to create new, or to improve existing, milk tanker routes.

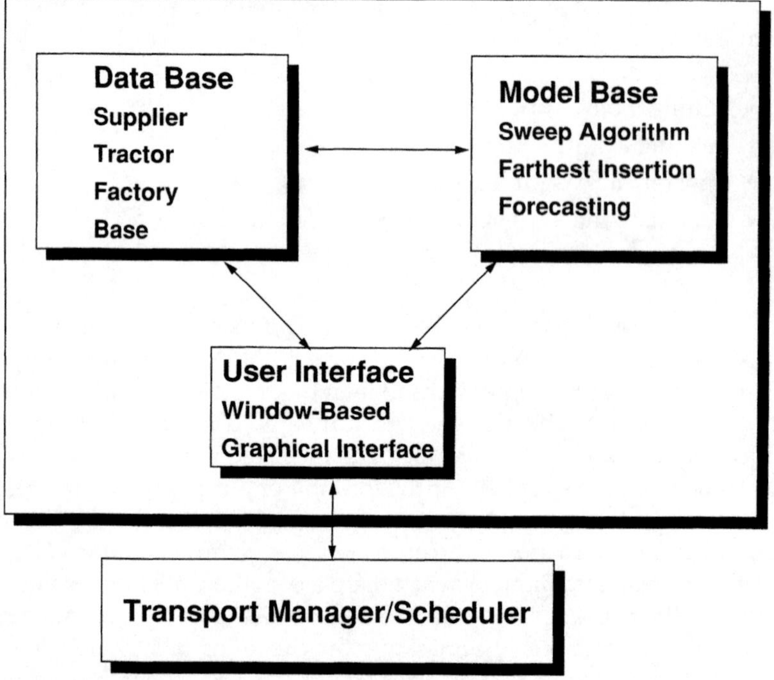

Figure 10–1 The Components of FleetManager

The assignments of suppliers to milk tanker runs can be automatically generated and then manually fine-tuned to meet users' specific needs. The system makes its recommendation to the scheduler by displaying the information on a digitized map of the area of operations of the dairy company, which shows all the relevant locations and roads. The system displays the map containing all relevant locations and roads and the scheduler modifies runs by clicking with a mouse on the locations of suppliers. When a schedule has been decided upon, the final assignments (run sheets) to be used by the tanker drivers can be printed. Additional summary information about suppliers and scheduled tanker runs is provided, as are warnings of possible routing oversights such as unscheduled suppliers and overfull tankers. Various statistics are automatically generated, such as the percentage of vehicle capacity utilized and the distance traveled.

Database and Model Base Components

The system maintains a database of suppliers, tankers, roads, factories, and base information that can be interactively entered and updated. This includes such information as supplier name, location, milk tank capacities, current output rate, tanker capacities, and road segment coordinates. This database can be easily accessed and manipulated through a File module. The database is initially created by the scheduler using this module. However, the digitized coordinates of the supplier locations and the road segments were supplied by the Department of Survey and Land Information of the New Zealand Government. Schedules can also be saved and recalled for use in future routing. The information on the actual milk output collected from each supplier is lodged with the company wide mainframe database. The mainframe writes this out to a file. FleetManager accesses this file to prepare an estimate of the milk output of suppliers. Models are used by FleetManager to suggest schedules to the user. The Sweep Algorithm of Gillet and Miller [3] is available to form the runs. Suppliers with sufficient milk in their tanks are first identified using estimates and preset criteria. This algorithm then forms clusters of these suppliers. Each cluster is allocated to a tanker. A cluster is formed by rotating a vertical plane around the factory. As long as the tanker capacity is not exceeded, any supplier swept by the plane is included in the cluster. The Farthest Insertion Algorithm [8] is available to determine the sequence of suppliers in a run to minimize the distance traveled. In this algorithm, the run is successively formed by adding to the current run a supplier which is farthest from the suppliers in the current run. Every time a supplier is added, it is inserted in such a position in the run that the total distance is minimized. A linear interpolation scheme is used to forecast the milk output. In this scheme, a gradient is established by looking at the previous output and the current output. This gradient is then used to forecast milk output for the next shift. These estimates can be altered by the schedulers based on their subjective judgment and experience concerning such factors as the amount of rainfall, and the passage of time since the beginning of the milk producing season.

User-Interface Component

The interface component has three subsystems: (1) the window-based user interface; (2) graphical user interface; and (3) automatic schedule creation.

The window-based user interface. The DSS is composed of five modules: ABOUT, FILE; AUTO; SCHEDULE; VIEW; and OPTIONS. The window-based user interface is illustrated in Figure 10–2. The pull-down menus give access to the modules. Each module includes a secondary menu of procedures. All procedures are independent and can be used in any order. All data can easily be stored for further processing. A short description of the modules and their procedures follows.

The FILE module provides file manipulations, exit, and DOS-shell functions. FleetManager automatically loads the supplier, tanker, factory, roads, and base files. These files are used in the routing process and can be viewed and edited using the File Open menu command.

The AUTO module provides for the use of FleetManager to generate automatically all schedules and to examine the effects of changes in milk yield. The schedule is constructed for all current suppliers using the tankers available for that shift.

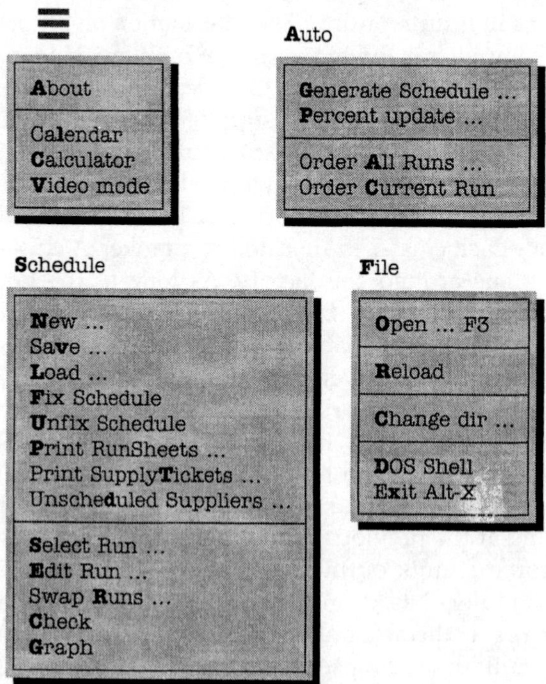

Figure 10–2 Menu Functions

FleetManager also allows users to edit manually supplier outputs. The SCHEDULE module provides most of the schedule manipulation functions. There are provisions for looking at a summary of the schedule, to edit a run (including swapping of suppliers between runs), and to check the performance of the schedule. The system also provides the scheduler with a summary of all runs of a schedule for a given shift. It also allows the users to print the run sheets as well as supply tickets (a list of runs with a corresponding supplier number). The SCHEDULE module also allows the user to view a summary of the tanker runs currently scheduled and the total milk to be collected by each tanker. For every run, a list of suppliers currently assigned to it, the capacity of the tanker, the total of milk assigned and the total distance to be traveled are presented. Runs in which total milk collection exceeds a user-specified percentage of the tanker capacity are displayed in red. Additionally, supplier vat estimates which exceed the user-specified percentage are also displayed in red.

The user can also modify the schedule by moving suppliers from one run to another. The system is also able to modify and fine-tune existing schedules including the transfer of suppliers between runs and shifts. The system allows the user to remove a supplier from a run and not schedule it on any other run. . Using the SWAP RUNS function, the system also allows the user to swap the complete set of suppliers on one run with the suppliers currently assigned to another run.

FleetManager also has a VIEW menu which allows the user to query the DSS about the suppliers. The system displays sets of suppliers which satisfy certain user-selectable criteria. The user can specify the following criteria: display all suppliers; display only those suppliers whose current uncollected total output exceeds a user-specified percentage of their milk holding tank (vat); display only those suppliers that are estimated to have less than a certain user-specified percentage of their vat size or with less than a specified litre vat estimates; or display only those suppliers which have been split between two or more runs or whose vat estimates have been only partially assigned to a run.

The graphical user interface. A second user interface is the graphical user interface. Both, the graphical user interface and the window-based interface can be accessed from each other at the touch of a button. The graphical interface displays a road map of the area and the location of the suppliers. The interface has provisions for zooming and panning. In order to build up a run, the user successively selects the supplier locations. Suppliers may be removed from runs or the output may be split between different runs. Information on current run and current supplier is continually updated and displayed.

Automatic schedule creation. FleetManager contains the option of automatically creating the runs. It can automatically generate a schedule using information from the user or a database, provide a schedule without the intervention of the user, and display or print the schedule or an individual run in a way that can easily be understood by most schedulers. Because users are often reluctant to use the solution of a model they do not understand (Turban [9] and Sprague and Carlson [6] listed "understandable model-base" as a desirable DSS characteristic), it was proposed that the system provide suggested schedules, which can be modified by the user. This option is also useful as a planning tool, where the system allows the user to have the "what-if" queries by examining the effect of changes in the milk yield, factory demands, shifts, and tanker capacities. The automatic creation of routes involves the following steps: the assignments of suppliers to factories, the assignments of tankers to factories, the creation of an initial run for each tanker and the assignment of subsequent runs to each tanker from a factory.

We should stress that our models do not generate schedules satisfying all the various constraints while recognizing the complicating factors that were mentioned earlier. Rather, the use of our models is to suggest an initial schedule. This schedule may then be modified by the scheduler in the light of those complicating factors. Automatic schedule generation may also be used as a strategic planning tool in which various options can be tested and the costs of those can be compared.

In summary, the proposed DSS (FleetManager) can accommodate the following:

- Multiple shifts;
- Supplier vat size limitation;
- Suppliers that are visited on less than a daily basis and the capability of judging how often a supplier should be visited;
- Tanker capacity;
- The ability to identify suppliers of various output sizes not yet visited;
- The ability to identify tankers with spare capacity during run construction;
- The ability to modify and fine-tune existing schedules including the transfer of suppliers between runs and shifts, a summary of all runs of a schedule for a given shift;
- The allocation of the total output of each shift among various destinations; and
- Warnings concerning illogical outcomes, such as unvisited suppliers and overloaded tankers.

FleetManager includes all of the characteristics of an effective DSS from the generic DSS framework of Sprague and Carlson [7] and Turban [9]:

- It supports but does not replace the decision maker. It should therefore neither try to provide the "answers" nor impose a predefined sequence of analysis;

- It supports semistructured decisions, where parts of the analysis can be systematized for the computer, but where the decision maker's insight and judgment are needed to control the process;
- It combines modeling techniques with database and presentation techniques;
- It emphasizes ease of use, user friendliness, user control, and flexibility and adaptability;
- It supports all phases of decision making;
- It interacts with other computer-based systems, mainly with the company mainframe system to download and upload information.

DEVELOPMENT METHODOLOGY

FleetManager has been implemented on IBM-PC compatible with a Super VGA monitor. It was developed using a prototyping approach ("The iterative (prototyping) approach is most common in DSS since the information requirements are not known precisely" [9, p. 304]). The core of the DSS was written in a general-purpose programming language—a set of Pascal subroutines and library functions. Systematic testing assured that each process was error-free before the next layer of complexity was added. Implementation enabled the team to work on both the model building and the interface between other components of the systems, allowing for periodic testing of their enhancements and progress and checks on performance of the whole system. The need for involvement and participation of the potential users was recognized right from the beginning.

Version 1.0 was first developed and following users' feedback and reaction, the system was refined, expanded, and modified. The changes have largely occurred in the area of transferring information from other systems to FleetManager and in the implementation of the graphical interface. Minor changes have also been made to other areas. The layout of the files that make up the FleetManager system has also been improved.

ILLUSTRATION OF USAGE

We now give an example to illustrate the use of FleetManager by the dairy companies. Figure 10–3 shows a window displaying a summary of all the generated runs (the top window). All the runs can be modified. If the scheduler wants to edit a particular run (say run 2 of tanker 14), the scheduler needs to select it by double-clicking on it. The system then automatically displays the bottom part of Figure 10–3 (the run window). At this point, the output of a supplier can be removed from the run or partly or wholly transferred to another run. This is a very important feature of the DSS, making it a useful tool to respond to different circumstances.

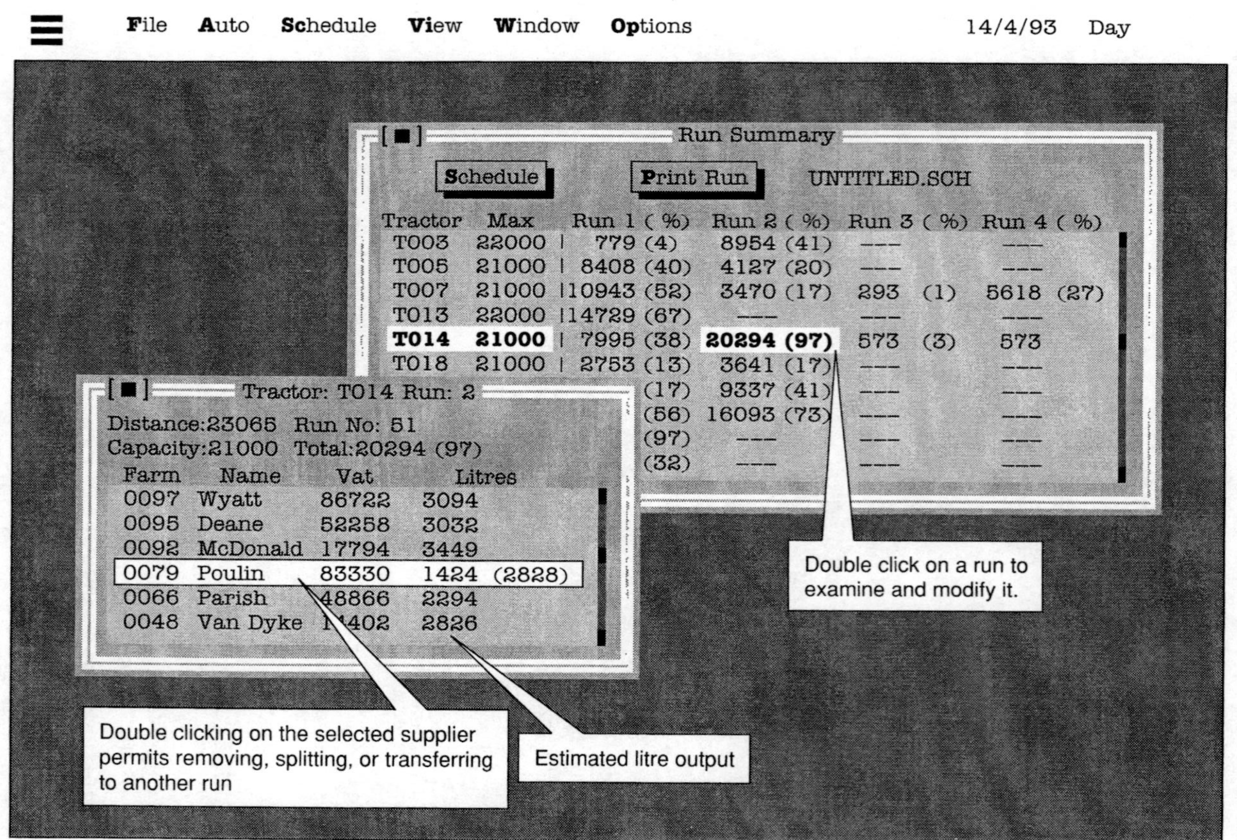

Figure 10–3 Modifying a Tanker Run

Figure 10–4 presents the run sheet for a particular run to be given to the tanker driver concerned. It shows the number and the name of the suppliers in the order they have to be visited, and the estimates of the suppliers' output. Tanker drivers are required to complete the sheet by filling in the actual milk collected from each vat of the supplier, total milk collected, and the temperature of the collected milk. This sheets is used to update the record of milk collections.

Figure 10–5 shows the window that permits the user to query the DSS regarding suppliers and a schedule. The scheduler can generate reports by spec-

Daily Milk Weight Sheet

Driver: __________ Run No. 003

Date: 14/4/93 Day Shift Checked: __________

Tractor No. T005 Entered: __________

SUP. No.	NAME	COMMENTS	VAT1 WT	VAT2 WT	TOTAL	TEMP	ESTIMATE
0178	Climo						2012
0162	Duindam						557
0160	Struthers						831
0158	McGrath						410
0146	Flemming						348
0157	Sullivan						399
0124	Foster						1706
	Hash Totals:						

Run No.	Start Factory	Delivery Factory	Last Pickup	Hash Total

Hubometer Readings:

Tractor No. ________	Semi No. ________	Trailer No. ________
End ________	End ________	End ________
Start ________	Start ________	Start ________
Total ________	Total ________	Total ________

Vehicle Maintenance Required:

Figure 10–4 A Run Sheet

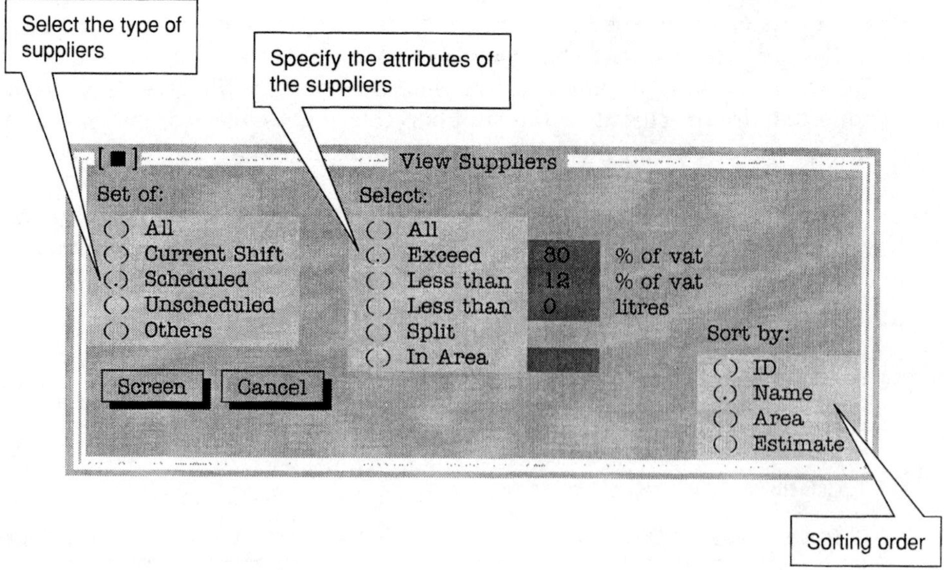

Figure 10–5 A Query Window

ifying the type of suppliers (display all suppliers; suppliers usually collected in the current shift; scheduled suppliers; unscheduled suppliers; or others) and the attributes of these suppliers (all; estimated milk exceeding x% of their vat capacity; less than x% of their vat capacity; less than x litres; suppliers whose output is split between tankers; or in a particular area). The report can be sorted by the milk suppliers' ID, name, area, or estimate of the milk.

The system can also display the deficiencies of a schedule. Figure 10–6 illustrates a warning window. In this example, there are four types of warning characteristics: some suppliers which exceed 80 percent of their vat capacity have not been scheduled; some suppliers which have less than 12 percent of their vats full are scheduled for collection; some tankers runs have more than 80 percent of their capacities; and some tankers runs have less than 3 percent of the tanker capacities. When one of the four is selected, the system displays a corresponding list of suppliers or tankers.

An example of the use of the graphical interface screen is shown in Figure 10–7. The information about the current tanker run is displayed at the top left and the current supplier information is shown underneath. FleetManager displays the suppliers' locations using the following color scheme:

RED	Unscheduled or partially scheduled suppliers
GREEN	Scheduled (including fully scheduled split) suppliers

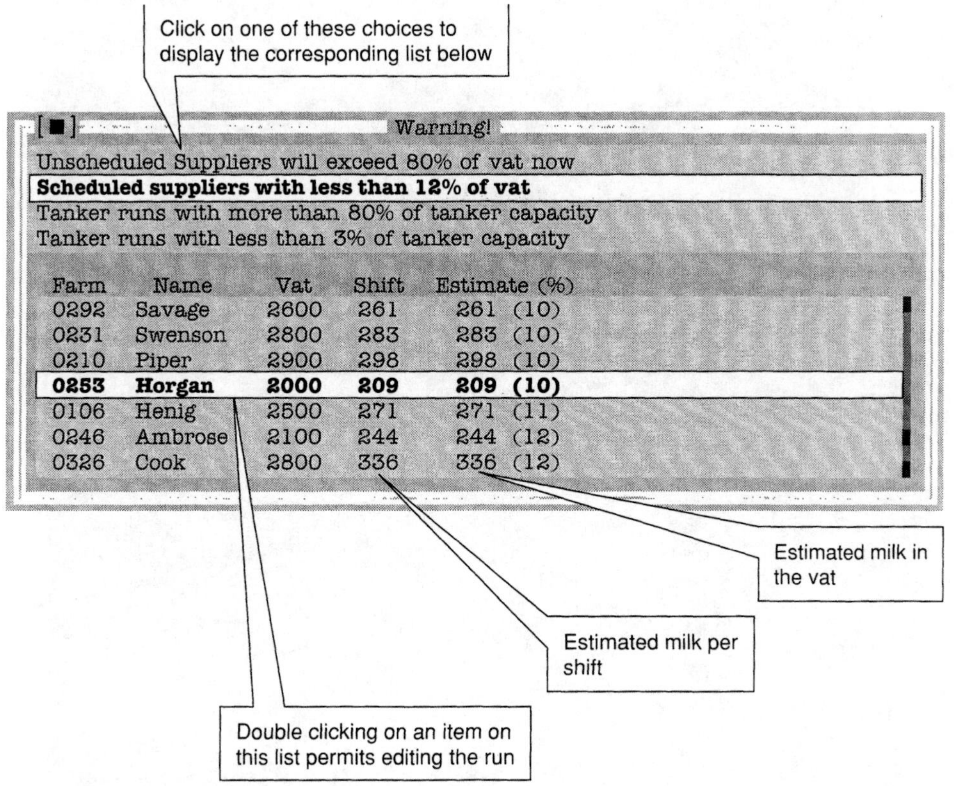

Figure 10–6 A Warning Window

PINK Suppliers scheduled on the current run

BLACK Other suppliers This display with color aims to simplify the system and emphasize the ease of use and flexibility and adaptability of the system.

The DSS has been in use in a dairy company over a year. Initially, teething problems were encountered and some bugs were discovered. There were gaps in our perception of the functions of the DSS and the desires of the users. There were also gaps in communicating the instructions to be followed. After a year of usage, the schedulers have expressed satisfaction with the DSS. The time spent by the schedulers in preparing the schedules has been cut significantly and the boredom of the task has been reduced, thus freeing the schedulers for more creative tasks. However, it is too early to gather evidence of actual savings of transportation costs.

Figure 10–7 The Graphical Interface

CONCLUSION

We introduced a DSS, called FleetManager, which is designed to address issues concerning milk tanker routing that commonly occurs within the New Zealand dairy industry. A conceptual model for providing a decision support system for vehicle routing has been presented. FleetManager was designed to assist vehicle schedulers in every step of the vehicle routing process. It does not automate the decision-making process but helps vehicle schedulers by providing powerful tools to create schedules, choose between plans, generate alternative plans, and to assess alternative plans with respect to given criteria. The system allows the scheduler to create vehicle routes automatically, minimize the total distance traveled, and to manually override created routes. It allows for more than one source or destination, skip a-day clients, multiple shifts, as well as fine tuning.

In general, DSS benefits are often uncertain and are difficult to assess. In our case, with the prototyping approach, where development is evolutionary, this is especially the case. The on-going schedule changes and changing environments make it even more so. The true value of a DSS is whether it improves a manager's decision making, which is not easily measured. Therefore, the traditional cost-benefit analysis will not be able to capture all DSS benefits [5,9]. Actually in some cases, it may not be well suited to the DSS. However, some of the benefits in our case can be measured, such as a reduction in milk collection costs. The use of FleetManager as a DSS may also result in a reduction in labor costs. The system also has tangible and intangible benefits. It can benefit the schedulers in the fine tuning of existing schedules, creation of entirely new schedules, strategic planning for new sites, efficient fleet utilization, and the flexibility to plan for and cope with unexpected situations. The DSS also allows the scheduler to carry out ad hoc analysis through "what-if?" queries. It also provides the scheduler with a better understanding of the business, where the system can alert users concerning illogical outcomes such as unvisited suppliers and overloaded tankers. In summary, this chapter shows that the milk tanker routing problem is a complex management process involving subjective and objective information and judgments. FleetManager is designed to deal with such complex situations.

QUESTIONS

1. Summarize the capabilities of FleetManager in each of the three major components of the architecture: the data component, the dialog component, and the modeling component.
2. Why is a DSS necessary? Why does this problem need anything more than good management science models?

3. What is the primary value of the graphical interface display?
4. What development methodology was used to build FleetManager? What are its advantages?

REFERENCES

1. C.B. Basnet, D.N. Clark and L.R. Foulds, "A Decision Support System Approach to Milk Tanker Routing, Control and Cybernetics" (Forthcoming, 1994).
2. L.D. Bodin, "Twenty Years of Routing and Scheduling," *Operations Research* 38, No. 4 (July–August 1990), 571–579.
3. B. Gillet and L. Miller, "A Heuristic Algorithm for the Vehicle Dispatch Problem," *Operations Research* 22, No. 2 (March–April 1974), 340–349.
4. B. Golden, L. Bodin and T. Goodwin, "A Microcomputer-based Vehicle Routing and Scheduling Software," *Computers and Operations Research* 13, No. 2/3 (1986), 277–285.
5. P.G.W. Keen, "Value Analysis: Justifying Decision Support Systems," *MIS Quarterly* 5, No. 1 (March 1981), 1–16.
6. R.H. Sprague and E.D. Carlson, *Building Effective Decision Support Systems* (Prentice Hall, Englewood Cliffs, NJ, 1982).
7. R.H. Sprague and H.J. Watson (Eds.), *Decision Support Systems: Putting Theory Into Practice*, Third Edition (Prentice Hall, Englewood Cliffs, NJ, 1994).
8. M.M. Syslo, N. Deo and J.S. Kowalik, *Discrete Optimization Algorithms* (Prentice Hall, Englewood Cliffs, NJ, 1983).
9. E. Turban, *Decision Support and Expert Systems: Management Support Systems*, Third Edition (Macmillan Publishing Company, New York, NY, 1993).

11

GUIDELINES FOR DESIGNING EIS INTERFACES

From the user's perspective, the user interface *is* the system. Most users care little about which hardware or software is used, where data reside, or which communications protocols are used. They focus their attention on what they must know in order to use the system, how the system's actions are directed, and how the system's output is presented. If a user interface is poorly designed there are two possible consequences: (1) the system is not used; or (2) the system is used (possibly because it is a job requirement), but with low user satisfaction, efficiency, and effectiveness.

In Chapter 7, it was pointed out that there is always a trade-off between simplicity and flexibility. Systems that are simple to use tend to be less flexible and vice versa. It is always important to consider the characteristics of the user (e.g., computer skills) and the task being supported (e.g., the analysis required) when designing an interface. The right balance between simplicity and flexibility must be achieved.

This chapter focuses on the design of user interfaces for executives. With this user group, simplicity of use is a primary concern. They seldom have the background, skills, time, or patience to deal with complex systems.

It is important to recognize that everyone appreciates an easy to use interface—not just executives. As a result, many of the user-interface features that were developed with executives in mind are finding their way into other kinds of applications. As you read this chapter, keep in mind that the guidelines that

This chapter is adapted from Hugh J. Watson and John Satzinger, "Guidelines for Designing EIS Interfaces," *Information Systems Management*, Vol. 11, No. 4, Fall 1994, pp. 46–52.

are given for designing EIS interfaces apply to other decision support applications as well.

THE DEVELOPMENT OF EISs

Building a successful EIS is challenging. A myriad of technical, organizational, and managerial issues must be addressed. Of utmost importance is creating an EIS that is easy to use. Consequently, system designers should pay careful attention to the design of the user interface for the system.

Definition of EIS User Interface. The term *user interface* refers to how the user directs the operation of the system (e.g., keyboard, mouse, or touchscreen; question/answer, command language, or menus) and how the output is given to the user (e.g., graphical, tabular, or textual; color or monochrome; paper or on-line). For the system to be easy to use, the user must know how to make it work and what the output means. A user interface must be designed to make operating the system and interpreting the output as easy as possible.

Designing an EIS user interface is somewhat different from designing other information systems. Because of the nature of executive users, the system must be more than user friendly; it must be user intuitive, even user seductive. Another difference is the flexibility the system must have, because it is difficult to determine how a particular executive will use an EIS. Also, because of advances in hardware and software, system designers have many new options to choose from when implementing an EIS.

A successful EIS often benefits other users in addition to executives. For this reason, it has been argued that EIS also stands for "everybody's information system" (Friend, 1990). These users are more likely to accept complex user interfaces than senior executives and may be willing to trade off simplicity for flexibility. In many instances, however, the more complex applications created for lower-organizational-level users are not given to executives. For example, an executive may not need an application that provides advanced query capabilities to analyze sales data. The focus of attention in this chapter is on the design of user interfaces for executives rather than for lower-level organizational personnel.

DESIGN GUIDELINES

Developers of an EIS are typically building their first system of this type. EIS users, information content, and software are often different from previous systems development projects. Although developers will learn how to better build EISs, poor initial choices can undermine or even eliminate the chances for successful implementations. Some EISs have not been as successful as they might be or have even failed because of poor user interface designs.

The following eight guidelines on designing an EIS interface should help developers successfully implement an EIS:

1. Involve executives in the design of the user interface.
2. Set standards for screen layout, format, and color.
3. Use of the system should be intuitive.
4. Use standard definitions of terms.
5. Design the main menu as a gateway to all computer use.
6. Design the system for ease of navigation.
7. Strive to make response time as fast as possible.
8. Expect preferences in user interfaces to change.

In the following sections these guidelines are examined and illustrated with examples from successful EIS implementations.

Involving Executives in the Design of the User Interface

Although user involvement in the systems development process is critical for all types of information systems, executive involvement in the design of an EIS user interface is especially important. Executives might have limited experience working directly with a computer, and if they do have some computer experience, the EIS will look and feel quite different from any other organizational information systems the executives might know. Designers should be prepared to show a variety of prototype screens and navigation approaches because the executive might have limited knowledge of what an EIS can actually do. Evaluating these prototypes is also likely to get apprehensive executives more committed to the EIS as they begin to see the system's potential. For this reason, it is important to involve all executive users in the process, not just the executive sponsor.

Prototyping Approaches. Early prototyping should be used to help decide on the basic look and feel of the system. Two fundamental approaches should be presented:

- A full-screen interface with large buttons and icons.
- A multiple window interface with pull-down menus and dialog boxes.

The first approach might be less intimidating, but the second approach conforms to the popular interface design standards. The preferred look and feel should be used to finalize the development environment that will be used (e.g., Windows), as some development environments might more easily accommodate one or the other type of system. Additionally, differences in preference for the look and feel reveal early in the development process the amount of individual tailoring for each executive that might be required.

Most of the commercial EIS products are designed to run in a Windows environment and to take advantage of the functionality of Windows. It is usually not safe to assume that executives have experience with Windows and can easily operate Windows-based applications. When users are not proficient with Windows, there are two options. The first is to train them in Windows and then in the application. The second is to design the EIS in such a way that the features of Windows are not used. Experience has shown that an application can fail, not because it is poor, but because it incorrectly assumes a proficiency in Windows.

Although rapid prototyping and extensive user feedback are quite important, the prototypes do not have to be computer-based. Paper screen mock-ups (i.e., storyboards) can be quite effective because the executive can review the screens as time permits and consider the alternatives before providing feedback to the designer. Computer-based prototypes, however, are quite useful when showing the executive the potential of the technology and when exploring navigation approaches the executive might prefer.

Executives also must be involved in the design of the interface, because preferences for screen prototypes can provide clues about the importance of screen content and design. This aids a designer in uncovering additional information requirements. The relationships among importance of data, the level of detail desired, and the frequency of need for the information can help a designer understand the way an executive will actually use the EIS.

Because of the almost endless number of possible screens that can be provided, it is important for the designer to narrow the number down to the most important screens for each executive. This not only reduces development time and system overhead, but also makes it possible to provide a system that makes it easy for the executive to find the information that is actually needed.

Any later changes to the interface of an EIS should be discussed with its users. This is especially true when a designer considers deleting seldom-used screens. It is not easy to tell the value of a particular screen just by tracking usage. An executive may have looked at a particular screen only once, but that screen could have provided critical insight that day. Months later, the same screen might be needed once again when the same critical need arises.

Setting Standards for Screen Layout, Format, and Color

Currently available EIS software offers an array of screen design alternatives. Screens can display graphs, tables, and text in hundreds of formats and colors. Unfortunately, this cornucopia of choices can be detrimental. There is a temptation to use many of these alternatives to add sizzle to the screens, but yielding to this temptation can create displays that are confusing. Designers should carefully develop screen design standards that use only a few layouts, formats, and colors.

The EIS at Lockheed illustrates the use of screen design standards; a sample screen is presented in Figure 11–1. The top of the screen presents the screen number, a title for the screen, and the date of the last update. The right-hand corner gives the names of those who are knowledgeable about the information and their work telephone number. This information makes it easier for users to go directly to the person who is best able to answer any questions about the information. Some EISs allow users to click on the person's name to have the telephone number dialed automatically.

Layout Standards. Lockheed's standard layout is to present graphical information at the top of the screen, more detailed tabular data below it, and textual information at the bottom of the screen. The graph provides a quick visual presentation of a situation, the table gives specific numbers, and the text provides explanations, assessments, actions being taken, and other such information.

Graph Standards. Graphs of historical and current data always use bar charts. When actuals are compared against plans or budgets, paired bar charts such as those shown in Figure 11–1 are used. The bars are of different widths to

Figure 11–1 Sample Screen from the Lockheed Aeronautical Systems EIS

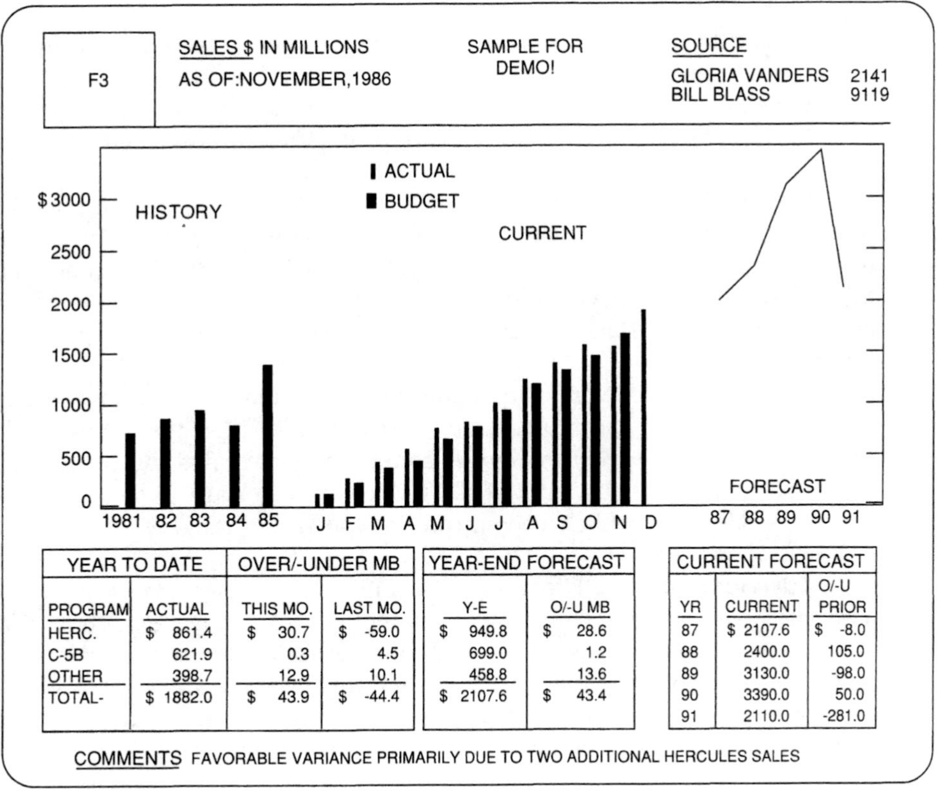

allow users with color perception problems to correctly identify each bar. Projections into the future use line graphs. Pie or stacked bar charts are used to depict parts of a whole. On all charts, vertical wording is avoided and abbreviations and acronyms are limited to those on an authorized list. All bar charts are set to zero at the origin to avoid distortions, scales are set in prescribed increments and are identical within a subject series, and bars that exceed the scale have numerical values shown.

Color Standards. Lockheed's EIS uses only a few carefully selected colors. Yellow is used to show actual performance, cyan (i.e., light blue) is used for company goals and commitments to the corporate office, and magenta represents internal goals and objectives. A traffic-light pattern is used to highlight comparisons: green is good, yellow is marginal, and red is unfavorable. For example, under budget or ahead of schedule is in green, on budget or on schedule is in yellow, and over budget or behind schedule is in red. Organization charts use different colors for the various levels of management. Colors have been selected to minimize color differentiation problems—about 6 percent of all men and less than 1 percent of all women have color perception problems—and all displays are designed to be effective with black-and-white hard copy output.

Standard layouts, formats, and colors offer many advantages. They provide a consistent look and feel for the system. Users are less likely to misinterpret or misunderstand the information presented. Standard displays require less cognitive effort on the part of the user and take less time to understand.

Use of Text. Textual material is entered by the EIS support staff to make the information displayed more useful. The information itself may not reveal the full story, but the purpose of the commentary is to add value to the information displayed. Although Lockheed's EIS presents commentary information on the same screen to which it applies, other EISs place it on a separate screen.

The power of a textual commentary is illustrated by the following example from Lockheed: Both a graph and tabular data indicated that actual cash flow was below budget by $20 million. A commentary revealed, however, that payment for a plane in the amount of $20 million was en route from a foreign country and would be in a Lockheed account by the end of the day.

Advanced Capabilities. A few EISs allow voice commentaries to be associated with screens. This is an appealing feature because executives are used to receiving information verbally and voice is richer for communications than printed words. Voice annotations to screens are currently the best accepted of the multimedia enhancements to EISs. Other possibilities such as video and personal teleconferencing have good potential, but the business case for them has yet to be made.

Using the System Should Be Intuitive

Ideally, an executive should be able to use an EIS without training. At the most, no more than 15 minutes of instruction should be required to teach how to use the basic information-retrieval capabilities. Systems more complex than this are unlikely to be used.

Most successful EISs are operated by point-and-click technology. By picking from among menus, icons, or buttons, an executive navigates through the system to a desired capability (e.g., e-mail or information). Experience with decision support systems has shown that most executives will not use a command language with a verb-noun syntax because it is too time-consuming to use and difficult to learn and remember (Hogue, 1987).

In one easy-to-use EIS, 35-inch monitors were installed in executives' offices; each can simultaneously display up to 10 windows of information. What is shown is customized for each executive and varies with the day of the month. This EIS is essentially a ticker tape of relevant information.

User Documentation. Systems developers are typically expected to write user documentation for new applications. However, this is usually unnecessary or inappropriate for EISs. The system should be sufficiently intuitive that instruction manuals are not needed. Even more so than with other types of users, executives do not read documentation. If an executive is having a problem using the system, it is best if the user calls the EIS support staff to correct the difficulty.

Users may request documentation, and in this case, it should be provided, either within the system and or as hard copy. Ideally, the instructions should fit on a single page or a few screens.

Using Standard Definitions of Terms

Most organizations have data dictionaries that include definitions for the data elements used in transaction processing applications. There are other terms that are widely used throughout organizations and are very important to EISs that are not as precisely defined. Everyone in a company uses these words and has a general understanding of their meaning but slight differences exist and can cause misunderstandings.

For example, the term *sign-up* at Lockheed had different shades of meaning. A sign-up involves a company interested in purchasing an aircraft. To marketing personnel a sign-up occurred when customers said they were going to make a purchase. The legal department, however, recorded a sign-up only when a signed contract was received. Finance waited until a down payment was received. Each group generally knew what the term meant, but slight differences based on their organizational perspective led to timing differences as to when a sign-up was recorded. Because an aircraft can cost between $20 to $30 million, such differences can result in considerably different impressions as to how the organization is doing. A sign-up has now been defined as a signed contract with a down payment.

A Dictionary of Terms. Lockheed has an executive data dictionary that contains definitions for all of the terms used in its EIS. The definitions can be accessed through the EIS and are available to all users. Creating an executive data dictionary is useful because it makes executives consider what terms are being used inconsistently and to develop definitions that reflect an organizationwide rather than functional-area perspective.

Designing the Main Menu as a Gateway

Most organizations have a variety of applications designed to support executives: e-mail, electronic filing, decision support, and access to external news and stock prices. It is common for many of them to require their own access procedures and passwords. This requirement, and the resulting difficulty and inconvenience, discourages hands-on computer use. The development of an EIS provides an excellent opportunity to deliver all of these capabilities in a single, integrated system. An EIS provides the logical and physical umbrella under which all of the executives' computer applications are placed.

A number of EISs use their main menus to display all information and applications available through picks (i.e., menus, icons, or buttons). The kinds of information usually provide one set of options. For example, there may be screen picks for financial, production, marketing, and human resources information. Separate picks may exist on the basis of products, geographical location, and organizational units (e.g., corporate, division). The choices reflect the information contained in the EIS and how it is organized. Lower-level menus let users move to specific information desired within a general category.

Access to these applications should be transparent to the user and not require any additional log-on procedures or passwords; these activities should be handled automatically by the system.

Designing the System for Ease of Navigation

Vendors' demos often show executives moving easily through a system, looking at current status information and drilling down to more detailed information when a problem or item of interest is identified. This scenario is possible in practice, but only if careful attention is given to navigation issues early in the system's design.

Navigation problems may be masked when there are few screens in the system. As the number of screens grows, as they inevitably do, users find it more difficult and time-consuming to move through a system. For example, an executive is looking at financial information and wants to move to operational production data. In a poorly designed system, the user will have to back out of the financial application, screen by screen, until the main menu is reached, and then enter the production xapplication, and move through screens to the desired information.

The starting point in designing navigation for an EIS is understanding the mental models that executives have of the organization. If the structure of the information does not match their mental models, users will have a difficult time finding the information they want. For example, do executives look at the firm in terms of geographical location, products, functional areas, or divisions? Each view of the organization may call for a pick on the main menu and a set of related screens.

A complicating factor is when one or a few executives have unique mental models. During the development of one EIS at a hospital, designers found that the director of nursing wanted information structured much differently than other users. Her view of the hospital could be accommodated but required custom designing the system for her use. The decision of whether to do this was a business rather than a technical one.

Navigation Features. There are features that can be included in an EIS to make navigation easier. Some systems have a screen that shows where the user is in the system. Often, users get lost and are uncertain about how to move elsewhere, short of turning off the system and starting over. Another feature is to have a home key or pick that takes the user directly back to the main menu. Some systems provide a retrace capability that allows users to easily backtrack to screens viewed previously. Another helpful feature is to include a pick on the main menu that takes the user to a screen that lists the user's most popular screens. From this screen, a user can go directly to any screen on a personalized menu.

Also, a single menu can be created that provides direct access to a large number of screens. For example, a company has five plants; each produces 20 products and there is work-in-process and finished goods inventory. The various combinations result in 200 screens (i.e., $5 \times 20 \times 2 = 200$). A single menu where the user picks the plant, the product, and the type of inventory provides direct access to the desired screen.

Lockheed switched recently from custom developed to commercial EIS software. Before Lockheed signed the contract, however, the vendor had to agree to support keyboards as an input device to the system, largely for navigation reasons. Lockheed's executives were accustomed to point-to-point navigation in the system. Each screen could be accessed from any place in the system by simply entering its screen number. Most executives remembered or kept a list of the screen numbers of their favorite screens.

Response Time as Fast as Possible

When incorporating text and graphics, internal and external data, hundreds of individually tailored screens and views, and multiple navigational paths through the system, EIS developers must continually monitor the response time of the system. Executives are intolerant of slow response times. A recent survey of EIS development practices found that response times for EISs had actually degraded from an average of 2.8 seconds in 1988 to 5.3 seconds in 1991 despite the increased use of powerful desktop computers and local area networks (Watson, Rainer, and Frolick, 1992). Although the same survey found satisfaction with ease of use and the effectiveness of the EISs to be relatively high, satisfaction with response times was extremely low.

Response time problems can be anticipated when the EIS must dynamically build a screen each time it is requested by searching corporate data bases. Response time can be much faster if the screens are static and updated each night, though designers must evaluate the trade-off between timeliness of data on the screens and response time. Response time can also be affected by the narrow bandwidth of today's networks.

When Speed Counts. Generally, executives expect very fast response times when flipping through their usual set of screens each morning. One EIS developer suggested thinking of the maximum acceptable time to move from screen to screen as the time it takes the executive to turn a page of *The Wall Street Journal.*

Executives can usually tolerate a slow response to ad hoc queries. When an executive is used to waiting several days for the staff to gather information for a specific question, several minutes may be an acceptable wait for directly retrieving the same information through the EIS. The differences between predefined screens and ad hoc query screens should be made clear to the executive, however. In either case, when any system function takes more than a few seconds, a message should always provide feedback that the system is processing the executive's request.

USER PREFERENCES MAY CHANGE

Almost all aspects of an EIS, including the user interface, change in time. Several examples illustrate this point. So much information is displayed on a screen in the Lockheed EIS that a first-time viewer may be confused. However, this is what Lockheed's executives prefer. They want information on a single screen rather than having to page through several screens. This approach also better supports the making of comparisons, such as when an executive wants to check graphical against numerical presentations of data.

Lockheed's screens were not originally designed this way; rather, they have evolved in response to executives' requests. This same phenomenon has been noted in other, but not all, organizations as their EISs have matured.

Often, organizations developing an EIS order touchscreens for technophobic executives. These users quickly discover the disadvantages of touchscreens and also find that using a mouse is easy after a little practice. Although touch-screens may help sell the idea of an EIS to some executives, these executives will probably prefer mouses eventually.

As an EIS evolves, the number of its users usually increases. Quite possibly, training given to first-time users will have to change. For example, more time may have to be spent discussing how to interpret the information presented on the most complex screens. Another approach is to include less complex screens in the system. This was done in one manufacturing firm where the new CEO had a strong background in engineering and production but was relatively weak in finance. Recognizing this fact, the EIS staff developed a number of simple screens that displayed key financial information. Within a few months, after the CEO had become experienced in finance, the special screens were phased out of the system.

QUESTIONS

1. Review the eight guidelines for designing an interface for EIS. Since trade-offs are often needed in design, which do you think are most important? Which are least important? Explain your opinion.
2. The importance of design guidelines such as those discussed in this chapter is decreasing because of the growing popularity of Windows as a de facto interface standard. Agree or disagree? Discuss.
3. Why are the screens in the Lockheed EIS so full? What are the advantages and disadvantages of this feature of their interface?

REFERENCES

DAVID FRIEND, "EIS and the Collapse of the Information Pyramid," *Information Center* (March 1990), pp. 22–28.

JACK T. HOGUE, "A Framework for the Examination of Management Involvement in Decision Support Systems," *Journal of Management Information Systems* 14, no. 1 (1987), pp. 96–110.

HUGH J. WATSON, R. KELLY RAINER, and MARK N. FROLICK, "Executive Information Systems: An Ongoing Study of Current Practices," *International Information Systems* (April 1992), pp. 37–56.

12

DOCUMENT-BASED DECISION SUPPORT

INTRODUCTION

Incalculable amounts of information are generated, disseminated and stored away in organizations daily. One estimate has it that American businesses and government agencies produce 900 million pages of paper information daily! U.S. companies now store approximately 1.3 trillion paper documents (Myers-Tierny), sometimes taking up to 50 percent of office floor space (Meall and Price, 1993). Companies have estimated that only about 5 percent to 10 percent of their paper-based information is accessible (Meall and Price, 1993; Myers-Tierny). Yet, with all of the technological advances and large corporate expenditures made with the goal of improving accessibility to information, very little (only 2 percent to 5 percent) of an organization's information base is actually computerized (Wallace, 1990). An even smaller percentage of this information is accessible on-line for managers and decision makers, even though 40 to 60 percent of an office worker's time entails working with documents (Frappaolo, 1992).

Why is this? Part of the reason can be ascribed to the fact that the information needed by managers is not predisposed to a generic definition. That is, it is not easily molded or manipulated in the simple record format required by most information systems. Although Decision Support Systems (DSS) were conceived to provide decision-making support to managers faced with semistructured problems, the data model underlying their data bases comprises a series of well-defined

This chapter was written specifically for this book by Jane Fedorowicz, Bentley College, Waltham, Mass.

fields and relationships. It is the analytical engine, or model base, that provides the user with greater flexibility of analysis. In spite of this limitation on the type of data that DSS can work with, DSS have become very powerful tools in a decision maker's arsenal. Recently, document management standards have been adopted by many vendors to provide some structure to the unstructured document, paving the way for documents to be accessed and analyzed with similar ease.

The information needs of senior level managers and executives, in particular, do not conform to the traditional conception of data base querying. Much of their information acquisition activity is centered on external and personal sources, many of which are not numeric or text-based (Fedorowicz, 1989). These individuals gather information from various formal and informal sources. Information may come from written reports, letters from customers, internal memos, news items, electronic mail messages, conversations with a golf partner, or video clips. Some of these data are so informal that they may never be captured, stored, and made available through a DSS. Most of them, however, have been excluded from traditional DSS only because it has been technologically difficult or impossible to include them. Now there are technological advances that are making it increasingly desirable to store and manage this data. We will call any stored form of information a "document."

We define "document" rather broadly here. It is a "chunk" of information, usually dealing with a relatively limited topic or subject area. It may contain numbers, but it is predominantly non-numeric, including text, graphics, image, voice, and video. DSS that expand the data component to gather, store, manipulate, manage, and provide access to these kinds of data are called document-based DSS (DDSS).

Traditional DSS failures in handling document-based data may be ascribed to the limitations and distinctive features of its underlying technology. These limitations may finally be dissipating. Client/server networks, telecommunications, mass storage, and other technologies provide the tools with which to make the information accessible. A document base also requires different internal representation and access schemes than a traditional database. Artificial intelligence (AI) can aid in improving the ability of technology to understand, interpret and classify the information itself. The technological demands of a DDSS must be determined in light of advances in these and many related areas. This will become possible with the *integration* of new techniques in AI, object-oriented data base management, groupware, information retrieval, electronic mail, and representation standards. We know how to build many of the component pieces of the DDSS, but progress is still needed on their merger.

In these and other areas, technological advances are now moving into the mainstream to enable the management of document-based data in DSS, making it accessible to managers, executives, and other decision makers. Figure 12–1 depicts the information sources and transformations of the Data Subsystem component of a DDSS. In this chapter, we examine advances in hardware, software, and application areas that will provide the basis for the development of this integrated subsystem.

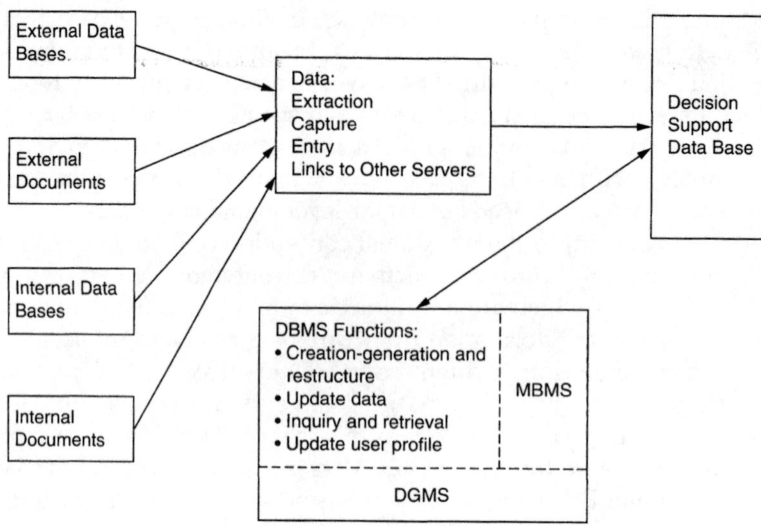

Figure 12–1 The Data Subsystem

TECHNOLOGY PLATFORMS

Decreased cost and increased processing speed are obvious technology indicators for pursuing DDSS, which inherently process large amounts of stored data. But these alone will not suffice for handling the volume of documents that a document base will contain. Indeed, since not all documents are amassed using traditional keyboarding options, alternative input and access mechanisms are required. Key to DDSS success are accompanying improvements in client-server technology, storage technology, and standards for inputing and storing this type of data.

Parallel processing machines are beginning to be used to analyze large amounts of data for decision support. Several processors running the same or concurrent programs cut down processing time dramatically, sometimes by several orders of magnitude. Marketing information systems, with their enormous POS data sets, have greatly benefited from parallel processing technology. However, these machines do not yet run software that is well matched to the unstructured nature of documents.

Client/server technology supports a network of small computers by giving seamless access to distributed data and processing at any site by another, remote site. Client/server (C/S) hardware incorporates powerful workstations, personal computers and special-purpose servers in local- and wide-area networks. The challenge of C/S is the need for seamless access to distributed data and processing by end users who only interact with the network through a GUI (graphical user interface). Several GUI vendors, including Easel, provide the interface to the multi-platform, distributed data needed for C/S-based decision support, including multimedia documents.

Relational database vendors have long been the mainstay data repository for DSS. Many relational databases (including market leaders Oracle, SyBase, DB2, and Informix) now offer C/S support and integration. C/S networks must be able to access data from multiple vendors and storage mechanisms. Relational vendors have built links to their competitors' products and other business mainstays (like word processing documents, spreadsheets, and e-mail) to comply with the needs of the C/S environment.

Several Executive Information Systems vendors, including Pilot Software, Comshare Inc., and IRI Software, have banded together to propose an alternative to the relational data base model as the basis for their decision support products. The OLAP (Online Analytical Processing) Model provides multidimensional data modeling, which is better suited for manipulating decision support data. These products also support links to many relational database products and provide object-oriented design tools. In a current release of Pilot's Lightship line, data or data links work along with maps to populate objects that can be manipulated onscreen. Although relatively small, the market for multidimensional databases is growing rapidly. See Chapter 9 for more detail.

Several newer object-oriented database vendors have recently become successful in competing with the relational products because of the perceived match between the object-oriented paradigm and the need for seamless data and processing access. Distributed, heterogeneous data bases are ideally suited to object technology because of the ability of object technology to treat any entity (data, database, procedure, message, etc.) as independent, yet with the capacity to link to other objects as needed. Market leaders of OODBMS include ObjectStore by Object Design, ONTOS, GemStone by Servio, Versant Object Technology, and Objectivity.

Object-oriented technology also enhances the ability to incorporate multimedia documents into C/S applications, although the limited availability of broadband networks restricts the wide distribution of multimedia documents. More and more companies are increasing bandwidth by installing fibre optic wiring, or connecting to commercial broadband networks. Wireless networks are beginning to crowd fibre optics as the communications mechanism of choice, given their inherent portability and unobtrusiveness. Wireless networks based on cellular and radio dispatch frequencies are now in limited operation.

An alternative method for distributing data and documents relies on the high capacity and high reliability of optical disks. New storage options that can store video, audio, graphics and full-motion video on a single optical disk are burgeoning in the marketplace. The technologies include the market leader, CD/ROM (compact disk read-only memory), WORM (Write Once Read Many), and laser discs, all of which enable large amounts of information to be stored relatively cheaply. CD/ROMs that can be written to are beginning to appear, and their superiority to WORM disks will soon lead to WORM's demise. Laser discs do not have the portability or immense published base as CD/ROMs.

CD jukeboxes residing on a C/S network increase the amount of data that can be stored and retrieved efficiently and with high reliability. Jukeboxes can contain up to 500 disks accessible by one or more drives for reading the data. Retrieval of data is slowed by the need to share the drives. Several vendors include recordable drives with their jukeboxes, including Pioneer New Media Technologies, which sells a 500-unit recording jukebox that can write up to 2,400 bytes of data per second. An alternative technology, the CD tower, stores up to seven disks, but each has a separate drive, giving multiple users fast access to stored documents.

These technologies store and access high volumes of data, but at a slower rate than magnetic disk technology. Few of them can be rewritten or changed after data are initially placed on them, so that historic and reference data are better suited for their use than data that change frequently. The low cost of reproducing large quantities of CDs promotes regular or frequent updates of data that do not need to reflect real-time changes.

Real-time stock market quotations, for example, are still better suited to magnetic disk or remote access. Now, recent advances in circuit board technology and compression standards permit compression of digitized images, including video, enabling them to be stored and updated quickly on a hard disk. This technology has the potential for supporting real-time updating and access needs.

A DDSS must integrate a variety of storage and processing technologies to provide a complete range of document retrieval. Magnetic disks or newer content addressable storage mechanisms, whether at a workstation or on a server, should be used for time-sensitive corporate data. On-line database services can be tied in to gather timely external information. Graphics, audio, and video images can be linked to more conventional relational or object-oriented databases. CDs can be used for historical records, including minutes of meetings, digitized voice, videotapes of teleconferences, copies of memos, external databases and search algorithms, and other documents that a decision maker might normally retain.

Imaging technology, initially marketed in the desktop publishing arena, enables the DDSS user to incorporate legacy pictorial or textual documents. Image scanners can copy any image into the PC. An appealing aspect of some of these scanners is that they will input a textual document in a format manipulable by word processing software, and pictorial images in digitized form that can be linked to the text component of a document. The document can then be indexed for ease of retrieval. Thus, any printed document can be included in the DDSS almost as if it had been input by hand. Although few products exhibit error-free scanning quality today, advances in intelligent character recognition (ICR) can provide automatic indexing to make this an imperative component of a "paperless" environment.

These storage and input technologies, in conjunction with powerful workstation processing and telecommunications, are vital components for DDSS. They provide the ease of use, flexibility, and speed of access that decision makers demand. The next sections will present an overview of the software advances that will make the system feasible.

ELECTRONIC MAIL

In order for documents to be disseminated and shared in a timely manner, a DDSS must include a suitable communications component. It is not enough, however, to tie decision makers to a central server or to put them on an electronic mail network. The shear amount of information content in organizational documents will require the DDSS to sort and route documents to those who need them, and also prevent them from burdening those who do not.

Electronic mail provides a medium for sending mail messages privately over a local area network, or worldwide using a public-access network such as the Internet. Over 20,000 companies are currently registered on the Internet, up from only 93 in 1990. The number of individual Internet users is sometimes estimated in the 2 to 3 million range, or even as high as 20 to 30 million.

Many companies rely on internal e-mail systems, with many turning to the mainframe IBM offering, PROFS, Hewlett Packard's OpenMail, or PC products such as Lotus' cc:Mail, Microsoft Mail, Novell Groupware, and Banyan's BeyondMail. Lotus Notes is also frequently used for e-mail, although it is actually a groupware product capable of attaching documents to messages.

These systems do not typically permit receivers of mail to sort messages based on the meaning of their contents prior to reading them. A number of development projects are currently under way to augment these systems with the capability of filtering messages based on their content or header information. BeyondMail offers filtering capabilities based on criteria such as the sender's identity, or message topic. These features will make sharing documents through some type of e-mail system a viable alternative for enterprise-wide computing.

Systems incorporating filters and intelligent agents demonstrate the application of AI techniques as a way of providing a meaningful interpretation of document contents in a DDSS. The filtering techniques can be adapted to other types of documents as well, and extended to applications not normally found in the electronic mail area. Agents and filters can be viewed as a type of personal search profile, or at least as a part of a more generic profile.

ON-LINE DATABASES

Competitive analysis through environmental scanning has become an essential element in the strategy of today's organizations (Weston, 1991). These are formal methods of monitoring the competitive environment to assess an organization's posture in the marketplace. One way to obtain this intelligence is by searching the data available on external databases. These are a key source of external information favored by managers and executives.

Companies are retrieving more and more information from databases such as Bloomberg, Dow Jones News Retrieval, Compuserve, Dialog Information Service, and Mead Data Central. For individuals, Compuserve, America Online, and Prodigy have brought cheap and easy database access onto the PC.

The increased reliance on external market indicators and improved sources of information have dramatically boosted the demand for on-line database services. One source estimates that there are over 7,000 online databases available worldwide (Reed, 1989). Another survey identified 5,183 on-line databases in 1993, with 490 of them listed for the first time (Hawkins, 1993).

Typically, users of these systems had been trained librarians who provide a service within their company, or PC users, who tie in to general purpose databases. Most of the time, the results of the search are hard copy reports of bibliographic, financial, or other stored information. Many DSS, groupware, and Executive Information Systems provide links to external data bases and display the results of prespecified searches on the screen.

Databases are rarely distributed through only a single, on-line channel. They can also be leased, downloaded, printed, or purchased on CD/ROM. The increasing number of CD/ROM installations has constituted the low-cost alternative for accessing these data bases. A 1994 survey of database title listings showed over 8,000 CD/ROM titles available, far exceeding the current number of on-line databases. The relatively low price and easy accessibility of this option appears to compensate for the fact that many of these are updated infrequently. This media also permits the storage and rapid retrieval of multimedia documents.

The mechanisms for searching textual databases have improved over time. Techniques for information retrieval are the subjects of the next sections.

INFORMATION RETRIEVAL

Document bases have their roots in the field of bibliographic information retrieval. Bibliographic searching to produce lists of citations and abstracts based on keyword selection has been successfully applied to large indexed files for over 25 years. These mechanisms provide the sorting and searching techniques used in querying large, external databases.

Commonly in information retrieval, keywords are linked by Boolean operators (e.g., AND, OR, NOT) to detect the documents that best match the characterization specified by the searcher. These services had been the domain of librarians, as they have been used predominantly as a research support mechanism for academics, corporate researchers, and practitioners who want to be apprised of new developments in their field. Now, home computer users of on-line services can perform searches from home. These techniques are also finding their way into many integrated business intelligence applications.

Bibliographic retrieval comprises a number of issues related to document management, including effective and efficient index term assignment, keyword search schemes, free text search algorithms, inverted file design, specification of adjacency conditions for free text terms, and the use of truncation and synonyms to improve the efficiency of retrieval (Salton, 1986). Improvements in retrieval effectiveness have been attained through the application of probabilistic indexing (Kwok, 1985), clustering of documents (van Rijsbergen, 1979), non-Boolean tree configurations of keywords (Appleton, 1992), signature files (Zezula et al., 1991) and cognitive modeling of users. Cognitive models are a user profiling technique that may simplify the interaction of individuals with DDSS.

Cognitive modeling has been incorporated into a number of expert systems that adapt knowledge about a user into a personalized retrieval tool. Models can be explicit, demanding answers to a list of questions by the user before the retrieval process can begin. Alternatively, implicit user modeling is based on the answers to a few preliminary questions, after which the system reverts to knowledge about stereotypical users. User models, in any case, will need to encompass static models reflecting permanent information about the user, and dynamic models, which depend on the particular interaction with the system.

Additionally, AI techniques have been advanced as a way to increase the effectiveness of the retrieval process. For example, fuzzy set theory has been applied to documents to represent the extent that a document is "about" an index term (Buell, 1985). Other expert systems have also been developed to provide intelligent interfaces for document retrieval systems.

Other systems combine hypertext with an expert system to monitor results from a traditional user query of a data base of citations, and help the user to broaden or narrow the search. To expand a query that is too narrow, a natural language component aids in suggesting additional keywords or classifications. An overly broad search is reduced in scope by using various classifications or subdivisions of subfields (Micco, 1991).

Advances in information retrieval will prove invaluable for DDSS search activities. Frustration with current DDSS centers on the difficulty of identifying relevant documents (Appleton, 1992). A DDSS will probably consist of large-scale collections of bibliographic, encyclopedic, reference, historical, informal notes or other types of text, image, and audio documents. Combined, these would be available in on-line and CD/ROM databases. For example, current financial data, interoffice memos, and newspaper clippings could be retrieved using artificially intelligent keyword profiles and user models. Multimedia documents would require the more sophisticated indexing of signature files.

If user profiles were sufficiently sophisticated, passive retrieval activities employing intelligent agents could be incorporated to provide environmental scanning facilities for executives. New concerns could be added or modified from existing profiles when new opportunities or problems arise, making this an active support tool as well. Simple versions of this type of facility are available in several commercial systems.

HYPERMEDIA

Recent advances in hypertext and multimedia have combined to make DDSS a commercially viable opportunity. Multimedia employs imaging, digital, and audio technology to store and retrieve graphics, photography, full-motion video, sound, and animation along with more traditional text and data. Standards for data compression have been adopted in these areas to promote the interchange of data among different commercial products, and to reduce the storage demands of these media.

Hypertext is the web that connects these disparate documents together in a way that imitates human cognitive maps. Hypertext links together various computer documents based on user-specified associations. Thus, a spreadsheet pertaining to an e-mailed report could be linked together by associative labeling, so that one could easily recall one when referring to the other. Graphs and drawings on the same subject could also be tied in, in line with the user's thought processes. The ability to associate different types of documents in a free-form manner provides the flexibility many decision makers need for ad hoc information retrieval.

Hypermedia results from coupling hypertext with multimedia. Multimedia computing allows for efficient collection and distribution of organizational documents of all types. Without a governing mechanism such as hypertext, these documents are jointly retrievable only after time-consuming indexing and keyword assignment activity. Document management systems employing SGML standards (to be discussed in a later section) provide the mechanism to make documents internally searchable. Hypertext gives them the ability to link across otherwise disparate documents.

More sophisticated retrieval techniques (as outlined earlier), coupled with the flexibility of hypertext links, will lead to increased growth in the multimedia market. The installed base of multimedia systems on business personal computers has grown rapidly, from 800,000 in 1991 to 7,500,000 in 1995. One estimate has it that one in every five newly purchased computers now contains a CD/ROM drive.

Hypermedia has become deeply embedded in many CD/ROM products, such as encyclopedias, interactive games, and commercial databases. It is also essential for connecting on-line wide-area network links, such as those provided by the World Wide Web or Compuserve. Although it is rarely advertised as an independent software product, it is an enabling technology for many of today's document-based products. Hypermedia is thus the preeminent technique for integrating assorted documents in a way that will make them accessible to, and therefore usable by, decision makers in organizations. The ability to annotate and transport these documents provides the expanded capabilities needed by executives and other decision makers who feel limited by current data base support. Hypermedia also augments traditional methods of communication in the organization, by allowing individuals to append notes to formal reports, audio messages to written documents, or pictures to text. Video clips will give a better sense of product dynamics than any spreadsheet ever will. In short, the ability to cut, paste, and link up a variety of source documents will make computer-supported analysis and communication an organizational imperative. See page 196 for more on hypermedia documents and the Web.

GROUPWARE

Groupware products are designed for collaborative work, and include a wide range of technologies to support various groupwork functions, many of which are not pertinent to a discussion of documents. Groupware products focused on enhancing the conduct of meetings do not provide any unique capabilities germain to a document management system. However, two successful products, Lotus Notes and Collabra Share, promote group collaboration based on the concept of shared documents. Notes enjoys a big lead in this market, although Collabra's aggressive pricing policy and links to other systems are gaining market share for them.

In these systems, versions of documents are maintained, indexed, and linked together to form new documents, which can then be shared with others. They employ form templates, but can also access documents from word processors, spreadsheets or relational databases. E-mail is a crucial component of the shared environment. The main drawback for these products is the lack of control over the collection of documents, which also adds to its attraction as a flexible system.

A DDSS will need to provide somewhat more control than the current groupware offerings. If DDSS will truly incorporate extensive internal and external documents with the ability to share among internal and external users, at least some part of the document base will require a searchable structure that can scale up to the requirements of an enterprise repository without demanding excessive computer resources. One emerging option is document management systems, which may provide the solution to the problems of storing and accessing documents more efficiently.

DOCUMENT MANAGEMENT SYSTEMS

Several commercial database vendors now provide capabilities for storing and retrieving documents, and some can also handle images and voice. These multimedia databases are typically upgraded versions of relational databases. One of the earliest competitors in this arena was Empress Software, which combined multimedia, relational, and object-oriented database management capabilities in a distributed environment.

Many other existing relational database or document processing products now incorporate document retrieval mechanisms. Among these are Rdb from

Digital Equipment Corporation, Informix from Informix Software, Hewlett Packard's NewWave Office software, NCR's Cooperation office automation system, IBM's Office Vision, SQL Text from Oracle, and Lotus Notes. These systems treat documents as blobs or objects that can be retrieved in their entirety based on stored keywords or descriptors.

The "object-oriented relational data base management system" is a very popular vehicle for storing documents, as a field in such a system could contain a document object of any size. It has become a premier storage technique for documents, both because of its leading market share for other data warehousing activity, and for the relative ease with which legacy documents (created by word processing, scanning or any other source) can be incorporated for widespread access. A major drawback to this strategy is that the document object must be accessed in its entirety, as there are no sophisticated retrieval techniques available to select only the relevant parts of such a document. Thus, these products are better suited for storing and retrieving smaller documents, such as memos, or accessing complete reports than for searching large manuals for a relevant passage.

Interleaf sells the Relational Document Manager (RDM), which is a general purpose object server that runs on top of commercial relational databases. It operates like a library, employing a "card catalog" to monitor which documents are checked out. One client, Barclays Law Publishers, uses RDM to produce personalized weekly legal newsletters for thousands of individual customers (Walter, 1994). Other products that search attributes about the document without exploring the contents are PCDocs by SoftSolutions, Mezzanine by Saros, and Documentum.

A long-overlooked vendor community has begun to gain visibility as hardware advances begin to make content-searchable large, multimedia documents a viable option. What had long been considered "information retrieval" products have been reborn as Document Management Systems, gaining additional functionality. One advancement that has aided in the growth of this market has been careful adherence to a standard for document definition and access mechanism called SGML (Standard General Markup Language). SGML provides a hierarchical structure for storing and retrieving documents, and for producing a dynamic table of contents tailored to the user's current search goals. Hypertext links can be used to tie in figures, tables, footnotes, animation sequences, sound, and video. These products are an important first step toward comprehensive DDSS.

A common method of providing this increased functionality is to incorporate sophisticated search capabilities into existing products that themselves have been extended to include multimedia documents. Leading competitors in the area of full text search and retrieval software are TOPIC by Verity Inc. and Ful/Text by Fulcrum Technologies. TOPIC provides object-oriented, "concept-based" searches, ranked by relevance to a search. It incorporates hypertext links to multimedia documents. User profiles filter and distribute feeds from on-line database services. Other products are considered to be content browsers, giving an information module view of the document, including EBT's Dynatext Browser, Oracle Book, HTML viewers for the World Wide Web, and Hal Orias Browser.

Dynatext by Electronic Book Technologies can be searched using full text, Boolean, proximity, wildcard, and SGML structure-aware searching techniques. It also allows for the use of bookmarks and electronic sticky notes for user notation. The product is designed for documents requiring tens of thousands of pages. DynaWeb, another EBT product, supports the HTML standard representation favored by the World Wide Web, thus facilitating this electronic bookserver over a wide-area network.

A fully functional DDSS must allow for multiple types of documents to be represented. Linkages should be made among relevant objects or documents, so that associative browsing among documents and document types is supported. As in Lotus Notes and Collabra Share, new documents can be constructed from bits and pieces of existing documents, permitting generation of multi-formatted output. They will likely incorporate artificial intelligence to carry out these complex activities. AI can govern the storage and retrieval patterns of the document-based systems.

They will also need to accommodate distributed data in a client-server or wide-area network. Most of today's DMS rely on a centralized database for routing, document updates, and control of the links between the document components.

Because of the huge number of legacy documents in today's corporations, a move to truly manipulable documents will be expensive and time consuming. A combination of methods may be called for, with static paper documents being scanned into the system as non-manipulable objects, and dynamic documents, or those expected to change, being converted to SGML representation. The difference in cost is significant, with estimates of scanning costing from $.50 to $1.00 per page, compared to an average of $5.00 per converted SGML page.

The role of document management systems in DDSS is obvious. The ability to integrate and link multimedia documents is vital to the success of a DDSS. These technological advancements demonstrate the intricacies and magnitude of a DDSS project. These systems permit the active access and reconstruction of many types of documents. In combination with advanced information retrieval profiling mechanisms that promote system-generated associations within and between documents, the document-based system will become the basis of a valuable decision support tool. The addition of analytical capabilities, communications, and group support mechanisms would expand their usefulness beyond the "office system" world, to supporting higher-level decision makers and teams.

CONCLUDING REMARKS

Where do we go from here? It is apparent that commercial efforts to produce a document based management system are well under way, and that a document-based decision support environment is not far behind. Over half of the Fortune 1000 companies surveyed in 1992 already have some form of DMS (Frappaolo,

1992). Many of these are Lotus Notes installations, which do promote the sharing and communication of internal documents, although so far they are frequently used primarily for enhanced e-mail.

The hardware technology, long a stumbling block for large document bases needing fast retrieval time, has progressed to a point where workstation and storage systems are inexpensively available, and are linked together in client/server configurations. Information retrieval techniques have advanced as well, with sophisticated search algorithms and expert system components providing efficient and effective searching. Electronic mail and hypermedia systems provide the technological foundations for augmenting passive retrieval techniques.

The missing element in successfully deploying DDSS is not the technology. It is the knowledge of how to effectively employ the technology in such a way that managerial decision makers will want to benefit from it. The U.S. paper industry is shipping 51 percent more office paper in 1994 than in 1993. It is clear that the elusive paperless office has not yet arrived, and is moving away from our grasp at an alarming rate!

Further study is needed to ascertain whether managers have not used available technology because it has been cumbersome and inappropriate to their needs, or if the inherent "impersonal-ness" of an information system as a source of information will persist as a deterrent to its use (Trevino et al., 1987). Only after determining its potential usefulness and, ultimately, its role in the decision-making process, will a DDSS become successful.

QUESTIONS

1. Why is it so important to develop document-based DSS?
2. What are the advances in basic technologies that are making it more feasible to include documents in DSS? Explain why each advance is valuable.
3. Identify and describe the software advances that are making DDSS more feasible. For each, explain why it is so important.

REFERENCES

Information Sources

FEDOROWICZ, JANE, "The Future of Decision Support: An Examination of Managers' Decision Making Needs," in *Proceedings of the Twenty-second Annual Hawaii International Conference on Systems Sciences,* Kona, Hawaii, January 1989, Vol. IV, pp. 167–174.

MEALL, LESLEY and ASHLEY PRICE, "Conquering the Paper Mountain," *Accountancy,* November, 1993, pp. 65–67.

MYERS-TIERNY, LINDA, "An Introduction to Text Management," *Office Computing Report,* Vol. 14, No. 10.

TREVINO, LINDA KLEBE, ROBERT LENGEL, and RICHARD L. DAFT, "Media Symbolism, Media Richness, and Media Choice in Organizations: A Symbolic Interactionist Perspective," *Communication Research*, Vol. 14, No. 5, October 1987.

WALLACE, S., "Desktop Spectaculars," *CIO Magazine*, October 1990, pp. 114–120.

Hardware

Business Week, "The Keys to the Future," Special Issue, *The Information Revolution*, July 1994.

PAUL, LAUREN GIBBONS, "Jukeboxes Can Harmonize Storage in Net Environment," *PC Week*, Dec. 26, 1994/Jan. 2, 1995, pp. 83–85.

WETMORE, TIM, "The Multimedia Challenge," *Information Week*, January 13, 1992, pp. 22–30.

On-line Databases

HAWKINS, DONALD T., "Growth Trends in the Electronic Services Market: Part 2: Technotrends," *Online*, September 1993, Vol. 17, No. 5, p. 105.

REED, NICHOLAS, "On-line Databases: Can They Help Your Business?," *Australian Accountant*, Vol. 59, No. 8, Sept. 1989, pp. 70–72.

WESTON, DIANE MCGINTY, *Best Practices in Competitive Analysis*, SRI International, Spring, 1991.

Information Retrieval

APPLETON, ELAINE L., "Smart Document Retrieval," *Datamation*, Vol. 38, No. 2, January 15, 1992, pp. 20–23.

BUELL, DUNCAN A., "A Problem in Information Retrieval With Fuzzy Sets," *Journal of the American Society for Information Science*, Vol. 36, No. 6, November 1985, pp. 398–401.

KWOK, K.L., "A Probabilistic Theory of Indexing and Similarity Measure Based on Cited and Citing Documents," *Journal of the American Society for Information Science*, Vol. 36, No. 5, September 1985, pp. 342–351.

MICCO, MARY, "The Next Generation of Subject Access Systems: Hypermedia for Improved Access," *Information Today*, Vol. 8, No. 7, Jul./Aug. 1991, p. 36.

SALTON, G., "Another Look at Automatic Text-Retrieval Systems," *Communications of the ACM*, Vol. 29, No. 7, July 1986, pp. 648–656.

VAN RIJSBERGEN, C. J., *Information Retrieval*, second edition, London: Buttersworth Publishers, 1979.

ZEZULA, P., F. RABITTI, and P. TIBERIO, "Dynamic Partitioning of Signature Files," *ACM Transactions on Information Systems*, Vol. 9, No. 4, October 1991, pp. 336–369.

Document-Based Systems

Electronic Book Technologies, Product literature, 1994.

FRAPPAOLO, CARL, "The Promise of Electronic Document Management," *Modern Office Technology*, October 1992, pp. 58–66.

WALTER, MARK, "Interleaf's Relational Document Manager: Ready to Stand on Its Own," *Seybold Report on Publishing Systems*, Vol. 23, No. 13, March 14, 1994, pp. 3–23.

13

INTELLIGENT SUPPORT SYSTEMS

INTRODUCTION

We're all familiar with the current business context. Virtually all enterprises face increasing global competition. This competition puts tremendous pressures on enterprises in every industry to substantially reduce their product cycle times, increase their product quality, and respond to the varied requests of individual customers. To handle this competition and the concomitant pressures, enterprises are reorganizing both their structures and operating processes. Rightsized, horizontal, team-based, learning-based, seamless, networked, virtual, and re-engineered are some of the terms used to describe the organizational changes taking place. Regardless of the term, the basic ideas are the same. Enterprises are becoming smaller, flatter, and more decentralized in order to reduce coordination costs, to improve communication flow, and to move decision making out to the edges of the business in order to quicken responses to a rapidly changing environment.

To support or stimulate these new, globally distributed organizational forms and processes, enterprises are rebuilding their information infrastructures. In the past 15 years we have witnessed a rapid shift from "host" to "desktop" to "client/server" computing. Now, we're in the midst of a move to "network" and "mobile" computing. Part of the goal is to provide individuals and teams with access to data, information and knowledge at any time and any place.

For executives, managers, analysts and other knowledge workers in the enterprise, the shift toward network computing is proving to be a mixed blessing. In the

This chapter was written specifically for this book by David King, Senior Research Fellow, Comshare, Inc.

words of Paul Saffo [1], a Director at the Institute for the Future, networked computing has brought us only "half the information revolution—access and volume." This means that knowledge workers are facing a qualitative jump in both the quantity and complexity of data needed to run the enterprise, while simultaneously experiencing a reduction in the amount of time they have to analyze, understand, interpret, and act on these data. Since the mid-80s, many of these knowledge workers have relied on executive information systems (EIS) to deliver management data and information in a highly reduced form that can be easily investigated in a point and click fashion. The systems have permeated the enterprise to such an extent that "EIS" has come to stand for "everyones' information system" or "enterprise intelligence system." No matter what the interpretation, the increasing volume and diversity of data and information available means that even with EIS, there may be too much data reaching the desktop, the data may not be processed into meaningful information, and there may be no time to navigate all the data sources each time they're updated in search of problems and opportunities.

What remains for the knowledge workers of the enterprise is the "other half of the revolution—reducing the flood (of data) to a meaningful trickle." For years experts have predicted that "software agents" will be at the core of this data reduction. Software agents have also been called software robots, knowbots, mediators, cyberservants, digital butlers, and intelligent assistants just to name a few. In the business world, the word "agent" has been applied to everything from a simple stored software procedure that backs up a hard disk at night to a system that, once informed of a staff member's intention to make a business trip, secures the necessary plane, hotel, and car reservations, keeps an eye on the weather forecast at the destination, and prepares a summary of existing corporate knowledge about customers to be visited on the trip [2].

Somewhere between the extremes of an automated procedure and an all encompassing intelligence are software processes that can routinely and automatically seek out and filter data according to user defined rules and proactively deliver this data in a packaged format to the desktops of interested users. These "software filtering" or "watcher" agents are being applied in a variety of managerial applications. It is this type of agent that will be the focus of this chapter. In particular this chapter will explore the general concept behind software filtering agents and examine the use of these agents in a series of managerial support applications.

INFORMATION OVERLOAD

Today, most EIS provide a "point and click," graphical front end to summary level numerical data aimed at discovering, locating, or monitoring trends or deviations from the plan. The data are usually presented in a multi-dimensional, hierarchical format so that users can examine the data from several perspectives (comparing products, locations, periods, and the like) and at different levels of detail (consolidated, country, region, state, territory, branch, etc.). A well-designed EIS makes it easy for users to sort the data, perform additional calculations, rotate they data to compare different factors, and drill up and down levels of the data hierarchy searching for various problems and opportunities.

Because the data in an EIS mirrors the enterprise, it's easy to see why the volume and complexity of data in a global company has the potential to overwhelm the users of an EIS. In the past, the data were often focused on a few levels of consolidation for a small set of dimensions and reported quarterly and monthly. The numbers of interest ranged in the thousands. As enterprises have becomes more complex, so have the data requirements for their EIS. Now, the drive is toward increasing levels of detail and real-time analysis.

Frito Lay is a well-known example. "Updated daily on handheld terminals by 10,000 Frito-Lay salespeople, information on 100 Frito Lay product lines in 400,000 stores appears on company computer screens in easy-to-read charts." [3] A little mathematics shows that this presentation compresses 400 billion numbers. And that's only one day! What if they make comparisons between the actual numbers and their plans? That's at least 800 billion numbers. Or, what about a trend analysis from one week to the next? It's easy to get the picture.

Mervyns, a retailer of moderate-priced clothing and home fashions, is another example [4]. Their system is designed to keep inventory managers and buyers appraised of the units sold and sales prices for some 300,000 stock items in 286 stores throughout the southern and western United States and to perform trend analysis across a minimum 60-week time period. Their decision support database, which originates from 270 point of entry systems (POS) and is uploaded daily to a centralized location, occupies several hundred gigabytes of disk space. Again, the potential number of comparisons runs in the billions of numbers.

But there's more to the operation of an enterprise than just the numbers. Recall that return on investment (ROI) has a numerator—net income—and a denominator—investment, net assets, or capital employed. As Hamel and Prahalad [5] note, managers have long focused on management of the denominator. Under intense pressure from global competition, the quickest way to improve performance is to cut the denominator. This is done primarily through downsizing, decluttering, delayering, divesting, and other forms of expense control. Where do we find information about the denominator? It often comes from internal numerical data that is readily available. This is why most EIS take a numerical slant.

What about the numerator? How do we grow net income? Again, as Hamel and Prahalad suggest,

> Managers . . . know that raising net income is likely to be a harder slog than cutting assets and headcount. To grow the numerator, top management must have a point of view about where the new opportunities lie, must be able to anticipate changing customer needs, must have invested preemptively in building new competencies, and so on.

Mintzberg [6] was one of the first management scientists to point out that for a variety of reasons hard data is not likely to tell the enterprise how to "grow the numerator." Instead, the answer often comes from staying abreast of "soft" or "qualitative" data originating from inside and outside the enterprise—like rumors, speculation, field intelligence, press releases, market research, industry publications, and government pronouncements. A case in point is the story behind Vistakon, Inc.'s purchase of the rights to the technology underlying their Acuvue disposable lenses [7]. Vistakon is a subsidiary of Johnson & Johnson that specializes in contact lenses. In 1983 the President of Vistakon received a tip from an employee working out of Belgium about a Copenhagen opthamologist who had conceived of a method for manufacturing disposable lens. If Vistakon had relied solely on the numbers, they would have probably dismissed the idea. Instead, they acted quickly, obtained the rights, and brought their Acuvue product quickly to market. The move caught their competitors off guard. In four years Vistakon went from a $20 million to a $225 million company and captured 25 percent of the disposable lens market. The moral of the story is not that one form of information—hard or soft—is preferable. Instead, full-equation management requires ready access to both.

In the past most of this soft data was handled in a fairly informal and haphazard fashion with much of the data being passed face-to-face or over the phone. Recognizing the growing import of this kind of information, many enterprises are beginning to treat qualitative data in the same systematic manner that they treat their numbers. In part this explains the exploding use of mail-enabled applications, groupware applications, on-line services like Compuserve, and global networks like the Internet by executives, managers, and knowledge workers.

This explosion in the use of soft data has exacerbated the problem of information overload. Companies like Verifone and Sun Microsystems report that employees receive on the average over 100 e-mail messages a day [8]. For Sun, that's a million and a quarter messages a day. You've probably read about the astonishing growth experienced over the past few years in the Internet [9]. There are over 35,000 networks on the Internet. A new network is added every 10–30 minutes. The Internet also has over 3 million host computers connected through these networks. Hosts are added at the rate of over 1000 per day. The amount of data traffic on the Internet grows at over 200 percent per year.

While there is no valid way to quantify the impacts of information overload on an enterprise, the Gartner Group [10], a well-known market research firm, has at least attempted to place the resulting issues in perspective. According to Gartner Group estimates:

- The amount of data collected by large enterprises doubles every year.
- Knowledge workers can analyze only about 5% of this data.
- Most of their efforts are spent in trying to discover important patterns in the data (60% or more), a much smaller percentage is spent determining what those patterns mean (20% or more), and very little time is spent (10% or less) actually doing something about the patterns.
- Information overload reduces our decision-making capabilities by 50%.

Whether their figures are correct is unimportant. What is important is the general pattern. With current systems there is virtually no way for executives, managers, and knowledge workers to navigate through and discover the problems and opportunities buried within those billions of numbers and words, especially when the volume is growing exponentially and product and decision cycles are rapidly shrinking toward real time.

Saffo was right. Our EIS and other managerial support systems have succeeded in bringing the "first half of the information revolution"—volume and access—to the desktops of executives, managers, and other knowledge workers in the enterprise. What's missing is the second half—reducing the flood (of data) to a meaningful trickle.

SOFTWARE AGENTS

Alan Kay, a senior research fellow at Apple Computer, who is acknowledged as the father of notebook computing and one of the originators of object-oriented programming, has long argued that the solution to information overload will not be found in the current generation of "point and click" graphical user interfaces, no matter how elegant. As he puts it [11],

> . . . the icon-and-mouse based interfaces are good for a few hundred objects. Now imagine a trillion objects. At some point the whole metaphor breaks down, just as it does when you go into the Library of Congress and the card catalog is larger than your whole hometown library. Most of us believe that when you're dealing with that many resources, any hand-tool metaphor [like the mouse] is not going to work. So you're going to require something that's like the people in the Library of Congress who try to find out what your [research] goals are, and then can work on your behalf even when you're working on other things.

More recently, Nicholas Negroponte, the Director of MIT's Media Lab, expressed the same idea this way [12]:

> Future human-computer interface will be rooted in delegation, not the vernacular of direct manipulation—pull down, pop up, click—and mouse interfaces. "Ease of use" has been such a compelling goal that we sometimes forget that many people don't want to use the machine at all. They want to get something done.
>
> What we today call "agent-based interfaces" will emerge as the dominant means by which computers and people will talk with one another.

The electronic equivalent of Kay's research librarian is known by a number of names. In this chapter we will stick with the term "software agent."

The concept of software agency is an old one. Some trace its origins to Vannevar Bush's 1945 vision of a machine called the memex that enabled users to navigate through oceans of information [1]. Others see signs of the concept in John McCarthy's Advice Taker, an idea he introduced in the later 1950s ([11],[13]). What McCarthy envisioned was a "soft robot" living and working in a computer network of information utilities (much like today's Internet). When given a goal, the soft robot could perform appropriate actions and ask for and receive advice from the user when it reaches a dead-end. Of the two, McCarthy's Advice Taker is what most researchers and practitioners have in mind when they use the term.

While the concept is an old one, there is still no agreed upon definition [14]. Even without consensus, there is some commonality among the various renditions. Most agree that a software agent is a computer program that [15]:

- *Operates in the background*—An agent is a program to which a users assigns a task. The whole idea is that once a task has been delegated, it's up to the agent to work in the background until the task is complete. We label this attribute "set and forget."
- *Supports conditional processing*—Most agents utilize rule-based, pattern-matching logic to make decisions in the face of changing contexts. The types of rules are similar to those employed in rule-based expert systems. The rules that an agent uses are typically supplied by the end user.
- *Focuses on a single set of tasks*—Even though agents utilize pattern-matching logic, they're less ambitious than their expert system counterparts. An agent typically focuses on a single task such as filtering e-mail. When a task becomes more complex, the "intelligence" of the agent is not increased. Instead, the task is broken into smaller subsets which are distributed among a group of agents who coordinate their efforts by communicating with one another. Substantial work has been done on the languages used for agent communication.
- *Automates repetitive tasks*—Much of the work done by agents does not require sophisticated logic. Instead, the work often involves simple repetitive tasks that could be performed by a person, if that person had the time or inclination to do so. Even if a person had time, there is no assurance that the person could perform it with the same accuracy as the agent, no matter how weak the agent's intelligence. If you were asked to check by hand the numbers in a million-cell spreadsheet to determine which were greater than 5, you could certainly do so, although the speed and accuracy with which you performed the task are likely to suffer in comparison to an agent. Now, what if you were asked to read 1000 business articles looking for the name of a particular company (say Johnson & Johnson). Because of the different ways that a company can be referenced—in this case it might be J&J or possibly a reference to one

of its products like Acuvue rather than to the company name—a person could probably do a more accurate job than an agent. But, is it worth your time, especially when an agent might do it with 90% accuracy?

If a "batch program" has conditional logic and is run at scheduled intervals, does it qualify as a software agent? The answer is possibly. If the program runs in the background in a multi-tasking operating environment, then it possesses the minimal set of attributes. While most purists would answer "no," it is good to remember that many applications and programs that are labeled "agent-based" aren't much smarter than this batch program.

Agents are called "intelligent" if they have the capacity to learn [15]. At present, few commercially available agents possess learning capabilities. There are, however, research prototypes. For example, Pattie Maes and other researchers at MIT's Media Lab [16] have created a variety of "advisory" agents that learn from their users' habits, interests, and behaviors. We will discuss some of this work in later sections. Although "intelligent" agents have garnered a great deal of attention, critics argue that most people don't want "smart" agents watching over their shoulders [14]. They contend that agents built with rule-based or script-based languages provide enough utility for the average user.

Within the world of executive and management support, there are a variety of applications where agents have been and will be employed. Most of these applications are of the "non-intelligent" variety and rest on a common foundation where

- The focus is typically on monitoring, filtering, and summarizing large or frequently changing data sets and automatically distributing or broadcasting the results to end users
- The applications are architected from a series of cooperative processes of which the agent is only one.
- The primary function of the agent is to provide background intelligence and to pass the results of its pattern matching efforts on to other processes.
- The agents derive their "intelligence" from a relatively small set of expert-system like "if/then/else" rules.

In these business applications a common definition arises. Here, a software agent is defined as a background process that utilizes a set of detection rules to automatically and routinely monitor a data set—either hard or soft—for patterns defined by those rules and to inform interested users when the patterns arise. Agents of this sort have also been called "software filtering" agents or "watcher" agents [17]. The basic components of this type of agent are depicted in Figure 13–1 where the agent is represented by the robot figure.

The definition says nothing about how these software filtering or watcher agents are implemented. In most cases a "client/server" or "messaging middle-

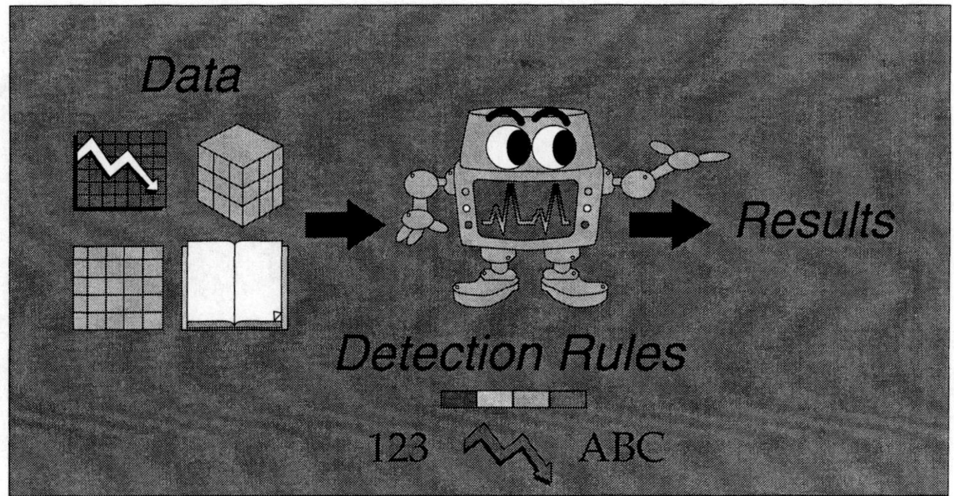

FIGURE 13–1 Software Filtering Agent

ware" architecture is employed [15]. In the client/server architecture the rules are created with a client application and stored in such a way that they can be accessed by the agent running on a server machine. The agent is set up to routinely evaluate the rules against a data set at scheduled intervals and to return its results to the same or a different client. In some cases, the connection to the agent on the server machine is established via e-mail. In this case, the rule is dropped in the e-mail by the client application and the agent retrieves it for later evaluation. After the evaluation has been performed, the results are sent back through e-mail where they are retrieved by the client. Software agents architectured as client/server applications are sometimes called "non-mobile" [18] because the agent remains stationary on the server. Figure 13–2 displays the elements of a c/s architecture.

There is another architecture for implementing agent-based applications. It is called remote programming [19]. A diagram of this architecture is shown in Figure 13–3. Under this approach, one computer sends a message containing both data and procedures to a receiving computer which executes those procedures. This is the basic idea underlying General Magic's Telescript technology, which runs on personal digital assistants (PDAs) and the AT&T PersonalLink network and can be summarized by the statement, "Agents go to places." Here, you can think of an agent as a "beneficial" computer virus. Agents based on the remote programming environment have also been implemented under Unix utilizing interpreted languages Tcl and Safe Tcl [20]. Because of the prevelance of Microsoft Windows on enterprise desktops and the general lack of support for remote programming under this operating environment, virtually none of the current executive or managerial applications are implemented with this architec-

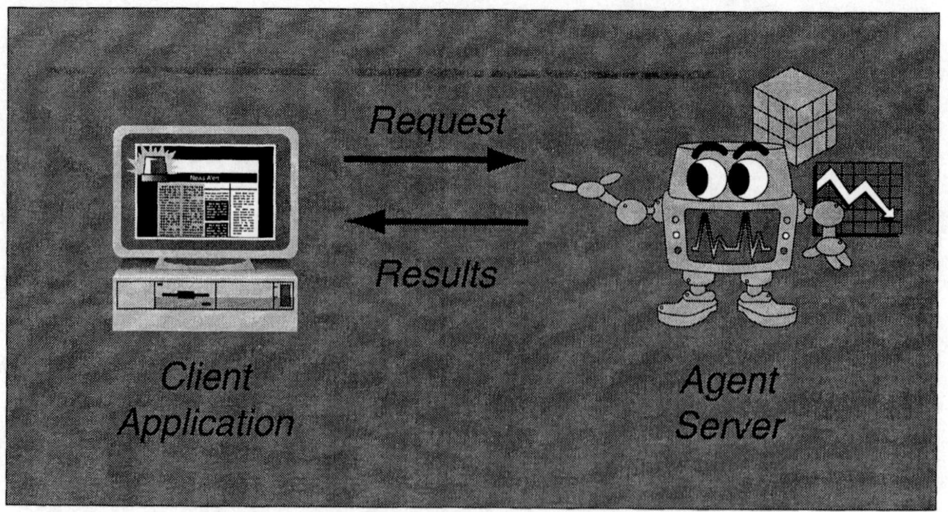

FIGURE 13–2 Client/Server Agent

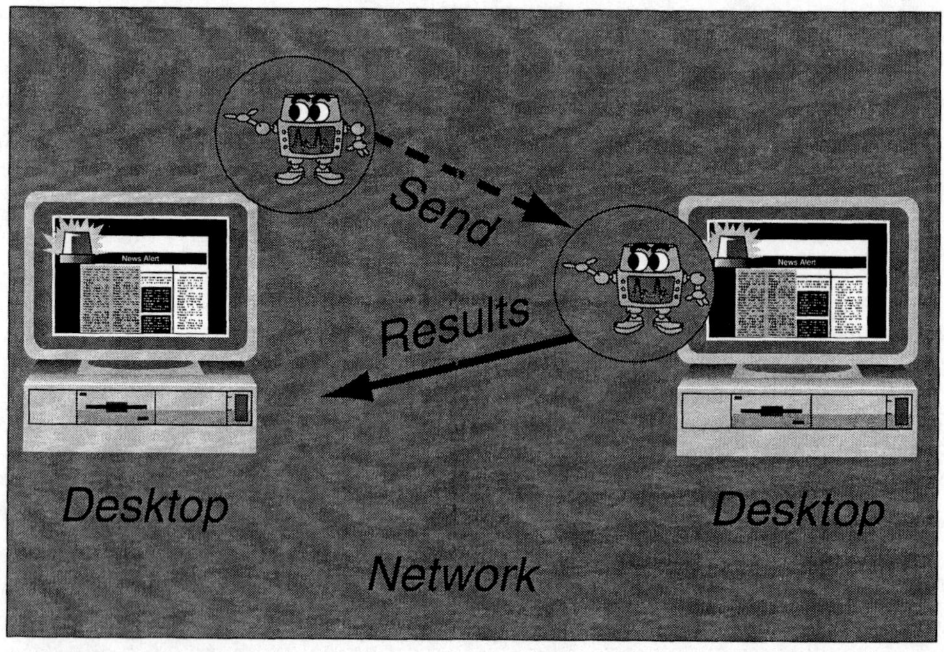

FIGURE 13–3 Remote Agent

ture. With the coming of distributed object-oriented operating systems, this will certainly change in the future. We will have more to say about this in our closing statements.

In the remainder of this chapter we will explore some of the executive and managerial applications where "software filtering agents" are being used. In particular we will examine their use in intelligent e-mail, active databases, competitive intelligence on the Internet, and personalized newspapers.

AGENT APPLICATIONS

E-Mail Filtering Agents

One of the earlier commercial applications of software agents was "e-mail filters." Most of these filtering agents can trace their origins to the work done by Thomas Malone and others ([21],[22]) on the "Information Lens." The Information Lens was a research prototype that assisted the senders and readers of electronic mail messages. It employed artificial intelligence rules and a graphical user interface to create intelligent e-mail assistants that could automatically sort and store incoming messages, alert readers when urgent messages arrived, and respond to messages based on the content of the message. Today, virtually every PC-based e-mail system has facilities of this sort.

Like a database record, an e-mail message consists of a series of fields including the "From," "To," "Cc," "Subject," "Date," and "Message" fields. In an e-mail filtering agent end users specify keywords or phrases for one or more these fields and designate the actions to be taken by the filtering agent if the fields in an incoming or outgoing message match the keywords or phrases. Most e-mail filtering agents can only perform a small repertoire of actions. They can automatically send replies, forward incoming messages, store a message in an external file, and sort messages into mail folders. The following illustrates, in "if/then" syntax, the types of pattern matching and actions that can be performed by a filtering agent:

IF Subject is "Weekly Meeting"

THEN Store in Folder "Meetings"

IF Date is Between (Next Monday and Next Friday)

THEN Store in File "c:\vacation.txt" and Send "Vacation_Msg" To Field "From"

For instance, the first rule says that if the "Subject" field in the e-mail message contains the keywords "Weekly Meeting," then store the message in an e-mail folder called "Meetings." Similarly, the third rule says that if the "Date" field of a message is between next Monday and next Friday, then store the message in an external file "c:\vacation.txt" and send a canned reply titled "Vacation_Msg" to the person(s) whose name(s) appeared in the "From" field of the incoming message.

There seems to be agreement among many experts that e-mail filters are one of the few successful applications of agent technology. The reason for this success rests on two facts—the "fielded" nature of e-mail messages and the limited repertoire of actions. These facts mean that [14]:

- It is easy for users to specify rules.

  Users don't have to know any special logic or syntax to accomplish the task. Instead rules are created with the aid of a form or template which mirrors the form or template used to create a regular e-mail message. Here, the user either types or simply selects from a pre-specified list the field values that are to be used in filtering the messages and the actions to be taken if the message matches the fields. This makes the creation of rules similar to "query-by-example" in the database world.
- It is easy to develop an agent to filter messages.

  Relative to other areas of artificial intelligence, creating a program to filter messages and perform a limited set of tasks is straightforward. If the e-mail system is "open" and there is a need to expand the power of an e-mail filter beyond its limited repertoire, this can be accomplished by having the agent invoke a macro, script or external program.
- It is potentially easier to create an "intelligent" e-mail filtering agent.

  As noted earlier, Pattie Maes and other researchers as MIT [16] have developed intelligent agents that learn by "watching over the shoulder of the user." One of their prototypes is an e-mail filtering agent called Maxims. Each time a user uses e-mail, Maxim records all the "situation-action" pairs. Situations are described by the fielded information in the message and the actions are the actions that the user performs on the message. When a new situation occurs Maxim uses the stored pairs to predict the action to take. Based on the user's desires, Maxim will either offer a suggestion to the user or will perform the action automatically. In this way the user isn't required to build their own rules. Here, the "learning" process is simplified by the fact that the number of fields and the number of actions are limited.

E-mail filtering agents were designed primarily to ease the problem of e-mail overload faced by many executives, managers, and other knowledge workers. They have also been used to help these same individuals stay informed about the enterprise. If an enterprises has a "public" mail box where staff send messages of general interest, then filters can be established to automatically distribute those messages to other interested staff members. For instance, a rule might be established to automatically forward "public" messages to the marketing team if the "Subject" or "Message" fields contain the names of competitive companies or products.

E-mail filters have the potential to be adapted to a variety of other applications. If you think of an e-mail message as a short document headed by a simple set of identifying fields, then it's easy to envision some of the possibilities. In all enterprises documents are ubiquitous. They're distributed everywhere. Many of these documents are being stored or archived in databases and indexed by keywords so they can be easily retrieved. Clearly, an e-mail filtering agent could be extended to pro-actively perform a number of actions depending on the document's keywords and content. For example, the agent could automatically distribute the document to interested readers. At Lotus Corporation e-mail filtering agents have been and are being incorporated not only in their document database product Lotus Notes but also in other workgroup applications like scheduling [14].

ACTIVE DATABASES

Much of the enterprise data used to support executives, managers, and analysts is being moved from core transaction processing databases to "data warehouses" where it is cleansed, organized, integrated, and optimized for decision support applications. Access to the data in a warehouse is provided through various client/server (c/s) applications. In a c/s application the client is a process or program that requests a service and the server is a process or program that responds to the request. In the database world clients are usually graphical front ends for issuing queries to and receiving results from the database server which executes the query against the data. In most c/s applications the client resides on the desktop, while the server resides on a high-end workstation or host computer.

In his book the *Database Factory* [23], Stephen Schur classifies database servers as "active" or "passive" depending on whether they perform their operations under external or internal control. An active server incorporates its own control logic. It operates on and is operated on by clients, other servers, and system events (which are surrogates for business or market events). In contrast a passive server only performs the operations specifically requested by a client.

To understand the distinction between an active and passive database, consider a sample scenario. A sales account manager wants to track volatile or problematic customer accounts. For instance, a volatile account might be defined as one where a customer complaint remains unresolved for some pre-defined period of time (say 5 days). Many enterprises keep customer data of this sort in a relational database. Assuming that the data are stored in a relational table or view with fields like CustomerID, the Type of complaint, the Status of the complaint (open or closed), a Description of the complaint, and the DateIssued and DateResolved, a list of volatile customers could be obtained by issuing an SQL query like

```
Select CustomerID, Type, Status, Description, DateIssued, DateResolved
From Complaints
Where Status = 'Open' And (SYSDATE - DateIssued) > 5
```

In this query SYSDATE represents the date the query was issued. This date is automatically provided by the database system. In this query the SYSDATE is compared to the date the complaint was issued to determine which of the "Open" complaints have been unresolved for more than 5 days.

If the manager used a passive database, then he or she would connect to the server through a client application, issue the query, and wait for the result. But, what if the table or view were large and the query took 30 minutes or more to run, tying up the desktop for the duration? Or, what if the manager were on a trip and couldn't establish a remote connection between the client and the server? The answer in both cases is: "tough luck." In a passive database queries are transient, the results can't be delayed, and the server has no "mind" of its own. It can only do what it is asked to do by a client application.

Contrast this with an active database server. In an active database, the manager might issue a query, ask that it be executed at a later point in time or on a periodic basis, and request that the results be delivered to his or her e-mail. Additionally, the query itself might be sent through e-mail (e.g., this is the basic idea underlying products like Oracle Mobile Agents and Collabra's Query-By-Mail). How is all this accomplished? It would be cleaner if the database could do it alone. However, it is usually accomplished through a cooperative venture. For instance, an e-mail agent might pick up the query and store it in a special table in the database. The table might have a field for the user's mail address, the text of the query, and a series of fields for the schedule. A second filtering agent might be responsible for actually invoking the query at the scheduled times, collating the results, and either storing the results or handing them back to the e-mail agent who would then deliver them to the user's e-mail box.

This is how, for example, Comshare's software "Robot for OLAP" works. OLAP stands for on-line analytical processing to distinguish it from on-line transaction processing (OLTP) [24]. In an OLAP application the data are stored in a multidimensional database as opposed to a relational database. An OLAP database is optimized for multi-dimensional comparisons. The Robot for OLAP is designed to search for trends and patterns within an OLAP database, to pinpoint the cells where matches occur, and to deliver the results to the end user's desktop via e-mail.

Hertz, the car rental company, uses this robot for pricing analysis [25]. They use the robot to quickly respond to the pricing moves of their competitors. Their stated goal is to be the price leader, offering the lowest price of any competitor in a given location, car class, and market segment while still maintaining a profit margin. Hertz has thousands of locations, a variety of competitors, rents cars for a range of classes, and services a number of market segments. This is where the problem occurs. There are so many possible combinations and the prices change so frequently, it is impossible for their pricing managers to shift through the data by hand in order to determine where prices need to be adjusted. Instead, what the pricing managers do is create a series of detection rules specifying the pricing trends and patterns to monitor. A simple rule might be: "For all the airport locations in the Western region, find those competitors whose prices are $5 lower than ours." The rules are given to the Robot for OLAP whose job it is to run all the rules on a daily basis against the OLAP pricing database and to deliver the results to the desktops of the pricing managers. A couple of the screens that a pricing manager might see are shown below in Figure 13–4. The number of data points any pricing manager must consider is reduced from several thousand to just a few.

Just like an e-mail filter, active database agents serve to filter numerical data and ensure that even the most minute detail can be proactively monitored on a routine basis. Active databases are also designed to support the "asynchronous" tasks of a mobile work force. For example, when used in conjunction with an e-mail agent, it can easily support queries issued by sales personnel and other staff

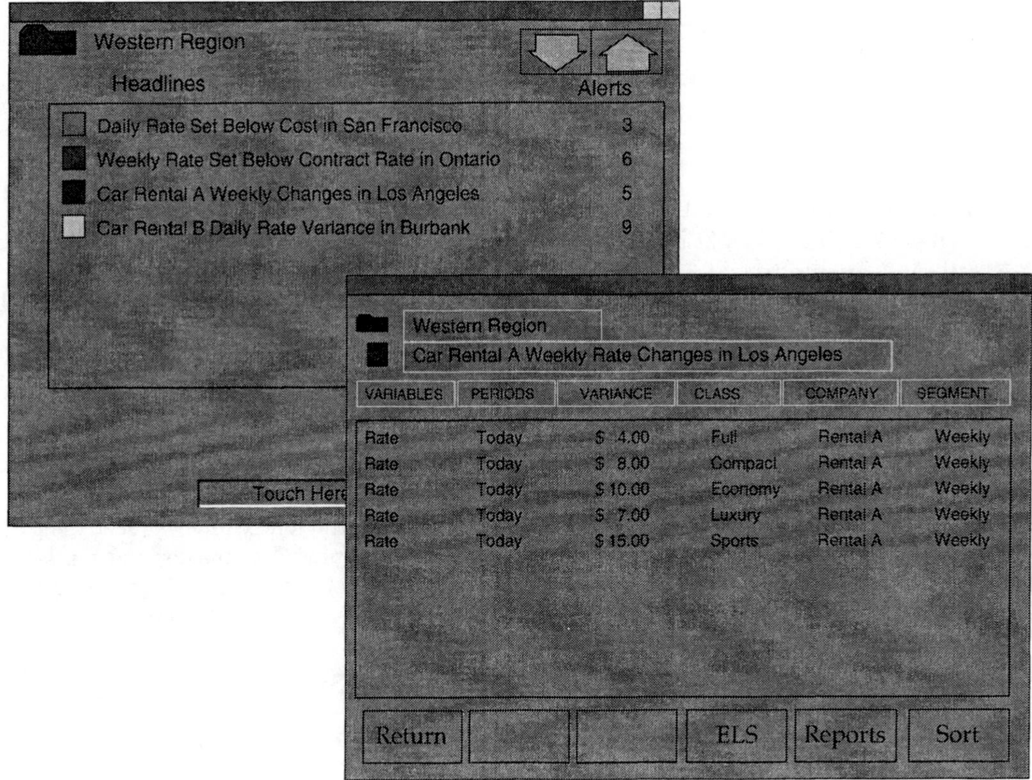

FIGURE 13–4 Pricing Results from Robot for OLAP

who spend the bulk of their time away from the office and disconnected from the network. In the future, more sophisticated data mining techniques may be used to find problems and opportunities. This way there will be no need for end users to issue queries in the first place. The agents will simply inform users when anomalies arise.

COMPETITIVE INTELLIGENCE FROM THE INTERNET

Trade journals and newspapers are replete with stories about the Internet. A few years ago there were about 30 stories a year. Now, there are over 300 a month. The fastest growing segment of the Internet is the World Wide Web. The Web is a globally distributed system of hypermedia documents [26]. On the Web the documents are called "pages." The pages are stored on Web servers located throughout the Internet and thus throughout the world. Each page consists of text and images, some of which are "hot spots" that link the page to other pages. When the user clicks on a hot spot he or she gets the feeling that they are being transported from one location in the Web to another. Actually, when a hot spot is clicked, the page referenced by the hot spot is digitally transported through the Internet from the Web server where it is located and brought to the user's machine. Web pages are viewed and traversed with tools called "browsers." The best known of these is Mosaic and its various commercial incarnations.

Because of it multimedia quality, enterprises view the Web as a new media for sales and marketing. Enterprises are rushing to turn their sales, product, and other promotional literature into Web pages where readers throughout the globe can access them. While most of the hype about the Internet has been generated by these promotional uses, the Web and other less glamourous Internet services may prove to be more valuable as a source of competitive intelligence for executives, managers, and other knowledge workers.

As Benjamin Gilad reminds us, "competitive intelligence is not competitor intelligence" [27]. Instead,

> Competitive intelligence is based on learning, which is based on the ability to listen to customers, to consumers, to partners, to competitors, to industry experts, and most importantly to ones own enterprise. The competitive environment sends out messages all the time: signals about change, trends, prospects, threats, and weaknesses. Early on these signals are weak, ambiguous, and hidden. Tapping them and then learning from them is an art that requires open eyes, ears and minds.

You can think of the Internet in general and Web in particular as a global nervous system [28], increasing an enterprise's access to the competitive messages sent by its environment. In terms of competitive intelligence the Internet offers:

- Direct access to many of the commercial on-line data providers (e.g., Dow Jones and Reuters)

- Cheaper access to many of the same sources provided by the commercial only data providers (e.g., the SEC Edgar database of quarterly and annual financial filings from all public companies)
- Timely access to many governmental data sources (e.g., procurement announcements from *Commerce Business Daily* and weekly listings of patents in the Patent News Service)
- Broad (and often unique) access to the discussions and assessments of products, competitors, customers and market, social, and technical trends (afterall if a company puts its product literature on the Web, this literature becomes a source of intelligence about that company).

Unfortunately, the Internet has been likened to Borge's fictional description of the Library of Babel [29], where all information presentable in the world's human languages is stored but where no one can find what they desire. In short, because of its distributed, uncontrolled nature, the Internet is completely disorganized, has too much information, is too hard to use (even with tools like Mosaic), and is growing too fast. Fortunately, researchers have been aware of these problems for some time and have been creating tools that ease the burdens. Most of these are query tools that enable a user to search indexes of various Internet data sources. Archie is a tool for searching an index of all the directories and subdirectories of those servers on the Internet that allow public transfer of files (e.g., shareware programs) from the server to the user's machine. These servers are known as FTP sites. Veronica is a tool for searching an index of all the Gopher menus on the net. Gopher is a browser that provides a hierarchical set of menus for navigating and accessing various Internet services (like the FTP sites indexed by Archie). Finally, there are a set of experimental indexes being created for the Web. The programs and processes used to create the indexes have names like "spiders," "wanders," and "worms." [26] Some of these programs simply index the titles and hot spot addresses contained in the Web pages they know about (e.g., the index created by the World Wide Web Worm). Other programs not only index this information but also the remainder of the text contained in the pages they know about (e.g., the index created by the Web Crawler). Regardless of how it works, the idea is to enable users to search for Web pages based on their content.

In most cases the search is performed via a Web page like the one shown below in Figure 13–5. In this case the user enters a list of keywords and then selects the content to be searched.

Web spiders, wanders, and worms have been likened to software agents. While these indexes and the other Internet indexes are invaluable, they all treat the Internet as a "passive" database. In every case the onus is on the user to invoke the query tool, type in the search criteria, and submit the query. The user must stay connected to the net in order for the query to be completed.

In order to qualify as an agent, the index and its associated query tool would have to enable a user to submit a query and come back later for the results. While not as glitzy as the Web, this is the basic idea behind "mailing list" servers on the

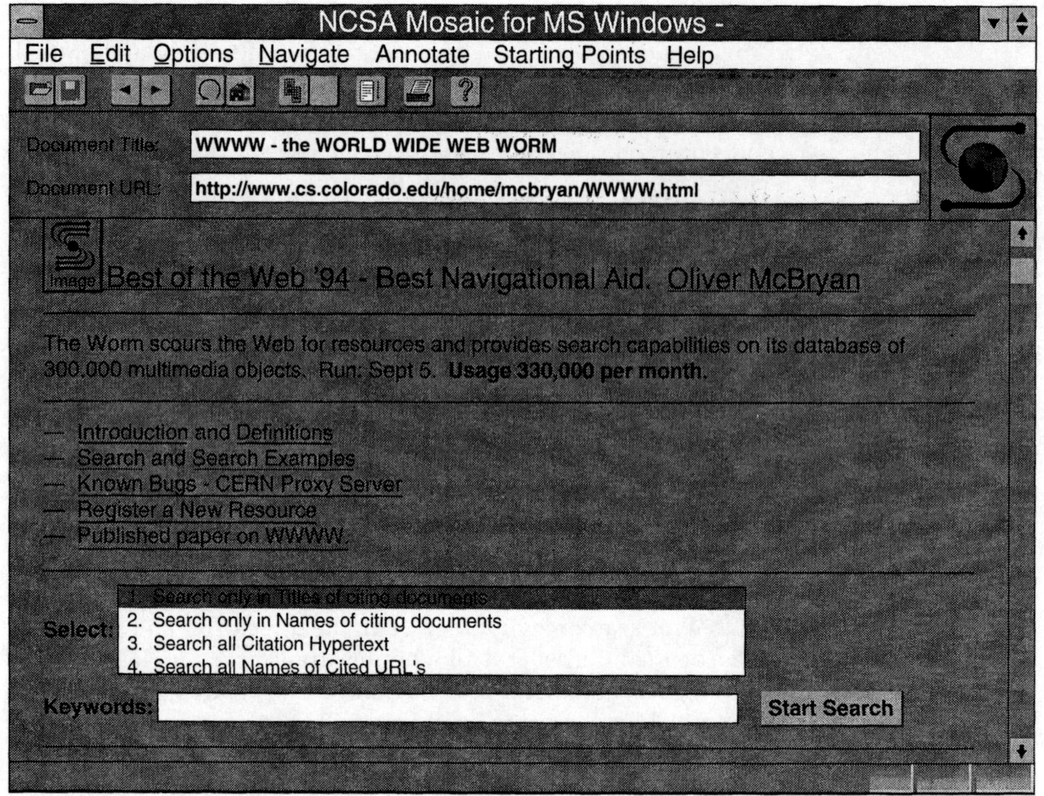

FIGURE 13–5 Searching with the World Wide Web Worm

Net. A mailing list server is a program that automatically sends a message about a particular subject to the e-mail boxes of a list of subscribers. A user can subscribe by sending an e-mail message to the server requesting that he or she be added to its list. For example, there is a mailing list server that automatically distributes on a daily basis a summary of all the White House press releases issued the previous day. In order to subscribe to this list the user sends an e-mail message to the e-mail address "almanac essuda.gov" with the keywords "subscribe wh-summary" in the body of the message. Some of the mailing list servers front end indexed databases of documents and allow end users to issue queries that are stored and executed on a routine basis with the results returned at a later time via e-mail. These servers qualify as software filtering agents.

One example is the Stanford Netnews Filtering Service [9] that automatically tracks postings to Usenet newsgroups. Most of us are familiar with electronic bulletin boards or forums (as on Compuserve) where an individual can post a message and others can respond. In Usenet these forums are called "newsgroups" and the postings are called "articles." There are over 10,000 newsgroups, each devoted to a particular subject area. Some of these newsgroups have several hundred articles per day. These are too many to monitor by hand. What the Stanford service does is create a special WAIS index [29] of all the articles for most of these groups. Individuals can monitor particular subjects by sending a "profile" to the service. The profile takes the form of a WAIS query. For instance, if the following profile were sent:

subscribe OLAP multidimensional
period 1
expire 60
threshold 80

then everyday (period 1) for the next 60 days (expire 60) the service would look for articles containing the keywords "OLAP" and "multidimensional" (subscribe OLAP multidimensional). The service computes a score for each article depending on how well the article matches the keyword list. The service will e-mail the user a list of articles whose scores exceed the threshold setting (threshold 80). The user can then request the complete text of any article that appears to be of interest.

Farcast is another filtering agent that operates much like the Stanford service, although it costs real money [30]. Farcast monitors news feeds including API, UPI, Businesswire, PR Newswire, and stock quote feeds for the NY, American, and Nasdaq exchanges. In Farcast the profiles or queries are called "droids." Unlike the Stanford service, Farcast handles boolean queries and can return results as they happen or in batch several times throughout the day. For example, the following "droid"

To: newstand@farcast.com
Subject: bill clinton not hillary or gore in the News

would retrieve articles from domestic newspapers that contain the words "bill" and "clinton" but not the words "hillary" or "gore."

In the future we can expect similar "asynchronous" queries to be available for various Web indexes. In this case the filtering agent would watch the index created by one or more spiders, wanders, or worms, looking for new pages matching a user's profile(s). A summary Web page listing the matching pages as "hot spots" would then be made available to the user. When the user activated his or her favorite Web browser, the summary page would automatically appear.

PERSONALIZED NEWSPAPERS

As early as 1996, a study conducted by TRW [31] forecasted that by 1978 newspapers would be printed on home facsimile machines and by 1980 these machines would print newspapers with information tailored to individual needs.

While somewhat off the mark, their forecasts have come to pass. Several major newspapers, magazines, and specialized trade journals and newsletters are available through CompuServe, Prodigy, America Online (AOL), and now the World Wide Web [32]. Some of these, like *Time* magazine on the Web, *U.S. News and World Report* on CompuServe, and *Business Week* on AOL retain the graphic quality of their paper counterpart. Most, however, bear no resemblance to the printed edition. Instead, users are presented with a menu of headlines from which they can download the text of selected stories.

Increasingly, executives, managers, and other knowledge workers are relying on electronic news for gleaning data and information about the competitive environment faced by their enterprises. Several filtering agents are available for creating personalized newspapers which "ease the burden of poring through the hyperabundance of newspapers, magazines, newsletters and trade journals." [1] The Farcast service described above is one example. Other examples include the Mercury Newshound [33], SandPoint's Hoover [34], Individual's First [1], Apple Search [15], and the "clipping" facilities offered by the on-line providers. All of these services automatically and routinely cull news stories from a variety of sources, select those matching the user's profile of interest, and deliver them to users via fax, e-mail, the Web, or Lotus Notes. The stories appear in summary format or as a collection accessed through a menu of headlines.

With the exception of Hoover, all of these filtering agents track external news. But, much of the news of interest to executives, managers, and knowledge workers comes from inside the enterprise and is generated from both hard and soft sources, like the field intelligence contained in a discussion database or query results produced by an active database. Commander NewsAlert is a managerial application that treats all filtering agents—internal and external, hard and soft—as potential electronic reporters who can deliver filtered stories to the desktop where they are displayed in a personalized electronic newspaper.

As shown in Figure 13–6, a NewsAlert paper retains much of the look and feel of a paper newspaper. Like its paper counterpart, a NewsAlert paper has a front page and a series sections. The sections that appear, the agents that report to those sections, and the rules that they use to filter data are customized to the individual reader. Where a standard newspaper might have sections on local news, business, sports, and living, a NewsAlert paper might have sections devoted to company vital signs, competitors, and customers.

The front page displayed in Figure 13–6 contains stories generated from a variety of sources including Dow Jones, Reuters, the Robot for OLAP (discussed in the section on active databases), and Lotus Notes discussion groups. Combining the stories in this manner yields a more complete picture of the overall status of a problem or opportunity. The paper also provides users with a set of Exploratory Tools (see the button at the top right of Figure 13–6) for further analyzing the data and context behind a story.

In part NewsAlert is derived from ideas contained in the NewsPeek prototype developed earlier at the MIT Media Lab [35]. The MIT prototype drew infor-

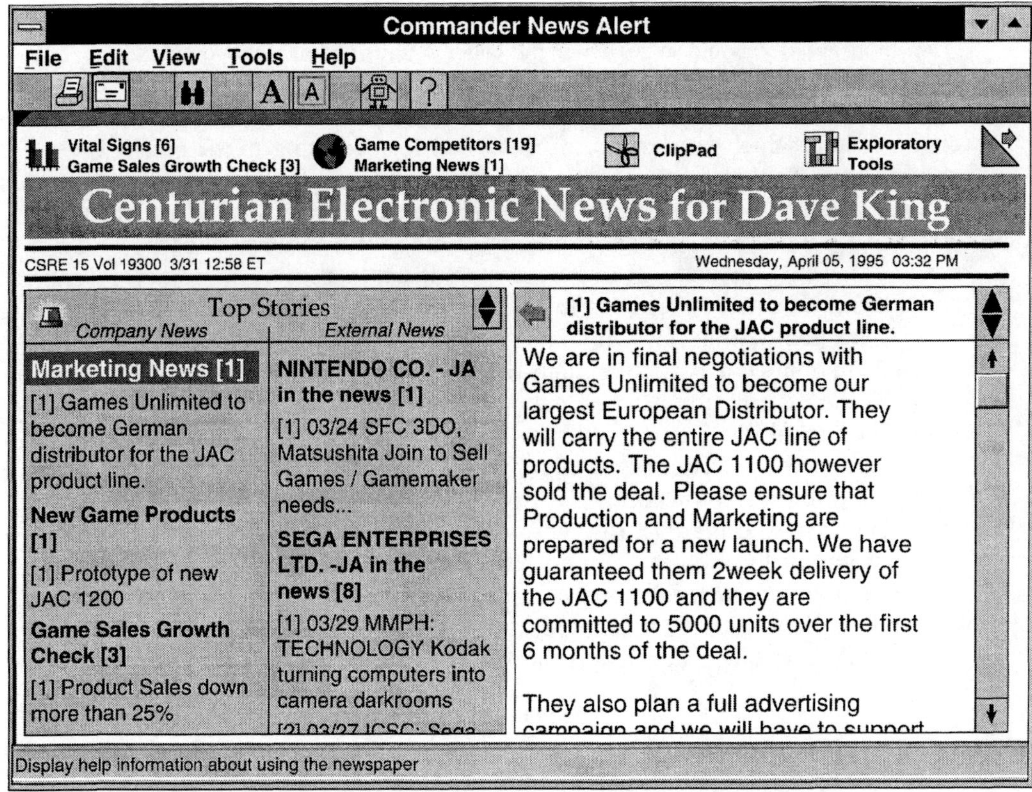

FIGURE 13–6 Front Page for NewsAlert

mation from Dow Jones, Nexis, Xpress, the wire services, and TV newscasts according to the interests of individual readers. The newspaper also supported the inclusion of videotape images, as well as audio and video clips from TV news stories. The headlines, graphical images, and certain highlighted words in the various stories act as "hot spots" which, when touched by the user, link to underlying detail or related stories.

One of the stated aims of the NewsPeek prototype was to create "prescient" agents that could learn about user preferences and interests by watching the user as she or he reads the paper. Negroponte [36] provided a simple example of the process

> Suppose you are reading this electronic paper on line. The system could infer from the time you dwell on particular stories how much of an interest you have in various subjects. So maybe you've been reading articles about government policy toward advanced television research. You might find that the system starts feeding you stories about rulings by the Federal Communications Commission, even though you

never explicitly exhibited interest in the FCC. And over time, it would learn more and more about you and so get better and better at figuring out what you want.

Fischer and Stevens [37] have implemented prescient agents in their Infoscope system, which is a graphical front end for browsing messages in Usenet newsgroups. As they note, these agents are loosely based on Anderson's *Rational Analysis of Human Memory* [38]. His analysis forms the base for a series of indicators that are employed to measure the probability of future usage based on prior usage patterns. Of particular importance are the measures of frequency, recency, and spacing. Frequency refers to the number of times a particular item or type of item is needed within a given time period. Recency refers to the amount of elapsed time since a particular item or type of item was needed, and spacing refers to the distribution across time of exposure to a particular item or type of item. The probability that a particular type of item will be needed in the future increases when the frequency is high, when recency is high and when usage is evenly distributed. By keeping track of these measures, prescient agents in the InfoScope system can adjust the types of messages that are shown to a user and the grouping or location of the messages in the browser. Similar measures could also be employed with personal newspapers to adjust the types of stories that were being displayed, the location of the stories (e.g., moving certain types from the front page to later pages), and the linkages among the stories.

CONCLUDING REMARKS

The past few years have witnessed tremendous organizational and technological change. Of particular importance have been the

- move toward team-based, globally distributed, and decentralized enterprises
- shortened product life cycles
- blurring of the boundaries between enterprises and their environments including distributors, suppliers, customers, partners, and the like
- increased mobility of knowledge workers
- heightened use of computers for purposes of communication rather than computation
- explosive rise of global computer networks, especially the Internet

All of these have impacted the work of managers and executives, resulting in a(n)

- explosion in the amount of data available for decision-making and problem-solving work
- intensified need to access these data at virtually any time and any place

- concomittant reduction in the amount of time and staff available for analyzing and understanding the data.

These have heightened the demand for software agents that have the potential to alleviate the time pressures faced by executives and managers by providing asychronous access and filtering the glut of data to a "meaningful trickle."

A couple of years ago I observed that many discussions about agent-based systems begin with the phrase "In the future . . ." [39] This still holds true. The phrase implies that today's agents continue to be "limited editions" of future generations. The agents that are used in today's managerial applications tend to (1) work alone, not in concert with other agents; (2) focus on single and relatively simple tasks; (3) employ basic reasoning capabilities (i.e., rule-based reasoning); and (4) exhibit only modest learning capabilities. The intelligence of future generations will certainly benefit from work being done on distributed artificial intelligence [40], data mining [41], and "over the shoulder" user interfaces.

At the same time I made this observation, I also noted the dangers in extrapolating from the present to the future—in saying that the future of agent-based systems will be more of the same, only better. As Stan Davis and Bill Davidson remind us [42], economies, industries, businesses, products, and technologies—like people—have life cycles. As one era matures, the seeds of another begin. Often the slow demise of the old era and the appearance of the new era is imperceptible. This is what makes the future so difficult to predict, because it's not more of the same.

Imagine a networked computing and communications environment where all the information utilities—computers, cable, and telephone—are interconnected, access and communication occur at gigabyte speeds, everything on the network is an object encapsulating data and programs, and all objects are capable of moving throughout the network. This is the environment where the next generation of agents will be developed. In this environment all applications will be created by combining the services of objects located throughout the network in much the same way that we organize teams and workgroups of people to accomplish particular aims. There is little doubt that we organize teams and workgroups of people to accomplish particular aims. There is little doubt that the next generation of agents will evolve out of the work being done on "mobile" agents, distributed artificial intelligence, and distributed object-oriented operating systems. What remains a mystery are the new organizational forms and types of enterprise work this next generation of agent-based applications will have to support.

QUESTIONS

1. What is the other half of the information revolution and what contribution can be made by software agents?

2. What are the differences between a software filtering agent, a client/server agent, and a remote agent?
3. For each of the four application areas discussed in the Chapter, give the key role of the software agent.
4. Will software agents "dehumanize" the decision making process of managers? Will they be limited to relatively mundane decision making support? Discuss.

REFERENCES

1. HAFNER, K. "Have Your Agent Call My Agent," *Newsweek*, February 27, 1995, 76–77.
2. Technological Partners. "Getting Good Help," *Computer Letter*, August 30, 1993, 1–6.
4. DEMAREST, M. "Leading Edge Retail," *DBMS*, December 1994, 78–84.
5. HAMEL, G. and C.K. PRAHALAD. *Competing for the Future*. Cambridge, Mass.: Harvard Business School Press, 1994.
6. MINTZBERG, H. *The Rise and Fall of Strategic Planning*, New York: Free Press, 1994.
7. TREACY, M. and F. WIERSEMA. *The Discipline of Market Leaders*. New York: Addison Wesley, 1995.
8. PETERS, T. *Crazy Times Call for Crazy Organizations*, New York: Vintage, 1994.
9. SAVEN, K. *Your Internet Consultant*. New York: Sams, 1994.
10. DRESNER, H. "Data Deluge: Users May Be Drowning in Data," *Gartner Group Research Note*, January 18, 1995.
11. KAY, A. "Computer Software," *Scientific American*, Vol. 251, Sept. 1984, 52–59.
12. NEGROPONTE, N. *Being Digital*, New York: Alfred Knopf, 1995.
13. KAY, A. "User Interface: A Personal View," in *The Art of Human-Computer Interface Design*, ed. B. Laurel, New York: Addison Wesley, 191–207.
14. GREIF, I. "Desktop Agents in Group-Enabled Products," *Communications ACM*, July 1994, 100–105.
15. MILEY, M. "Agent Technology," *MacWeek*, April 19, 1993, 41–44.
16. MAES, PATTIE, "Agents that Reduce Work and Information Overload," *Communications ACM*, July 1994, 31–40.
17. BOOKER, E. "Verity Outlines Strategy for Cross-Platform Application," *Computerworld*, April 19, 1994, 64.
18. EDWARDS, J. "Searcher Serfs," *CIO*, September 15, 1994, 60–64.
19. DAVIS, A. "The Digital Valet, or Jeeves Goes Online," *Educom Review*, May/June, 1994, 44–46.
20. WAYNER, P. "Free Agents," *Byte*, March 1995, 105–114.
21. MALONE, T., K. GRANT, F. TURBAK, S. BREBET, and M. COHEN. "Intelligent Information Sharing Systems," *Communications ACM*, Vol. 30, May 1987.
22. ROBINSON, M. "Through the Lens Smartly," *Byte*, May 1991, 177–187.

23. SCHUR, S. *The Database Factory: Active Database for Enterprise Computing.* New York: Wiley, 1994.
24. DEJESUS, E. "Dimensions of Data," *Byte,* April 1995, 139–148.
25. WILDER, C. "Intelligent Agents: Important Information Fast," *Information Week,* November 14, 1994.
26. DECEMBER, J. and N. RANDALL. *The World Wide Web Unleashed.* New York: Sams, 1994.
27. GILAD, B. *Business Blindspots.* New York: Dow Irwin, 1994.
28. MCKENNA, REGIS. "Stalking the Information Society," *Upside,* January 1995, 37–45.
29. GILSTER, P. *Finding It on the Internet.* New York: Wiley, 1994.
30. ANKER, A. "Tomorrow's Print News Today," *Wired,* April 1995, 145.
31. SCHNAARS, S. *Megamistakes: Forecasting and the Myth of Rapid Technological Change,* New York: Free Press, 1989.
32. NOVAK, D. "The Cyber Papers," *Sky Magazine,* February 1995, 112–118.
33. EAGER, W., L. DONAHUE, D. FORSYTH, K. MITTON, and M. WATERHOUSE. *net.search.* Indianapolis, IN: Que Corporation, 1995.
34. INDERMAUR, K. "Baby Steps," *Byte,* March 1995, 97–104.
35. BRAND, S. *The Media Lab: Inventing the Future at MIT,* New York: Viking, 1987.
36. BRODY, H. "Machine Dreams: An Interview with Nicholas Negroponte," *Technology Review,* Vol. 95, Jan. 1992, 33–40.
37. FISCHER, G. and STEVENS, P. "Information Access in Complex, Poorly Structured Information Spaces," *CHI Conference Proceedings: Human Factors in Computing Systems,* ACM Press, 1991, 63–70.
38. ANDERSON, J. *The Adaptive Character of Thought,* Hillsdale, N.J.: Lawrence Erlbaum Associates, 1990.
39. KING, DAVID "Intelligent Support Systems: Art, Augmentation and Agents." In R. Sprague and H. Watson (eds.), *Decision Support Systems: Putting Theory into Practice* (3rd Edition), Englewood Cliffs, N.J.: Prentice Hall, 1992.
40. RASMUS, D. "Intelligent Agents: DAI Goes to Work," *PC AI,* January/February 1995, 27–32.
41. HEDBERG, S. "The Data Gold Rush," *Byte,* October 1995, 83–88.
42. DAVIS, S. and DAVIDSON, B. *2020 Vision,* New York: Simon & Schuster, 1991.
43. ORFALI, R., D. HARKEY, and J. EDWARDS. "Intergalactic Client/Server Computing," *Byte,* April 1995, 108–122.

Part 4

CREATING THE DECISION SUPPORT ENVIRONMENT

It was not uncommon in the early days of DSS for companies to develop and launch specific DSS projects that had high impact and great success. This became known as "cherry-picking," or more generally, using a strategy to "pick the low hanging fruit." But on-going development and use of DDS depends on the right kind of *environment* to support it. Even the growth and evolutionary development of these cherry systems depends on a good environment.

In Chapter 1 we described the importance of the environment for the development and use of DSS. Part 4 of the book consists of two chapters which describe the two most important aspects of that environment: the organizational environment and the technology environment.

The process of building and using DSS can be supported in a variety of ways in an organization. At one extreme, an individual champion may build decision support systems on an entrepreneurial basis, promoting development and use primarily with enthusiasm and zeal. At the other extreme, the organization may commit itself to supporting and encouraging DSS as part of its corporate strategy after careful analysis of benefits. Whatever approach is taken, there normally comes a time when management realizes that a systematic approach must be used in order to create an appropriate DSS environment. This endeavor is a major undertaking that involves human as well as physical resources.

The organizational environment is described in Chapter 14. The focus of this chapter is on the primary element of the organizational environment—the organizational unit(s) which must take the responsibility for building and nurturing DSS and their use. Defining these units and their responsibilities is frequently an important and difficult process. Two reasons are because DSS are so different from traditional computer systems, and because the users have a much different role than in traditional systems development.

Chapter 15 discusses the primary element of the technology environment—the software. The software environment for DSS is crucial because it provides the ability to create DSS applications quickly and change them frequently. Chapter 15 presents an approach to selecting the heart of the software environment—the DSS generator—using an expanded set of evaluation criteria. The approach allows for the possibility of building the software environment without a generator, and building specific DSS directly from DSS tools.

14

ORGANIZATIONAL STRATEGIES FOR SUPPORTING DSS

Global competition with shorter product cycles has radically changed the complexity and speed of decision making in organizations. Decision support systems (DSS) offer a number of analytic capabilities to extract competitive intelligence from this data rich world. The diffusion of end-user computing has facilitated the building of limited scope DSS by end users. In many situations, however, institutional support is needed for DSS development, operation, and maintenance. Users often lack the technical expertise or necessary resources to develop and operate DSS on their own.

A recent study examined the formal, institutional mechanisms for supporting DSS activity. Although DSS activity may occur without such support, a formal DSS support group usually is needed to advance DSS activity beyond small-scale, ad hoc applications [20]. A DSS Group [22] is defined as an organizational unit which plans, supports, and controls DSS activities as an important element of its mission. DSS groups can provide conventional end-user computing support services such as training, consulting, hardware/software evaluation, and access to corporate data [3], [7], [23]. In addition to these services, DSS groups often develop, maintain, and operate DSS for users [23].

A number of options exist for providing DSS institutional support. Expanding on Sprague and Carlson's [20] organizational placement alternatives, Watson and Carr [22] identify the following possibilities:

This chapter is adapted from Stephen R. Hawk and Martin L. Bariff, "An Examination of Organizational Strategies for Supporting DSS," *Information & Management*, 1995.

1. Traditional applications development group
2. Operations research or management science group
3. Planning department or staff analysis group within a functional department
4. A stand-alone, formally chartered DSS group
5. A DSS group within end-user services
6. Information center

Table 14–1 (pages 212–213) discusses each of these alternatives.

Specialized staff groups frequently evolve within planning or functional area departments. The formally chartered DSS group is a stand-alone unit within the MIS department. A DSS group located within an end-user services group is similar to the formally chartered DSS group, except that it is located in a group which houses other end-user support groups, such as an information center. Although an information center might seem to be limited to providing conventional end-user computing support services, many information centers have expanded their service offerings to include systems development and project management [15].

Early research addressing organizational support for DSS shows that DSS using departments usually play a leading role in the development and management of DSS, while the MIS department's role is often limited to providing hardware or technical support [9], [10], [21]. More recent research indicates that information centers and formally chartered DSS groups have become widespread, and that most DSS groups provide services that go beyond supporting end-user DSS development [23].

Although DSS has been a major information systems research area for the past 15 years, our knowledge of DSS support practices is fairly limited. The goal of the study was to provide a better understanding of the different organizational practices for providing DSS support services. An approach that was taken in investigating this issue was to examine the support characteristics of a sample of DSS groups. DSS support characteristics, such as staff backgrounds [8] [13], formalization [5] [17], types of services offered [22], and DSS development methodology [11], [14], [20] have been proposed as key elements of an organization's strategy for supporting DSS. The study investigated practices of different organizations with respect to these characteristics.

A second approach taken in examining this issue was to assess the characteristics of DSS groups in different organizational locations. Some authors have suggested that a DSS group's organizational location can have a substantial impact on the group's effectiveness [1], [8], [18], [22]. Watson and Carr [22] for instance, argue that information centers may not be the best alternative for providing DSS support since they tend to be understaffed, and the staff may have an inappropriate mix of backgrounds. DSS groups in planning and functional area departments, on the other hand, will likely have staff who understand the area of application, but may be weak in terms of their technical capabilities. An additional problem with placing DSS support staff in a non-MIS department is that the staff may show favoritism to clients in that department. Formally chartered DSS groups and DSS groups in an end-user services group are expected to be able to develop a staff with the appropriate mix of skills for DSS support. The second approach taken in the current study, therefore, was to examine the differences among groups with respect to these support characteristics. Although this study is descriptive in nature, examining the similarities and differences of DSS groups in different locations can be useful in understanding the potential strengths and weaknesses of the various organizational placement options.

RESEARCH METHOD

Twenty-three Midwest organizations participated in a cross-sectional field study to provide information related to the research hypotheses. Fifty-seven organizations were contacted by the researchers to discuss their participation in the current study. The potential existence of DSS groups in these organizations was suggested by the following resources: A top computer executive directory [11] (21 of the contacted organizations), a listing of DSS-87 through DSS-89 conference attendees (13 of the contacted organizations), a customer list provided by a DSS software vendor (8 of the contacted organizations), and the authors' personal contacts (15 of the contacted organizations). Phone calls made on the basis of these leads eventually led to a conversation with the manager of a DSS group, or a determination that no DSS group existed in an organization.

There was an attempt to include groups in the sample which represented the organizational placement options described by Watson and Carr [22]. The DSS criteria described by Hogue and Watson [9] were used in the initial discussions with firms. Groups were included in the sample if an important element of their mission was to provide services related to the development and operation of DSS to users. Of the fifty-seven contacted organizations, 29 did not meet the selection criteria. Organizations were excluded from the sample if they had no DSS group, or if they provided very limited DSS services such as formal classroom training, data downloading, or hardware installation. Four of the nonparticipating organizations had recently dissolved their DSS group, while three others were in the process of establishing one. Five out of the 28 groups that met the selection criteria declined involvement in the study, citing policy, workload, or confidentiality concerns. The number of participating groups were suggested by the four resources as follows: The top computer executive directory (8 groups), the DSS-8X conference attendee lists (6 groups), DSS software vendor's customer list (2 groups), the researchers' personal contacts (7 groups). Industries of the sampled organizations are shown in Table 14–2 (page 214). The average number of employees in these organization was 20,300, with an average annual sales of $5.2 billion.

Unfortunately, it was not possible to involve groups that represented all of the organization placement options. No groups in corporate planning departments were located. The only two firms contacted which provided DSS support

TABLE 14-1 Organizational Placement Alternatives for Providing DSS Support

Alternative 1: Traditional Applications Development Group

This choice involves placing DSS support in the hands of data-processing professionals. There are several advantages to this choice. Personnel in these groups are skilled in the use of computer hardware and software technology, are experienced in developing computer applications, and are capable of providing strong technical support.

There are also disadvantages with this selection. Data-processing professionals tend to be oriented toward traditional information systems (IS) methods and applications, and their training and experience may have limited transferability to DSS work. Also the group does not contain the mix of personnel with the skills needed for supporting DSS activities. They may only have a limited understanding of the nature of the decisions faced by managers and functional area personnel. They may speak in jargon alien to many potential users. For these reasons, they do not enjoy the confidence of management and functional area users. For most organizations, the disadvantages of this alternative outweigh the advantages.

Alternative 2: Operations Research or Management Science Group

Operations research/management science (OR/MS) groups are highly skilled in modeling and providing computer-based decision support. Unfortunately, many OR/MS groups are not held in high regard by management. The OR/MS people and their methods seem remote from the problems and decisions in the functional areas. In fact, the trend in many organizations is to distribute rather than centralize OR/MS talent. Traditional OR/MS approaches are best suited for structured decision making rather than the semistructured and unstructured decision making which characterizes DSS. Their organizational ties to data services may be loose, and OR/MS personnel also are frequently criticized for their specialized jargon.

Once again the disadvantages outweigh the advantages. However, we should point out that the OR/MS field is reconsidering its usefulness and organizational role. These deliberations may produce a new orientation more closely associated with the DSS approach. If this happens, the disadvantages associated with the OR/MS alternative would decrease.

Alternative 3: Planning Department or Staff Analysis Group within a Functional Area

These alternatives (planning departments or staff analysis groups) are similar in that both are specialized staff groups. Both are also popular choices for housing DSS activities. They have the advantage of being where many of the potential DSS applications are located. They have frequent contact with management and functional area personnel. Their mindset is that of an end user, and they speak in the language of potential DSS users.

There are also disadvantages associated with this choice. The interest of planning departments and staff analysis groups in DSS may be greater in their own applications than in the applications of other potential users. They may have trouble perceiving themselves as a DSS support group and, hence, ready to accept the full range of DSS support responsibilities. They are likely to be relatively weak in their ability to provide technical support and may have only weak ties to the data services department.

Though these are popular choices for housing DSS work, there are significant problems with these alternatives. The most serious are a possible lack of support for DSS efforts outside of the group and the group's low visibility as a focal point for DSS activities.

Alternative 4: A Stand-Alone, Formally Chartered DSS Group

Some organizations have created new, formally chartered organizational units responsible for DSS activities. This approach has a number of appeals. A staff can be assembled with the correct combination of skills necessary for DSS work, including the ability to communicate effectively with users. A range of DSS support responsibilities is easily assigned to the group, and they can take an organizationwide approach to DSS.

The disadvantages are less obvious than with the other alternatives, but they do exist. As a new, small, specialized staff group, they may not have a strong base of political support. Depending on their placement in the organization's structure, they may not be highly visible to potential users. In an ideal arrangement for fostering DSS, the DSS group should be placed high in the organization's structure and support upper man-

TABLE 14–1 *(continued)*

agement. However, this arrangement is not always easy to sell to top management because management may be uncertain about what DSS has to offer and may feel that DSS is just another set of computer applications. Also, the appealing nature of their work and their potential contacts with top management and other important organizational personnel may foster resentment from the data services group.

The separate DSS group has considerable appeal. Safeguards need to be installed, however, to minimize disadvantages.

Alternative 5: A DSS Group within End-User Services

Another alternative is the end-user services (EUS) group. With this organizational arrangement, the DSS group becomes a department within EUS along with the IC and other user support staffs. This alternative has many advantages, overcomes most of the disadvantages associated with the other alternatives, and is compatible with current trends in providing computer services. EUS advantages include high visibility, accessibility, a formal organization charter, support for fast application development, a management and a functional area orientation, a firm base of support, and close ties to data services.

Separating DSS from the IC eliminates many of the disadvantages of an IC placement. The DSS group would not be affected by the existing workload of IC staffs. The DSS staff would have the right mix of education, skills, and experience. This staff could possess an exceptionally strong management and functional area orientation. They would have the time, opportunity, and charter to stay current with DSS developments.

There are some disadvantages to this placement alternative. Because placement of an end-user services group in the overall organization structure is relatively low, upper management may not fully perceive and utilize this support. This problem might be reduced, however, by aggressive promotion of DSS services. Another potential problem is how the data services group treats the DSS group. There may be jealousy within the application development department because of the attractiveness of DSS work and the contacts that such work provides throughout the organization. Data services management might fail to recognize the contribution of DSS to the organization because of the difficulty of measuring many of the benefits of DSS. One key to managing this potential problem is to make data services management understand the role and value of DSS to an organization. Another is to protect the DSS group.

Alternative 6: Information Center

Many organizations have created information centers (IC) to formally support end-user computing. Their responsibilities are similar to those listed for an EUC group. Both groups have administrative responsibilities, provide consulting services, supply technical support, evaluate hardware and software products, and provide training. Consequently, it makes sense to consider placing DSS activities in the information center. There are other points in favor of this placement alternative. It is more efficient to have a single group. Information centers are well received, highly visible, and familiar with organizationwide information needs. They tend to be service-oriented and capable of serving a variety of computing and information needs.

The use of the information center has disadvantages that, like those of the formally chartered DSS group, may not be obvious immediately. Information centers tend to be understaffed relative to the amount of work and customer base they support. The backgrounds, educational levels, and training of IC and DSS groups differ. IC staff support to top management may be limited, and they may be more familiar with tools than with potential applications.

Information centers ultimately may be an attractive home for DSS activities. To date, there is little evidence about how well this alternative is working. There is another alternative, however, that has the advantages of the IC but fewer of the disadvantages.

Source: This table is adapted from Hugh J. Watson and Houston H. Carr, "Organizing for Decision Support System Support: The End-User Services Alternative." *Journal of Management Information Systems*, Vol. 4, No. 1 (Summer 1987), pp. 83–95.

TABLE 14-2 Industries of the Sampled Organizations

Industry of the Organization	Number of Organizations
Industrial/commercial products manufacturer	7
Consumer products manufacturer	6
Insurance	2
Banking	4
Transportation	1
Utility	1
National Industry Organization	1
Health Care	1
Total	23

through the conventional systems development area were among the five that chose not to participate. A management science group was excluded from the sample since their role was primarily one of recommending actions to management. In this case, they were the users of the systems they developed.

During an in-person structured interview, DSS group managers provided background information about their organizations, their groups' organizational placement, policies, development methodology, staff backgrounds, services, and client locations. Since data were collected in an interview setting, it was possible to ensure that questions were understood. This data collection approach also allowed respondents to provide comments and qualitative explanations that were useful in interpreting the results.

RESULTS

The staff backgrounds, development methodology, formality, services provided, and clients of the groups' services for the entire sample are presented first. This is followed by a comparison of characteristics by group location. The location of the groups, and some basic group characteristics are shown in Table 14–3. Sixteen of the groups reported within the MIS department. Of these, seven were information centers. Of the nine that were identified as decision support groups, seven were formally chartered groups, and two were part of an end user services group within MIS. One of these groups, for instance, developed DSS, while other end-user support groups conducted formal classroom training, or assisted clients in using Lotus 1-2-3 and dBASE III. Seven groups were located in functional area departments.

Staff Background

Two different backgrounds have been suggested as being important to the success of a DSS groups. First, staff members should have in-depth technical, systems development expertise in order for the group to have the capability to

TABLE 14-3 Characteristics of the DSS Groups

	Number of groups	Staff size	Number of clients	Staff/client ratio	Year of formation
DSS Groups Reporting to the MIS Department					
Information Center	7	11.1	1492	0.011	83.4
Stand-alone DSS Group	7	4.1	71	0.088	84.0
DSS Group in "End User Services"	2	16.5	663	0.025	83.5
Means for MIS Groups		8.75	718	0.049	83.7
DSS Groups Reporting to Non-MIS Departments					
Reporting to Marketing	3	7.3	225	0.069	83.3
Reporting to Operations	1	4.0	50	0.080	85.0
Reporting to Accounting/Finance	3	6.3	117	0.054	84.3
Means for Non-MIS Groups		6.4	154	0.064	84.3
Means for All Groups		8.0	539	0.054	83.9

develop the complex or large-scale DSS which are beyond the capabilities of most end users [8], [22]. DSS groups also need some staff with a good understanding of the clients' area of application. By hiring staff with backgrounds similar to the areas served, groups should tend to be more oriented to the needs of their clients [3], [17], and should be able to better understand their clients' DSS requirements [13].

DSS managers were asked to identify each staff member's most recent previous occupation prior to being hired into the group. The backgrounds of DSS staff are shown in Table 14–4. By far, the most common background was traditional, data processing systems development. Only 3 of the 23 groups in the sample (one in MIS, and two outside of MIS) had no staff with a traditional data processing background. The next most common staffing approach was to hire people who had work experience in the functional areas served by the group (e.g., finance, marketing, operations). In the case of groups located in non-MIS departments, this often occurred as a natural outgrowth of the groups' evolution. Prior

TABLE 14-4 Backgrounds of DSS Staff

	Mean	Std. dev.	Range
Conventional Systems Development	34.9%	29.0%	0-100%
Functional Area Management	14.9	24.3	0-75
Information Center	13.3	19.1	0-73
Recent College Graduates	10.4	16.2	0-67
Corporate Planning	10.0	11.7	0-50
OR/MS Groups	1.9	6.5	0-25
Other	14.6	19.9	0-72

to the establishment of these groups, a core of managers became their department's experts on using the DSS software. They continued in this role when their groups became formally established. In other cases, a conscious effort was made to hire staff with backgrounds matching those of their clients into the group. Included in the "other" category were MIS trainers, secretarial/administrative staff, systems programming and data center staff, consultants, and computer maintenance.

Formalization

DSS groups may adopt policies that govern how various DSS support activities are performed. By establishing standards of good conduct related to the planning, delivery, and evaluation of DSS services, formalization should help to increase the quality and consistency of DSS services [1], [5]. DSS group managers were asked to identify whether a policy was in place to prescribe how ten DSS planning, control, and service delivery issues should be handled. Policy issues covered by the items in this measure were suggested by prior discussions of DSS group/end-user computing formalization [1], [2], [3], [5], [17], [19]. For each issue, DSS group managers were asked to identify whether it was:

a. governed by a formal, written policy.
b. governed by an informal, well-known policy. In this case, no formal, written policy existed.
c. handled on an ad hoc basis.

In the event the issue was handled on an ad hoc basis, DSS managers were also asked whether having no formal/informal policy caused problems.

The issues and the number of groups with formal/informal policies governing them are shown in Table 14–5. As can be seen in Table 14–5, DSS groups tended to be managed in a fairly informal manner. The mean number of formal policies for the sample was 2.7. Only three groups had more than 5 formal policies related to the issues in the formalization measure. DSS managers tended to be unconcerned by the relative informality. This may partly be due to the fact that the clients and DSS staff of many groups had an informal understanding concerning the handling of certain issues. For instance, most groups had a good sense of the types of systems they dealt with, and their role in supporting these systems even though most groups did not formally define the range of services to be provided.

The issues that had the most responses indicating a problem with a lack of formal or informal policy were DSS group evaluation (9), DSS planning (5), and prioritization of client requests (4). The difficulty of evaluating DSS group performance may be a reflection of the general problem of evaluating DSS [12]. Many of the DSS managers expressed frustration at not being able to determine the success or impact of their group. In those cases where formal evaluation took

TABLE 14-5 Formalization of DSS Groups

	Formal, written policy	Informal policy	Handled on an ad hoc basis	Lack of formal or informal policy is a problem
1. Job descriptions for DSS staff	21	1	1	1
2. Procedure for clients to request DSS services	9	6	8	1
3. Hardware/Software selection	8	7	8	2
4. Methodologies used by DSS staff	6	8	10	1
5. Range of services provided	5	13	5	0
6. DSS service planning	5	7	11	5
7. Determining whether the DSS group is the best group to meet client's request	4	6	13	1
8. Justification of client requests	2	8	13	2
9. Evaluation of the DSS group	2	5	16	9
10. Prioritization of client requests	1	8	14	4

place, DSS groups employed a self-developed survey which was completed by their clients. The combination of these three issues suggests that a common problem for DSS groups may lie in determining what they should be doing, and following up with an evaluation of whether they were successful in carrying out this plan. In only a few organizations did the DSS planning involve a long-term DSS development plan.

Services Provided by the DSS Groups

DSS group managers were also provided with a list of services, and were asked to determine the percentage of their group's effort that was devoted to providing each service. In order to make this a manageable task, the number of categories needed to be relatively small. The services included in this list were:

Training—both classroom training and individual instruction

Selecting appropriate software—helping the clients determine which software tool is appropriate for their problem

Conceptual DSS design—helping clients formulate a DSS solution at the conceptual level, (e.g., what data are needed, where will the data come from, what sort of retrieval and analysis routines are needed).

DSS building—implementing the DSS design, including data base creation, development of methods for maintaining data, programming of retrieval/analysis routines, and constructing interfaces between different software tools.

Technical support—includes data base maintenance, data downloading, network support, hardware/software troubleshooting, and hardware repair.

DSS operation—running the DSS applications.

The percentage of effort devoted to each of the service categories is shown in Table 14–5. The support service that consumes the most time is DSS building, followed by technical support, DSS design, and DSS training. Most groups did not operate DSS for clients, and those that did were involved primarily in running batch applications and distributing output.

The distinction between designing a DSS and building one is similar to the distinction between systems analysis and design and implementation. In some cases, DSS staff consult with users to develop a DSS design. The users then do most or all the work involved in implementing the design. In other cases, DSS staff also do most of the work involved in implementing the design. A common division of responsibilities is for the DSS staff to create the DSS data base and the associated methods for maintaining it, leaving to users the work of developing the procedures for accessing and analyzing the data. In several cases where the DSS staff also programmed the access and analysis routines, DSS managers hoped that users would eventually learn how, or be willing to do most of this, on their own. Also shown in Table 14–6 is the effort spent on DSS development, defined as the combination of conceptual DSS design and DSS building.

An issue related to DSS development services is the DSS development methodology. The use of an evolutionary methodology has been widely recommended for DSS development [4], [13], [16]. Proponents of this approach claim that a sequential life cycle approach does not work well for DSS, because users have difficulty specifying DSS requirements prior to actual system use [11], [20]. DSS managers were asked to estimate the proportion of the DSS developed by their group using an evolutionary approach versus the proportion of DSS developed using a sequential life cycle approach. A score of 0 percent indicates complete reliance on a sequential methodology, and a score of 100 percent indicates

TABLE 14–6 Proportion of Time Spent Providing Different Support Services

	Mean	Std. dev.	Range
Education and Training	15.0%	9.4%	5-40%
Selecting appropriate DSS software	7.1	5.3	0-20
Designing DSS at the Conceptual Level	15.5	12.3	2-45
Building ("programming") DSS	26.0	17.0	0-70
Technical support	25.8	16.3	0-65
DSS Operation	5.8	9.2	0-30
Other	4.8	6.3	0-25
DSS Development (Combination of Conceptual Design and DSS building)	41.5	21.0	10-95

that all DSS are developed using an evolutionary approach. The average proportion of DSS developed in an evolutionary manner was 70 percent. Only one group used a sequential, life cycle approach for all DSS development. Five groups developed all DSS in an evolutionary manner.

Managers of DSS groups which used both approaches were asked to explain why they would choose the life cycle approach over the evolutionary approach for a given project. The most common response, provided by five managers, was that the life cycle approach was more appropriate for larger scale DSS projects. They felt it is important to use a more formal development approach for developing the necessary infrastructure from which subsequent, smaller-scale DSS could be developed, or for defining a common set of requirements that would satisfy the needs of various user departments.

Location of Clients

Table 14–7 shows the percentage of clients in different locations. As can be seen in Table 14–7, the marketing/sales and accounting/finance areas had the largest percentage of clients, followed by corporate planning and production/operations. Included in the "other" category are users in engineering, R & D, and senior executives. Except for some differences in categories, these results are similar to those of Watson et al. [23]. That is, marketing, finance, and accounting tended to be the major users of DSS services, while human resources and data processing tend to be minor users. Also, corporate planning departments were significant users of DSS services.

A Comparison of Group Characteristics

In discussing group similarities and differences, the focus will be on comparing information centers, formally chartered DSS groups, and groups reporting outside of the MIS department (There were seven sampled groups in each of these locations, but only two in an end-user services department). The results shown in Table 14–2 suggest that groups in the different locations differed in terms of staff size, number of clients, and in their staff to client ratios. Information centers

TABLE 14-7 Percent of Clients in Different Locations

	Mean	Std. Dev.	Range
Marketing/Sales	30.5%	26.1%	0-85%
Accounting/Finance	22.1	17.7	0-70
Production/Operations	13.3	19.0	0-80
Human Resources/Personnel	4.3	5.2	0-16
Information Systems Management	6.0	9.4	0-40
Corporate Planning	17.2	24.3	0-90
Other	5.6	6.4	0-20

tended to have the largest staffs, and served the greatest number of clients of all the DSS group types. An exception to this was one group located in an end-user services department that had a staff of 25. Information centers also had smaller staff to client ratios than formally chartered groups or non-MIS groups. No systematic differences in date of establishment were found among the group locations.

Table 14–8 shows how the groups differed in their staffs' backgrounds. Information centers had a lower proportion of staff with functional area background than did formally chartered DSS groups or groups in non-MIS departments. Although the average proportion of staff with functional area backgrounds was higher for non-MIS groups than it was for formally chartered DSS groups, this difference was not significant. Formally chartered DSS groups had a higher proportion of staff with a conventional systems development background than did information centers or functionally located groups.

The time spent providing the four most time consuming services (as indicated in Table 14–6) is shown by group location in Table 14–9. Information centers devoted less effort to DSS building than either formally chartered DSS groups or groups in non-MIS departments. The results also show that information centers devoted less effort to DSS development (DSS design and building combined) than either formally chartered DSS groups or groups in non-MIS departments. The only other significant difference in service emphasis was that information centers spent more of their time providing technical support than formally chartered DSS groups.

The client percentages found in different locations, broken down by DSS group location, are shown in Table 14–10. No discernable pattern emerges in the

TABLE 14-8 Staff Backgrounds—by DSS Group Location

	Conventional systems development	Functional area mgmt.	Info. center	Recent college grads.	Planning dept.
DSS Groups Reporting to the MIS Department					
Information Center	26.1%	2.9%	21.4%	10.8%	7.5%
Stand-alone DSS Group	50.0	14.3	11.9	9.5	3.8
DSS Group in "End-User Services"	55.3	0.0	8.0	26.5	8.0
Means for MIS Groups	40.2	7.5	15.6	12.2	5.9
DSS Groups Reporting to Non-MIS Departments					
Reporting to Marketing	12.5%	22.2%	10.4%	2.1%	27.8%
Reporting to Operations	0.0	75.0	0.0	0.0	0.0
Reporting to Accounting/Finance	37.5	26.4	8.3	12.5	17.7
Means for Non-MIS Groups	21.4	31.5	8.0	6.2	19.5
Means for All Groups	34.9	14.9	13.3	10.4	10.0

TABLE 14-9 Proportion of Time Spent on Different Services—by DSS Group Location

	Training	Technical support	DSS design	DSS building	DSS devel-opment
DSS Groups Reporting to the MIS Department					
Information Center	16.7%	37.9%	13.4%	11.0%	24.4%
Stand-alone DSS Group	14.6	12.9	17.9	32.4	50.3
DSS Group in "End-User Services"	12.5	21.5	19.5	39.5	59.0
Means for MIS Groups	15.3	24.9	16.1	23.9	40.0
DSS Groups Reporting to Non-MIS Departments					
Reporting to Marketing	11.7%	31.7%	17.3%	25.0%	42.3%
Reporting to Operations	5.0	40.0	15.0	25.0	40.0
Reporting to Accounting/Finance	20.0	20.0	10.0	38.3	48.3
Means for Non-MIS Groups	14.3	27.9	13.9	30.7	44.6
Means for All Groups	15.0	25.8	15.5	26.0	41.5

TABLE 14-10 Percent of Clients in Different Locations—by DSS Group Location

	Marketing/ sales	Account-ing/ finance	Produc-tion/ opera-tions	Human re-sources	Info. systems mgmt.	Corpo-rate plan-ning
DSS Groups Reporting to the MIS Department						
Information Center	17.0%	28.1%	14.4%	8.1%	13.7%	10.1%
Stand-alone DSS Group	25.7	22.9	2.1	2.1	2.1	34.3
DSS Group in "End-User Services"	36.5	13.0	25.5	10.5	5.5	0.0
Means for MIS Groups	23.2	23.9	10.4	5.8	7.6	19.4
DSS Groups Reporting to Non-MIS Departments						
Reporting to Marketing	68.3%	10.0%	3.3%	0.0%	3.3%	15.0%
Reporting to Operations	0.0	5.0	80.0	5.0	5.0	5.0
Reporting to Accounting/Finance	41.7	30.0	16.6	0.0	0.0	11.7
Means for Non-MIS Groups	47.1	17.9	20.0	0.7	2.1	12.1
Means for All Groups	30.5	22.1	13.3	4.3	6.0	17.2

number of clients found in different locations when the groups reporting within MIS are examined. It was expected that groups located in non-MIS departments would tend to concentrate their services on clients within their department. This was true for groups in marketing and operations. The groups in accounting/finance, however, tended to support a greater number of clients outside their departments. All groups located in non-MIS departments supported users outside their own department.

Finally, no significant differences were found in the groups' use of an evolutionary development methodology, or in the number of formal or informal policies adopted.

The results in Tables 14–3, 14–8, and 14–9 partially confirm the disadvantages of information centers when compared to formally chartered DSS groups and staff analysis groups [22]. Because information centers supported a larger number of clients per staff member, DSS users would be less likely to receive the same level of service provided by the other groups. This apparently was reflected in the relatively low level of effort spent by information centers on DSS development. A second point of confirmation is found in differences in staff backgrounds. The low level of staff with functional area backgrounds found in information centers suggests that these staffs would be less likely to understand the functional areas being supported.

Other results suggest that some of the potential weaknesses of groups in non-MIS departments may be less than expected. Five of the seven groups in non-MIS departments had at least one staff member with conventional data processing systems development background. This suggests that these groups were able to compensate for the supposed technical weakness of other staff members. It also did not appear that the staff with non-technical backgrounds in these groups were as technically weak as one might presume. First, DSS support work was the sole occupation of most the staff in these groups. This provided them with the opportunity to develop the necessary technical skills. With increasingly easy to use fourth generation tools, the time required to become technically proficient is becoming fairly short. Second, the staff with functional-area backgrounds usually had a fairly good set of technical skills prior to their being hired into the group. Many were reported to be the local computer experts in their area before becoming DSS staff members.

The results concerning the locations of clients indicates that groups in non-MIS departments were willing to support the DSS needs of clients outside their departments. This was especially so for groups in the accounting/finance area. Although this study did not directly attempt to assess favoritism in the support provided, this suggests that these DSS groups at least see their mission as one that extends beyond departmental boundaries.

SUMMARY

Twenty-three organizations participated in a field study to explore alternative approaches to supporting DSS activity. The following summarizes the general findings of this study:

- Some DSS are developed solely by end users, others by DSS staff, and in many cases they are developed by both parties.
- Many DSS managers would like to see DSS become more of an end-user computing activity.

- DSS tend to be developed using an iterative methodology.
- Conventional systems development continues to be the predominant background of DSS staff. Despite recommendations to the contrary, people with functional area backgrounds tend to account for a relatively small proportion of DSS staff.
- DSS groups are managed in a fairly informal manner. With a few exceptions, this is not viewed as a problem by DSS managers.
- Few DSS groups engage in long-range planning. Planning tends to be reactive, done in response to client requests for DSS development. Few groups have enacted mechanisms for evaluating the impact or client satisfaction with their services.
- Developing DSS and providing technical support are the primary responsibilities of DSS groups.

This study confirmed many of the expected differences between groups placed in different locations. Although this study was descriptive in nature, it tended to confirm prior thinking about the potential strengths and weaknesses of the different DSS support locations [22]. To the extent that having a high staff to client ratio and having staff with backgrounds matching those of clients is important for providing DSS support, the results suggest that the use of an information center to provide DSS support services may have some limiting consequences. The high number of clients per staff member tends to strain staff resources so that little time will be available to develop DSS for end users. Lack of staff with backgrounds similar to those of their clients is likely result in a limited ability to understand the problems to be supported by DSS. According to Keen [13], this tends to result in support being limited to helping clients understand how to use the DSS tools. Such staffs are less capable of taking a more active role, such as suggesting how the tools could be used to solve the clients' problems. The likely result of these two factors is that the DSS supported by information centers tend to be developed by end users. The sort of applications developed by end users are more likely to be ad hoc, small-scale applications than would be the case if the DSS group became involved in designing and building the DSS [20].

The results indicate only a few differences exist between DSS groups in functional area departments and formally chartered DSS groups in the MIS departments. Both:

- have relatively few staff members.
- serve a small number of clients.
- have a relatively high staff to client ratio.
- have a higher proportion of staff with functional area backgrounds than information centers.
- place greater emphasis on DSS development than information centers.

These factors suggest that these groups tend to have a more appropriate mix of staff for supporting DSS and are better able to concentrate on providing a full set of DSS support services than information centers. As a result, organizations may wish to consider the creation of DSS groups in these locations if small-scale, ad hoc DSS are not an adequate solution to the decision-making needs of their managers. Although the charter of some information centers has evolved over the years to include systems development, they continue to emphasize applications development by end users.

QUESTIONS

1. List one advantage and one disadvantage for each of the 6 options for the organizational location of the DSS group.
2. What implications do you draw from the fact that there are twice as many groups reporting to MIS Departments as to non-MIS Departments? Do you think that is still true today? Why or why not?
3. You would expect the DSS support personnel with the most technical backgrounds to provide the more technical kinds of support services? Is that what the data show? Explain.
4. Based on the overall summary of the study, which of the placement options is best, in your opinion? Give support for your choice.

REFERENCES

1. D. Amoroso, "Organizational issues of end user computing," *Data Base*, vol. 19, no. 3/4, pp. 49–58, 1988.
2. F. Bergeron, and C. Berube, "The management of the end-user environment: An empirical investigation," *Inform. Manag.*, vol. 14, pp. 107–113, 1988.
3. H. Carr, *Managing End User Computing*, Englewood Cliffs, NJ: Prentice Hall, 1988.
4. R. P. Cerveny, E. J. Garrity, and G. Lawrence Sanders, "The application of prototyping to systems development: A rationale and model," *J. MIS*, vol 3., no. 2, pp. 52–62, 1986.
5. P. W. Cheney, R. I. Mann, and D. L. Amoroso, "Organizational factors affecting the success of end user computing," *J. MIS*, vol 3, no. 1, pp. 65–80, 1986.
6. *Directory of Top Computer Executives—West Edition*, Phoenix, AZ: Applied Computer Research, Spring 1989.
7. L. W. Hammond, "Management considerations for an information center," *IBM Systems J.*, vol. 21, no. 2, pp. 131–161, 1982.
8. G. Houdeshel, and H. Watson, "The management information and decision support (MIDS) system at Lockheed-Georgia," *MIS Quart.*, vol. 11, no. 1, pp. 127–140, 1987.

9. J. T. HOGUE, and H. J. WATSON, "Management's role in the approval and administration of decision support systems," *MIS Quart.*, vol 7, no. 2, pp. 15–26, 1983.
10. S. L. HUFF, S. RIVARD, A. GRINDLAY, and I. P. SUTTIE, "An empirical study of decision support systems," *INFOR*, vol. 22, no. 1, pp. 21–39, 1984.
11. P. G. W. KEEN, and M. S. SCOTT-MORTON, *Decision support systems: An organizational perspective*, Reading, MA: Addison-Wesley, 1978.
12. P. G. W. KEEN, "Value analysis: Justifying decision support systems," *MIS Quart.*, vol 5, no. 1, pp. 1–14, 1981.
13. P. G. W. KEEN, "Decision support systems: The next decade," *Decision Support Systems*, vol. 3, pp. 253–265, 1987.
14. G. B. LANGLE, R. L. LEITHEISER, and J. D. NAUMANN, "A survey of systems prototyping in industry," *Inform. Manag.*, vol. 7, pp. 273–284, 1984.
15. B. C. MCNURLIN, and R. H. SPRAGUE, JR., *Information systems management in practice* (second edition), Englewood Cliffs, NJ: Prentice Hall, 1989.
16. J. D. NAUMANN, and A. M. JENKINS, "Prototyping: The new paradigm for systems development," *MIS Quart.*, vol. 6, no. 3, pp. 29–42, 1982.
17. R. D. NEAL, and M. RADNOR, "The relationship between formal procedures for pursuing OR/MS activities and OR/MS group success," *Operations Res.*, vol. 21, pp. 451–474, 1973.
18. J. F. ROCKART, and L. S. FLANNERY, "The management of end user computing," *Commun. ACM*, vol. 26, no. 10, pp. 776–784, 1983.
19. J. C. SIPIOR, and G. L. SANDERS, "Definitional distinctions and implications for managing end user computing," *Inform. Manag.*, vol. 16, pp. 115–123, 1989.
20. R. H. SPRAGUE, JR., and E. D. CARLSON, *Building Effective Decision Support Systems*, Englewood Cliffs, NJ: Prentice Hall, 1982.
21. G. R. WAGNER, "Decision support systems: The real substance," *Interfaces*, vol. 11, no. 2, pp. 77–86, 1981.
22. H. WATSON, and H. CARR, "Organizing for decision support system support: The end-user services alternative," *J. MIS*, vol. 4, no. 1, pp. 83–95, 1987.
23. H. J. WATSON, A. LIPP, P. Z. JACKSON, A. DAHMANI, and W. FREDENBERGER, "Organizational support for decision support systems," *J. MIS*, vol. 5, no. 4, pp. 87–109, 1989.

15

DSS SOFTWARE SELECTION

INTRODUCTION

The DSS Software Selection Problem

Recent publications devoted to evaluating decision support systems (DSS) software [19, 21, 22, 28, and 32] have identified criteria, especially user-related ones, which are critical in selecting a suitable DSS generator. However, these authors have not suggested how to incorporate multiple user criteria, as well as technical attributes, into a complete and thorough evaluation and selection process. Furthermore, Lynch [16, 17] suggests that inadequate examination of prospective software packages leads to serious difficulties if not failures when implementing information systems.

Although a number of approaches to selecting application software for transaction processing and MIS have been proposed [3, 4, 6, 9, 18, 25, 33], some critical factors were omitted. These factors include assuring that the selected software package is superior to a custom alternative, or that a screening process is provided to reduce the number of packages subjected to detailed evaluation.

DSS Terminology

A number of key terms and expressions that will be used throughout the chapter are now defined. A *DSS Generator* is a "package of related hardware and software

This chapter is a reprint of DSS Software Selection. Reprinted by special permission of *Information & Management*, Volume 17, 1989.

which provides a set of capabilities to build specific DSS quickly and easily" [26]. Examples of such generators include IFPS [8], Prefcalc [15], Expert Choice [7], and Lightyear [29]. A DSS generator constitutes one of the three technological levels that make up the DSS development framework suggested by Sprague [26]. The other two levels are: *Specific DSS*, which are systems that actually support the manager (user) to solve specific sets of related decision problems; and *DSS Tools*, which are hardware and software elements built by a toolsmith to facilitate the development of both specific DSS and DSS generators (see respectively (1) and (2) in Figure 15–1). Examples of such DSS tools include procedural programming languages, graphics and color subroutines, and other dialog-handling software.

Figure 15–1 (adapted from [26]), shows the three technological levels defined above, the relationships between them, and the manager/technician roles associated with each level. Notice that specific DSS can be developed either directly from tools or by adapting the DSS generator to satisfy the application requirements. In the latter case, the DSS builder may use the *iterative design approach* [5] to add capabilities to the ones available in the DSS generator (or delete unnecessary features) as needed by the specific DSS. This approach can be represented by the iterative cycling between the DSS generator and the specific DSS (see (3) in Figure 15–1).

To emphasize the importance of evaluation and selection of DSS software (as compared to that of other information systems), it should be noted that DSS generators are used to develop *multiple* application systems, while MIS software is employed only for a *single* application. To efficiently develop specific DSS using the iterative design approach, a generator needs to be available. Hogue and

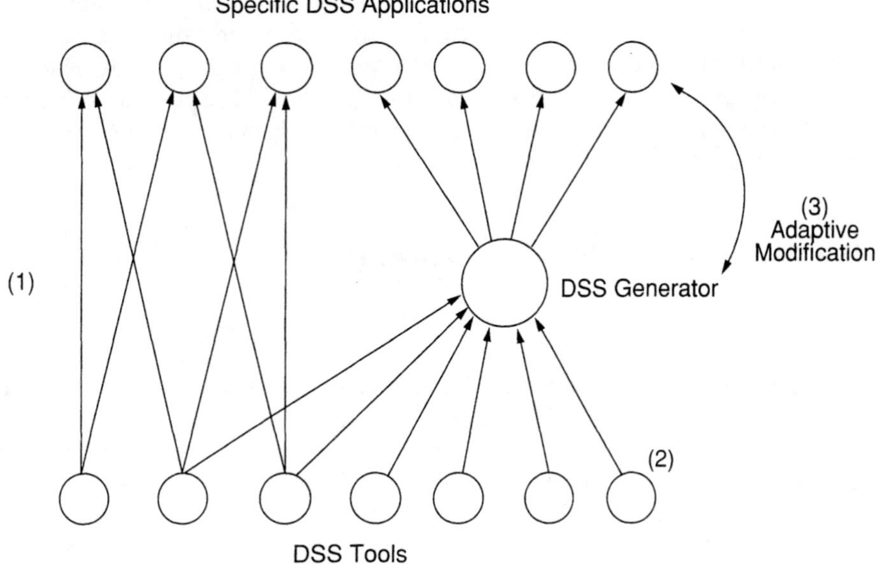

FIGURE 15–1 DSS Technology Levels and Development Framework

Watson [10] reported that 50 percent of the firms that they studied developed specific DSS applications with a generator. The very critical software evaluation and selection process for DSS generators should take place prior to any systems analysis and design efforts.

This chapter illustrates a method to select the most appropriate DSS generator where multiple criteria exist not only from functional requirements but also from technical and vendor support perspectives. As an essential part of the methodology, an initial stage determines whether a DSS software product is even suitable for a particular enterprise, or whether a specific DSS should be developed from available tools.

The proposed selection process in this chapter also ensures that, at each successive stage of the methodology, a DSS generator is superior to a DSS application custom-built from tools. It continually reduces the number of DSS software products under consideration until a final selection of a generator is made or constructing a specific DSS from tools is chosen as the best alternative (see Figure 15–2).

Structure of the Paper

This chapter is primarily addressed to academics interested in software selection methodologies as well as practitioners faced with DSS-related problems. The second section outlines DSS developments affecting information systems (IS) planning. In particular, the enterprise software policy and the implications that DSS generators might have are discussed. The third section suggests a multiple criteria methodology for DSS software selection. The three stages of the methodology—DSS software screening, DSS generator evaluation, and specific DSS design—are described. Then, the fourth section presents a case example that demonstrates the applicability of the proposed methodology. The fifth section covers the impact of DSS software on specific DSS development from systems analysis and design, installation, and operating support viewpoints. The sixth section concludes with some final remarks.

DSS DEVELOPMENTS AFFECTING IS PLANNING

The increased use and availability of DSS software has greatly influenced IS planning [34]. Questions such as the following ones have been raised. What is the organization's strategy concerning the use of packaged software? What types of criteria should be used? Are packages easy to maintain?

These questions and others must be directly addressed by IS management, since many applications requirements can be effectively satisfied by DSS software packages. One major consideration is the degree to which DSS generators are compatible with the enterprise's technical architecture for information processing. For example, if multiple DSS generators and vendors are used, how effectively can a common database be employed throughout the organization?

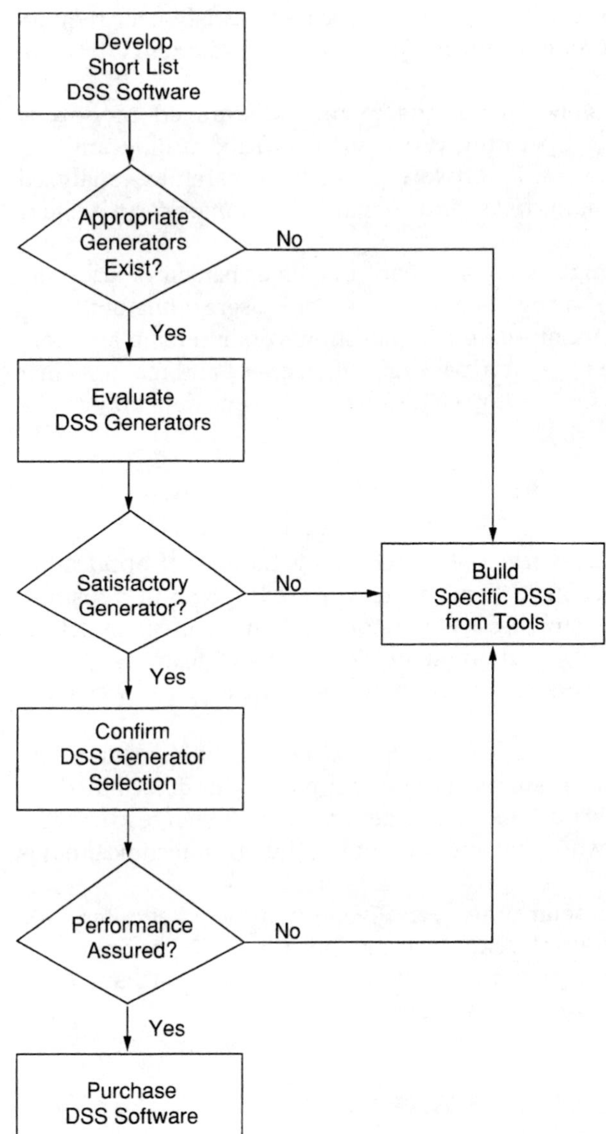

FIGURE 15–2 A Multiple Criteria Decision Methodology for DSS Software Selection

Implications of DSS Generators

With the greater availability of DSS generator software and its improved quality, it appears that, for most organizations, DSS packages may be preferred over custom development from DSS tools. While there are obvious benefits to using generator packages, they are not necessarily "off-the-shelf" solutions. Generator selection should be a careful and well-organized process to satisfy user requirements and to meet generally accepted information processing standards for quality and performance.

The selection of a DSS generator needs to be a disciplined process of matching package options with operating procedures, and reconciling any differences. Modifications to the DSS software should be carefully analyzed before they are made to consider risks and jeopardizing longer-term vendor support.

The use of DSS generators may conflict with the major benefit of adopting a corporate database—that is, sharing data among several users while enforcing a unique way to define it and manipulate it in addition to minimizing and controlling data redundancy. Since generator packages often create and manage their own data, this may lead to having multiple versions of the same data and can be a source of inconsistencies.

Enterprise Software Policy

The importance of an enterprise-wide policy regarding the use of application software cannot be overemphasized. This means a stated "going-in" position concerning the desirability of using DSS generators and the manner in which it should be used. Such a policy statement guides a project team as it considers the compromises that users might have to make to employ DSS technology.

The hardware and software policy of the firm has a direct relationship to the choice of DSS products. Normally, such a policy will have been determined by the enterprise IS strategy. The evaluators of DSS generators will then restrict their search to vendors offering software that will operate in the given technical environment.

The organization needs to determine overall vendor and market criteria for DSS software evaluation. For example, each package must meet 85 percent of the application's functional requirements; and each DSS generator must have been previously installed in at least five organizations.

A DECISION METHODOLOGY FOR DSS SOFTWARE SELECTION

There are three principal stages in the proposed DSS evaluation and selection methodology: (1) screening of prospective candidates and development of a short list of DSS software packages; (2) selecting a DSS generator, if any, which best suits the application requirements; and, (3) matching user requirements to the features of the selected generator and describing how these requirements will be satisfied through the building of prototypes for specific DSS. The detailed procedures involved in each state of the selection process are described in the following sections.

DSS Software Screening

During the first stage of the evaluation and selection methodology, three key issues must be addressed: (1) Is there DSS software that can be used or should a specific DSS be developed from tools?; (2) What DSS generators are available?; and, (3) Which DSS software packages should be seriously considered and evaluated in detail? Examples of commercially available mainframe- and microcomputer-based DSS software packages are given in Table 15–1.

The purpose of developing a short list of generator products is to narrow the field of available DSS software for consideration during generator evaluation. A short list of software (two or three) eliminates any unnecessary effort or confusion which might result because too many alternative DSS products are evaluated.

Identify Candidate Software. The project team must first identify available DSS products that operate within the enterprise's specific computer hardware and are compatible with its operating system and database management system (DBMS). To accomplish this task, there are several publications (e.g., *Datapro Directory* and *ICP Directory*) which provide profiles of DSS software vendors and the products they offer.

Screening Criteria. At this point in the process, since a detailed analysis of user requirements has not likely been performed, screening criteria should be kept to a rather high level. Otherwise, these criteria will become so specific that

TABLE 15–1 Representative DSS Software Products

Product	Vendor
Mainframe Packages	
EXPRESS	Information Resources, Inc.
IFPS	Comshare, Inc.
SYSTEM W	Comshare, Inc.
SIMPLAN	Simplan Systems, Inc.
INSIGHT	Insight Software
PLATO	OR/MS Dialogue, Inc.
PC or Client/Server Packages	
FOCUS/PC	Information Builders, Inc.
NOMAD 2 PC	D&B Computing Services
ENCORE	Ferox Microsystems
PC ANALECT	Dialogue, Inc.
PC EXPRESS	Information Resource, Inc.
PREFCALC	Euro-Decision
ENABLE	Software Publishing Group
SYMPHONY	Lotus Development
FRAMEWORK	Ashton-Tate

it might become impossible to meet them with any commercially available DSS generator. The list of criteria will contain relatively few items and should concentrate on functional requirements not commonly provided by DSS packages and which are very specific to the organization evaluating DSS software.

Some of the screening criteria are requirements that cannot be compromised and are easy to define objectively, such as compatibility with a particular operating system. However, other criteria are less definite, such as a vendor's ability to adequately support the software. Screening criteria can be categorized into four major types: (1) technical requirements; (2) functional requirements; (3) documentation and training; and (4) vendor information.

Technical Requirements. An organization's hardware and software strategy will likely dictate the high-level criteria in the technical area. To be considered, a package must fit the framework of the proposed system; it must be compatible with the hardware and software direction already identified (usually IS planning). The operating system is clearly a strict technical requirement. Others could include programming languages, peripherals, memory needs, or data communication capabilities. If relatively high transaction and report volumes are required, then the technical architecture of the DSS software package must support efficient processing.

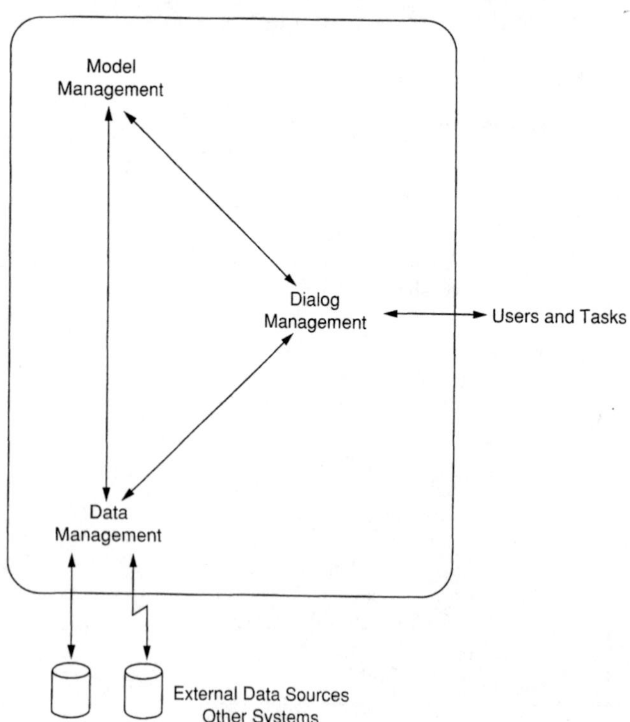

FIGURE 15–3 Functional Components of a Decision Support System

Functional Requirements. The functional requirements of a DSS generator can be classified according to the following system components (see Figure 15–3 adapted from [2]): (1) Dialog Management; (2) Data Management; and (3) Model Management. The functional requirements associated with each of these three system components readily distinguish DSS generator evaluation and selection from other software appraisal efforts [27], where functional requirements are less unique to the IS type.

The dialog component of a DSS is the software and hardware that provides the user interface for the system. It presents the process outputs to the users and collects the inputs to the DSS. Building a DSS without databases and associated DBMS will be extremely difficult, since this component provides the data needed for decision making. The modeling component gives decision makers the ability to analyze a problem by developing and comparing alternative solutions.

Table 15–2 lists several examples of functional criteria to conduct the first-cut screening according to the DSS components. High-level criteria for the dialog management component would be that the DSS generator offers several dialogs (e.g., command language, menu, question/answer, and object oriented) to accommodate different cognitive styles of various users. The data management component could call for both relational and hierarchical DBMS. Model management criteria might require the availability of multiple optimization models, such as linear, dynamic, and integer programming models.

Documentation and Training. DSS software packages normally include the documentation required to install and support the DSS generator. It should be detailed, complete, and easy to understand. Poor documentation makes it more difficult for personnel to understand the package, and would also increase the

TABLE 15–2 High-Level Screening Criteria of DSS Components

Dialog Management	Data Management	Model Management
Multiple Dialog Styles	Variety of Logical Data Views	Library of Optimization Models
Command Language	Relational DBMS	Linear Programming
Menu	Hierarchical DBMS	Dynamic Programming
Question/Answer	Network DBMS	Integer Programming
Object Oriented	File Management System	

time to modify it, if necessary. The availability of vendor-developed training sessions and materials may be very important, especially when the organization's personnel are inexperienced in implementing software.

Vendor Information. A vendor's ability to support its package through training, consultation, installation, and maintenance assistance is an important consideration in evaluating DSS software packages. Whenever the extent of a vendor's support for a generator package is unclear, the vendor should be contacted so the point can be clarified. He should also be able to refer an evaluation team to a user who is willing to talk to them about the DSS package and the accompanying support.

The financial stability of a vendor can also be an important consideration. Financially successful vendors that have been in existence for more than a few years are more likely to adequately support their packages initially and in the future. Such vendors attract and retain competent personnel, so that, in addition to having the funds available for support, they also have the personnel.

It is important to remember, however, that financial success alone does not ensure adequate, continued support. Vendor image, package reputation, the unit price, and the number of installations are also important considerations. Either the vendors themselves or the users to whom they directed the prospective buyer should be able to provide the needed information in these areas. Vendor support should always be carefully investigated.

Pick Finalists. The matching of the screening criteria against the list of DSS software and their capabilities will cause the elimination of many (but hopefully not all) generators. The following are typical reasons to eliminate potential DSS software candidates: (1) a vendor has only three employees and has been in business less than a year; (2) operating systems software and hardware is not supported by a vendor; and, (3) system documentation is inadequate.

By reducing the number of DSS software packages under consideration from as many as twenty to two or three, a project team can more effectively devote its attention to the critical details that can make the difference between selecting an adequate DSS and selecting a superior one. Moreover, by determining what DSS software packages are available for the application, the screening process also determines whether a DSS generator can be used or if a specific decision support system should be constructed from DSS tools (see Figure 15–2).

DSS Generator Evaluation

This second stage focuses on the two or three DSS generators that were identified in the screening of DSS software. The objective is to evaluate in detail the DSS generator finalists and select the one software product that best meets the needs of the organization. The primary tasks of DSS software selection are:

(1) to further define the detailed evaluation criteria; (2) obtain generator product information; and, (3) evaluate the DSS software finalists and pick one as the best alternative.

Expand Evaluation Criteria. The screening criteria are expanded in more detail and fall into the same four categories: (1) technical requirements; (2) functional requirements; (3) documentation and training; and (4) vendor information. Although all categories are expanded during generator evaluation, the *functional requirements* receive the majority of attention and are related to the dialog, data, and model management components of the DSS generator.

The purpose of this task is to develop a rather comprehensive functional view of the proposed system and to summarize the requirements that must be satisfied by the DSS. The definition of functional requirements must be detailed enough to provide users and management with a complete view of the proposed system. This task should emphasize how the new system will work in the business environment. As the project team defines the functional criteria, they should also document the levels of importance and need to the user. The following functional requirements for DSS software, identified in [19, 22, and 27], are those for a hypothetical firm: (1) user friendliness; (2) hardware and operating system considerations; (3) variety of dialog styles; (4) data handling functions; (5) management of internal and external databases; (6) logical data models; (7) analysis; (8) forecasting and statistics; and, (9) graphics. These categories represent an outline for the extended functional criteria of the DSS generator. Table 15–3 exhibits an expansion of the above summary list of functional generator requirements categorized by the DSS as dialog, data, and model management components.

Obviously, some criteria are more important or critical to users than others. To reflect the relative importance of each criterion, the users must weight or assign a level of importance (such as "3" for essential, "2" for important, or "1" for optional) to each criterion. To demonstrate this element of the evaluation and selection methodology, an example of the weighting procedure is given below using the "Analysis" criteria from Table 15–3 for a hypothetical enterprise.

Analysis	Weight
What-If	1
Goal Seeking	3
Monte Carlo	2
Optimization	2

The purpose of this weighting process will be discussed in more detail in a later section (Evaluate DSS Generators).

TABLE 15-3 Detailed Functional Criteria for DSS Software

Dialog Management Component
User Friendliness
Consistent, natural language commands
"Help" command and error messages
Novice and expert modes
Hardware and Operating System Elements
Printer and plotter support
Variety of input device support
Variety of Dialog Styles
Menu
Command language
Object oriented
Question/Answer
Graphics
Basic plots and charts
Multicolor support
Previewing of output
Data Management Component
Data Handling Functions
Dictionary
Creation, deletion, update, and query
Management of Internal and External Databases
Extraction
Capture
Integration of data sources
Logical Data Views
Record
Relational, Hierarchical, and Network DBMS
Rule
Model Management Component
Analysis
What-if
Goal Seeking
Monte Carlo
Mathematical optimization
Forecasting and Statistics
Basic statistical functions
Time series with seasonal adjustment
Multivariate statistics

Criticism levied against weighting schemes for software selection decisions [14] can be minimized through the screening process and development of a short list. Naumann and Palvia [20] successfully applied weighting and scoring measures to select a systems development tool from a relatively short list (4) of candidate techniques. By weighting criteria for only two or three packages rather than for a dozen (in which case the forementioned criticism is probably valid), the proposed evaluation process allows for a very detailed and focused inspection of just the few best alternative DSS software products.

The proposed approach is an efficient, pragmatic, and managerially oriented evaluation and selection procedure. The advantages of using a DSS generator may be reduced significantly by a lengthy evaluation and selection process which often delays the prompt installation of the software and postpones the benefits available from rapidly producing a specific DSS from a generator.

Obtain Package Information. Once the system requirements have been established, and the criteria have been reviewed and weighted, the capability of each DSS generator to satisfy the requirements must be measured. Several techniques may be used to gather enough information to determine how well each package meets the requirements.

In many cases, the project team can meet directly with the vendor sales and support personnel and discuss each requirement. But if requirements are so comprehensive and detailed that a more formal procedure should be followed, a request for proposal (RFP) can be submitted to vendors. In situations where requirements are less detailed and complex, the RFP can be replaced by a less formal and more direct procedure, for example a basic letter of request.

Evaluate DSS Generators. Once the vendors' responses to requirements have been received, the actual evaluation process can begin. The review is very detailed at this point, since the project team is looking for specific strengths and weaknesses of each package.

The project team is searching for deciding factors—not only *what* DSS software packages have and how well they provide it, but also what they *don't* have. Detailed information is desired on the functions of the DSS software and its related processing, including if and how functions that are not included in the DSS generator could be implemented.

Evaluation Matrix. An evaluation matrix should be constructed to organize and assimilate all necessary information. The first step in constructing this matrix is to set up a rating scale that indicates, for each evaluation criterion (i.e., technical, functional, documentation, and vendor-related), how easily each package is able to meet that specific criterion. These rating scores are then multiplied by the weight factor for that criterion. The weights reflect the relative importance of each of the criteria, while the rating scores show how well a given package meets each user criterion.

Using the previous example of the "Analysis" criteria, a project team might employ a scale of 0–3: "3" if the DSS package totally meets the requirements; "2" when the product does not meet the requirement completely but enough so that tailoring is not warranted; "1" if the criterion would be met with some tailoring; and, "0" when the package does not meet the criterion at all. (Other rating, scoring, or evaluation methods (e.g., [23, 24, and 31]) could also be appropriate depending on the particular user requirements.)

Using this scale, two prospective DSS software packages, ABC and XYZ, were scored:

Analysis	ABC	XYZ
What-If	1	3
Goal Seeking	3	3
Monte Carlo	3	2
Optimization	2	3
Subtotal	9	11

These results would indicate that XYZ meets the hypothetical requirements better. However, these may not be accurate! The detailed requirements for "Analysis" (an element of the model management component in the DSS generator) are probably not equal. The weighting factors, which were established earlier, are absent from these calculations.

If the scores are adjusted by multiplying the rating score for each "Analysis" criterion by the corresponding weight factor, then the figures would appear as the following:

	ABC Generator					XYZ Generator				
Analysis	Weight		Rating		Total	Weight		Rating		Total
What-If	1	×	1	=	1	1	×	3	=	3
Goal Seeking	3	×	3	=	9	3	×	3	=	9
Monte Carlo	2	×	3	=	6	2	×	2	=	4
Optimization	2	×	2	=	4	2	×	3	=	6
Total					20					22

Note that the weight scores for each "Analysis" criterion are the same for both DSS generators, reflecting the user's decision about the relative importance of each of the criteria. On the other hand, the rating scores indicate how well each DSS software package meets each criterion established by the users.

A "total possible points" column could represent an ideal package meeting 100 percent of requirements. The "constant" weight factor would be multiplied by the highest possible rating score for each of the "Analysis" criteria. An ideal package would have all of the analysis features (i.e., what-if, goal seeking, Monte Carlo, and optimization) as standard. This would mean a score of "3" in the example.

This scoring by matrix is a small part of the DSS software evaluation process; but this exercise or calculation must be completed for each criterion, such as those listed in Table 15–3. The total points of each criterion for each DSS software package would then be recorded in a large matrix. A partially completed matrix for the hypothetical example follows:

Functional Requirements	ABC	XYZ	Total Possible Points
1. User Friendliness	23	21	24
2. Hardware and Operating System Elements	13	13	16
3. Variety of Dialog Styles	20	22	24
4. Data Handling Functions	15	14	18
5. Extraction from Internal or External Data Base	22	20	22
6. Logical Data Views	18	17	20
7. Analysis	20	22	24
8. Forecasting and Statistics	12	10	15
9. Graphics	26	21	30
Subtotal	169	160	193

As established in an enterprise software policy, hurdle scores ensure that DSS generators provide adequate coverage of requirements. A policy for software selection might be that all DSS generators must satisfy at least 80 percent of the requirements. In the prior partial matrix, the "ABC Generator" satisfied 88 percent of the criteria, while "XYZ" covered only 83 percent. Both DSS software packages met the minimum hurdle.

In this instance, where both packages exceed the hurdle percentage scores, an index would be constructed by dividing the cost of each respective package by its score, giving the price in dollars per requirement point. For example, if the ABC package sold for $100,000 and XYZ costs $75,000, the respective indices would be $591.72 and $468.75. This indicates that the XYZ package would provide more than the minimum functional requirements and almost equal coverage of these requirements as the alternative DSS software package but at considerably less cost per requirement.

Additional Selection Requirements. The matrix scores are not necessarily the determining factor for selecting a particular DSS generator. The matrix should be used as a decision tool—a means for organizing and summarizing the significant quantity of information that the project team has collected. The highest score on the evaluation matrix may not always indicate the best DSS generator. The matrix scores may not accurately reflect certain intangible factors such as the cosmetic appearance of reports and screens, how easy it will be to use the DSS software, etc.

Tailoring. The matrix may not indicate how much time or the level of technical expertise needed to "tailor" the DSS generator. Tailoring can be either costly if it is relatively extensive, or difficult if the internal structure of the software is complex. The importance of the technical processing architecture will depend on how much tailoring is anticipated. Furthermore, the architecture of the DSS generator also determines how much modification is even possible.

Documentation. A decision to use a particular DSS generator should not be made on the basis of functional requirements alone. The DSS software's documentation is a very important nonfunctional factor. Its accuracy and level of detail can affect the time it will take to evaluate and modify the package.

Comparing documentation is sometimes very difficult at this stage of the evaluation process due to differences in format, style, etc. Still, it is important to review the vendors' documentation and to reconfirm that the information collected on maintenance and support, for instance, is accurate and correct. At this stage, the vendor should be able to refer the project team to current users of his software. The comments of these customers should prove invaluable. Site visits and demonstrations of the DSS software in operation may be helpful.

Specific DSS Design

Assuming that DSS software which is anticipated to provide satisfactory performance has been selected (see Figure 15.2), the project team is ready to confirm the selection by developing some specific DSS prototypes based on the chosen generator. The primary reasons for this stage are to ensure that the DSS package can be used effectively and to provide one last chance to reconsider the DSS software design.

It is often difficult to determine the degree of user satisfaction until the design process has begun for specific applications utilizing the selected DSS software. Therefore, this stage involves the design of demonstration prototypes of specific DSS built from the DSS generator [11, 19]. Such prototypes can provide significant benefits before finalizing the selection decision [1, 11, 12, 13]. These benefits afford much information for the evaluation and selection process [19], including: (1) estimates of programmer productivity; (2) measures of computer resource utilization; (3) personnel requirements for the DSS software; (4) performance of the documentation under actual working conditions; and, (5) experience with the iterative development process using the DSS generator for building specific DSS applications.

In addition to prototyping specific DSS with the selected DSS software before actual purchase, Meador and Mezger [19] suggest conducting "benchmark evaluations" which would be undertaken during this stage of the proposed evaluation and selection process. A benchmark evaluation is a series of simulated tests for a comprehensive set of the DSS software's features. The simulations attempt to determine the level of computer system resources utilized by the various capabilities of the DSS package. Resources include CPU cycles, main memory, input/output activity, and response time. The programs or models to be tested are specifically designed to execute the features or capabilities of the DSS generator, rather than to solve specific DSS application problems.

Alter Functional Requirements. Based on the capabilities of the selected DSS generator as experienced in the prototyping exercise of specific DSS and benchmark testing, the definition of user requirements might be altered to include package features not previously considered, or to change or eliminate others. The modified requirements should be reviewed with the users. The effect of DSS software deficiencies perhaps can be minimized by altering user procedures or postponing the implementation of some requirements until generator enhancements could be made.

DSS Software Modifications and Supporting Programs. Typically, the specific DSS being developed requires certain functions and interfaces not provided by the software. If a DSS generator does not meet all the functional requirements of a system, the following alternatives should be considered: (1) persuade the vendor to include additional features; (2) develop supplemental software; and, (3) modify the vendor's software. The chosen alternative will depend on the extent of the DSS generator's deficiencies, the potential costs and benefits of altering the software, and the size and technical skills of the programming staff.

Vendor-Supplied Enhancements. If possible, the vendor should be persuaded to do the modification for the purchaser. This is often the best alternative, since the vendor will usually update and maintain the software on a routine basis.

Supporting Programs. Developing software to supplement the vendor's DSS package is often the most practical alternative. The vendor will normally continue to service the DSS generator; but if this alternative is selected, the supplemental software should conform to the standards used by the vendor in developing the DSS generator.

Alter Code. Modifying a DSS generator is usually not recommended. If the software is modified, the vendor may be reluctant or may even refuse to service the package. Updates to the software may not be compatible with the modifications effected.

In some cases, this may not even be an option, since the purchaser of the DSS generator does not have (or cannot get at any price) a copy of the source code. In this instance, all that the purchaser can do is to build a front end or back end to the software package.

Finalize DSS Generator Selection. It is not unheard of for an organization to complete the last stage of the evaluation and selection process for DSS software, only to realize that the DSS generator selected is not the best choice. Perhaps too many compromises have been made and users are no longer satisfied. Possibly, the tailoring effort has become so extensive that a custom DSS (i.e., specific DSS application built from tools) would be a better choice (see Figure 15–2). Therefore, a final commitment to using a particular DSS generator should be avoided until the design of specific DSS using the potential software package has progressed to the point where user satisfaction is ensured.

The following section provides an illustrative example of how the DSS software evaluation and selection methodology works. It uses a real-world case, the Wildlife and Fisheries Department, to demonstrate the applicability of the proposed methodology.

CASE EXAMPLE: THE WILDLIFE AND FISHERIES DEPARTMENT

The Wildlife and Fisheries Department (WFD) is a state government office responsible for developing a strategy to manage its state's deer population. Each year, the Department chooses to either maintain, increase, or decrease the deer population in each county. Population regulation may be achieved through the selective issuance of hunting permits. Therefore, it is essential that WFD be able to accurately predict deer population levels within each of the state's counties.

Case Background

Deer hunting regulations require that each successful hunter report his kill to a check station within 24 hours. Within the state of Indiana, for example, there are approximately 240 such check stations. When a hunter brings his deer to a check station, the deer is tagged and the hunter is required to fill out a form listing the county of kill, date of harvest, and the sex of the deer taken. A copy of this form is then forwarded to the WFD on a weekly basis for the duration of the hunting season.

Once the WFD receives the data, it must sort it by county. Certain statistical analysis, such as the percentage of yearling, must also be calculated. Once the data is adequately prepared, it is ready for use in a predictive model. With data, such as population fecundity and survivorship by age class, a spreadsheet model could produce estimates of the state's deer population. The harvest number can then be varied to show its effects on the deer population within each county of interest. In this way, the WFD can determine the number of permits to issue within each county. The spreadsheet output along with recommendations for management are then incorporated into an annual report which is presented to the WFD's "administrator" who makes the final decision.

The professional construction and presentation of the report may also influence the "administrator." Therefore, it is to the advantage of the WFD staff to have its report neatly processed. For illustrating the calculated trends in the deer population, graphical and tabular summaries should also be incorporated into the report.

DSS Generator Screening

While practically any spreadsheet program could perform the mathematical requirements of the population forecasting model, the production of the complete report requires additional software capabilities. A functional and technical analysis of the procedures to be used by the WFD revealed the following list of requirements (i.e., screening criteria).

IBM-PC Compatibility. This was essential for interfacing with the corresponding systems of neighboring states which would provide relevant input data. As a base level operating system, DOS was chosen.

Database. The database must be large enough to incorporate all of the data from the approximately 50,000 individual kill reports received each year. One hundred characters were needed for each record. Also, the maintenance of a five-year database was recommended.

Statistical Analysis. Functions such as mean, standard deviation, relative percentages and to a lesser extent regression analysis, were necessary for the data analysis.

Spreadsheet. The dimensions of the spreadsheet should be large enough to accept data from all 92 state counties and perform the necessary computations. In addition, the spreadsheet functions must link individual county spreadsheet models into a comprehensive statewide summary.

Word Processor. This component required both spelling and grammatical checks to assist the biologists in preparing their reports.

Graphics. The software had to produce good quality line, grouped line, and bar charts for showing trends and supporting quick information assimilation by the WFD users.

File Import/Export. In addition to exchanging files from other computer programs, the chosen software package must be able to accept data from existing files which contain a significant amount of needed historical data. The acceptance of this material by the new system without major modification would allow for considerable savings in time and money.

Documentation. The documentation had to be detailed, organized and precise. Both external documentation (books, manuals, videotapes) and internal (on-screen help) should be available. On-line documentation should be context sensitive, and external documentation might include videotape sessions.

Two classes of potential "commercial" DSS software, namely basic and integrated spreadsheets, were identified by the WFD. It should be noted here that these packages are commercially available products which might differ from the "ideal" DSS generator defined in the first section. The list of spreadsheet packages available in this market is very long, ranging from the most simplistic to the very sophisticated. A preliminary list, based on the two potential classes of DSS software, follows. From this roster, a short list of three DSS generators was developed by applying the forementioned screening criteria (i.e., functional and technical criteria, etc.) and eliminating those packages which were not considered adequate for more detailed inspection.

Basic Spreadsheets	Integrated Spreadsheets
Lotus 123	Enable
Quattro	Symphony
Excel	Framework
Multiplan	Smart
Supercalc	Electric Desk

A brief evaluation of the main characteristics of the basic spreadsheets uncovered the following attributes: (1) good features in terms of mathematical abilities; (2) lack of graphical components (except in Lotus and Quattro); (3) none of them has a word processing component; and, (4) none of them can handle the necessary database size.

The functional and technical environment described earlier in this section documented the crucial nature of the graphical, word processing, and database capabilities. Consequently, the basic spreadsheet packages were eliminated and would not be included in the final evaluation. While separate software products may be combined into one DSS to perform the necessary functions, the number of possible combinations was too large to consider.

The further matching of screening criteria against the list of integrated spreadsheet packages eliminated all but the following potential DSS generators: Symphony (Lotus Development), Framework (Ashton-Tate), and Enable (Software Group). The other potential DSS generators failed to be included in the short list since they did not meet one or more of the screening criteria (i.e., database size or spreadsheet linking functions).

DSS Generator Evaluation and Selection

Based on the aforementioned list of screening criteria, a scheme for the detailed evaluation and selection of the generator software was based upon the following categories: (1) technical criteria; (2) functional criteria; (3) documentation criteria; and, (4) vendor criteria.

Technical Criteria. The primary technical requirement for the WFD computing environment is IBM and DOS compatibility. A version of DOS 3.0 or higher was also considered a necessity.

Functional Criteria. The functional requirements of the WFD application include the database, statistical, spreadsheet, word processing, graphics creating, file handling and exchange, and documentation criteria which were listed in the initial phase (DSS Generator Screening).

For purposes of evaluating the three commercial DSS generators listed before, the preceding criteria were weighted according to their relative importance to the WFD operations. The following scale was used: "3" expressing a crucial function; "2" meaning significant; and "1" noting optional. Table 15–4 describes the relative importance assigned to each criterion.

In addition to the weighting scale, a rating system was used to indicate the respective software's performance on each of the criteria. This rating was based on a four-point scale (3 = good, 2 = fair, 1 = poor, and 0 = not available).

Table 15–4 depicts both the weights and the total scores (weights multiplied by rating scores) developed for each DSS generator. The matrix totals give Enable the edge over the other DSS software packages evaluated. However, the tabulated scores were rather close (i.e., Enable = 91, Framework = 85, Symphony = 76).

While scores were close, Enable was the best performer in the most critical areas. Of the criteria considered to be the most crucial, Enable received a perfect

TABLE 15–4 WFD Case: Evaluation Matrix for DSS Software

		DSS Generator Scores		
Criteria	Weight	Symphony	Framework	Enable
Technical				
IBM Compatibility	3	9	9	9
Functional				
Data base Size	3	3	3	9
Basic Statistics	3	9	9	9
Regression Analysis	1	0	0	0
Spreadsheet Size	3	3	6	6
Spelling Check	2	0	6	6
Grammar Check	1	0	0	0
Graphics	3	6	6	6
Spreadsheet Linking	2	6	6	4
File Import/Export	2	2	6	6
Combine Graphics and Text	2	2	4	6
Menu Dialog	2	6	6	6
Common Dialog	2	4	2	6
Documentation				
External Documentation	2	2	4	6
On-Line Help in Context	3	9	9	9
Vendor				
Reputation	3	9	9	3
Total		76	85	91

(3) rating in four of them. Perhaps the most important criterion was database size. Enable was the only DSS generator capable of handing the required 50,000 records. Enable was also superior in both internal and external documentation, which was critical since non-computer personnel would be directly involved in the operation of the DSS software. However, Enable was relatively inferior in two areas, namely its spreadsheet linking function and its vendor reputation (i.e., lack of market prominence compared to the other vendors).

Overall, Framework had the best word processing features, Enable offered the most useful database module, and Symphony's spreadsheet capabilities were exceptional. However, the superior package at providing comprehensive functionality in spreadsheet, database, and word processing in a single package was Enable.

Specific DSS Applications

At this point in the evaluation and selection process, specific DSS applications were constructed with Enable, the chosen DSS generator. Representative prototypes were built to evaluate the DSS software's ability to handle not only functional requirements but also appraise its operating efficiency. If satisfactory performance was achieved by the DSS generator, then multiple copies would be purchased or a site license acquired. In the event that performance was less than satisfactory, the methodology prescribes construction of the specific DSS application from tools as needed to achieve the application requirements and user expectations.

Case Summary

It is important to note that no package provided a perfect fit for the WFD case. For example, none of the software offered regression analysis as a standard feature. A grammar check was also not available in any package.

As described by Sprague [26], an "ideal" DSS generator does not likely exist. The ideal generator would be developed over a long period of time in a fairly narrow problem domain. In practice, however, most specific DSS applications are being developed with general purpose DSS generators such as FOCUS, IFPS, and Lotus 1-2-3 [31, p. 205].

THE IMPACT OF DSS SOFTWARE ON SPECIFIC DSS DEVELOPMENT

Because DSS software can reduce the costs of developing specific decision support systems, organizations should investigate the possibility of using DSS generators during the systems planning process. Obviously, this may increase the personnel requirements of systems planning. However, such an investigation is valuable even if a custom approach to developing specific DSS from tools is determined to be more appropriate.

The evaluation process will help familiarize personnel with the functional requirements of proposed DSS applications. Furthermore, the availability of good DSS packages may have a significant effect on the organization's hardware and software strategy. Although the evaluation of DSS products can increase the cost of systems planning, the use of a DSS generator can clearly reduce overall development costs for specific DSS.

The following subsections discuss the effects that DSS software may have on developing specific DSS applications. In particular, the impact on system analysis and design, installation, and operating support is assessed.

DSS Software Impact on Systems Analysis and Design

DSS software selection often precedes the design of a specific DSS since the latter will be based on the chosen DSS package(s). Therefore, DSS software evaluation and selection is usually an additional effort that would not be required (or at least not to the same extent) for building specific DSS from tools.

While using DSS generators will often reduce the time and effort needed to complete the preliminary design, this reduction is frequently offset by the amount of work involved in evaluating and selecting a DSS package. Therefore, the overall effort for systems analysis and design may remain fairly constant regardless of whether users decide to use DSS generators or develop specific DSS from tools.

User Requirements and Application Design. The systems analysis activity for developing specific DSS determines whether or not the user's requirements are met by DSS software. While the effort needed to define these requirements is not reduced when a DSS generator is used, specific DSS design usually requires fewer personnel than when a specific system is custom developed from tools.

If user requirements are not satisfied by a DSS software package, the investment in time and effort depends on the amount of analysis and design that is necessary to meet the user's needs. This might involve developing manual procedures, interface capabilities, as well as additional software modules.

Technical Design. The work required for technical design is significantly reduced when DSS software is used. This is apparent because the technical architecture, database, and system processes for the DSS generator have already been defined by the vendor. However, what is necessary here is a confirmation by the project team that the architecture of the DSS package is compatible with the organization's technical environment.

The personnel requirements for designing security and control mechanisms will vary according to the particular DSS software package being used. For many packages, however, security and control is a weak area that requires additional work.

The operating performance of the system can be affected by the use of DSS software. It may suffer especially if many options are used, since the generalized software logic could require longer execution times than specific DSS developed from tools. Therefore, operating performance should not be overlooked during systems design just because DSS software is being used. This underscores the need for benchmark testing as previously mentioned.

DSS Software Impact on Systems Installation

Clearly, the greatest savings in developing specific DSS from a DSS generator are realized during installation. When a DSS package is installed, detailed systems design, programming, and debugging should require less effort than they would in the installation of a custom developed, specific DSS. Computer programs have already been designed, and coding and testing completed when DSS software is utilized.

Detailed Design and Programming. The primary purpose of using DSS software is to reduce the work performed for detailed design and programming. If the user requirements are not completely met by the DSS generator, some tailoring may be necessary. Any modification at this point needs thorough documentation which should be made available (by the system support group) for ongoing maintenance of the DSS software.

Even if no program code changes to the DSS software are necessary, there is usually some detailed design, programming, and testing required. Other production systems (e.g., transaction processing) might need to be changed, or interface programs be developed. Data conversion facilities are commonly needed to load the initial production (raw) files.

Systems Testing. The reduction of effort in detailed design and programming does not imply that system testing is less critical when DSS software is used. It is just as important as for specific DSS built from tools, if not more. A combination of conditions could be unique to a particular user and may not have been system tested by the vendor.

Some additional effort is required to perform physical installation of the DSS package. The project team should verify that the software delivered by the vendor is complete and operates in the company's technical environment. Some vendors provide a limited test case to be executed during what is often called the "acceptance test." All other segments of systems installation are still required and usually are not materially affected by DSS software.

Operating DSS Software Support

The amount of support work involved with installed DSS software usually depends, to a large degree, on the quality of the vendor support. DSS generator packages are more difficult to maintain if vendor support is poor.

The type of necessary maintenance also determines the extent of the impact DSS software has on supporting installed decision support systems. Maintenance of a DSS generator is categorized as follows: (1) maintenance of the code performed by the vendor, including new releases, temporary program fixes in response to bugs or code changes requested by the user; (2) maintenance of the code performed by in-house personnel, which refers to modifying the DSS software's program code; and, (3) maintenance of existing parameters and selected options (i.e., most parameter-driven software is designed to be maintained by the user).

When vendor modifications are implemented to an installed DSS generator, it is very important to maintain a listing of updates made to the DSS software, and to keep track of specific modifications and who made them. It is very useful for the vendor to know the status of the software when he is asked to investigate problems.

When implementing new vendor releases, several levels of modification and testing may be necessary: (1) acceptance testing of the new release; (2) modification of the new release to reflect prior user changes and parameters; (3) testing the modified release with acceptance data; and (4) testing the modified release with a system model. The net effect of installed generator effort varies with the particular package, the quality of vendor support, and the extent of maintenance. With a DSS generator, the number of necessary maintenance changes is often fewer than for custom-built specific DSS.

If the DSS software is well designed, it incorporates additional functions that can be activated as needed. The activation and testing effort required in this case would be far less than the effort to add the same functions to a specific DSS built from tools. If the DSS generator is well coded and tested, the number of bugs occurring immediately after conversion should be substantially fewer than with custom-developed specific DSS.

CONCLUDING REMARKS

Using DSS generators for the development of specific decision support systems will reduce personnel requirements and development costs. Conducting the evaluation of DSS software increases the effort necessary for developing specific DSS, but this undertaking is offset by the advantages of using a generator package. Despite the promises offered by DSS software, the performance of some DSS generators is much less than expected. Weak or nonexistent selection procedures may explain most of this poor implementation record. The methodology proposed in this chapter will hopefully reduce the risks associated with decision support systems software and facilitate success in developing specific DSS from generators.

The most critical phases of the methodology are the first (the development of a short list) and the third (design of specific DSS with the selected generator). Initially, the screening process determines whether a generator is feasible and reduces the number of DSS software packages to be evaluated in detail. Finally, the development of specific DSS with the selected generator ensures that the DSS software can be used effectively and provides a last chance to consider building specific DSS from tools.

As stated in the first section, while prior work provided partial guidelines for DSS software evaluation and selection, no unified and comprehensive methodology (as presented herein) was suggested. It is the author's belief that this methodology is quite easy to use and pragmatic. Its intent is to efficiently choose a DSS generator that meets the application needs and user expectations from the employment of packaged software.

QUESTIONS

1. What is the purpose of the DSS software screening phase of the methodology? Give some examples of the criteria used in this phase.
2. The second phase of the methodology, which evaluates DSS generators, uses an evaluation matrix. What is the purpose of this matrix? What are its rows and columns?
3. The third phase of the methodology calls for the development of some specific DSS. Is this a proper part of the selection process for a DSS generator? Why or why not?

REFERENCES

1. ALAVI, M. "An Assessment of the Prototyping Approach to Information Systems Development," *Communications of the ACM*, 27, no. 6 (June 1984), 556–563.
2. ARIAV, G., and M. J. GINZBERG "DSS Design: A Systemic View of Decision Support," *Communications of the ACM*, 28, no. 10 (October 1985), 1045–1052.
3. BERST, J. "The ABC's of Evaluating Packaged Software," *Interface Age* (February 1983), 35–38.
4. BRESLIN, J. *Selecting and Installing Software Packages*. Westport, CT: Quorom Books, 1986.
5. COURBON, J. C., J. GRAJEW, and J. TOLOVI, JR. "Design and Implementation of Decision Supporting Systems by an Evolutive Approach." Unpublished working paper, University of Grenoble, France, 1980.

6. CURRY, J. W., and D. M. BONNER, *How to Find and Buy Good Software: A Guide for Business and Professional People,* Englewood Cliffs, NJ: Prentice Hall, 1983.
7. DECISION SUPPORT SOFTWARE, INC. *EXPERT CHOICE User's Manual.* McLean, VA, 1983.
8. EXECUCOM SYSTEMS CORPORATION, *IFPS User's Manual.* Austin, TX, 1982.
9. GRAY, C. D. *The Right Choice: A Complete Guide to Evaluating, Selecting, and Installing MRP II Software.* Essex Junction, VT: Oliver Wight Limited Publications, 1987.
10. HOGUE, J. T., and H. J. WATSON, "Current Practices in the Development of Decision Support Systems," *Proceedings of the Fifth International Conference on Information Systems,* 117–127. Houston, TX, 1984.
11. JANSON, M. "Applying a Pilot System and Prototyping Approach to Systems Development and Implementation," *Information And Management,* 10, no. 4 (1986), 209–216.
12. KEEN, P. G. W. "Adaptive Design for Decision Support Systems," *Data Base,* 12, no. 3 (1980), 15–25.
13. KEEN, P. G. W. "Value Analysis: Justifying Decision Support Systems," *MIS Quarterly,* 5, no. 2 (1981), 1–15.
14. KLEIN, G., and P. O. BECK, "A Decision Aid for Selecting among Information System Alternatives," *MIS Quarterly,* 11, no. 2 (June 1987), 177–185.
15. LAUER, T. W., and M. T. JELASSI, "PREFCALC—A Multi-Criteria Decision Support System: A User Tutorial," Indiana University Institute for Research on the Management of Information Systems, Working Paper #714, December 1987.
16. LYNCH, R. K. "Implementing Packaged Application Software: Hidden Costs and New Challenges," *Systems, Objectives, Solutions,* 4, no. 4 (1984), 227–234.
17. LYNCH, R. K. "Nine Pitfalls in Implementing Packaged Applications Software," *Journal of Information Systems Management,* 2, no. 2 (1985), 88–92.
18. MARTIN, J., and C. MCCLURE "Buying Software off the Rack," *Harvard Business Review,* 61, no. 6, (November-December 1983), 32–47.
19. MEADOR, G. L., and R. A. MEZGER "Selecting An End User Programming Language For DSS Development," *MIS Quarterly,* 8, no. 4 (December 1984), 267–281.
20. NAUMANN, J. D. and S. PALVIA "A Selection Model for Systems Development Tools," *MIS Quarterly,* 6, no. 1 (March 1982), 39–48.
21. REIMANN, B. C. "Decision Support for Planners: How To Pick The Right DSS Generator Software," *Managerial Planning,* 33, no. 6 (May/June 1985), 22–26.
22. REIMANN, B. C. and A. D. WAREN "User-Oriented Criteria for the Selection of DSS Software," *Communications of the ACM,* 28, no. 2 (February 1985), 166–179.
23. SAATY, T. *The Analytic Hierarchy Process.* New York, NY: McGraw-Hill, 1981.
24. SAATY, T. *Decision Making for Leaders,* Belmont, CA: Lifetime Learning, 1982.
25. SANDERS, B. L., P. MUNTER, and R. O. REED "Selecting A Software Package," *Financial Executive,* 50, no. 9 (September 1982), 38–46.
26. SPRAGUE, R. H., JR. "A Framework for the Development of Decision Support Systems," *MIS Quarterly,* 4, no. 4 (June 1980), 1–26.
27. SPRAGUE, R. H., JR. and ERIC D. CARLSON *Building Effective Decision Support Systems.* Englewood Cliffs, NJ: Prentice Hall, Inc., 1982.
28. SUSSMAN, P. N. "Evaluating Decision Support Software," *Datamation,* 30, no. 17 (October 15, 1984), 171–172.

29. THOUGHTWARE, INC. *LIGHTYEAR User's Manual,* Coconut Grove, FL, 1984.

30. TIMMRECK, E. M. "Computer Selection Methodology," *Computing Surveys,* 5, no. 4 (December 1973), 199–222.

31. TURBAN, E. *Decision Support and Expert Systems.* New York, NY: Macmillan Publishing Company, 1988.

32. WAREN, A. D., and B. C. REIMANN "Selecting DSS Generator Software: A Participative Process," *Policy and Information,* 9, no. 2 (December 1985), 63–76.

33. WELKE, L. A. "Buying Software," in *Systems Analysis and Design: A Foundation for the 1980's,* edited by W. W. Cotterman, J. D. Couger, N. L. Enger, and F. Harold. New York, NY: Elsevier North Holland, Inc., 1981, 400–416.

34. YOUNG, O. F. "A Corporate Strategy for Decision Support Systems," *Journal of Information Systems Management,* 1, no. 1 (Winter 1984), 58–62.

Part 5

EXECUTIVE INFORMATION SYSTEMS

Executive information systems (EISs) are one of the fastest growing applications in organizations today. Most larger and even smaller firms have developed them. They provide senior executives with current status information about events internal and external to the firm. This information is typically related to the executives' critical success factors—those things that must be done right if the executives and the organization are to be successful. Most EISs contain additional features such as e-mail or decision support system capabilities that further support the performance of executives' job responsibilities.

An EIS contains a wide variety of information—internal and external, hard and soft. It is presented in graphical, tabular, and textual formats, often on the same screen. The system should be so easy to use that it requires little or no training to use. Using a variety of navigation methods, the user accesses needed information.

Although EISs offer great potential, they are high-risk systems. There is a myriad of potential organizational, development, and technical problems that have to be overcome. For example, they serve users who often have little previous computer training and experience, have been successful without using computers in the past, and may feel that they have little need to use computers now. Developers may have a limited understanding of executive work and information needs, little prior experience in developing applications of this kind, and typically must work with new technology.

A successful EIS, however, can generate a variety of benefits. It can provide information that is timely, accurate, relevant, concise, and in an attractive format. It can support strategic business objectives such as improving the firm's competitive position or improving the quality of goods and services provided. It may even facilitate downsizing the organization.

The three chapters in this part should enhance your understanding of what EISs are, how they are developed, current organizational practices, and their potential benefits.

One of the oldest and most successful EISs has been in operation at Lockheed-Georgia since 1978. Chapter 16 describes how it is used; how it has evolved over time; its component parts, features, and capabilities; its benefits; and the keys to its success. It should give you an enhanced understanding of what an EIS is like.

Chapter 17 presents an EIS development framework consisting of a structural perspective, which covers the key elements of an EIS and their interactions; the development process; and the user-system dialog. The development framework provides a roadmap for creating an EIS. Also presented are survey data collected from fifty organizations that describe current EIS practices.

Executives base many of their decisions on soft rather than hard information. Recent advances in information technology have made it increasingly possible to deliver soft information in information systems. Chapter 18 presents a definition of soft information, its characteristics, several taxonomies, and basic understandings; the findings from thirty-two telephone interviews with EIS developers about current practices in regard to including soft information in EISs; a set of fifteen propositions about soft information; and a look at current technology for including soft information in EISs.

16

THE MANAGEMENT INFORMATION AND DECISION SUPPORT (MIDS) SYSTEM AT LOCKHEED-GEORGIA

INTRODUCTION

The first computer-based executive information systems (EISs) were developed in the late 1970s. These systems were truly on the "bleeding edge" of technology because special-purpose EIS software did not become available until the mid-1980s. Developers had to create their systems by either "kludging" together existing software or developing their own. While many of these systems failed, there were a few notable successes. One of these was the management information and decision support (MIDS) system at Lockheed-Georgia. It has survived the test of time and is still in operation more than 15 years after it was originally built. In 1986 it was an award winner in the Society for Information Management's International Paper Competition for outstanding IS practice. Many of the features of MIDS have become standards for EIS designers. The description of MIDS which follows provides an excellent understanding of what an EIS is, how it is developed and used, and what the benefits are.

This chapter is adapted from George Houdeshel and Hugh J. Watson, "The Management Information and Decision Support (MIDS) System at Lockheed-Georgia," *MIS Quarterly*, Volume 11, Number 1, March 1987, pp. 127–140.

MIDS AT LOCKHEED-GEORGIA

Senior executives at Lockheed-Georgia are hands-on users of MIDS. It clearly illustrates that a carefully designed system can be an important source of information for top management. Consider a few examples of how the system is used.

- The president is concerned about employee morale which for him is a critical success factor. He calls up a display which shows employee contributions to company-sponsored programs such as blood drives, United Way, and savings plans. These are surrogate measures of morale, and because they have declined, he becomes more sensitive to a potential morale problem.
- The vice president of manufacturing is interested in the production status of a C-5B aircraft being manufactured for the U.S. Air Force. He calls up a display which pictorially presents the location and assembly status of the plane and information about its progress relative to schedule. He concludes that the aircraft is on schedule for delivery.
- The vice president of finance wants to determine whether actual cash flow corresponds with the amount forecasted. He is initially concerned when a $10 million unfavorable variance is indicated, but an explanatory note indicates that the funds are en route from Saudi Arabia. To verify the status of the payment, he calls the source of the information using the name and telephone number shown on the display and learns that the money should be in a Lockheed account by the end of the day.
- The vice president of human resources returns from an out-of-town trip and wants to review the major developments which took place while he was gone. While paging through the displays for the human resources area, he notices that labor grievances rose substantially. To learn more about the situation so that appropriate action can be taken, he calls the supervisor of the department where most of the grievances occurred.

These are not isolated incidents; other important uses of MIDS occur many times a day. They demonstrate that computerized systems can have a significant impact on the day-to-day functioning of senior executives.

Our purpose is to describe aspects of MIDS which are important to executives, information systems managers, and information systems professionals who are the potential participants in the approval, design, development, operation, and use of systems similar to MIDS. As a starting point, we want to discuss MIDS in the context of various types of information systems (i.e., MIS, DSS, and EIS), because its positioning is important to understanding its hands-on use by senior Lockheed-Georgia executives. We will describe how it was justified and developed, because these are the keys to its success. While online systems are best seen in person to be fully appreciated, we will try to describe what an executive experiences when using MIDS and the kinds of information that are available. Any computer system is made possible by the hardware, software, personnel, and data used and these will be described. Then we will discuss the benefits of MIDS. An organization considering the development of a system like MIDS needs to focus on key factors of success, and we will describe those factors that were most important to MIDS' success. As a closing point of interest, the on-going evolution of MIDS will be discussed.

MIS IN CONTEXT

Management information systems (MIS) were the first attempt by information systems professionals to provide managers and other organizational personnel with the information needed to perform their jobs effectively and efficiently. While originators of the MIS concept initially had high hopes and expectations for MIS, in practice MIS largely came to represent an expanded set of structured reports and has had only a minimal impact on upper management levels [11].

Decision support systems (DSS) were the next attempt to help management with its decision-making responsibilities. They have been successful to some extent, especially in regard to helping middle managers and functional area specialists such as financial planners and marketing researchers. However, their usefulness to top management has been primarily indirect. Middle managers and staff specialists may use a DSS to provide information for top management, but despite frequent claims of ease-of-use, top managers are seldom hands-on users of a DSS [4, 5].

With hindsight it is understandable why DSSs have not been used directly by senior executives. Many of the reasons are those typically given when discussing why managers do not use computers: poor keyboard skills, lack of training and experience in using computers, concerns about status, and a belief that hands-on computer use is not part of their job. Another set of reasons revolves around the trade-off between simplicity and flexibility of use. Simpler systems tend to be less flexible while more flexible systems are usually more complex. Because DSS are typically used to support poorly structured decision-making tasks, the flexibility required to analyze these decisions comes at the cost of greater complexity. Unless the senior executive is a "techie" at heart, or uses the system enough to master its capabilities, it is unlikely that the executive will feel comfortable using the system directly. Consequently, hands-on use of the DSS is typically delegated to a subordinate who performs the desired analysis.

Executive information systems (EIS), or executive support systems as they are sometimes called, are the latest computerized attempt to help satisfy top management's information needs. These systems tend to have the following characteristics which differentiate them from MIS and DSS:

- They are used directly by top managers without the assistance of intermediaries.

- They provide easy online access to current information about the status of the organization.
- They are designed with management's critical success factors (CSF) in mind.
- They use state-of-the-art graphics, communications, and data storage and retrieval methods.

The reportings of EIS suggest that these types of systems can make top managers hands-on users of computer-based systems [2, 10, 12]. While a number of factors contribute to their success, one of the most important is ease-of-use. Because an EIS provides little analysis capabilities, it normally requires only a few, easy to enter keystrokes or clicks of a mouse. Consequently, keyboard skills, previous training and experience in using computers, concerns about loss of status, and perceptions of how one should carry out job responsibilities are less likely to hinder system use.

MIDS is an example of an EIS. It is used directly by top Lockheed-Georgia managers to access online information about the current status of the firm. Great care, time, and effort go into providing information that meets the special needs of its users. The system is graphics-oriented and draws heavily upon communications technology.

THE EVOLUTION OF MIDS

Lockheed-Georgia, a subsidiary of the Lockheed Corporation, is a major producer of cargo aircraft. Over 19,000 employees work at their Marietta, Georgia plant. Their current major activities are production of the C-5B transport aircraft for the U.S. Air Force, Hercules aircraft for worldwide markets, and numerous modification and research programs.

In 1975, Robert B. Ormsby, then President of Lockheed-Georgia, first expressed an interest in the creation of an online status reporting system to provide information which was concise, timely, complete, easy to access, relevant to management's needs, and could be shared by organizational personnel. Though Lockheed's existing systems provided voluminous quantities of data and information, Ormsby thought them to be unsatisfactory for several reasons. It was difficult to quickly locate specific information to apply to a given problem. Reports often were not sufficiently current, leading to organizational units basing decisions on information which should have been the same but actually was not. This is often the case when different reports or the same report with different release dates are used. Little action was taken for several years as Ormsby and information services personnel waited for hardware and software to emerge which would be suitable for the desired type of system. In the fall of 1978, development of the MIDS system began.

The justification for MIDS was informal. No attempt was made to cost-justify its initial development. Ormsby felt that he and other Lockheed-Georgia executives needed the system and mandated its development. Over time, as different versions of MIDS were judged successful, authorization was given to develop enhanced versions. This approach is consistent with current thinking and research on systems to support decision making. It corresponds closely with the recommendation to view the initial system as a research and development project and to evolve later versions if the system proves to be successful [7]. It also is in keeping with findings that accurate, timely and new kinds of information, an organizational champion, and managerial mandate are the factors which motivate systems development [6].

A number of key decisions were made early in the design of the system. First, an evolutionary design approach would be used. Only a limited number of displays would be created initially. Over time they would be modified or possibly deleted if they did not meet an information need. Additional screens would be added as needed and as MIDS was made available to a larger group of Lockheed-Georgia managers. Ease-of-use was considered to be of critical importance because of the nature of the user group. Most of the Lockheed-Georgia executives had all of the normal apprehensions about personally using terminals. In order to encourage hands-on use, it was decided to place a terminal in each user's office, to require a minimum number of keystrokes in order to call up any screen, and to make training largely unnecessary. Response time was to be fast and features were to be included to assist executives in locating needed information.

Bob Pittman was responsible for the system's development and he, in turn, reported to the vice president of finance. Pittman initially had a staff consisting of two people from finance and two from information services. The finance personnel were used because of their experience in preparing company reports and presentations to the corporate headquarters, customers, and government agencies. Their responsibility was to determine the system's content, screen designs, and operational requirements. The information services personnel were responsible for hardware selection and acquisition and software development.

Pittman and his group began by exploring the information requirements of Ormsby and his staff. This included determining what information was needed, in what form, at what level of detail, and when it had to be updated. Several approaches were used in making these determinations. Interviews were held with Ormsby and his staff. Their secretaries were asked about information requested of them by their superiors. The use of existing reports was studied. From these analyses emerged an initial understanding of the information requirements.

The next step was to locate the best data sources for the MIDS system. Two considerations guided this process. The first was to use data sources with greater detail than what would be included in the MIDS displays. Only by using data which had not already been filtered and processed could information be generated which the MIDS team felt would satisfy the information requirements. The second was to use data sources which had a perspective compatible with that of

Ormsby and his staff. Multiple organizational units may have data seemingly appropriate for satisfying an information need, but choosing the best source or combination of sources requires care in order that the information provided is not distorted by the perspective of the organizational unit in which it originates.

The initial version of MIDS took six months to develop and allowed Ormsby to call up 31 displays. Over the years, MIDS has evolved to where it now offers over 700 displays for 30 top executives and 40 operating managers. It has continued to be successful through many changes in the senior executive ranks, including the position of president.

MIDS FROM THE USER'S PERSPECTIVE

An executive typically has little interest in the hardware or software used in a system. Rather, the dialog between the executive and the system is what matters. The dialog can be thought of as consisting of the command language by which the user directs the actions of the system, the presentation language through which the system provides the response, and the knowledge that the user must have in order to effectively use the system [1]. From a user's perspective, the dialog *is* the system, and consequently, careful attention was given to the design of the dialog components in MIDS.

An executive gains access to MIDS through a PC on his or her desk. Entering a password is the only sign-on requirement, and every user has a unique password which allows access to an authorized set of displays. After the password is accepted, the executive is informed of any scheduled downtime for system maintenance. The user is then given a number of options. He can enter a maximum of four keystrokes and call up any of the screens that he is authorized to view, obtain a listing of all screens that have been updated, press the "RETURN/ENTER" key to view the major menu, access the online keyword index, or obtain a listing of all persons having access to the system.

The main menu and keyword index are designed to help the executive find needed information quickly. Figure 16–1 shows the main menu. Each subject area listed in the main menu is further broken down into additional menus. Information is available in a variety of subject areas, including by functional area, organizational level, and project. The user can also enter the first three letters of any keywords which are descriptive of the information needed. The system checks these words against the keyword index and lists all of the displays which are related to the user's request.

Information for a particular subject area is organized in a top-down fashion. This organization is used within a single display or in a series of displays. A summary graph is presented at the top of a screen or first in a series of displays, followed by supporting graphs, and then by tables and text. This approach allows executives to quickly gain an overall perspective while providing backup detail when needed. An interesting finding has been that executives prefer as

MIDS MAJOR CATEGORY MENU

- TO RECALL THIS DISPLAY AT ANY TIME HIT 'RETURN-ENTER' KEY.
- FOR LATEST UPDATES SEE S1.

A MANAGEMENT CONTROL
MSI'S; OBJECTIVES;
ORGANIZATION CHARTS;
TRAVEL/AVAILABILITY/EVENTS SCHED.

CP CAPTURE PLANS INDEX

B C-5B ALL PROGRAM ACTIVITIES

C HERCULES ALL PROGRAM ACTIVITIES

E ENGINEERING
COST OF NEW BUSINESS; R & T

F FINANCIAL CONTROL
BASIC FINANCIAL DATA; COST REDUCTION; FIXED ASSETS;OFFSET; OVERHEAD; OVERTIME; PERSONNEL

H HUMAN RESOURCES
CO-OP PROGRAM,EMPLOYEE STATISTICS & PARTICIPATION

M MARKETING
ASSIGNMENTS; PROSPECTS; SIGN-UPS; PRODUCT SUPPORT; TRAVEL

O OPERATIONS
MANUFACTURING; MATERIAL; PRODUCT ASSURANCE & SAFETY

P PROGRAM CONTROL
FINANCIAL & SCHEDULE PERFORMANCE

MS MASTER SCHEDULING MENU

S SPECIAL ITEMS
DAILY DIARY; SPECIAL PROGRAMS

FIGURE 16–1 The MIDS Main Menu

much information as possible on a single display, even if it appears "busy," rather than having the same information spread over several displays.

Executives tend to use MIDS differently. At one extreme are those who browse through displays. An important feature for them is the ability to stop the generation of a display with a single keystroke when it is not of further interest. At the other extreme are executives who regularly view a particular sequence of displays. To accommodate this type of system use, sequence files can be employed which allow executives to page through a series of displays whose sequence is defined in advance. Sequence files can either be created by the user, requested by the user and prepared by the MIDS staff, or offered by MIDS personnel after observing the user's viewing habits.

All displays contain a screen number, title, when it was last updated, the source(s) of the information presented, and a telephone number for the source(s). It also indicates the MIDS staff member who is responsible for maintaining the display. Every display has a backup person who is responsible for it when the primary person is on leave, sick, or unavailable for any reason. Knowing the information source and the identity of the responsible MIDS staff member is important when an executive has a question about a display.

Standards exist across the displays for the terms used, color codes, and graphic designs. These standards help eliminate possible misinterpretations of the information provided. Standard definitions have also improved communications in the company.

The importance of standard definitions can be illustrated by the use of the word "signup." In general, the term refers to a customer's agreement to buy an aircraft. However, prior to the establishment of a standard definition, it tended to be used differently by various organizational units. To marketing people, a signup was when a letter of intent to buy was received. Legal services considered it to be when a contract was received. Finance interpreted it as when a down payment was made. The standard definition of a signup now used is "a signed contract with a nonrefundable down payment." An online dictionary can be accessed if there is any question about how a term is defined.

Color is used in a standard way across all of the screens. The traffic light pattern is used for status: green is good; yellow is marginal; and red is unfavorable. Under budget or ahead of schedule is in green; on budget or on schedule is in yellow; over budget or behind schedule is in red. Bar graphs have a black background and yellow bars depict actual performance, cyan (light blue) is used for company goals and commitments to the corporate office, and magenta represents internal goals and objectives. Organization charts use different colors for the various levels of management. Special color combinations are used to accommodate executives with color differentiation problems, and all displays are designed to be effective with black and white hard copy output.

Standards exist for all graphic designs. Line charts are used for trends, bar charts for comparisons, and pie or stacked bar charts for parts of a whole. On all charts, vertical wording is avoided and abbreviations and acronyms are limited to those on an authorized list. All bar charts are zero at the origin to avoid distortions, scales are set in prescribed increments and are identical within a subject series, and bars that exceed the scale have numeric values shown. In comparisons of actual with predicted performance, bars for actual performance are always wider.

Comments are added to the displays to explain abnormal conditions, explain graphic depictions, reference related displays, and inform of pending changes. For example, a display may show that signups for May are three less than forecasted. The staff member who is responsible for the display knows, however, that a down payment from Peru for three aircraft is en route and adds this information as a comment to the display. Without added comments, situations can arise which are referred to as "paper tigers," because they appear to require managerial attention though they actually do not. The MIDS staff believes that "transmitting data is not the same as conveying information" [8].

The displays have been created with the executives' critical success factors in mind. Some of the CSF measures, such as profits and aircrafts sold, are obvious. Other measures, such as employee participation in company-sponsored programs, are less obvious and reflect the MIDS staff's efforts to fully understand and accommodate the executives' information needs.

To illustrate a typical MIDS display, Figure 16–2 shows Lockheed-Georgia sales as of November 1986. It was accessed by entering F3. The sources of the information and their Lockheed-Georgia telephone numbers are in the upper right-hand corner. The top graphs provide past history, current, and forecasted sales. The wider bars represent actual sales while budgeted sales are depicted by the narrower bars. Detailed, tabular information is provided under the graphs. An explanatory comment is given at the bottom of the display. The R and F in the bottom right-hand corner indicates that related displays can be found by paging in a reverse or forward direction.

Executives are taught to use MIDS in a 15-minute tutorial. For several reasons, no written instructions for the use of the system have ever been prepared. An objective for MIDS has been to make the system easy enough to use so that written instructions are unnecessary. Features such as menus and the keyword

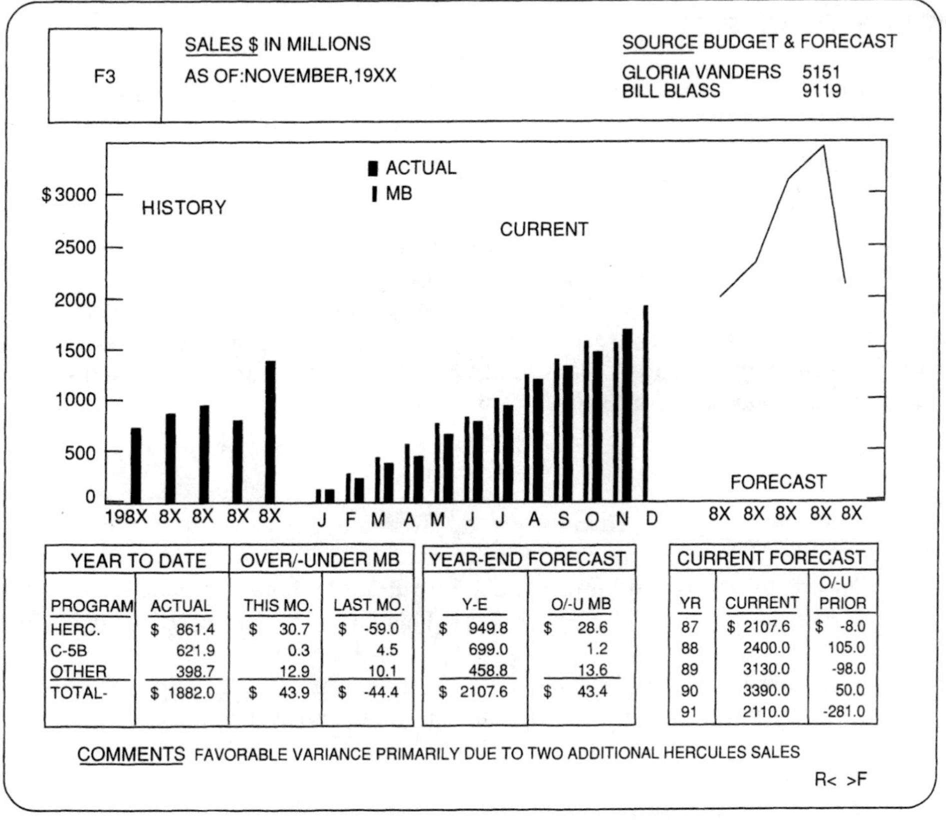

PROGRAM	ACTUAL	THIS MO.	LAST MO.	Y-E	O/-U MB
HERC.	$ 861.4	$ 30.7	$ -59.0	$ 949.8	$ 28.6
C-5B	621.9	0.3	4.5	699.0	1.2
OTHER	398.7	12.9	10.1	458.8	13.6
TOTAL-	$ 1882.0	$ 43.9	$ -44.4	$ 2107.6	$ 43.4

YR	CURRENT	O/-U PRIOR
87	$ 2107.6	$ -8.0
88	2400.0	105.0
89	3130.0	-98.0
90	3390.0	50.0
91	2110.0	-281.0

FIGURE 16–2 Lockheed-Georgia Sales

index make this possible. Another reason is that senior executives are seldom willing to take the time to read instructions. And most importantly, if an executive has a problem in using the system, the MIDS staff prefers to learn about the problem and to handle it personally.

The PC on the executive's desk is useful for applications other than accessing MIDS displays. It can be used off-line with any appropriate PC software. It is also the mechanism for tying the user through MIDS to other computer systems. For example, some senior executives and even more middle managers want access to outside reference services or internal systems with specific data bases. Electronic messaging is the most common use of the PC for other than MIDS displays. The executive need only request PROFS from within MIDS and the system automatically translates the user's MIDS password to a PROFS password and transfers the user from the DEC VAX host to the IBM mainframe with PROFS. After using PROFS' electronic mail capabilities, the transfer back to MIDS is a simple two-keystroke process.

THE COMPONENTS OF MIDS

A number of component parts are essential to the functioning of MIDS: hardware, software, MIDS personnel, and data sources.

Hardware

A microcomputer from Intelligent Systems Corporation was used for the initial version of MIDS. Each day MIDS personnel updated the floppy disks which stored the displays. As more executives were given access to MIDS, it became impractical to update each executive's displays separately, and the decision was made to store them centrally on a mainframe where they could be accessed by all users. This arrangement continues today.

Software

At the time that work on MIDS began, appropriate software was not commercially available. Consequently, the decision was made to develop the software in-house. The custom-built software was used until 1992 when a decision was made to switch over to commercial EIS software. This change is discussed later in the chapter.

The custom-built software was used for three important tasks: creating and updating the displays: providing information about the system's use and status; and maintaining system security.

Creating and Updating the Displays. Each display has an edit program tailored to fit its needs. Special edit routines have been developed for graph drawing, color changes, scale changes, roll-offs, calculations, or drawing special characters such as airplanes. These edit functions are then combined to create a unique edit program for each display. This approach allows MIDS personnel to quickly update the displays and differs from off-the-shelf software which requires the user to answer questions for all routines, regardless of whether they are needed.

The edit software has other attractive features. There are computer-generated messages to the information analyst advising of other displays which could be affected by changes to the one currently being revised. Color changes are automatically made to a display when conditions become unfavorable. When the most recent period data is entered, the oldest period data is automatically rolled off of all graphs. The edit software has error checks for unlikely or impossible conditions.

Providing Information about the System's Use and Status. Daily reports are generated at night and are available the next morning for the MIDS staff to review. A daily log of system activity shows who requested what, when, and how. The log indicates everything but "why," and sometimes the staff even asks that question in order to better understand management's information needs. The log allows MIDS personnel to analyze system loads, user inquiry patterns, methods used to locate displays, utilization of special features, and any system and/or communication problems. Another report indicates the status of all displays, including the last time each display was updated, when the next update is scheduled, and who is responsible for the update. Yet another report lists all displays which have been added, deleted, or changed.

Weekly reports are generated on Sunday night and are available Monday morning for the MIDS staff. One report lists the previous week's users and the number of displays viewed by each executive. Another report lists the number of displays with the frequency of viewing by the president and his staff and others.

A number of reports are available on demand. They include an authorization matrix of users and terminals; a count of displays by major category and subsystem; a list of users by name, type of terminal, and system line number to the host computer; a list of displays in sequence; a list of display titles with their number organized by subject area; and a keyword exception report of available displays not referenced in the keyword file.

Maintaining System Security. Careful thought goes into deciding who has access to which displays. Information is made available unless there are compelling reasons why it should be denied. For example, middle managers might not be allowed to view strategic plans for the company.

System access is controlled through a double security system. Users can call up only displays which they are authorized to view and then only from certain terminals. This security system helps protect against unauthorized users gaining access to the system and the unintentional sharing of restricted information. As an example of the latter situation, a senior executive might be allowed to view sensitive information in his office, but be denied access to the information in a conference room or the office of lower management.

Personnel

The MIDS staff grew from five to its current size of nine. Six of the staff members are classified as information analysts, two are computer analysts, and there is the manager of the MIDS group. The information analysts are responsible for determining the system's content, designing the screens, and keeping the system operational. Each information analyst is responsible for about 100 displays. Approximately 170 displays are updated daily by the MIDS staff. The computer analysts are responsible for hardware selection and acquisition and software development. While the two groups have different job responsibilities, they work together and make suggestions to each other for improving the system.

It is imperative that the information analysts understand the information that they enter into the system. Several actions are taken to ensure that this is the case. Most of the information analysts have work experience and/or training in the areas for which they supply information. They are encouraged to take courses which provide a better understanding of the users' areas. And they frequently attend functional area meetings, often serving as an important information resource.

Data

In order to provide the information needed, a variety of internal and external data sources must be used. The internal sources include transaction processing systems, financial applications, and human sources. Some of the data can be transferred directly to MIDS from other computerized systems, while others must be rekeyed or entered for the first time. Access to computerized data is provided by in-house software and commercial software. External sources are very important and include data from external databases, customers, other Lockheed companies, and Lockheed's Washington, D.C., office.

MIDS relies on both hard and soft data. Hard data comes from sources such as transaction processing systems and provides "the facts." Soft data often comes from human sources and results in information which could not be obtained in any other way; it provides meaning, context, and insight to hard data.

BENEFITS OF MIDS

A variety of benefits are provided by MIDS: better information; improved communications; an evolving understanding of information requirements; a test-bed for system evolution; and cost reductions.

The information provided by MIDS has characteristics which are important to management. It supports decision making by identifying areas which require attention, providing answers to questions, and giving knowledge about related areas. It provides relevant information. Problem areas are highlighted and pertinent comments are included. The information is timely because displays are updated as important events occur. It is accurate because of the efforts of the MIDS staff, since all information is verified before it is made available.

MIDS has also improved communications in several ways. It is sometimes used to share information with vendors, customers, legislators, and others. MIDS users are able to quickly view the same information in the same format with the most current update. In the past, there were often disagreements, especially over the telephone, because executives were operating with different information. PROFS provides electronic mail. The daily diary announces major events as they occur.

Initially identifying a complete set of information requirements is difficult or impossible for systems which support decision making. The evolutionary nature of MIDS' development has allowed users to better understand and evolve their information requirements. Having seen a given set of information in a given format, an executive is often prompted to identify additional information or variations of formats that provide still better decision support.

The current system provides a test-bed for identifying and testing possible system changes. New state-of-the-art hardware and software can be compared with the current system in order to provide information for the evolution of MIDS.

MIDS is responsible for cost savings in several areas. Many reports and graphs which were formerly produced manually are now printed from MIDS and distributed to non-MIDS users. Some requirements for special reports and presentation materials are obtained at less cost by modifying standard MIDS displays. Reports that are produced by other systems are summarized in MIDS and are no longer printed and distributed to MIDS users.

THE SUCCESS OF MIDS

Computer-based systems can be evaluated on the basis of cost/benefit, frequency of use, and user satisfaction considerations. Systems which support decision making, such as MIDS, normally do not lend themselves to a quantified assessment of their benefits. They do provide intangible benefits, however, as can be seen in the following example.

Lockheed-Georgia markets its aircrafts worldwide. In response to these efforts, it is common for a prospective buyer to call a company executive to discuss a proposed deal. Upon receipt of a phone call, the executive can call up a display which provides the following information: the aircraft's model and quantity; the dollar value of the offer; the aircraft's availability for delivery; previous purchases by the prospect; the sales representative's name and exact location for the week; and a description of the status of the possible sale. Such a display is shown in Figure 16–3. All of this information is available without putting the prospective customer on hold, transferring the call to someone else, or awaiting the retrieval of information from a file.

When a user can choose whether or not to use a system, frequency of use can be employed as a measure of success. Table 16–1 presents data on how the number of users and displays and the mean number of displays viewed per day by each executive changed over time. The overall picture is one of increased usage; an average of 5.5 screens were viewed each day by the 70 executives who had access to MIDS. Unlike some systems which are initially successful but quickly fade away, the success of MIDS has increased over time.

Frequency of use can be a very imperfect measure of success. The MIDS group recognizes that a single display which has a significant impact on decision making is much more valuable than many screens which are paged through with passing interest. Consequently, frequency of use is used as only one indicator of success.

MIDS personnel have felt no need to conduct formal studies of user satisfaction. The data on system usage and daily contact with MIDS users provide

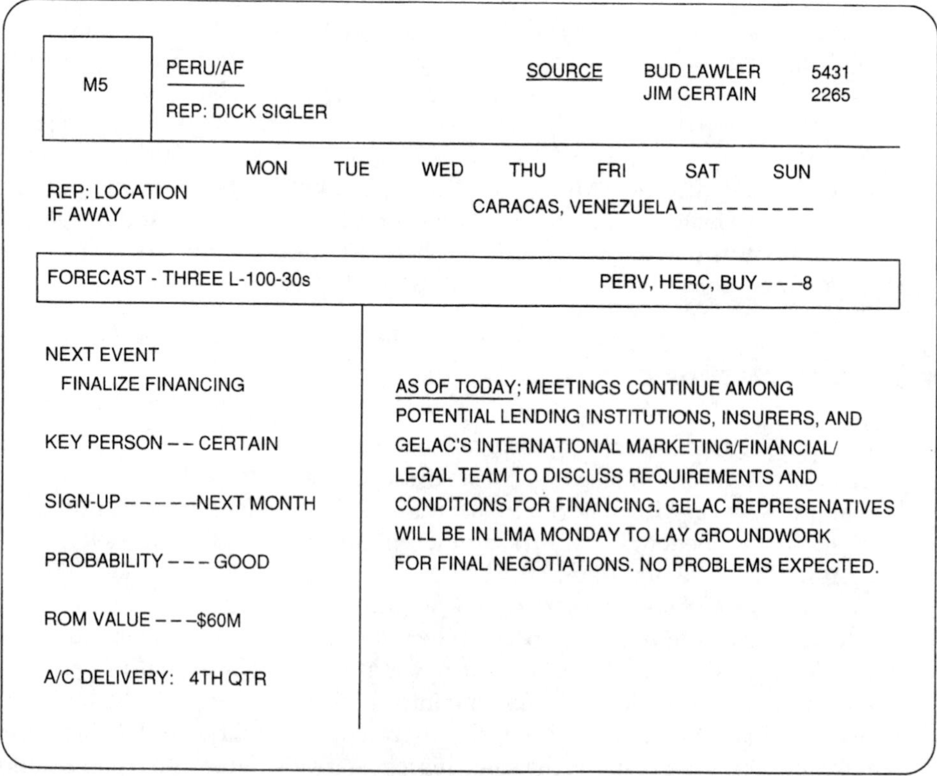

FIGURE 16–3 The Status of a Sale.

TABLE 16–1 MIDS Users, Displays, and Displays Viewed

Year	Number of Users	Number of Displays	Mean Number of Displays Viewed Per User/Per Day
1979	12	69	*
1980	24	231	*
1981	27	327	*
1982	31	397	3
1983	31	441	4
1984	49	620	4.2
1985	70	710	5.5

*Figures not available.

ample information on how satisfied users are with MIDS. User satisfaction can be illustrated by the experience of Paul Frech who was vice president of operations in 1979. When MIDS was offered to him, he had little interest in the system because he had well-established channels for the flow of information to support his job responsibilities. Shortly afterwards, Frech was promoted to the corporate headquarters staff in California. When he was again promoted to become the president of Lockheed-Georgia, MIDS had become a standard for executive information and he was reintroduced to the system. He has stated:

> I assumed the presidency of the Lockheed-Georgia Company in June 1984, and the MIDS system had been in operation for some time prior to that. The MIDS system enabled me to more quickly evaluate the current conditions of each of our operational areas and, although I had not been an advocate of executive computer systems, the ease and effectiveness of MIDS made it an essential part of my informational sources.

Because Frech and other senior executives have come to rely on MIDS, middle managers at Lockheed-Georgia and executives at other Lockheed companies want their own versions of MIDS. Within Lockheed-Georgia there is the feeling that "If the boss likes it, I need it." Currently, MIDS personnel are helping middle functional area managers develop subsystems of MIDS and are assisting other Lockheed companies with the development of similar systems.

KEYS TO THE SUCCESS OF MIDS

Descriptions of successful systems are useful to people responsible for conceptualizing, approving, and developing similar systems. Perhaps even more important are insights about what makes a system a success. We will identify the keys to MIDS' success here, but it should be remembered that differences exist among executive information systems, organizations, and possibly the factors that lead to success.

1. *A Committed Senior Executive Sponsor.* Ormsby served as the organizational champion for MIDS. He wanted a system like MIDS, committed the necessary resources, participated in its creation, and encouraged its use by others.
2. *Carefully Defined System Requirements.* Several considerations governed the design of the system. It had to be custom-tailored to meet the information needs of its users. Ease-of-use, an absolutely essential item to executives who were wary of computers, was critical. Response time had to be fast. The displays had to be updated quickly and easily as conditions changed.
3. *Carefully Defined Information Requirements.* There has been a continuing effort to understand management's information requirements. Displays have been added, modified, and deleted over time. Providing information relevant to managements' CSFs has been of paramount importance.
4. *A Team Approach to Systems Development.* The staff that developed, operates, and evolves MIDS combines information systems skills and functional area knowledge. The computer analysts are responsible for the technical aspects of the system while the information analysts are responsible for providing the information needed by management. This latter responsibility demands that the information analysts know the business and maintain close contact with information sources and users.
5. *An Evolutionary Development Approach.* The initial version of MIDS success fully addressed the most critical information needs of the company president and strengthened his support for the system. There is little doubt that developing a fully integrated system for a full complement of users would have resulted in substantial delays and less enthusiasm for the system. Over the years, MIDS has expanded and evolved as more users have been provided access to MIDS, management's information requirements have changed, better ways to analyze and present information have been discovered, and improved computer technology has become integrated into the system.
6. *Careful Computer Hardware and Software Selection.* The decision to proceed with the development of MIDS was made when good color terminals at reasonable prices became available. At that time graphics software was very limited and it was necessary to develop the software for MIDS in-house. The development of MIDS could have been postponed until hardware and software with improved performance at reduced cost appeared, but this decision would have delayed providing management with the information needed. Also affecting the hardware selection was the existing hardware within the organization and the need to integrate MIDS into the overall computing architecture. While it is believed that excellent hardware and software decisions have been made for MIDS, different circumstances at other firms may lead to different hardware and software configurations.

MIDS II: THE ONGOING STORY

In 1990, after 12 years of successful MIDS operations, it became necessary to update the hardware technology used with Lockheed's executive information system. This change was required because the Intelligent Systems Company (ISC) graphics computers that were used by the MIDS support staff to design and update the screens were no longer in production and replacement parts were becoming increasingly difficult to find. The MIDS staff faced the real possibility of not being able to maintain the system because of a lack of hardware. Faced with this situation, it was decided to undertake a comprehensive review of the hardware and software options that were available for EIS.

After a review of the software alternatives, it was decided that it was more economical to purchase commercial EIS software than to develop another system in-house. Several commercial products were evaluated and Comshare's Commander EIS was ultimately chosen. This product offers a large number of capabilities that facilitate the development and maintenance of an EIS; see Table 16–2. Two important changes to the Comshare software were requested, however, before a contract was signed. The changes retained capabilities that were in MIDS but not in Commander EIS. It was deemed important to the MIDS staff that the changes be made to the basic Comshare product and not to just a special version for Lockheed in order to ensure compatibility with later releases of the Comshare software.

TABLE 16-2 Capabilities of Commander EIS

- Support for multiple user interfaces
- Online, context-dependent help screens
- Command files
- Multiple methods for locating information
- Access to external databases (e.g., Dow Jones News Retrieval)
- Interfaces to other software (e.g., Profs, Lotus 1-2-3)
- Integrated decision support (e.g., System W, IFPS)
- Easy screen design and maintenance
- Screen design templates
- Application shells
- Data extraction from existing organizational data bases
- Graphical, tabular, and textual information on the same screen
- Integration of data from different sources
- Security for data, screens, and systems
- Support for rapid prototyping
- Support for multiple computing information
- Support for hard-copy output (e.g., paper, overhead transparencies, 35-mm slides)

The two changes permitted users to operate the system through a keyboard (in addition to a mouse or touch screen) and provided for monitoring the use of the system. Lockheed executives had enjoyed the MIDS system advantage of going from any screen to any other screen without retracing a path or returning to a predetermined point. This capability was retained by allowing executives to enter the number of the desired screen. Monitoring of system usage had always been performed by the MIDS system management and it had become invaluable in keeping the MIDS system up to date. With these changes, Commander EIS became the development environment for MIDS II.

Even though commercial EIS software was selected for MIDS II, the original screen designs were retained. In fact, when Lockheed asked vendors to prepare demonstration prototypes, they requested screens that looked like those currently in use. Considerable thought and experimentation had gone into screen design over the years, Lockheed's executives were familiar with them, and MIDS II was to continue the look and feel of the original system.

In addition to a new software, hardware improvements were made to take advantage of state-of-the-art technology and to position MIDS II in Lockheed's long-range computing plans. The Comshare software helped make this possible because of its ability to run on a mixed platform of IBM and Macintosh computers. The executives use IBM PCs and screens are developed and maintained on Macintoshes by the support staff. A Novell local area network was installed to improve the system's response time and reliability.

MIDS II was developed and rolled out to users in 1992 and provides a variety of benefits over the original system: faster response time, easier navigation through the system (drilldown to related, more detailed information), better links to other resources (internal and external data bases), reduced maintenance costs (automatic update of some screens), shared EIS techniques with other Commander EIS users, and a state-of-the-art technology platform that permits future improvements and growth within information system's long-range plans. It has also allowed for a significant reduction in the size of the MIDS support staff. The original MIDS system has served Lockheed very well since 1978 and MIDS II is designed to carry this tradition into the future.

QUESTIONS

1. Why have many senior executives not become hands-on users of a DSS? What raises the hopes for EIS?
2. What screen design features of the MIDS system might be appropriate for any EIS?
3. What methods have been used to document the success of the MIDS system? Are any other methods feasible and desirable? Discuss.
4. What led to the development of MIDS II?

CASE: AN EIS FAILURE AT GENERICORP

Bill Perry, vice-president of information systems at Genericorp, had advocated the development of an executive information system (EIS) to support the information needs of the firm's senior executives. From trade writings, conferences and conversations with other information systems managers, Perry had heard of EIS successes at firms such as Xerox Corp., Phillips Petroleum and Lockheed-Georgia. Perry believed that besides helping top management, an EIS would also improve the image of the IS department. For too many years, company executives had approved multimillion-dollar budgets without much IS support. An EIS would change that situation, however.

Perry arranged for one of the EIS vendors to present a demonstration to the chief executive officer and other senior executives. The demonstration was very well received. With a touch of the screen, charts and reports quickly appeared in a rich variety of formats and colors. The executives were impressed and, after a brief meeting, authorized the development of an EIS. The project was allotted a budget of $250,000.

The next step was to put together a team of people to develop the EIS. Sam Johnson, who had worked at Genericorp for 20 years in a variety of areas, was recruited to head the project. Johnson was a good choice because of his knowledge of the business, executives, and politics of the organization. Perry also assigned two of his best systems analysts to the project.

After reviewing the software and hardware alternatives, the EIS team chose what they thought would be a good approach. A major EIS vendor's software would be used. The product was designed around the co-processing concept, in which the personal computer performs graphics functions and the mainframe handles data storage. The executives would have IBM Personal System/2 Model 50 machines connected to an IBM 4381 by a Token-Ring network. Most of the hardware was already in place.

Getting the initial set of executive users to specify their information requirements proved to be a problem. The EIS staff found it difficult to arrange time with the executives because of the latters' travel and job requirements. Even when they did meet, the executives were often vague and uncertain about their information needs. Consequently, the executive's staff and secretaries became important sources for determining what should go into the EIS.

Three months later, the initial version of the system was rolled out to five users. The 50 screens provided key financial reports that were previously available only in paper form. The system also provided information on key performance indicators that had been identified in Genericorp's strategic planning processes. The screens were efficiently updated by automatic downloading of data from existing data bases.

This case is adapted from Hugh J. Watson, "Avoiding Hidden EIS Pitfalls," *Computerworld*, June 25, 1990, pp. 87–91.

The executives' initial reaction to the system was generally positive. One executive said, "I've never been able to get my hands on this information this quickly before." Several of the executives seemed proud to finally be able to use a computer. Only one older executive seemed to have little interest in the EIS.

Having delivered the system, the focus turned to maintenance. Johnson was assigned to another project. The systems analysts were given responsibilities for developing a new, important transaction processing application. Two maintenance programmers were assigned the task of handling the evolution and spread of the system to more users, with additional screens and new capabilities.

Little happened with the system during the next few months. It took the maintenance programmers a while to learn how to use the EIS software. Even after they knew how to develop screens, the programmers discovered that this activity always seemed less critical than working on other applications. Besides that, the executives seldom requested additional screens. To some extent, the maintenance programmers viewed the EIS as an "executive toy."

Nine months after the introduction of the EIS, little evolution had occurred. There were no new users, and usage-tracking software revealed that three of the five executives were not using the system at all. Few new screens had been added, and there were no new system capabilities.

At about this time, Genericorp began to encounter financial troubles. To maintain a healthy bottom line, any nonessential expenditures were eliminated. At a key meeting, the executive who had never taken to using the EIS proposed that it be terminated. "We've put a lot of time and money into this system, and I don't see that we have gotten much out of it," he said. "If we are honest with ourselves, all we are getting is the same information that we used to get before—except now it is on a screen with fancy graphs and colors. We can save money by trashing the system and not lose much." After discussion, the executives agreed that the system had turned out to be a disappointment that should be scuttled.

When Perry learned of the decision, he was crushed. The EIS had seemed so promising, and things seemed to have been going so well. What had gone wrong? He'd gotten executive support, assembled a good staff, selected appropriate hardware and software, and quickly delivered an initial version of the system. These were frequently mentioned keys to success. Maybe the executives just weren't ready to use computers. One thing Perry did know, however, was that the EIS experience smeared his reputation, as well as that of his department.

QUESTIONS

1. What factors contributed to the failure of the EIS at Genericorp?
2. What actions might be taken at this point to save the EIS?

REFERENCES

1. BENNETT, J. "User-Oriented Graphics, Systems for Decision Support in Unstructured Tasks," in *User-Oriented Design of Interactive Graphics Systems*, S. Treu, (ed.), Association for Computing Machinery, New York, New York, 1977, 3–11.
2. De LONG, D. W., and J. F. ROCKART "Identifying the Attributes of Successful Executive Support System Implementation," *Transactions from the Sixth Annual Conference on Decision Support Systems*, J. Fedorowicz (ed.), Washington, D.C., April 21–24, 1986, 41–54.
3. EL SAWY, O. A. "Personal Information Systems for Strategic Scanning in Turbulent Environments: Can the CEO Go On-Line?" *MIS Quarterly*, 9, 1, March 1985, 53–60.
4. FRIEND, D. "Executive Information Systems: Success, Failure, Insights and Misconceptions," *Transactions from the Sixth Annual Conference on Decision Support Systems*, J. Fedorowicz (ed.), Washington, D.C., April 21–24, 1986, 35–40.
5. HOGUE, J. T., and H. J. WATSON "An Examination of Decision Makers' Utilization of Decision Support System Output," *Information and Management*, 8, 4, April 1985, 205–12.
6. HOGUE, J. T., and H. J. WATSON "Management's Role in the Approval and Administration of Decision Support Systems," *MIS Quarterly*, 7, 2, June 1983, 15–23.
7. KEEN, P. G. W., "Value Analysis: Justifying Decision Support Systems," *MIS Quarterly*, 5, 1, March 1981, 1–16.
8. McDONALD, E. "Telecommunications," *Government Computer News*, February 28, 1986, 44.
9. ROCKART, J. F. "Chief Executives Define Their Own Data Needs," *Harvard Business Review*, 57, 2, January–February 1979, 81–93.
10. ROCKART, J. F., and M. E. TREACY. "The CEO Goes On-Line," *Harvard Business Review*, 60, 1, January–Feburary 1982, 32–88.
11. SPRAGUE, R. H., JR. "A Framework for the Development of Decision Support Systems," *MIS Quarterly*, 4, 4, December 1980, 10–26.
12. SUNDUE, D. G. "GenRad's On-line Executives," *Transactions from the Sixth Annual Conference on Decision Support Systems*, J. Fedorowicz (ed.), Washington, D. C. April 21–24, 1986, 14–20.

17

A FRAMEWORK FOR DEVELOPING EXECUTIVE INFORMATION SYSTEMS

In Chapter 16, the highly successful MIDS system at Lockheed-Georgia was described. Embedded in the case study were many examples of how an EIS should be developed. In this chapter, we look at EIS development more carefully. An EIS definition is given along with a set of characteristics. Next, an EIS development framework is introduced. Then, the findings of the survey are discussed in the context of the framework. Finally, conclusions are drawn from the study. After reading this chapter you should have a better understanding of EIS development practices.

EIS DEFINITION AND CHARACTERISTICS

There are a variety of definitions for EIS (Paller and Laska, 1990; Turban and Watson, 1989). For our purposes, an EIS is defined as a computerized system that provides executives with easy access to internal and external information that is relevant to their critical success factors. While a definition is useful, a richer understanding is provided by describing the characteristics of EIS. Research (Burkan, 1988; Friend, 1986; Kogan, 1986; Zmud, 1986) shows that most executive information systems:

This chapter is adapted from Hugh J. Watson, R. Kelly Rainer, and Chang E. Koh, "Executive Information Systems: A Framework for Development and a Survey of Current Practices," *MIS Quarterly*, Volume 15, Number 1, March 1991, pp. 13–30.

- are tailored to individual executive users;
- extract, filter, compress, and track critical data;
- provide online status access, trend analysis, exception reporting, and "drill-down" (drill-down allows the user to access supporting detail or data that under lie summarized data);
- access and integrate a broad range of internal and external data;
- are user-friendly and require minimal or no training to use;
- are used directly by executives without intermediaries;
- present graphical, tabular, and/or textual information.

The EIS and ESS terms are sometimes used interchangeably. The term "executive support system," however, usually refers to a system with a broader set of capabilities than an EIS (Rockart and DeLong, 1988). Whereas the EIS term connotes providing information, the ESS term implies other support capabilities in addition to information. Consequently, we find it useful to conceptualize an ESS as including the following capabilities:

- support for electronic communications (e.g., e-mail, computer conferencing, and word processing);
- data analysis capabilities (e.g., spreadsheets, query languages, and decision support systems);
- organizing tools (e.g., electronic calendars, automated rolodex, and tickler files).

These additional capabilities are typically made available as options on a system's main menu or by the ability to "hot key" the workstation into a PC mode of operation.

The distinctions between an EIS and an ESS are not particularly important for our purposes other than to recognize that an ESS influences and increases system requirements. For example, many systems include e-mail; hence, e-mail software and a keyboard must be available. The materials provided here apply equally well to EIS or ESS, even though the EIS term is used throughout.

WHY PREVIOUS EFFORTS FAILED

There are many reasons why previous efforts to bring computer support to senior executives have failed. Understanding these reasons is important because they provide insights into what problems must be overcome if an EIS is to be successful.

One of the difficulties involves the executives themselves. Many of today's senior executives missed the computer revolution. Consequently, they may feel uncomfortable using computers, have poor keyboarding skills, or believe that "real" executives do not use computers.

When the decision was made in 1988 to restore the Michigan State Senate chamber, many of these tasks had to be performed by legislative aids. The chamber was to look much as it did in 1879 when the Capitol building was built, but extensive information display and communications capabilities were to be added. Both executive information systems and group support systems were to be literally at the senators' fingertips.

The decision to automate many senate activities and processes was driven by a few senators who were computer users. They saw the potential and opportunity to make more information available, improve communications, and enhance the senators' efficiency and effectiveness.

Bill Snow, the secretary of the Senate, served as the system's executive sponsor. He brought in Decision Resources Corp., a Washington, D.C.-based consulting firm to help design the system. To maintain esthetics, the workstations were placed in rolltop desks so that the chamber would retain its original look when the PCs were not in use. A little more than a year and $800,000 later ($495,000 in application development and implementation and $322,000 on workstations and network hardware) the system was made available to the 38 senators.

The system is used in everyday work and during legislative sessions. At their desks on the floor, senators can use the system to cast votes, request to speak, find out what bill is under consideration, view the text of the current amendment, send e-mail, and perform other legislative functions. Through local area networks connected to the senators' offices, they can also query the status of bills, view reports and analyses, and communicate with others outside the chamber, particularly with their own staff, without having to leave the floor. In the past, many of these tasks had to be performed by legislative aids. The system integrates the voting and debate activities for the senate leaders. Even members of the press are not left out—workstations in the two press areas on the floor let reporters view votes and see the text of amendments.

Another difficulty involves the nature of executive work. Previous studies provide a better understanding of what senior executives do and insights into how computer support must be delivered (Isenberg, 1984; Kotter, 1982; Mintzberg, 1975). Executives' busy schedules and travel requirements are not amenable to long training sessions, do not permit much uninterrupted time for system use, and do not allow a system to be employed on a daily basis (Albala, 1988). The result is that senior executives are unlikely to employ systems that require considerable training and regular use to be learned and remembered. Because senior executives have ready access to staff personnel to fulfill their requests for information, any system must prove to be more responsive than a human (Rockart and DeLong, 1988).

Another problem in providing computer support includes technology that is difficult to use, at least from most executives' perspective. Powerful workstations, improved micro-to-mainframe software, high-quality color graphics, and touchscreens are just some of the technological developments that now make it possible to deliver appealing systems to senior executives.

Finally, many previous systems have contained little information of value to senior executives, which is a problem related to a lack of understanding of executive work. This lack was exacerbated by systems designers who often possessed excellent technical knowledge but little business knowledge (Reck and Hall, 1986). This condition is improving as organizations recognize that business skills and the ability to interact with executives are critical.

Three broad guidelines for developing a successful EIS can be gleaned from these failures. First, the EIS must meet the information needs of senior executives. Second, in order to do this, the EIS must be developed by personnel with both business and technical skills. Finally, the EIS must be so easy to use that it might be considered to be "intuitive" or "user seductive." Even though it is challenging to implement an EIS that meets executive information needs and is extremely easy to use, a number of EIS have achieved these objectives (Applegate and Osborn, 1988; Houdeshel and Watson, 1987).

AN EIS DEVELOPMENT FRAMEWORK

According to Sprague (1980), a *development framework* is "helpful in organizing a complex subject, identifying the relationships between the parts, and revealing the areas in which further developments will be required" (p. 6). It guides practitioners in developing systems and provides insights for academicians in identifying where research needs to be performed. Gorry and Scott Morton's (1971) framework for MIS and Sprague's (1980) for DSS are two of the best known and most useful frameworks. Turban and Schaeffer (1987) suggest the need for an EIS development framework. This chapter provides such a framework based on the EIS literature, our experiences in developing EIS, and discussions with vendors, consultants, and EIS staff members.

The EIS development framework introduced here is illustrated by the structural perspective depicted in Figure 17–1. With this perspective, there are key elements and interactions among the elements that are important when developing an EIS. The elements include executives, functional area personnel (e.g., line managers, staff personnel, and data suppliers), information systems personnel, vendors, data, and information technology. The interactions are in the form of pressures, human interactions, and data flows.

The development of an EIS is a dynamic process that places the key elements and interactions in motion. In order for this to be successful, an appropriate development process must be used. This consideration is another important part of the framework.

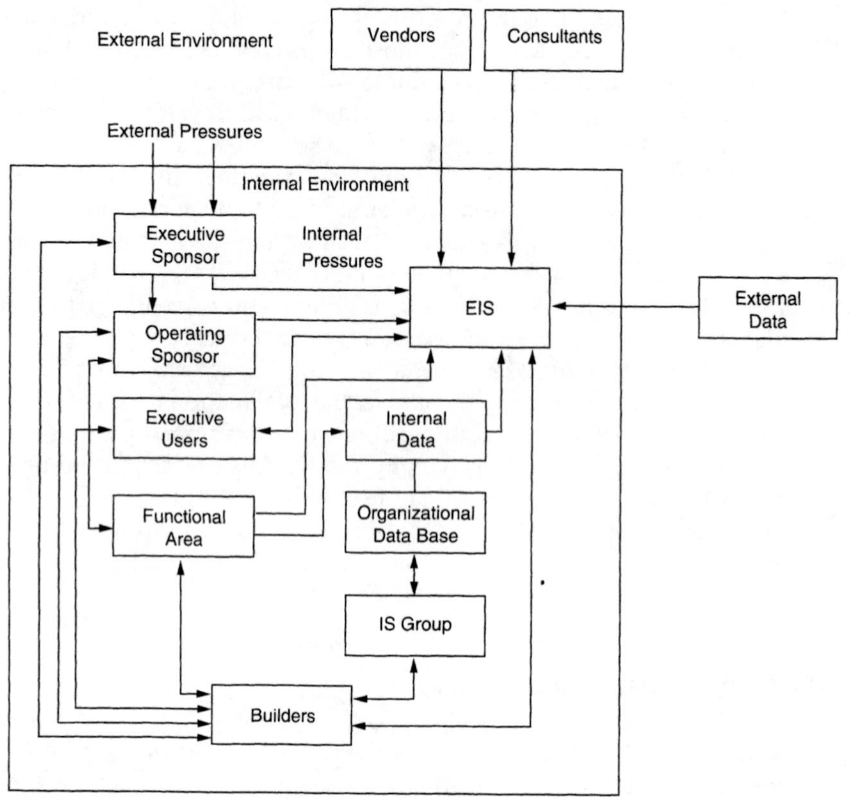

FIGURE 17–1 Structural Perspective of the EIS Development Framework

From the users' perspective, the dialog with the system is of fundamental importance. It includes what must be known in order to use the system, how to direct the system's actions, and how the output is presented by the system (Bennett, 1977). The dialog is another important part of the framework.

In summary, the EIS development framework includes a structural perspective, the development process, and the user-system dialog. There are a number of aspects associated with each. Those that are explored in this research are identified in Table 17–1.

THE STUDY

The research study was begun in the spring of 1988 to investigate current EIS practices. The authors mailed a multipart questionnaire to a large sample of geographically dispersed firms. The first part of the questionnaire defined an execu-

TABLE 17-1 Aspects of the EIS Development Framework

Structural

- Personnel
  - EIS Initiator
  - Executive Sponsor
  - Operating Sponsor
  - EIS Builder/Support Staff
  - EIS Users
  - Functional Area Personnel
  - IS Personnel
- Data
  - Internal
  - External

Development Process

- External and Internal Pressures
- Cost/Benefit Analysis
- Costs
  - Development Costs
  - Annual Operating Costs
- Development Time
- Development Methodology
- Hardware
- Software
- Spread
- Evolution
- Information Provided
- EIS Capabilities

User-System Dialog

- Knowledge Base
  - Training
  - User Documentation
  - System User
- Action Language
  - User-System Interface
  - System Response Time
- Presentation Language
  - Multiple Information Formats
  - Color

tive information system. The definition is important because EIS are the most recent computer-based information system to evolve, and, therefore, a precise definition of EIS is not universally accepted among academicians and practitioners. The second part of the questionnaire gathered demographic data on each organization. Finally, the questionnaire sought data concerning the development, operation, support, and capabilities of the EIS in the organization. Suggested changes made after two pretests were incorporated into the final survey instrument.

The survey population was chosen from three groups. The first group attended either the DSS-87 or DSS-88 conferences. One hundred and eighty-five questionnaires were sent to this group. Questionnaires were not sent to attendees from educational institutions or consulting firms. The second group, all of whom received questionnaires, consisted of the 100 firms identified by a *Computerworld* survey as having invested the most effectively in information systems. The authors believed that organizations that are leaders in the use of information systems (IS) are likely candidates to have an EIS. The third group consisted of 19 firms known by the authors to have an EIS but were not included in the first two groups. Each firm was carefully checked to ensure that the firm was not included in more than one group. Because 18 firms appeared more than once, a total of 286 questionnaires were mailed. The survey was not a random sample. Because most firms had not developed an EIS at this point in time, a frame was used that maximized the likelihood of contacting firms with an EIS.

Initially, the authors received 72 usable responses, with 30 of the firms indicating that they had an EIS, and 42 indicating that they did not. Five weeks after the first mailing, another questionnaire was mailed to non-respondents. This follow-up resulted in responses from 20 additional firms with an EIS and 20 with none. The profile of responses from the second group corresponded closely with the profile of the initial responses. A total of 112 usable responses was received for a response rate of 39.1 percent. The number of companies with an EIS was 50, which provides the "n" on which percentages are based when describing current practices in this chapter. In some cases, the respondents did not answer every question. In such instances, the percentages calculated are based on the number of responses received.

FINDINGS AND DISCUSSION

Demographics

Organizations in this survey represent a variety of industries located in widely dispersed geographic areas (see Figure 17–2). Their total corporate assets average $5.37 billion, with only three firms reporting total assets of less than $1 billion. Forty-eight respondents listed their positions in their firms (see Figure 17–2). The largest number of respondents are IS managers, followed by executives and IS staff members. The respondents averaged 18.74 years of work experience, 13.78 years of IS work experience, and 2.77 years of EIS experience.

Forty-seven firms (94 percent) had an operational EIS, and three firms (6 percent) were far enough along in developing one that they were able to partially answer the questions on the survey. The latter three firms all indicated that they would have an operational EIS in less than one year.

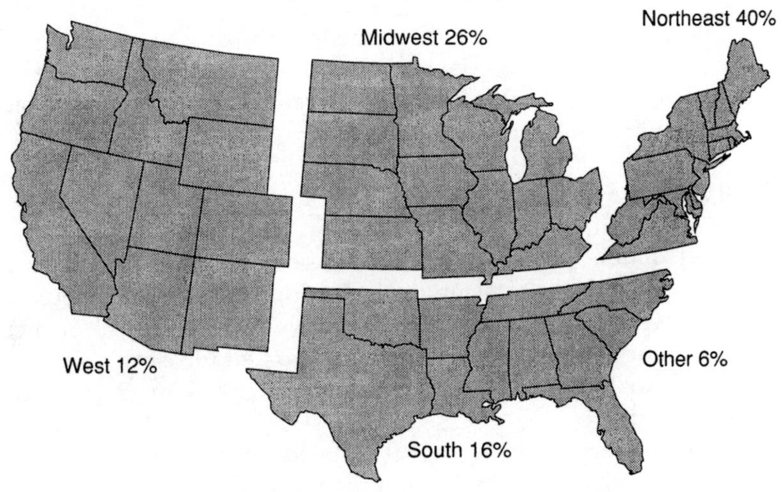

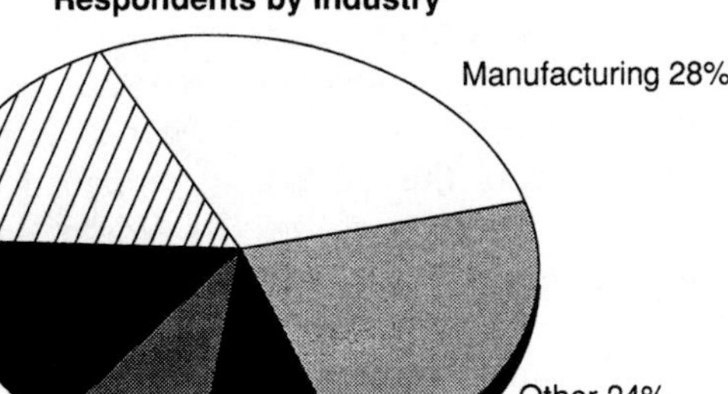

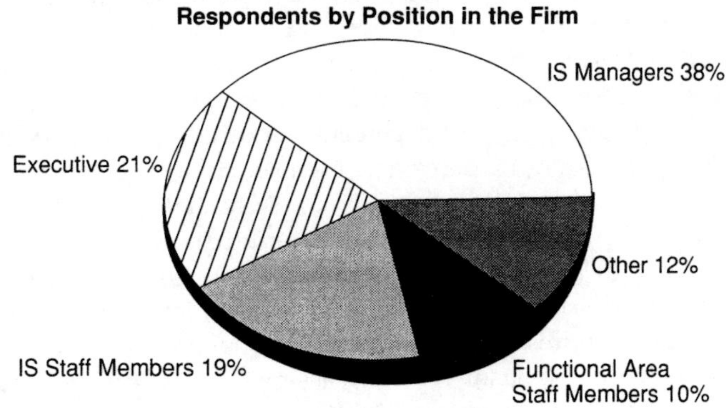

FIGURE 17–2 Respondents by Location, Industry, and Position

While some EIS date back to the late 1970s (Houdeshel and Watson, 1987), most of them are recent. The survey findings support this statement as 40 firms (80 percent) indicated that their EISs were less than three years old. The average age of an EIS in this survey is two years.

A Structural Perspective

Personnel. Thirty-four firms (68 percent) indicated that a company executive(s) served as the *initiator* of the development of the EIS. Survey respondents were allowed to define the term "executive" in the context of their own organizations. Information systems personnel initiated EIS development in 14 firms (28 percent). Finally, the information center in one firm (2 percent) initiated EIS development.

The finding that IS personnel initiated EIS development in 14 firms is somewhat surprising because the literature indicates that executives initiate EIS development (Houdeshel and Watson, 1987; Stecklow, 1989). However, 11 of these 14 firms (79 percent) had EIS that were less than two years old. Of the 34 firms with EIS initiated by executives, nineteen (56 percent) had EIS that were less than two years old. These numbers suggest that executives motivated EIS development when these systems first evolved. Few IS departments had the confidence of management and/or the risk-taking propensity to push for an EIS. However, as the number of EIS success stories has grown, more IS departments are taking the lead in advocating EIS development by keeping abreast of technological developments and communicating the potential benefits of the technology to senior executives (Volonino and Drinkard, 1989).

EIS development is spurred by a highly placed senior executive who serves as the system's *executive sponsor* (Barrow, 1990; Rockart and DeLong, 1988). This person is typically the president or vice president of the company. Rockart and DeLong (1988) suggest that three major responsibilities of the executive sponsor include making the initial request for the system; staying on top of the system's development and providing direction and feedback about proposed applications; and communicating strong and continuing interest to those with a stake in the system, such as key staff groups and line managers supplying data.

In this study, 42 firms (84 percent) reported having executive sponsors for their EIS. Interestingly, 62 percent of the executive sponsors hold positions other than CEO or president (see Table 17–2). A partial explanation for this finding relates to the scope of the EIS. While it is not explored in this survey, the authors are familiar with a number of EIS that serve a functional area rather than the entire organization. In these situations, it is logical that the executive sponsor would be the vice president from the functional area served.

The executive sponsor typically assigns an *operating sponsor* to manage the day-to-day development of the EIS (Rockart and DeLong, 1988). The operating sponsor is often a senior executive who has an interest in having an EIS for his or her own purposes. An information systems project manager may serve as the

TABLE 17-2 Positions Held by Executive Sponsors

Position	Percent of firms
Chief Executive Officer	21
President	17
Chief Financial Officer	14
Vice President	42
Controller	6

operating sponsor. The operating sponsor works with executives, specialized staff, functional area personnel, IS personnel, and vendors in creating the EIS.

Forty-five firms (90 percent) reported having an operating sponsor, and 42 firms listed the operating sponsor's position. The operating sponsor held a variety of positions, the most prevalent being the manager or director of IS (42 percent of firms) (see Table 17–3). This finding is different from what might be expected because the literature suggests that the operating sponsor is typically a senior executive (Rockart and DeLong, 1988).

The *EIS builder/support staff* is responsible for creating and maintaining the EIS (Paller and Laska, 1990; Rockart and DeLong, 1988). The staff may be either newly created or an existing organizational unit given a new charge. For example, a unit that provides specialized information and presentation materials to senior management can be given EIS responsibilities (Houdeshel and Watson, 1987). It is likely that an existing group will require help with technical matters. This lack of technical skills is not the case when IS personnel are responsible for the EIS, but IS personnel are often judged to be out of sync with the needs of senior management or too busy with other activities. Consultants and vendors can also be involved, especially during initial development.

All firms in this survey had EIS builder/support teams, with 37 firms (74 percent) indicating that their group consisted of five or fewer full-time people. The average size of the team was four people. Table 17–4 shows that the four categories of personnel most commonly found on the EIS team are end-user support personnel (58 percent of firms), systems analysts (54 percent), programmers (44 percent), and executive staff support personnel (40 percent). Only seven firms (14 percent) reported using vendor personnel when developing their EIS.

TABLE 17-3 Positions Held by Operating Sponsors

Position	Percent of firms
Manager or Director of IS	50
Manager or Director of Functional Areas	14
Vice President	12
Analyst	10
Staff	7
Consultant	7

TABLE 17–4 EIS Development Team Members

Category	Percent of firms
End-user support personnel	58
Systems analysts	54
Programmers	44
Executive staff	40
Executive	22
Vendor personnel	14
Others	14

The builder/support team should include personnel with a mixture of business and technical skills because the team must work closely with many different people in the firm (e.g., executives, the IS department, and functional area personnel) (Reck and Hall, 1986; Rockart and DeLong, 1988). The business skills typically come from people who have experience in the company. The technical skills often come from IS personnel, either by virtue of being assigned to the staff or given specific responsibilities for supporting EIS activities.

Respondents were asked to rank the top five skills in order of importance. Five points were awarded to the most important skill, four points to the second most important skill, and so on. The ability to work well with executives was found to be the most necessary skill for a development team member, followed by knowledge of the business and interpersonal skills (see Table 17–5). Technical skills ranked only fourth.

While it was not explored in the survey, it is worth noting that the EIS builder/support group can have a variety of organizational structures. One approach is to have a centralized group that reports to IS or a functional area. Another approach is to have a small, centralized group with functional area personnel working on a part-time basis performing tasks such as identifying information requirements and supplying data. These tasks are in addition to other job responsibilities. This arrangement matches up well with the skills that the support group needs in order to work effectively with executives.

TABLE 17–5 Important Skills for the EIS Development Team

Skill	Total Points
Ability to work well with executives	161
Knowledge of the business	143
Interpersonal skills	141
Technical skills	133
Ability to organize data	115
Other	12

The executive sponsor, operating sponsor, and EIS staff identify the *users* of the EIS. This group is usually small initially and expands over time. A key to the success of the EIS is identifying the system and information requirements of the executive users (Stecklow, 1989). A variety of methods can be used, including participation in strategic planning sessions, formal CSF sessions, informal discussions, monitoring executive activities, discussions with staff support personnel, software tracking of system usage, and others (Watson and Frolick, 1988).

Functional area personnel are an important source of data for the EIS, and an implementation strategy should be pursued that encourages their cooperation and support for the system. Before implementation of an EIS, much of the needed data are already being gathered but often only for the executives of the functional area in which the data originate. Two of the major organizational resistances to EIS are staff personnel who feel threatened by the possibility of a diminished role in supplying information to executives and subordinate line managers who fear that their operations will be too visible to top management (Argyris, 1971; Carroll, 1988; Rockart and DeLong, 1988).

Information systems personnel may not lead the EIS project, but their support, cooperation, and assistance are critical (Leibs, 1989). Helping select and install hardware and software, providing maintenance, trouble-shooting problems, and providing access to machine-resident data are some of the support responsibilities that fall to IS personnel. In organizations where IS personnel have the attention and confidence to top management, they may be able to create an interest in the creation of an EIS (Volonino and Drinkard, 1989). This task is accomplished by demonstrating what an EIS is and the kind of information it provides. Possible demonstration strategies include showing a potential executive sponsor an EIS in another company; arranging a vendor-provided demonstration, ideally using company data important to the executive; or prototyping an EIS in-house.

Data. Data play a critical role in an EIS because they are the basis for the information provided (Houdeshel and Watson, 1987; Rockart and DeLong, 1988). The data can come from internal or external sources and can be hard or soft. The EIS can require that new data be collected and stored. Much of the *internal data* is extracted from existing organizational databases that are used by transaction processing systems and functional area applications. This tends to be hard data. The use of this hard data in an EIS is not as straightforward as it might seem, however, because of different reporting and updating cycles, functional area feelings of data ownership, and multiple, incompatible databases (e.g., inconsistent data definitions). Other internal data come from human sources and often are soft in nature and are critical to understanding complex problems (Mintzberg, 1975; Zmud, 1986). Included can be news, rumors, opinions, ideas, predictions, explanations, and plans. Collecting, analyzing, and entering these data to an EIS tends to be very labor-intensive but adds considerably to the richness of the information provided.

Firms in the survey listed a variety of internal data sources. The corporate data base is a common source of internal data for most (82 percent) of the firms. Other internal data sources include the functional areas of the firm (62 percent), documents (38 percent), and humans (34 percent). These data indicate the richness and variety of data sources that can be used by an EIS. Further, the data illustrate the extensive data access requirements associated with an EIS.

External data are also important to an EIS (Runge, 1988). Like internal data, they can be hard or soft and can come from existing data bases or require special collection efforts. Data sources include external data bases (e.g., Dow Jones News Retrieval), published data, customers, and suppliers. External data sources primarily noted in this survey include news services (56 percent of firms), stock markets (46 percent), and trade/industry data (34 percent).

The Development Process

The executive sponsor's interest in the development of an EIS can be the consequence of external and internal pressures (Gulden and Ewers, 1989; Houdeshel and Watson, 1987; Rockart and DeLong, 1988). The *external pressures* come from the firm's external environment and can include environmental turbulence (e.g., rapidly changing costs of raw materials), increased competition, and increased government regulations. *Internal pressures* include the need for new, better, or more timely information; having to manage organizations that are increasingly complex and difficult to run; and the need for more efficient reporting systems.

The study asked respondents to rank order the three most important external pressures and the three most important internal pressures. Three points were awarded to the most important pressure in each category, two points to the second most important pressure, and one point to the third most important pressure.

The most critical external pressure is an increasingly competitive environment. Other critical external pressures, in descending order, include the rapidly changing external environment and the need to be more proactive in dealing with the external environment (see Table 17–6).

The survey findings for internal pressures (see Table 17–6) reveal that respondents consider the need for timely information to be most critical. Other internal pressures include the need for improved communication, the need for access to operational data, and the need for rapid status updates. An interesting finding is that respondents place the need for more accurate information as the least critical internal pressure. This seems to indicate that EIS users already consider the information they receive to be accurate.

Many researchers observe that *cost/benefit analyses* are difficult to perform on EIS because of the difficulty in quantifying many of the benefits (Houdeshel and Watson, 1987; Moad, 1988; Rockart and DeLong, 1988; Rockart and Treacy, 1982). These researchers suggest that there is simply an intuitive feeling that the system will justify its costs. After the system becomes operational, specific benefits and cost savings may be identifiable (Wallis, 1989). Forty-four firms answered this

TABLE 17-6 Pressures Leading to EIS Development

	Total Points
External Pressures	
Increasingly competitive environment	113
Rapidly changing external environment	59
Need to be more proactive in dealing with external environment	46
Need to access external data bases	25
Increasing government regulations	15
Other	8
Internal Pressures	
Need for timely information	61
Need for improved communication	39
Need for access to operational data	35
Need for rapid status updates on different business units	34
Need for increased effectiveness	27
Need to be able to identify historical trends	27
Need for increased efficiency	25
Need for access to corporate database	25
Other	17
Need for more accurate information	15

questionnaire item. Their responses support these assertions; forty-two respondents (95 percent) indicate that their firms assessed potential benefits of their EIS through intuitive feelings about improved decision making. Only two firms (5 percent) assessed hard dollar benefits.

Costs

Even though most firms do not measure hard dollar benefits, many firms do consider the costs involved before undertaking EIS development. Most firms estimate software costs (79 percent), hardware costs (68 percent), and personnel costs (68 percent). Fewer firms (32 percent) estimate training costs, perhaps because training costs are anticipated to be minimal.

In conjunction with data on firms that estimated EIS costs before development, this study gathered data on actual EIS development costs and operational costs. *Development costs* are those costs incurred creating the first version of the EIS. Thirty-three firms provided development costs for their EIS. The firms averaged $128,000 on software, $129,000 on hardware, $90,000 on personnel, and $18,000 on training. These firms also supplied *annual EIS operating costs,* which were found to average $117,000 on personnel, $46,000 on software, $29,000 on hardware, and $16,000 on training. These numbers suggest that an EIS is expensive and, consequently, may be limited to larger firms with considerable financial resources.

Of note is that annual operating costs for personnel appear to be higher than personnel development costs. A possible explanation for this finding is that companies may need additional people to handle increases in the number of users, screens, and system capabilities.

The *time to develop* the initial version of an EIS is important. As with other systems that support decision making, the first version of an EIS should be developed quickly and presented to users for their reactions (Moad, 1988; Runge, 1989). Forty-six firms (92 percent) developed their EIS using an *iterative, prototyping methodology* and four firms (8 percent) used a formal systems development life cycle approach.

The *hardware* and especially the *software* used in developing the first version may or may not be what are used in later versions. At one extreme, a few screens can be designed using existing software to run on workstations already in place (Rinaldi and Jastrzembski, 1986). Information for the screens can be entered manually. This approach minimizes development time and cost. At the other extreme, a commercial EIS package can be purchased and installed. The EIS builders use the package to create the initial screens and to supply them with information. This approach minimizes the difficulties of moving to later versions if the EIS proves to be successful.

There are several hardware configurations possible with an EIS (Paller and Laska, 1990; Rockart and DeLong, 1988). Forty-eight companies indicated the hardware configuration used for their EIS. Forty firms (83 percent) use a mainframe approach. The mainframe approach includes 18 firms (37 percent) that employ a shared mainframe, 17 firms (35 percent) that use a PC network connected to a mainframe, and five firms (11 percent) that employ a dedicated mainframe. Eight firms (17 percent) use a PC network with a file server for their hardware configuration. More vendors have been offering local area network-based EIS products (e.g., Lightship from Pilot) since this study was conducted.

The availability of commercial software has contributed considerably to the growth of EIS. Products from vendors such as Comshare (Commander EIS) and Pilot (Command Center) facilitate the development and maintenance of an EIS. These products support ease of use (e.g., mouse or touch screen operation), access to data, screen design and maintenance, interfaces to other software (e.g., Lotus 1-2-3), and other system requirements.

An EIS can be developed using in-house developed software, vendor-supplied software, or some combination of the two (Paller and Laska, 1990; Rockart and DeLong, 1988). Twelve firms (24 percent) developed their EIS using custom-built, in-house software; 12 firms (24 percent) used vendor-supplied software; and 26 firms (52 percent) used a combination of in-house and vendor software. Of the 38 firms that employ at least some vendor-supplied software, nine firms (24 percent) use Pilot's Command Center, seven firms (18 percent) use Comshare's Commander EIS, five firms (12 percent) use Interactive Image's EASEL, and the remaining 17 firms (46 percent) use a wide variety of other vendor software. These results are not surprising; Pilot and Comshare are generally recognized to be the two leading vendors of EIS software.

Over time an EIS evolves in terms of the number of users, the number of screens, the content and format of the screens, and EIS capabilities (Houdeshel and Watson, 1987; Rockart and DeLong, 1988). In some cases the EIS may be "pushed" on users, but a more desirable approach is to allow "demand pull" to occur. The latter normally occurs as subordinates learn that their superiors have access to certain information and they "want to see what their bosses are looking at." Still, some executives may legitimately have little interest in using the EIS because it contains little information relevant to them, or they have well-established alternative sources of information.

Executive information systems usually spread over time. *Spread* refers to the increase in the number of users who have access to the EIS (Rockart and DeLong, 1988). It can be argued that an EIS that does not spread is likely to fail (Friend, 1990). The survey question about spread referred only to the number of users over time and did not specify that the users be executives. Therefore, the users could include executives, executive staff, and other organizational personnel. This study found that the EIS supported an average of 7.75 users initially, with a steadily increasing number of users over time, as can be seen in Figure 17–3. The "n"s shown in Figure 17–3 are the number of respondents who provided data for the various points in time.

Evolution refers to additional capabilities and information provided by an EIS over time (Rockart and DeLong, 1988). This study gathered data on the number of screens available to users over time. An average of 55.8 screens were available initially, and the number of available screens increased in each time period (see Figure 17–3). This increase implies that users usually want more information as time passes and they become familiar with the system.

Even though the data show that the number of screens consistently increases, outdated screens must be deleted and other screens modified. Adding, modifying, and deleting screens is an important responsibility of the EIS support staff. Software tracking of system use is very helpful in identifying screens that may need to be changed. Screen content and format can change over time. As an example of this change, screens may become denser in content as users become more familiar with them (Houdeshel and Watson, 1987). Information that was spread over several screens may be placed on a single screen, which can result in format changes.

To be most effective in supporting executives, an EIS must *provide information* from many areas (Houdeshel and Watson, 1987; Rockart and DeLong, 1988). It can supply information about the industry in which the firm competes, company information, work unit information, and information that may be of interest to only a single executive. The information can span subsidiaries, divisions, functional areas, and departments.

The surveyed firms reported that their EIS provided information by strategic business unit (88 percent), functional area (86 percent), key performance indicator (71 percent), product (67 percent), and location (53 percent). These percentages demonstrate that EIS are able to supply information for various perspectives, thus allowing users flexibility in the information they can access.

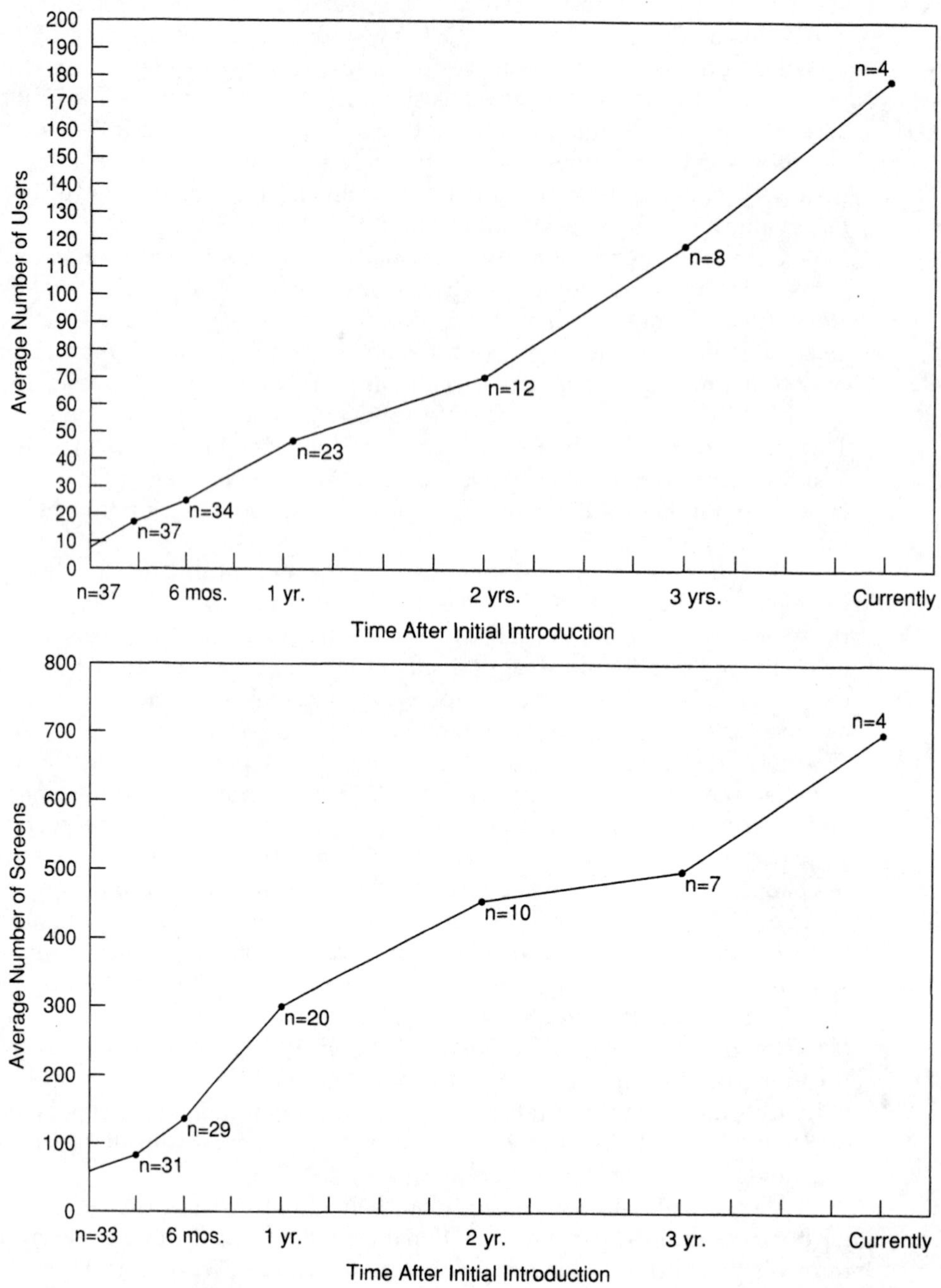

FIGURE 17–3 EIS Spread

An EIS can have a variety of *capabilities* (Friend, 1986; Kogan, 1986). Eighty-eight percent of the firms in this study state that their EIS provides access to current status information about the company. Other capabilities provided in a majority of firms are electronic mail, external news access, and access to other external databases (see Table 17–7).

Executives may want access to the EIS while at home (Wallis, 1989). Executives who are traveling may also want to access the EIS. This off-site use creates special communications, security, and support responsibilities. This is just one example of a system requirement that can evolve over time.

The Dialog

From the executive's perspective, the dialog with the EIS is the most important component of the system (Zmud, 1986). As was pointed out previously, because of the nature of executives and executive work, the system should be quite user-friendly. It should avoid elaborate logon procedures. Movement among EIS components should be seamless (e.g., e-mail might be a main menu option and not require a separate user ID). The system should provide context-dependent online help. Menus and a keyword index for locating screens should be included to help the executive find information. Sequence or command files should be created that allow executives to page through regularly viewed screens. The inclusion of a "drill-down" capability allows executives to go into more detail when an exceptional situation is encountered. The screens can provide the names and telephone numbers of people who can discuss the information presented.

Training on the use of the EIS should be one-on-one. Any system that requires more than a few minutes of training probably does not satisfy ease-of-use requirements (Carroll, 1988). *User documentation* should not be necessary for a well-designed EIS. If documentation is provided, it should be kept to a single page.

The *system user* of the EIS may be the executive, or it may be operated by an intermediary (Rockart and DeLong, 1988). Forty-eight respondents answered this item on the questionnaire. Forty-three firms (89 percent) report that their execu-

TABLE 17-7 Capabilities Available on the EIS

Capability	Percent of Firms
Access to current status	88
Electronic mail	65
Other external data base	57
External news access	56
Spreadsheet	37
Word processing	34
Automated filing	22
Other	14

tives use the EIS directly, and five firms (11 percent) report that intermediaries operate the system.

In keeping with the fact than an EIS must be highly user-friendly, the *user interface* and *response time* of the EIS are critical (Houdeshel and Watson, 1987; Rockart and DeLong, 1988). Ninety-two percent of the EIS employ a keyboard interface, one-half a mouse, and one-fourth a touch screen. These percentages indicate that there are multiple interfaces available in many of the EIS in this sample. The mean response time of the EIS in this survey was 2.8 seconds, with 42 firms (84 percent) reporting average response times of less than five seconds.

The EIS can provide a variety of capabilities for selecting screens. Keystrokes can be employed to move through menus or to identify particular screens. Even though some executives are adverse to using keyboards, this typically is not a major problem if the required skills are not too great. A keyboardless system can be provided by using a mouse or a touchscreen. Most vendor-supplied software offer these methods of system operation as options. Icons are commonly used to make the system more intuitive.

Screens should include graphical, tabular, and textual presentation of information. Most supplied software provides a large variety of screen design capabilities. Standards should be established for any terms used, color codes, and graphic designs (Smith and Mosier, 1984; Tullis, 1981). These standards help to avoid misunderstandings and reduce the amount of mental processing required to interpret information.

Executive information systems should be able to present information to the user in *multiple formats* (e.g., graphical, tabular, and textual) (Friend, 1988; Houdeshel and Watson, 1987; Rockart and DeLong, 1988). Ninety percent of the EIS in this study have graphical formats available, 90 percent use textual formats, and 88 percent employ tabular formats. These percentages suggest that many EIS present information in multiple formats.

Executive information systems make extensive use of *color* in presenting information (Friend, 1988; Houdeshel and Watson, 1987; Rockart and DeLong, 1988). Out of 47 respondents who answered this question, 39 EIS (83 percent) in this study employ color displays and eight (17 percent) do not.

CONCLUSION

This study has presented a framework for the development of executive information systems and data related to this framework from 50 organizations. In most cases, the data support the "conventional wisdom" found in the literature:

- EIS are a recent development.
- EIS development is typically driven by a senior executive.
- An EIS has an executive sponsor, and this person is normally a CEO or a vice president.

- The development of an EIS is approved with little formal cost/benefit analysis.
- EIS development groups include a variety of personnel with a mixture of business and technical skills.
- An EIS obtains data from multiple internal and external sources.
- An EIS provides broadly based information.
- Pilot's Command Center and Comshare's Commander EIS are the two most popular vendor products for creating an EIS.
- The initial version of an EIS is developed quickly.
- Most EIS are mainframe-based.
- An EIS is created using an iterative, prototyping development methodology.
- The number of users and the number of screens of an EIS increase over time.
- Nearly all EIS are used directly by executives without intermediaries.
- An EIS presents information in graphical, textual, and tabular formats.
- Most EIS use color in presenting information.

The study also provides insights about areas where little is previously reported:

- The increasingly competitive environment and the need for timely information are the main external and internal pressures that lead to the development of an EIS.
- On average, the total costs of developing an EIS are $365,000, and the annual costs to maintain one are $208,000. It should be noted that the firms in this study are large, and smaller companies might develop more limited, and therefore less expensive, EIS due to cost considerations.
- The average size of an EIS development group is four people.
- On average, about one-fourth of the EIS are created using in-house developed software, one-half with vendor supplied plus in-house software, and one-fourth with only vendor-supplied software.
- On average, it takes 4.9 months to develop the initial version of an EIS.
- On average, 92 percent of all EIS employ a keyboard interface, one-half a mouse, and one-fourth a touchscreen.

And finally, there were a few surprising findings:

- In some firms, EIS development is initiated by IS, and this seems to be a growing trend.
- A vice president is most often the executive sponsor for an EIS.
- An IS manager or director is most often the operating sponsor for an EIS.

While this and other studies provide information about EIS, there is much that still needs to be learned. After reading the MIS literature, one is surprised by how little academic research has been conducted on EIS. Most of the literature only provides glowing descriptions of specific EIS and how they are being used. In conducting this research, a variety of interesting and important EIS research questions surfaced.

- Is the organizational position and level of commitment of the executive sponsor related to EIS success?
- What considerations are most important when selecting an operating sponsor?
- How can the benefits of an EIS be assessed in advance?
- How does the software used in building an EIS affect the development process and system success?
- What level of staffing and organization structure are best for the EIS builder/support staff?
- What methods can be most effectively used to identify executives' information requirements?
- What are the major EIS data management problems and their solutions?
- What impact does the inclusion of soft data have on EIS success?
- What are the major problems associated with EIS "spread" and its evolution?
- How can EIS functionality be increased while maintaining ease-of-use?
- What emerging technologies (e.g., voice, optical disc) can be effectively used with EIS?
- What are the most effective screen presentation formats for an EIS?

Currently, the technology for EIS is evolving rapidly, and future systems are likely to be different from those that are in use today. A number of interesting and promising changes that can be anticipated include:

- Better integration with other applications. For example, better support can be provided by integrating EIS with decision support systems, group decision support systems, and expert systems. A DSS can provide analysis capabilities when problems are identified using an EIS; an EIS can be used to provide information in a decision room setting; and an expert system can be created to help guide executives in using the EIS effectively.
- Better commercial EIS software. Some of the advances to expect include better interfaces to organizational data and other organizational systems, enhanced capabilities for monitoring system usage, industry-specific template screens, and expanded sets of builders' tools (e.g., icons for use in screen development).

- Better executive-system interfaces. While keyboards are required for e-mail and most decision support applications, mouse and touchscreens are attractive alternatives for other types of system use. Animation is likely to be increasingly used to "add life" to information. Television may be available in a window. Voice may be used to direct the system.

An EIS is a high-risk system, and many failures have occurred (Watson and Glover, 1989). By following the EIS development framework, however, the likelihood of having a failure should be reduced. Over time, as more experience is gained, better products emerge, and more research findings are available, the chances for having an EIS success should grow.

QUESTIONS

1. What is the relationship between executive information systems and executive support systems?
2. Why are executive information systems succeeding when most previous attempts to supply senior executives with computer-generated information have failed?
3. Assume that a senior executive has asked you to prepare a summary description of what might be expected if the firm develops an EIS. Prepare such a description based on the study findings presented in the reading.

REFERENCES

1. ALBALA, M. "Getting to the Pulse of the Company," *Personal Computing* (12:10), October 1988, 196–98.
2. ALEXANDER, M. "Executive Information Systems Catch On," *Computerworld,* February 27, 1989, 31.
3. APPLEGATE, L. M., and C. S. OSBORN "Phillips 66 Company: Executive Information Systems," Harvard Case (9-189-006), Harvard Business School, Boston, MA, December 1988.
4. ARGYRIS, C. "Management Information Systems: The Challenge to Rationality and Emotionality," *Management Science* (17:6), June 1971, B275–292.
5. BARROW, C. "Implementing an Executive Information System: Seven Steps for Success," *Journal of Information Systems Management* (7:2), Spring 1990, 41–46.
6. BENNETT, J. "User-Oriented Graphics Systems for Decision Support in Unstructured Tasks," in *User-Oriented Design of Interactive Graphics Systems,* S. Treu (ed.), Association for Computing Machinery, New York, 1977.

7. Burkan, W. C. "Making EIS Work," *DSS 88 Transactions*, The Institute of Management Sciences, Providence, RI, 1988, 121–136.
8. Carroll, P. B. "Computerphobe Managers," *The Wall Street Journal*, June 20, 1988, 21.
9. *Computerworld* "The Premier 100," Special Supplement, September 12, 1988, 9.
10. Friend, D. "Executive Information Systems: Successes, Failures, Insights, and Misconceptions," *DSS 86 Transactions*, The Institute of Management Sciences, Providence, RI, 1986, 35–40.
11. Friend, D. "EIS and the Collapse of the Information Pyramid," *Information Center* (6:3), March 1990, 22–28.
12. Gorry, G. A., and M. S. Scott Morton "A Framework for Management Information Systems," *Sloan Management Review* (13:1), Fall 1971, 51–70.
13. Gulden, G. K., and D. E. Ewers "Is Your ESS Meeting the Need?" *Computerworld*, July 10, 1989, 85–91.
14. Houdeshel, G., and H. J. Watson "The Management Information and Decision Support (MIDS) System at Lockheed-Georgia," *MIS Quarterly* (11:1), March 1987, 127–40.
15. Isenberg D. J. "How Senior Managers Think," *Harvard Business Review* (62:6), November–December 1984, 81–90.
16. Kogan, J. "Information for Motivation: A Key to Executive Information Systems That Translate Strategy into Results for Management," *DSS 86 Transactions*, The Institute of Management Sciences, Providence, RI, 1986, 6–13.
17. Kotter, J. P. "What Effective General Managers Really Do," *Harvard Business Review* (60:6), November–December 1982, 156–57.
18. Leibs, S. "EIS: It's All Down Hill From Here," *Information Week*, May 1989, pp. 44–46.
19. Main J. "At Last, Software CEOs Can Use," *Fortune* (119:6), March 13, 1989, 77–83.
20. Mintzberg, H. "The Manager's Job: Folklore and Fact," *Harvard Business Review* (53:4), July-August 1975, 49–61.
21. Moad, J. "The Latest Challenge for IS Is in the Executive Suite," *Datamation*, May 15, 1988, 43.
22. Paller, A., and R. Laska *The EIS Book*, Dow Jones-Irwin, Homewood, IL, 1990.
23. Reck, R. H., and J. R. Hall "Executive Information Systems: An Overview of Development," *Journal of Information Systems Management* (3:4), Fall 1986, 25–30.
24. Rinaldi, D., and T. Jastrzembski "Executive Information Systems: Put Strategic Data at Your CEO's Fingertips," *Computerworld*, October 27, 1986, 37–50.
25. Rockart J. F., and M. E. Treacy "The CEO Goes On-Line," *Harvard Business Review* (60:1), January-February 1982, 84–88.
26. Rockart, J. F., and D. W. DeLong *Executive Support Systems: The Emergence of Top Management Computer Use*, Dow Jones-Irwin, Homewood, IL, 1988.
27. Runge, L. "On the Executive's Desk," *Information Center* (4:6), June 1988, 34–38.
28. Smith S. L. and J. N. Mosier "Design Guidelines for User-System Interface," Software Report (ESD-TR-84-190), The MITRE Corporation, Bedford, MA, September 1984.
29. Sprague, R. H. "A Framework for the Development of Decision Support Systems," *MIS Quarterly* (4:4), December 1980, 1–26.
30. Stecklow, S. "The New Executive Information Systems," *Lotus*, April 1989, 51–55.

31. TULLIS, T. S. "An Evaluation of Alphanumeric, Graphic, and Color Information Displays," *Human Factors* (23:5), October 1981, 541–50.

32. TURBAN, E., and D. M. SCHAEFFER "A Comparative Study of Executive Information Systems," *DDS 87 Transactions,* The Institute of Management Sciences, Providence, RI, 1987, 139–48.

33. TURBAN, E., and H. J. WATSON "Integrating Expert Systems, Executive Information Systems, and Decision Support Systems," *DSS 89 Transactions,* The Institute of Management Sciences, Providence, RI, 1989, 74–82.

34. VOLONINO, L., and G. DRINKARD "Integrating EIS into the Strategic Plan: A Case Study of Fisher-Price," *DSS 89 Transactions,* The Institute of Management Sciences, Providence, RI, 1989, 37–45.

35. WALLIS, L. "Power Computing at the Top," *Across the Board* (26:1–2), January–February 1989, 42–51.

36. WATSON H. J, and M. FROLICK "Determining Information Requirements for an Executive Information System," unpublished working paper, Department of Management, University of Georgia, Athens, GA, 1988.

37. WATWON, H., and H. GLOVER "Common and Avoidable Causes of EIS Failure," *Computerworld,* December 4, 1989, 90–91.

38. ZMUD, R. W. "Supporting Senior Executives Through Decision Support Technologies: A Review and Directions for Future Research," in *Decisions Support Systems: A Decade in Perspective,* E. R. McLean and H. G. Sol (eds.), Elsevier Science Publishers B. V., North-Holland, Amsterdam, 1986, 87–101.

18

INCLUDING SOFT INFORMATION IN EIS

INTRODUCTION

Information systems have traditionally provided hard information such as monthly financials, sales orders, inventory levels, and headcounts. This information is typically delivered through scheduled, summary reports; demand reports; and queries, and is from the organization's transactions processing data base. It is valuable to lower-level managers but normally has limited usefulness to executives.

No executive wants to be accused of making "soft" decisions, but truth told, much of executive decision making is based on soft information. Predictions, opinions, news, ideas, and even rumors influence the actions of executives. The importance of this kind of information is seen in the hours executives spend every day, networking with people inside and outside the organization, reading, attending meetings, making phone calls, and "managing by walking around." The importance of soft information is well recognized in the literature as can be seen by the quotes in Table 18–1.[1]

Because soft information is valuable to executives, it is logical to include it an organization's EIS. To do so, however, involves many differences when compared to providing hard information. For example, the data sources (e.g., people, newspapers, and television) are different. So too is how it is collected and processed, because it tends to be non-machine resident and textual. Careful thought also has to be given to how it should be delivered (e.g., annotations to

Hugh J. Watson, Margaret O'Hara, Candice Harp, and Gigi Kelly contributed to the writing of this chapter. A version of it will be published in *Information Systems Management*. Used with permission of Auerbach Publishers.

TABLE 18-1 Quotes about Soft Information

Mintzberg	"Managers seem to cherish soft information. . . . A great deal of the manager's inputs are soft and speculative—impressions and feelings about other people, hearsay, gossip, and so on."
Brookes	"The role that soft information can play in providing additional support to the executive decision-making processes is dependent on the close integration between the report of hard and soft information."
Zmud	"One thing that is known about executive communication is that much of it involves 'soft,' rather than hard, information."
Jones and McLeod	"Evidence suggests that managers identify decision situations and build mental models not with the aggregated historical abstraction that a formal management information system (MIS) provides but with specific tidbits of informal or soft data."
Lester	". . . executive data requirements can vary quite significantly, ranging from a need for hard data, such as market research and management information systems, to 'fuzzy' or soft data, such as external news items or internal mail."
Huber	"Except for their systems that routinely index and store 'hard' information organizations tend to have only weak systems for finding where a certain item of information is known to the organization. . . . What about 'soft' information? Much of what an organization learns is stored in the minds of its members. . . . Thus, . . . as the friendliness and capabilities of expert systems increase the proportion of an organization's 'soft' and local information that is computer resident increases."

screens, electronic bulletin boards, and e-mail), because there is usually limited experience in providing this kind of information. In many ways, it represents a paradigm shift in terms of how executives and other workers can be supported by information technology.

In this chapter, a definition of soft information, its characteristics, several taxonomies, and basic understandings are provided. Next, the findings from 32 structured telephone interviews with EIS developers about current practices in regard to including soft information in EISs is presented. A set of 15 propositions about soft information are given and the chapter concludes with a brief look at current technology for including soft information in EISs.

WHAT IS SOFT INFORMATION?

Before discussing the inclusion of soft information in EIS, it is helpful to have a better understanding of exactly what soft information is. Interestingly, there is no well-accepted definition. Often it is simply contrasted with hard information. Hard information is "definite, certain, official, factual, clear, and explicit," while soft information is "fuzzy, unofficial, intuitive, subjective, nebulous, implied, and vague." For our purposes, the following definition is useful:

> **Soft information** enhances the understanding of past, current, and future events, often by adding value to factual data. Its accuracy and usefulness is assessed by the individual and depends on the timeliness and source of the information and how well the information matches existing understandings. It can be conveyed in multiple forms—text, graphics, image, and voice—and through multiple channels—formal and informal and internal and external to the organization.

Consider this definition in an EIS context. To manage effectively, executives must understand what has happened in the past, what is occurring now, and what might take place in the future, both inside and outside the firm. Often this is best accomplished by combining hard and soft information. For example, an EIS screen may show that a project is running behind its estimated completion date (hard information). A commentary added to the screen may describe what corrective steps are being taken and predict when the project will return to the schedule (soft information). Presented together, the information gives the executive a much clearer understanding of the situation than the hard information alone would have provided.

An executive assesses the accuracy and usefulness of soft information in light of its timeliness, source, and how well it corresponds with existing mental models. Recent information is often more trusted and valued than older information. Because executives often ask, "When did you hear this?" or "When did it happen?", EIS screens typically indicate when the information was last updated.

The executive's knowledge of its source influences the soft information's credibility. Consequently, it is considered good EIS design practice to identify information sources on screens. Telephone numbers are also usually given so that executives can obtain answers to any questions. While soft information that agrees with existing mental models is more believable than that which does not, disconfirming information often has the greatest value because it makes executives reevaluate existing understandings.

Soft information can be communicated through a variety of media. For example, voice annotations can be added to screens, full-motion video can be shown, and personal teleconferencing can be conducted.

An EIS expands and enhances the formal and informal, and internal and external channels used to gather soft information. For example, the inclusion of e-mail and an electronic bulletin board can facilitate the sharing of soft information. Access to news databases such as the Dow Jones News Retrieval helps executives keep in touch with the external environment. An EIS can be viewed as a broad band channel in which carefully prepared information in a rich variety of forms is communicated.

Because hard and soft information are often contrasted, one way to better understand soft information is to consider its relationship to hard information. With this approach, hard and soft information form a continuum. For example, a financial report would generally be considered at the "hard" end of the continuum, while a rumor would be placed on the "soft" end. With this perspective, information has varying degrees of hardness and softness. Just as there are many shades of gray between black and white, there are many shades of information between hard and soft.

While the positioning of a particular type of information along a hard/soft continuum is subjective, certain characteristics guide its placement. Figure 18–1 presents a number of characteristics that are helpful for this purpose. The characteristics are related to the content or source of the soft information. Executives receive many different kinds of information. Figure 18–2 groups various types at points along the hard/soft information continuum. The placements are subjective but reflect the differentiating characteristics of hard and soft information shown in Figure 18–1.

A STUDY OF SOFT INFORMATION

Despite numerous references to soft information in the literature, it has not been formally studied. This is perhaps not surprising because until recently information systems had limited capabilities for handling soft information. Thus, while

Characteristics of Information	Hard Information		Soft Information
Source	Machine resident	----------►	Human
	Often internal	----------►	Often external
Accuracy	High	----------►	Questionable
Degree of certainty	High	----------►	Low
Subject to interpretation	Generally accepted	----------►	Individually assessed
Timeliness	Historical	----------►	Current or future
Availability	Regularly	----------►	Ad hoc
Standardization of presentation	High	----------►	Low
Richness	Low	----------►	High
Knowledge of its existence	Generally known	----------►	Often unknown
Ownership	Generally available	----------►	Often tightly held
Lifetime	Long	----------►	Short
Communication channel	Formal	----------►	Informal

FIGURE 18–1 Hard/Soft Information Characteristics

HARD						SOFT
Financial Statements	News Reports	Schedules	Explanations	Predictions	Opinions	Rumors
Operational Reports	Industry Trends	Formal Plans	Justifications	Speculations	Feelings	Gossip
Historical Information	Survey Data		Assessments	Forecasts	Ideas	Hearsay
			Interpretations	Estimates		

FIGURE 18–2 Information Along the Hard/Soft Continuum

executives', need for soft information is well established, its inclusion in EIS has not been explored.

To learn more about the use of soft information in EIS, 32 EIS developers were asked the following questions:

- What types of soft information are included in your EIS?
- How is the soft information entered?
- How is the soft information made available to users?
- Is soft information ever intentionally excluded and, if so, why?
- What are the most popular applications of soft information?
- What important business decisions have been impacted by soft information?
- What is the relationship between the inclusion of soft information and the perceived value of the EIS?
- What factors influence the inclusion of soft information?
- What are companies' future plans for including soft information?

For the study, soft information was operationalized as any information other than the "hard" end of the hard/soft information continuum. Consequently, financial statements, operational reports, and historical reports were treated as hard information while, for example, news reports, schedules, explanations, predictions, opinions, and rumors were considered to be soft information.

The sample was selected from The University of Georgia's EIS data base. The structured interview was pilot tested with three EIS developers, which resulted in questions being added, deleted, and modified. A second pilot test led to additional minor refinements in the wording of questions. Thirty-two EIS developers agreed to be interviewed for the study.

STUDY FINDINGS

Demographics

The organizations included in the study represent a variety of industries located in geographically dispersed areas; see Figure 18–3. The total corporate assets and gross revenues for the companies surveyed ranged from $25 million to over $5 billion, with the majority of companies having over $1 billion in gross assets and revenues. Sixteen (50.0 percent) of the respondents (see Exhibit 1) classified themselves as EIS managers. Respondents averaged 13.5 years of computer experience, 10.3 years with their current company, and 3.3 years with their company's EIS.

Types of Soft Information, How They Are Entered, and How They Are Presented

The study participants were asked whether or not their EISs contain various types of soft information. The types explored were the points along the hard/soft information continuum in Figure 18–2. Figure 18–4 shows the percentages of EISs that include each type of soft information. The participants also were asked how each type of soft information is entered into the system and how it is made available to users. These issues are most easily discussed by considering each type of soft information separately.

Rumors, gossip, and hearsay. Only three systems (9.4 percent) contain rumors, gossip, and hearsay. The methods for sharing this information include e-mail and electronic bulletin boards. Because the study was limited to soft information in EISs, this count includes only those organizations where e-mail is embedded in the EIS. In many firms, e-mail and voice mail are stand-alone applications. E-mail messages may be entered by the executives or the executives' support staff (e.g., secretary). In firms where rumors, gossip, and hearsay are communicated through an electronic bulletin board, either the executives or the EIS support staff enters the information.

Opinions, feelings, and ideas. Five respondents (15.6 percent) indicated that opinions, feelings, and ideas are included. The means for communicating this type of information includes e-mail, electronic bulletin boards, and text annotations to screens. Three respondents said that this information is entered by the EIS support staff, one indicated that it is entered by executives, and one said that it is entered by both executives and the EIS support staff.

Predictions, speculations, forecasts and estimates. Twenty-five respondents (78.1 percent) indicated that their EIS includes predictions, speculations, forecasts, and estimates. This information may be about internal operations or

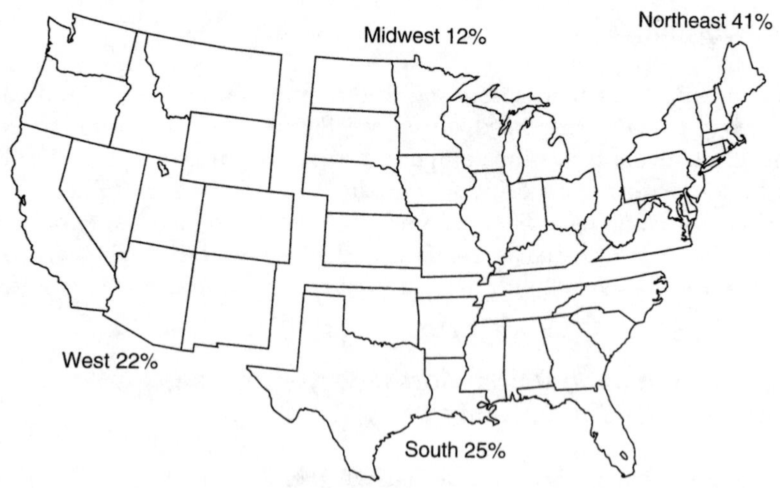

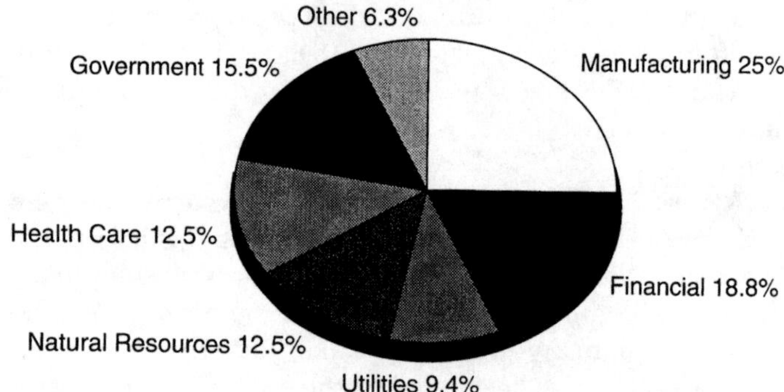

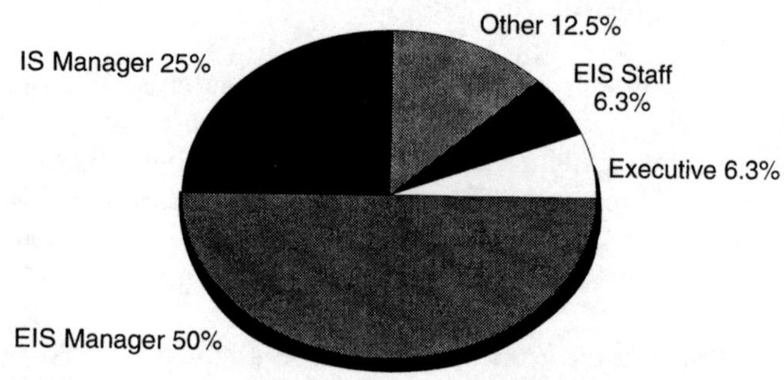

FIGURE 18-3 Respondents by Location, Industry, and Position

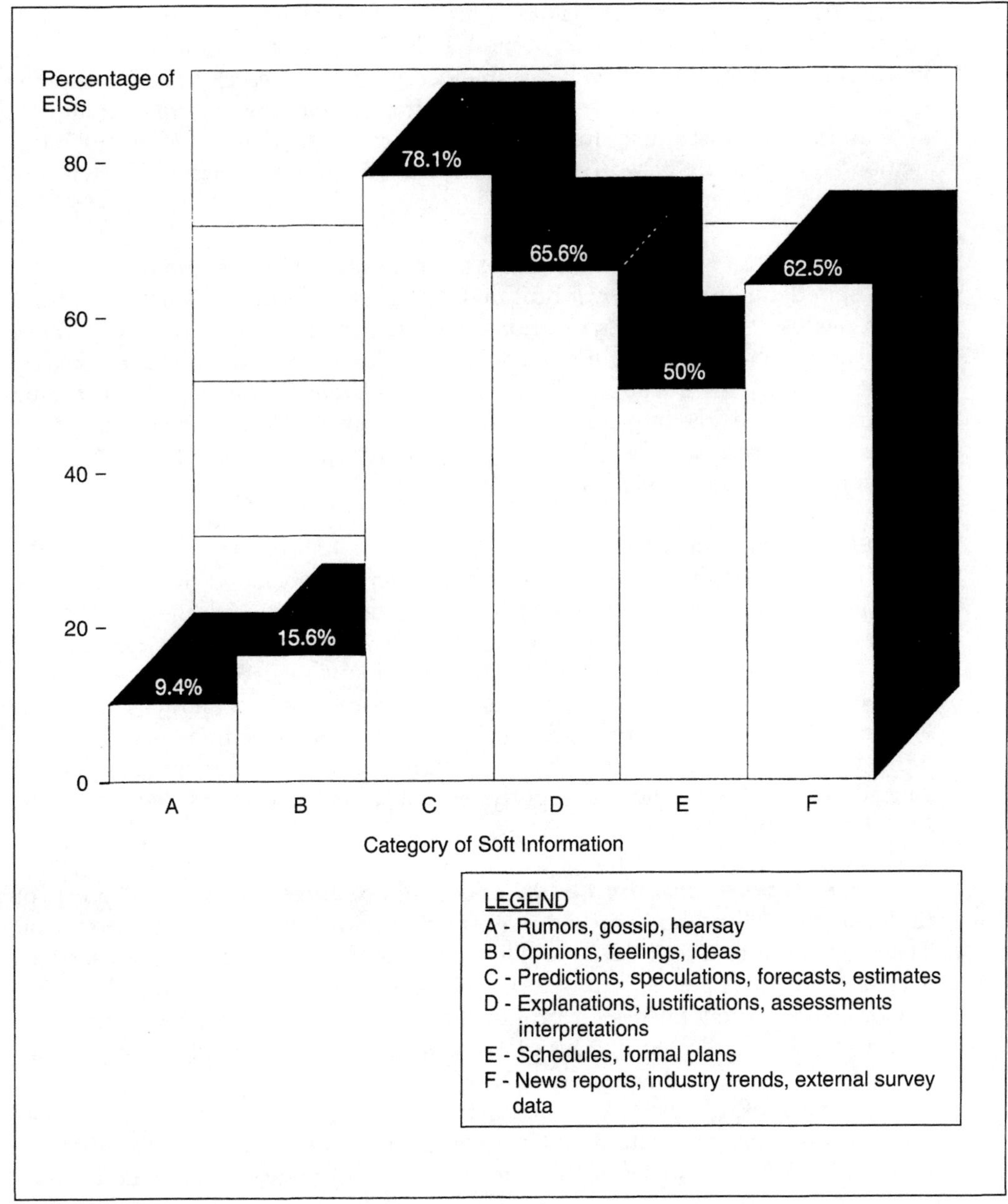

FIGURE 18-4 Types of Soft Information in EISs

the external environment and is often important for planning purposes. This category of information is included in more EISs than any of the other types, and its importance to executives is well documented by other research.[2] The EIS support staff, executives, and executives' support staff may enter this information into the system. In some cases (e.g., forecasts), the computer system generates the information automatically based on historical data. Textual information is often provided as an annotation to a screen.

Explanation, justification, assessments, and interpretations. Twenty-one respondents (65.6 percent) indicated that they included explanations, justifications, assessments, or interpretations. This information helps executives "make sense" about what is happening inside and outside the firm. It may be entered by executives or by the EIS support staff. In some systems, comments are placed on the same screen as the information to which they apply. Other systems have comments on separate screens. These comments are accessed by "clicking" on the "hot spot" or "button" displayed on the screen.

Schedules and formal plans. Exactly one half of the respondents (50.0 percent) indicated that schedules or formal plans are included in their systems. Examples included production schedules, product rollout schedules, and strategic plans. This information is entered by both executives and the EIS support staff. The ability to make textual annotations about deviations from schedules was noted as a key feature in several systems. Some systems allow users to add electronic Post-it™ notes to a screen. Deviations from schedules may be highlighted by color coded dates. The traffic light metaphor, where green indicates "ahead of schedule," yellow is slightly "off schedule," and red is "behind schedule," is frequently used.

News reports, industry trends, and external survey data. A majority of the systems (62.5 percent) provide information about the external environment. The most common approach is to allow users to access electronic news services such as Dow Jones News Retrieval. The executive can either direct the search online or create a predefined user profile and have stories delivered automatically. One respondent indicated that his system supports "TV in a window" and allows executives to monitor the news on CNN.

Fourteen of the systems include external survey data. Competitive information and demographic data about the company's market are two examples. As with external news data bases, this information is normally entered electronically.

The Exclusion of Soft Information

Some types or specific instances of soft information may be excluded intentionally. This is particularly true of rumors, gossip, and hearsay. Some respondents made a special point of saying that gossip has no place in an EIS. There is some concern that "putting it in writing" formalizes or legitimizes this information. There is also some hesitancy to include opinions, feelings, and ideas. One reason for this is that including the information tends to put its source on record. Many people prefer to be accountable only for information about which they are reasonably certain. As one respondent said, "People don't want to go out on a limb." For the same reason, some people are hesitant to enter subjective predictions, speculations, forecasts, and estimates.

Our interviews suggest that a variety of factors affect the types of soft information and whether the soft information is included in an EIS. In addition to the factors stated above, hardware and especially the software are also likely to have an impact. For example, some EISs do not make it feasible for users to enter soft information. The size of the EIS support staff is also a factor. Providing some types of soft information, such as preparing commentaries for screens, is very labor intensive. The firm's culture is an additional consideration. In some organizations, soft information such as rumors and gossip is not deemed appropriate for electronic distribution. These and other factors are discussed in greater depth later.

Most Popular Soft Information Applications

Many respondents indicated that enhancing hard information with explanations is the most popular application. In addition to this general assessment, several specific applications were identified as being popular.

An oil company's EIS provides information about important visitors and guests each day. As a result, the firm's executives have a better understanding of what is going on and are better able to greet visitors by name. An aerospace firm maintains an on-line schedule for the corporate jet. Executives who need to travel can check flight schedules for available space and scheduled travelers, and some use the flight as an opportunity to meet with other executives. Several firms' EISs contain personal information about key customers, such as their birthdays, spouses' and childrens' names, hobbies, and clubs. Other EISs provide their executives with access to current stock prices.

Important Decisions Impacted by Soft Information

Most respondents knew of specific instances where soft information significantly affected an important business decision. Often, they were unable to discuss them fully because of confidentiality concerns. However, two of the more interesting instances are presented.

A manufacturing firm received a large order from a foreign government. Soft information in the EIS indicated that the country might have difficulty paying for the goods. Consequently, the shipment was delayed until payment was guaranteed.

In another example, an oil company's refineries were ice bound. The EIS contained an assessment of whether the Coast Guard would be able to clear paths for the company's tankers. Based on this information, management was able to plan and make arrangements for a steady flow of oil.

Soft Information and the Value of EIS

The study's participants included several EIS managers with many years of EIS experience who expressed a belief that soft information increases the value of an EIS. There is also limited empirical support for this position. The respondents were asked what kinds of soft information are included in their systems (i.e., variety), and what percentage of the screens contain soft information (i.e., amount). They also were asked to assess their users' perceived value of the EIS. Positive correlations were found to exist between the variety of soft information and perceived value, and the amount of soft information and perceived value.

Future Plans for Including Soft Information

Study participants named three areas in which they plan to concentrate efforts with respect to soft information: external news services, competitor information, and the ease of entering soft information. Access to external news services was the most frequently cited extension to what is currently being done. A number of firms also plan to add more information about competitors, either through access to external data bases or from primary data collection efforts, such as drawing on input from the sales force. A few firms intend to make it easier for executives to add soft information themselves. The methods mentioned include voice and handwritten annotations to screens, video (e.g., news clips), and pre-formatted screens for entering soft information, much like e-mail.

PROPOSITIONS ABOUT SOFT INFORMATION

The inclusion of soft information in information systems is a recent phenomenon. While much still needs to be learned about what kinds of soft information are most valuable, how to capture it, and how to best deliver it, the potential of soft information is great.

The study provided insights about soft information in EISs that are believed to be true and are of potential value to EIS developers. The ordering of the propositions is from the most general to the most specific.

Proposition #1: The nature of executive work requires the use of soft information.

Executives rely heavily on verbal communication. Many of their activities involve gathering and disseminating soft information. For example, one-on-one meetings, private phone conversations, and social activities with colleagues demonstrate several traditional methods for sharing soft information.

Executives who are credited with having good intuition and judgment use (consciously and unconsciously) soft information to influence their actions. As one EIS manager said, "If you probe why an executive wants to pursue an action based on his feelings, you often get a statement such as 'This fits with the industry projections that I saw in *The Wall Street Journal*' or 'Sam and Rita will like this decision, because it ties in with their comments at the party last night'."

Proposition #2: The culture of a firm affects the inclusion of soft information in the company's EIS.

A strong organizational culture can control the behavior of individuals within the organization and affect all aspects of the firm. Thus, the inclusion of soft information in an EIS is affected by the corporate culture. If the culture favors traditional hard data more than less traditional soft information, the firm's EIS is unlikely to contain much soft information. If providers of what turns out to be incorrect soft information are either embarrassed or have their abilities questioned, the soft information pipeline will evaporate.

One EIS manager described a new application that illustrates his organization's willingness and desire to solicit and share soft information. In this organization, the EIS has spread to many users in middle and lower management positions. The new application allows users to employ the system's e-mail capability to submit questions to the firm's senior executives. The questions and the executives' answers are posted on an electronic bulletin board that is available to all users. Anonymity is provided by removing the questioner's name, which has led to questions being asked that would otherwise not be. To illustrate, it was recently asked, "Why are the senior executives still flying first class when we are trying to cut costs?" Only an open corporate culture would support an application such as this one.

Proposition #3: Executives may be unwilling to share soft information in an EIS.

Power in an organization is often associated with an individual who has information that others need. If executives feel that the power they have will be threatened by sharing the soft information they possess, they are unlikely to share it; thus, soft information in an EIS will be absent.

Furthermore, information politics can have a significant impact on executives' willingness to share information. Because information acts as the key organizational "currency," it becomes too valuable to exchange freely. If the reward structure fosters competition rather than cooperation, executives will be less likely to share valuable soft information. When the reward structure encourages the sharing of soft information, the executive information miser will no longer be rewarded for hoarding information.

Several steps can be taken to affect the willingness to share information. One is to identify the source of the information. If the executives are given credit for providing it, they are more likely to share soft information. Another step is for the executive sponsor to mandate (either directly or indirectly) using the EIS as a medium for exchanging soft information. In one company, the CEO told other executives that he expected them to read and to respond to his e-mail messages. Over time, e-mail has become an important source of soft information.

Proposition #4: Soft information in an EIS increases executives' awareness of critical issues.

Many executives rely on personal contacts to obtain opinions, rumors, and other soft information. When soft information is included in the EIS, executives have faster, easier access to it. Instead of waiting to contact a person, the executive may simply access the EIS to obtain the information. This can be especially helpful in companies where personal contact is uncommon, for example, in firms that are geographically dispersed. One EIS manager told us that the system provides an important means of exchanging soft information because the executives rarely see one another. Another EIS manager in a multinational firm said that the soft information makes expatriate executives feel more "connected" to what is taking place at headquarters.

Although environmental scanning is common among upper-level managers, executives who actively seek soft information from external sources often find that personal scanning is neither effective nor efficient. External scanning is time consuming, and executives may miss critical information simply because they cannot scan enough information. This is where an EIS can be especially useful.

Proposition #5: Including soft information in the EIS enhances the corporate grapevine.

Including soft information in an EIS helps manage, structure, and enhance the corporate grapevine. Unmanaged rumors can lead to lower productivity and added stress for employees. The EIS can provide a mechanism for addressing rumors by providing more information, in a more timely manner, to more people. Where the soft information is inaccurate, it is more likely to be detected and corrected. The net effect is to reduce the deficiencies of the corporate grapevine.

Proposition #6: The inclusion of soft information varies with the industry.

While a comprehensive picture of the relationship between industry type and the inclusion of soft information is not available, it appears that for a variety of reasons some industries are more or less likely to include soft information in their EISs than others and the type of soft information included varies as well. Hospitals and governmental organizations are prime examples.

Hospital EISs tend to contain relatively little soft information. Most hospitals have limited IS staffs, and senior hospital management tends to have small support staffs. As a result, unless the data are already machine resident—and most soft information is not—or is entered by executives, it is not likely to be included in the EIS. Recognizing the difficulty of supporting labor intensive applications in hospital EISs, vendors and consultants to hospitals have focused on financial applications that draw on summarized transaction data.

Because government organizations are affected by external events, public opinion, election outcomes, and funding appropriations, their EISs often contain soft information about current and potential developments in these areas. One state government's EIS contains video clips taken from the previous evening's news shows. A federal government agency's EIS contains assessments of which candidates are likely to win upcoming elections and the potential impact on funding levels. An EIS for a state senate contains information about how different voting groups feel about pending legislation.

Proposition #7: Soft information about competitors is highly valued.

The competitive pressures posed by deregulation, foreign competition, and changes in technology have increased for most firms in recent years. To deal with these pressures, firms employ a variety of methods to obtain competitive information. In firms where soft information about competitors is included in their EIS, this information is often considered to be very important. For many firms, the sales force, acting as the eyes and ears of the executives, is the biggest source of competitor information. As sales representatives call on clients, they pick up useful information about competitors which is disseminated by the EIS.

Several study participants said that soft information involving a competitor's forthcoming product announcement had a significant impact on their business. Knowing that a competitor was about to launch a new product allowed the firm to pour more resources into their own similar product to meet the competition's product launch date. The success and use of an EIS is often reliant on the information it contains and how executives are able to exploit this information for their benefit as well as the benefit to the organization.

A few firms are very creative in their collection and use of soft information. In one company, an employee is sent out to count the number of cars in a competitor's parking lot. If the number of cars is up, it suggests that business is good. This information is entered into the EIS and is useful in competitive bid situations. The firm's executives have learned that the competitor is less likely to give a low bid if business is good and vice versa.

Proposition #8: Some soft information may be excluded intentionally from the EIS.

For a variety of reasons, some firms deliberately exclude certain soft information from their EISs. Some firms are concerned about the security of sensitive information. A hospital, for example, may choose to exclude information about hospital caused mortalities because the potential for a lawsuit is too great. Several companies deliberately exclude human resources information because of Equal Employment Opportunity Commission and confidentiality concerns. One company excludes steering committee reports because the information is considered to be too sensitive.

Some government agencies are unlikely to include certain types of soft information. Many states have "sunshine" laws that make government agencies more subject to public scrutiny than their private sector counterparts. It is not surprising, then, that potentially sensitive information is unlikely to find its way into governmental EISs.

Proposition #9: The value of soft information depends on its timeliness.

Yesterday's news is of little value to executives in today's high velocity environments. The difference between being a leader and being a follower often depends on how responsively a company reacts to change. An EIS that delivers valuable information to executives quickly is likely to be perceived as valuable.

An example of the importance of timely delivery of soft information was described by an EIS manager with a large oil company. During the Gulf War, the EIS provided access to CNN. The constant monitoring of news through the EIS provided up-to-date information that was used to make critical business decisions. Although access to CNN was available by other methods, the EIS provided the executives with "one-stop" shopping for their needed information.

Proposition #10: Increasing the quantity and variety of soft information in an EIS increases the support staff requirements.

The inclusion of soft information in an EIS usually means additional work for the EIS support staff. Soft information is often presented as commentaries to screens. Obtaining this information typically involves investigative work, and the soft information must then be entered to the system. Providing external soft information can also increase the staff's workload. In one company, for example, the public relations department scans news stories and prepares summary descriptions that are entered into the system by the EIS support staff. Because collecting and entering soft information is labor intensive, its inclusion increases EIS staffing requirements.

Proposition #11: The variety and quantity of soft information increases the value of an EIS.

There seems to be a positive relationship between the amount and variety of soft information and the perceived value of the EIS. Because executives use soft information, it is logical that they would value an EIS that provides such information more than one that does not. When executives have access to soft information in the EIS, they can often reduce their reliance on extensive networking (either face-to-face or via telephone) to uncover the latest information or focus their networking on specific issues. This saves the executives valuable time, and consequently, increases their perceived value of the EIS.

Proposition #12: Organizations increase the variety and quantity of soft information over time.

The amount and variety of soft information in older EISs is usually greater than in newly established ones. The reasons for this phenomenon are clear when one considers the evolution of a typical EIS. Once executives commit to the development of an EIS, the system needs to be rolled out quickly while executive interest is high. Consequently, the first applications are often extensions of existing reports with a new format or minor enhancements. This early version becomes the foundation for the iterative and adaptive approach that is typical of EIS development. In order to better satisfy the information requirements of executives, the hard information is supplemented later with soft information. As executives receive the benefits from soft information, they are likely to request additional soft information. As one EIS manager succinctly stated, "Soft information breeds over time."

One EIS manager said that when his firm's EIS was first installed, the executives focused their attention on hard information that they could not obtain previously. After the EIS was available for some time, the executives began to think about other types of information that would be beneficial. The executives' focus changed from historical to visionary, and they began asking the EIS staff what else was possible with the system. What started as simple annotations to graphs blossomed into more sophisticated and detailed explanations.

Proposition #13: Identifying the source enhances the value of the soft information in an EIS.

Anonymity in an EIS is usually inappropriate. Many EIS applications (e.g., e-mail) automatically attach the author's name to the information being entered. Even in instances where input is not tagged, the author is often obvious. While hard information is usually taken at face value, soft information may require a source for verification, and the identity of this source may be the crux to the perceived accuracy of the information.

Proposition #14: The delivery of soft information by the EIS depends on the technology employed.

The inclusion of soft information is impacted by currently available EIS technology. For example, some EIS products allow executives to easily add commentaries to screens while others do not. Vendors are aggressively moving forward to include applications and features in their products that facilitate the inclusion of soft information.

Multimedia technology may further support the inclusion of soft information in EISs. One firm that deals in resort properties places video tapes of properties that are being considered for purchase in its EIS. The videos convey information about the properties that the numbers cannot. A grocery store chain conducts spot checks of its stores by video taping the conditions within the stores and making the tapes accessible through their EIS. In addition to helping monitor store conditions, the tapes are used in store manager performance evaluations. More multimedia applications in EISs will undoubtably follow the rapidly expanding set of multimedia products in the marketplace.

Proposition #15: Rumors, gossip, and hearsay are the least likely of soft information to be included in an executive information system; predictions, forecasts, and estimates are the most likely.

As discussed previously, only 9.4 percent of the respondents in our study indicated that rumors, gossip, or hearsay were entered into their EIS, whereas 78 percent of the respondents indicated including predictions and forecasts. The absence of the softest of soft information is not surprising. Projecting next month's budget and predicting next year's sales are common and encouraged business practices, but propagating and amplifying rumors and gossip are not. The integration of harder information such as forecasts with softer information such as personal feelings provides richer information. For example, one financial investment firm includes predictions about market prices that are based on facts as well as intuition and experience.

TECHNOLOGY FOR HANDLING SOFT INFORMATION

Firms currently include soft information in their EISs in a variety of ways: e-mail, voice mail, electronic bulletin boards, text annotations to screens, and access to external data bases. A smaller number of firms have voice annotations to screens and video. Appearing recently, however, are several developments that should increase the inclusion of soft information.

A considerable amount of soft information exists in text-based documents such as news stories, e-mail, letters, and reports. With the exception of news stories that can be accessed by many EISs from commercial data bases, locating needed information can be very time consuming and difficult. A relatively new product is NewsAlert™ offered by Comshare for use with its Commander EIS product. Used for both hard and soft information, it employs software robots that constantly monitor data sources—textural and numeric, internal and external—for changing patterns and trends. When the robots detect a significant trend, they send out alerts to the users' desktops. Alerts are displayed in a personalized electronic newspaper, along with background tools needed for analysis.

Although EIS and groupware evolved separately, they have had the common objective of sharing information. Recognizing the opportunity to enhance their products and increase sales, vendors have recently taken steps to provide integrated EIS and group support capabilities. Cyril Brookes and others at the University of New South Wales in Australia have developed grapeVine, a data base collection, dissemination, and browsing system for soft information. It combines business intelligence, executive alerting, and information filtering functions that can be used to augment an EIS. Within its Command Center product, Pilot Software includes its Impact application which allows executives to delegate issues that require action. Project tracking features monitor what is being done. IRMS and PSR have graphical interfaces to Lotus Notes as part of their OnTrack and TRACK products. These and other products are likely to increase the inclusion of soft information in EISs over time.

A few firms are going beyond providing an interface to Lotus Notes applications and are making Notes part of the EIS software. One of Notes' attractive features is its text handling ability. In one firm that is planning to use Notes, the EIS will maintain departmental objectives and commentaries about their status, and departmental personnel will be responsible for keeping the commentaries current. The application will be developed in Notes because of its capabilities for entering, maintaining, and updating textual information. Our conversations with EIS developers reveal considerable interest in the possibility of using Notes in their EISs.

Another interesting technology-driven EIS enhancement is EIS software that automatically generates certain types of soft information. This is already common with integrated forecasting models that make projections beyond current conditions. A less common capability was noted by one of the study participants, whose system automatically generates on-screen explanations for occurrences. The system was built using EXECUCOM's Executive Edge with IFPS. IFPS contains an AI-based EXPLAIN capability that provides a textual explanation for changes that have taken place. It is important to recognize, however, that all the explanations are based on the variables and relationships expressed in the underlying IFPS models. Many explanations are exogenous to these models and must be provided to the system by other means.

CONCLUSION

The importance of soft information to executives is well recognized. Until recently, information systems did little to include it. This is changing rapidly, however, due in large part to improvements in information technology (e.g., multimedia). It may well become the rule rather than the exception when an application includes soft information. This development will require careful thought about what information should and should not be included, how to capture and present it, and its impacts.

QUESTIONS

1. Are hard and soft information best viewed as binary states or as endpoints that form a continuum? Discuss.
2. What factors contribute to the perceived accuracy of soft information? Do they apply equally well to hard information? Discuss.
3. What kinds of soft information are most frequently found in EISs?
4. What are the barriers to including soft information in EISs?

REFERENCES

1. These quotes appear in: H.D. MINTZBERG, "The Manager's Job: Folklore and Fact," *Harvard Business Review,* (July–August 1975) pp. 49–61; C.H.P. BROOKES, "Soft Information: An Underutilized Resource for the Executive," Executive Seminar, Atlanta, GA, 1988; R.W. ZMUD, "Supporting Senior Executives through Decision Support Technologies: A Review and Directions for Future Research," In E.R. MCLEAN and H.G. SOL (eds.), *Decision Support Systems: A Decade in Perspective,* Elsevier Science Publishers B.V., Amsterdam: North-Holland, 1986, pp. 87–101; J.W. JONES and R. MCLEOD, Jr., "The Structure of Executive Information Systems: An Exploratory Analysis," *Decision Sciences,* (Spring 1986), pp. 220–249; C. LESTER,"Europe's Information Seekers," *Datamation,* (July 1, 1989), pp. 17–18; and G. HUBER, "Organizational Learning: The Contributing Processes and the Literature, " *Organization Science,* (February 1991), pp. 88–115.
2. D.W. STRAUB and J.C. WETHERBE, "Information Technologies for the 1990's: An Organizational Impact Perspective," *Communications of the ACM,* (November 1989), pp. 1328–1339.

Part 6

GROUP SUPPORT SYSTEMS

Group support systems (GSS) are the newest of the computer-based applications to support decision making. These systems are designed to provide computer support for groups of people who work together on collaborative endeavors. They are sometimes referred to as group decision support systems, collaborative work support systems, or groupware. Applications of this technology include support for strategic planning sessions, focus groups, determining information requirements, setting budgets, and sales tracking.

People spend large quantities of their workday in group activities. For example, it has been found that managers spend 25 to 80 percent of their time in meetings, with the highest percentages being associated with senior executives. It should be clear that anything that can make group activities more effective and efficient can have a significant impact on organizational and individual productivity.

Many organizations are downsizing and redesigning business processes. Normally the use of information technology is a key ingredient in making this possible, and GSS can play an important role. Depending on the kind of GSS technology used, it can support broader spans of control, keep people better in touch, and directly connect the company with customers and suppliers.

GSS products have now found their way into the marketplace and business organizations. The four chapters in this part of the book should give you a good understanding of what GSS are, what has been learned about them to date, how they are currently being used, and what their future potential is.

A wide variety of products fall under the groupware label. They vary from products like GroupSystems which is used for electronic meetings to Lotus Notes which supports electronic communications and workflow applications. Chapter 19 discusses these products, how they are used, the benefits realized, and their limitations.

Meetings are often not as effective or efficient as they should be. One kind of groupware is designed to improve meetings through the use of specialized software, hardware, procedures, and group facilitators. Chapters 20 and 21 focus on this type of groupware and they include a discussion of the technology, a description of how it is used, and lessons learned.

Lotus Notes is the most popular groupware product. It combines a variety of capabilities that allow work groups to share information and communicate better. Chapter 22 describes and illustrates the use of Lotus Notes.

19

A REVIEW OF GROUPWARE PRODUCTS

Ever been in a meeting where ideas start flowing so fast everybody wants to talk at once? Boeing and other companies have found a radical new way to harness that creative energy. Their brainstormers still sit around a table, but instead of shouting, they type their thoughts on networked personal computers using a new kind of software that keeps track of what everyone has to say. Participants can sift through far more material and act faster than they could in an ordinary meeting.

In fact, after years of complaints that investment in desktop computing doesn't pay off in productivity, this new software—called groupware—has produced dramatic results. Boeing has cut the time needed to complete a wide range of team projects by an average of 91%, or to *one-tenth* of what similar work took in the past. In one case last summer, a group of engineers, designers, machinists, and manufacturing managers used TeamFocus software from IBM to design a standardized control system for complex machine tools in several plants. Managers say such a job normally would take more than a year. With fifteen electronic meetings, it was done in 35 days.

Boeing's data come from the largest and most rigorous study yet of the cost-saving impact of groupware—computer software explicitly designed to support the collective work of teams. Productivity gains around a conference table have so far been most obvious. But groupware's ultimate promise is larger—linking departments, or colleagues in different locations, or even entire corporations in ways that vastly improve the efficiency and speed of collaborative projects.

This chapter is a reprint of David Kirkpatrick, "Here Comes the Payoff from PCs," *Fortune,* Volume 125, Number 6, March 23, 1992, 93–102.

The software has piqued the interest of many company problem solvers because the typical American manager spends 30% to 70% of the day in meetings. The setup that Boeing and others are finding so successful seems absurd at first: a conventional conference room with a computer at every place. "Why can't we just look each other in the eye and talk?" you wonder. The answer: because you seldom elicit all the best ideas, and many potentially valuable contributors remain silent. In many meetings, 20% of the people do 80% of the talking. Those who are shy, junior, intimidated, or just too polite typically shut up.

Meeting software uses several techniques to loosen the lips of the silent majority. Everyone speaks at once, via the keyboard. (In most cases, plenty of outloud interaction happens too.) As you type in your ideas and comments—hunt and peck is okay—they accumulate on your screen alongside everyone else's. Most people can read much faster than they can listen, so they can deal with far more material in a given period. Says Jay Nunamaker, who helped pioneer the concept at the University of Arizona in the early 1980s and is now CEO of Ventana Corp., a Tucson firm that markets systems based on his work: "In a typical hour-long meeting of 15 people, everybody's got an average of only four minutes of air time. With computer support, everybody's got the potential to talk for 60 minutes. That's a big increase in productivity."

Also important, most systems keep the author of a given comment anonymous. That can be a powerful incentive to speak. Go ahead and disagree with your boss. He won't know it was you. Explains a market researcher at a Fortune 500 company who has begun conducting all meetings electronically: "It's generally unacceptable in a culture like ours to say your most private thoughts on a matter. You might be embarrassed or considered silly. But once a thought is on the screen it becomes something to be seriously considered by the group, and otherwise secret thoughts can be very useful. The processes of the mind become open to the group." The software uses a voting system, again anonymous, to rate ideas.

Groupware is already having a major impact on companies willing to move toward the new form of organization futurist Alvin Toffler calls "ad-hocracy," in which individuals decide what needs to be done and form teams to do it. These pioneers—which include Boeing, Dell Computer, GM Europe, IBM, Marriott, MCI Communications, J. P. Morgan, Pacific Gas & Electric, Price Waterhouse, Southern New England Telecommunications, and Texaco—are using technology to push toward flatter, faster, more team-focused organizations.

Proponents believe in what could be called the democratization of data: the flow of knowledge to wherever it is needed. Groupware enables team members to stay abreast of one another's progress whether they are in a meeting room or scattered at PC keyboards from Boston to Bangkok. Companies can more quickly find connections among disparate pieces of information and disparate people whose expertise might otherwise be overlooked.

Many of these companies use a unique product from Lotus Development called Notes, which Robert Johansen, a senior fellow at the Institute for the

Future in Menlo Park, California, calls "the bellwether groupware product out there." Introduced in late 1989, Notes is starting to show how the remarkable possibilities of groupware go well beyond meetings. Users type into the system vast amounts of their written work, which creates a set of data bases that can be organized and searched in whatever way a user finds most convenient.

Price Waterhouse was Lotus's first Notes customer and now has 9000 employees hooked up (see Figure 19–1). Sheldon Laube, who has responsibility for all technology in the accounting and consulting firm's U.S. operations, required virtually everyone to have a PC powerful enough to handle the Notes network. Says he: "This is a revolutionary piece of software that will change the way people think about computers."

In many companies, leaders of teams trying to improve customer service have been among the first to embrace groupware. Technology consultants at Boeing used TeamFocus to better identify their customers' needs and to set a strategic direction for themselves. They estimated the process would normally have taken six weeks but with the help of two half-day electronic meetings were finished in one.

At Marriott, human resources executive Carl Di Pietro started using meeting software five months ago. He has run meetings for groups from all across the company, and his enthusiasm is boundless: "In my 30 years, it's the most revolutionary thing I've seen for improving the quality and productivity of meetings. It gets you closer to the truth." A group is able to reach a genuine consensus, he says, and members leave much more committed to decisions than they would have been with conventional methods.

By definition groupware requires groups of PC users wired into a network. That knitting together is happening so fast in the Nineties that Steve Jobs of Next Computer suggests rechristening the machines "*inter*personal computers." Already 38% of corporate PCs are tied into networks, many spanning whole companies.

Computer networks not only connect machines but also make employees feel connected to the organization. Researchers find that electronic mail users are more likely to feel committed to their jobs than do the unplugged. No similar data yet exist for groupware, but anecdotal evidence so far suggests it creates an even more powerful sense of belonging.

Managers have been frustrated for years by their inability to prove that office computing increases productivity. Morgan Stanley senior economist Stephen Roach flatly asserts that there has been *no* productivity payoff. His primary evidence: While service companies spent about $800 billion on information technology in the past decade, service productivity growth over that period has been a measly 0.7%. One problem, Roach says, is that service companies have not made the staff reductions that the new hardware should have made possible.

Others make a similar point about manufacturing. Economist Gary Loveman at the Harvard Business School studied comprehensive five-year cost and productivity data for 60 large manufacturing enterprises and found no evidence that information technology improved productivity.

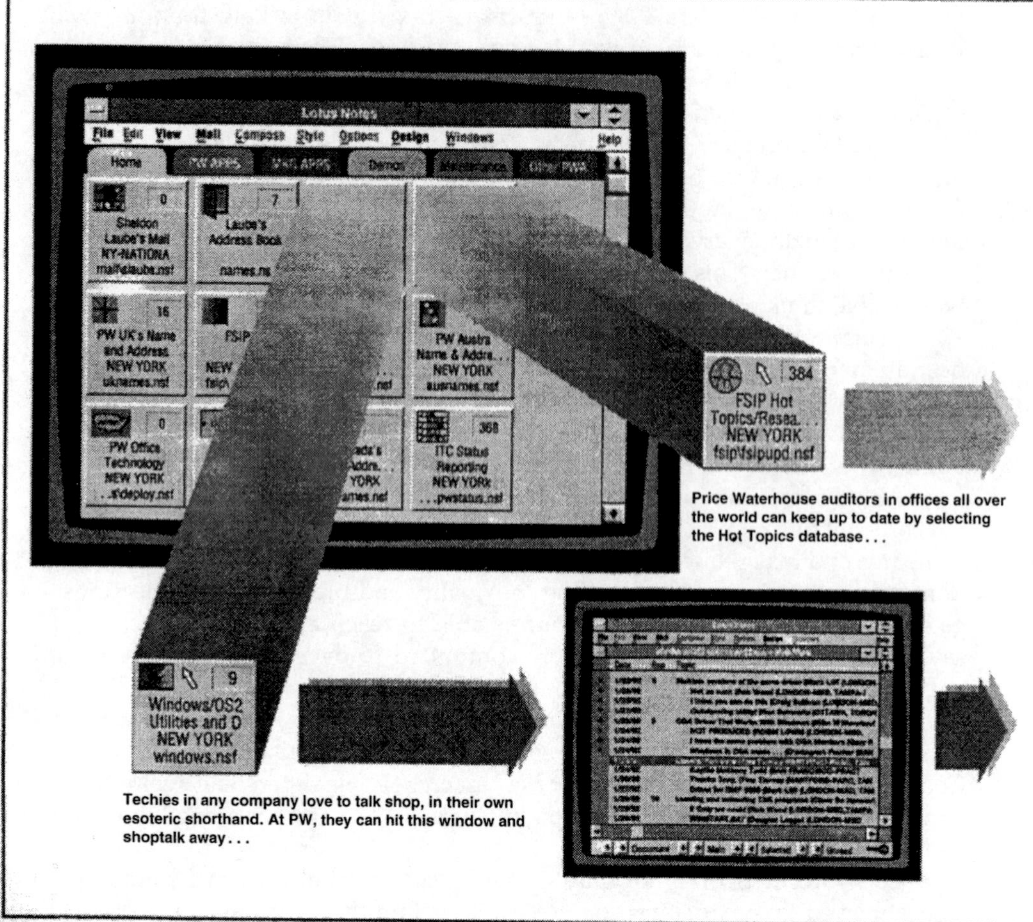

FIGURE 19–1 Groupware can get everybody into the act
While groupware generally aims to help established teams work more efficiently, Lotus's Notes helps create ad hoc teams. It provides interlinked electronic bulletin boards that allow people in a company who have insights or expertise on a particular problem to find one another. At Price Waterhouse a Notes user logs on and sees a screen with lists of different data bases (large screen below). Need to know who in the firm is an expert on nonferrous mining? The box called FISP Resumes will tell you. (The initials, which also appear in the Hot Topics box, stand for Financial Service Industry Practice, an internal PW designation.)

Neither Roach nor Loveman thinks computers are the fundamental problem. "I don't blame the machines," says Roach. "It's a managerial problem. Call it ineptitude. They haven't had the guts to trade machines for bodies." Loveman concurs: "I don't think most organizations have thought about what information does to authority, job structures, decision-making, and allocation of people's time."

FIGURE 19–1 *(continued)*
The Notes Program differs significantly from electronic mail, where senders must select the recipients of a message. With Notes, anyone with an interest in a subject can read the information. It's not uncommon for a Notes conversation to include people from five or six cities around the world. A query from London may be answered by someone in Toronto, who may be challenged in turn by someone else in Los Angeles. Before Notes, only four members of Price Waterhouse's 15-person senior executive committee used PCs at all. Now they all do.

Lotus CEO Jim Manzi agrees that evidence of productivity gains is paltry—so far. "Nobody can demonstrate a return on investment for stand-alone computing," he says. (By contrast, CEO Bill Gates of Microsoft argues that productivity gains do exist but are just extremely difficult to measure.) Manzi thinks progress will come with groupware. Says he: "We think productivity can be improved if we use work group computing to integrate people into teambased organizations." He adds that Notes demonstrates the difference between "information processing" and "information sharing."

IBM was the first company to install an electronic meeting room in a real business situation—a manufacturing and development facility in Oswego, New York. A team from the University of Arizona led by Nunamaker designed the software and in the fall of 1987 visited Oswego to measure its impact. They found that meeting time was cut by 56%. Subsequent research by IBM itself at a corporate administrative center found similar results.

Boeing's study late last year is the most comprehensive followup to the IBM research. It closely replicated the Oswego results with a larger sample over a longer period. It also demonstrated cost benefits for the first time. Boeing studied 64 meetings with 1,000 participants, tracking what managers did compared with what they said they would have done without the software. Boeing saved an average of $6,700 per meeting, mainly in employee time. Says TeamFocus project manager Brad Quinn Post, who ran the study, "The data show there are very clear opportunities to use these products to significantly improve business processes, to make our work cheaper, faster, and better."

In 1989, IBM signed a licensing agreement with Nunamaker's Ventana that allowed Big Blue to install more meeting rooms in its own offices and to sell the software to outside clients. IBM now has more than 50 such rooms all over the world. It rents some to outsiders for $2,000 to $7,000 a day, and will license its TeamFocus software—a version of Ventana's system—for one meeting room for $50,000. Ventana charges $25,000 to license its product, called GroupSystems.

One other program is on the market: VisionQuest, developed by tiny Collaborative Technologies of Austin, Texas. IBM has deliberately proceeded slowly, wanting to establish TeamFocus internally and refine the software before pushing it hard on customers. Collaborative Technologies, on the other hand, recently reorganized in order to market its product more aggressively. The company sells a VisionQuest license for $29,000.

All three are elegantly designed and user-friendly. Collaborative Technologies has taken the simplest path: It requires no equipment other than a network of PCs. The competing systems designed and sold by Ventana and licensed to IBM add a big display screen at the front of the room. While a professional meeting facilitator is helpful at any electronic meeting, Ventana and IBM virtually require one. That makes their systems costlier to operate, though they do offer a wider range of features, including a way for groups to collaborate on writing letters or documents.

Some gleanings from the experience of companies already seriously committed to groupware follow.

At Marriott's Bethesda, Maryland, headquarters recently, seven executives from one of the company's large Washington-area hotels sat in a room full of PCs equipped with VisionQuest. None had ever taken part in an electronic meeting.

A sign at the front warned: "Enter this room ONLY if you believe the ideas and opinions of others have value."

Their challenge was to find new ways to improve guest satisfaction. After a lot of laughing and a few silly suggestions on screen, the room was silent. Occasionally someone left briefly. The hotel's general manager ate a cookie. After 25 minutes, the group had generated 139 ideas. Then they rated them on a scale of one to five: once according to the likely impact of each idea on guests, and again according to what each would probably cost. A consensus emerged that, among other things, more thorough training of hotel employees was essential.

A market researcher, who asked not to be identified because he doesn't want his competition to start using groupware, has been running all his meetings with VisionQuest for six months. They typically include scientists, product developers, sales and marketing people, and often ad agency staffers. Says he: "While I thought I was a good facilitator, I'm convinced I was actually missing about 75% of the information I could have got out on the table." He installed the software in a room his company had designed for PC training, where 15 networked PCs often sat unused.

Southern New England Telecommunications installed IBM's TeamFocus in an electronic meeting room in its New Haven, Connecticut, headquarters in June 1990 and has just added a second. The company used the rooms to develop a new customer relations strategy in seven weeks that it figures would have taken about a year using focus groups or surveys of employees who deal with the public.

J. P. Morgan installed a handsomely appointed thirteen-seat room equipped with TeamFocus last March. Since then it has been in almost constant use for meetings devoted to strategic planning, organizational changes, auditing, and employee surveys, among other subjects. Morgan will soon install TeamFocus rooms in its Wilmington, Delaware, and London offices. Says Lynn Reed, a vice president in Morgan's global technology and operations group: "The software works best for a meeting that is going to take more than an hour and that is intended to achieve a group decision. It's not beneficial for status-checking meetings, where each participant has to give a report, or for meetings with a single speaker."

Dell Computer started using VisionQuest last May for strategic planning meetings. The company found it could include more people in the process and still finish faster. Says Bruce Ezell, manager of business development: "That went so well we've started using it for any type of project that requires groups of people to work together—like product planning and developing marketing strategies."

In one case, Dell used the system to name a new product. In the past, names were developed by asking product team members to send in suggestions by electronic mail. Then meetings were called to consider lists of names on flip charts. "Whoever screamed loudest would be heard," says Ezell. "It was still up to the product manager to make a decision, but there was no way to get consensus." With VisionQuest, a group of marketing and sales managers met for two hours, proposed and rated 75 names, and reduced them to five finalists. It would have taken two months to get there the old way.

Ezell says groupware is a natural for Dell since everyone in the company has good computer skills. More important, the PC industry is experiencing brutal price cutting and going through faster technological change than perhaps any other industry in history. Says Ezell: "When we detect a major change in the market, we need to pull our management team together immediately. We can't tolerate meetings that hash things out all day and end without consensus." Strategic planning meetings that used to last two days now take four hours.

Di Pietro of Marriott is convinced that meeting software can also enhance cultural diversity, a company priority. "It's a room of nondiscrimination," he says. "You don't know if that idea you're reading comes from a woman or a man, part of the minority or majority, or a senior or junior person. People begin to say, 'Hey, we've got a lot in common with each other.'"

Many experts caution, however, that a repressive boss or a dysfunctional group will probably remain so with or without electronic help. Says Bob Bostrom, who teaches at the University of Georgia and consults with companies on using meeting software: "The technology doesn't make people equal in terms of power but in terms of being heard." Some bosses defeat its purpose by walking around the room glaring at people's terminals or loudly bullying everyone to put in ideas that resemble their own, says Geraldine DeSanctis, a professor of information systems at Duke University. "The group has to decide it wants to get more out of meetings," she observes. "It's like an alcoholic has to want to stop drinking."

The next step is to enable people to meet without being in the same room—or even the same city. The three meeting software products are all designed to work among distant participants, and a few companies, including Dell Computer, are already reporting early success with this approach. Nunamaker, however, says his research has found obstacles. Without the nonverbal cues and other stimuli that come from seeing others in the same room engaged in a common task, people's attention easily wanders.

Groupware has other potential drawbacks. Notes, for example, may prove threatening to some managers because employees can independently identify and connect with others working on similar tasks. These new working relationships may improve efficiency, but they may also upset organizational hierarchies. Says Natasha Krol, an analyst at the Meta Group, a Westport, Connecticut, consulting firm: "You can start your own subculture in Notes. Managers often have very little to do with that, and the process may even help identify which managerial layers are obsolete."

The flip side of Notes is that putting so much employee activity on the network gives management the potential to monitor exactly what is going on in the organization. At Price Waterhouse, some departments use Notes as a kind of electronic filing cabinet, with all written documents inserted in the data base. The boss can see every memo anybody writes.

Some new types of groupware on the horizon could increase management control still further. Later this year NCR expects to release an enhancement to Cooperation, its program that ties together office activities now conducted on different computer systems from PCs to mainframes. The new feature can, among other things, keep track of documents that must be passed from person to person for processing. It will alert managers to logjams or other inefficiencies.

The payoff from groupware could be huge. John Oltman, CEO of SHL Systemhouse, a large Ottawa firm that manages computer systems for clients, predicts that some big insurance companies could reduce their claims-processing work force by as much as 50% over the next five years.

Groupware that allows teams to communicate using video will open entirely new productivity horizons. Researchers are already working on various ways to conduct what they call "virtual meetings," in which videoscreens would allow people in various places to interact as if they were face to face. Jay Nunamaker has a plan that calls for groups of four people to sit at terminals in front of giant screens in four different rooms. The screens create the illusion that all 16 participants are in the same room.

At AT&T Bell Laboratories, researcher Sid Ahuja is working on a way to accomplish the same thing from individual offices. His system would display live video images of each participant on a desktop terminal, and allow them to share software, graphics, and other data as easily as if they were all together.

If groupware really makes a difference in productivity long term, the very definition of an office may change. You will be able to work efficiently as a member of a group wherever you have your computer. As computers become smaller and more powerful, that will mean anywhere. Paul Saffo, a researcher at the Institute for the Future, thinks networked computing may well lead to drastic population dispersal. Says he: "For the first three-quarters of the century our cities were shaped by developments in transportation and telecommunications, but now the influence is shifting to computers and communications." And all we really wanted was a little boost in productivity.

QUESTIONS

1. What are some of the ways that groupware can affect how people in groups act?
2. Summarize how companies have used various groupware products.
3. What are the potential obstacles to the use of groupware in organizations?
4. Describe a potential use of groupware in an organization that you belong to.

20

GROUP DECISION SUPPORT SYSTEMS

INTRODUCTION

At the First International Conference on Decision Support Systems, Peter G. W. Keen [7] pointed out that the fundamental model of DSS—the lonely decision maker striding down the hall at high noon to make a decision—is true only in rare cases. In real organizations, be they public or private, Japanese, European, or American, most decisions are taken only after extensive consultation. Although it is possible on occasion for decision makers to go counter to the consensus of their organization, this is not a viable long-term position for them.

In this chapter we consider group decision support systems, usually referred to as GDSS.[1] GDSS is a subfield within DSS in which there has been significant activity since the mid-1980s. The evolution of GDSS has been rapid. To a first approximation, the evolution can be characterized in terms of a chronology having some very short time intervals:

1981–1983	Initial papers describing group decision support systems
1982–1985	Survey papers and research agendas

This chapter was written by Paul Gray and Jay F. Nunamaker.

[1]The term GDSS is not the only one used for these systems. Other terms include: group support systems (GSS) based on the argument that more than decision making is being supported, and electronic meeting systems (EMS) to indicate the computer-based nature of these systems. We have chosen GDSS in this chapter to indicate that the systems described and the lessons learned apply in particular to decision support systems designed for groups.

1982–1986	Initial experimentation and experimental results
1987–1990	Building of advanced facilities in universities
1988–	Commercial versions of hardware introduced by IBM and other vendors
1990–	Commercial versions of software introduced by Ventana Corporation Lotus Notes, Collabra, and others

As indicated by this chronology, GDSS was in a laboratory stage throughout the 1980s. In the past, when these systems were installed in industry and government, they often behaved like shooting stars. They were put in by one senior executive and used during his or her tenure. However, as soon as that individual was replaced, the system was dismantled or fell into disuse. The classic "not-invented-here" syndrome held sway. As we moved into the 1990s, the systems became commercial in the United States. The move to commercialization became possible because we found out

- how to use these systems effectively; and
- how to design systems so that people (particularly middle-aged executives) do not require significant training.

Group decision support systems are now a mature branch of decision support. There is growing evidence that group decision support systems are able to improve both the efficiency and the effectiveness of organizational group processes.

THE NATURE OF GROUP DECISION MEETINGS

Although most business organizations are hierarchical, decision making in an environment involving choices among alternatives and assessment of risks is usually a shared process. Face-to-face meetings among groups of senior executives (or boards of directors) are an essential element of reaching a consensus. The group may be involved in a decision or in a decision-related task such as creating a short list of acceptable alternatives or creating a recommendation for approval at higher level. These group meetings are characterized by the following activities and processes:

- The meetings are a joint activity, engaged in by a group of people of equal or near equal status[2] typically 5 to 20 or more individuals;
- The activity, as well as its outputs, is intellectual in nature;

[2]However, the use of group systems has proven to be effective as a way of holding meetings whose members may cross many levels of an organization.

- The product depends in an essential way on the knowledge, opinions, and judgments of its participants; and
- Differences in opinion are settled either by fiat by the ranking person present or, more often, by negotiation or arbitration. The results lead to action within the organization.

Another way of looking at group decision meetings is in terms of what groups do. Specifically, groups:

- Retrieve (or generate) information;
- Share information among members;
- Draft policies and procedures; and
- Use information to reach consensus or decision.

DEFINITION

Definitions of GDSS have been offered by both Huber [5] and DeSanctis and Gallupe [3]. These definitions serve our purpose well.

- "A GDSS consists of a set of software, hardware, and language components and procedures that support a group of people engaged in a decision-related meeting." (Huber [5])
- "An interactive, computer-based system which facilitates the solution of unstructured problems by a set of decision makers working together as a group." (DeSanctis and Gallupe [3])

An important point to note is that the group using the GDSS may not make the ultimate decision. It may be creating and/or reviewing alternatives to be submitted as a short list to the next level in the organizational hierarchy. For this reason, the term group support systems (GSS) mentioned at the beginning of this chapter is often used rather than GDSS.

GDSS TECHNOLOGY

Although almost all group decision meetings today are face-to-face, technology is starting to be applied to make it possible for participants to be separated in space and/or time. These electronic meeting systems include computer conferences (either on-line or extended in time) and audio and video teleconferences. Figure 20–1 shows the four possible combinations of proximity and separation in space and in time. In this chapter we will concentrate on one form of electronic meeting system, the "decision room" in which the participants are in the same room at the same time.

	Same Time	Different Times
Same Place	EXAMPLE: Decision Room Need: Face-to-Face Meeting Private Displays Public Displays Networks Copyboards	EXAMPLE: Team Room Need: Administration, Filing, Filtering Private Workstations Shift Work Kiosks Group Displays
Different Place	EXAMPLE: Video Conference Need: Cross-Distance Meeting Conference calls Screen Sharing Video	EXAMPLE: Computer Conference Need: Ongoing Coordination Group conversations Group writing Group Voice Mail

FIGURE 20–1 Forms of Electronic Meeting Systems Based on Separation in Space and Time

The motivation for creating a decision room comes from the observation that in almost all organizations office automation resulted in personal computers (PCs) being ubiquitous in work areas. However, as soon as one stepped into a conference room, the only technology available was a telephone and high technology was a speakerphone. The personal and networked computer capabilities used routinely elsewhere were not available.

In a typical decision room, personal computers are provided at some or all of the seating positions at a conference table. Input to these terminals is by keyboard, mouse, touchscreen, bit pad, or some combination of these devices. Participants can do "private work" at their individual displays. One member of the group (either the group leader or a staff member acting as a "chaffeur") operates the software needed to create the "public" display (e.g., a projection TV) which can be seen by everyone. In some rooms, multiple public screens are provided where one screen is used for the current discussion and the others for reference or slowly changing information.

Because decision rooms are designed for senior managers, they tend to have an "executive feel" to them. Even the experimental laboratories have plush carpeting and quality furnishings.

The computer and communications equipment in the decision room typically includes file servers to act as dedicated storage, local area networks to interconnect the terminals and the servers, and connection to a central computer (usually a minicomputer) and to peripheral equipment including printers to provide hard copy and (sometimes) electronic blackboards. Whiteboards, overhead and slide projectors, and other audio-visual support are also provided.

GDSS SOFTWARE

GDSS provide software to support the individual and to support the group. To allow each individual to do private work, the usual collection of text and file creation, graphics, spreadsheet, data base, and help routines are provided at the individual workstations. For the group as a whole, in addition to providing information retrieval and display, a GDSS provides software for summarizing the group's opinion. Thus, for example, the public screen can be used to present a cumulative list of all suggestions (such as from a nominal group technique session) or to show the aggregated results of voting and ranking or ratings of alternatives. Votes and preferences can be either identified by individual or aggregated so that individuals need not expose themselves if they hold views contrary to the consensus or to those of the senior person present. This anonymity feature allows managers to obtain a truer set of advice, since people need not fear retribution if they do not follow the prevailing group opinion.

GDSS software has become a major business. For groups working in the same room, the GroupSystems software developed by the University of Arizona and marketed by Ventana Corporation of Tucson, Arizona, has become the standard. This software, described in the appendix, can also be used by people separated in space, in time, or both. Software designed for workgroups which has some or most of the features of GDSS includes Lotus Notes and Collabra.

As discussed later in this chapter, introducing GDSS hardware and software into a conference changes the content of the discussions. By being able to do private work, a participant can examine an alternative (e.g., a "what if") on his/her private screen and, if it is good, send it to the public screen for discussion. However, if the alternative is poor, it can be quietly buried without embarrassment. The recording of information on the public screen reduces the redundancy of the conversation. People do not keep bringing the same ideas up over and over if they are displayed. As a result, communication focuses on what participants know and on the rationale that led them to hold their views. Recording of information also provides group memory by recording all electronic comments. In many systems it is possible for participants to walk out of the room at the end of the meeting with a complete record of what happened.

GDSS COMMUNICATIONS

A GDSS must have a communications base as well as the model base, data base, and interface required in conventional DSS (Bui and Jarke [2]). This is particularly true for a GDSS distributed in time and space. However, even in a decision room where everyone is present at the same time, communications links are required. For example, a participant may want to send you a message "for your eyes only." These links provide electronic mail among participants, access to remote computers, and the ability to send information from a workstation to the public screen via the chauffeur.

GDSS MEETING STYLES

GDSS software and hardware in full service facilities is sufficiently flexible that it can be used in any of three styles:

- Chauffeured;
- Supported; or
- Interactive.

As shown in Table 20–1, in the chauffeured style, only one person uses the software, either a group member or the meeting leader. A workstation is connected to the public screen to provide the electronic version of the traditional blackboard. The group discusses the issues verbally, with the public screen used as a group memory to record and structure information.

The supported style is similar to a chauffeured style, but differs in that each member has access to a computer workstation that provides a parallel anonymous electronic communication channel with a group memory. The meeting proceeds using a mixture of verbal and electronic interaction. Each member is able to enter items that appear on the public screen.

In the interactive style, the parallel, anonymous, electronic communication channel with a group memory is used for almost all communication. Virtually no one speaks. While a public screen may be provided, the group memory is typically too large to fit on a screen and thus is maintained so that all members can access it electronically at their workstation.

In practice, GDSS meetings involve use of two or all three of these styles.

TABLE 20–1 GDSS Meeting Styles

Chauffeured	Supported	Interactive
One person enters group information	All group members can enter comments	All Group members can enter comments
Public screen can provide group memory	Public screen can provide group memory	Group memory accessible via workstations
Verbal communications predominates	Both verbal and electronic communications	Electronic communication predominates

A TYPOLOGY OF GDSS FACILITIES

GDSS facilities can be characterized by the delivery mode and the range of tasks supported. Delivery modes are

1. *Permanent installations at the user's site.* Here a conference room is equipped with PCs and dedicated to GDSS use. For such a system to be successful, it must be used frequently; otherwise, it is not cost-effective and typically falls victim to one of the periodic cost-cutting efforts in organizations.
2. *Portable installations brought to the user's site on an on-call basis.* The equipment and the services of support staff to run the meeting are rented from a vendor. The skills of the vendor's staff in facilitating meetings is often as important as the equipment in such arrangements.
3. *Permanent installation at the vendor's site.* Here the group travels to the vendor site to hold its meeting. The vendor supplies the software, hardware, and support staff for a fee. The support staff usually acts as the chauffeur.
4. *Facilities designed and sold by commercial firms.* IBM installed over 50 group decision support centers in its own facilities by 1991 and began marketing these facilities to other companies. Two organizations in England, ICL (a computer manufacturer) and Metapraxis (a consulting firm and software house) have designed and developed permanent GDSS facilities that they installed at company locations.

The range of tasks supported can be for one or a few, to a "full service" GDSS. An example of the former is the room provided by SUNY-Albany which

> Universities have been at the forefront of creating decision rooms. These rooms are used to conduct research and to generate revenue by making them available to the public. At the University of Auckland in New Zealand, the Decision Support Centre is being used by industry sector groups to generate ideas and plans that will enable their industries to become more competitive in global markets. Each group is composed of twenty-five business leaders, government planners, and politicians. They meet in sessions called "Advantage New Zealand Meetings," which begin with participants entering ideas on what they see as the strengths and weaknesses in their industry. A voting tool is used to help identify which of the ideas are the best. Next, the participants identify initiatives that will capitalize on the industry's strengths. Once again the voting tool is used to help select the best initiatives. These are then developed into action plans. Follow-up sessions have shown that the plans are being implemented.
>
> Source: The example is based upon R. Brent Gallupe and William H. Cooper, "Brainstorming Electronically," *Sloan Management Review*, Fall 1993, pp. 27–36.

supports primarily interactive decision analysis sessions that allow users to create decision trees and utility functions and in which the system does the Bayesian statistics. A full service GDSS contains a broad range of software and the ability to support a diversity of tasks from financial decision making to crisis management, to personnel selection, to project review, to long-range planning, and forecasting. Facilities using the GroupSystems software developed at the University of Arizona (see Appendix for capabilities) are typical of full service facilities.

RELATION OF GDSS TO DSS

GDSS can be viewed as subsuming conventional DSS within it. That is, the concepts of model base, data base, and human interface (see, Sprague and Carlson [10]) all apply. Thus, as group size shrinks to one, a GDSS reduces to a DSS. Conversely, in moving from a DSS to a GDSS, some new requirements are introduced:

1. the addition of communications capabilities;
2. enhancement of the model base to provide voting, ranking, rating, and so on for developing consensus;
3. greater system reliability;
4. enhanced physical facilities; and
5. increased setup before use of the system.

The first two of these have already been discussed. System reliability must be much greater for a GDSS than for a DSS. If a GDSS fails, many people are affected, not just one. Since these people are high-level executives and well paid, there is a much greater loss both in terms of financial costs and trust in the system. A GDSS requires much more setup time and effort before the system can be used because both the people and the facility must be scheduled, an agenda must be prepared, participants must be able to prepare for the meeting by seeing its data files and models, and so forth and, if necessary, create any additional knowledge bases that are needed.

A GDSS requires capital investment in physical facilities. If the GDSS is located in a decision room, the room has to be elegantly furnished and have the feel of the executive conference room that it is. A GDSS also requires much more display and communications hardware.

APPLICATIONS

GDSS have been used principally for tasks involving idea generation, planning, competitive analysis, and consensus building. Typical tasks include developing a mission statement, strategy formulation, evaluations of senior managers, and information systems planning. In addition to these standard managerial tasks, GDSS has been used in a variety of innovative ways. Among these applications are the following:

- Gaming for risk assessment and crisis management. Gaming is a form of training that improves both the intuition and skills of a manager in facing real-life high stress, high stakes situations. The experience and data gained from extensive gaming of a particular situation under laboratory condition provide a basis for understanding how to cope with "surprise" and with outcomes of low probability.
- Supporting negotiations. For example, in international situations two or more groups that speak different languages and have different cultural backgrounds are negotiating a contract,
- Supporting business teams involved in design work, quality control reviews, and such relatively new tasks as reengineering and concurrent engineering.
- Supporting visual decisions such as selecting packaging for a new product or locating facilities or designing school districts. In visual decision making, the 2-dimensional display capabilities of GDSS are exploited. In packaging selection, people can see alternative package designs. In location or districting problems, the public screen is used to display maps from a geographic information system (GIS).
- Determining senior managers' requirements for information to be included in their executive information system. Using a decision room reduced this requirements assessment from the usual six months to two weeks for three different sets of hospital executives.

WHAT HAS BEEN LEARNED

Experimentation with the use of decision rooms has been undertaken since the mid-1980s. A large number of papers have appeared which report observations, field research, action research, and laboratory experiments. These papers indicate the high potential for the contribution of computer and communication-based mediation, facilitation, and support in creating effective group decision support. The following summary of what has been learned in over ten years of GDSS is based on these papers and our own observations.[3]

[3]Additional information on GDSS facilities and what has been learned from them can be found in Bostrum et al. [1] and Jessup and Valacich [6].

The research results have underscored the need to review and examine the theories and hypotheses on group decision making that have been developed in the past. There is reason to believe that many previously held assumptions about the conduct of group deliberation are subject to review in the new electronically based forum. Factors such as speed, anonymity, recording of group processes, voting, participation levels, group size, and other facilitated activities change the group environment significantly.

Analysis of the available data shows that using decision rooms can improve group work in many situations because it:

- Enables all participants to work simultaneously (human parallel processing), thereby promoting broader input into the meeting process and reducing dominance of the meeting by a few people;
- Provides equal opportunity for participation (through anonymity);
- Triggers additional points to be made;
- Enables larger group meetings which can effectively bring more information, knowledge, and skills to bear on the task;
- Provides process structure to help focus the group on key issues and discourages irrelevant digressions and nonproductive behaviors; and
- Supports the development of an organizational memory from meeting to meeting.

In the following sections, we describe these and other findings in more detail.

GROUP SIZE AND COMPOSITION

Groups numbering from 3 to 30 or more of differing composition have used GDSS facilities to accomplish a variety of tasks. One finding is clear; individual satisfaction increases with the size of the group. Computer support assists groups in building toward a consensus. Larger groups appreciate the inherent structuring that keeps the group from becoming bogged down or subject to domination by personalities. Small groups find that the fixed overhead associated with using the computer-based systems eats up the gains from using the system. Small groups are less likely than large groups to conclude that the computer-aided support is more effective or efficient than an unstructured face-to-face meeting. The various electronic brainstorming approaches do not work effectively with groups of less than four. Such techniques are more effective for groups of 8 or more persons. Many other techniques, such as stakeholder identification and assumption surfacing, also increase in satisfaction with group size. The implication of this finding is that different tools are required for different group sizes.

The increase in satisfaction with group size is due, in part, to "human parallel processing." That is, in many situations, participants are entering information into the computer simultaneously. They are functioning in parallel rather than in sequence. In a typical meeting that follows, say, Roberts Rules of Order, verbal input is sequential. As a result, if a group of 10 meets for an hour, each participant has the floor for only 6 minutes on the average. In parallel processing, each individual (even slow typists!) can make a larger individual contribution. Furthermore, people do not lose track of their own ideas while listening to someone else, nor do they lose track of what others are saying while trying to remember what they want to say when they get the floor.

Studies of groups using electronic meeting systems have consistently measured increases in productivity, with the gain in productivity increasing with group size. Large meetings can be supported. For example, former President Jimmy Carter used an electronic meeting system to run several meetings of nearly 300 people from all walks of life in Atlanta, Georgia to develop ideas for improving the economic conditions there. Large groups have also been shown to generate more ideas of higher quality than groups of the same size that do not use electronic support.

Anonymity

The anonymity facilitated through use of nominal group technique (Van de Ven and Delbecq [11]) and other tools for electronic brainstorming is a positive factor in encouraging broad-based participation. Anonymity is important when sensitive issues being discussed can easily be confounded with personalities in the group. Anonymity also provides a sense of equality and encourages participation by all members in the group, independent of perceived status. Problems of "group think," pressures for conformity, and dominance of the group by strong personalities of particularly forceful speakers are minimized even though the participants are face-to-face. Group members can contribute without the personal attention and anxiety associated with gaining the floor and being the focus of a particular comment or issue. As a result, issues are discussed more candidly.

Anonymity does tend to heighten conflict within the group because members tend to become more blunt and assertive in their written comments and often are not as polite as when speaking face-to-face. (However, people are more accepting of written criticism than verbal criticism because it does not carry with it the same level of embarrassment. Written comments become more polite with age and rank in the organization). Further, in any written medium, the richness of voice inflections and facial expressions is lost, which can lead to misunderstanding. Occasional face-to-face discussions as well as breaks and social time are important as issues become more politically charged and sensitive.

Finally, false promises of anonymity are damaging. Any attempt to observe input or find out who said what defeats the purpose of anonymity. That does not mean that people will not try to figure out the sources of comments. However, experience has shown that such guesses are most often incorrect.

Distributed Groups

Distributed groups are groups that are not located in the same place at the same time. These groups require special attention to group incentives and to providing feedback to overcome observed problems such as:

- Lower involvement by remote participants, because they do not have visual and non-verbal cues and often have low accountability; and
- Distributed groups tend to lose momentum whereas face-to-face groups use peer pressure to keep people moving.

Voting

In many organizations, formal voting is a rare event and is used only to close or decide a matter once and for all. However, as corporations rely more on teams, with increasing emphasis on participative management, their need to create and measure consensus grows. Electronic voting tends to inspire a "vote early, vote often" approach. Because it is so fast, teams use electronic voting to measure consensus and focus subsequent discussion on unresolved issues. Thus, voting overcomes the often observed problem that groups spend their time discussing what they agree on, rather than facing the difficult choices they must make. Furthermore, electronic voting clarifies communication, surfaces issues that remain buried during direct conversation, and facilitates decisions (such as where to downsize) that are too painful to face using traditional methods.

Leadership

Technology does not replace leadership style but can help to support it. When working with cross-functional teams, democratic leadership is needed to coordinate communications, facilitate the group process, and make sure that resources are available. GDSS enhances a leader's ability to move a group forward in a given set of circumstances.

Satisfaction

Individual satisfaction is reflected in user reports on the positive aspects of the group decision-making process in a computer-based support environment. Group participants conclude that they are not blocked out of the group and, as a result, they support the group solution with increased confidence.

Bottom-Line Benefits

Studies conducted at IBM and at Boeing show that significant savings are achieved through the use of GDSS (Grohowski [4], Post [9]). These savings result from much shorter project elapsed times, great reductions in labor costs, improved decision quality, and improved buy-in to the decision.

Implementation

Like all information systems that change the way people do business, careful planning is needed to ensure implementation success. For example, powerful stakeholders must participate in the planning for early sessions. Busy, powerful people are tempted to delegate these planning activities to others, but choices that appear arbitrary to others may turn out to be critically negative to the stakeholders. An electronic meeting system is neutral with respect to power shifts. They can be used in ways that reinforce the current structure or in ways that change power relationships. Sometimes a shift is desirable, but changes in power can cause resistance. These issues must be carefully weighed or the benefits of the technology to the organization may be lost.

HARDWARE AND SOFTWARE DESIGN CONSIDERATIONS

In addition to learning about how GDSS affects outcomes, considerable knowledge had been gained about how to create hardware and software. This sidebar describes these findings.

Facility Design

The lighting and physical organization of the decision room affect outcomes. Better results are obtained when the facility has aesthetic appeal and provides a comfortable, familiar setting for executives. Carpeting, wall coverings, executive style furniture, and quality acoustics provide an atmosphere that is well suited to long sessions over a number of days.

The seating configuration should map expected group activities and group size. A variety of seating arrangements from conference tables, to U-shaped, to round tables, to tiered classrooms have been used. All seating configurations require trade-offs. The design must consider the primary purpose of the facility, the relative importance of group focus, public display screen access, and support for large group size.

Adequate lighting control and arrangement of lights are needed to assure results legibility of both the public and the individual workstation screens. For example, front screen projector images are "washed out" by fluorescent lighting and can reduce the effectiveness of a meeting.

Adequate work surfaces must be made available to participants so they can spread papers about and have privacy for their own work screen. The work screens should be partially recessed in the table so people can see one another. If they are put on the table, people do not have line-of-sight. If they are completely buried under a glass panel in the desktop, the viewing area is cluttered by papers and lights create glare.

Multiple Public Screens

More than one public screen increases group productivity. Not all information can be displayed adequately in the standard 25 line by 80 character format of current computer screens. Windowing on a single screen allows presenting multiple sets of data but further reduces the amount of information that is shown about individual items. In a multiple screen setup, the group can view both the current information being discussed and reference information (e.g., sales trends, financials) at the same time. They can see the existing version and the proposed alternative side by side. In rank ordering, they can see the unordered and ordered items simultaneously.

Knowledge Bases and Data Bases

The documentation of meeting activities, the creation of working papers, and the recording of decisions and commitments are particularly useful byproducts of GDSS. These outputs are provided without detracting from meeting activities. File servers handle the knowledge bases and data bases, facilitate coordination and management of input from individual decision makers, and serve as "organizational memory" from session to session. The file server functions as a knowledge base repository and provides access to organizational data that are relevant to a particular meeting. A key to effective use of GDSS in supporting planning is the continuity from planning session to planning session provided by an on-going, expanding knowledge base which is integrated through the output from software tools. This continuity and integration provide the opportunity for analysis from multiple perspectives.

Communication Network Speed

Users become impatient if they must wait more than one or two seconds for a screen. Experience has shown that users expect to receive subsecond response for all activities. A wide bandwidth local network (LAN) is needed to maintain these high levels of network response.

Fixed versus Customized Tools

In planning, groups usually start with idea generation, followed by the development of alternatives, and conclude by converging on a course of action through forming a consensus. A group can go through this process in either of two modes:

1. It can create a customized methodology from the set of available tools or
2. It can follow a standard sequence for using the tools.

Some groups prefer to adopt a standard methodology whereas others feel that their needs are very different from everyone else's and therefore prefer to generate the sequence. Both approaches have given excellent results.

Software Design: Ease of Use and User Friendly

The best GDSS software helps rather than frustrates individual users. It supports a continuum of modes of working ranging from electronically based, self-directed participation to facilitator-directed discussion. However, a minimum amount of instruction and direction is still required. In the software designed by the University of Arizona (see Appendix), for example, it takes less than a minute to explain how to use each software tool. Efforts to increase software ease of use are particularly worthwhile. Techniques that use color, overlays, windowing, consistent interfaces, and on-demand help screens all help the user (particularly the novice and the computerphobic user) master the software. One or two group members who have difficulty with the software can affect the productivity of the entire group.

Consistency in the dialog interface protocols permits effective dialog management, ease of introduction of participants to new support tools, and ease of tool building. Common keystroke assignments, window layouts, use of color, messaging, and icon semantics facilitate this dialog management.

Screens sharing across, and among, participants opens new opportunities for particular decision tasks. Activities such as local editing of shared screens, help and monitoring activities, and personal messaging create alternative forms of communication. Using the keyboard as an input device has not proven to be an inhibitor of active participation.

Group support tools must integrate with individual desktop applications. It is now possible for individuals to bring their own applications (e.g., word processor, spreadsheet, presentation graphics) and their internal and external data sets and use them in conjunction with the group support software. The software must also be capable of knitting multiple meetings on a topic together by providing transcripts of previous sessions.

MEETING ENVIRONMENTS OF THE FUTURE

Technology exists today to permit team members to work any time, any place, and nearly any way they want. Electronically supported groups can work as individuals linked by electronic media in a virtual meeting; they can be located in several meeting rooms that are connected electronically; they can work at the same time, or different members can work at different times. They can work in small groups of four or five, or they can work in very large groups of 50 or more people. However, today many of these technologies are developing independently of one another. To date there is no single environment that combines individual and group support, remote and face-to-face collaboration, text, graphics, video and voice links, and shared computer applications. Each working mode requires electronic tools specifically tailored to the situation. Each kind of collaboration requires different kinds of information. For example, some information is formal, as with corporate reports. Other information is less formal, as with hallway conversations or notes on the back of a placemat. As we move toward the future, all group support technologies will be integrated into the same working environment.

New experimental environments are now under development at a number of places. Three of these developments are taking place at the University of Arizona: The Multimedia Collaboration Center, TeamRoom 2000, and the Mirror Project. Research in these facilities focuses on the integration of many technologies to support group work, including automating traditional group processes, real-time video and audio through the computer, and intelligent information retrieval and group support.

The Multimedia Collaboration Center, which opened in November 1993, is the current state of the art. It combines audio and video teleconferencing technology with GroupSystems and other electronic meeting support. It supports 29 users each with 21-inch screens on their workstations and three 10-foot public display screens. It also provides a full arsenal of multimedia display equipment and gives users on-line access to an electronic library and other external data bases. Phase Two of this project will include desktop audio and video links at every station. This center will also be fully integrated with the two other environments, the TeamRoom 2000 and the Mirror Project.

TeamRoom 2000 extends the capabilities of existing group support facilities to create an anytime/anyplace meeting environment. TeamRoom 2000 combines pen, voice, and wireless network technology so that distributed groups can work in a virtual team space. A dedicated facility with a network of pen- and voice-based notepad computers is the hub of this team environment, but users will move in and out with their portable computers as their needs dictate. TeamRoom 2000 extends the Multimedia Collaboration Center concept beyond the four walls.

The Mirror Project extends the concept of single groups to group-to-group interactions. Current audio and video teleconferencing technology does not support the rich and subtle communication possible in face-to-face meetings. Where the TeamRoom 2000 project focuses on the interface between the individual and the group, the Mirror facility focuses on creating the illusion of presence that is lost when groups use today's video teleconferencing facilities. The Mirror facility features floor-to-ceiling high-resolution video display walls and addresses optical, mechanical, and human issues to enhance the connection between remotely collaborating groups.

THE FUTURE OF GDSS

The foregoing discussions were based on the assumption that GDSS is an emerging technology that will become pervasive in many organizations. Certainly, the commercialization of GDSS by IBM and others is an important indicator of its long-term success. People meeting in a group need to have a free flow of ideas and the technology—with its typing, pointing of mice and other mechanical interruptions—can act as a barrier and a delayer rather than a facilitator of thought. Certainly the present technology could be made even more user friendly and transparent. New technologies (such as pen-based systems and voice recognition) should help in this regard. One of the dangers in the development of GDSS is that, like many other computer-based solutions offered previously, it may overpromise and underperform in its early stages, resulting in user expectations that are too high for what GDSS can deliver. The research programs and the commercial experience now under way should increase the long-term viability of GDSS.

What can we expect? Group decision support systems today use relatively standard computer, communications, and display technology. Physically, existing decision rooms look very much like conventional conference rooms with terminals and projection screens added. This is to be expected. When a new technology is introduced into an existing situation, it tends to look like and be used in the same way as the technology it replaces. The early automobile looked like and was used in the same way and over the same roads as the carriage, with only the horse replaced by a motor. GDSS provides an enhanced environment for performing existing tasks and will, in the short term, be used the way conference rooms are used now. As understanding of GDSS develops, the nature of group decision making itself can be expected to change. The idea of human parallel processing is such a change.

One potential new direction comes from the changes going on in the workplace. As large companies decentralize more and more and as computer and communications costs continue to decrease relative to transportation costs, we can expect that many people will "telecommute" (e.g., Nilles [8]) to meetings just as they telecommute to work. That is, they will stay where they are and will be brought into the decision conference electronically—through video and computer conference. It is also possible to use these technologies to call experts on a particular subject into the meeting, obtain their advice, and let them go without their ever leaving their place of work. The Mirror project described above is a first step in this direction.

Another potential direction of change comes from the expert/knowledge-based system realm. As expert systems become more pervasive, one or more of them will be brought into meetings to assist in deliberations. In effect, they become the $(n + 1)$st person in a meeting of n people. Their role can range from retrieving information to synthesis of new alternatives to helping resolve conflicts of opinions.

The present approach of using the technology to mechanize group processes such as voting, Delphi, and nominal group techniques is relatively crude and rudimentary. We can anticipate that new ways of gaining group interaction and group consensus will be developed that take advantage of the capabilities offered by GDSS.

We are at a very early and a very exciting point in GDSS. The level of activity is building as firms start to explore the possibilities. The years ahead should bring additional innovation and lead to maturity.

APPENDIX: GROUPSYSTEMS TOOLS DEVELOPED AT THE UNIVERSITY OF ARIZONA PLANNING LABORATORY

The Planning Laboratory established in 1985 at The University of Arizona's Management Information Systems Department was specifically constructed to aid groups in planning and decision making. A GDSS software toolkit known as GroupSystems was developed for use in the Planning Laboratory. The elements of this toolkit, shown in Table A–1, are similar to a DSS model base. The toolkit provides tools in three areas:

1. Session planning and management;
2. Group interaction and;
3. Organizational memory.

Groupsystems is the leading tool used in in decision rooms throughout the world.

TABLE A-1 Groupsystems Tools Developed at the University of Arizona*

Tool	Function
Idea Generation	
Brainstorming	Anonymous entry of new ideas. Allows rapid generation of a free flow of ideas.
Topic Commenter	A set of electronic index cards for simultaneous entry of information on multiple topics. Allows people to assign ideas to "file folders" or topics.
Idea Organization	
Idea Organizer	Categorizing comments from idea generation.
Group Outliner	Organizing ideas according to a structured outline form. Allows a group to explore issues and develop action plans using a tree or outline structure.
Issue Analyzer	Identifying and consolidating comments from idea generation into issues.
Group Writer	Joint authoring of a document by meeting participants.
Prioritizing	
Vote Selection	Choice of voting method (e.g., yes/no, multiple choice, ranking), voting, and vote result presentation. Helps in evaluating ideas, measuring consensus, and making choices.
Alternative Evaluation	Compares a set of alternatives according to multiple criteria developed by the group.
Questionnaire	An electronic questionnaire form that allows the group to provide its inputs to specific questions.
Group Matrix	Ratings on a two-dimensional matrix. Supports analysis of interrelationships between information sets.
Policy Development	
Policy Formation	Structured support for reaching consensus on policy statements and action plans.
Stakeholder Identification	Helps the group analyze the impact of actions or policies on identified stakeholders and on fundamental assumptions.
Session Planning	
Session Manager	Pre-session planning, in-session management, and post-session organization of results.
Organization Memory	
Enterpriser Analyzer	Structuring and analysis of group information in a semantic net.
Graphical Browser	"Zoom-in" and "zoom-out" on nodes of enterprise analyzer.
Group Dictionary	Allows the group to develop and store formal definition of common definitions for critical concepts.
Brief Case	Immediate read-only access to any stored text file; also provides productivity tools including calculator, notepad, and calendar functions from windows.

*These tools are now marketed by Ventana Corporation of Tucson, Arizona, under the name Groupsystems for Windows and Groupsystems V for DOS. At the beginning of 1995, this set of tools was installed at over 400 sites worldwide.

QUESTIONS

1. Do you believe that GDSS has high or low potential for use in organizations? Why?
2. What are the various types of GDSS facilities? What are the keys to their success?
3. What has been learned from the GDSS experiments that have been conducted?

REFERENCES

1. BOSTROM, R. P., R. T. WATSON, and S. T. KINNEY, *Computer Augmented Teamwork, A Guided Tour,* New York: Van Nostrand Reinhold, 1992.
2. BUI, T. and M. JARKE, "Communications Requirements for Group Decision Support Systems," *Proceedings of the 19th Hawaii International Conference on Systems Sciences,* Honolulu, HI (January 1986) 524–533.
3. DeSANCTIS, G. and R. B. GALLUPE, "Group Decision Support Systems: A New Frontier," *Data Base* (Winter 1985) 3–10.
4. GROHOWSKI, R., C. McGOFF, D. VOGEL, B. MARTZ, and J. F. NUNAMAKER, "Implementing Electronic Meeting Systems at IBM: Lessons Learned and Success Factors," *MIS Quarterly* (December 1990) 369–384.
5. HUBER, G. P., "Group Decision Support Systems as Aids in the Use of Structured Group Management Techniques," *Transactions of the Second International Conference on Decision Support Systems,* San Francisco, CA (June 1982) 96–108 (Reprinted in P. Gray (ed.), *Decision Support and Executive Information Systems,* New York: Prentice Hall, 1994).
6. JESSUP, L. W. and J. S. VALACICH, *Group Support Systems: New Perspectives.* New York: Macmillan Publishing Company, 1993.
7. KEEN, P. G. W., Remarks at the closing plenary session, First International Conference on Decision Support Systems, Atlanta, GA (June 1981).
8. NILLES, J. M., *Making Telecommuting Happen: A Guide for Telemanagers and Telecommuters,* New York: Van NostrandReinhold, 1995.
9. POST, B. Q. "Building the Business Case for Group Support Technology," *Proceedings of the 25th Annual Hawaii International Conference on Systems Sciences,* Kauai, HI (January 1992) 34–45.
10. SPRAGUE, R. H. JR. and E. D. CARLSON, *Building Effective Decision Support Systems,* Englewood Cliffs, NJ: Prentice Hall, 1982.
11. VAN de VEN, A. H. and A. L. DELBECQ, "Nominal Versus Interacting Group Processes for Committee Decision Making Effectiveness," *Academy of Management Journal* (1971) 203–212.

21

BRAINSTORMING '90s STYLE

If people are to achieve some degree of happiness in their work, the 19th-century British critic John Ruskin wrote, "they must be fit for it. They must not do too much of it. And they must have a sense of success in it."

All of which points to the dreaded meeting as the toothache of corporate life. According to a study by the University of Southern California, in Los Angeles:

- The average meeting takes place in the company conference room at 11 a.m. and lasts an hour and 30 minutes.
- It is attended by nine people—two managers, four co-workers, two subordinates and one outsider—who have received two-hour prior notification.
- It has no written agenda, and its purported purpose is completed only 50 percent of the time.
- A quarter of meeting participants complain they waste between 11 and 25 percent of the time discussing irrelevant issues.
- A full third of them feel pressured to publicly espouse opinions with which they privately disagree.
- Another third feel they have minimal or no influence on the discussion.
- Although 36 percent of meetings result in a "complete" resolution of the topic at hand, participants considered only one percent of those conclusions to be particularly "creative."

This chapter is a reprint of Alice Laplant, "'90s Style Brainstorming," *Forbes ASAP,* Volume 152, Number 10, October 25, 1993, pp. 44–61.

- A whopping 63 percent of meeting attendees feel that underlying issues outside the scope of the official agenda are the real subjects under discussion.
- Senior executives spend 53 percent of their time in meetings, at an average rate of $320 per person per hour.

Happily, help is on the way.

"ELECTRONIC BRAINSTORMING"—HERE'S HOW IT WORKS

A new type of software—labeled, awkwardly enough, GDSS, for group decision support system—promises to change all of this. Here's the scenario: A U-shaped conference table contains between 12 and 20 "meeting stations" made up of PCs or Macintosh computers and their associated point-and-click devices (such as mice) or drawing tools (such as light pens). A large—usually 60-inch—color monitor is located at one end of the table where it can be easily viewed by everyone in the room. A facilitator calls the meeting to order, and instead of talking (whispering, shouting), participants type their ideas, comments, or reactions on their keyboards. Their input appears simultaneously on every screen in the room, as well as on the monitor at the head of the table. Input is anonymous. Everyone gets a chance to contribute. No one can dominate the airspace—because there is none. With everyone typing simultaneously, it's virtually impossible for someone to grab the floor and hold onto it to the dismay of the other participants.

Public relations giant Hill & Knowlton raves about the results. A key H&K client had suddenly initiated Chapter 11 bankruptcy proceedings; the client needed to spin the news in such a way that the stock price would not be disastrously affected or thousands of suppliers and distributors frightened off until the reorganization was complete. Timing was critical. "This was an urgent situation. We were under a very tight deadline to come up with a plan," says Mayer G. Becker, an H&K vice-president. Becker had seen a demo of VisionQuest, a GDSS package from Innovative Solutions Inc., at a computer trade show. Becker liked what he saw. Last November, he took nine of his account team colleagues to the Chicago offices of Lante Corp., a systems design firm that had built a dedicated electronic brainstorming room for its own use.

The H&K account team members sat down around the conference table at networked PCs and began typing their thoughts into the system. "Within 10 minutes, we had 47 excellent ideas," says Becker. "By the end of the hour, we had discussed them, voted on them, ranked them in order of priority and walked out with printed documentation in hand."

As Hill & Knowlton discovered, GDSS offers myriad benefits. Personal and organizational influence go out the window. One person can't dominate this type of meeting. You can't raise your voice. You can't stare down an underling who says something you don't like. It's no wonder that more ideas—and more surprising conclusions—can be generated in a much shorter time. Studies show that computer-assisted meetings substantially cut down on meeting time, according to Virginia Johnson, director of human relations at 3M Co. and a member of the 3M Management Institute in Austin. She adds that "many major companies are in the experimental phase of using these technologies."

Just ask Carl DiPietro, a consultant specializing in computer-assisted meetings who first introduced the idea to the Marriott Corp. in 1992 while he was vice-president of human resources there. He claims to have held more than 5,000 electronically enhanced meetings with more than 100 different clients since starting his own meeting consulting firm last year in Bethesda, Md. DiPietro carries with him to customer sites 12 to 20 notebook computers equipped with Ethernet networking packs, a more powerful "lunch box" portable to act as a Novell LAN server, and VisionQuest software. Within minutes, he is able to transform a conventional conference room into a wired forum, ready to untangle deadlocked management teams.

HOW TO AVOID THE "ABILENE PARADOX" AND THE "FOOTBALL PHENOMENON"

One of the strengths of meetingware is that it helps organizations avoid what DiPietro calls the "Abilene paradox." "We've all heard this type of saga," he says. A Texas family gathers one Sunday morning to decide what to do for the day. No one has any ideas—or if they do, they're afraid to speak up. "Finally, the patriarch of the family suggests going to Abilene—which is 100 miles away—on the hottest day of a Texas summer. Everyone agrees, with relief, and they take a long, hot, joyless trip there and back." At the end of the day it turns out that no one wanted to go to Abilene—not even the person who suggested it. "But everyone just fell in line with the suggestion. This happens all the time. We make decisions by observing other people's behaviors rather than based on our own ideas or beliefs."

Another conference room scenario is one DiPietro characterizes as the "football phenomenon." All hell breaks loose during the last five minutes of a meeting, and grand conclusions are reached that bear little resemblance to the discussions of the preceding three hours. Worse still is the case of the person who volunteers to write up the minutes of the meeting, walks off with the flip chart and two months later sends around a memo that reflects nothing of what the participants thought occurred.

Indeed, anyone who has used a GDSS generally gets around to expressing amazement at its tremendous power to disarm the "meeting bully."

"With the anonymity, the ideas become more important than who said them or how they were said," says Susanna Opper, president of Susanna Opper and Associates, a New York-based consulting firm that focuses on groupware, such as Lotus Notes, and meetingware, such as VisionQuest. "Someone lower down in an organization, who might not be as respected because of his job or minority status, or because she is a woman, is someone who isn't normally listened to. This technology gives them a voice."

BUT IS IT FOR YOU?

All of this sounds good, even terrific—so what's the catch?

For one thing, it's easy for this type of technology to disrupt or even dominate a meeting. Johnson, of 3M's Meeting Management Institute, warns that "for the most part, this technology is well ahead of the acceptance level of the average meeting-goer."

Walter Parrish, a facilitator for Tulsa, Okla.-based Texaco, uses GroupSystems V, a GDSS from Ventana Corp., Tucson, Ariz., in approximately 25 percent of the meetings he coordinates, but he doesn't recommend it for shorter conferences involving high-level executives. "When people aren't very computer literate—which includes some of upper management—there's a bias against these tools. You have to fight for it," he says.

For this reason, some consultants and meeting facilitators prefer to bypass full-blown GDSS products in favor of scaled-down technologies. Westinghouse Electric Corp., for example, prefers a simple electronic voting keypad for its ease of use.

Hudi Cantrell, an information technology manager at Hewlett Packard Co., has noticed that extroverts tend to "drop out" of electronic meetings because they are so dismayed with their inability to use their strong verbal skills. "You tend to get much more input from shyer people, but you also lose others." Cantrell says balanced use of these tools is the answer. In most HP meetings where GroupSystems V is used the electronic portion represents between only 25 and 50 percent of the meeting, she says.

Mark Tebbe, president of Lante Corp., which assisted Hill & Knowlton with its initial VisionQuest session, agrees: "The best meetings are a combination of the two. You use these tools to brainstorm and prioritize ideas, then you discuss them in the usual way."

Will an old-style manager be comfortable with this? "Probably not," says Opper. "We're talking about leveling the hierarchy, and that's a scary thing." But opening up a meeting in this way doesn't imply that a senior manager is going to opt for democratic rule. "People simply want their day in court. They can understand if the decision-making authority still resides elsewhere," says DiPietro.

In the brainstorming session Lante conducted for Hill & Knowlton, participants used VisionQuest's voting tools to get a sense of how the group ranked the ideas that had been generated, but in the end the results—and final decision-making authority—were left to the three managers who headed the account. Old-fashioned leadership still counts, in other words.

CALCULATIONS, WEIGHTINGS, AND GRUNT WORK

One of GDSS's nicest features is its voting and calculation mechanism. DiPietro can ask participants to prioritize a list of projects using a scale of, say, one to 10. "Or I'll say, 'You have $1 million in your budget; allocate the money among these projects.' The computer does all the calculations, weightings and grunt work. It displays the results on the screen. You have a clear picture of what everyone thinks."

Be aware, however, that people will undoubtedly find ways to manipulate the technology to suit their own purposes. Lante's Tebbe, who uses VisionQuest or GroupSystems V every other week with his 10-member management team, realized that one meeting participant—a fast typist—was pretending to be more than one person when he vehemently agreed or disagreed with an idea being discussed. "He'd type 'Oh, I agree,' and then 'Ditto, ditto' or 'What a great idea' all in quick succession, using different variations of upper-case and lower-case letters and punctuation," recalls Tebbe. "He tried to make it seem like a lot of people were concurring, but it was just him." How did Tebbe discover this ploy? "The person sitting next to him got suspicious and began watching his screen," he says.

Meeting experts also say to be wary of the productivity numbers bandied about by meetingware vendors. According to Lisa Neal, a senior research engineer with Electronic Data Systems' Center for Advanced Research, Cambridge, Mass., a lot of the hype surrounding computer-assisted meetings is meaningless. "People say, 'We generated so many more ideas in so much time, so we had 50 percent time savings.' That's meaningless because it says nothing about the quality of those ideas."

Indeed, it's often difficult to define a successful meeting, says Dave Hoffman, an information systems programmer who works in organizational development for Texaco, in Houston, on meeting technologies. Texaco uses GroupSystems V and in the last two years has spent approximately $300,000 to build a room for electronically facilitated meetings. It's equipped with a U-shaped table that contains embedded networked PCs, letting participants see each other and their personal screens easily. A large monitor mounted at the front of the room also displays group output.

"We'd had meetings where people walked out extremely satisfied, yet they hadn't accomplished anything," says Hoffman. "At other times, people would leave a meeting room very frustrated and unhappy, yet in my opinion they had accomplished a lot." How do you initially determine a solution's quality? Only time will tell.

Still, EDS's Neal has discovered that people place more value on the result of electronic brainstorming. She asks participants to fill out questionnaires immediately after a meeting, and then again two to three weeks later. When asked why they are more satisfied, respondents often say they feel they've moved forward—even if they haven't accomplished what they set out to. "But something happened, even if it's just identification of the next step," says Neal.

Last words of advice? When experimenting with this technology, say Opper and others, "forget about the demos that the vendors want to show you. Take a real business problem to one of these electronic meeting rooms, bring a real work team eager to discuss something that matters, and prepare to be amazed."

CASE STUDY: HOW GE RATES THE BOSS — SAFELY

A year ago, Bob Flynn's boss read an article about electronic brainstorming. Intrigued, he asked Flynn, information services manager at General Electric Co.'s Capacitor and Power Protection unit in Fort Edward, N.Y., to investigate. Flynn brought in VisionQuest for a three-month trial run.

One project in particular had loaded consequences. At the direction of Joe McSweeney, the plant general manager, Flynn divided the plant's 45 work group leaders into six groups and led them through a no-holds-barred evaluation of the plant's management. The outline revealed that the employees viewed McSweeney as creative, entrepreneurial and "a bureaucracy basher," eager to remove organizational barriers to innovative and good ideas, says Flynn.

On the downside, it emerged that "people felt he was so impatient to get things done that he interceded in a decision that should have been theirs to make." A week after the electronic ratings were completed, McSweeney stood before his management team and responded, point by point, to the comments. "He was absolutely sincere about really wanting this feedback," says Flynn.

McSweeney and other GE managers were so impressed by this new type of software that they made VisionQuest a standard tool for many important meetings at the site. "This takes the mechanics out of arriving at a consensus," says Flynn. "We don't need flip charts, we don't need tape recorders, we don't need someone writing down their version of what's happening."

However, VisionQuest is not a panacea for every meeting, says Flynn. "We have one guy—a very strong personality—who tends to dominate traditional meetings. Because he can't do that using VisionQuest, he isn't terribly inclined to participate or use this tool." Instead of typing his comments on the keyboard, Flynn says, the backslider calls things out, starts a discussion, changes the topic and leads everyone down a different path. How should facilitators respond when confronted with this type of behavior? "Let it go; then eventually steer people back to the matter at hand," he says—especially when, as is the case with this example, the person happens to be a valuable and active contributor. With people like this, "you have to be flexible until they become more comfortable with the tool," says Flynn.

CASE STUDY: HOW HEWITT ASSOCIATES BALANCES DECISIONS BETWEEN OPPOSING INTERESTS

Today, discussions of benefit packages often require the input of the CEO, CFO, and other senior executives. Surprised at the upper-level involvement? Don't be. "After capital expenditures and direct pay, benefits are the largest single expense

PROFILE OF A FACILITATOR

Until a year-and-a-half ago, Walter Parrish was a technical trainer for Tulsa, Okla.-based Texaco. Intrigued by the activities of a newly formed department within Texaco's business services consulting group—created to help make Texaco meetings more productive—Parrish made a career jump. Now, as one of nine facilitators spread among Texaco's U.S. operations, Parrish travels from site to site, helping executives and line workers conduct more effective meetings. Here's his accumulated wisdom.

Cultivate the ability to "read" the room during a brainstorming session. "You need to allow participants enough time so that they feel they've expressed their ideas, but not so much time that they are grasping for things to type," says Parrish. If the suggestions and ideas start sounding frivolous or silly, "it's probably gone on too long."

Carefully define all questions or issues to be discussed, and set time limits on brainstorming sessions. Otherwise, you'll end up with more information than the group can reasonably process.

Don't go overboard on the technology. "When you first get this tool, there's a tendency to overuse it because it can be very productive and exciting," says Parrish. "But there are times you want to step away from it. Have a traditional discussion, do some role playing or perform some other exercise that doesn't involve the keyboard."

Give participants lots of breaks and time off. They're working harder than in traditional meetings, so they'll become exhausted if you push too hard.

Smoke out hidden agendas. Try to get all ideas on the table so that everyone feels a decision has been reached in an unbiased manner.

Be alert to hostility. "Electronic tools allow people to put out a lot of information very quickly, and things can heat up," says Parrish. "You need to be able to defuse such situations and slow down the pace, perhaps do some team-building exercises. Always make it clear that even if people have opposing viewpoints, there's room for everyone to be heard."

many employers have," says Jack Bruner, flexibility compensation practice leader for Hewitt Associates, an international firm of consultants and actuaries specializing in employee benefit and compensation programs.

Getting top managers in a room necessitates that complex negotiations be conducted quickly. "We need to be as efficient as possible," says Bruner, who uses VisionQuest to facilitate meetings with clients. "This tool allows them to dump all of their best ideas with amazing quickness, take a preliminary vote, then discuss the top 10 of those 50 ideas before coming to a consensus."

Founded in 1940, the $357 million Lincolnshire, Ill.-based Hewitt employs more than 3,500 associates in 60 offices worldwide, and has provided benefits consulting services to 75 percent of America's largest companies. About half of the clients work with electronic brainstorming tools like VisionQuest.

The first time Bruner used VisionQuest was with client Kraft General Foods to help brainstorm ideas for a new employee benefits program that would later be presented to Kraft's senior managers. Bruner sat the 12 middle managers down in front of networked PCs in the Hewitt VisionQuest conference room, and within an hour they had come up with "some very different answers than if we had simply talked about possible benefits programs," he recalls.

The tool helped "free up the thinking," Bruner says. Instead of talking about medical insurance carriers or retirement plans, "we heard things like, 'I'd like to be able to send my kids to college, buy a house, get my finances under control, improve my health.'" Once these ideas were on the table, Bruner's staff was able to guide the meeting participants to the next step—dividing company resources among benefits programs structured around those needs.

You could do this in the traditional way, says Bruner, but he believes that the anonymity allows for a more open-ended and creative discussion. He recalls doing this same sort of brainstorming exercise manually with another client: When it came time to vote on the ideas raised, no one was willing to commit, says Bruner. *"No one,"* he reiterates. "I asked them what the problem was." It turned out that the manager of the group—a vice-president—had left the room for a moment, and no one wanted to vote before understanding how the manager felt about the issues. "It's really true: The anonymous format makes people feel freer to say what they think," says Bruner.

Hewitt has been so impressed with the results that it's put VisionQuest on the enterprise network that connects its IBM and Amdahl mainframes with LANs in a wide-area network of 30-odd regional offices throughout the United States. The VisionQuest file server resides in Lincolnshire, and any regional office can log onto the server and use the software remotely.

Hewitt has used the technology in two virtual meetings to date—that is, meetings in which participants are separated by time, distance, or both. One such virtual meeting was held by 16 members of the Hewitt consulting team to define contribution recordkeeping. According to Larry Hebda, IS consultant for Hewitt, the participants logged onto VisionQuest from their individual PCs at 9 on a designated morning, and discussed and voted on the agenda items. He points out that although that meeting was considered highly successful, the group found it necessary to hold a traditional meeting later in the day to go over the results of the electronic discussion.

Hewitt had to learn the most effective way to use this technology. According to Hebda, it's easy to get overloaded with too many ideas. He remembers one early VisionQuest session—before he understood the importance of carefully directing brainstorming sessions—in which participants generated 100 ideas in less than 10 minutes. It was overkill, admits Hebda, "too much to digest."

Despite the usual learning glitches, the benefits of such systems far outnumber the drawbacks, says Bruner. He estimates that with VisionQuest, his staff can finish a consulting project in 60 percent of the time it would take them with traditional methods. "When you're on a per-hour basis, that means you can deliver more to your clients for less. And you can't argue that we're getting better results."

CASE STUDY: HOW WESTNGHOUSE USES VOTING AS A DISCUSSION STIMULANT

Jeff Jury remembers getting an urgent call from the head of a $150 million manufacturing division of Westinghouse Electric Corp. The division had reached a critical juncture in its 12-year history, but was deadlocked in its attempts to formulate a new strategic business plan.

Jury, a senior consultant at the Productivity and Quality Center, an internal management consulting group within Westinghouse, called a meeting of the division's top managers. He took his 386-based laptop out of his briefcase, along with a dozen small electronic voting keypads, and within minutes had distributed one of the devices to every executive in the room. The keypads were linked via thin wire cables to his laptop, which was running a voting application called OptionFinder.

Jury began probing the group's attitudes by asking questions about the division's fundamental strategy. Participants answered his questions by pressing the keypads in front of them. Questions included: "Are you trying to be a low-priced competitor? Differentiate on value? Serve the entire market or just a niche?" Then he showed the executives the results, displayed in full-color graphs on an overhead projector. The group was stunned to find that "answers were scattered across the board, with absolutely no agreement or consensus," says Jury. "Yet if I'd asked them this question vocally, we probably wouldn't have gotten any challenge."

Calculation is instantaneous. And results are displayed graphically—not just averages but distribution of votes as well. You immediately see not only which issues "won" but by how much—and whether the group is splintered. You can even calculate subgroups of agreement and disagreement according to preset demographics of attendees. And because the process is truly anonymous, people feel freer to vote their own minds.

Westinghouse spent just $15,000 to equip as many as 100 people with OptionFinder keypads and software. Usually, however, the device is used in much smaller meetings of between 15 and 25 people. "I'll put a list on a flip chart of 10 or 15 key issues, and we'll prioritize that list in just minutes," says Jury.

ELECTRONIC BRAINSTORMING GUIDE

Do use a meeting facilitator to manage the process.

Do decide upon a clear "deliverable," or goal, for the meeting.

Do make it clear who has ultimate decision-making power when all of the input has been collected.

Do vote early and often, and use the results to open up further discussion.

Do be prepared to change gears if something isn't working.

Do be aware when things aren't working.

Do turn off the machines and talk for at least 50 percent of the meeting time.

Don't use GDSS for simple information-sharing.

Don't assume the results of voting activities are statistically valid. Instead, use them to probe conflicting attitudes and opinions.

Don't call a meeting unless you have a firm goal in mind.

Don't allow brainstorming sessions to spin out of control. Take charge of both the time allotted and the scope of the discussion.

Don't use GDSS with too few (less than four) or too many (more than 20) participants.

Don't impose GDSS on nontechnical employees without allowing adequate "familiarity" time and exercises.

QUESTIONS

1. What are the potential benefits of electronic over traditional meetings?
2. What are the characteristics of people who are prone to (1) like or (2) dislike electronic meetings?
3. What role does a facilitator play in electronic meetings?
4. How might the effectiveness and efficiency of electronic meetings be judged?

22

HOW LOTUS NOTES SUPPORTS WORKGROUPS

Lotus Notes flies high. Way high. And the wonder of it is how close it gets to the sun.

This network application aspires to be nothing less than a total working environment for business groups. The Notes frontier is a "place" beyond the usual limits of time and space, where workgroups can create, store, distribute, and share information in ways no one has tried before.

Remarkably, the program actually achieves some of its lofty goals. Although it has flaws, Notes represents the shape of things to come in PC computing. It's the first program to infuse the concept of groupware with pulsing, practical vitality.

Notes stands apart from other early forays into the unexplored territory of group-oriented software because it displays a unique understanding of the information-centered work users long to do on office PCs. In the past, people had no choice but to approach their business work in groups—staff meetings, committees, teams, departments—and their PC tasks as individuals. And local-area networks failed to change this reality: LANs linked the machines, but the users remained locked into largely stand-alone applications.

Lotus Notes creates an application structure that accommodates a group without wresting control from individual users. Any Notes user can create an application data base and become its manager—with complete control over what it does, how it works, who can use it, and even whether it lives or dies. Notes is democracy in action, an effective balance between the divergent aspirations of individuals and the confederating power of MIS.

This chapter is a reprint of David DeJean, "Sky High Notes," *PC Computing*, March 1990.

Because of its success at maintaining this delicate balance, Notes stands a strong chance of becoming the first group-oriented package to be a major force in the PC marketplace. Lotus hopes to make this happen by selling the product through direct sales calls to *Fortune* 500 company MIS departments. But chances are excellent that despite its group flavor, Notes will be championed in corporations by individuals, gaining acceptance via the underground railroad of user word of mouth.

Manufacturers Hanover Trust is one of the most active beta sites for Notes. Pat Sziklai, vice president for information services there, has already witnessed the first signs of grassroots user mania. "Notes is addictive," she says. "People who aren't technical use it and feel empowered. They move to another group and pretty soon that group wants to be hooked up to Notes." And so Notes, by being both formal and free-form, may ring in a new era of PC populism in corporate computing.

What exactly is Notes? Even Lotus has had problems describing its new product. Before the official product announcement, late last year, Notes was a "document management system." At the unveiling, it was dubbed "group communication software." In fact, Notes is both these things—and more.

IS NOTES GROUPWARE?

Lotus has also called Notes "groupware"—but cautiously. The term *groupware* is so fuzzy that it doesn't do much to describe Notes, and it may even obfuscate the matter further by focusing attention on what Notes doesn't do, rather than what it does do.

The few applications that have begun to define groupware have been based on coordinating the activities of a group. Packages like The Coordinator, WordPerfect Office, and Syzygy are built around electronic mail, shared calendars, group scheduling, or project management functions. Because Notes doesn't come with appointment-calendar functions or a scheduling application, at first glance it doesn't look like what we've come to think of as groupware.

The lack of a calendar in Notes might be a mistake, says Susanna Opper, a consultant based in New York City who works on groupware issues for corporate clients. "As I watch people use these products, they want to do that kind of coordination, the logistical stuff of scheduling meetings and distributing agendas." But scheduling is only one category of groupware. There are many more of them, says Opper. "It isn't like spreadsheets, where there are different brands but they all do pretty much the same thing. Notes is a different category of groupware."

Notes begins to look more familiar when compared with other categories of groupware products. Its e-mail features are strong. Its data management capabilities make it look something like a contact management package. With its strengths in tracking and indexing messages and responses, it resembles a computer conferencing application. In fact, Notes is something of a chameleon: where other groupware products tend to shape the organizations that adopt them, Notes is shaped by its users.

The trade-off lies between the short-term work needed to develop Notes applications and the long-term usability of groupware applications that aren't customizable.

THREE FUNCTIONS, TWO PARTS

Notes is built on three major functions: information management, document formatting, and wide area communication. It aims to make all aspects of all three functions available to every member of a group, in a high-confidence, high-security environment and across any standard PC local area network.

Architecturally, Notes comes in two parts. The server piece runs on a networked PC that manages a group's data and communications. The client piece runs on all other PCs in the group. It handles requests from group members to the server for data and other services. This setup represents one of the first real-world implementations of client-server architecture, a widely ballyhooed but little understood computer industry catchphrase. For this achievement alone, Lotus Notes deserves honor.

Notes runs on any NetBIOS-compatible LAN, including Novell NetWare, 3Com, and IBM's PC LAN. Notes' server software can support either DOS or OS/2 clients. The Notes client software runs on PCs with either DOS and Windows or OS/2 and Presentation Manager. Both the server and client programs are sizable (the Windows version of the client application, for instance, takes up 490K).

NOTES AT WORK

To the user, Notes begins as an icon on the PC's Notes screen. This very simple initial view of the program borrows most of its appearance from the Windows/Presentation Manager graphical interface. Drop-down menus list the program's commands, and individual application data bases appear as icons with their names beside them.

A mouse click on an icon opens a "view" into the documents it represents, and this view looks much like a traditional data base report. Information from fields in the documents is arranged in columns, and each row represents a document in the application data base. The presentation definitions for the columns and the rules for document selection are written in a macro language that uses the familiar 1-2-3- @ functions, yet few of these scripts will look familiar to 1-2-3 users.

Creating views for a Notes application takes a significant chunk of the user's or manager's development effort. Shortcuts are few in Notes application development—no ad hoc query, no "watch-me" keystroke recorder to build definitions and formulas, no menu-driven application generator. All formulas involving @ functions have to be written out like program code. This may appear to be a bother, but it makes sense. Building a Notes application is a programming task that requires keeping more than one person in mind, so individual code-writing has to be careful and complete before it can become part of the system.

An example of the macro-building price exacted in a group-oriented environment comes from comparing similar tasks in Notes and its Lotus cousin, the personal information manager Agenda. Both Notes and Agenda use "categories," "views," "templates," and the like, but Agenda lets you randomly pound in data, then organize it as you wish later. Notes requires more formal structure up front. Data has to have a place to go—a field (in a form) or a category (in a view)—before it can be entered into Notes. A Notes application data base needs careful planning to determine which fields, which forms, which views, and which access controls to use.

Despite the detail required, users will write Notes applications—probably lots of them, and probably some of the best user-derived programs ever. Notes rewards clear understanding of a business problem by allowing a straightforward script to deliver a clear, easy-to-use application. And the software makes it easy for users to get started. Templates for basic applications such as computer conferencing, client contact-tracking, and problem reporting are included with the program. At the same time, the Notes development environment is powerful enough that extremely complex applications are possible.

Building Notes applications is worth the effort because it produces programs that are tailored to the needs of their user/developers and are therefore easier for their true customers to understand. For users, success with Notes doesn't depend on mastering an outside report-writing package or learning an independent command language. All the elements for success dwell within the Notes environment.

Confidentiality and security are two of Notes' most strikingly original characteristics. Most current applications leave security to the underlying operating system; Notes guarantees the sanctity of its own documents.

LOTUS' OWN TEST

Perhaps the best way to explain Notes is to show how it actually works for a corporate group. One of the most ambitious Notes applications at this early stage is a sales activity reporting system used at Lotus. Like a doctor who has developed a new medicine, Lotus conducted extensive in-house Notes experiments before prescribing the product for the public. After gathering field information from sales and marketing staff, the system consolidates it into reports for upper management at Lotus headquarters.

Private views and access controls play a major part in the Lotus sales sys-

Private views and access controls play a major part in the Lotus sales system. Views in Notes can be restricted for use only by individuals or members of group lists. Only sales department managers can view personnel information in Lotus's sales-activity data base, for instance. Evaluations and other sensitive documents are hidden from users in other departments.

The basic building blocks of Lotus's sales activity are the salespersons' monthly reports, which detail contacts and customer feedback and pass along ideas and marketplace information. Each report is a separate document in the Notes data base, and each individual document is based on a group-consistent form.

Forms are created by laying out named fields onscreen and assigning attributes to them. A field may represent numbers, text, or Rich Text—text formatted much the way a word processor formats a document (in fact, Notes' Rich Text Format is borrowed from Microsoft Word). Field types are specialized as well: an "Author" field is automatically filled with the name of a document's creator; a "Date" field can correctly interpret entries like "today" and "3/6"; a keyword field can be turned into a selection list of check boxes or radio buttons.

A form can also be graphic. Graphics files, such as company logos, can be positioned on forms. And Notes supports varied text fonts, sizes, and colors. Even an application's icon can be edited, and the icons on the templates distributed with Notes give a hint of the hours that pixel Picassos will spend developing miniature masterpieces in shops that adopt the product.

Some of these features will look more than fleetingly familiar to users of HyperCard for the Macintosh. The workspace with its icons looks something like the Home Card, and the individual forms, with their heavy formatting capabilities, check boxes, and radio boxes, are far more Mac-like than PC-like.

Lotus's sales activity application replaced a paper-based system that produced a 200-page report once a quarter. That process had some major problems that Notes has resolved, according to Ron Turcotte, who created the application and now administers it. For example, the quarterly production schedule was too long. After three months, every problem had grown into a crisis. Three months' worth of bulky reports also proved difficult to digest. The daunting paper reports would lie in an in-basket unread until they were thrown out to make room for new reports. And the paper reports presented only two cuts of the information: sales contacts and market intelligence. It wasn't easy to look at the contents in any other configuration—by competitor, for example.

The great value of the Notes application has been in the amount of time saved, says Jim Manzi, CEO of Lotus. The salespeople and management can now do in hours what once took days, and three weeks have been cut off the report's production cycle. "The work is more valuable because it's more current and more accessible," says Manzi. "It's a win on time and quality for sure, and on capacity to respond."

A key to building a successful system in Notes, creator Turcotte says, is training. The training time for a user to become functional in Notes is about half an hour, but it's necessary training. Training programs and continuing user support earned Lotus's system a better reception than earlier (failed) sales reporting efforts received, according to Turcotte.

It's not surprising that Lotus should be able to mine value from its own product. The more important question is whether potential Notes users in other organizations can catch the wave.

Lotus is fielding a brand-new direct sales force to provide the missionary selling and ongoing support that Notes needs. It's an impressive commitment on Lotus's part. Unfortunately it requires an impressive commitment on the customer's part: although Notes' price per user is reasonable, to meet the high cost of the direct-sales approach Lotus has set the minimum purchase at $62,500 for a 200-user site license, including training, documentation, and tech support.

BRILLIANT COMPROMISES

Notes' potential can probably best be judged by considering the alternatives: How much of what Notes does can be duplicated by other programs? On a function-by-function basis, little about Notes is dazzlingly original. Its electronic mail, for example, isn't much different from that of standalone e-mail packages, whereas its ability to provide access to external mail systems is woefully weak compared with most of those offerings. Similar comparisons could be made on a function-by-function basis of Notes versus data base managers, word processors, presentation graphics packages, executive information systems, newswire services, and a variety of more specialized packages that do things like client tracking and document management.

The genius of Notes lies in the number of such comparisons it evokes. All products it can be compared with do what they do as well as or better than Notes does. But none of them handles as much in so many functional areas. The integration of previously disparate tasks in Notes means that no e-mail package can match its message-formatting capabilities, and no word processor can rival its document-management skills. What other data base manager can turn a data-entry form into an e-mail message just by adding a field named "SendTo"? Notes is a brilliantly programmed collection of compromises, and that makes the whole much greater than the sum of its parts.

Just how good is this unified working environment for you? That depends on how wedded you are to your current working environments, one of which is the patchwork of applications and utilities you run on your PC; the other is the real world where you deal with real people.

Notes probably won't compete well in the first situation. If your company already has an electronic mail system that reaches people Notes doesn't, you'll leave Notes to use it. If you make extensive use of the multiple columns or tables features in a word processor, you'll abandon Notes for that. If you spend most of your day in Lotus 1-2-3, you'll visit Notes only occasionally. (Despite its nascent abilities to import and export data, Notes is still pretty much a functional island. Things can be automated *within* Notes, but it has no tool for automating big data-transfer jobs with the outside world—using terminal emulation to pull data from a mainframe, for instance.)

But if e-mail is your life and everybody you interact with is on Notes, you'll pick up the Notes text editor quickly (there's not that much to pick up) and visit your word processor less often as time goes by. If you write short notes and fill out forms all day—memos, call reports, requests for purchase orders—you're a likely candidate for an advanced degree in Notes form design. Notes can soak up a high percentage of your in-house phone calls and those discussions that begin, "Just a quick question. . . ." And Notes can manage the distribution of a dozen copies of a report without trips to the copy machine and the mailroom. And six months later, Notes will remember that a copy went to Sam in production, no matter what he says.

THREE CONDITIONS FOR SUCCESS

Because Notes works at the intersection of the PC environment and the real world, its chances for success will be greater if three basic business conditions are met. First, all the workers and departments affected by what happens in the Notes environment need access to Notes. Second, the Notes applications must be built to a critical mass, so that most of the data that most people want is easier to find within Notes than outside it. Third, everybody expected to use Notes should have a PC capable of running it.

This may sound obvious, but it's not. The Notes client software will run under Windows on a 640K 286 machine, but the performance is awful. A fast 286 with a couple of megabytes of RAM is the minimum acceptable hardware platform for a Notes workstation. Performance is much improved by OS/2 and 4MB of RAM. But equipping everybody to run OS/2 and a graphical interface ups the ante considerably for organizations that might benefit from Notes. They may have to invest in anything from the major sticker shock of more powerful PCs to the easily overlooked cost of adding mice to all their machines.

Still, the costs of upgrading users' hardware to run advanced operating systems will be quickly repaid. Both Windows and OS/2 are becoming more capable: Windows 3.0 or higher fixes much of the worst of Windows. OS/2 2.0 (the 386-specific version of OS/2) is due later this year. And Notes itself is a moving target: Lotus has a list of improvements in the works that will make it more capable.

At its introduction, Lotus officials were talking about fixes to minor annoyances, like the 64K limit on the size of graphics files that can be imported into documents, and major upgrades, like an application programming interface (API) that will enable programmers to write extensions in the C language to handle such chores as automatic data conversions for proprietary file formats and access to external e-mail systems such as IBM Profs. Also high on Lotus's list is support for the MHS (Message Handling Services) protocol to provide access to the many e-mail systems, such as Da Vinci eMail, Higgins, and cc:Mail, that support this message format. In the longer term, Lotus plans a complete gateway toolkit for constructing customized communications gateways to other systems.

INSTALLATION AND MANAGEMENT

While application-building punch and a sense of freedom will matter most to individual Notes users, network installation and management issues will play a major role in determining whether Notes captures the hearts and minds of systems professionals. Overall, Notes appears to have no more drawbacks than other network software, and it boasts a few alluring advantages.

Getting a Notes installation up and running is straightforward. Creating user and server IDs takes some work because Notes' security features rest on the system's ability to validate the user. Each ID includes public and private encryption keys, for instance, which can generate an electronic signature that a remote server can use to verify that a message that says it came from John Smith really did come from John Smith.

The system manager's control over replication of applications across Notes servers, or servers and remote users, is one of the most interesting and innovative aspects of the package.

A Notes application and all its associated data can reside on any number of Notes servers, and Notes manages the process of keeping those multiple copies in sync. A document added on one server will be added on any other server the next time those two servers connect and trade information on the state of applications they know they share. If the two servers are on the same network, they can connect that way. More typically, replication is done via telephone lines.

The administrator sets the replication list and schedule for each application, and the servers become a sort of virtual wide area network that can adopt any of several distribution schemes. One server can be a hub and replicate with every other server on the list, or changes can propagate through a chain of servers. Servers can replicate applications as frequently or infrequently as is tolerable. Heavy e-mail traffic between two locations may mean a replication every 15 minutes, while the corporate policy manual may need replicating only once a month.

Notes allows for admirable configuration flexibility. One Notes beta tester, Corporate Software, has three Notes sites: one in Massachusetts, one in England, and one in Germany. The U.S. server replicates with its British counterpart, which in turn updates with Germany. One system administrator says that this two-hop configuration was the best solution to the problems of connecting foreign phone systems.

So flexible is the Notes system that individual PC users who aren't on networks can still replicate applications with Notes servers or connect via modem to a remote Notes server and use applications resident on that server.

THE OVERWRITING PROBLEM

The way Notes runs on a network leaves room for some interesting interactions among users—and for some potential fistfights, if two users make simultaneous changes to the same document and one wipes out the work of the other.

Notes can't prevent users from simultaneously editing the same document, because the same data may exist in replicated files on servers and on users' PCs.

Two users may open the same document and edit it without either being aware of the other's actions. Even when User A saves her edited version, she is left blissfully unaware of User B's existence.

If both users are clients of the same server, User B will be warned when he tries to save his changes: "Another copy of this document was saved while you were editing it. Overwrite it?"

If User A and User B are clients of separate servers, User B won't even get a warning. User B's version will be replicated to other servers even while User A thinks the boss is seeing *her* work. This "last edit wins" rule isn't hard and fast, because Notes also checks to see which version of the document has been edited most often since the last replication and passes on that one instead of the most recent version. (The "last edit wins" rule may fail for another reason: Notes applies it based on the computers' system clocks. If the last edit was saved on a machine whose clock was an hour or a week slower than the other, it won't be treated as the last edit.)

Whether permitting concurrent access to data is a major problem for Notes depends on the application—and on corporate culture, because the best solutions are as much cultural as technical. The alternative, some kind of record-locking or more elaborate user notification, would impose performance-degrading overhead on the system, and even if it could be made to work, it would work for only one server.

MANY ROLES FOR NOTES

Notes' ability to exchange strictly limited amounts of information in a secure environment has vast implications for how the product may be used. For example, it holds the potential for sharing application data bases not just within a company but between companies. A single workgroup might even comprise people from several companies. Consultants can share dedicated applications with their clients.

Notes may also have a role as a smart publishing medium. Reuters is already delivering its newswire services via Notes, which can add value at each client location with filters and views that customize the information for each customer.

Will Notes succeed? We don't know. We do know that it's the first group-oriented application that has a chance to make good—it's the first to offer in software a useful reflection of practical business reality. And even if the product doesn't catch on, or if it has a painfully elongated takeoff curve, à la OS/2, it still represents the initial iteration of a form and style that will become common in the PC software of tomorrow.

By aiming high, Notes lifts everyone's sights to a more distant horizon.

QUESTIONS

1. Write a description of Lotus Notes for someone who is not familiar with it.
2. Describe how a Lotus Notes data base is created, updated, and shared by users.
3. Discuss the role of templates and forms in Lotus Notes.
4. What makes Lotus Notes a unique product?

Part 7

EXPERT SYSTEMS

Artificial Intelligence (AI) is concerned with having computers perform in an intelligent manner, where the standard for intelligence is human intelligence. This has been an area of interest to researchers since when computers were first introduced. The classic test for AI was provided by the noted, eccentric British mathematician Alan Turing. Turing's test calls for questions to be submitted by an interrogator to both a human and a computer. Based on the responses to the questions, if it is impossible for the interrogator to determine whether the computer or the human provided the response, AI has been realized. Obviously, Turing's test is very demanding. Only limited progress has been made in developing generalized computer programs that can respond to a range of questions.

AI is a broad field with many categories of applications. For example, robotics involves the use of machines that move and relate to objects as humans do. They are heavily used in repetitive production processes. Vision systems provide machines with the ability to "see" using a camera connected to a computer. Natural language processing focuses on having machines understand and respond to human commands. This is an area with tremendous potential, and while significant progress is being made, we are still far from being able to communicate with a computer using everyday speech. Yet another AI area is software agents, and they were described in Chapter 13.

This part of the book explores expert systems, which is an AI application area that focuses on decision support and is widely used in business organizations. An expert system is a computer application that contains the knowledge, experience, and judgment of skilled professionals. It suggests the decisions that experts make and often the reasoning behind them. Whereas many organizations once viewed expert systems as intriguing possibilities, many are now actively using them. The applications range from the simple to the complex. The four chapters in this part describe what expert systems are, how they are developed, organizational strategies for introducing expert systems, and several descriptions of expert systems.

Chapter 23 provides an introductory look at expert systems. It discusses what they are, their component parts and how they function, and a framework for understanding how expert systems fit into the information systems constellation of applications. It also describes their benefits, problems, risks, and other important issues.

Navigating ships in congested waters is becoming increasingly difficult. In response to this problem, an expert system was developed to assist maritime pilots. Chapter 24 discusses the navigation problem, the piloting expert system that was developed, and how it was evaluated using a simulation.

Organizations that want to develop expert systems should have a strategy for doing so. Different strategies can be successfully employed, as discussed in Chapter 25. The experiences of DuPont and Digital Equipment Corporation are used to illustrate how two companies took different approaches. Insights are provided for how a company can develop a strategy appropriate for it.

Bar code scanners generate millions of records of data of great potential value to marketing managers. The problem is making sense out of the data. Organizations are increasingly wanting to "mine" this data for valuable nuggets of information. Chapter 26 describes CoverStory, an expert system developed for Ocean Spray Cranberries that serves this purpose.

23

EXPERT SYSTEMS: THE NEXT CHALLENGE FOR MANAGERS

Winston defines artificial intelligence (AI) as "the study of ideas which enable computers to do the things that make people seem intelligent."[1] AI systems attempt to accomplish this by dealing with qualitative as well as quantitative information, ambiguous and "fuzzy" reasoning, and rules of thumb that give good but not always optimal solutions. Another way to characterize artificial intelligence is not in terms of what it attempts to do, but in terms of the programming techniques and philosophies that have evolved from it. Specific AI techniques such as "frames" and "rules" allow programmers to represent knowledge in ways that are often much more flexible and much more natural for humans to deal with than the algorithmic procedures used in traditional programming languages.

There are at least three areas in which AI, in its current state of development, appears to have promising near-term applications: robotics, natural language understanding, and expert systems. In this chapter, we will focus on the realistic potential for the use of expert systems in business. To emphasize our main point about appropriate ways of using these systems, we will exaggerate a distinction between expert systems, as they are often conceived, and a variation of expert systems, which we will call expert support systems.

This chapter is a reprint of Fred L. Luconi, Thomas W. Malone, and Michael S. Scott Morton, "Expert Systems: The Next Challenge for Managers," *Sloan Management Review,* Volume 27, Number 4, Summer 1986, pp. 3–14.

WHAT DO EXPERT SYSTEMS DO?

Preserve and Disseminate Scarce Expertise

Expert systems techniques can be used to preserve and disseminate scarce expertise by encoding the relevant experience of an expert and making this expertise available as a resource to the less experienced person. Schlumberger Corporation uses its Dipmeter Advisor to access the interpretive abilities of a handful of their most productive geological experts and to make it available to their field geologists all over the world.[2] The program takes oil well log data about the geological characteristics of a well and makes inferences about the probable location of oil in that region.

Solve Problems Thwarting Traditional Programs

Expert systems can also be used to solve problems that thwart traditional programming techniques. For example, an early expert system in practical use today is known as XCON. Developed at Digital Equipment Corporation in a joint effort with Carnegie-Mellon University, XCON uses some 3,300 rules and 5,500 product descriptions to configure the specific detailed components of VAX and other computer systems in response to the customers' overall orders. The system first determines what, if any, substitutions and additions have to be made to the order so that it is complete and consistent. It then produces a number of diagrams showing the electrical connections and room layout for the 50 to 150 components in a typical system.[3]

This application was attempted unsuccessfully several times using traditional programming techniques before the AI effort was initiated. The system has been in daily use now for over four years and the savings have been substantial, not only in terms of saving the technical editor time, but also in ensuring that no component is missing at installation time—an occurrence that delays the customer's acceptance of the system.[4]

WHAT ARE EXPERT SYSTEMS?

With these examples in mind, we define expert systems as *computer programs that use specialized symbolic reasoning to solve difficult problems well*. In other words, expert systems (1) use specialized knowledge about a particular problem area (such as geological analysis or computer configuration) rather than just general purpose knowledge that would apply to all problems, (2) use symbolic (and often qualitative) reasoning rather than just numerical calculations, and (3) perform at a level of competence that is better than that of nonexpert humans.

Expert systems can, of course, include extensive numerical calculations, but a computer program that uses *only* numerical techniques (such as a complex optimization program) would not ordinarily be called an "expert system." The kinds of nonnumerical symbolic knowledge that expert systems use include component/subcomponent relationships and qualitative rules about causal factors.

One of the most important ways in which expert systems differ from traditional computer applications is in their use of heuristic reasoning. Traditional applications employ algorithms, that is, precise rules that, when followed, lead to the correct conclusion. For example, the amount of a payroll check for an employee is calculated according to a precise set of rules. Expert systems, in contrast, often attack problems that are too complex to be solved perfectly; to do this, they use heuristic techniques that provide good but not necessarily optimum answers.

In some ways, of course, all computer programs are algorithms in that they provide a complete set of specifications for what the computer will do. Heuristic programs, however, usually search through alternatives using "rules of thumb" rather than guaranteed solution techniques. A program might consider many different types of geological formations before deciding which type best explains the data observed in a particular case.

WHAT ARE EXPERT SUPPORT SYSTEMS?

While expert support systems and expert systems use the same techniques, expert support systems help *people* (the emphasis is on people) solve a much wider class of problems. In other words, *expert support systems are computer programs that use specialized symbolic reasoning to help people solve difficult problems well.* This is done by pairing the human with the expert system in such a way that the expert system provides some of the knowledge and reasoning steps, while the human provides overall problem-solving direction as well as specific knowledge not incorporated in the system. Some of this knowledge can be thought of beforehand and made explicit when it is encoded in the expert system. However, much of the knowledge may be imprecise and will remain below the level of consciousness, to be recalled to the conscious level of the decision maker only when it is triggered by the evolving problem context.

COMPONENTS OF EXPERT SYSTEMS

To understand how expert systems (and expert support systems) are different from traditional computer applications, it is important to understand the components of a typical expert system (see Figure 23–1). In addition to the *user interface,* which allows the system to communicate with a human user, a typical expert system also has (1) a *knowledge base* of facts and rules related to the problem and (2) a set of reasoning methods—an *"inference engine"*—that interacts with the information in the knowledge base to solve the problem. As these two

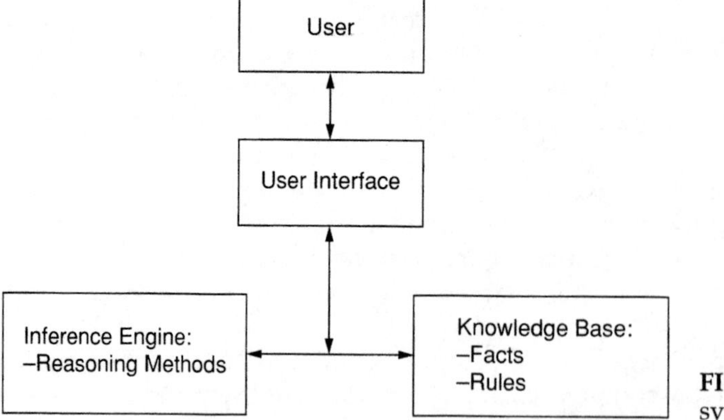

FIGURE 23–1 Expert systems Architecture

components are separate, it makes it much easier to change the system as the problem changes or becomes better understood. New rules can be added to the knowledge base in such a way that all the old facts and reasoning methods can still be used. Figure 23–1 shows in detail the elements of the expert systems architecture.

Knowledge Base

To flexibly use specialized knowledge for many different kinds of problems, AI researchers have developed a number of new "knowledge representation" techniques. Using these techniques to provide structure for a body of knowledge is still very much an art and is practiced by an emerging group of professionals sometimes called "knowledge engineers." Knowledge engineers in this field are akin to the systems analysts of data-processing (DP) applications. They work with the "experts" and draw out the relevant expertise in a form that can be encoded in a computer program. Three of the most important techniques for encoding this knowledge are (1) production rules, (2) semantic networks, and (3) frames.

Production Rules. Production rules are particularly useful in building systems based on heuristic methods.[5] These are simple "if-then" rules that are often used to represent the empirical consequences of a given condition or the action that should be taken in a given situation. For example, a medical diagnosis system might have a rule like:

If: (1) The patient has a fever, and
(2) The patient has a runny nose,
Then: It is very likely (.9) that the patient has a cold.

A computer configuration system might have a rule like:

If: (1) There is an unassigned single port disk drive, and
(2) There is a free controller,
Then: Assign the disk drive to the controller port.

Semantic Networks. Another formalism that is often more convenient than production rules for representing certain kinds of relational knowledge is called semantic networks or "semantic nets." To apply the rule about assigning disk drives, for example, a system would need to know what part numbers correspond to single port disk drives, controllers, and so forth. Figure 23–2 shows how this knowledge might be represented in a network of "nodes" connected by "links" that signify which classes of components are subsets of other classes.

Frames. In many cases, it is convenient to gather into one place a number of different kinds of information about an object. Figure 23–3 shows how several dimensions (such as length, width, and power requirements) that describe electrical components might be represented as different "slots" in a "frame" about electrical components. Unlike traditional records in a data base, frames often contain additional features such as "default values" and "attached procedures." For instance, if the default value for voltage requirement of an electrical component is 110 volts, then the system would infer that a new electrical component required 110 volts unless explicit information to the contrary was provided. An attached procedure might automatically update the "volume" slot, whenever "length," "height," or "width" is changed (see Figure 23–3).

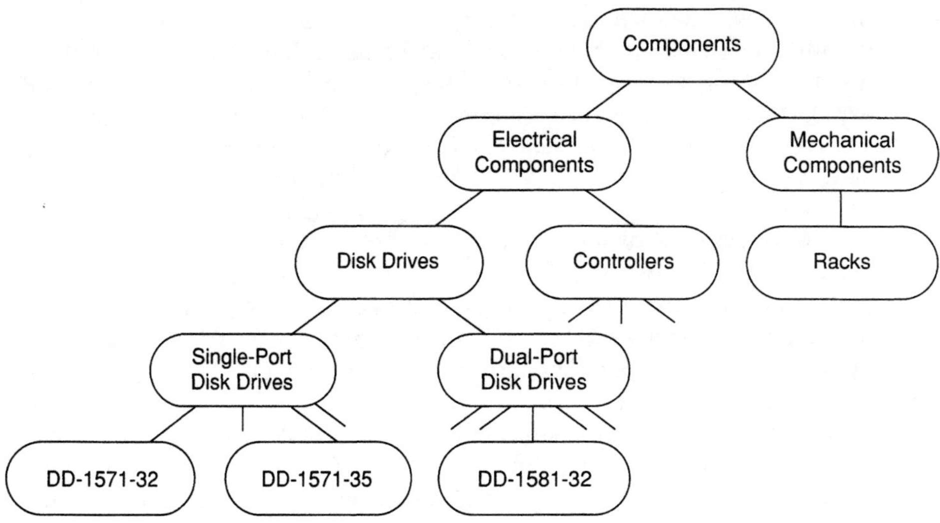

FIGURE 23–2 Semantic Network

Electrical Component	
Part No.	
Length	
Width	
Height	
Volume	
Voltage	

FIGURE 23–3 Frame

These three knowledge representation techniques—production rules, semantic networks, and frames—have considerable power in that they permit us to capture knowledge in a way that can be exploited by the "inference engine" to produce good, workable answers to the questions at hand.

INFERENCE ENGINE

The inference engine contains the reasoning methods that might be used by human problem solvers for attacking problems. As these are separate from the knowledge base, either the inference engine or the knowledge base can be changed relatively independently of the other. Two reasoning methods often employed with production rules are *forward chaining* and *backward chaining*.

Forward Chaining. Imagine that we have a set of production rules like those shown in Figure 23–4 for a personal financial planning expert system. Imagine also that we know the current client's tax bracket is 50 percent, his liquidity is greater than $100,000, and he has a high tolerance for risk. By forward chaining through the rules, one at a time, the system could infer that exploratory oil and gas investments should be recommended for this client. With a larger rule base, many other investment recommendations might be deduced as well.

Backward Chaining. Now imagine that we want to know only whether exploratory oil and gas investments are appropriate for a particular client, and we are not interested in any other investments at the moment. The system can use exactly the same rule base to answer this specific question more efficiently by backward chaining through the rules (see Figure 23–4). With backward chaining, the system starts with a goal (e.g., "show that this client needs exploratory oil and gas investments") and asks at each stage what subgoals it would need to reach to achieve this goal. Here, to conclude that the client needs exploratory oil and gas investments, we can use the third rule (indicated in Figure 23–4) if we know that risk tolerance is high (which we already do know) and that a tax shelter is indicated. To conclude that a tax shelter is rec-

Forward Chaining

If: Tax bracket = 50%
and liquidity is greater than $100,000

Then: A tax shelter is indicated.

If: A tax shelter is indicated
and risk tolerance is low

Then: Recommend developmental oil
and gas investments.

If: A tax shelter is indicated
and risk tolerance is high

Then: Recommend exploratory oil
and gas investments.

Backward Chaining (Subgoaling)

What about exploratory oil and gas?

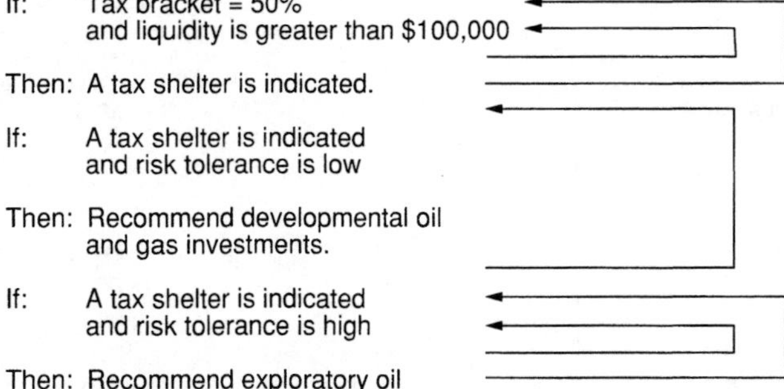

FIGURE 23–4 Inference Engine

ommended, we have to find another rule (in this case, the first one) and then check whether its conditions are satisfied. In this case, they are, so our goal is achieved: we know we can recommend exploratory oil and gas investments to the client.

Keeping these basic concepts in mind, we now turn to a framework that puts expert systems and expert support systems into a management context.

THE FRAMEWORK FOR EXPERT SUPPORT SYSTEMS

The framework developed in this section begins to allow us to identify those classes of business problems that are appropriate for data processing, decision support systems, expert systems, and expert support systems. In addition, we can clarify the relative contributions of humans and computers in the various classes of applications.

This framework extends the earlier work of Gorry and Scott Morton [6] in which they relate Herbert Simon's seminal work on structured vs. unstructured decision making [7] to Robert Anthony's strategic planning, management control, and operational control.[8] Figure 23–5 presents Gorry and Scott Morton's framework. They argued that to improve the quality of decisions, the manager must seek not only to match the type and quality of information and its presentation to the category of decision, but he or she must also choose a system that reflects the degree of the problem's structure.

In light of the insights garnered from the field of artificial intelligence, Figure 23–6 shows how we can expand and rethink the structured/unstructured dimension of the original framework. Simon separated decision making into three phases: intelligence, design, and choice.[9] A structured decision is one

	Operational Control	Management Control	Strategic Planning
Structured	Accounts Receivable	Budget Analysis – Engineered Costs	Tanker Fleet Mix
	Order Entry	Short–term Forecasting	Warehouse and Factory Location
	Inventory Control		
Semistructured	Production Scheduling	Variance Analysis – Overall Budget	Mergers & Acquisitions
	Cash Management	Budget Preparation	New Product Planning
Unstructured	PERT/COST Systems	Sales and Production	R&D Planning

FIGURE 23–5 The Original Information Systems Framework. Reprinted from G. A. Gorry and M. S. Scott Morton, "A Framework for Management Information Systems," *Sloan Management Review,* Fall 1971, p. 62.

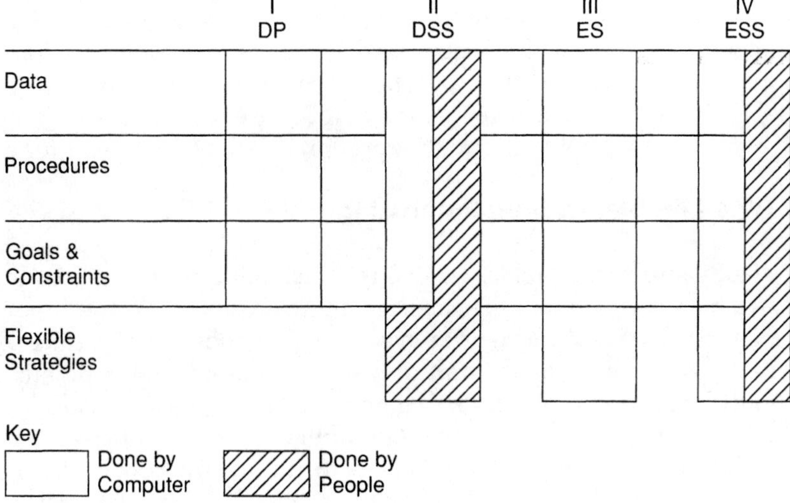

FIGURE 23–6 Problem Types

where all three phases are fully understood and "computable" by the human decision maker. As a result, the decision is programmable. In an unstructured decision, one or more of these phases are not fully understood.

For business purposes, we can extend this distinction by taking Alan Newell's insightful categorization of problem solving, which consists of goals and constraints, state space, search control knowledge, and operators.[10] We relabel and regroup these problem characteristics into four categories (see Figure 23–6):

1. *Data:* the dimensions and values necessary to represent the state of the world that is relevant to the problem (i.e., the "state space");
2. *Procedures:* the sequence of steps (or "operators") used in solving the problem;
3. *Goals and Constraints:* the desired results of problem solving and the constraints on what can and cannot be done; and
4. *Strategies:* the flexible strategies used to decide which procedures to apply to achieve goals (i.e., the "search control knowledge").

For some structured problems, we can apply a standard procedure (i.e., an algorithm or formula) and proceed directly to a conclusion with no need for flexible problem-solving strategies. For example, we can use standard procedures to compute withholding taxes and prepare employee paychecks, and we can use the classical formula for "economic order quantity" to solve straightforward inventory control problems.

In other less structured problems, no straightforward solution techniques are known. Here, solutions can often be found only by trial and error, that is, by trying a number of possibilities until an acceptable one is found. For instance, for a manager to determine which of three sales strategies to use for a new product, he or she might want to explore the probable consequences of each for advertising expenses, sales force utilization, revenue, and so forth. We will discuss the range of these different types of problems and the appropriate kinds of systems for each.

Type I Problems: Data Processing

A fully structured problem is one in which all four elements of the problem are structured: We have well-stated goals, we can specify the input data needed, there are standard procedures by which a solution may be calculated, and there is no need for complex strategies for generating and evaluating alternatives. Fully structured problems are computable and one can decide if such computation is justifiable given the amount of time and computing resources involved.

Such problems are well suited to the use of conventional programming techniques in that virtually everything about the problem is well defined. In effect, the expert (i.e., the analyst/programmer) has already solved the problem. He or she must only sequence the data through the particular program. Figure 23–6 represents pictorially the class of decision problems that can be solved economically using conventional programming techniques. This class is referred to as Type I Problems—that is, problems historically thought to be suited for data processing.

It is interesting to note that the economics of conventional programming are being fundamentally altered with the provision of new tools such as an "analyst's workbench."[11] These tools include professional workstations used by the systems analyst first to develop flow chart representations of the problem and then to move automatically to testable running code. The more advanced stations use AI techniques, thereby turning these new techniques into tools to make old approaches more effective in classical DP application areas.

Type II Problems: Decision Support Systems

As we move away from problems that are fully structured, we begin to deal with many of the more complicated problems organizations have to grapple with each day. These are cases where standard procedures are helpful but not sufficient by themselves, where the data may be incompletely represented, and where the goals and constraints are only partially understood. Traditional data-processing systems do not solve these problems. Fortunately, in these cases, the computer can perform the well-understood parts of the problem solving, while, at the same time, humans use their goals, intuition, and general knowledge to formulate problems, modify and control the problem solving, and interpret the results. As Figure 23–6 shows, human users may provide or modify data, procedures, or goals, and they may use their knowledge of all these factors to decide on problem-solving strategies.

In many of the best-known decision support systems,[12] the computer applies standard procedures to certain highly structured data but relies on human users to decide which procedures are appropriate in a given situation and whether a given result is satisfactory. Investment managers, for instance, who used the portfolio management system (PMS)[13] did not rely on the computer for either making final decisions about portfolio composition or deciding on which procedures to use for analysis: they used the computer to execute the procedures they felt were appropriate, say for calculating portfolio diversity and expected returns. In the end, the managers themselves proposed alternative portfolios and decided whether a given diversification or return was acceptable. Many people who use spreadsheet programs today for "what-if" analyses follow a similar flexible strategy of proposing an action, letting the computer predict its consequences, and then deciding what action to propose next.

Type III Problems: Expert Systems

We call the problems where essentially all the relevant knowledge for flexible problem solving can be encoded Type III Problems: the systems that solve them are expert systems. Using AI programming techniques like production rules and frames, expert systems are able to encode some of the same kinds of goals, heuristics, and strategies that people use in solving problems but that have previously been very difficult to use in computer programs. These techniques make it possible to design systems that don't just follow standard procedures, but instead use flexible problem-solving strategies to explore a number of possible alternatives before picking a solution. A medical diagnosis program, for example, may consider many different possible diseases and disease combinations before finding one that adequately explains the observed symptoms.

For some cases, like the XCON system, these techniques can capture almost all of the relevant knowledge about the problem. As of 1983, less than 1 out of every 1,000 orders configured by XCON was misconfigured because of missing or incorrect rules. (Only about 10 percent of the orders had to be corrected for any reason at all and almost all of these errors were due to missing descriptions of rarely used parts.)[14]

It is instructive to note, however, that even with XCON, which is probably the most extensively tested system in commercial use today, new knowledge is continually being added and human editors still check every order the system configures. As the developers of XCON remark: "There is no more reason to believe now than there was [in 1979] that [XCON] has all the knowledge relevant to its configuration task. This, coupled with the fact that [XCON] deals with an ever-changing domain, implies its development will never be finished."[15]

If XCON, which operates in the fairly restricted domain of computer order configuration, never contained all the knowledge relevant to its problem, it appears much less likely that we will ever be able to codify all the knowledge needed for less clearly bounded problems like financial analysis, strategic planning, and project management.

In all of these cases, there is a vast amount of knowledge that is *potentially* relevant to the problem solution: the financial desirability of introducing a proposed new product may depend on the likelihood and nature of a competitor's response; the success of a strategic plan may depend as much on the predispositions of the chief executive as it does on the financial merit of the plan; and the best assignment of people to tasks in a project may depend on very subtle evaluations of people's competence and motivation. While it is often possible to formalize and represent any *specific* set of these factors, there is an unbounded number of such factors that may, in some circumstances, become important. Even in what might appear to be a fairly bounded case of job-shop scheduling, often there are many continually changing and possibly implicit constraints on what people, machines, and parts are needed and available for different steps in a manufacturing process.[16] What this suggests is that for many of the problems of practical importance in business, we should focus our attention on designing systems that *support* expert users rather than on replacing them.

Type IV: Expert Support Systems

Even where important kinds of problem-solving knowledge cannot feasibly be encoded, it is still possible to use expert systems techniques. (This dramatically extends the capabilities of computers beyond previous technologies such as DP and DSS.) What is important, in these cases, is to design expert support systems with very good and deeply embedded "user interfaces" that enable their human users to easily inspect and control the problem-solving process (see Figure 23–6). In other words, a good expert support system should be both *accessible* and *malleable.* Many expert support systems make their problem solving accessible to users by providing explanation capabilities. For example, the MYCIN medical diagnosis program can explain to a doctor at any time why it is asking for a given piece of information or what rules it used to arrive at a given conclusion. For a system to be malleable, users should be able to easily change data, procedures, goals, or strategies at any important point in the problem-solving process. Systems with this capability are still rare, but an early version of the Dipmeter Advisor suggests how they may be developed.[17] The Advisor is unable by itself to automatically detect certain kinds of complex geological patterns. Instead it graphically displays the basic data and lets human experts detect the patterns themselves. The human experts then indicate the results of their analysis, and the system proceeds using this information.

An even more vivid example of how a system can be made accessible and malleable is provided by the Steamer Program, which teaches people how to reason in order to operate a steam plant.[18] This system has colorful graphic displays of the schematic flows in the simulated plant, the status of different valves and gauges, and the pressures in different places. Users of the system can manipulate these displays (using a "mouse" pointing device) to control the valves, temperatures, and so forth. The system continually updates its simulation results and expert diagnostics based on these user actions.

SUMMARY OF FRAMEWORK

This framework helps clarify a number of issues. First, it highlights, as did the original Gorry and Scott Morton framework, the importance of matching system type to problem type. The primary practical points made in the original framework were that traditional DP technologies should not be used for semistructured and unstructured problems where new DSS technologies were more appropriate; and secondly that interactive human/computer use opened up an extended class of problems where computers could be exploited. Again, the most important practical point to be made is twofold: first, "pure" expert systems should not be used for partially understood problems where expert support systems are more appropriate; and second, expert systems techniques can be used to dramatically extend the capabilities of traditional decision support systems.

Figure 23–7 shows, in an admittedly simplified way, how we can view expert support systems as the next logical step in each of two somewhat separate progressions. On the left side of the figure, we see that DSS developed out of a practical recognition of the limits of DP for helping real human beings solve complex problems in actual organizations. The right side of the figure reflects a largely independent evolution that took place in computer science research laboratories. This evolution grew out of a recognition of the limits of traditional computer science techniques for solving the kinds of complex problems that people

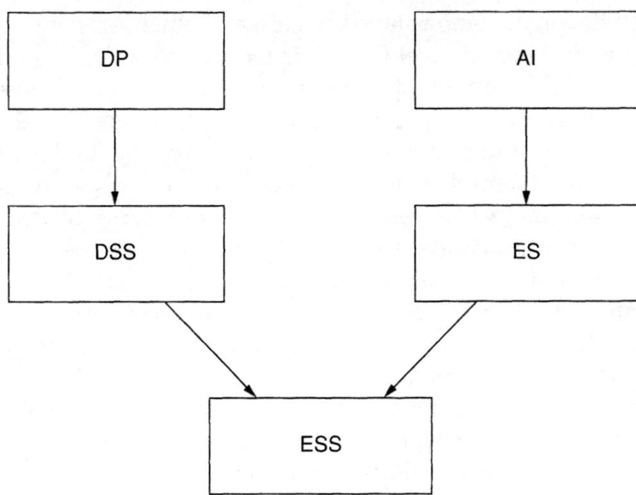

FIGURE 23–7 Progressions in Computer System Development

are able to solve. We are now at the point where these two separate progressions can be united to help solve a broad range of important practical problems.

THE BENEFITS OF ESS TO MANAGERS

The real importance of ESS lies in the ability of these systems to harness and make full use of our scarcest resource: the talent and experience of key members of the organization. There are considerable benefits in capturing the expert's experience and making it available to those in an organization who are less knowledgeable about the subject in question. As organizations and their problems become more complex, management can benefit from initiating prototypes ES and ESS. However, the questions now facing managers are when and how to start.

When to Start

The "when" to start is relatively easy to answer. It is "now" for exploratory work. For some organizations, this will be a program of education and active monitoring of the field. For others, the initial investment may take the form of an experimental low-budget prototype. For a few, once the exploration is over, it will make good economic sense to go forward with a full-fledged working prototype. Conceptual and technological developments have made it possible to begin an active prototype development phase.

Where to Start

The second question is "where" to start. A possible beginning may be to explore those areas in which the organization stands to gain a distinct competitive advantage. Schlumberger would seem to feel that their ES used as a drilling advisor is one such example. Digital Equipment Corporation's use of an expert system for "equipment configuration control" is another example. It is interesting that of the more than twenty organizations that we know are investing in ES and ESS, almost none would allow themselves to be quoted. The reasons given basically boil down to the fact that they are experimenting with prototypes that they think will give them a competitive advantage in making or delivering their product or service. Examples of where we can quote without attribution are cases in which an ESS is used to support the cross selling of financial services products (e.g., an insurance salesman selling a tax shelter), or to evaluate the credit worthiness of a loan applicant in a financial services organization.

It is clear that there are a great many problem areas where even our somewhat primitive ability to deal with expert systems can permit the building of useful first generation systems. The development of expert support systems makes the situation even brighter: by helping the beleaguered "expert," the organization will get the desired leverage in the marketplace.

PROBLEMS, RISKS, AND ISSUES

It would be irresponsible of us to conclude without acknowledging that expert systems and expert support systems are in their infancy, and researchers and users alike must be realistic about their capabilities. Already there is an apparent risk that an expert system will be poorly defined and oversold: the resulting backlash may hinder progress.

There is also a danger of proceeding too quickly and too recklessly, without paying careful attention to what we are doing: We may very well embed our knowledge (necessarily incomplete at any moment in time) into a system that is only effective when used by the person who created it. If this system is used by others, there is a risk of misapplication: holes in another user's knowledge could represent a pivotal element in the logic leading to a solution. While these holes are implicitly recognized by the creator of the knowledge base, they may be quite invisible to a new user.

The challenge of proceeding at an appropriate pace can be met if managers treat artificial intelligence, expert systems, expert support systems, and decision support systems as a serious topic, one that requires management attention if it is to be exploited properly. To this end, managers must recognize the differences between Types I and II problems, for which the older techniques are appropriate, and the new methods available for Types III and IV.

CONCLUSION

Although there are some basic risks and constraints that will be with us for some time, the potential of AI techniques is obvious. If we proceed cautiously, acknowledging the problems as we go along, we can begin to achieve worthwhile results.

The illustrations used here are merely a few applications that have been built in a relatively brief period of time with primitive tools. Business has attempted to develop expert systems applications since 1980 and, despite the enormity of some of the problems, has succeeded in developing a number of simple and powerful prototypes.

The state of the art is such that everyone building an expert system must endure this primitive start-up phase to learn what is involved in this fascinating new field. We expect that it will take until about 1990 for ES and ESS to be fully recognized as having achieved worthwhile business results.

However, expert systems and expert support systems are with us now, albeit in a primitive form. The challenge for managers is to harness these tools to increase the effectiveness of the organization and thus add value for its stakeholders. Pioneering firms are leading the way, and once a section of territory has been staked out, the experience gained by these leaders will be hard to equal for those who start later.

QUESTIONS

1. How do expert systems differ from other types of computer applications?
2. What are the component parts of an expert system? Briefly discuss each component.
3. Do expert systems *replace* humans in the decision-making process or *support* humans in decision making? Discuss.
4. What are some of the potential benefits of expert systems to managers?

REFERENCES

1. WINSTON, P. H. *Artificial Intelligence,* 2d ed. (Reading, MA: Addison-Wesley, 1984), p. 1.
2. R. DAVIS ET AL. "The Dipmeter Advisor: Interpretation of Geological Signals," *Proceedings of the 7th International Joint Conference on Artificial Intelligence* (Vancouver: 1981), pp. 846–849.
3. J. BACHANT and J. MCDERMOTT. "RI Revisited: Four Years in the Trenches," *AI Magazine,* Fall 1984, pp. 21–32.
4. J. MCDERMOTT. "RI: A Rule-based Configurer of Computer Systems," *Artificial Intelligence,* 19 (1982).
5. WINSTON (1984).
6. G. A. GORRY and M. S. SCOTT MORTON. "A Framework for Management Information Systems," *Sloan Management Review,* Fall 1971, pp. 55–70.
7. H. A. SIMON. *The New Science of Management Decision* (New York: Harper & Row, 1960).
8. R. N. ANTHONY. "Planning and Control Systems: A Framework for Analysis" (Boston: Harvard University Graduate School of Business Administration, 1965).
9. SIMON (1960).
10. A. NEWELL. "Reasoning: Problem Solving and Decision Processes: The Problem Space as a Fundamental Category," in *Attention and Performance VIII,* ed. R. Nickerson (Hillsdale, NJ: Erlbaum, 1980).
11. B. SHEIL. "Power Tools for Programmers," *Datamation,* February 1983, pp. 131–144.
12. P. G. W. KEEN and M. S. SCOTT MORTON. *Decision Support Systems: An Organizational Perspective* (Reading, MA: Addison-Wesley, 1978).

13. Ibid.
14. BACHANT and MCDERMOTT (Fall 1984).
15. Ibid, p. 27.
16. M. S. FOX. "Constraint-Directed Search: A Case Study of Job-Shop Scheduling" (Pittsburgh: Carnegie-Mellon University Robotics Institute, Technical Report No. CMU-RI-TR-83-22, 1983).
17. DAVIS (1981).
18. J. D. HOLLAN, E. L. HUTCHINS, and L. WEITZMAN. "Steamer: An Interactive, Inspectable Simulation-based Training System," *AI Magazine*, Summer, 1984, pp. 15–28.

24

AN EXPERT SYSTEM FOR MARITIME PILOTS

THE PROBLEM

A considerable change in the size and structure of marine traffic has taken place in the maritime world of the last two decades. From 1960 to 1980, the number of tankers has doubled, and their tonnage has increased sevenfold (Kwik 1986). New types of ships have evolved, such as fast container ships, as have medium-speed vessels for the carriage of dangerous cargo, such as gas and chemical carriers. In addition, numerous structures for oil and gas production have been erected in inland waters, which complicates marine traffic flow. These changes make the pilot's and ship's officers' task of navigating vessels in congested waters considerably more complicated.

Shipboard crew reductions have also occurred over the same period, making work that was previously the task of 33–39 crew members now the responsibility of 14–18 crew members (Grove 1989). These smaller shipboard complements are responsible for an increasing number of tasks; the traditional tasks of navigation, cargo loading and discharge, and propulsion plant maintenance are now coupled with vessel management, voyage planning and provisioning, outfitting, and logistics tasks. These changes reflect the trend for ship's officers to become shipboard managers, performing an increasing number of tasks in shorter time periods (National Academy of Sciences 1990).

This chapter is a reprint of Martha Grabowski and William A. Wallace, "An Expert System for Maritime Pilots: Its Design and Assessment Using Gaming," *Management Science*, Volume 39, Number 12, December 1993, pp. 1506-1520.

These organizational changes have been accomplished in shipboard environments which are traditionally stressful workplaces. Personnel are exposed to noise and vibration, excessive heat, fatigue, and disruption of normal sleeping and waking cycles. They stand lengthy cargo watches followed by stressful navigational bridge watches, often with little opportunity for rest. Consequently, stress and fatigue are important components of the maritime work environment (National Academy of Sciences 1990). The result is a vigilance decrement. In one study (Schmidtke 1966, cited in Parasuraman 1987), experienced radar operators were studied as they stood watch, alone and in pairs, and monitored a simulated maritime navigation and collision avoidance system. Operators were increasingly slow to detect critical targets on collision paths over a four-hour watch period. Response times had slowed to such a point that had ships been on a collision course, there would not have been sufficient time for the operators to take preventive action (Parasuraman 1987).

In addition, officers on ship's bridges are more effective at monitoring radars early in a watch than later (Parasuraman 1987). Even in well-rested, healthy laboratory subjects, the tendency of monitoring efficiency to decrease with time is well attested; fatigue and other sources of stress can amplify it. The vigilance decrement is especially critical during bridge watches, when even a few moments of inattention can result in a casualty.

DECISION SUPPORT FOR SMALLER BRIDGE WATCH TEAMS

Most vessels navigate with three people on or about the bridge: the watch officer, the helmsman, and a lookout. Some shipping companies have eliminated the lookout in normal navigational circumstances, with good visibility (Froese 1989). At night or in conditions of poor visibility, a lookout is added to the team.

Integrated bridge systems are being developed by a number of nations—the United States, Norway, West Germany, Japan, and the United Kingdom (Grove 1989). These integrated systems project the wheelhouse as the operational center for navigational and supervisory tasks aboard the ship. These bridges in many cases become "ships' operations centers," incorporating controls and monitors for all essential vessel functions—navigation, engine control, and communications. Many routine navigational tasks, such as chart updating, position plotting, and steering may be automated. The integrated ship's bridge is modeled as a unified federation of subsystems supporting vessel navigation, communications, steering, administration, collision avoidance, safety, and ship's systems monitoring and control functions.

Single-handed bridges—those on which the watch officer serves also as a helmsman and a lookout—are also being introduced by some non-U.S. flag shipping operators, and the certificating authorities of some nations have permitted some vessels to operate in this manner, provided they have some automated equipment (Vail 1988). Many other vessels operate in this way without permission, even in restricted waters (Beetham 1989). In most cases where integrated and single-handed bridges are introduced, bridge equipment is automated and decision aids are added (Schuffel et al. 1989, Kristiansen et al. 1989, Grabowski 1989). However, decision aids which have been developed within the context of these systems have often been standalone systems, not integrated with existing bridge designs. The system described in this chapter is one example of such a standalone system. Some empirical research shows that officers serving single-handed watches aboard such "Ship of the Future" bridges were significantly better at maintaining the vessels' course than traditional watches aboard conventional bridges (Schuffel et al. 1989, Kristiansen et al. 1989). These improvements were attributed to attentive ergonomic design and the provision of robust decision aids. They were also reported to have been accomplished with no accompanying information overload.

Introduction of bridge automation can be effective in combatting shipboard stress and fatigue, by removing the noncritical monitoring task from the human decision maker. However, integrated bridge systems may be distracting enough to degrade performance on the most critical task: keeping the vessel on course while avoiding collision. Thoughtful introduction of bridge technology can work to alleviate stress and fatigue on watch by embedding simulation and functional team training capabilities in automated systems, so as to provide nondistracting, stimulating exercises (National Academy of Sciences 1990).

We have been reminded recently of how these factors—smaller shipboard crews working long hours in stressful conditions, a highly automated ship being piloted by an inexperienced officer—can combine and result in disastrous consequences. On March 24, 1989, the tanker *Exxon Valdez* collided with Bligh Reef, outbound from Valdez, Alaska. As a result of the collision, the *Valdez's* oil tanks were breached and oil spilled into Prince William Sound, eventually oiling more than 350 miles of coast. This maritime casualty and oil spill renewed interest in on-board decision support for pilots and officers on watch, as the government and industry investigated ways of improving decision making and shipboard organizational structures (Harrald et al. 1990).

Previous research focused on the design and evaluation of maritime decision aids which provided support for the perceptual and motor activities involved in controlling a vessel. Typically, these aids used enhanced graphics and visual representations of actual and expected ship's position, in addition to steering assistance. These decision aids provided good support for the lower-level cognitive skills of piloting—trackkeeping and maneuvering—but provided little help in supporting the higher-level cognitive tasks which are an important component of good piloting and navigation, specifically collision avoidance and qualitative ship management skills known collectively as the "practice of good seamanship."

The present research complements the previous work by developing and evaluating a decision aid for the cognitive skills of piloting: maneuvering and collision avoidance, and the practice of good seamanship. The system provides decision support to (1) senior ship's pilots training junior pilots, as it provides an efficient means of distributing piloting heuristics; (2) ship's masters training junior deck officers in the essentials of good piloting and shiphandling; and (3) watchstanding deck officers utilizing the system's on-line reminder and assist capabilities, or off-line simulation and contingency planning capability.

This chapter describes (1) the design of a decision aid that employs expert systems technology to assist ship's masters, mates on watch, and pilots navigating in close waters, and (2) an assessment, using gaming, of the decision support value of the aid.

THE ART AND SCIENCE OF PILOTING

On the high seas, where there is no immediate danger of grounding, navigation is comparatively leisurely. Courses and speeds are maintained over relatively long periods and fixes (determinations of ship's position) are obtained at convenient intervals. Under favorable conditions, a vessel might continue for several days using positions determined by dead reckoning (by estimate) as errors in position can usually be detected and corrected before danger threatens.

In the vicinity of shoal water, however, the situation is different. Frequent or continuous positional information is usually essential to the safety of the vessel. An error, which at sea may be considered small, may in pilot waters be intolerably large. The proximity of other vessels increases the possibility of collision. Navigation under these conditions is called piloting.

In piloting, positions are commonly obtained by reference to nearby landmarks or to the harbor bottom. Pilots also use range and bearing techniques, electronic navigational aids, and radar navigation to fix the vessel's position during the harbor transit. Because the time element is often of vital importance in piloting, adequate preparation for navigating in close waters is essential. Long-term preparation includes the acquisition of a thorough knowledge of the methods and techniques of piloting, most often through an oral tradition which is handed down from one generation of pilots to the next. The more immediate preparation includes a study of the charts and publications of the area to familiarize oneself with the channels, shoals, tides, currents, and aids to navigation of the area.

Piloting is largely a visually dependent activity involving a continuous series of actions and reactions to the transit situation. Most of the essential navigational tasks are performed by the pilot's use of visual sightings of navigational aids and prominent landmarks. Vessel control, or track-keeping actions, are taken to maintain a known course or to move the vessel from its present position to a desired position. In order to process this visually acquired data, a pilot needs knowledge, i.e., cognitive representations which are used to interpret data. Three types of knowledge are necessary in piloting: local knowledge, transit-specific knowledge, and knowledge of shiphandling (Huffner 1978).

Local knowledge provides the port and harbor context that permits the pilot to maintain his orientation in the harbor, to accurately fix the vessel's position and track, and to understand and anticipate the dynamic characteristics of the environment.

Transit-specific information is acquired before and during a particular transit. It includes processing data on the environment (wind, weather, current, tide, drift), the harbor, the ship (ability to respond to orders, communications, propulsion, navigation and communications suite on board, steering system), and their interactions under the conditions of a specific transit.

Pilots acquire their *shiphandling knowledge* primarily through observing and performing during their apprenticeship transits. Shiphandling is the essence of piloting, but is not the totality of piloting. For instance, a ship's captain has a great deal of experience in shiphandling, but cannot pilot his own ship in a port without acquiring the local knowledge and transit-specific knowledge that comprises the other essential element of piloting (Farnsworth and Young 1983). The accuracy of a pilot's local knowledge and the transit-specific data he processes are determinants of the quality of his piloting (Huffner 1978). Errors from these sources can contribute to undesirable piloting performance that is often confusingly labeled as "shiphandling error."

A pilot, therefore, accesses data and uses local, transit-specific, and shiphandling knowledge in order to gain the information needed to perform the three piloting tasks: trackkeeping; maneuvering and collision avoidance; and adherence to procedures and good practice developed over the years, referred to as the "practice of good seamanship." Each of these activities requires different human information processing skills to be done well.

Trackkeeping, the process of determining the actual ship's position compared to an intended track, requires perceptual and motor skills to fix and follow a ship's position through the harbor. *Maneuvering and collision avoidance* estimates the present and projected positions of harbor traffic, and, in compliance with the International and Inland Rules of the Road, sets the course or track of the vessel. Maneuvering and collision avoidance require both perceptual and motor skills, and cognitive abilities to apply the Rules of the Road in the context of the particular harbor. The *practice of good seamanship* involves compliance with proper procedures, determination of how to proceed in usual circumstances, and management of the watch team—those responsible for the navigation of the vessel.

These tasks form a hierarchy (Figure 24–1), with the need for cognitive skills increasing as one proceeds from trackkeeping to good seamanship, while the requirement for perceptual and motor skills decreases.

Adherence to procedures of good seamanship is the most cognitively complex task, since one needs the cognitive ability to make decisions in both usual and unusual situations (reduced visibility, exceptional weather, and other potentially disastrous conditions). This decision making is congruent with the "ordinary practice of seamen" (Farnsworth and Young 1983). However, little training

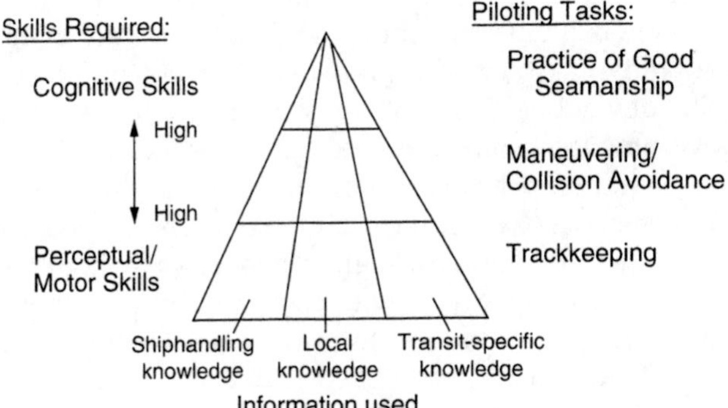

FIGURE 24–1 Ship's Piloting Requirements

in developing good piloting practice is provided, other than piloting organizations' apprenticeship programs and some ship simulator exercises.

DECISION SUPPORT FOR PILOTING

Ship's masters, mates, and pilots navigating in congested waters are inundated with data from a variety of sources, and are required to make crucial piloting decisions in real time (MTRB 1976). These decisions take place in a stressful maritime environment, often after lengthy cargo watches, and are increasingly made by smaller bridge watch teams. These conditions frequently cause information overload, which results from a pilot's inability to interpret large amounts of data rapidly. The result is the inability to match the data with the appropriate knowledge in time to provide the information needed to perform a piloting task.

Shortcomings of the human memory have been postulated as the cause of information overload (Simon 1981). In the model human processor (Card et al. 1983), the perceptual, motor, and cognitive systems each have their own processor and associated memories. The perceptual system takes sensory data from the environment and creates visual and audio image stores based on the data acquired. The perceptual system holds the output of the sensory system while the data are being symbolically coded. The cognitive system receives the symbolically coded data from the sensory image stores in working memory and also uses previously stored knowledge in long-term memory to make decisions about how to respond. The motor system carries out the desired response, based on input provided by the cognitive system.

In a simple transit scenario, the pilot takes data from the environment (ranges, bearings, distances from objects, lines of position) as he arrives on the bridge and begins the transit. If we interpret his internal processing in the language of the model, this data is stored in his perceptual processor and memory.

Lines of position, deviations from the channel centerline, and trackkeeping information are held in the sensory system's buffer memory while the data are symbolically coded. The pilot's cognitive system takes knowledge from long-term memory—past experience with deviations from the present track, procedures from the Rules of the Road governing the conduct of vessels, courses to steer and closest points of approach, and "good seamanship" recommendations—and sensory images stored in working memory. The resulting information is used to make decisions about how to conduct the vessel through the waterway—courses to steer, how to align the vessel in the waterway, how to compensate for current set and drift. The pilot's motor system affects the results of the decisions made as the commands, e.g., "Five left," "Steady on 160," and "Left to 272," are vocalized.

Previous work in piloting decision support systems focused on supporting the pilot's perceptual and motor systems by providing autopilots which automated trackkeeping (Veldhuyzen and Stassen 1977, Van Amerongen et al. 1978). Early autopilots provided visual representations of ship's actual position versus an intended track, without recommendations for course or speed changes. Present autopilots have the added capability to control ship movement and maintain a preset track. These autopilots are primarily designed for trackkeeping in the open sea, where maintaining a desired heading and applying efficient rudder control for fuel conservation are the goals (Hwang et al. 1989).

The present research concentrates on the development of a decision aid which supports the cognitive tasks of piloting. Such a piloting decision aid should (1) represent internally local, transit-specific, and ship-handling knowledge, (2) support the appropriate level of piloting cognitive skills, and (3) provide recommendations for effecting the piloting tasks of trackkeeping, maneuvering and collision avoidance, and the practice of good seamanship. In addition, the decision aid must provide support in situations where the pilot would encounter information overload. The decision aid should also provide mental rehearsal capabilities, allowing masters, mates, and pilots to practice typical and atypical inbound and outbound transits. The system's on-line capabilities may prove most useful to ship's officers after the pilot has disembarked and the vessel is headed to sea (the case of the *Exxon Valdez*), or when deck officers are assuming the bridge watch after lengthy or strenuous cargo handling watches. Off-line, the decision aid's voyage planning capability mirrors the way senior ship's officers and pilots encourage their junior officers to plan and mentally rehearse transits prior to assuming a watch. Thus, the system could be expected to impact piloting in two ways: improved vessel performance (trackkeeping) and improved bridge watch team performance (maneuvering, collision avoidance, and the practice of good seamanship skills).

THE PILOTING EXPERT SYSTEM

The Piloting Expert System (PES) was developed using a Symbolics machine with the Knowledge Engineering Environment (KEE), an Intellicorp product (Fikes and Kehler 1985). This expert system shell utilizes both frame- and rule-

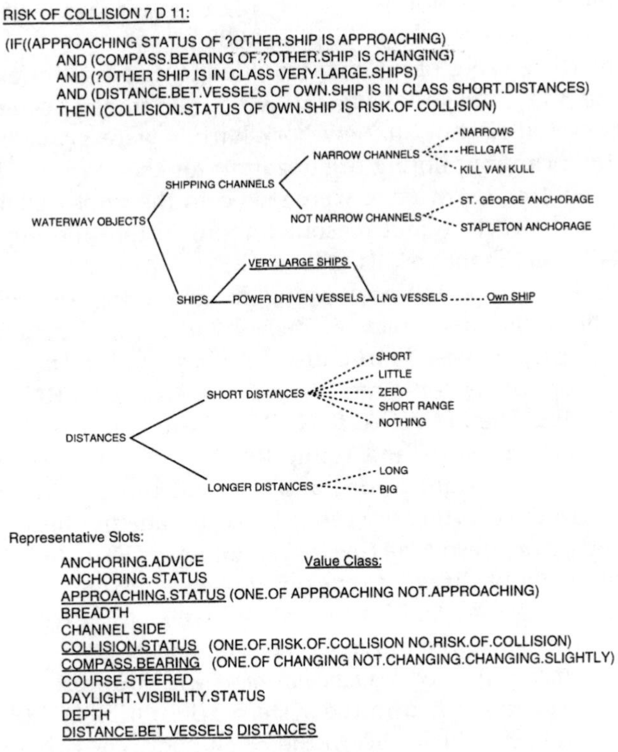

FIGURE 24–2 Frame Representation and Production Rule Example

based representation schemes. KEE frames provided the mechanism for both storing the objects in the piloting knowledge base (ships, channels, lighthouses, and buoys) and for propagating reasoning about these objects. For example, in the knowledge base, the generic class SHIPS (see Figure 24–2) is broken into the subclasses VERY.LARGE.SHIPS and POWER.DRIVEN.VESSELS. Attributes of SHIPS ("breadth," "depth," "height," "freeboard," etc.) may be inherited by all SHIPS subclasses or may be peculiar to different types of ships and thus, not universally inherited. The objects and attributes of the SHIPS class are reasoned about in the production rules, like the one shown on top of Figure 24–2.

Structure of the Piloting Expert System

In order to construct the system, a model of the information flows and concomitant decisions was developed into a reasoning hierarchy. This process required rudimentary knowledge of piloting, obtained from the International and Inland Rules of the Road. In addition, the authors had previous piloting experience—both as naval watch officers and one in the merchant marine. A user interface was constructed which facilitated gathering and formalizing the judgment of experienced pilots. The prototype knowledge base was reviewed and edited by New York harbor pilots (Grabowski 1987, 1988).

The three types of piloting knowledge discussed previously form the foundation of the PES knowledge base. Local, transit-specific, and shiphandling knowledge for piloting in New York harbor were provided by the Sandy Hook pilots, the primary piloting organization for this harbor. Once elicited, the three types of piloting knowledge were stored in the piloting knowledge base using a frame-based structure and reasoned about in the piloting production rules. For full details, see Grabowski (1987).

The PES supports trackkeeping, maneuvering and collision avoidance, and the practice of good seamanship tasks by utilizing the information stored within its rule-and frame-based structure. *Trackkeeping, maneuvering, and collision avoidance task* support is contained, within the 45 META.RULES and 120 NAVIGATION.RULES. The NAVIGATION.RULES are comprised primarily of the Rules of the Road (Farnsworth and Young 1983)—rules for the conduct of vessels in any visibility, those in sight of one another, and those in restricted visibility. These rules govern the conduct of vessels who are meeting head-on and are crossing at right angles, or are overtaking one another. META.RULES provide procedural information about different types of vessels—power driven vessels, fishing vessels, and sailing vessels, for instance—as well as control and maneuvering information particular to the different types of vessels.

The *practice of good seamanship tasks* are supported by the piloting heuristic information contained in the system's SHIPPING.OBJECTS and in the NAVIGATION.RULES which govern their behavior. These heuristics pertain to transit-specific information (how to position the vessel to pass under the Verrazano-Narrows bridge, for instance); local conditions (i.e., the impact on the vessel of adverse weather in the harbor); and watchstanding procedures for the vessel.

The PES knowledge base contains procedures and heuristics for when a vessel encounters *changing conditions*. Responses to and reasoning about these situations are invoked by using a series of electronic menus and checklists. Through this menu, the user can (1) change parameters about which the system reasons (in response to changing conditions or emergencies), (2) establish baseline parameters for off-line simulation exercises, or (3) change on-line or off-line system reasoning parameters in order to conduct "what if" analyses. These changing conditions include restricted visibility, loss of critical ships systems (steering, propulsion, navigation, communications, etc.), anchoring, arrivals, departures, as well as on-line and off-line scenarios for emergency procedures (fire, flood, abandon ship, etc.).

The problem faced by maritime pilots is typical of what has been called "situation assessment": a person or machine gathers new data about the decision situation and reasons about its implications. Reasoning in the PES is accomplished by moving "forward" or top to bottom, through the hierarchical rule structure. Figure 24–3 is an example of the forward chaining piloting rules.

```
CROSSING.POV.RULE.15

(IF((?OTHER.SHIP IS IN CLASS POWER.DRIVEN.VESSELS)
    AND (LOCATION OF ?OTHER.SHIP IS NOT.IN CLASS NARROW.CHANNELS)
    AND (LOCATION OF OWN.SHIP IS NOT.IN CLASS NARROW.CHANNELS)
    AND (VESSEL.STATE OF OWN.SHIP IS (NOT.ONE OF RESTRICTED.IN
        ABILITY.TO.MANEUVER FISHING CONSTRAINED.BY.HER.DRAFT
        NOT.UNDER.COMMAND)
    AND (VESSEL.STATE OF ?OTHER.SHIP IS (NOT.ONE.OF RESTRICTED.IN.
        ABILITY.TO.MANEUVER FISHING CONSTRAINED.BY.HER.DRAFT
        NOT.UNDER.COMMAND)
    AND (VESSEL.IN.SIGHT.STATUS OF OWN.SHIP IS VESSEL.IN.SIGHT.OF.
        ONE.ANOTHER)
    AND (COLLISION.STATUS OF OWN.SHIP IS RISK.OF.COLLISION)
    AND (VESSEL.STATE OF OWN.SHIP IS CROSSING)
    AND (SHIP.ON.SIDE.STATUS OF OWN.SHIP IS STBD)))))))))
    THEN (RIGHT.OF.WAY.STATUS OF OWN.SHIP IS GIVE.WAY)
        (EVASIVE.ACTION.TAKEN OF OWN.SHIP IS ALTER.COURSE.TO.STBD
        AND NOT.CROSS. AHEAD))

WHISTLE.SIGNAL.A/C.TO.STBD.RULE

(IF((?ANY.SHIP IS IN CLASS SHIPS)
    AND(EVASIVE.ACTION.TAKEN OF ?ANY.SHIP IS ALTER.COURSE.TO.STBD))
    THEN (WHISTLE.ACTION.TAKEN OF ?ANY.SHIP IS BLOW.ONE.SHORT.BLAST)))

WHISTLE.HEARD.RULE.1

(IF(?ANY.SHIP IS IN CLASS SHIPS)
    AND.(WHISTLE.ACTION.TAKEN OF ?ANY.SHIP IS IN CLASS BLOW.WHISTLE.
        ACTIONS)
    AND (DISTANCE.BET.VESSELS OF OWN.SHIP IS SHORT))))
    THEN (WHISTLE.HEARD.STATUS OF OWN.SHIP IS WHISTLE.HEARD))))
```

FIGURE 24–3 An Example of Forward Chaining—Cascading Rules

The User Interface

The user interface was constructed to facilitate user interaction with the system. The input device was a mouse, with menus used for inputting data on changing conditions (i.e., visibility, traffic conditions, or status of ship's equipment). Menus were also used to do contingency voyage planning—different piloting approaches could be experimented with or potential voyage changes could be anticipated and planned for. Figure 24–4 gives an example of how inputs cause new information to be propagated through the system. A series of cascading menus accept more detailed data and invoke the forward-chaining reasoning process. Figure 24–5 provides a detailed view of the PES recommendations for a particular transit.

Piloting information needs to be presented in a highly specialized format in order to be of use. Research has been done in the maritime field on representing ship-handling and piloting information (Goldberg 1980a, b, NTSB 1981, Gotebiowski 1983). All conclude that such information must be presented to ship's captains and pilots in a familiar format, and most recommend that some form of a chart representation be utilized in order to mirror the users' mental representa-

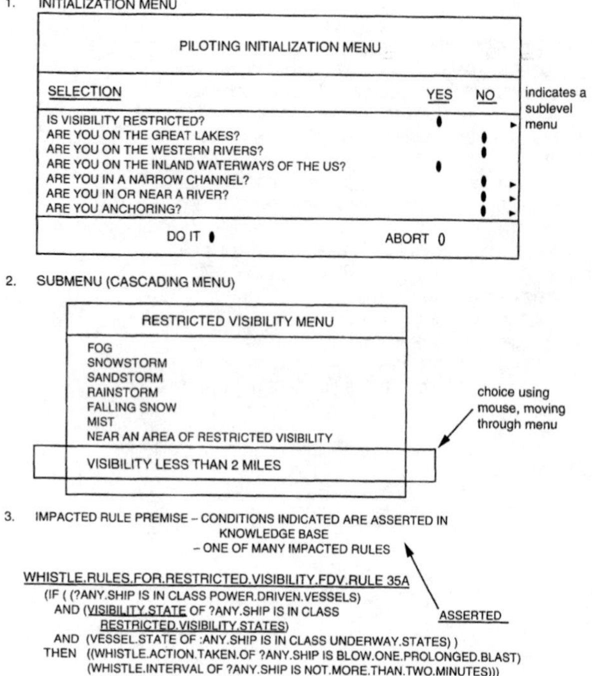

FIGURE 24–4 Menu Driven User Interface

tions of the problem space. Thus, the user interface is divided into three sections (Figure 24–6). The left-hand side of the screen contains a digitized chart of a portion of New York harbor. The center portion of the screen contains the static and dynamic system recommendations, which reflect the system's inferencing (Figure 24–5); the right-hand side of the screen provides access to input changing conditions—speed, visibility, traffic, or emergency conditions.

The recommendations provided to the user in the center of the screen were of two types: general ship-handling knowledge, which was transit-specific and generally static ("recommended course 347 for 1.94 miles; half ahead (60 rpm's)," as seen in Figure 24–5) and dynamic recommendations about maneuvering, collision avoidance, and the practice of good seamanship ("If visibility closes, reduce speed to the minimum required to maintain way"; "Approaching vessel is the stand-on vessel; you are required to keep clear by altering course to starboard and blowing one short blast."), reflecting inputs by the user and system responses to changing conditions.

The PES was constructed as a standalone system; thus, it was not connected to sensors providing data on the ship's position or steering. As a consequence, the trackkeeping capabilities of the PES were limited and not as robust as those which would be found in piloting expert systems that are part of an integrated ship's bridge system.

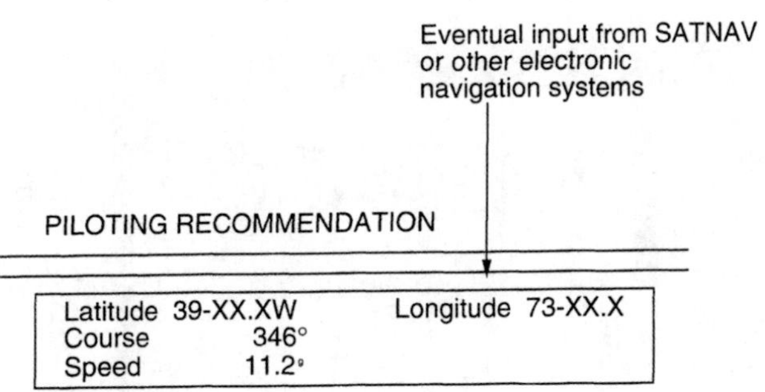

Based on the information provided.

- Recommend course 347° for 1.94 miles
  Half Ahead (60 RPM's)

Until pass buoys 13,14 –0– (N. end, Ambrose Channel)

Coney Island Light Ø's	013°
West Bank Light Ø's	092°
Great Kills Light Ø's	264°
Old Orchard Shoals Lt. Ø's	247°

- Then A/C to 348°, for 2.3 miles
- If visibility closes (expected weather),
  - reduce speed accordingly
  - sound appropriate whistle signals
  - notify docking master of delayed arrival.
- To make gangs at 0800, you must pass Stapleton Anchorage by 0615

FIGURE 24–5 Sample Output for Leg D, Inbound NY

AN EVALUATION USING GAMING

The purpose of the evaluation was to assess the decision support contribution provided by a cognitive decision aid to one of the three classes of intended users: inexperienced junior deck officers (represented by bridge watch teams of three senior cadets from the U.S. Merchant Marine Academy). Evaluation occurred at the Computer-aided Operations Research Facility (CAORF), an operational ship's simulator on the grounds of the United States Merchant Marine Academy, at Kings Point, New York.

The Experiment

Subjects who participated in this experiment were fourth-year (senior) cadets at the U.S. Merchant Marine Academy. These cadets were in the third quarter of their senior year at the Academy and were preparing to be licensed by the U.S. Coast Guard as Third Mates, the entry-level bridge officer certification required of all officers sailing aboard U.S. flag merchant ships.

Subjects had also completed a ten-week "Bridge Watchstanding Simulation Training" course at the Computer-aided Operations Research Facility. This course

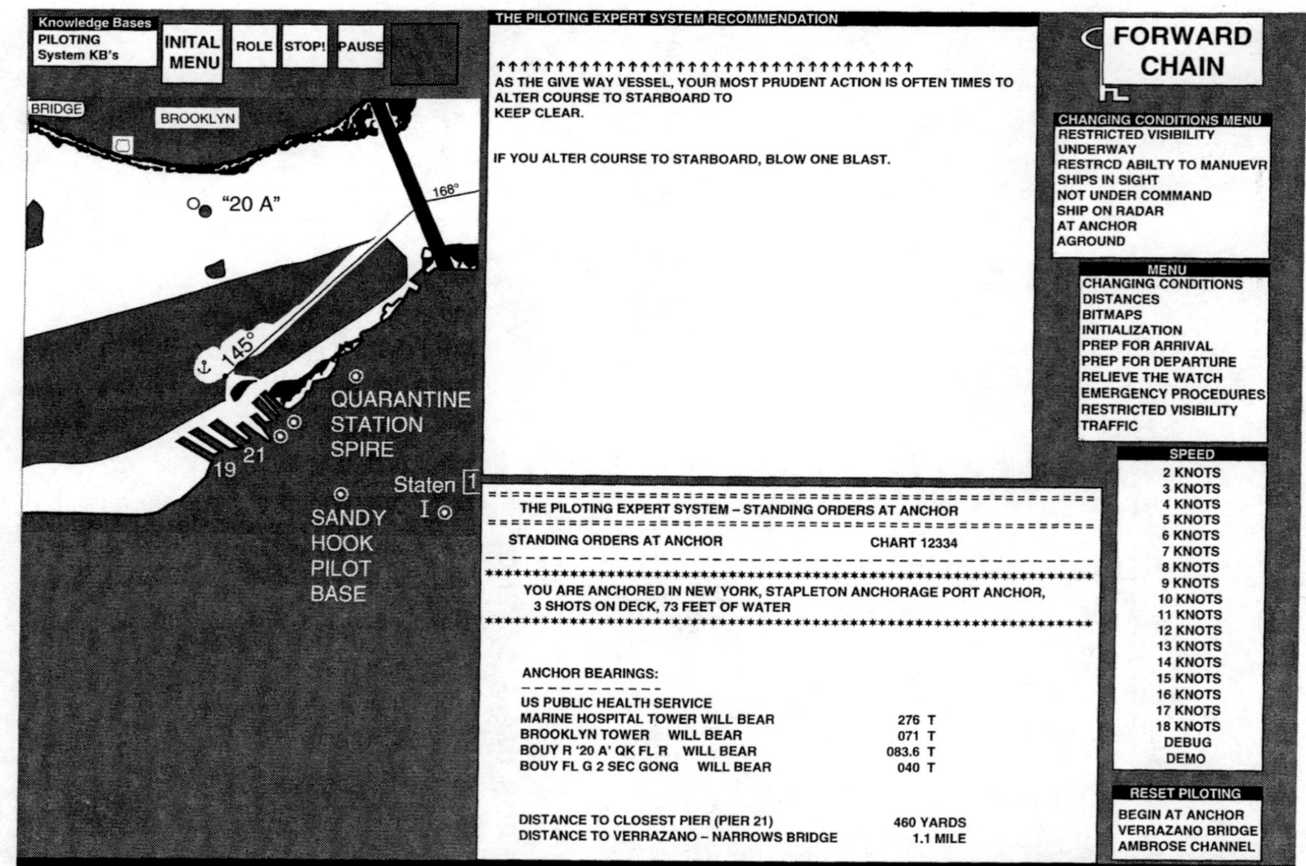

FIGURE 24–6 Piloting Expert System—User Interface

is the capstone in the navigation curriculum at the Merchant Marine Academy. During the course, subjects participated in a "Departure New York" scenario identical to the scenario used in this experiment. In addition, many subjects had participated in actual transits of New York harbor sailing as cadets aboard merchant vessels.

Subjects were divided into eight watchstanding crews of three members each. Each crew was run through the simulation scenario a total of three times. The first run (pretest) for all eight crews was completed in clear visibility without the use of the expert system. Subjects "piloted" a 30,000 deadweight ton vessel with which they were already familiar. There was no wind; light traffic (meeting traffic within the navigational channel—no risk of collision); and the current was steady at 0.5 knots. Although this does not represent a typical passage in New York, this set of initial conditions was sufficient to refamiliarize the subjects with the ship and New York harbor area.

For the second run, visibility was reduced to 0.5 nautical miles. Traffic patterns within Ambrose Channel were typical of those normally encountered during passages. The combination of reduced visibility and expected traffic patterns resulted in a simulated passage of moderate difficulty, with the possibility of collision. The expert system was available to three of the eight teams. During the third run, also conducted under reduced visibility, the expert system was made available only to those watchstanding teams that had not previously used it. All groups, whether or not they had PES on the bridge, had available to them the full CAORF ship's bridge configuration.

The setting was New York harbor, from Stapleton Anchorage through Ambrose Channel to Ambrose Light, at the seaward end of the navigation channel. The visual scene and radar presentation included all major shoreline features, prominent landmarks, and navigational aids found in these parts of New York harbor. The data base included accurately modeled tidal currents in the channels, as well as shallow water and passing ship effects. The channel depth was kept constant at 35 feet. The simulated transit was divided into five segments or legs. Prior to the experiment, subjects were familiarized with the PES and given instruction in operating the system. Each bridge watch team participating in the research was told that the purpose of the project was to determine the amount of simulator training necessary for Third Mates to become familiar with the port of New York. Groups were also told that they would be evaluated relative to their performance and that their relative rankings would be provided to them at the conclusion of the experiment.

Watch teams were to depart from the port of New York, from Stapleton Anchorage, and were given an accurate chart of the area. The experiment was a variation on the "pretest-posttest" design. The pretest was followed by two posttests, so that PES was introduced to the bridge watch teams at different times. This scheme had the advantage of allowing two sources of extraneous variation to be minimized. First, the pretest allowed preexisting differences in proficiency among the bridge watch teams to be accounted for with an analysis of covariance. Second, the staggered introduction of the expert system made it possible to assess the effects of the system, independent of learning which was expected to occur with repetition of the same simulator exercise.

Subjects used the system in on-line reminder and assist mode. As the vessel made the transit, subjects continually referred to the PES for course and speed recommendations, reminders to contact vessel traffic and the Coast Guard on VHF radio, and, when visibility closed, instructions on proper restricted visibility procedures (i.e., calling the captain, sounding fog signals, reducing speed, and posting a lookout).

Two sets of performance measures were gathered and used to assess the bridge watch teams' performance: *watch team performance* measures and *vessel performance* (trackkeeping) measures.

Watch team performance was assessed in two ways. First, a form used by the Merchant Marine instructors in their regular grading of bridge watch teams, the Voyage Arrival/Departure Evaluation Checklist, was used to determine subjects' compliance with the captain's departure and night orders; to assess their use of communications and voyage plans; to assess bridge watch team coordination; and to ascertain compliance with the Rules of the Road and proper use of all navigational aids.

In addition to this evaluation sheet, the watch team's "bells" (rudder orders, wheel commands, communications, changes in speed or position) were kept by independent observers, and cross-checked with videotapes of the experiment from three different vantage points—from outside the bridge, looking inward (to cover the entire bridge); from the centerline aft of the bridge, looking directly forward (to record the harbor position and the view which the helmsman had); and on the port side of the bridge, looking forward, focused on the PES (so as to record use of the PES).

These measures were "mapped" to ship's position every 30 seconds, using data by CAORF on ship's position and weather, tide, current, and other environmental factors. These plots provided graphical representations of vessel's track vs. an intended track, and were visual depictions of each watch teams' vessel performance. An example of these 30-second plots is shown in Figure 24–7.

Vessel performance measures were assessed by using several variables related to the motion of the vessel and its position relative to the centerline and boundaries of the shipping channel (Grabowski 1987). These vessel performance variables were also reported at 30-second intervals for the duration of each exercise, and were summarized for each leg of the transit by maximum, mean, and standard deviation. The entire transit was summarized by overall mean and standard deviation values.

The most desirable position of one's vessel is on the centerline of the inbound or outbound navigational channel. Accordingly, variables based on distance from the centerline were the primary performance measures used in the study. The vessel deviation measures gathered for all trials included: (1) mean

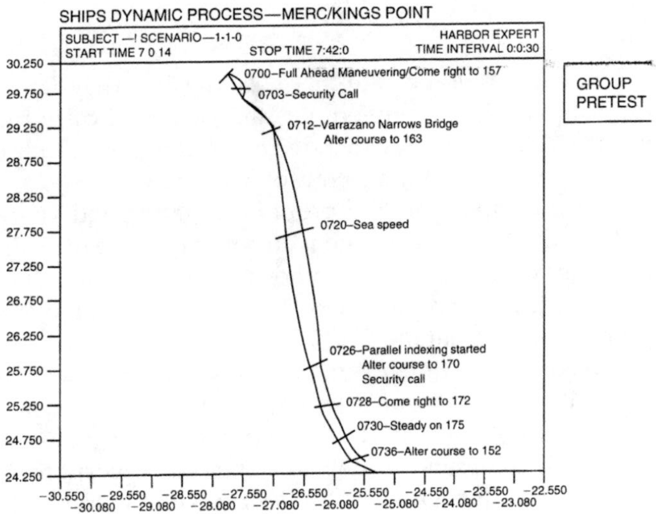

FIGURE 24–7 An Example of the Ship Pilot Data for CAORF

off-track deviation, (2) maximum deviation (port and starboard), (3) mean deviation (port and starboard), (4) maximum swept path, and (5) mean swept path and standard deviation of swept path.

The maximum deviation from centerline to port and to starboard represent the closest point of approach of the vessel to the boundaries of the channel. These measures were therefore indicative of extreme values, and not of overall position in the channel. These values are important in that they reflect the danger of grounding.

The mean deviation from centerline to port and starboard represent the vessel's average distance left or right of the centerline of the channel without regard to the direction of the deviation. These values provide a summary of the vessel's position relative to the centerline over the entire leg (or entire transit). These variables do not, however, indicate the extent to which the vessel's distance from centerline changed within a leg. The standard deviation of off-track deviation represents the variability of the distance from centerline. Low values indicate that the vessel was moving parallel to the centerline of the channel, while high values reflect motion across the channel.

Swept path is a function of the difference between the vessel's heading and the course made good. In the absence of any wind and current, a swept path in excess of the beam of the ship is indicative of pilot-induced swing. The maximum swept path is indicative of the severity of the maneuvers undertaken in a particular leg (or overall); the mean swept path can be taken to represent the amount of swing, while the standard deviation of swept path indicates the variability of the swept path.

Results

Tables 24–1 through 24–4 indicate that with the expert system, *watch team performance* was significantly improved. In almost every case, introduction of the expert system was correlated with a decreased number of rudder orders (indicating a higher degree of piloting control with fewer course corrections) and a greater degree of compliance with proper navigation and safety procedures.

With the expert system, bridge watch teams completed all required security calls; communicated properly with other vessel traffic and the New York harbor maritime authorities; and, as evidenced by their ratings on the "Voyage Arrival/Departure Evaluation Checklist," focused on the essence of piloting. Table 24–3 was collapsed to perform an estimate of the effect that the presence of the expert system had on subjects' communications, and a one-sided test of equality in proportions was used. The hypothesis that the presence of the expert system resulted in a significant decrease in communications (indicating greater piloting control) was supported at the 95 percent confidence level. The effect of the expert system on completion of external vessel communications was most pronounced for all subjects in legs 3 and 4, where 100% of all required communications were effected with the expert system, versus 81% of all required communications effected without the expert system.

During the experiment, as visibility closed, teams with the PES effected proper restricted visibility procedures to a greater degree than those without the expert system. In Table 24–4, the same one-sided test of equality in proportions was made and found to be significant at the 95% confidence level. Presence of the expert system did not guarantee 100% compliance with proper navigation and safety procedures, but of the eight bridge watch-standing teams, five performed all required restricted visibility procedures and the remaining three groups main-

TABLE 24–1 Watch Team Performance: Voyage Arrival Departure Checklist

Group	Pretest	Overall Score Without PES*	With PES*
1	78	82	91
2	92	93	96
3	90	89	92
4	94	93	95
5	91	91	90
6	88	92	93
7	90	83	84
8	86	89	90
Average	89	89	91

*Piloting Expert System.

TABLE 24–2 Watch Team Performance: Number of Rudder Orders

		Leg of Transit				
Group	Test	1	2	3	4	5
1	Pretest	4	3	1	3	3
	Without PES*	4	2	4	4	3
	With PES	2	2	1	2	1
2	Pretest	2	3	1	3	2
	Without PES	1	1	2	3	1
	With PES	1	1	1	2	1
3	Pretest	2	4	2	3	4
	Without PES	1	3	2	3	1
	With PES	1	2	1	3	2
4	Pretest	3	2	3	4	3
	Without PES	2	2	3	3	3
	With PES	2	3	2	2	1
5	Pretest	4	4	3	4	3
	Without PES	1	3	4	3	1
	With PES	1	2	3	1	2
6	Pretest	1	2	3	3	2
	Without PES	2	1	2	2	2
	With PES	2	2	3	2	3
7	Pretest	1	2	2	2	2
	Without PES	1	2	3	2	2
	With PES	2	1	2	2	3
8	Pretest	3	2	4	2	2
	Without PES	2	2	2	2	3
	With PES	2	3	2	3	2

*Piloting Expert System.

tained their percentage level of compliance with the procedures, or slightly improved them.

In contrast, measured effect of the PES on *vessel performance* (i.e., centerline trackkeeping) was not statistically significant, either positively or negatively. Considerable variation existed among teams with individual data marked by a number of outliers. The result was rather large variance in the measurements, and this, coupled with a sample size of eight teams, made the measurements relatively insensitive. An anticipated learning effect of progressively better performance over the three runs did not appear. Thus, we cannot say with statistical confidence that PES improved (or worsened) the performance.

The observation that PES contributed minimally to trackkeeping performance of the inexperienced bridge watch teams was confirmed with statistical analysis. The analysis of covariance (those without the PES vs. those with the PES with performance at pretest the covariate) failed to detect any significant effect of the expert

TABLE 24-3 Watch Team Performance: Comparison of Required and Effected External Communications

		Leg of Transit				
		1	2	3	4	5
		No. Required				
Group	Test	1	0	1	1	0
1	Pretest	1	0	1	0	0
	Without PES*	0	1	1	0	0
	With PES	1	0	1	1	0
2	Pretest	0	0	0	0	0
	Without PES	1	0	1	1	0
	With PES	1	0	1	1	0
3	Pretest	0	1	1	0	1
	Without PES	1	0	1	1	0
	With PES	1	0	1	1	0
4	Pretest	0	1	1	0	1
	Without PES	0	1	1	0	1
	With PES	0	1	1	1	1
5	Pretest	1	0	1	1	1
	Without PES	1	0	1	1	0
	With PES	1	0	1	1	0
6	Pretest	0	0	1	1	1
	Without PES	0	0	1	1	1
	With PES	1	0	1	1	1
7	Pretest	1	0	1	1	0
	Without PES	1	0	1	1	0
	With PES	1	0	1	1	0
8	Pretest	0	0	0	0	0
	Without PES	0	0	0	1	1
	With PES	0	0	1	1	1

*Piloting Expert System.

system on any of the vessel performance variables. In retrospect, this may not be surprising since the PES provided no support for the motor and perceptual skills traditionally provided by a ship's trackkeeping autopilot. The videotapes showed that the novice pilots had difficulty in maintaining track and tended to overreact to various course and speed changes recommended by the expert system.

Interestingly, subjects committed errors in two cases: (1) when subjects failed to consult the PES and relied on their memory of proper watch procedures, and (2) when subjects failed to properly effect the PES piloting recommendations. Since one video camera was dedicated to capturing the PES screen and user interactions with the system (and was synchronized with the other two video cameras

TABLE 24-4 Watch Team Performance: Compliance with Proper Navigation and Safety Procedures

Group	Test	Percentage Complete (With 100% = Five Procedures)
1	Without PES*	40%
	With PES	100%
2	Without PES	60%
	With PES	100%
3	Without PES	60%
	With PES	60%
4	Without PES	20%
	With PES	60%
5	Without PES	80%
	With PES	100%
6	Without PES	60%
	With PES	80%
7	Without PES	40%
	With PES	100%
8	Without PES	20%
	With PES	100%

*Piloting Expert System.

recording the bridge and environmental situations), we were able to ascertain that proper PES recommendations had been consistently provided to the subjects for each voyage leg.

As noted before, the PES was not an autopilot and thus, was not provided with real-time vessel position information. Vessel course and speed information was provided for legs of the transit, and was computed algorithmically for the 30,000 deadweight ton vessel along the transit legs, but was not cross-checked or corrected by referencing on-line navigational and position information (from the simulator's radars or satellite navigation systems, for instance). This feature limits the usefulness of the system as a trackkeeping aid, and is an area important for future research. However, we collected trackkeeping data in order to determine whether a system, as developed, had any utility as an aid for the motor skills of piloting.

DISCUSSION

The results indicate that the contribution of the PES to novice pilots in the simulated operational setting lies in the improved performance of the bridge watch team—by providing timely, accurate, expert-level protocols with a graphic display. The teams performed efficient emergency procedures, communicated as required with other vessels and the maritime authorities, and fully complied with proper safety and navigational procedures. These are all procedures which are part of the local, transit-specific, and shiphandling knowledge of a pilot in New York harbor. This knowledge is used to process data in collision avoidance and maneuvering, and to a limited extent, contributed to the practice of good seamanship.

In contrast, the PES did not, within the accuracy of our measurements, improve the novice pilots' trackkeeping. Possibly this should have been anticipated, since the PES did not support the motor and perceptual skills of trackkeeping. However, some teams were surprisingly erratic. We conjecture that without these basic types of skills, operational performance in piloting cannot be helped by an expert system designed solely to support the higher end cognitive skills. This is particularly true with novice subjects.

We can also refer to the model of human information processing discussed previously. The contribution of the PES was to make available to the user knowledge that was presumed to be either not stored or not readily accessible in long-term memory (i.e., the knowledge base) to support the memory, and the interface to provide the cues. We can conjecture, perhaps, that one of two problems caused the poor trackkeeping. The novice pilots either had difficulty in forming the correct visual image—a perceptual skill—or could not perform the motor activity needed for the proper response. It was difficult for us to recognize the perceptual problem on the videotapes. As previously noted, however, we saw poor (in terms of over- or under-correction) course and speed responses. But we could not find a consistent pattern with respect to the recorded data on trackkeeping.

This conclusion leads us to suggest that prior to the development of a decision aid employing constructs that seek to represent judgment and knowledge, the task, problem, and decision situation must be studied with care in order to determine the relevant skills. In addition, one must ascertain the degree of dependency between the motor, perceptual, and cognitive skills used in performing a task or in solving a problem. We might consider that financial analysis requires predominantly cognitive skills. However, many experienced analysts rely on perceptual skills in recognizing patterns in financial data. An expert system that cannot support that aspect of the analysis task will not achieve the anticipated gains in performance.

The problem of measuring performance is certainly not unique to this study. It plagues many attempts at assessing expert systems (O'Keefe et al. 1987). It is suggested that by careful task analysis, one can develop ways of measuring how the technology supports cognition—the purpose of an expert system. By breaking the process down, we have identified the contribution reflected in the improved nontrackkeeping activities. It is the performance of these activities that is vital under extreme or emergency conditions, when a decision aid may reduce stress by improving human information processing (Belardo et al. 1984).

Following the *Exxon Valdez* oil spill, the first author began development of a Shipboard Piloting Expert System (SPES) for U.S. tankers transiting the Gulf of Alaska. This continuation of the previous work addresses the challenges of transitioning from a prototype to an operational environment, as well as it provides an opportunity to answer many of the questions which arose during the prototype's development.

The SPES is being developed for operational use in both on-line and off-line modes. The SPES will be one node in an integrated bridge system, as part of the maritime industry's move to develop one-man bridge systems. The prototype Piloting Expert System needs to be transferred from a laboratory hardware and software configuration (Symbolics 3600 series processor running Genera 6.0 and KEE 2.1) to an implementation appropriate for shipboard deployment. The PES is presently being transferred to an 80386/80486 microprocessor-based machine running the Unix operating system with a run-time version of the expert system shell KEE as one process in the multitasking environment.

In addition, the PES software architecture is being revised. When originally constructed, the system was a stand-alone system requiring manual input of most situational data. This input mode, and the system's stand-alone nature, are sufficient for prototype training systems, but unreasonable configurations for shipboard implementations. Consequently, the SPES will be but one node in a distributed shipboard network of cooperating hardware and software systems—an implementation which reflects a systems engineering approach to shipboard systems design. Thus, the SPES will reason about data provided by a variety of shipboard sensors (navigation, engine, meteorological, and steering systems, i.e.), reason about this information as it is available on the shipboard local area network, and share information with the other distributed systems on the shipboard network.

Incorporation of real-time position and trackkeeping data is an important challenge for the SPES. In the fully-integrated SPES, input from the electronic bridge equipment will be fed digitally into the SPES microprocessor. Thus, the system will reason about the implications of the real-time position and trackkeeping data, and provide recommendations to the users in real time. Autopilot information, available from the attached shipboard network and shipboard steering systems, will also be reasoned about. The receipt and use of real-time data from a distributed shipboard network is a significant reasoning challenge for the SPES.

The objective of the SPES is to develop and demonstrate an operational shipboard piloting expert system which will provide decision support to ships' officers while piloting large vessels in restricted waters. The system is intended to reduce the information overload under which these officers labor, by providing the requisite decision support in a timely fashion. One of the research issues that will be addressed during the development of the SPES is whether or not officers using the SPES can handle higher information loads (supporting the use of fewer bridge watchstanders). It is anticipated that this research will evaluate more precisely the contribution of a full piloting expert system—one incorporating local, transit-specific, and shiphandling knowledge in support of both the motor and cognitive skills of piloting—to naive and experienced decision makers using the system in both on-line and off-line modes.

QUESTIONS

1. What kinds of knowledge are required in piloting? What are the sources of this knowledge?
2. How is knowledge represented in the piloting expert system?
3. What factors influenced the design of the user interface for the piloting expert system?
4. Discuss the results from the evaluation of the piloting expert system.

REFERENCES

BEETHAM, E. H., "Bridge Manning," *Seaways,* February (1989), 19–20.

BELARDO, S., R. KARWAN and W. A. WALLACE, "Managing the Response to Disasters Using Microcomputers," *Interfaces,* 14 (1984), 29–39.

CARD, S. K., T. P. MORAN and A. NEWELL,. *The Psychology of Human-Computer Interaction,* Lawrence Erlbaum Associates, Hillsdale, NJ, 1983.

FARNSWORTH, B. A., and L. C. YOUNG, *Nautical Rules of the Road: The International and Unified Inland Rules* (2nd ed.), Cornell Maritime Press, Centreville, MD, 1983.

FIKES, R. and T. KEHLER, "The Role of Frame-Based Representation Reasoning," *Communications of the ACM,* 28 (1985), 904–920.

FROESE, J., "Training for Advanced Ships," *Proceedings of the Training Forum Europe '89,* Amsterdam, 1989.

GOLDBERG, J., A. D'AMICO, M. GILDER, and K. WILLIAMS, "The Effectiveness of Active vs. Passive Trainee Participation and Segmented vs. Integrated Training Structure on the Acquisition of Shiphandling Skills," National Maritime Research Center, Kings Point, NY, CAORF-50-7918-02, 1980a.

——, —— and K. WILLIAMS, "Transfer of Training from Low to High Fidelity Shiphandling Simulators," National Maritime Research Center, Kings Point, NY, CAORF 50-7919-02, 1980b.

GOTEBIOWSKI, P. and W. MCILROY, "Experimental Identification of Human Control Functions on Simulated Tankers in Restricted Waterways," Computer Aided Operations Research Facility, National Maritime Research Center, Kings Point, NY, CAORF-26-7911-01, 1983.

GRABOWSKI, M.R., "Prototyping as a Design Strategy and as a Means of Knowledge Acquisition: As Assessment Using the Piloting Expert System," Ph.D. Thesis, Rensselaer Polytechnic Institute, NY, 1987.

——, "Knowledge Acquisition Methodologies: Survey and Assessment," *Proceedings of the Ninth International Conference on Information Systems,* Association for Computing Machinery, Minneapolis, MN, 1988.

——, "Decision Aiding Technology and Integrated Bridge Design," *Proceedings of the Society of Naval Architects and Marine Engineers Spring Meeting/Ship Technology and Research Symposium,* New Orleans, LA, 1989.

GROVE, T. W., "U.S. Flag of the Future: Concepts, Features, and Issues, *Proceedings of the Society of Naval Architects and Marine Engineers Spring Meeting/Ship Technology and Research Symposium,* Society for Naval Architects and Marine Engineers, New Orleans, LA, 1989.

HARRALD, J., H. MARCUS, and W. A. WALLACE, "The Exxon Valdez: An Assessment of Crisis Prevention and Management Systems," *Interfaces,* 20 (1990), 14–30.

HUFFNER, J. R., "Pilotage in the Port of New York," Washington, DC, U.S. Department of Transportation, U.S. Coast Guard, Office of Research and Development, CG-D-81-78, 1978.

HWANG, W., E. GUEST, E. PIZZARIELLO, and W. BROWN, "Factors to Consider in Developing a Knowledge-Based Autopilot Expert System for Ship Maneuvering Simulation," *Proceedings of the Society of Naval Architects and Marine Engineers Ship Technology and Research Conference,* Society for Naval Architects and Marine Engineers, New Orleans, LA, 1989.

KRISTIANSEN, S., E. RENSVIK, and L. MATHISEN, "Integrated Total Control of the Bridge," *Proceedings of the Annual Meeting of the Society of Naval Architects and Marine Engineers,* Society for Naval Architects and Marine Engineers, New York, 1989.

KWIK, K. H., "Collision Rate as a Danger Criterion for Marine Traffic," *J. Navigation* 39 (1986), 203–212.

Maritime Transportation Research Board (MTRB), Panel on Human Error in Merchant Marine Safety, *Human Error in Merchant Marine Safety,* National Academy Press, June 1976.

National Academy of Sciences, *Crew Size and Maritime Safety,* National Academy Press, Washington, DC, 1990.

National Transportation Safety Board (NTSB), "Major Marine Collisions and Effects of Preventive Recommendations," Bureau of Technology, NTSB-MSS-81-1, 1981.

O'KEEFE, R. M., O. BALCI, and E. P. SMITH, "Validating Expert System Performance," *IEEE Expert,* 2 (1987), 81–90.

Panel on Human Error in Merchant Marine Safety, "Human Error in Merchant Marine Safety," Maritime Transportation Research Board, National Academy of Sciences, June 1976.

PARASURAMAN, R., "Human Computer Monitoring," *Human Factors,* 29 (1987), 695–706.

SCHUFFEL, H. J., P. A. BOER, and L. VAN BREDA, "The Ship's Wheelhouse of the Nineties: The Navigation Performance and Mental Workload of the Officer of the Watch," *J. Institute of Navigation,* 42 (1989), 60–72.

SIMON, H. A., *The Sciences of the Artificial* (2nd ed.), MIT Press, Cambridge, MA, 1981.

VAIL, B., "Crew Cuts Please Ship Lines But Take Toll on Seafarers," *J. Commerce,* November 28 (1988), 3.

VAN AMERONGEN, J., H. R. VAN NAUTA LEMKE, and J. C. T. VAN DER VEEN, "Optimum Steering of Ships with an Adaptive Autopilot," *Proceedings of the Fifth Ship Control Systems Conference,* Annapolis, MD, 1978.

VELDHUYZEN, W. and H. G. STASSEN, "The Internal Model Concept: An Application to Modeling Human Control of Large Ships," *Human Factors,* 19 (1977), 478–487.

25

CHOOSING AN EXPERT SYSTEMS GAME PLAN

In the world of baseball, there are many ways to score a run. The brute force of a power hitter can certainly do the job in dramatic fashion. But so, too, can the individual efforts of players working their way down the bases with in-field hits and walks. By the ninth inning, it matters little how each team planned and plotted to rack up its runs. Only the total score—and who came out on top—really counts.

Choosing an expert systems strategy also involves making a series of choices from the beginning of the game. As in baseball, there is no right or wrong approach to winning with expert systems technology. But choosing a strategy that fits your company's culture and structure has a lot to do with your chances for ultimate success.

Five years ago, E. I. DuPont de Nemours & Co. opted to train its end users to develop their own small systems. Today, the more than 600 expert systems installed in DuPont's business units are cumulatively saving more than $75 million per year.

Over the last 10 years, Digital Equipment Corp. has evolved an equally successful program following an entirely different strategy. To begin its expert system efforts organization, Digital established the Artificial Intelligence Technology Center (AITC), in Marlborough, Mass. AITC has become a strategic resource for training highly skilled knowledge engineers. The result is a fast-growing number of operational and strategic systems affecting all its business processes. Digital now has 50 major expert systems in place, contributing $200 million in annual savings.

This chapter is a reprint of C. Lawrence Meador and Ed G. Mahler, "Choosing an Expert Systems Game Plan," *Datamation*, Volume 36, Number 15, August 1, 1990, pp. 64–70.

DuPont and Digital share a fundamental expert systems goal: to improve decision making throughout the corporation by putting relevant information and knowledge into the hands of those making the decisions. But the routes the companies have chosen in achieving this goal are very different.

DuPont uses a "dispersed" approach to expert systems development. End users develop their own systems using standard, low-cost tools.

The "specialist" approach used by Digital typically involves a centralized development center where specially trained programmers or knowledge engineers use custom tools to create systems. Generally, the systems are more complex and are used by more people than those created under the dispersed approach.

Each approach can vary in the way that it's controlled and deployed, and many companies are evolving systems that use elements of both approaches. In choosing an expert system for your company, you should ask questions in the following areas:

Knowledge: What are the critical points of decision making for the business? Is it critical to share knowledge between departments or is knowledge highly localized?

Resources: What is the state of your company's current information systems infrastructure? What is the computer literacy level of the employees? And what is your company's IS strategy?

At first glance, DuPont and Digital appear to have a lot in common. Both are global, highly decentralized organizations. Both have 120,000 employees and more than 100 plants worldwide. But that's where the similarity ends.

Digital's focus is on a single basic technology and a single architecture, with a primary emphasis on selling computer systems to end users. DuPont is a federation of businesses that produces products in almost every category found in a host of categories: fibers, plastics, chemicals, imaging systems, oil, coal, automotive products, electronics, agricultural products, and medical products. DuPont offers an array of product types that are typically several sales away from the end user. For instance the nylon it manufactures may ultimately end up in carpets made by Karastan and sold to the consumer by Sears Roebuck & Co.

THE KNOWLEDGE PROFILE

The term "knowledge profile" describes the patterns of information flow throughout a company. Some companies require a tight integration of information between departments, while others function well with localized wisdom.

Although Digital also has a vast array of products—namely, 43 computer families comprise some 30,000 parts—most of these products must function under the constraints of a single computer architecture. That's a fundamental corporate totem, the basic strategy through which Digital tries to differentiate itself. Each part must plug and play with all the others, and the knowledge possessed by each function must be aligned with the others to create the final product.

Sales, for example, must be able to propose systems that are technically correct, manufacturing must be able to verify that an order can be produced, and field service must know how and when to assemble the system at the customer's site.

At DuPont, the distribution of knowledge parallels the organizational structure—both are localized. The knowledge required to manufacture nylon in Seaford, Del., has nothing to do with the knowledge needed to sell Teflon in Hamburg, Germany. Fiber production is a world away from coal mining.

Furthermore, enormous disparity exists within each product line. Most of the company's 1,700 product lines each contain several hundred subtypes. Some, such as the electronics connectors business, range up to 500,000 items. Even within a single plant, the individual assembly lines may differ.

Such dispersed knowledge pushed DuPont to its roll-your-own approach to expert systems. So did the organization's culture. DuPont nurtures fierce independence and technical excellence throughout its federation—a prerequisite for a company trying to stay on the leading edge in so many arenas.

Another DuPont characteristic begs for the dispersed approach. At DuPont, big is not necessarily beautiful. Large problems can be broken into small pieces that an individual expert can tackle. If care is taken to create standard interfaces—in this case, between expert systems—each of those solutions can be linked later to solve bigger problems. In one plant, for example, an expert system for process-control troubleshooting is actually an agglomeration of smaller systems designed for troubleshooting various components.

Understanding the resource profile of an organization is critical to devising a strategy for implementing expert systems, no matter which approach is followed. First, an effective resource profile dictates that the company's information systems infrastructure—the hardware platforms, the networks, the data bases—must be in place. The decision makers, the users or user/developers of the systems must also have an adequate level of computer literacy. Without such a foundation, success will take a long time to achieve.

THE RESOURCE PROFILE

Digital's resource profile is blessed with a staff that's largely computer literate. This literacy level contributes to the company's success in spreading the use of expert systems throughout its organization and beyond. AITC has already trained 500 knowledge engineers throughout the world.

Another key aspect of Digital's resource profile is an IS strategy to integrate at all levels—business process, applications, and data. Driven by its need to align knowledge across functions, Digital's strategy mandates that expert systems adhere to all data and network standards. Like the products it sells, Digital's expert systems must be able to communicate with each other and with any data bases and applications.

DuPont, in contrast, works with various hardware platforms and global networks. A degree of applications and database integration exists at each major organizational level—corporate, department, and business unit—with most needs satisfied through four large IBM data centers. For example, an electronic mail system operates across all platforms: IBM mainframes, Digital and Hewlett-Packard Co. minicomputers, and PCs. The Digital VAXs and HP 3000s are used throughout DuPont's engineering and manufacturing facilities. And 15,000 IBM PCs and 15,000 Apple Macintoshes are used in DuPont offices worldwide.

More than 30,000 DuPont managers and professionals are Lotus literate today, a number that will grow to 60,000 before the decade is out. With this supporting infrastructure in place, DuPont's resource profile is naturally more oriented toward PC-based expert systems. More than 1,800 DuPont people are now using expert system shells as readily as they do spreadsheets, electronic mail, and other tools.

THE SPECIALIST APPROACH

Being a high-cost/high-payback effort, the specialist approach requires many of the same attributes of any major system development effort: senior management sponsorship, adequate funding and rigorous management control when it comes to project selection, prioritization, and development.

The human resource requirements can be a problem with the specialist approach. A knowledge engineer requires a mixture of normal programming skills, expert system language and tool skills, and a firm understanding of subject matter. Digital says that, for complex systems, it can take a year before a trained individual is fully up to speed. The company's knowledge engineers are put through an apprenticeship program ranging from 13 weeks to nine months, depending on the business problem and the level of training required. In some instances, AITC consultants may continue to work with the trainees back at their home sites.

The development and maintenance of complex systems require more than a group of knowledge engineers working together. A group at Digital responsible for the XCON and XSEL programs, which are used to configure systems for customers, includes a program manager, software systems integration engineers, and various experts providing information in terms of process and data content. For each quarterly release of these systems, Digital consults hundreds of experts in manufacturing and engineering. Moreover, 40% of the rules in the configuration systems change annually.

The possible options for getting started using the specialist approach are:

- Hire an outside firm to develop the first expert systems.
- Experiment internally, but team up with other companies to create a support group.
- Create a specialized shop.

In the late 1970s, when Digital decided on an expert system as the solution to its configuration problems, the technology was in its infancy. So the company joined with an academic artificial intelligence hotbed, Carnegie-Mellon University in Pittsburgh, to produce what became XCON. The AI Technology Center grew out of this effort, and subsequently so did Digital's entry into the expert systems market, providing tools, training, and consulting for customers wanting to leapfrog steps in the specialist approach.

AI CENTRAL

As its expert systems strategy evolved, Digital discovered that, in some cases, development and maintenance had to be controlled centrally. Yet this didn't prove to be true of the total expert systems program. Nor would the culture and organizational structure of the company allow for vesting such control in a single organization, says Jack Rahaim, manager of Digital's AI marketing and productivity shell programs. "From the beginning, we planned to disperse the technology throughout the organization," he says.

Digital's structure is not a simple one—a functionally decentralized organization integrated at the business process level and run under a matrix style of management. Even though the AI Technology Center is the locus for AI expertise at Digital, it doesn't run the entire expert systems show. Nor does its management plan or control the applications.

The Marlborough facility houses two basic expert systems groups. The first comprises 150 people involved in applications development for configuring systems, field service and manufacturing, and engineering. These professionals report to line managers, as do other expert systems developers scattered throughout the company.

The second is the core staff under AITC management—also 150 professionals—who are involved in services and products for both internal and external customers. They are responsible for distributing the technology they develop throughout the organization and to customers via marketing, training, and apprenticeship programs. They are also involved in establishing new training centers in Europe, Japan, and the United States.

Rahaim emphasizes that line managers and their staffs control the selection of applications, the tools they use for development and even the skills-training process. (AITC offers training, but it's not mandatory for employees to go there.)

The only rules are that applications meet the communications and data standards of the company if they are to be integrated at the business process, network, and data levels.

In short, although AITC has enormous influence over the Digital program, it does not pull all the strings, a fact that Rahaim feels has contributed to corporatewide acceptance and commitment.

THE DISPERSED APPROACH

The issues involved in implementing the dispersed approach are quite different. The key questions to ask are the following:

- Who will be the target developers—the ultimate end user, the user in concert with an IS professional, or a local guru?
- How can you build the user/developer's understanding and commitment?
- How can developers increase their programming skills?
- What standard tools should you select and sponsor, and how many of them will you need?
- How do you avoid reinventing the wheel?
- How do you find and maintain area management support?

The strength of this approach is that expert systems are often developed fast—from days to months—and for costs ranging from a few hundred to a few thousand dollars. At DuPont, training consists of a basic two-day course, plus a number of one-day, specialized courses.

Besides speed and low cost, the dispersed approach fosters user ownership and creates broad organizational support. If it's handled correctly, the successful user/developers will sell the concept to their colleagues.

To succeed in the dispersed mode, a company must move through three stages:

- **Maverick.** A few aggressive pioneers begin to create their own small systems.
- **Experimentation.** The mavericks' successes convince a group or a manager to address certain problems formally for a trial period.
- **Culture change.** A group decides to embrace the development of expert systems for a wide variety of applications.

With so many issues to resolve, don't expect shortcuts to culture change. Culture change means that many existing processes for resolving problems must be thrown out and new ones adopted. To make culture change work, the group must have a vision. And that vision must be supported by successful experiences, a sizable cadre of trained amateurs, and a plan that specifies each milestone for achieving a completed system and the rewards at the end of each milestone.

It's taken five years for DuPont to evolve through the maverick and experimentation stages. Eighteen hundred people have been trained to use expert system shells, and several business units are now ready for the culture change that lies ahead. Two of them are developing several hundred expert systems this year.

SUPPORT FROM THE TOP

The dispersed strategy does not mean no corporate guidance or support. Back in 1985, DuPont did not simply scatter a few expert systems shells on users' desks and tell its people to play with them. An AI task force led by Ed Mahler examined the idea of letting the experts—the decision makers—develop their own systems using existing expert systems shells. The task force approved 40 different packages that would run on DuPont's installed workstations and personal computers.

Although shells were still in their commercial infancy, the task force decided there was enormous opportunity for improving front-line decision making through a dispersed approach. Senior management agreed to experiment and provided $3 million in seed money.

Gradually, a consulting organization was put in place. The corporate AI group was to serve as the catalyst and change agent, selling the concept, selecting the standard tools, and establishing training programs. Under this group, a cadre of site coordinators (now numbering 200) have been assigned to user locations, arranging for training and supplying help when needed.

Recognizing the culture of fierce independence at DuPont, the AI Group knew the expert system movement had to grow by word-of-mouth advertising, rather than by edict. Group members began by calling their colleagues throughout the business units and giving talks, and then waited for the word to spread. As the successes piled up, area management support increased.

The standard tools that were selected were not stipulated by law—users could opt to use any tool that would run on their microcomputers or VAX workstations. The initial tools sponsored were Insight + from New York City-based Information Builders Inc. and RS Decision from BBN Software Products, a division of Cambridge, Mass.-based Bolt Beranek and Newman Inc. Because no shell is suited to all applications, the number of standard tools in use today has grown. The only hard and fast rule was that each system had to have a standard interface for linking into the network and the data files.

It didn't take long for results to come in. Typically, trainees developed their first systems within a few weeks. DuPont tried several routes to avoid reinventing the wheel with these systems. The first idea, to create a database of expert systems, was soon discarded. Besides the technical complexity involved, the AI Group recognized that human nature would not cope with the centralized data base idea. Could everyone be counted on to enter their expert systems into the central file? Not likely.

But people who were creating new systems could be counted on to find out if anyone had done a similar project. Fortunately, a vehicle for managing this type of fishing expedition was already in place. DuPont's global electronic mail network allows employees to put out a single call to all of DuPont's 1,800 expert systems developers.

The dispersed approach requires a lot of self-help and self-discipline. Novices will make mistakes, and they will sometimes develop systems that are not useful. Yet most mistakes quickly work themselves out, and whimsical projects usually fall into disuse because of the maintenance time involved. Just 50 systems have simply withered away at DuPont, while 600 have proven highly productive.

DuPont's expert systems generally fall into one of the following areas: troubleshooting and selection systems used from development to sales and delivery; production planning and scheduling; and remote process control.

Useful expert systems have been devised to help design products meeting specific customer needs. For example, the Packaging Adviser, used for designing rigid plastic food containers, helped DuPont break into the highly competitive barrier resin market. The company also tackled a critical problem, chemical spills occurring in transit, by developing a Transportation Emergency Response Planner to guide people in the field through the right procedures for diagnosing, controlling, and cleaning up a spill. A Maintenance Finish Adviser is used at trade shows to answer questions on high-performance paints and obtain sales leads. And a Confidentiality Document Adviser is used for preparing sections of legal documents.

Expert systems are widely used throughout DuPont's manufacturing processes for troubleshooting and quality control. So far, the company has developed 50 expert systems for diagnosing and correcting process control problems. A 600-rule expert system, built by two people in concert with the business team, has been integrated into one unit's production planning and scheduling system.

While DuPont continues to decompose large problems into parts addressable through small expert systems developed by individuals, the company realizes that there are economies of scale in creating centers to help tackle generic problems, such as real-time process control and production scheduling. These groups, called competency centers, are composed of IS and network professionals who work with business units wanting to develop such systems.

17,000 RULES

At Digital, the configuration systems today include six systems totaling more than 17,000 rules: XCON, used to validate the technical correctness of customer orders and guide the assembly of these orders; XSEL, used iteratively to assist sales in configuring an order; XFL, for diagramming a computer room for floor layout for the proposed configuration; XCLUSTER, to configure clusters; XNET, for designing local area networks; and SIZER, for sizing computing resources according to customer need.

Among the variety of other expert systems are inventory monitoring (CAN BUILD), truck scheduling (National Dispatch Router), manufacturing planning (MOC) and logic gate design (APES).

Digital's Rahaim notes that although enormous operational savings have been realized through the use of these systems, even greater benefits are evident, although difficult to quantify. "The configuration systems allowed us to pursue and extend our à la carte marketing strategy, which is what differentiates us."

The APES system has resulted in striking productivity gains. "Typically, a senior design engineer can create 200 logic gates per week," say Rahaim. "With APES, the number had gone to 8,000 per day. The first chip we designed this way sped up a computer introduction by six months. How do you quantify the strategic advantage of slashing the time to market?"

Besides day-to-day operational systems, Digital also has expert systems designed for senior management. One such system is called Manufacturing Operations Consultant (MOC), which helps managers examine the impact of major changes—in pricing, in resources, in market demand—on the capacity and work load of their plants worldwide. "That is an example of a strategic system and of a system that must integrate," says Rahaim. "You don't know about the plant in Ireland unless you can tap into the data bases there on their production load, the cost structures, etc." MOC is used for short-range planning, but other expert systems are being devised for modeling long-range plans.

Systems integration is extremely important to the evolution of strategic expert systems at Digital. For instance, Rahaim foresees the day when systems such as APES will be integrated with other design systems and business processes so that management can electronically simulate the final product and estimate the manufacturing costs and time to market.

What's the right approach for your organization? There is no simple answer. Analyzing the business environment and the technology readiness of your business are critical steps that can lead to the use of either or both approaches described here. Whatever method is chosen, managing the evolution of the effort must be handled carefully if the program is to achieve broad organizational commitment.

Becoming a world-class organization requires putting world-class knowledge, not just information, into the hands of decision makers. Expert systems technology is far from mature, but we already have the tools, methods, and approaches to use expert systems to begin to achieve that goal. Those still mulling over the question of whether to develop an expert system program will be outclassed by those already planning and implementing these systems.

QUESTIONS

1. Describe the strategy that DuPont used to introduce expert systems.
2. Describe the strategy that Digital used to introduce expert systems.
3. Discuss the factors that an organization should consider when developing an expert systems strategy.

26

COVERSTORY—AUTOMATED NEWS FINDING IN MARKETING

INTRODUCTION

Machine-readable bar codes on products in supermarkets have changed forever the way the packaged-goods industry tracks its sales and understands how its markets work. Although the codes were originally introduced and justified to save labor at check-out, the spin-off data produced by them provide marvelous opportunities for retailers and manufacturers to measure the effectiveness of their marketing programs and create greater efficiencies in their merchandising and promotion. We shall describe how one manufacturer, Ocean Spray Cranberries, Inc., has responded to these opportunities with an innovative decision support system designed to serve marketing and sales management.

Ocean Spray

Ocean Spray Cranberries, Inc., is a grower-owned agricultural cooperative headquartered in Lakeville-Middleboro, Massachusetts, with about nine hundred members. It produces and distributes a line of high quality juices and juice drinks with heavy emphasis on cranberry drinks but also with strong lines in grapefruit and tropical drinks. The company also has a significant business in cranberry sauces and fresh cranberries. About 80% of Ocean Spray products sell through supermarkets and other retail stores with lesser amounts flowing through food

This chapter is a reprint of John D. Schmitz, Gordon D. Armstrong, and John D. C. Little, "CoverStory—Automated News Finding in Marketing," *Interfaces,* Volume 20, Number 6, November–December, 1990, pp. 29–38.

service and ingredient product channels. Ocean Spray is a Fortune 500 company with sales approaching $1 billion per year.

Until the mid-1980s, Ocean Spray, like most grocery manufacturers, tracked the sales and share of its products with syndicated warehouse withdrawal and retail store data provided by companies such as SAMI and A. C. Nielsen. This data supplemented the companies' own shipments data by providing information on competitive products and the total market. Such databases have formed the cornerstones of useful and effective decision support systems in many companies (Little, 1979; McCann, 1988). For some time, however, it has been apparent that a radically new generation is on the way. By the mid-eighties, the penetration of scanners in supermarkets had reached a level such that data suppliers could put together valid national samples of scanning stores and provide much more detailed and comprehensive sales tracking services than previously. In 1987, Ocean Spray contracted for InfoScan data for the juice category from Information Resources, Inc. (IRI) of Chicago.

InfoScan

IRI's InfoScan is a national and local market tracking service for the consumer packed-goods industry. InfoScan follows consumer purchases of products at the individual item level as identified by the industry's universal product code (UPC). IRI buys data from a nationally representative sample of over 2500 scanner-equipped stores covering major metropolitan markets and many smaller cities. These provide basic volume, market share, distribution, and price information. Added to this are measures of merchandising and promotion collected in the stores and markets. These include retailer advertising in newspapers and flyers, in-store displays, and coupons. Most of the measures contain several levels of coding; for example, newspaper ads are coded A, B, or C, according to their prominence. In addition, the InfoScan service provides access to IRI's individual household purchase data collected from approximately 70,000 households across 27 market areas.

Data Explosion

The amount of data is almost overwhelming. IRI adds about 2 gigabytes per week to its master database in Chicago. Compared to the old tracking data, a company buying the InfoScan service receives increased detail by a factor of 4 to 6 because of dealing with individual weeks instead of multiweek totals, 3 to 5 because of UPC's instead of aggregate brands, 4 to 5 because of 50 individual markets instead of broad geographic regions, 2 to 3 because of more tracking measures, and 1 to 3 because of breakouts to individual chains within a market. Multiplying out the factors reveals that 100 to 1000 times as much data is being handled as previously.

Most packaged-goods manufacturers did not initially understand the implications of two to three orders of magnitude more data. And, in fact, this kind of change is difficult to comprehend. In terms of a management report, it means that, if a report took an hour to look through before, the corresponding report with all the possible new breakouts would take 100 hours to look through. In other words, the new detail will not be looked at.

The remarkable advances that have taken place in computing have helped conceal this issue. Today's technology certainly makes it feasible to store and retrieve all the new data and, although the hardware and software to do this are not cheap, they represent a small fraction of the sales dollars involved, so that, if using the data can lead to more effective marketing, a full scale DSS with on-line access to the database is certainly warranted. Indeed, it was clear in advance and even more clear after the fact that the detailed data contain much information of competitive value in running the businesses.

DSS Strategy

Packaged goods companies today have lean staffs. Many have been restructured and lost people. This is in the face of the huge data increases just described. Although Ocean Spray has not been restructured, its roots as an agricultural cooperative have always given it an internal culture of lean self-sufficiency. It has a small IS department for the organization as a whole.

This situation led Ocean Spray naturally to a strategy of a small marketing DSS organization running a decentralized system where the users do most of their own retrieval and analysis. The marketing DSS for syndicated data currently consists of one marketing professional plus the database administrators. The goal is to have a largely centralized database with workstations for sales and marketing in the business units. User interfaces must be easily mastered by busy people whose main jobs are in the functional areas. The role of the DSS organization is to acquire and develop tools with which the end users can do their own analyses. DSS consults with users to develop appropriate preprogrammed reports to be delivered as hard copy and/or online.

An important characteristic of the system must be growth potential. Not only should retrieval of specific numbers, tables, and graphs be easy now, but the system architecture and computing power should also be there for future calculations and analyses that are likely to be much more computationally intensive than simple retrieval.

Ocean Spray's InfoScan Database

Ocean Spray's syndicated database for juices is impressive, almost imposing, considering the change from the past and the level of human resources put against it. It contains about 400 million numbers covering up to 100 data measures, 10,000 products, 125 weeks, and 50 geographic markets. It grows by 10 million new numbers every four weeks. Finding the important news amid this detail and getting it to the right people in a timely fashion is a big task for a department of one.

Hardware and Software

The DSS architecture puts the database and CPU-intensive processing on an IBM 9370 mainframe with ten gigabytes of disk storage and puts user-interface tasks on eleven 386-level workstations located in the marketing and sales areas. The basic DSS software is IRI's DataServer, which manages data and mainframe computation in the fourth generation language EXPRESS and the user interface in pcEXPRESS. This provides menu-driven access to a family of flexible preprogrammed reports available on the workstations.

Unlike some other solutions used by packaged-goods manufacturers, this architecture provides easy access to mainframe computing power from the workstations as is needed, for example, to run applications like the CoverStory software to be discussed.

BASIC RETRIEVAL AND BASIC REPORTING

The basic retrieval, reporting, and analytic capabilities of Ocean Spray's DSS are extensive. Any particular fact from the database can be pulled out in a few steps with the help of pull-down menus and picklists. Much of the use comes from standard reports: a company top line report, and four business area reports (cranberry drinks, grapefruit, aseptic packages, and tropical drinks) showing status and trends including changes in share in aggregate and in detail, and changes in merchandising and distribution against a year ago or four weeks ago. Derived measures such as BDI (brand development indices) and CDI (category development indices) are available. Product managers can get a quick update of what is going on with their products. Standardized graphs can be called up and it is relatively easy to construct new ones. Similarly, users can readily construct measures that are ratios, differences, and other combinations of ones already in the database. Usage has been growing steadily since DataServer and the InfoScan database were installed.

Nevertheless, the introduction of the system has required as much learning for the DSS department as the end users. Some people, especially in sales, made little use of the system. Within marketing a few individuals took to the system quickly and did considerable analysis but there was also a feeling that you would not want to have a reputation for spending too much time pushing numbers around. In fact, within sales, the characteristic attitude has been: "Using the computer is not my job. Give me something that is already analyzed. Give me materials that are ready to use and will help me do my job."

In response to this the DSS department has developed (and continues to develop) tools and analyses that will help solve specific user problems. There are a number of approaches; CoverStory to be discussed below is one of the key directions. In addition a variety of reports oriented about selected issues have been developed, for example, reports that rank products and point out Ocean Spray strengths and identify markets where some Ocean Spray product is underdistributed relative to its inherent selling power. The intention is to help sales and marketing people identify market opportunities and product selling points.

FINDING THE NEWS: COVERSTORY

CoverStory is an expert system developed by IRI to tackle the problem of too much data; Ocean Spray has been a development partner and first client. CoverStory automates the creation of summary memoranda for reports extracted from the large scanner databases. The goal is to provide a cover memo, like the one a marketing analyst would write, to describe key events that are reflected in the database—especially in its newest numbers. The project began as a teaching exercise in marketing science—"How would you summarize what is important in this data?" (Stoyiannidis, 1987; Little, 1988)—and has developed into a practical tool.

CoverStory is undergoing continuing development as we gain experience with its use in new situations. We describe the following aspects of the system as it is now being used: (1) the role of marketing models, (2) the basic decomposition steps embodied in the search strategy, (3) the linearization and ranking processes used to decide what facts are most worth mentioning, and (4) methods for generating and publishing the output.

Marketing Models

CoverStory is rooted in the modeling tradition. However, by design, it does not directly present model results at this stage of development, but rather reports only database facts, such as share, volume, price, distribution, and measures of merchandising. The reason is to have the output and underlying processes as transparent and easy to understand as possible. The program assesses the relative importance of these facts, and selects them for presentation by using weights and thresholds which come from marketing models. However, the user is able to inspect and change these values.

Furthermore, in choosing measures of marketing effort for CoverStory to consider, we select a set of marketing variables from the scanner database that model-building experience has shown to be important for driving sales and share. Measures commonly used include:

Displays—percent of stores (weighted by size) that displayed a brand or item.

Features—percent of stores (weighted by size) that ran a feature ad on a brand.

Distribution—size-weighted percent of stores that sold a brand.

Price cuts—percent of stores that sold a brand at a price reduced by more than a threshold, such as 10%, from the regular price.

Price—Price can be represented by many data measures. CoverStory sometimes uses the overall average price paid at the register but often draws from a finer set of price measures that may include regular price, average merchandised price, and depth of discount. The regular price is the price of an item not undergoing special promotion; average merchandised price is the price of an item in stores where it is being promoted with feature ads or displays. Depth of discount is the difference between these two. In an InfoScan database, we can get even finer measures of price by breaking out average merchandised price and depth of price discount by type of merchandising.

Through a marketing model, we quantify the impact of each of these marketing levers on share or on sales volume and find their relative importance. For grocery items, among the measures described above, we usually (but not always) find the distribution is more important than price, displays, features, and price cuts in that order.

Flow of Analysis and Decomposition

Figure 26–1 shows the general flow of analysis in CoverStory. The central idea is to analyze the behavior of an aggregate product in an aggregate market by a series of decompositions or disaggregations. An aggregate product is a product which includes more than one UPC. The UPC (bar code on the package) is the lowest level of product detail available in a scanner database. An example of an aggregate product is Ocean Spray Cranberry Juice and Blends. It consists of many different sizes, package types, and flavors and blends. An example of an aggregate market is the total United States which can be disaggregated into regions or individual cities or even grocery chains within markets.

In doing decomposition, CoverStory follows a style which we have observed in the analytical marketing reports used in many companies. Analysis proceeds by answering the following series of questions. (1) What is going on overall in the aggregate product for the aggregate market? (2) What changes does this reflect in the components of the aggregate product? (3) What changes does this reflect in the aggregate market? (4) What is happening to competitive products? In CoverStory, we go through each of these in turn. Within each of these sections of the analysis, the program follows a standard series of steps:

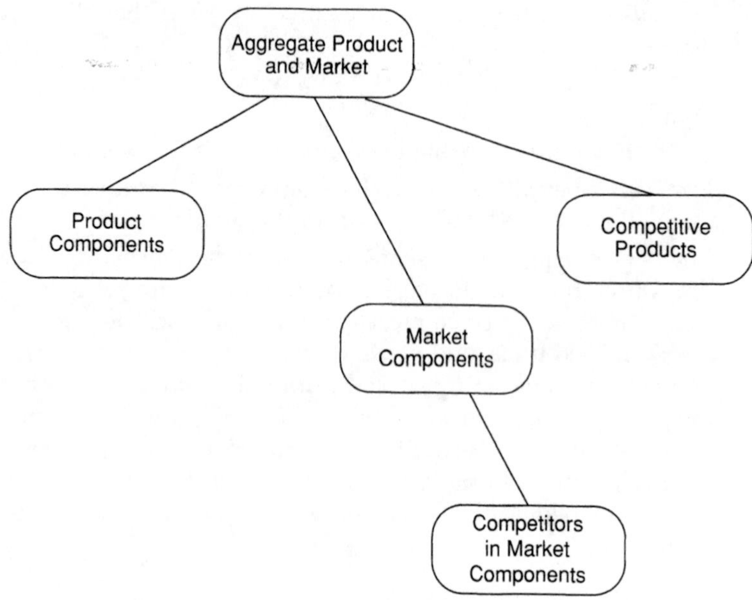

FIGURE 26–1 Structure of CoverStory Analysis

Rank the components (markets or products or market/product combinations) by some criteria.

Select the most noteworthy for mention and for further analysis.

Calculate causal factor changes for these top few markets, products, or combinations. Causal factor changes are distribution, price, and merchandising changes.

Rank these causal factors changes; then select the top few causal changes to include in the report.

The need to select "the top few" items from different lists is dictated by the size of the scanner database. The number of events that can be mentioned is enormous. Without strictly limiting the amount of information in a report, we found that the news drowned in the detail.

Ranking the Products or Markets

We nearly always rank component products or component markets by share or volume change. When we are looking at size groups within an aggregate product, for example, and we are analyzing share changes, size group ranks will be based on share changes. We have found this to be generally effective with one exception. If there has been a fundamental restructuring of the way a category is marketed, share changes may not be meaningful. (This happened, for example, in the coffee category when packaging switched from multiples of a pound (1-, 2-, and 3-pound cans) to multiples of 13 ounces (13, 26, and 39 ounces). This gave the appearance that a large amount of volume was switching into "new products" and, for a year, volume and share change calculations required special treatment.

Selecting the Top Few Products or Markets

The top few are the few that are the most noteworthy. We generally calculate which component products or markets are furthest away from average and retain these extremes for mention. Normally, this leads CoverStory to pick winners and losers. In some cases, however, when most of the products and markets are behaving in similar fashion, CoverStory will select only winners or only losers. This approach has been very effective and it closely mimics the way that human market analysts select individual segments of a product line or individual markets for mention.

Calculating Causal Factor Changes

When we point out share or volume changes, we also want to mention possible causes of these share or volume changes. To do so, we calculate the amount of change in marketing support in each of the marketing factors which affects the product. For example, a share change in CranApple sales in Boston may have been partially caused by distribution, price, display, feature, or price cut activity.

Ranking Causal Factor Changes

We can generate a large number of causal factor changes when we decompose the aggregate product and market behavior into components. If there are ten product components, fifty markets, and eight causal factors we are screening, we have four thousand causal changes which are candidates for mention. Trimming this down to a small number for inclusion in the CoverStory report requires a ranking procedure. The procedure we have chosen is similar in spirit to the evaluation functions used in evaluating positions in game-playing programs (Barr, 1981). We calculate a score for each of the causal measure changes. The score incorporates the market in which the change occurred, which causal factor changed, and the magnitude of the change. Symbolically:

$$\text{Score} = \text{Change} \times \text{Factor weight} \times \text{Market weight}$$

Change is the amount of change in the causal factor and is either a percent change or raw change depending on the factor. Factor weight is different for each of the marketing factors such as distribution, price, displays, featuring, and price cuts. These factor weights are intended, informally speaking, to make different marketing changes have the same score if their impact on sales is the same. We initialize factor weights based on analysis done outside of CoverStory based on logit models of the type described in Guadagni and Little (1983). Market weight is a term which makes it more likely that an event in a large market will be mentioned than an event in a small market. We originally used market size but found that this was to strong. Only events from New York, Chicago, and Los Angeles would be mentioned and so we have softened the impact of market size. One approach that has proven effective is to use the square root of market size as the market weight.

In all, this scoring method yields a ranked list of causal market changes where such a change can be described in terms of

What happened? (e.g., price went up by 20%)
Where did it happen? (e.g., in the Southeastern Region)
What product did it happen to? (e.g., the 32-ounce bottles)

The events that CoverStory describes are the ones that rank highest using this scoring mechanism.

Presenting the Results

We have experimented with several methods for presenting these results. Our present style is to produce an English-language report in distribution-quality format. This has been an important piece of overall effort and has had a dramatic effect on the acceptability of CoverStory reports to end users. The language generation is usually straightforward; it is based on sentence templates (Barr, 1981). We have considered but not yet implemented context and memory (Schank and Riesbeck, 1981) in our text generation. The use of some randomization of detailed wording through the use of a thesaurus keeps the CoverStory memo from sounding too mechanical. The memo is relatively short and structured so this simple language generation has not been a limitation on CoverStory.

The CoverStory results are published through a high-quality desktop publishing package or a word-processor with desktop publishing capabilities. Variation in typeface, use of graphic boxes, and sidebars are all intended to give the memo visual appeal and highlight the marketing facts which are contained in it.

CoverStory is very much a decision support system rather than a decision-making system. The user can adjust all major system parameters such as who competes with whom, what weights to use for the marketing factors, and how much information is to be reported. The final memo is published through a standard word processing package so it can be edited by the user, although this seldom happens. Because the memo is automated and easily set up (and then left alone) to meet the needs of specific managers, the appropriate "news" can quickly be distributed throughout the organizations when new data arrives.

The CoverStory memorandum shown in Figure 26–2 (page 434) illustrates the output. In this coded example, we present highlights about a brand called Sizzle in the Total United States. The recipient for this memorandum is the Sizzle Brand Manager and the brand management team. The series of decomposition in this report is

Breaking down total Sizzle volume into sales by size groups.
Looking at Sizzle's major competitors.
Looking at submarkets of the United States—cities in this database.
Looking at competitive activity in these submarkets.

The analysis is based on share change. A sample of a causal change shown by CoverStory is the increase of display activity to support 64-oz bottles of Sizzle.

BENEFITS

Ocean Spray's DSS design strategy has successfully solved several problems. The decision to put users in charge of their own basic retrieval and analysis has generally worked well and, where it has run into problems, the DSS organization has responded by providing increasingly customized tools. The DataServer interface has been easy to learn. Usage on the 386-level workstations located in the marketing area is many hours per week and rising.

The strategy casts the DSS organization in the role of acquiring and building tools to make the users more effective. Consultation with users has led to a set of hard copy reports that are circulated regularly to marketing, sales and top management and to customized reports that can be called up on line and printed locally on laser printers, if needed.

CoverStory is a particularly desirable development because, with very little effort, it provides users with top line summaries and analyzes across a wide variety of situations. Previously this required time-consuming intervention by a skilled analyst. Furthermore the technology is an extensible platform on which to build increasingly sophisticated decentralized analysis for the user community.

The information coming out of Ocean Spray's marketing DSS is used every day in planning, fire-fighting, and updating people's mental models of what is going on in the company's markets. Typical applications include such actions as taking a price increase and monitoring its effect; discovering sales softness in a particular market, diagnosing its causes, and applying remedies; and following a new product introduction to alert the sales department in case of weak results in certain markets compared to others. The DSS is totally integrated into business operations and it no longer seems possible to consider life without it.

FIGURE 26–2 Example of CoverStory Output

To: Sizzle Brand Manager
From: CoverStory
Date: 07/05/89
Subject: Sizzle Brand Summary for Twelve Weeks Ending May 21, 1989

Sizzle's share of type in Total United States was 71.3 in the C&B Juice/Drink category for the twelve weeks ending 5/21/89. This is an increase of 1.2 points from a year earlier but down .5 from last period. This reflects volume sales of 10.6 million gallons. Category volume (currently 99.9 million gallons) declined 1.3% from a year earlier.

Display activity and unsupported price cuts rose over the past year - unsupported price cuts from 38 points to 46. Featuring and price remained at about the same level as a year earlier.

Components of Sizzle Share

Among components of sizzle, the principal gainer is:

Sizzle 64 oz: up 2.2 points from last year to 23.7

and losers:

Sizzle 48 oz. -0.6 to 34.9

Sizzle 32 oz. -0.1 to 6.7

Sizzle's share of type is 71.3 - up 1.2 from the same period last year.

Sizzle 64 oz's share of type increase is partly due to 11.3 pts rise in % ACV with Display vs. yr. ago.

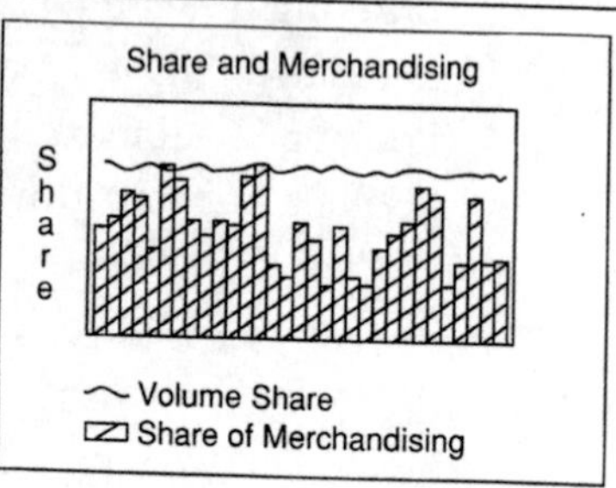

Competitor Summary

Among Sizzle's major competitors, the principal gainers are:

Shakey: up 2.5 points from last year to 2.6

Private Label +.5 to 19.9 (but down .3 since last period)

and loser:

Generic Seltzer -.7 to 3.5

Shakey's share of type increase is associated with 71.7 pts of ACV rise in ACV Wtd Dist versus a year ago.

Market Highlights

Sizzle showed significant gains relative to

Perhaps the easiest way to express the success of the system is that, with the help of marketing science and expert systems technology, the DSS has made it possible for a single marketing professional to manage the process of alerting all Ocean Spray marketing and sales managers to key problems and opportunities and of providing them with daily problem-solving information and guidance. This is being done across four business units handling scores of company products in dozens of markets representing hundreds of millions of dollars of sales.

QUESTIONS

1. In what ways has data generated by bar-code scanners caused both opportunities and problems?
2. Summarize how CoverStory works.
3. Is CoverStory an expert system? Discuss.

REFERENCES

1. BARR, A., AND E. A. FEIGENBAUM, eds. *Handbook of Artificial Intelligence.* Los Altos, CA: William Kaufman, 1981.
2. GUADAGNI, P. M., AND J. D. C. LITTLE. "A Logic Model of Brand Choice Calibrated on Scanner Data," *Marketing Science,* 2 (Summer 1983), 203–238.
3. LITTLE, J. D. C. "Decision Support Systems for Marketing Managers," *Marketing,* 43 (Summer 1979), 9–26.
4. LITTLE, J. D. C. "CoverStory: An Expert System to Find the News in Scanner Data," internal working paper, Sloan School of Management, M. I. T. (September 1988).
5. MCCANN, J. M. *The Marketing Workbench,* Homewood, IL. Dow Jones-Irwin, 1988.
6. SCHANK, R. C., AND C. K. RIESBECK, eds. *Inside Computer Understanding.* Hillsdale, NJ: Lawrence Erlbaum, 1981.
7. STOYIANNIDIS, D. "A Marketing Research Expert System," Sloan School Master's thesis, M.I.T., Cambridge, MA, June 1987.

Part 8

THE BENEFITS OF DECISION SUPPORT APPLICATIONS

Organizations are increasingly interested in measuring the return on their investments, especially in regard to expenditures on information technology (IT). The days when senior managers quickly approved information systems budgets are over. They are no longer willing to blindly accept statements such as "we need to keep technologically up-to-date" or "it isn't possible to measure the return on IT investments." The growth in outsourcing is related, in part, to managements' concern that they are not getting a good return from IT.

Investments in decision support are not escaping scrutiny. Consequently, managers are trying to figure out how to determine the benefits from these applications. The costs are not usually too hard to figure but the benefits are. There are exceptions, of course, as seen in Chapter 6 where the train dispatching system at Southern Railway was discussed. The most common problem in assessing decision support benefits is that it is usually impossible to know what decisions would have been made and the outcomes from those decisions if the information from the decision support application was not available.

Any discussion of decision support benefits includes "hard" and "soft" benefits. The former are those to which a dollar value can be assigned while the latter are not amenable to quantification. Most decision support applications include a mixture of each.

This final part of the book explores decision support benefits. Chapter 27 describes how executives at Xerox, Quaker Oats, and Beneficial have benefited from their companies' EIS. Often in their own words, they talk about how they use their systems and what they think the benefits are.

Chapter 28 begins with a description of a study that explored the benefits associated with EISs, how the costs and benefits are assessed, and factors that affect the assessment process. The findings provide insight into current practices. The chapter also includes a description of the award-winning methodology used to evaluate the EIS at Conoco. While the approach was developed for an EIS, it is general enough that it has potential use with other applications. The chapters make clear that developing hard benefits is a challenging, but not impossible undertaking, but that many important benefits are soft.

27

THE BENEFITS OF DECISION SUPPORT AT XEROX, QUAKER OATS, AND BENEFICIAL

Stories abound about the many senior executives who, while paying tribute to the contributions of computer technology to their companies, break out in a rash when they get within 10 feet of a computer terminal or personal computer.

This resistance is puzzling, since top executives have signed off on billions of dollars' worth of computers for their companies and must realize that their operations would grind to a halt if deprived, even temporarily, of these facilities. But translating that into their own work is another matter. They may note the computer's handling of millions of transactions for payroll, accounting, invoicing, plus word processing and other office automation. But they view their own work as vastly different, not at all susceptible to automation. Their jobs appear fundamentally different from those many layers below them, and they fail to see how their productivity could be improved by a computer system.

For them, productivity may not be the key issue. Jim Carlisle, a consultant who helped develop executive information systems for Xerox Corporation and Westinghouse Electric Corporation, observes: "Anyone who has made senior vice president probably can't have his personal productivity improved. However, he can have his vision and comprehension of the business improved."

Others say that many attempts at executive information systems have failed because they do not meet the highly individual needs of top managers. One skeptic is Henry Mintzberg, professor of management at McGill University in Montreal, who has observed that executives "are still forced to conform to the tech-

This chapter is a reprint of Lou Wallis, "Power Computing at the Top," *Across the Board*, Volume 26, Number 182, 1989, © 1989 by the Conference Board, Inc., pp. 42–51.

nology's capabilities, rather than being able to tailor it to their own needs. The mistaken assumption is that the technology is based on an understanding of what managers do, and it's not. The technology has simply been superimposed over the work."

Executives make important decisions, a lot of them. But as they grapple for the best outcomes, they can become exasperated, panning the dross and silt of corporate computer data bases, searching for nuggets of information. Too many information systems have been designed for everything and everybody in the company except for the high-level decision makers, who tend to find them "data rich, insight poor." The problem of providing adequate corporate data for executive decision makers is similar to that of the provident squirrel who intends to dine on acorns once the winter snows have arrived—that is, saving the treasure isn't the problem, it's finding where it's hidden.

But newer and better systems are designed especially for corporate decision makers and fit the way they actually work. One type that has worked well for many managers is called an executive support system (ESS). The powerful software is sold by vendors but usually has to be adapted to the needs of each company's top managers. ESS learns what executive users want, allows users to enter information and ask questions in informal English, delivers the results in a meaningful form, and, as far as possible, eliminates the need to make adjustments to the computer itself.

Computer systems have long been able to store and retrieve financial, production, marketing, and other essential measures of company performance. These are the conventional, recognizable output from electronic data processing or management information systems (MIS). The day-to-day output of these systems are garden-variety reports of weekly, monthly, year-to-date results intended for many different people and purposes. "The monthly reports are essentially background music," says Jim Carlisle, managing director of Office of the Future Inc. "They are 10 to 15 days old on arrival. If you're budgeting monthly sales of $50 million and in 15 days you've done $7 million, you need to know now—not 15 days later." With traditional computer systems, a patient analyst can sort and probe the various data bases and standard reports, draw up the comparisons, ratios, increases, and decreases, and, if familiar with the needs of the executive, produce the same kind of quality analyses offered by executive systems.

So, why should a company switch to ESS if traditional systems have worked for years? Some companies have turned to ESS because it is designed to help executives make decisions by giving them immediate access to any information that they deem helpful. ESS takes into account that one executive's needs are not necessarily another's, because analysis, reflection, and decision making are personal arts. By contrast, little of the costly and imposing structure of corporate computing run by MIS was especially designed for, or is very useful for, making decisions. Rosabeth Moss Kanter, of the Harvard Business School, reminds us: "Information quality requires focusing on what's important, not what's available. Stored information represents potential, but is useless unless it can be actively communicated to those who need it."

Many corporate leaders have tried to do something about the shortcomings of MIS, not just for themselves but for their entire organizations. Determined not to be outflanked by the upwardly techno-mobile, some chief executives have led the charge for installing flexible information systems and convincing people to use them.

Three executives who have had positive experiences with ESS are Paul A. Allaire, president of Xerox, William D. Smithburg, chairman and chief executive officer of the Quaker Oats Company, and Finn M. W. Caspersen, chairman and chief executive officer of Beneficial Corporation. Each has for some time been using an executive support system developed by his company, getting three kinds of support from it: 1) company performance data—sales, production, earnings, budgets, and forecasts; 2) internal communications—personal correspondence, reports, and meetings; 3) environmental scanning—for news on government regulations, competition, financial and economic developments, and scientific subjects.

What follows does not pretend to be a balanced appraisal of executive support systems, but rather conveys how three executives have profited from their use.

WHY XEROX STARTED AT THE TOP

Paul Allaire began by insisting that Xerox would not cram a new system down the throats of executives, telling them, "Use it or else." In 1983, Allaire returned from Britain where he had been managing director of Rank Xerox Ltd. and took over as corporate chief of staff. To begin development of ESS, Allaire brought Kenneth Soha to headquarters from the company's plant in Rochester, New York, where he had directed the information systems group. David T. Kearns, Xerox's CEO, had asked Allaire to reduce the cost of staff work at corporate headquarters and improve its effectiveness; Allaire believed that information technology had a major role to play. He thereby became the executive sponsor of ESS, and Soha became the operational sponsor and director of the system. Allaire describes their early actions: "We hired a consultant, Jim Carlisle, and looked at the state of the art of ESS. Looking at all of the systems that we could find in operation, we concluded that none were much good for us. So we decided to build our own."

In 1983, Xerox embarked on the development of its ESS, which was to serve more than 400 people at corporate headquarters in Stamford, Connecticut. It was to link strategic planning with electronic mail, changing the way top executives communicated and worked with one another. Soha's supporting operation grew to more than a dozen people with an annual budget of $1 million by 1988.

"We decided that ESS had to be evolutionary, not forced," says Allaire, who was promoted to president of the company in 1986. "But we had to start at the top, so we had to prove how it could help [executives] do their jobs. Bill Glavin, our vice chairman, at first said: 'I came from a systems environment, but I'm not going to use the system. I'll give it to my secretary.'" Allaire continues: "We said, 'Fine, we'll put it on your secretary's desk, and if you want a printout of anything, here's how you get it.'" Glavin eventually became one of the system's biggest fans.

"Compared with people, technology is cheap, and one of my objectives every year is to reduce spending on corporate staff," Allaire says. "We have some fairly stringent targets on that." He estimates that for each of the past three years, ESS has helped reduce staff expenses at headquarters by 5 percent. "I felt sure that technology could help reduce staff, the big expense item. But we realized we couldn't just present the system and say, 'Here's the answer to your prayers, and, by the way, take a 10 percent cut in your people.' You have to provide tools and let people decide how to use them most efficiently."

One explanation for the success of ESS at Xerox is that, early on, the principal developers, especially Allaire and Soha, did not just throw money at a vague set of problems. Improving communications and the planning process were always uppermost in their minds. Allaire explains: "Right away, we realized that electronic mail was going to be a big item. Here's an illustration: We have what's called the extended management committee meeting. When I was in Britain, I had to come to the United States for these meetings once a month. The reading material I had for the meeting was supposed to come a week in advance, but sometimes it was only three days. I still needed time to analyze it and comment on it, and have my staff go over it. So I sometimes faced the prospect of reading it in a hotel room the night before the meeting, which was clearly ridiculous. Now, it's all on the ESS. The manager in Britain may actually have the materials before it's available here. The meetings themselves are more productive because the action items that result from decisions go on the system and are likely to be waiting for the British manager upon his return from the United States."

One of the first things put on the system was the management data book, which contains information on sales, customer service, personnel, and finance, including items such as currency rates. Xerox ran into a stumbling block, however, with the data book. Although the data was on the system, executives had to proceed through it page by page, just as with a book. They had to conform their thinking to the structure of the data book, which was the opposite of what Allaire wanted ESS to do. Allaire reports a big breakthrough, just out and not yet generally available, that eliminates this structural problem. "Now, if I'm looking at a profit-and-loss statement and want to zero in on, say, a sales-expense item, I can point with the mouse and get more detail, perhaps geographical or historical, and plot it on a graph. I can look at it any way I want, rather than have a staff person tell me what I should be looking for. I can take a trend that concerns me, bring it up on the screen, put a note on it, and ask my marketing people, 'What's going on here?'"

Part of the pleasure of being president of a company must be to be able to pick up the phone and get anyone on the other end. Is Allaire more likely to use the system, instead of buzzing someone for the information? "Oh yes! In the past, one of the frustrations of managing has been that when you know you need some information and call someone—and we still do—they ask how soon you need the information. I say, 'Right away,' and they say, 'You'll have it this afternoon.' Now that's pretty responsive. But I find that, when you're working on a project this morning and in the afternoon you're out with a customer, then when you return to the office and get the information, you may end up asking yourself, 'What the heck was I thinking of when I asked for this?' So, ESS allows you to work on a project or a decision, complete it right away, and be less reliant on staff support. You have flatter lines of control, and you can be more effective because you have the information you need. You can be more creative as well."

How often Allaire turns to ESS depends on the job at hand. "The fact that it isn't turned on doesn't mean it isn't working," he says. "My secretary's system is on all the time, and she can pick up anything urgent for me. I would say that some days I may not use it at all, but other days I use it most of the day."

Strategic planning at Xerox turned out to be one of the applications of ESS that got executives involved because it performed an essential task better. Shortly after ESS development began, Xerox's new resource management statement (essentially, a five-page summary of each business unit's plan) was put on the system. David Bliss, as executive in Xerox's corporate-strategy office, said that Allaire asked his operation to find a way to improve the planning process and reduce the time spent on it. An obvious target was the different formats each business-unit manager used to present the unit's plans. This made it difficult to compare one plan with another and kept senior executives scrambling to understand the details of each plan (Kenneth Soha describes this as the executives having to play on each unit's home field).

Four of the five pages of the new computer-based planning format consist of a summary of a unit's plan, such as projected sales and earnings, while the final page is reserved for senior management to respond to the plan with decisions or comments. Top management receives the plans on the ESS for a "pre-reading" three to five days before a scheduled meeting. The pertinent information is greatly condensed, and senior executives can easily compare one plan with another because of the consistent format.

Paul Allaire also developed the business priority list, a 15-item list used by those who report to him. The list keeps Allaire's people focused on important programs and provides progress reports. It is used to set agendas for meetings and is the basis of the direct-action list that prioritizes short-term tasks. Allaire reflects: "The list would be much harder without the ESS. The system permits us to store the items on the list in different ways and follow deadlines. Could we do it without the system? Well, we didn't. It also helps us to discipline ourselves and document meetings immediately."

What has been the impact of ESS on meetings? "I'm not sure we have fewer meetings, but they are more productive," Allaire says. "If we feel that an issue can be decided on material already available, we don't have a meeting. If more information is needed, it's available before the meeting. The result is that we very rarely have a meeting at which we don't have enough information to make a decision."

One benefit of ESS is that when executives must travel they can still use it, wherever they are. "When you travel, it is very valuable," agrees Allaire. "If I need a document, I can tell my administrative assistant and have it sent. The bad part is that you can't hide. People can get messages to you anywhere! I don't use it much at home, frankly. I live only 10 minutes away from the office, and I have to go through a modem to reach the office system. So, if I'm going to work on something, I'll just come in."

The easy flow of information from person to person is another benefit of ESS. But confidentiality of communications is obviously necessary, too—especially at the senior-executive level. ESS has security safeguards to protect that confidentiality. At Xerox, "need to know" is still invoked, and executives see essentially what their bosses want them to see. Nevertheless, since those who report to Allaire are on his system and thus receive similar information, was he worried that he might be second-guessed, perhaps limiting his freedom to make decisions?

"No, that doesn't bother me at all," he replies. "I'm glad to have the information, some that I didn't have before. People have more confidence in the decision we make, confidence that the decision makers are using relevant information and aren't up there in an ivory tower, not knowing what's going on in the world."

VISION AND KNOWLEDGE AT QUAKER OATS

"It didn't take any particularly creative thought to realize that executives can enhance their information flow in a way that enhances their decision making," explains William Smithburg, CEO at Quaker Oats. "All businesses live and die with information, and historically, it's been in a stack of paper somewhere and in files and books."

Smithburg began his initiation into computers in 1982 when he asked that a PC be installed in his office and hooked up to the Dow Jones Service and The Source (an on-line public-access company offering an array of computer data bases and bulletin boards). But, he says, "It eventually took several years to master the idea of computerizing all the information that used to come into our offices on paper. We wanted it in a more digestible and accessible form. I wanted access to all the information without picking up the phone to call my controller. The problem is that the executive wants to describe the end result, 'Give me this, give me that,' rather than delving into the process, which is really what makes it productive in the end."

Smithburg continues: "I remember when one of my business-unit executives came into my office, saw my PC, and asked what I did with it. I proceeded to pull up all kinds of information on his operation, and he was stunned. He rushed back to his information-systems people and said, 'Do you realize what Smithburg has in his office, on his computer? I've got to have the same thing!' Actually, there has been a productive migration of systems, both up and down, within the company."

Using the system didn't come easy at first, Smithburg says. "The main source of slowness was that I had to get up to speed on what I needed. And information systems had to understand better what executives need from a data base; they needed to learn how executives use information to make decisions. The first year or so, my use of the PC was not particularly successful, because all I really used it for was accessing Dow Jones and similar things—valuable, but not worth the cost of putting it in my office. So we needed more. An information-systems person would say, 'Okay, you draw a chart and show us what you want and we'll get it in that box.' But that's not what you want. Then someone said, 'Why don't we ask planning to see what kind of information they want, and maybe we can enhance the flow from them to you.'

"That proved to be very beneficial. The ESS didn't really click until one or two people in information systems clearly understood my personal operating style and what I needed for decision making. Now they are very client oriented. They say, 'Tell us how you use information and make decisions, and we'll get you a product.'"

An article in *Advertising Age* noted that one of Quaker Oats' strengths was its ability to adapt to change in the marketplace. Frank Morgan, the president, was quoted as saying that Smithburg brought a visionary quality. Had ESS contributed? "I think so," Smithburg says. "I use ESS more for environmental scanning than for management and control. A vision for the future requires knowledge of the present and the recent past, and executives need to be able to get that at will. In days of drought in farming areas, for example, I can get into the ESS and find agricultural information quickly that will influence our costs for raw materials."

With ESS, Smithburg and other senior executives can dig deeply into marketing data to check into, say, sales of Quaker Extra cereal versus sales of Total Oats, a competitor's product. "Sometimes you just feel like wading into the data," Smithburg says. His purpose, however, is to improve his own decisions, not to second-guess another department's. "I might look at more data because curiosity gets the better of me, but not because I want to get involved in managing a business that others run. Quite often I go back and check my assumptions on the ESS, because I can't remember everything I see. I'll look to see if I'm correct and check on a few hunches."

ESS offers two valuable features: compression and freshness of information. Which means the most to Smithburg? "Freshness is important," he replies, "especially for financial data. But for me, compression is the plus. It really helps me focus on the broad issues."

ESS allows the creation and use of graphs to express data visually. Yet, although research has shown that use of graphs instead of numbers increases comprehension, it means a shift in habits for many executives. "Graphs are fine for presentations, but I don't use them on my computer much," Smithburg says. "I know what I'm looking for, and I get the numbers. When I was a brand manager I came up with presentations called super charts. These had everything on them: market shares, advertising expenses, advertising campaigns, and so on. Now I can get that completeness using ESS."

Overall, Smithburg thinks ESS has improved his productivity. "I pick up the phone less, a lot less, than I used to. There are times when you're curious about what's happening, but you don't want to meddle. When important people are freed from this, they can do the more valuable diagnostic work. It makes them more productive. I may be working at home on Sunday night preparing for our management committee meeting on Monday, and I need to check some backup material on products. If I couldn't access my ESS, I would have to phone my controller at home. The vast majority of my time is spent communicating, in meetings, at lunches and breakfasts, on the telephone. It's not reflection time or analysis time. The best time for thinking is at home."

Smithburg agrees that ESS can affect working relationships. "I view the company not as a holding company but an operating entity in which senior executives understand the businesses they run," he says. "I expect them to know what is going on. When I prepare for a meeting, if I can access the right information, I can be more responsive to the upward flow of communications. The presenters see executives who are well informed and up-to-date."

Business leaders must have persuasive powers. Does ESS diminish the need to persuade—do the numbers themselves create agreement? "We used to say that you could make data talk," Smithburg replies. "But there's good data and bad data. The difference now is that we are all looking at the same numbers and the emphasis is on analysis and decision making. In effect, the data can persuade because they are analyzed well."

Smithburg thinks better information is a competitive asset. "We now ask ourselves: 'Are we competitive with our information systems?' Twenty-five years ago we wouldn't have asked that. It's important now because it is a real asset. I can't pinpoint a decision for which I am sure ESS made a contribution. But I'm sure there are countless examples of when it has. It's become part of our culture. Like the car phone, I don't know how we ever lived without it. ESS is not magic, not a black box, but in general it has exceeded my expectations."

Business has come under heavy criticism for concentrating unduly on the short term, and ESS would seem to make that even easier, but Smithburg doesn't place the blame on the computers. "Business has been criticized for this. Like any fundamental contribution, computers have a dark side, and overemphasis on data has been one result. The information churned out by securities firms can be awesome, and even inhibiting. I was once in a meeting at a securities firm where they had all kinds of computers and began to throw all kinds of data on the screen. It was almost too much. It was approaching 'analysis-paralysis.' But you can't blame the computers, they just do what they're told."

Smithburg thinks the prospects for ESS are very bright. The better that senior executives understand the systems, and the better information systems understand the executives, he says, the better they can work together. "It's really an investment decision. You have to get what's useful and necessary, not pie in the sky," he says. "If you aren't careful, the expenses can go through the roof. You don't need a Rolls Royce to go to the grocery store. I can't overemphasize how necessary prioritizing is to get what you really want and need. It's very hard, very demanding work to do that."

A MILLION-DOLLAR SAVINGS AT BENEFICIAL

"If I get a hard copy of a memo, I send it back. I get 100 to 120 pieces of mail a day, nearly all of it electronic."

Finn Caspersen, the CEO at Beneficial, explains why neither "trickledown" nor "trickleup" ESS implementation was acceptable to him and why personal use of ESS by all of the company's executives is essential to make it work. "The system identifies whether the manager or the secretary answers my memos," says Caspersen. "I simply remind the sender that if I can trouble myself to send a memo, they can trouble themselves to answer it personally. That usually does the trick."

Caspersen admits that initially he underestimated the usefulness of ESS. "I thought it would be a nice tool to contain secretarial costs, but it has now got to the point that I don't think we could operate without it," he says. "I recently came into the office and the computer system was down between 7 and 8 A.M. That was not acceptable to me. You have to educate your systems people that downtime is unacceptable. Three hundred people depend on that system. Now someone comes in at 6 to be sure it's working.

"The system is really just a conduit for information. I don't type 'what-if' scenarios in the wee hours of the morning, and I don't do much primary analysis. The CEO's job is to maintain communication with individuals in the company, move decisions through committees or meetings in a timely fashion, and implement decisions. If I want to ask the senior-management committee for their advice, I only have to type 'SM' on my terminal, type the question, and out it goes to 18 people. I can do the same thing for the board of directors. This has really speeded up communications. Reliability and accuracy have grown tremendously. In only two instances in five years can I remember when a message I sent didn't reach the person intended, and that might have been my fault. I'm not sure."

Outside the office, the system can also be helpful. But Caspersen notes, "I have used the system traveling, and frankly, I've had problems with it. I used a lap-top computer and modem and found it hard to use in hotel rooms. The phone lines are too noisy and sometimes hard to connect. I don't use it that way anymore; I just call my secretary. I do have the ESS in my vacation home and have a dedicated phone line for that, it works fine. And when I visit other Beneficial offices, I often log onto the system."

Users claim that the rewards of networking go far beyond sending an electronic reminder of when the next meeting is going to take place. "ESS is useful in unanticipated ways," says Caspersen. "Let's suppose a broker calls in and says, 'I have a block of 100,000 shares of stock for sale. Would you like to buy it?' There might be five or six people in the company who would be interested. But reaching them by telephone could take half an hour. With electronic mail, we have the answer for the broker almost instantaneously."

Has ESS changed the way companies operate, the way they organize or structure their important functions? In many instances, it has simply automated activities, but in others it has been more fundamental. Caspersen thinks the latter applies to Beneficial. "I do think it has changed the way we do business. The system has an ingrained prejudice against long-winded memos and works best with terse, data-filled content. It has increased our executives' productivity tremendously. Most of them have the system at home, and as a result, they often work in the evening and on weekends. Most of the executives will be on-line with the system at least once each weekend. They can access files and communicate with other executives, who, if you tried to reach by phone, might not be there to receive the call."

The pace of change in today's world has become a cliché, but Caspersen sees a genuine need to make decisions faster "because competitors are making faster decisions." He continues: "The pace of new-product introductions is faster and profit margins are narrower, so the margin of error is smaller. As your business matures, your profit margins can go down and you have to make better decisions. You just can't afford to be the last to respond to important changes. We use the Lexis and Nexis on-line data bases for monitoring changes that can affect us. Lexis is for the legal department, and Nexis is for general news."

Executives invest heavily in meetings, some of which are unproductive. Beneficial uses ESS to eliminate some of the wasted time. "Meetings are more effective because of ESS," says Caspersen. "We have a meeting scheduling system that works well. If you want a meeting with six people who must attend and nine others who it would be nice if they attended, the system will round up their schedules and indicate the date. Not only can all the documents necessary for a decision at a meeting be prepared and distributed, you can tell if each person attending has received the material. You can also choose areas in which you may sacrifice some of the give-and-take of a meeting to make a quicker decision. For instance, I can send out a memo to six people and ask for their thoughts. All respond, and I make the decision. If someone objects, they can append it to the request and then we may have to have a meeting. Obviously, some of the meetings become unnecessary."

Some companies note "soft-dollar" benefits from ESS—such as nonmeasurable increases in the effectiveness and professionalism of their executives—but cannot easily document "hard-dollar" savings. Caspersen believes Beneficial realizes real savings. "We have actually decreased the number of secretaries. We had Deloitte Haskins & Sells do a study for us, and they found that there was a

$1 million savings in the first year that the system was in operation and a nine-month payback for the cost of the equipment. Now, I'm not sure if that is accurate, and we have spent more since, but I'm sure the system is helpful."

Beneficial is sufficiently convinced of the value of ESS to invest more money. "We are building a new system called Bencom III," Caspersen explains, "which will change the way we do business throughout the company. Not only will it make the field locations more efficient, but by pushing a button, I can inquire about the productivity of a single office if I need to."

Caspersen realizes that since others see a lot of his memos and decisions he is, to an extent, working in a fishbowl. But he sees a brighter side to this. "Some people may want to hide behind the statement that 'I have superior information that you don't have.' But I don't operate that way. I think it's an advantage for all to see the data that decisions are based on. I'd rather have people knock holes in my argument, and if you make a mistake, you make a mistake. The more people that have a chance to speak their piece, the less likely you are to make a wrong decision."

Is old-fashioned persuasion no longer necessary? Not according to Caspersen. "The facts alone won't make the decision or carry it out," he says. "People have to be motivated. As CEO, you have the power to send out a memo to 20 people and say, 'Do this,' and then you can relax and read *The Wall Street Journal*. But if you know someone has a tough job to meet a deadline, you don't just demand cooperation, you call and say it's important and, 'How can I help if you need it?' I find that you really have to lean over backward to avoid saying something in a cold, impersonal way because the system makes it so easy to do that."

Given Caspersen's ESS experience at Beneficial, what would he say to fellow CEOs thinking of acquiring an ESS? "I would tell them it's like getting another three or four secretaries, each with 20 years' experience, and a couple of MBAs thrown in. It's just great. I must admit that I cheated initially, in order to be able to lead and be experienced. I didn't want to look like a fool using it and making blunders. I had a system installed at home three months ahead of the others and worked on it every night until I felt comfortable with it."

If he could have known the benefits of the system beforehand, Caspersen says he would have pushed his managers to adopt the system even faster. "I would be very strict about getting all to use it and insisting that executives use it, not just their secretaries. You don't have to type, I don't type that well. I still believe that it must be done from the top down. There will always be a few who can't change—a secretary who finds long-standing methods comfortable and can't adapt, the executive who deigns not to type on a keyboard. It pays to find that out early rather than several years later. It is absolutely a leadership issue from the CEO on down."

"Those who kept an open mind learned to use it effectively, even if they were at first opposed to it. There's no place for the executive who calls his secretary, presents the document to her, she bows twice, retires, and prepares it. Frankly, we lost a few people who couldn't change, and it's just as well. Although there was both surprising acceptance from some quarters and surprising rejection from others, overall, it went better than I hoped. But it does require firmness. It's an open-and-shut case. There's a natural ambiguity about anything new, but I would probably push it faster if I had it to do again."

CEO-COMPATIBLE SYSTEMS

For executives such as Caspersen, Smithburg, and Allaire, ESS undoubtedly works. But how transferable are their personal and company experiences to others? The answer, some say, lies not just in the technology available or the executives' ability to describe their work and needs, but deeper in the company, in its information systems. To satisfy their ordinary computing requirements, companies have developed systems and attitudes that create inflexible structures, enforce conformity, and are intolerant of ambiguity. These are far from ideal qualities in an ESS. The work of top executives is fairly unstructured and nonroutine; facts are necessary but not sufficient to make good decisions. In addition, a lot of good ESS software is sold by outside vendors such as Execucom, Comshare, Inc., and Pilot Executive Software, which can lead to the not-invented-here syndrome.

Essentially, information systems should see ESS development not as catering to the personal whims of top management but as a means of enhancing their work, to the benefit of the whole company. Giving senior executives the information they need can have greater impact than automating the work of several hundred people below them. Top executives don't want their work to be easier—they thrive on difficulty. But they do want to be more effective, and ESS offers possibilities for doing that.

For some firms, the improved communications from ESS justifies use of the system. It's much harder to prove that better top-level decisions result. In the rarefied realm of decision making, art overshadows science. ESS may not change that. Do shortcomings of current ESS and their rate of improvement justify reluctance to use them now? Probably not.

QUESTIONS

1. What were some of the keys to EIS success at Xerox?
2. William Smithburg at Quaker Oats feels that the EIS has improved his personal productivity. What is the basis for this statement?
3. Finn Caspersen at Beneficial indicates that the EIS has changed the way the company operates. What changes has the EIS brought about?
4. What similarities and differences are there in the EIS experience at Xerox, Quaker Oats, and Beneficial?

28

ASSESSING EIS BENEFITS

Recent studies show little or no productivity gains or other measures of business performance improvements from investments in information technology (IT) (Loveman, 1991; Weill, 1992). These findings and the attention they have received are troubling for the information systems (IS) community because of their potential for undermining future IT investments. Although the findings may be the consequence of how economists measure productivity, they do reflect the continuing problem of documenting the returns from many IT investments (Panko, 1991).

While transaction processing applications usually are justified on the basis of reduced clerical expenses, decision support applications are more difficult to evaluate because benefits such as "better, more timely" information are hard to quantify. Often there is only an intuitive feeling that the value exceeds the cost (Hogue and Watson, 1983; Keen, 1981). Researchers routinely employ user satisfaction and frequency of use as surrogate measures when evaluating systems (Ives, et al., 1983; Srinivasan, 1985).

Economic conditions and competitive pressures are causing companies to closely scrutinize their IT capital and operating expenditures (Wilder and Hildebrand, 1992). There are growing pressures to evaluate IT investments like any other, using traditional financial measures such as return on investment, net dis-

This chapter draws from two sources: Hugh J. Watson, Jay E. Aronson, Ralph H. Hamilton, Lakshami Iyer, Murli Nagasundaram, Hamid Nemati, and James Suleiman, "Assessing EIS Benefits: A Survey of Current Practices," University of Georgia working paper, Terry College of Business, University of Georgia, Athens, Georgia 30602 and Lloyd W. Belcher and Hugh J. Watson, "Assessing the Value of Conoco's EIS," *MIS Quarterly*, Vol. 17, No. 3, September 1993, pp. 239–253.

counted present value, and benefit/cost analysis (Silk, 1990). Despite these pressures to use financial measures, there are strong feelings that the strategic and intangible nature of some IT benefits need to be recognized (Badiru, 1990; Davenport, 1989). However, there should always be an attempt to quantify as many benefits as possible, otherwise "there may be an absence of disciplined analysis, no real basis of objective measurement, and limited awareness of the true costs and benefits of IT investments" (Bacon, 1992, p. 338).

The value resulting from an investment in an EIS is arguably the most difficult of all to show. An EIS typically has a large number of users, including the organization's senior executives, who perform highly unstructured work; a large number of information applications (e.g., financial information, external news services); and a variety of capabilities (e.g., e-mail, decision support systems) (Watson, et al., 1991). Some of the more frequently mentioned benefits of an EIS are more timely information, enhanced mental models, improved communications, and more focused organizational attention (Gulden and Ewers, 1989; Rockart and DeLong, 1988; Watson, et al., 1991). It is not immediately obvious how to place a value on benefits such as these.

The decision to develop an EIS is usually based on executive mandate rather than on an analysis that shows that the benefits will outweigh the costs. Most companies estimate the costs of the proposed EIS but do not attempt to quantify the possible returns. The executive sponsor simply provides the support and resources necessary to undertake the project (Watson, et al., 1991).

Even though the initial decision to develop an EIS usually is not cost-justified, conventional wisdom encourages the documentation of benefits after the system is operational (Paller with Laska, 1990). Because the costs of maintaining an EIS are substantial (averaging over $200,000 per year), EISs tend to be attractive targets for cost-cutting organizations (Watson, et al., 1991). Even though there is a better feeling for the benefits once the system is in use, and there may be specific instances where the EIS led to quantifiable returns, it is still very difficult to place a value on it.

A STUDY OF HOW EISs ARE ASSESSED

A recent study explored the benefits being realized from EISs, the kinds of benefit/cost analysis being performed, and the factors that affect whether and how a benefit/cost analysis is conducted (Watson, et al., 1995). The study utilized both a mail survey and telephone interviews. The survey instrument was designed to collect data on the participating firms, the respondents, their EISs, and benefit/cost related issues. It was pretested by three EIS managers to help ensure content and external validity. After minor modifications, the instrument was mailed to 215 firms in the University of Georgia's EIS database. A follow-up mailing was sent to nonrespondents. A total of 72 responses were received from the two mailings, resulting in a response rate of 33.5 percent.

The participants in the telephone interviews were selected from survey respondents who were willing to discuss in-depth how the benefit/cost assessment was conducted at their company. An open-ended structure for the phone interview allowed the interviewer to probe for anecdotal information on how the benefit/cost analysis was performed. Sixteen people were interviewed and each interview typically lasted 15 to 20 minutes.

STUDY

Demographics

The organizations come from a variety of industries with finance, insurance, and real estate (28.8 percent) and manufacturing (25.8 percent) the most heavily represented (see Table 28–1). Almost 14 percent of them are governmental. The organizations are generally large, with 45.5 percent of them reporting annual gross revenues over $5 billion, while only 9.3 percent have revenues under $250 million (see Table 28–2).

The respondents are seasoned managers and professionals, and average three years of EIS, 13 years of IS, and 18 years of total work experience. Their job categories include EIS manager (32.4 percent), IS manager (23.9 percent), and IS staff (14.1 percent) (see Table 28–3).

The executive sponsors for the EISs included vice presidents (35 percent), CEOs or presidents (21.7 percent), other executives (36.7 percent), and IS managers (1.7 percent). On average (i.e., median), the EISs have 38 active users, 100 screens, and are three years old. Pilot's Command Center (21.6 percent) and Comshare's Commander EIS (18.3 percent) are the most commonly used EIS software products.

TABLE 28–1 Responding Companies by Industry

Industry	Percentage of Firms
Finance, Insurance, and Real Estate	28.8
Manufacturing	25.8
Government Agencies	13.7
Transportation, Communication, and Utilities	12.1
Services (e.g., hotels, personal services, health services)	4.6
Mining	1.6
Agriculture, Forestry, and Fishing	1.6
Other	12.1
Total	100.0

TABLE 28-2 Responding Companies' Assets and Gross Revenues

	Assets	Gross Revenues
Under $1 Million	0.0%	0.0%
$1 Million - $10 Million	0.0	0.0
$10 Million - $50 Million	5.2	2.4
$50 Million - $100 Million	1.8	2.4
$100 Million - $250 Million	5.2	4.5
$250 Million - $1 Billion	10.3	20.5
$1 Billion - $5 Billion	10.3	25.0
Over $5 Billion	39.7	45.4
Total	100.0	100.0

TABLE 28-3 Positions of Respondents

Position	Percentage of Respondents
EIS manager	32.4
IS manager	23.9
IS staff	14.1
EIS staff	11.3
Executive	5.6
Functional area staff	4.2
Other	8.5
Total	100.0

Expected Benefits

EISs offer many potential benefits. Drawing on the relevant literature, a long list of benefits was developed and respondents were asked to judge on a five-point anchored scale the expectation for each benefit in deciding whether to develop their EIS.

As Table 28–4 shows, the most highly anticipated benefits were faster access to information (a mean of 4.79), more timely information (4.58), and improved presentation of data (4.22). Other studies have found the need for more timely information is the primary motivation for developing an EIS (Watson, Rainer, and Koh, 1991). The other two top rated benefits reflect the improved access and presentation of data that are possible with EISs.

In a number of areas, the expected benefits were not great. Even though EISs are often touted for their ability to provide information about the external environment, improved access to external data (2.42), better environmental scanning (1.83), more competitive information (2.27), and being more responsive to changing customer needs (2.55), these factors were relatively unimportant. Providing better access to soft information (2.48) also was ranked low despite evi-

TABLE 28-4 Expected and Realized Benefits from the EISs

Benefit	Expected Benefits Mean	Realized Benefits Mean	(Realized - Expected Benefits)
More timely information	4.58	3.98	−0.60
Faster access to information	4.79	4.29	−0.50
More accurate information	3.81	3.53	−0.28
More relevant information	3.85	3.40	−0.45
More concise information	3.94	3.67	−0.27
Better access to soft information	2.48	2.36	−0.12
Improved communications	3.67	3.10	−0.57
Improved access to external data	2.42	2.34	−0.08
Better environmental scanning	1.83	1.56	−0.27
More competitive information	2.27	2.03	−0.24
Improved executive performance	3.31	2.61	−0.70
Save executive time	3.74	2.98	−0.76
Increased span of control	2.56	2.19	−0.37
Improved planning	3.39	2.60	−0.79
Improved decision making	3.97	3.03	−0.94
Better problem understanding	3.75	2.92	−0.83
Better development of alternatives	2.89	2.41	−0.48
Improved presentation of data	4.22	4.05	−0.17
Cost savings	2.44	2.60	0.16
Less paper	3.42	3.17	−0.25
Support TQM program	2.23	1.98	−0.25
More responsive to changing customer needs	2.55	2.11	−0.44
Support downsizing the organization	1.95	1.79	−0.16

dence that it adds to the value of an EIS (Watson, et al., 1992). There are several well-documented accounts of how EISs have facilitated increases in management's span of control and the downsizing of organizations (Paller with Laska, 1990), but these benefits were not a high expectation of most of the firms in the survey (as evidenced by means of 2.56 and 1.95, respectively). Finally, the better development of alternatives (2.89), cost savings (2.44), and support for a TQM program (2.55) received relatively low scores.

Realized Benefits

The mean benefits actually received from the EISs are also shown in Table 28–4. The highest marks go to faster access to information (4.29), improved presentation of data (4.05), and more timely information—the same benefits for which expectations were the greatest. The lowest benefits received include better environmental scanning (1.56), support for downsizing the organization (1.79), and support for a TQM program (1.98).

While there is a correlation between the expected and realized benefits (mean r = .76), the most dramatic finding is that with the exception of cost savings, where the expectations were low, the expected benefits were less than those received. This gap between expectations and reality highlights why so many EISs fail; they often do not live up to their promise (Watson and Glover, 1989). It should also be kept in mind that the data were collected from organizations in which the EISs are operational. One might speculate that this expectations/reality gap was even greater in those organizations with failed systems.

It is interesting to note that many of the benefits where the gap is the greatest are related directly to executive performance—improved decision making (–.94), better problem solving (–.83), improved planning (–.79), save executive time (–.76), and improved executive performance (–.70). These disappointments are even more significant when one considers that expectations were not especially great in these areas. In contrast, the EISs have almost lived up to their potential in terms of the faster (–.50) presentation (–.17) of timely (–.60), accurate (–.28), relevant (–.45), concise (–.27) information. It appears that the greatest problem with EISs today is their information contents rather than information delivery issues. This weakness is also indicated by the low levels of realized benefits in terms of the inclusion of soft information and information about the external environment—two areas in which executives value information.

Benefit/Cost Analysis

The respondents were asked what kind of benefit/cost analysis was performed prior to the implementation of their EISs (see Table 28–5). The majority of the firms (58.5 percent) reported that costs and an intuitive feeling for the benefits were determined. This finding is consistent with studies of decision support systems (Keen, 1981; Hogue and Watson, 1983) and suggests the difficulty of quantifying the benefits of decision support applications. In 19 percent of the firms, neither costs nor benefits were determined. In only 13.8 percent of the organizations were costs and tangible benefits determined.

The difficulty of quantifying EIS benefits was not the only reason why little was done about it, as the interviews revealed. In some firms, the position of the executive sponsor was a factor. One interviewee reported that the president was

TABLE 28–5 Benefit/Cost Analysis prior to Implementation

Analysis Method	Percentage of Respondents
Costs and "hard" benefits were determined	13.8
Costs and an intuitive feeling for the benefits were determined	58.5
Costs only were determined	3.4
Benefits only were determined	5.2
Neither costs nor benefits were determined	19.0
Benefit/Cost Total	100.0

the "chief EIS spokesperson" and that the project was therefore viewed very favorably; no benefit analysis was performed.

The cost of the system is a factor. It was found that the cost of developing an EIS varied from $10,000 to $1.5 million when hardware, software, personnel, and training costs are included. These differences are due to the nature of the EIS developed and whether additional hardware and software were acquired. Low-cost systems are less likely to be subjected to close scrutiny. One respondent from a federal government agency reported that the development of his system cost "little more than a box of floppies" because a portable system was available from another governmental agency. He also pointed out that a rigorous benefit/cost analysis in government agencies is a cumbersome process to be avoided if possible.

A formal EIS proposal was prepared in a bank which included a qualitative description of the potential benefits and cost estimates. Of particular interest was how the costs were framed. In addition to a breakdown by hardware, software, personnel, and training costs, they were subdivided on the basis of whether they were for the enhancement of executive information or for its presentation. Most of the cost of the system was for creating (e.g., collecting, processing, and interpreting) information rather than for its presentation on screens using EIS technology. In this context, it was obvious that it was an information tool rather than an expensive executive toy. The proposal also pointed out that most of the information creation costs already were being incurred by personnel feeding existing, inefficient, and ineffective systems. The development of the EIS was quickly approved.

Another company took an unusual approach to cost justifying its EIS. It required each business unit manager supported by the EIS to cut one business analyst from the staff. It was reasoned that the system would provide more support than the business analysts, and these personnel reduction savings more than covered the costs of the EIS.

Respondents also were asked about any benefit/cost analyses performed after the system was operational. The conventional wisdom is that benefits are easier to identify after the system is running and that significant benefits should be documented in case justification is necessary (Paller with Laska, 1990). The data presented in Table 28–6 suggests this advice is often ignored. In 40.7 percent

TABLE 28-6 Benefit/Cost Analysis after Implementation

Analysis method	Percentage of respondents
Costs and "hard" benefits were determined	7.4
Costs and an intuitive feeling for the benefits were determined	40.7
Costs only were determined	5.6
Benefits only were determined	5.6
Neither costs nor benefits were determined	40.7
Benefit/Cost Total	100.0

of the firms, neither costs nor benefits have been determined, and in 40.7 percent of the organizations, costs and an intuitive feeling for the benefits have been determined.

Moreover, the interviews revealed why formal assessments are uncommon after implementation. In some organizations, there is a staunch belief that the benefits are so significant that they justify the system's cost. As one participant said, "the benefits have been so obvious." There is also a sense in a few organizations that the system has become so embedded in management processes and critical to the success of the organization that its value is not subject to scrutiny.

The interviews found that several events can trigger an EIS evaluation. One condition is difficult economic times. An EIS manager said that business conditions led to significant cost-cutting efforts in his company. As part of an organizationwide examination of all costs, he conducted a thorough benefit/cost analysis which saved his EIS from the cost-cutting ax.

The loss of the executive sponsor may also lead to a new environment for an EIS. In another firm, the president was the executive sponsor for the EIS, and after he died, so did the EIS. The system had a heavy financial orientation and the new president chose not to manage that way.

ASSESSING THE VALUE OF CONOCO'S EIS

The most comprehensive methodology for assessing the value of an EIS was developed at Conoco (Belcher and Watson, 1995). It was judged to be the outstanding IS practice in the 1993 Society for Information Systems International Paper Competition. While the methodology was developed for an EIS, the approach can be used with other kinds of decision support applications. Specific lessons learned from Conoco's experiences are also given.

About Conoco and Its EIS

Conoco is a major international energy company. Founded in 1875 as the Continental Oil and Transportation Company, Conoco has a long-standing history of innovation in the energy industry. While others only sold kerosene and oil by the barrel, Conoco put spigots on horse-drawn tank wagons and sold fuels by the gallon. By 1950, Conoco was ranked as the eighth largest oil and gas producer in the nation, and in 1981 it became a subsidiary of DuPont. Today, Conoco is ranked among the world's 10 largest energy companies, with 1992 gross revenues of $16.1 billion and operations in more than 20 countries. In addition to involvement in most of the major oil fields in the United States, Conoco holds major business interests in Canada, Trinidad, the North Sea, onshore and offshore Europe, Africa, Asia, Australia, and the Middle East.

A computer-based EIS was begun in the early 1980s under the sponsorship of Constantine S. Nicandros, then president of Worldwide Petroleum Operations and, since 1987, president and CEO of Conoco. Nicandros requested the development of an EIS to help him and other senior managers obtain more effective information. Over the years, the EIS has grown into a very large system. It has 75 applications, hundreds of screens, and is used in some form by most senior managers as well as by over 4,000 employees located at corporate headquarters in Houston and throughout the world. With applications ranging from internal operating and financial information to coverage of external events that affect the petroleum industry, it reflects the diverse nature of Conoco's business.

Events Leading to the Evaluation of Conoco's EIS

Like most cost-conscious firms today, Conoco has made corporatewide efforts to eliminate unnecessary expenses. In this environment, Aivars "Ike" Krasts, vice president of External Affairs, Planning and Communications, suggested to EIS Manager Lloyd Belcher that he might want to "get ahead of the curve" and assess the value of Conoco's EIS. Belcher agreed and began seeking out potentially relevant literature and asking others in the EIS community about applicable evaluation methods.

Although no specific methodologies for evaluating an EIS were found, several useful ideas and concepts were identified. The evaluation should take a business and user perspective (Davenport, 1989). It should consider the business value of the EIS at the level at which the value is received, whether it be at the individual, departmental, or organizational level (Singleton, et al., 1988; Smith, 1983). As much as possible, the evaluation should incorporate the variety of benefits into the "bottom line" (Dixon and Darwin, 1989). Intangible benefits should be recorded because they exist with decision support-oriented applications and need to be considered in any comprehensive assessment (Melone and Wharton, 1984; Smith, 1983). The evaluation should take an incremental approach to the assessment of benefits and the associated costs (Smith, 1983). Conservative estimates for the benefits should be used in order to enhance the credibility of the evaluation (Litecky, 1981).

The Evaluation of Conoco's EIS

Three broad principles guided the evaluation process. First, benefits should be quantified as realistically as possible, but intangible benefits should also be recorded. Benefits include improvements in both efficiency and effectiveness as a result of the system. Second, costs should include both the direct costs associated with the EIS (e.g., the EIS support staff) and the indirect costs absorbed by the operating groups who provide personnel to perform EIS-related tasks such as data entry. Finally, benefits should be measured at the lowest logical level, most typically on an individual application basis. Most EIS benefits occur when a user accesses a specific application on the system.

Three business analysts and a technical specialist from the EIS support staff were assigned to the project. All the business analysts have MBA degrees and substantial work experience. Their support responsibilities include determining information requirements and designing specific applications. Their role in the evaluation process was to identify the EIS users within each group, the applications being used, the cost of the applications, and the value of the applications to users. The technical analyst provides technical support for the EIS. His role in the evaluation process was to compile system usage statistics and to place a value on the EIS software.

The evaluation methodology is shown in Figure 28–1. Its steps include determining objectives for the evaluation, gathering system usage statistics, interviewing users, assessing costs and benefits, and reporting the findings to management. The process evolved over time; many specific details, such as the specific data collection forms that were used, emerged as the evaluation went forward.

Objectives for the evaluation. An evaluation process should be driven by specific objectives. The evaluation of Conoco's EIS was designed to:

- Identify the users of the system;
- Identify user requirements;
- Identify and eliminate low-value applications;
- Identify applications that should be enhanced or added; and
- Result in a cost/benefit analysis.

Collection of usage statistics. Data about how the system was being used were collected over a 90-day period. The EIS recorded data by geographical area, department, user, and application. A statistical analysis of the data revealed which applications were being used in each department, who was using them, and how often. Prior to this effort, most departments had only a limited understanding of their overall use of the EIS.

Interviews of key users. It was not feasible to interview all users; therefore, criteria were established to identify "key users." These people were typically either department heads, performed critical jobs, utilized key information such as critical market data, or were frequent users. Most of the EIS benefits were expected to be found in this group. The interviews were designed to verify what information on the EIS was being used, how it was being used, whether it is essential to the work being performed, if it had replaced an existing process for providing the same information, if it was meeting the user's needs, and to assess the information's tangible and intangible benefits. The EIS User Interview Form is shown in Figure 28–2. The form structured the interview process, but users

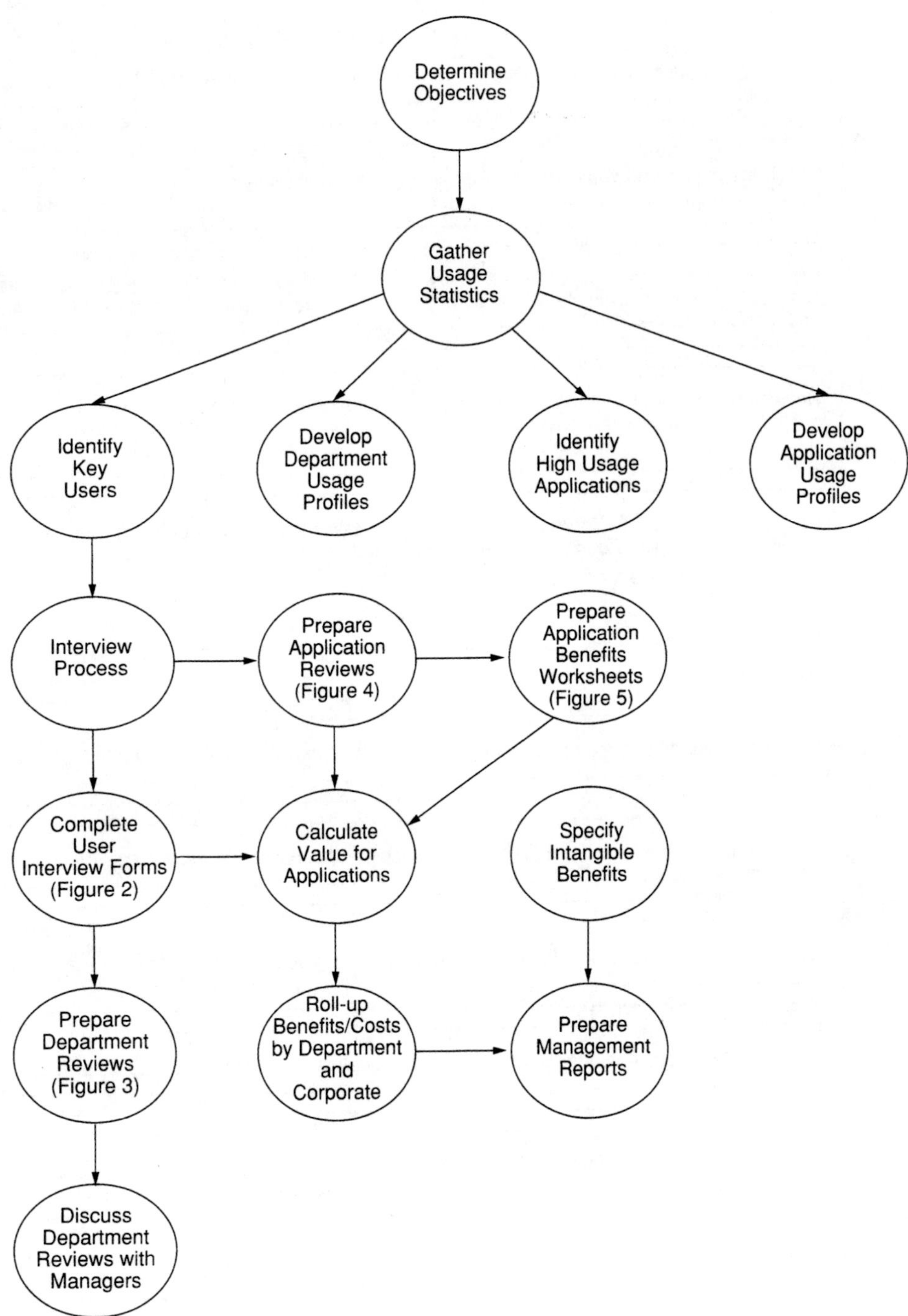

FIGURE 28–1 The EIS Evaluation Process

EIS INTERVIEW QUESTIONS

Of all the EIS applications, which are the most important to you personally? ______________

Which applications do you consider vital, as opposed to ancillary? ______________

Would you replace any applications if they were no longer available? For example, if API statistics graphs were not available, would someone in your department need to assemble the data and graphs each week? ______________

Do you consider the EIS to be your department's information transmitter to others within or outside of your department? Would you continue to distribute this data if the EIS did not? ______________

Have any features in the EIS helped you eliminate data handling procedures in your own job or department? (ISD,API,Postings Bulletin, prices, etc.) ______________

Does having the EIS at your desk give you productivity advantages you did not have before? ______________

Does your department use Megamenu? Bulletin? EnVision? DataVision? InDepth? ______________

Do you request data from the EIS database, such as spot prices, futures prices, API or DOE statistics, etc.? ______________

Do you forsee the EIS as a vehicle for future applications you or your department may need? ______________

Do you know any other system(s) in Conoco that duplicates the EIS? ______________

Can you put a value on what the EIS means to you? ______________

Other comments: ______________

FIGURE 28–2 The EIS User Interview Form

were encouraged to discuss other aspects of the EIS that they considered important. Interviews were typically 30–60 minutes in length, but if there was clear evidence that the system was heavily used or delivered significant value, the interviews probed more in-depth for benefits. Two problems were sometimes encountered during the interviews. A few users were either overly enthusiastic or critical of the system, which made it difficult to objectively assess its benefits.

Although it was not feasible to interview international users of the EIS, input was requested and received from them through e-mail. The comments revealed that many international users considered the EIS to be very important for communications purposes and for being kept up-to-date on company activities.

EIS use review. After the key users in each department were interviewed, a summary of that department's use of the EIS was prepared and discussed with the department's manager. Figure 28–3 shows the Department Review for a typical department, Refining, Marketing, Supply and Transportation (RMS&T) Planning and Finance. It includes the department's name, the permanent number of employees who are on the system, the average number of users per month, the average number of system accesses per month, the EIS software tools used by the department, the applications that the department "owns" (i.e., by either requesting the application, supplying the data, or as the primary beneficiary), EIS database usage, and the applications used by the department. This summary was important to the analysis of the benefits and to the department head's comprehension of the system's utility to the department.

Applications review. A profile was developed for each application or application suite (a set of related applications). Figure 28–4 shows the EIS Application Review that was prepared for the Industry Statistical Data application. The data were gathered from the usage statistics and the interviews. From these it was possible to identify the application's owner, purpose, function(s) replaced, exceptional support costs, average accesses per month, and tangible and intangible benefits. This worksheet provided a common structure for analyzing all of the applications.

Assessing the benefits and costs. In assessing the benefits and costs, the evaluation team looked for benefits and costs that would not have occurred without the system. This resulted in an incremental approach to the assessment of benefits and costs. Ultimately, this comparison provided a "bottom line" for the EIS.

The assessment of the benefits was primarily determined by the advantages various applications provided to individual users. Some of the benefits and costs were most appropriately analyzed at either the departmental or the corporate level.

DEPARTMENT REVIEW

Department: RMS&T Planning & Finance

Total permanent employees on network: 19

Average users per month: 18 *Average accesses per month:* 612

EIS software usage on local network: Megamenu

EIS applications developed with P&F:
RMS&T Financial Perspectives
RME Integrated Margins
RMS&T Vision Statement
Downstream Maps
RMS&T Quantitative Goals
RMS&T Calendar
RMS&T Long Range Plan Instructions
Cash & Earnings Forecast Notes

EIS database usage: Downloading crude and product prices using DataVision for presentations.
Retrieving API statistics from InDepth Applications.

Potential EIS applications/activities: Downstream metrics presentations

EIS APPLICATIONS VIEWED BY RMS&T, P&F IN MARCH/APRIL 1992

Crude Oil Hot Key
U.S. Products Hot Key
U.S. Light Oil Spread Hot Key
European Light Oil Spread Hot Key
Natural Gas Futures Hot Key
Stocks/Price Relation
RMS&T Industry Comparisons
Market Status
COS&T Crude Postings
API Detail
API Summary
RMNA Integrated Margin
Industry Statistical Data
Marketing Update
What's Hot on EIS?
Snapshot
Days Supply
API Refinery Capacity
Europe/Singapore Prices
WTI vs Postings
Organizational Bulletin
EP Earnings
RMS&T Earnings
Earnings Assumptions
Doe Statistics
Daily Market Update
Volumes History
RMS&T Vision Statement
RMS&T Additions
Product Price Analysis
Cash & Earnings Forecast Notes
RMS&T Financial Perspectives
Profit Objective
Safety
Exploratory Wells
Product Demand
Current Rack Prices
Historical Rack Prices
Refining Indicators
Downstream Maps
Short-Term Economic Prices
Downstream Key Indicators
External Earnings Reporting
Net Cash Flow
Crude Prices
Goldbook

FIGURE 28–3 A Department Review

EIS APPLICATION REVIEW

Application: *Industry Statistical Data*

Department/user owner: *EIS*

Type of software: *InDepth Graphics*

Maintained by: *EIS*

Basic purpose: *Accumulate important data for quick, efficient review.*

Original function replaced: *Paper booklets published weekly and distributed throughout the company*

Exceptional costs to support this application (fees,etc.): *None*

Dollar Value, Savings, Etc., based on:

Paper/Reproduction/Distribution: *60 weekly books at $2.00/book*

Productivity/time savings/better information: *1 minute/access saved at employee cost savings of $1.00/minute*

Alternate cost to provide same benefits: *Analyst: 4 days/week = $36,000/yr. + computer clearances of $5,000/yr.*

Improved decision making: *None*

Services replacement costs: *None*

Average accesses per month: *108*

Noteworthy "Intangibles": *Graphics can be customized for managers (e.g., Eurostocks).*

FIGURE 28–4 An EIS Application Review

The nature of the application influenced where the search for benefits was concentrated. To illustrate, if the information provided by an application was the result of considerable analysis, the focus was on what analytic processes may have been eliminated and whether the information was an improvement over what was available in the past (e.g., more rapid access of the information). If the application involved the distribution of textual information, the benefits might include efficiencies gained through electronic rather than paper-based distribution.

The data from the EIS Application Review Form (Figure 28–4) became the basis for the Application Benefits Worksheet (illustrated in Figure 28–5), which was prepared for each application. It was helpful in summarizing the application's benefits.

The following types of benefits and costs were included in the evaluation.

Improved Productivity. These benefits derive from work being done more efficiently. Perhaps the EIS has reduced the staff time needed to generate required information. This time savings can be converted into dollar benefits. For example, the Industry Statistical Data application provides a large number of analysts with quick access to current, consistent, and comprehensive market information. This application saved 80 percent of the time of an analyst who routinely updated the data, generated graphics and tables, and distributed the materials. This productivity increase provided benefits in the form of compensation savings.

The application may provide information that is needed now but was not available before the implementation of the EIS. Creating this information without the EIS would require additional staff. The benefits resulting from avoiding more staff time were estimated by multiplying the number of hours spent per year supporting the application by a standard hourly rate.

There can be productivity increases on the users' end, too. For example, the EIS may decrease the time that it takes users to access information. These savings can be estimated by multiplying the decreased average access time by the average number of accesses by a standard labor rate.

Improved Decision Making. Users were asked to put a value on any specific improvements in decision making that they could attribute to the EIS. Many improved decision-making benefits are subjective and thus, potentially viewed skeptically by top management; therefore, these benefits were estimated conservatively. Benefits were not attributed to the system without a strong user endorsement that the EIS had improved decision making. For example, one commodity trading group asserted that an EIS application enhanced its ability to analyze market supply and demand conditions. A set of graphs had been developed that compared inventories with prices for each commodity. The graphs were updated as soon as new data became available. The automated graphing made it possible to instantly identify areas of opportunity. During the initial use of this application, the trading group spotted a marketing region in which inventories were

EIS APPLICATION BENEFITS WORKSHEET

APPLICATION: *Industry Statistical Data*

IMPROVED PRODUCTIVITY

A. Decreased Information Creation Cost Savings:	$41,000
B. New Information Creation Cost Savings:	0
C. Reduced Information Access Time Savings	
(1) Average Access Time Reduction: *1 minute*	
(2) Average Number of Accesses: *108/week*	
(3) Employee Cost: *$1.00/minute*	
(4) Savings Per Year: *1 * 108 * 1 * 52*	$5,616
IMPROVED DECISION MAKING	0
INFORMATION DISTRIBUTION COST SAVINGS	
(1) Cost of Document: *$2.00*	
(2) Average Number of Copies: *60/week*	
(3) Savings Per Year: *2 * 60 * 52*	$6,240
SERVICES REPLACEMENT COST SAVINGS	0
TOTAL TANGIBLE BENEFITS	$52,856

FIGURE 28–5 An EIS Application Benefits Worksheet

decreasing steadily while prices remained level. This condition gave early warning of a price rise because low supplies usually predict higher prices. The traders' quick response to this anticipated price increase generated considerable, calculable savings for the company.

Information Distribution Cost Savings. A less exciting but still potentially important benefit is the reduction of hard-copy distribution costs. These savings result from cuts in expenses for paper and binders, handling, copying, mailing, and taxing. Cost estimates were made by the evaluation team for each document replaced; for example, a one-page memo may have been priced at $1 per copy, while a three-ring notebook with tabs used to transmit budget or planning instructions may have cost $10 a copy. The annual cost savings for each document was calculated by multiplying the savings per document times the number of documents distributed per year. Such calculations were made only for hard-copy documents that are no longer distributed because the EIS replaced them.

Services Replacement Cost Savings. These were benefits attributed to support from the EIS that the company otherwise would need to purchase. At Conoco, the major benefit comes from its EIS database. Some users query the database directly for information required in their jobs. If the EIS did not exist, many of them would subscribe to external database services.

In order to figure this replacement cost savings, users were asked to estimate the cost of the service. Vendors were asked also to bid on providing some of the services. An estimate of the internal costs of maintaining the EIS database was made and then compared to the outsourcing cost. The resulting net gain from having an in-house EIS database was credited as a benefit.

Software Replacement Cost Savings. Conoco's EIS software was developed in-house and includes component tools that can be used on a stand-alone basis for other applications. This software has been distributed freely to employees and has reduced the need to purchase commercial software (e.g., graphics software).

The systems support staff that maintains the networks tallied the number of copies of each software product that had been requested and distributed to users. The value of the software was estimated taking a conservative approach. The estimate reflected the following: the assumption that some of the software would have been ignored if it were not free; reduced costs that would have been associated with site licenses; and the need to amortize the cost of the software over a number of years (five in this instance).

Intangible Benefits. User feedback received during the review made it apparent that the value of a companywide information distribution system goes beyond quantifiable benefits. As the sample of comments in Figure 28–6 illustrates, the EIS weaves a unifying thread throughout this global company, helping people feel more connected and more informed. Because of its pervasive nature, the system is recognized as an essential link between management and employees. This embedding demonstrates an important transition from the traditional EIS to a successful enterprise information system.

Costs. In addition to the benefits, it was necessary to assess the annual costs associated with the EIS. Four cost categories were considered. The first included the direct costs associated with maintaining the EIS support staff. Any out-of-pocket costs related to this group were figured into the total. The second included the indirect costs associated with personnel in the business units who support the EIS part time. For example, those who supply data to the system were interviewed to determine the amount of time spent on EIS-related activities each year. An annual cost was calculated for each support person by multiplying the number of hours spent by a standard hourly rate. Third, the costs of the PCs and the networks were considered but not included as an EIS expense. This computing infrastructure is needed for other purposes and would exist without the EIS; consequently, the EIS was not considered to create incremental expenses.

The user feedback was used in quantifying the benefits of each application, but additionally was used in gauging the "intangible value" that the EIS was generating.

Sample feedback from users:

"We used the EIS graphics software to display our prices because no other product on the market can do it as well." ***—Manager, Operations Group***

"I don't see the kinds of things you are doing occurring anywhere else in the company." ***—Manager, Operations Group***

"I had EIS made accessible to my group so they would have the chance to feel a part of the operations. This has been a big boost to the morale of the group—an unquantifiable value." ***—Manager, Service Group***

"EIS has helped break down some of the traditional barriers to inter-departmental information sharing."***—Analyst, Information Systems***

"EIS gives us instant access to information that we need on a daily basis. Previously, getting what we needed was a long and painful process."***—Operations Group***

"Our department is committed to putting necessary work online as much as possible. I'm requiring all my new analysts to learn the EIS software tools."***—Operating Group***

"If we didn't have graphics provided by the EIS, we'd hire someone to do them. I value this tool at $100,000 annually. It has significantly increased our confidence in our trading decisions."***—Manager, Trading Group***

"Based on my use of the statistics in the database, and the decisions affected, I would put a value on the database of $500,000 per year."***—Senior Manager, Planning***

"EIS is a necessary information source that eliminates the need for widespread paper distribution of financial and operational information."***—Manager, Planning & Finance***

"EIS is Conoco expatriates' one consistent and timely link to what is going on in the world of Conoco."***—Manager, Foreign Operating Subsidiary***

FIGURE 28–6 Sample User Comments

Finally, EIS software costs also were not considered relevant because Conoco has in-house-developed software, and the costs of developing the software were captured in the EIS support staff costs. Other organizations may have relevant incremental costs in these last two categories.

Management report. After the evaluation was completed, a report was prepared for management. A spreadsheet was used to summarize all benefits by application, by department, along with costs, and then a total corporate net annual value for the EIS was determined. How the benefits and costs were rolled up is shown in Figure 28–7. The Xs in the matrix indicate at what level the different costs and benefits were assessed. On a corporate basis, the EIS benefits outweighed its costs by a factor of four or five to one. This ratio would have been higher if a less conservative assessment of some of the benefits (e.g., improved decision making) had been made. The report also included the intangible benefits identified in the user interviews.

Outcomes from the evaluation. The evaluation process met the five objectives that were established initially, and most importantly, management accepted the evaluation as being thorough and objective. While the benefit/cost ratio was impressive, management reacted just as favorably to the evidence that the EIS was being used, that it helped people do their jobs, and that it delivered value. Consequently, support for the EIS remains high.

Another outcome was that usage statistics and user interviews revealed that 15 percent of the applications were deemed questionable in value and therefore candidates for elimination. After further discussions with users, 90 percent of these weak applications were discontinued.

The evaluation also identified applications that needed to be added or enhanced. The most important finding was that the senior executives wanted a more consistent look and feel for some of the applications, faster response time, easier access to the most important applications, and more current information. Most of these problems are common as an EIS spreads to a large user base. An executive briefing book was added to address these needs.

After the evaluation, it was recognized that the EIS could be used as part of an on-going evaluation process. This is now occurring regularly with the applications in Conoco's EIS. When an application undergoes an evaluation, the first time users access that application, a screen with a set of questions appears. Questions currently asked are: Is this an important application to you? Is it what you need? Is this information available elsewhere? Can someone call you? Users'

	Benefits						Costs	
Level Analyzed	Improved Productivity	Improved Decision Making	Information Distribution Cost Savings	Services Replacement Cost Savings	Software Replacement Cost Savings	Intangible	Direct	Indirect
Application	X	X	X	X				X
Department					X		X	X
Corporate	X	X	X	X	X	X	X	X

FIGURE 28–7 Roll Up of Benefits and Costs

answers are returned electronically. The questions only appear the first time that the application is accessed so that they are unintrusive.

Lessons learned. A number of generalizable lessons were learned from evaluating Conoco's EIS.

Lesson 1. A comprehensive evaluation can renew interest and support for an EIS. Prior to the evaluation there was the possibility that Conoco's EIS could have been scaled back substantially. Instead, the interviews and documented benefits resulted in a greater awareness of the system's current and potential value. Users more readily appreciate how much the EIS supports them in performing their job responsibilities.

Lesson 2. A comprehensive evaluation can identify which applications deliver value and where enhancements or new applications are needed. Sometimes there is a difference between a subjective appraisal of an application and the findings from an objective analysis. Until the evaluation was made, it was unclear which applications were paying for themselves. The interviews also were useful for identifying needed changes and additions to the system. The evaluation, therefore, helped to identify new information requirements.

Lesson 3. Both usage statistics and user interviews are needed. Usage statistics are invaluable in determining who uses which applications. Nonetheless, derived benefits can be identified only through interviews with the users. It is also important during the interviews to ask about other users who may be receiving considerable benefits from the system. In some cases, users who were not identified initially as "key users" needed to be interviewed, too.

Lesson 4. Focus attention on mission-critical applications. Some applications are more important than others. Those that are crucial to job performance are likely to generate the greatest benefits; consequently, they require the most careful evaluation. Specifically, the greatest improvements in decision making are likely to be found here.

Lesson 5. EIS benefits should be assessed at the level at which they occur. It is not possible to place a total value on an EIS by comparing the firm's "bottom line" before and after its implementation because too many exogenous factors (e.g., national economy, actions of competitors) affect the firm. Only by investigating each type of benefit at the organizational level at which it occurs can a meaningful analysis be performed.

Lesson 6. Quantify benefits as much as possible and record intangible benefits. With sufficient effort, more EIS benefits can be quantified than first thought. Hopefully, these are sufficient to cost justify the EIS. On the other hand, some of the existing benefits may not lend themselves to quantification. These intangible benefits should be recorded and presented as part of the management report.

Lesson 7. Discount benefits by an amount commensurate to their degree of uncertainty. Benefits are seldom completely "hard and certain" or "soft and uncertain." Rather, they contain varying degrees of "hardness and softness." The softer the benefits, the more likely they are to be discounted by senior management. It is best to make conservative estimates because this makes the numbers more credible. Benefits should not be claimed unless they can be supported.

Lesson 8. Do not confuse the size or complexity of an application with its significance. Some applications contain many screens while others have only one. Some applications are complex; others are simple. Applications come in many sizes and shapes; a small or simple one may provide considerable value.

Lesson 9. The assessment should be as open and objective as possible. It is important that users feel that the evaluation team is honestly trying to gather information to assess and improve the system. Avoid the impression that the purpose of the evaluation is to justify the system's existence. Management's acceptance of the evaluation depends ultimately on how objectively it is perceived to have been done.

Lesson 10. Keep the interview structure relatively open. Some structure to the user interviews is needed in order to fully cover the benefit categories. Users may want to take the discussions into other areas, however, and this should be encouraged because unanticipated benefits may be divulged.

Lesson 11. The interviews should be conducted by people who understand the business. There are three reasons for this: to have credibility with users, to be able to understand and evaluate the benefits, and to see opportunities for improving the system.

Lesson 12. A comprehensive assessment requires considerable time and effort. Working on a part-time basis, it took the EIS manager and four staff members three months to complete the evaluation of Conoco's EIS. An EIS with fewer users and applications should be easier to review, but interviews with users will still be time-consuming.

Lesson 13. The assessment should be an on-going process. Conoco's evaluation had many beneficial outcomes: renewed interest and support for the system; the identification of applications that should be eliminated; the identification of applications that should be enhanced or added. An on-going rather than an ad hoc review process helps ensure that the system remains valuable.

Lesson 14. There is no single way to evaluate an EIS. An EIS may be developed for a variety of reasons: to provide more timely information, to be more responsive to changing customer needs, to support a total quality management initiative, or to improve organizational communications. The assessment should be done with the objectives for the system in mind. Top management may feel that the system is successful even if the benefits are largely intangible if they believe that the EIS supports important organizational objectives. Research has shown that support of explicit business objectives is the most important criterion in selecting IT investments (Bacon, 1992).

CONCLUSION

The fundamental objective of the evaluation was to assess whether Conoco's EIS was delivering business value. This was achieved by studying the system application by application all the way to the corporate level. The process described and illustrated in this article provided a framework for the evaluation. In the final analysis, an EIS is meant for the business, and thus it is the individual users who must determine its business value. The analysis demonstrated that the system helped to achieve organizational objectives, which resulted in management's continued support. Even if it is not possible to prove the benefits of an EIS quantitatively, the positive benefits resulting from this process may warrant its use by others.

Even though the evaluation methodology was developed to assess an EIS, there is an intriguing possibility that the approach could be appropriate for other kinds of computer applications, perhaps providing a meta model or framework for assessing other IT investments. On the benefits side, the methodology explores a spectrum ranging from improved decision making to reduced information distribution costs.

QUESTIONS

1. Why is it usually easier to estimate the costs rather than the benefits of a decision support application?
2. Identify and discuss the five "hard" benefit categories that were used in assessing the value of Conoco's EIS. Are these categories broad enough to cover any decision support application? Discuss.
3. Is it really difficult to assess the value of decision support applications or are people who make this claim copping out from doing their homework? Discuss.
4. Should investments in decision support applications be subjected to the same financial measurements (e.g., return on investment, payback period) that are commonly applied to other kinds of corporate investments? Discuss.

REFERENCES

BACON, C. J. "The Use of Decision Criteria in Selecting Information Systems/Technology Investments," *MIS Quarterly* (16:3), September 1992, pp. 335–350.

BADIRU, A. B. "A Management Guide to Automation Cost Justification," *Industrial Engineer* (22:2), February 1990, pp. 27–30.

BAKOS, J. Y. and KEMERER, C. F. "Recent Applications of Economic Theory in Information Technology Research," *Decision Support Systems* (8:5), September 1992, pp. 365–386.

BELCHER, L. W. and WATSON, H. J. "Assessing the Value of Conoco EIS," *MIS Quarterly* (17:3), September 1993, pp. 239–253.

DAVENPORT, T. H. "The Case of the Soft Software Proposal," *Harvard Business Review* (89:3), May-June 1989, pp. 12–24.

DIXON, P. J. and DARWIN, A. J. "Technology Issues Facing Corporate Management in the 1990s," *MIS Quarterly* (13:3), September 1989, pp. 247–255.

GULDEN, G. K. and EWERS, D. E. "Is Your ESS Meeting the Need?" *Computerworld* (23:28), July 10, 1989, pp. 85–91.

HOGUE, J. T. and WATSON, H. J. "Management's Role in the Approval and Administration of Decision Support Systems," *MIS Quarterly* (7:2), June 1983, pp. 15–26.

IVES, B., OLSON, M. H., and BAROUDI, J. J. "The Measurement of User Information Satisfaction," *Communications of the ACM* (26:10), October 1983, pp. 785–793.

KEEN, P. G. W. "Value Analysis—Justifying Decision Support Systems," *MIS Quarterly* (5:1), March 1981, pp. 1–14.

KRIEBEL, C. H. and MOORE, J. "Economics and Management Information Systems," in *Proceedings of the International Conference on Information Systems*, E.R. McLean (ed.), available from ACM, New York, NY, December 1980, pp. 19–31.

LITECKY, C. R. "Intangibles in Cost/Benefit Analysis," *Journal of Systems Management* (32:2) February 1981, pp. 15–17.

LOVEMAN, G. "Cash Gain, No Gain," *Computerworld* (25:48), November 25, 1991, pp. 69–72.

MELONE, N. P. and WHARTON, T. J. "Strategies for MIS Project Selection," *Journal of Systems Management* (35:2), February 1984, pp. 27–33.

PALLER, A. with LASKA, R. *The EIS Book*, Dow Jones-Irwin, Homewood, IL, 1990.

PANKO, R. R. "Is Office Productivity Stagnant?" *MIS Quarterly* (15:2), June 1991, pp. 191–203.

POWELL, P. "Information Technology Evaluation: Is It Different?" *Journal of the Operations Research Society* (43:1), January 1992, pp. 28–42.

ROCKART, J. F. and DELONG, D. W. *Executive Support Systems: The Emergence of Top Management Computer Use*, Dow Jones-Irwin, Homewood, IL, 1988.

ROCKART, J. F. and TREACY, M. E. "The CEO Goes Online," *Harvard Business Review* (60:1), January-February 1982, pp. 84–88.

SILK, D. J. "Managing IS Benefits for the 1990s," *Journal of Information Technology* (5:4), December 1990, pp. 185–193.

SINGLETON, J. P., MCLEAN, E. R., and ALTMAN, E. N. "Measuring Information Systems Performance: Experience With the Management By Results System at Security Pacific Bank," *MIS Quarterly* (12:2), June 1988, pp. 325–337.

SMITH, R. D. "Measuring the Intangible Benefits of Computer-Based Information Systems," *Journal of Systems Management* (34:9), September 1983, pp. 22–27.

SRINIVASAN, A. "Alternative Measures of System Effectiveness: Associations and Implications," *MIS Quarterly* (9:3), September 1985, pp. 243–253.

STRASSMAN, P. A. *Information Payoff: The Transformation of Work in the Electronic Age*, Free Press, New York, NY, 1985.

WATSON, H. J., HARP, C. G., KELLY, G. G., and O'HARA, M. T. "Soften Up!" *Computerworld* (26:42), October 19, 1992, pp. 103–104.

WATSON, H. J. and GLOVER, H. "Common and Avoidable Causes of EIS Failure," *Computerworld* (23:48), December 4, 1989, pp. 90–91.

WATSON, H. J., ARONSON, J. E., HAMILTON, R. H., IYER, L., NAGASUNDARAM, M., NEMATI, H., and SULEIMAN, J. "Assessing EIS Benefits: A Survey of Current Practices," University of Georgia working paper, Terry College of Business, University of Georgia, Athens, Georgia, 1995.

WATSON, H. J., RAINER, R. K., and KOH, C. E. "Executive Information Systems: A Framework for Development and a Survey of Current Practices," *MIS Quarterly* (15:1), March 1991, pp. 13–30.

WEILL, P. "The Relationship Between Investment in Information Technology and Firm Performance: A Study of the Value Manufacturing Sector," *Information Systems Research* (3:4), December 1992, pp. 307–333.

WILDER, C. and HILDEBRAND, C. "Faster! Better! Cheaper! Now!" *Computerworld* (26:1), January 2, 1992, pp. 2–6.

DECISION SUPPORT BIBLIOGRAPHY

A large body of decision support writings has been published in books, articles, conference proceedings, trade publications, and the like. This diversity can be seen in the varied sources of materials included in this book of readings. To help you find other materials of interest, the following decision support bibliography is provided. Although it contains references to what the authors feel are the most important, interesting, and accessible materials on decision support, it includes only a small percentage of what has been written. There are many other excellent decision support writings, with more appearing daily. This bibliography should provide assistance, however, as you strive to learn more about decision support.

This bibliography includes books and articles. The articles have been categorized by their major topic(s): (1) general overview; (2) relationship with OR/MS and MIS; (3) decision support framework; (4) development process; (5) software interface; (6) model subsystem; (7) database subsystem; (8) integrating the software interface, models, and data; (9) integrating decision support into the organization; (10) evaluation of decision support; (11) applications of decision support; (12) executive information systems; (13) expert systems; (14) group decision support systems; (15) future of decision support; and (16) decision support benefits.

BOOKS

1. ALTER, STEVEN, L. *Decision Support Systems: Current Practices and Continuing Challenges.* Reading, Mass.: Addison-Wesley, 1980.

2. BENNETT, JOHN L., ed. *Building Decision Support Systems.* Reading, Mass.: Addison-Wesley, 1983.

3. BOSTROM, ROBERT P., RICHARD T. WATSON, and SUSAN T. KINNEY, *Computer Augmented Teamwork: A Guided Tour.* New York: Van Nostrand Reinhold, 1992.

4. GRAY, PAUL *Decision Support and Executive Information Systems.* Englewood Cliffs, N.J.: Prentice Hall, 1994.

5. JESSUP, LEONARD M., and JOSEPH S. VALACICH, *Group Support Systems.* New York: Macmillan, 1993.

6. KEEN, PETER G. W., and MICHAEL S. SCOTT MORTON *Decision Support Systems: An Organizational Perspective.* Reading, Mass.: Addison-Wesley, 1978.

7. MALLACH, EFREM G. *Understanding Decision Support Systems and Expert Systems.* Burr Ridge, Ill.: Irwin, 1994.

8. MOCKLER, ROBERT J. *Knowledge-based Systems for Management Decisions.* Englewood Cliffs, N.J.: Prentice Hall, 1989.

9. SCOTT MORTON, MICHAEL S. *Management Decision Systems: Computer Support for Decision Making.* Boston: Harvard University Press, 1971.

10. SILVER, MARK *Decision Support Systems.* Chichester, N.Y.: John Wiley, 1991.

11. SPRAGUE, RALPH H., and ERIC D. CARLSON *Building Effective Decision Support Systems.* Englewood Cliffs, N.J.: Prentice Hall, 1982.

12. STRASSMAN, PAUL A. *Information Payoff: The Transformation of Work in the Electronic Age.* New York: Free Press, 1985.

13. TURBAN, EFRAIM *Decision Support and Expert Systems.* Englewood Cliffs, N.J.: Prentice Hall, 1995.

14. WATSON, HUGH J., RAINER R. KELLY, and GEORGE HOUDESHEL, *Executive Information Systems.* New York: John Wiley, 1992.

REFERENCES

1. ABDOLMOHANNADI, M. H. "Decision Support and Expert Systems in Auditing: A Review and Research Directions," *Accounting and Business Research,* 17, no. 3 (Spring 1987), 173–185.

2. ADELMAN, L. "Involving Users in the Development of Decision-Analytic Aids: The Principal Factor in Successful Implementation," *Journal of the Operational Research Society,* 33, no. 4 (April 1982), 333–342.

3. AIKEN, M. W., O. R. L. SHENG, and D. R. VOGEL "Integrating Expert Systems With Group Decision Support Systems," *ACM Transactions on Information Systems,* 9, no. 1 (January 1991), 75–95.

4. AKOKA, J. "A Framework for Decision Support System Evaluation," *Information and Management,* 4 (July 1981), 133–141.

5. ALAVI, M., and J. C. HENDERSON "Evolutionary Strategy for Implementing a Decision Support System," *Management Science,* 27, no. 11 (November 1981), 1309–1323.

6. ALAVI, M., "An Assessment of Electronic Meeting Systems in a Corporate Setting," *Information and Management,* 25, no. 4 (October 1993) 175–182.

7. ALBRECHT, M., N. J. BELKIN, L. FUSCO, P. G. MARCHETTI, S. SKOGVOLD, H. STOKKE, and G. TROINA, "User Interfaces for Information Systems," *Journal of Information Science,* 17, no. 6, (1991) 327–344.

8. ALTER, S. L. "Development Patterns for Decision Support Systems," *MIS Quarterly,* 2, no. 3 (September 1978), 33–42.

9. ALTER, S. L. "Why Is Man-Computer Interaction Important for Decision Support Systems?" *Interfaces*, 7, no. 2 (February 1977), 109–115.
10. ALTER, S. L. "A Taxonomy of Decision Support Systems," *Sloan Management Review*, 19, no. 1 (Fall 1977), 39–59.
11. ARINZE, B. "A Contingency Model of DSS Development Methodology," *Journal of Management Information Systems*, 8, no. 1 (Summer 1991), 149–166.
12. BACON, C. J. "The Use of Decision Criteria in Selecting Information Systems/Technology Investments," *MIS Quarterly*, 16, no. 3 (September 1992), 335–350.
13. BAHL, H. C., and R. G. HUNT "Decision Making Theory and DSS Design," *Data Base*, 15, no. 4 (Summer 1984), 12–19.
14. BAKER, D. S., S. C. CHOW, M. T. HENNEN, T. P. LUKEN, G. J. ROBINSON, and H. L., SCHEURMAN "An Integrated Decision Support and Manufacturing Control System," *Interfaces*, 14, no. 5 (September–October 1984), 44–52.
15. BARBOSA, L. C., and R. G. HERKO "Integration of Algorithmic Aids into Decision Support Systems," *MIS Quarterly*, 4, no. 1 (March 1980), 1–12.
16. BEAUCLAIR, R. A., and D. W. STRAUB "Utilizing GDSS Technology: Final Report on a Recent Empirical Study," *Information & Management*, 18 (1990), 213–220.
17. BELARDO, S., K. R. KARWAN, and W. A. WALLACE "Managing the Response to Disasters Using Microcomputers," *Interfaces*, 14, no. 2 (March–April 1984), 29–39.
18. BENBASAT, I., and A. S. DEXTER "Individual Differences in the Use of Decision Support Aids," *Journal of Accounting Research*, 20 (Spring 1982), 1–11.
19. BENBASAT, I., and R. N. TAYLOR "The Impact of Cognitive Styles on Information Systems Design," *MIS Quarterly*, 2, no. 2 (June 1978), 43–54.
20. BENDERS, J., and F. MANDERS, "Expert Systems and Organizational Decision Making," *Information and Management*, 25, no. 4 (October 1993) 207–213.
21. BERRISFORD, T., and J. WETHERBE "Heuristic Development: A Redesign of Systems Design," *MIS Quarterly*, 3, no. 1 (March 1979), 11–19.
22. BLANNING, R. W. "What Is Happening in DSS?" *Interfaces*, 13, no. 5 (October 1983), 71–80.
23. BOIES, S. J., J. D. GOULD, and J. P. UKELSON, "User Navigation in Computer Applications," *IEEE Transactions on Software Engineering*, 19, no. 3 (March 1993) 297–306.
24. BONCZEK, R. H., C. W. HOLSAPPLE, and A. B. WHINSTON "Computer Based Support of Organizational Decision-Making," *Decision Sciences*, 10, no. 2 (April 1979), 268–291.
25. BONCZEK, R. H., C. W. HOLSAPPLE, and A. B. WHINSTON "The Evolving Roles of Models in Decision Support Systems," *Decision Sciences*, 11, no. 2 (April 1980), 337–356.
26. BONCZEK, R. H., C. W. HOLSAPPLE, and A .B. WHINSTON "Future Directions for Developing Decision Support Systems," *Decision Sciences*, 11, no. 4 (October 1980), 616–631.
27. BRENNAN, J. J., and J. J. ELAM "Understanding and Validating Results in Model-Based Decision Support Systems," *Decision Support Systems*, 2 (1986), 49–54.
28. BRIGHTMAN, H. "Differences in Ill-Structured Problem Solving Along the Organizational Hierarchy," *Decision Sciences*, 9, no. 1 (January 1978), 1–18.
29. BUNEMAN, O. P., and OTHERS "Display Facilities for DSS Support: The DAISY Approach," *Data Base*, 8, no. 3 (Winter 1977), 46–50.
30. BYRD, T. A., "Expert Systems in Production and Operations Management: Results of a Survey," *Interfaces*, 23, no. 2 (March–April 1993).

31. CALE, E. G., and S. E. ERICKSEN, "Design & Implementation Issues for a Banking Decision Support System," *IS Management* (April 1994) 18–21.
32. CANNING, R. G. "What's Happening with DSS," *EDP Analyzer,* 22, no. 7 (July 1984), 1–12.
33. CANNING, R. G. "Interesting Decision Support Systems," *EDP Analyzer,* 20, no. 3 (March 1984), 1–12.
34. CARLIS, J. V., G. W. DICKSON, and S. T. MARCH "Physical Database Design: A DSS Approach," *Information and Management,* 6 (August 1983), 211–224.
35. CARLSON, E. "Decision Support Systems: Personal Computing Services for Managers," *Management Review,* 66, no. 1 (January 1977), 4–11.
36. CARLSON, E. D., B. F. GRACE, and J. A. SUTTON "Case Studies of End User Requirements for Interactive Problem Solving Systems," *MIS Quarterly,* 1, no. 1 (March 1977), 51–63.
37. CONHAGEN, A. E., and OTHERS, "Decision Support Systems in Banking," *Bankers Magazine,* 165 (May–June 1982), 79–84.
38. COOPER, D. O., L. B. DAVIDSON, and W. K. DENISON, "A Tool for More Effective Financial Analysis," *Interfaces* (February 1975), 91–103.
39. CRESCENZI, A. D., and G. K. GULDEN, "Decision Support for Manufacturing Management," *Information and Management,* 6 (April 1983), 91–95.
40. CULLUM, R. L. "Iterative Development," *Datamation,* 31 (February 1985), 92–98.
41. CURLEY, K. F., and L. L. GREMILLION, "The Role of the Champion in DSS Implementation," *Information and Management,* 6 (August 1983), 203–209.
42. DAFT, R. L., and N. B. MACINTOSH, "New Approach to Design and Use of Management Information," *California Management Review,* 21, no. 1 (Fall 1978), 82–92.
43. DAVENPORT, T. H. "The Case of the Soft Software Proposal," *Harvard Business Review,* 89, no. 3 (May–June 1989), 12–24.
44. DAVIS, R. "A DSS for Diagnosis and Therapy," *Data Base,* 8, no. 3 (Winter 1977), 58–72.
45. DE, P., and A. SEN "Logical Data Base Design in Decision Support Systems," *Journal of Systems Management,* 32 (May 1981), 28–33.
46. DENNIS, A., J. F. NUNAMAKER, and D. R. VOGEL "A Comparison of Laboratory and Field Research in the Study of Electronic Meeting Systems," *Journal of Management Information Systems,* 7, no. 3 (Winter 1990–91), 107–135.
47. DENNIS, A., J. GEORGE, L. JESSUP, J. NUNAMAKER, and D. VOGEL, "Information Technology to Support Electronic Meetings," *MIS Quarterly,* 12, no. 4 (December 1988), 591–619.
48. DESANCTIS, G., and B. GALLUPE, "Group Decision Support Systems: A New Frontier," *Data Base,* 16, no. 4 (Winter 1985), 3–10.
49. DESANCTIS, G., and G. GALLUPE "A Foundation for the Study of Group Decision Support Systems," *Management Science,* 33, no. 5 (May 1987), 589–609.
50. DICKSON, G. W., and M. A. JANSON "The Failure of a DSS for Energy Conservation: A Technical Perspective," *Systems, Objectives, Solutions,* 4, no. 2 (April 1984), 69–80.
51. DOKTOR, R. H., and W. F. HAMILTON "Cognitive Style and the Acceptance of Management Science Recommendations," *Management Science,* 19, no. 8 (April 1973), 884–894.

52. DONOVAN, J., and S. MADNICK "Institutional and Ad Hoc DSS and Their Effective Use," *Data Base*, 8, no. 3 (Winter 1977), 79–88.

53. DURAND, D. E. and S. H. VAN HUSS, "Creativity Software and DSS," *Information and Management*, 23, no. 1 (July 1992), 1–6.

54. EASON, K. D. "Understanding the Naive Computer User," *Computer Journal*, 19, no. 1 (February 1976), 3–7.

55. EBENSTEIN, M., and L. I. KRAUS "Strategic Planning for Information Resource Management," *Management Review*, 7 (June 1981), 21–26.

56. EDEN, C., and D. SIMS "Subjectivity in Problem Identification," *Interfaces*, 11, no. 1 (February 1981), 68–74.

57. ELAM, J. J., and J. C. HENDERSON "Knowledge Engineering Concepts for Decision Support Design and Implementation," *Information and Management*, 6 (April 1983), 109–14.

58. EL SAWY, O. A. "Personal Information Systems for Strategic Scanning in Turbulent Environments: Can the CEO Go On-Line?" *MIS Quarterly*, 2, no. 1 (March 1985), 53–60.

59. ERICKSEN, D. C. "A Synopsis of Present Day Practices concerning Decision Support Systems," *Information and Management*, 7 (October 1984), 243–252.

60. ETGAR, M., S. LICHT, and P. SHRIVASTA "A Decision Support System for Strategic Marketing Decisions," *Systems, Objectives, Solutions*, 4, no. 3 (August 1984), 131–140.

61. FARWELL, D. C., and T. FARWELL "Decision Support System for Ski Area Design," *Journal of Systems Management*, 33, no. 3 (March 1982), 32–37.

62. FERGUSON, R. L., and C. H. HONES "A Computer Aided Decision System," *Management Science*, June 1969, B550–B561.

63. FINDLAY, P. N. "Decision Support System and Expert Systems: A Comparison of Their Components and Design Methodologies," *Computers Operations Research*, 17, no. 6 (1990), 535–543.

64. FRANZ, L. S., S. M. LEE, and J. C. VAN HORN "An Adaptive Decision Support System for Academic Resource Planning," *Decision Sciences*, 12, no. 2 (April 1981), 276–293.

65. FRIEND, DAVID "Executive Information Systems: Successes and Failures, Insights and Misconceptions," *Journal of Information Systems Management*, 3 (Fall 1986), 31–36.

66. FROLICK, M. N., and S. JEANINGS, "EIS Software Selection at Georgia Power: A Structured Approach," *Information Strategy: The Executive Journal*, 9, no. 3 (Spring 1993), 47–52.

67. FUERST, W. L., and P. H. CHENY "Factors Affecting the Perceived Utilization of Computer-Based Decision Support Systems in the Oil Industry," *Decision Sciences*, 13, no. 4 (October 1982), 554–569.

68. GERRITY, T. P. "Design of Man-Machine Decision Systems: An Application to Portfolio Management," *Sloan Management Review*, 12, no. 2 (Winter 1971), 59–75.

69. GINZBERG, M. J. "Finding an Adequate Measure of OR/MS Effectiveness," *Interfaces*, 8, no. 4 (August 1978), 59–62.

70. GINZBERG, M. J. "Redesign of Managerial Tasks: A Requisite for Successful Support Systems," *MIS Quarterly*, 2, no. 1 (March 1978), 39–52.

71. GORRY, G. A., and M. S. SCOTT MORTON "A Framework for Management Information Systems," *Sloan Management Review*, 13, no. 1 (Fall 1971), 55–70.

72. GRACE, B. F. "Training Users of a Decision Support System," *Data Base*, 8, no. 3 (Winter 1977), 30–36.

73. GROHOWSKI, R., D. R. VOGEL, B. MARTZ, and J. A. NUNAMAKER "Implementing Electronic Meeting Systems at IBM: Lessons Learned and Success Factors" *MIS Quarterly*, 14 (December 1990) 369–382.

74. HACKATHORN, R. D., and P. G. W. KEEN "Organizational Strategies for Personal Computing in Decision Support Systems," *MIS Quarterly*, 5, no. 3 (September 1981), 21–26.

75. HAMILTON, W. P., and M. A. MOSES "A Computer-Based Corporate Planning System," *Management Science*, 21, no. 2 (October 1974), 148–159.

76. HAMMOND, J. S., III "The Roles of the Manager and Management Scientists in Successful Implementation," *Sloan Management Review*, 15, no. 2 (Winter 1974), 1–24.

77. HASEMAN, W. D. "GPLAN: An Operational DSS," *Data Base*, 8, no. 3 (Winter 1977), 73–78.

78. HEHNEM, M. T. ET AL. "An Integrated Decision Support and Manufacturing Control System," *Interfaces*, 14, no. 5 (September–October 1984).

79. HENDERSON, J. C., and P. C. NUTT "Influence of Decision Style on Decision Making Behavior," *Management Science*, 26, no. 4 (April 1980), 371–386.

80. HENDERSON, J. C., and P. C. NUTT "On the Design of Planning Information Systems," *Academy of Management Review*, 3, no. 3 (October 1978), 774–785.

81. HOGUE, J. T., and H. J. WATSON "Managements' Role in the Approval and Administration of Decision Support Systems," *MIS Quarterly*, 7, no. 2 (June 1983), 15–26.

82. HUBER, G. P. "The Nature of Organizational Decision Making and the Design of Decision Support Systems," *MIS Quarterly*, 5, no. 2 (June 1981), 1–10.

83. HUBER, G. P. "Cognitive Style as a Basis for MIS and DSS Designs: Much Ado about Nothing?" *Management Science*, 29, no. 5 (May 1983), 567–579.

84. HUBER, G. P. "Issues in the Design of Group Decision Support Systems," *MIS Quarterly*, 8, no. 3 (September 1984), 195–204.

85. HUFF, S. L. "DSS Development: Promise and Practice," *Journal of Information Systems Management*, 3 (Fall 1986), 8–15.

86. IVES, B., M. H. OLSON, and J. J. BAROUDI, "The Measurement of User Information Satisfaction," *Communications of the ACM*, 26, no. 10 (October 1983), 785–793.

87. KEEN, P. G. W. "Value Analysis-Justifying Decision Support Systems," *MIS Quarterly*, 5, no. 1 (March 1981), 1–14.

88. KEEN, P. G. W. "Adaptive Design for Decision Support Systems," *Data Base*, 12, nos. 1 and 2 (Fall 1980), 15–25.

89. KEEN P. G. W. "Computer-Based Decision Aids: The Evaluation Problem," *Sloan Management Review*, 16, no. 3 (Spring 1975), 17–29.

90. KEEN, P. G. W. "Decision Support Systems: The Next Decade," *Decision Support Systems*, 3 (1987), 253–265.

91. KEEN, P. G. W. "Decision Support Systems: Translating Analytic Techniques into Useful Tools," *Sloan Management Review*, 21, no. 3 (Spring 1980), 33–44.

92. KEEN, P. G. W. "Interactive Computer Systems for Managers: A Modest Proposal," *Sloan Management Review*, 18, no. 1 (Fall 1976), 1–17.

93. KEEN, P. G. W. and G. R. WAGNER "DSS: An Executive Mind-Support System," *Datamation*, 25, no. 12 (November 1979), 117–122.

94. KIMBROUGH, S. O., C. W. PRITCHETT, M. P. BIEBER, and H. K. BHARGAVA "The Coast Guard's KSS Project," *Interfaces*, 20, no. 6 (November–December 1990), 29–38.

95. KING, W. R., and D. I. CLELLAND "Decision and Information Systems for Strategic Planning," *Business Horizons* (April 1973), 29–36.

96. KING, W. R., and J. I. RODRIQUEZ "Participative Design of Strategic Decision Support Systems," *Management Science*, 27, no. 6 (June 1981), 717–726.

97. KLAAS, R. L. "A DSS for Airline Management," *Data Base*, 8, no. 3 (Winter 1977), 3–8.

98. KLING, R. "The Organizational Context of User-Centered Software Designs," *MIS Quarterly*, 1, no. 4 (December 1977), 41–52.

99. KOESTER, R., and F. LUTHANS; "The Impact of the Computer on the Choice Activity of Decision Makers: A Replication with Actual Users of Computerized MIS," *Academy of Management Journal*, 22, no. 2 (June 1979), 416–422.

100. KOSAKA, T., and T. HIROUCHI, "An Effective Architecture for Decision Support Systems," *Information and Management*, 5 (March 1982), 7–17.

101. LARRECHE, J., and V. SRINIVASAN "STRATPORT: A Decision Support System for Strategic Planning," *Journal of Marketing*, 45 (Fall 1981), 39–52.

102. LITTLE, J. D. C. "Decision Support Systems for Marketing Managers," *Journal of Marketing*, 43 (Summer 1979), 9–26.

103. LOCANDER, W. B., A. NAPIER, and R. SCAMELL, "A Team Approach to Managing the Development of a Decision Support System," *MIS Quarterly*, 3, no. 1 (March 1979), 53–63.

104. LOVEMAN, G. "Cash Gain, No Gain," *Computerworld*, 25, no. 48 (November 25, 1991), 69–72.

105. LUCAS, H. C., JR. "Experimental Investigation of the Use of Computer Based Graphics in Decision Making," *Management Science*, 27, no. 7 (July 1981), 757–768.

106. LUCAS, H. C., JR. "Empirical Evidence for a Description Model of Implementation," *MIS Quarterly*, 2, no. 2 (June 1978), 27–42.

107. LUCAS, H. C., JR. "The Evolution of an Information System: From Key-Man to Every Person," *Sloan Management Review*, 19, no. 2 (Winter 1980), 39–52.

108. MACINTOSH, N. B., and R. L. DAFT, "User Department Technology and Information Design," *Information and Management*, 1 (1978), 123–131.

109. MCCLEAN, E. R. "End Users as Application Developers," *MIS Quarterly*, 3, no. 4 (December 1979), 37–46.

110. MCCLEAN, E. R., and T. F. RIESING, "MAPP: A DSS for Financial Planning," *Data Base*, 3, no. 3 (Winter 1977), 9–14.

111. MCKENNY, J. L., and P. G. W. KEEN, "How Managers' Minds Work," *Harvard Business Review* (May–June 1974), 79–90.

112. MEADOR, C. L., and D. N. NESS, "Decision Support Systems: An Application to Corporate Planning," *Sloan Management Review*, 16, no. 2 (Winter 1974), 51–68.

113. METHLIE, L. "Data Management for Decision Support Systems," *Data Base,* 12, nos. 1 and 2 (Fall 1980), 40–46.

114. MEYER, M. H., and K. F. CURLEY "Putting Expert Systems Technology to Work," *Sloan Management Review,* (Winter 1991), 21–31.

115. MINTZBERG, H. "Managerial Work: Analysis from Observation," *Management Science,* 18, no. 2 (October 1971), B97–B110.

116. MINTZBERG, H., D. RAISINGHANI, and A. THEORET "The Structure of `Unstructured' Decision Processes," *Administrative Science Quarterly,* 21, no. 2 (June 1976), 246–275.

117. MOSES, M. A. "Implementation of Analytical Planning Systems," *Management Science,* 21, no. 10 (June 1975), 1133–1143.

118. NAYLOR, T. H. "Effective Use of Strategic Planning, Forecasting, and Modeling in the Executive Suite," *Managerial Planning,* 30, no. 4 (January–February 1982), 4–11.

119. NAYLER, THOMAS H. "Decision Support Systems or Whatever Happened to M.I.S.?" *Interfaces,* 12, no. 4 (August 1982), 92–97.

120. NELSON, C. W., and R. BALACHANDRA "Choosing the Right Expert System Building Approach," *Decision Sciences,* 22 (1991), 354–367.

121. NESS, D. H., and C. R. SPRAGUE "An Interactive Media Decision Support System," *Sloan Management Review,* 14, no. 1 (Fall 1972), 51–61.

122. NEUMANN, S., and M. HADASS "Decision Support Systems and Strategic Decisions," *California Management Review,* 22, no. 2 (Spring 1980), 77–84.

123. NOUR, M. A., and D. YEN, "Group Decision Support Systems (Towards a Conceptual Foundation)," *Information and Management,* 23, no. 2 (August 1992). 55–64.

124. NUNAMAKER, J. F., A. R. DENNIS, J. S. VALACICH, D. R. VOGEL, and J. R. GEORGE "Electronic Meeting Systems to Support Group Work," *Communications of the ACM,* 34, no. 7 (July 1991), 40–61.

125. NUNAMAKER, J. F., L. M. APPLEGATE, and B. R. KONSYNSKI "Facilitating Group Creativity: Experience with a Group Decision Support System," *Journal of Management Information Systems,* 3, no. 4 (Spring 1987), 5–19.

126. NUNAMAKER, J. F., A. R. DENNIS, J. S. VALACICH, and D. R. VOGEL, "Information Technology for Negotiating Groups: Generating Options for Mutual Gain," *Management Science,* 37, no. 10 (October 1991), 1325–1346.

127. NYWEIDE, J. O. "Decision Support through Automated Human Resource Systems," *Magazine of Bank Administration,* 62, no. 5 (November 1986), 60–62.

128. OSBORN, P. B., and W. H. ZICKEFOOSE "Building Expert Systems from the Ground Up," *AI Expert* (May 1990), 28–33.

129. PARTOW-NAVID, P. "Misuse and Disuse of DSS Models," *Journal of Systems Management,* 38, no. 4 (April 1987), 38–40.

130. PRASTACOS, G. P., and E. BRODHEIM "PBDS: A Decision Support System for Regional Blood Management," *Management Science,* 26, no. 5 (May 1980), 451–463.

131. RAYMOND, L., and F. BERGERON, "Personal DSS Success in Small Enterprises," *Information and Management,* 22, no. 5 (May 1992) 301–308.

132. RECK, R. H., and J. R. HALL "Executive Information Systems: An Overview of Development," *Journal of Information Systems Management,* 3 (Fall 1986), 25–30.

133. REMUS, W. E., and J. KOTTERMAN "Toward Intelligent Decision Support Systems: An Artificially Intelligent Statistician," *MIS Quarterly*, 10, no. 4 (December 1986).

134. RICHMAN, L. S. "Software Catches the Team Spirit," *Fortune*, September 1985, 125–136.

135. ROBEY, D., and D. FARROW "User Involvement in Information System Development," *Management Science*, 28, no. 1 (January 1982), 73–85.

136. ROBEY, D., and W. TAGGART "Human Information Processing in Information and Decision Support Systems," *MIS Quarterly*, 6, no. 2 (June 1982), 61–73.

137. ROBEY, D., and W. TAGGART "Measuring Managers' Minds: The Assessment of Style in Human Information Processing," *Academy of Management Review*, 6, no. 2 (July 1981), 375–383.

138. ROCKART, J. F., and M. E. TREACY "The CEO Goes On-Line," *Harvard Business Review*, 60, no. 1 (January–February 1982), 32–38.

139. ROLAND, R. "A Model of Organizational Variables for DSS," *Data-Base*, 12, nos. 1 and 2 (Fall 1980), 63–72.

140. ROY, A., A. DEFALOMIR, and L. LASDON "An Optimization Based Decision Support System for a Product Mix Problem," *Interfaces*, 12, no. 2 (April 1982), 26–33.

141. RUCKS, A. C., and P. M. GINTER "Strategic MIS: Promises Unfulfilled," *Journal of Systems Management*, 33 (March 1982), 16–19.

142. SANDERS, L. C., J. F. COURTNEY, and S. L. LOY "The Impact of DSS on Organizational Communication," *Information and Management*, 7 (June 1984), 141–148.

143. SCHMITZ, J. D., G. D. ARMSTRONG, and J. D. C. LITTLE "CoverStory—Automated News Finding in Marketing," *Interfaces*, 20, no. 6 (November–December 1990), 29–38.

144. SEABURG, R. A., and C. SEABURG "Computer-Based Decision Systems in Xerox Corporate Planning," *Management Science*, 20, no. 4 (December 1973), 575–584.

145. SILVER, M. S. "Decision Support Systems: Directed and Nondirected Change," *Information Systems Research* (March 1990), 47–70.

146. SILVER, M. S. "On The Restrictiveness of Decision Support Systems," *Organizational Decision Support Systems* (1988), 259–270.

147. SIMARD, A. J., and J. E. EENIGENBURG "An Executive Information System to Support Wildfire Disaster Declarations," *Interfaces*, 20, no. 6 (November–December 1990), 53–66.

148. SINGLETON, J. P., E. R. MCLEAN, and E. N. ALTMAN, "Measuring Information Systems Performance: Experience with the Management by Results System at Security Pacific Bank, *MIS Quarterly*, 12, no. 2 (June 1988) 325–337.

149. SMITH, R. D. "Measuring the Intangible Benefits of Computer-Based Information Systems," *Journal of Systems Management*, 34, no. 9 (September 1983), 22–27.

150. SPRAGUE, R. H., JR. "Conceptual Description of a Financial Planning Model for Commercial Banks," *Decision Sciences*, 2, no. 1 (January 1971), 66–80.

151. SPRAGUE, R. H., JR. "The Financial Planning System at the Louisiana National Bank," *MIS Quarterly*, 3, no. 3 (September 1979), 1–11.

152. SPRAGUE, R. H., JR. "Systems Support for a Financial Planning Model," *Management Accounting*, 53, no. 6 (June 1972), 29–34.

153. SPRAGUE, R. H. JR. and H. J. WATSON "Bit by Bit: Toward Decision Support Systems," *California Management Review*, 22, no. 1 (Fall 1979), 60–68.

154. SPRAGUE, R. H., JR., and H. J. WATSON, "A Decision System for Banks," *Omega: The International Journal of Management Science*, 4, no. 6 (1976), 657–671.

155. SPRAGUE, R. H., JR., and H. J. WATSON, "MIS Concepts: Part I," *Journal of Systems Management*, 26, no. 1 (January 1975), 34–37.

156. SPRAGUE, R. H., JR., and H. J. WATSON, "MIS Concepts: Part II," *Journal of Systems Management*, 26, no. 2 (February 1975), 35–40.

157. SRINIVASAN, A. "Alternative Measures of System Effectiveness: Associations and Implications," *MIS Quarterly*, 9, no. 3 (September 1985), 243–253.

159. STEFIK, M. ET AL. "Beyond the Chalkboard: Computer Support for Collaboration and Problem Solving in Meetings," *Communications of the ACM*, 30, no. 1 (January 1987), 32–47.

159. STOTT, K. L., JR., and B. W. DOUGLAS "A Model-Based Decision Support System for Planning and Scheduling Ocean Borne Transportation," *Interfaces*, 11, no. 4 (August 1981), 1–10.

160. SUSSMAN, P. N. "Evaluating Decision Support Software," *Datamation*, 30 (October 1984), 171–172.

161. SVIOKLA, J. J. "An Examination of the Impact of Expert Systems on the Firm: The Case of XCON," *MIS Quarterly* 44, no. 2 (June 1990) 127–140.

162. TRIPPI, R. "Decision Support and Expert Systems for Real Estate Investment Decisions: A Review," *Interfaces*, 20, no. 5 (September–October 1990) 50–60.

163. TURBAN, E., and P. R. WATKINS "Integrating Expert Systems and Decision Support Systems," *MIS Quarterly*, 10, no. 2 (June 1986), 121–136.

164. VIERCK, R. K. "Decision Support Systems: An MIS Manager's Perspective," *MIS Quarterly*, 5, no. 4 (December 1981), 35–48.

165. WAGNER, G. R. "Decision Support Systems: Computerized Mind Support for Executive Problems," *Managerial Planning*, 30, no. 2 (September–October 1981), 9–16.

166. WAGNER, G. R. "DSS: Dealing with Executive Assumptions in the Office of the Future," *Managerial Planning*, 30, no. 5 (March–April 1982), 4–10.

167. WAGNER, G. R. "Decision Support Systems: The Real Substance," *Interfaces*, 11, no. 2 (April 1981), 77–86.

168. WATKINS, P. R. "Perceived Information Structure: Implications for Decision Support System Design," *Decision Sciences*, 13, no. 1 (January 1982), 38–59.

169. WATKINS, P. R. "Preference Mapping of Perceived Information Structure: Implications for Decision Support Systems Design," *Decision Sciences*, 15, no. 1 (Winter 1984), 92–106.

170. Watterson, K. "The Changing World of EIS" *Byte* 19, no. 6, (June 1994) 183–193.

171. WATSON, H. J., and M. M. HILL "Decision Support Systems or What Didn't Happen with MIS," *Interfaces*, 13, no. 5, (October 1983), 81–88.

172. WATSON, H. J., and R. I. MANN "Expert Systems: Past, Present, and Future," *Journal of Information Systems Management*, 5 (Fall 1988).

173. WEITZ, R. R., and A. DEMEYER "Managing Expert Systems: A Framework and Case Study," *Information & Management*, 19 (1990), 115–131.

174. WETHERBE, J. C., "Executive Information Requirements: Getting It Right,: *MIS Quarterly*, 15, no. 1 (March 1991).

175. WHITE, K. B. "Dynamic Decision Support Teams," *Journal of Systems Management*, 36, no. 6 (June 1984), 26–31.

176. WILL, H. J. "MIS—Mirage or Mirror Image?" *Journal of Systems Management* (September 1973), 24–31.

177. WYNNE, B. "Decision Support Systems—A New Plateau of Opportunity or More Emperor's New-Clothing?" *Interfaces*, 12, no 1 (February 1982), 88–91.

178. WYNNE, B., AND G. W. DICKSON "Experienced Managers' Performance in Experimental Man-Machine Decision System Simulation," *Academy of Management Journal*, 18, no. 1 (March 1975), 25–40.

179. WYNNE, B. "A Domination Sequence—MS/OR, DSS, and the Fifth Generation," *Interfaces*, 14, no. 3 (May–June 1984), 51–58.

180. ZALUD, B. "Decision Support Systems—Push End User in Design/Build Stage," *Data Management*, 19, no. 1 (January 1981), 20–22.

CATEGORIES OF DECISION SUPPORT ARTICLES

GENERAL OVERVIEW
36, 93, 121, 142, 154, 156, 159, 164, 167, 168, 178

RELATIONSHIP WITH or/ms AND mis
22, 25, 127, 156, 159, 175

DECISION SUPPORT FRAMEWORK
10, 52, 71, 85, 123, 154

DEVELOPMENT PROCESS DESIGN: 21, 31, 40, 56, 63, 88, 108, 135
User involvement: 2, 8, 70, 96, 98, 103, 109, 136, 180
Organizational variables: 28, 42, 79, 98, 108, 115, 140
Others: 8, 26, 85, 103, 174

SOFTWARE INTERFACE
Impact of cognitive style: 19, 51, 79, 83, 139
Impact on decision making: 18, 99, 105, 139
Others: 7, 23, 29, 53, 66, 92, 98, 154, 159

MODEL SUBSYSTEM
Modeling of decision making: 13, 24, 28, 56, 111, 116
Human information processing: 137, 169, 171
Others: 15, 25, 27, 100, 119, 154, 156, 159, 167

DATABASE SUBSYSTEM
25, 34, 45, 100, 119, 154, 156, 159

INTEGRATING THE SOFTWARE INTERFACE, MODELS, AND DATA
100, 156, 158

INTEGRATING DECISION SUPPORT INTO THE ORGANIZATION
Implementation: 2, 5, 8, 41, 54, 67, 69, 76, 91, 106, 117, 118, 179
Training: 70, 72

INDEX